FACES OF THE INFINITE

For over 100 years the *Proceedings of the British Academy* series has provided a unique record of British scholarship in the humanities and social sciences. These themed volumes drive scholarship forward and are landmarks in their field. For more information about the series and guidance on submitting a proposal for publication, please visit www.thebritishacademy.ac.uk/proceedings

PROCEEDINGS OF THE BRITISH ACADEMY • 240

FACES OF THE INFINITE

NEOPLATONISM AND POETRY AT THE CONFLUENCE OF AFRICA, ASIA AND EUROPE

Edited by
STEFAN SPERL AND YORGOS DEDES

Published for THE BRITISH ACADEMY
by OXFORD UNIVERSITY PRESS

Oxford University Press, Great Clarendon Street, Oxford OX2 6DP

First edition published in 2022

British Library Cataloguing in Publication Data
Data available

Library of Congress Cataloging in Publication Data
Data available

Typeset by NewgenPublishing UK
Printed in Great Britain by TJ Books Ltd, Padstow, Cornwall

ISBN 978-0-19-726725-7
ISSN 0068-1202

In memoriam
Trevor J. Dadson

Contents

Notes on Contributors x
Acknowledgements xvii
Note to the Reader xx

Introduction: 'A Thing All Living Faces' 1
STEFAN SPERL AND YORGOS DEDES
1. Why Plotinus? 6
2. The Pre-Modern Poems (4th to 17th Centuries) 14
3. A Neoplatonic Poetics? 27
4. The Modern Poems 36
5. The Birth of Love 42

Part I: From Paganism and Eastern Christianity to the Islamic World (4th to 17th Centuries CE) 51

1 Neoplatonism and Poetics in Ancient Greek and Byzantine Literature 53
DAVID HERNÁNDEZ DE LA FUENTE

2 Stages of Ascent: Neoplatonic Affinities in Classical Arabic Poetry 93
STEFAN SPERL

3 What are Neoplatonic Poetics? Allegory; Figure; Genre 131
ALEXANDER M. KEY

4 Beauty Stings: Plotinus and Rūzbihān Baqlī on Beauty 148
KAZUYO MURATA

5 Ottoman Poetry: Where the Neoplatonic Dissolves into an Emotional Script for Life 169
WALTER G. ANDREWS

6 Mihrî Hatun and Neoplatonic Discourse: Legitimation of Women's Writing in Early Modern Ottoman Poetry 188
DIDEM HAVLIOĞLU

7 Poetry and Ishraqi Illuminationism among the Esoteric Zoroastrians of Mughal India 203
CARL W. ERNST

Part II: Jewish Neoplatonism and Hebrew Poetry in Muslim and Christian Realms (11th to 17th Centuries CE) 215

8 Andalusian Hebrew Poems on the Soul and their Afterlife 217
ADENA TANENBAUM

9 Karaite Poems about the Nature of the Soul from the Muslim East, Byzantium and Eastern Europe 237
JOACHIM YESHAYA

Part III: Christian and Jewish Neoplatonism in Italy and Spain (14th to 17th Centuries CE) 253

10 '*Nostro intelletto si profonda tanto*': The Philosophical Background of Dante's *Paradiso* I, 1–12 and IV, 22–60 255
CRISTINA D'ANCONA

11 Agathon Redivivus: Love and Incorporeal Beauty in Ficino's *De Amore*, *Speech V* 276
SUZANNE STERN-GILLET

12 'A Man within a Woman, or even a God': Vittoria Colonna and 16th-Century Italian Poetic Culture 292
ABIGAIL BRUNDIN

13 The Ascent of the Soul: Neoplatonic Themes in the Literature of Golden Age Spain 306
COLIN P. THOMPSON

14 The Christian Neoplatonism of Francisco de Aldana in the *Carta para Arias Montano* 323
TERENCE O'REILLY

15 A Poetics of Difference: Neoplatonism and the Discourse of Desire in the Early Modern Spanish Love Lyric 336
JULIAN WEISS

Part IV: Neoplatonism in Modern Poetry: Splintered but Vibrant 353

16 An Equivocal Echo: Eugenio Montale 355
PETER ROBINSON

17 Eroticism of the Infinite: Neoplatonism, Kabbalism and Sufism in the Work of José Ángel Valente 373
CLAUDIO RODRÍGUEZ FER

18 Body and Soul in the Arabic Literature of the Americas 392
ROBIN OSTLE

19 Neoplatonist Echoes in Modern Arabic Poetry: The Case of Muḥammad ʿAfīfī Maṭar 404
FERIAL J. GHAZOUL

20 Shards of Infinitude: Neoplatonist Relics in Modern Persian Poetry 419
AHMAD KARIMI-HAKKAK

21 The New Image of the Beloved in the Old Mirror: Reflections on the Neoplatonic Tradition in Modern Turkish Poetry 433
NESLIHAN DEMIRKOL AND MEHMET KALPAKLI

22 Neoplatonists in Modern Greek Poetry 454
DAVID RICKS

Index of References to the Enneads *of Plotinus* 469
Index of Citations from the Qur'an 471
Index of Names and Places 472
Index of Subjects 477

Notes on Contributors

Walter G. Andrews was Professor Emeritus of Turkish and Ottoman literature in the Department of Near Eastern Languages and Civilization at the University of Washington. He has published books, translations, articles and edited works on Ottoman literature, modern Turkish literature, the history of emotions and literary theory in English and Turkish. He was also co-director of the Ottoman Texts Archive Project (OTAP), a web-based resource developing digital tools and methods for the archiving and analysis of Ottoman texts and Co-Director of Newbook Digital Texts, a collaborative web-based publishing house devoted to the multimedia publication of primary source texts and digital humanities studies.

Abigail Brundin specialises in the literature and culture of Renaissance and Early Modern Italy. She has written on many aspects of the period, from female convents to the Grand Tour, and is above all known for her work on the poet Vittoria Colonna, as the translator of the *Sonnets for Michelangelo* (2005) and author of *Vittoria Colonna and the Spiritual Poetics of the Italian Reformation* (2008). A Fellow of St Catharine's College, Brundin is Professor of Italian at the University of Cambridge and, since September 2021, Director of the British School at Rome.

Trevor J. Dadson was Professor Emeritus of Hispanic Studies at Queen Mary University of London, having previously held chairs at Queen's University, Belfast and the University of Birmingham. He is the author of numerous books, articles and book chapters on Spanish Golden Age literature, textual criticism and socio-cultural history. He has published an anthology of the poetry of Diego de Silva y Mendoza, Count of Salinas (1985) and edited the complete works of Gabriel Bocángel y Unzueta (2001), on whom he has also published an extensive biography (1991). Among his more recent publications are *Tolerance and Coexistence in Early Modern Spain. Old Christians and Moriscos in the Campo de Calatrava* (2014); *Diego de Silva y Mendoza, Conde de Salinas, Marqués de Alenquer* (2015); *La princesa de Éboli. Cautiva del rey: Vida de Ana de Mendoza y de la Cerda (1540–1592)* (with Helen Reed, 2015); and *Conde de Salinas. Obra completa. I. Poesía desconocida* (2016). He was President of the Asociación Internacional 'Siglo de Oro' (1999–2002), President of the Association of Hispanists of Great Britain & Ireland (2011–15) and for many years Editor-in-Chief of the Journal of Hispanic Research. In 2008 he was elected a Fellow of the British Academy, and in 2015 he was awarded the 'Encomienda de la Orden de Isabel la Católica' by King Felipe VI of Spain for his services to Spanish culture. In 2016 he was elected a Corresponding Fellow of both the Real Academia Española and the Real Academia de la Historia.

Cristina D'Ancona is Associate Professor at the Dipartimento di Civiltà e forme del sapere of the University of Pisa. Her teaching includes Late Antique and Medieval philosophy (Arabic and Latin). In 2010–15 she acted as the Principal Investigator of the project *Greek into Arabic. Philosophical Concepts and Linguistic Bridges* funded by the European Research Council. Her fields of research include Greek Neoplatonism and Medieval Philosophy, both Arabic and Latin. Among her numerous publications is *Plotino. L'immortalità dell'anima. IV 7[2]. Plotiniana Arabica, pseudo-Teologia di Aristotele, capitoli I, III, IX* (2017).

Yorgos Dedes is Senior Lecturer in Turkish at the Department of the Languages and Cultures of Near and Middle East at SOAS. His teaching includes courses on Ottoman and Modern Turkish language, literature and culture. For the last ten years he has also been teaching at the Intensive Ottoman and Turkish Summer School in Cunda. His research interests focus on Ottoman literature and Turkish culture with special reference to frontier epic traditions and relations with Byzantium and Greece. Another area of interest is the *aljamiado* literature of the Greek-speaking Muslims of the Ottoman empire. His recent publications include a book chapter on Bursa in *Europe: A Literary History*, edited by David Wallace (Cambridge University Press, 2015), an edition of the Greek *aljamiado* translation of Süleymân Çelebî's *Mevlid-i nebî* (*Journal of Turkish Studies*, 2013) and an article on Ottoman poetry with Stefan Sperl ('"In the rose-bower every leaf is a page of delicate meaning": An Arabic perspective on three Ottoman kasides', in *Eski Edebiyat Çalışmaları VIII*, Istanbul 2013).

Neslihan Demirkol is a research associate of the Corpus Musicae Ottomanicae (CMO) project, based within the University of Münster, Germany. She holds an MA and Ph.D. from Bilkent University. She worked as an assistant professor between 2016 and 2019 in the Department of Turkish Language and Literature at the Social Sciences University of Ankara, Turkey. She spent one year in the Islamic Studies Department within the Institute for Asian and Oriental Studies at the University of Zurich, for her postdoctoral studies as a Swiss Government Excellence Scholarship holder for the academic year 2018–19. Her research and teaching interests are modern Turkish literature, literary theories, literary history, translation studies, adaptations and translations of *A Thousand and One Nights* in Turkish and their influences on Turkish literature. Neslihan was a member of the Expert Committee for Intercultural Dialogue of the Turkish National Commission for UNESCO between 2008 and 2013. She has been a member of ÇEVBİR (Professional Association of Translators) since 2006. She has been on the editorial board of *Kebikeç* since 2011, a peer-reviewed academic journal in the field of humanities and social sciences; and *fe journal*, an international peer-reviewed academic journal in the field of feminist critique and gender studies since 2018.

Carl W. Ernst is a scholar who writes on critical issues of Islamic studies (West and South Asia), pre-modern and contemporary Sufism, and Muslim encounters with

Hinduism. He has received research fellowships from the Fulbright programme, the National Endowment for the Humanities and the John Simon Guggenheim Foundation, and he has been elected a Fellow of the American Academy of Arts and Sciences. He studied comparative religion at Stanford University (BA 1973) and Harvard University (Ph.D. 1981). He is now William R. Kenan, Jr., Distinguished Professor of Religious Studies at the University of North Carolina at Chapel Hill.

Ferial J. Ghazoul is Professor of English and Comparative Literature at the American University in Cairo. She is the editor of the tri-lingual annual *Alif: Journal of Comparative Poetics* and is the co-translator of the award winning *Quartet of Joy* by Muḥammad ʿAfīfī Maṭar and the *Chronicles of Majnūn Laylā* by Qāsim Ḥaddād. She is the author of *Nocturnal Poetics: The Arabian Nights in Comparative Context*. She has published studies on the Orient in Western imagination including the works of Shakespeare, Flaubert, Joyce and Proust. She has also published extensively on postcolonial literatures, women studies, translation studies and literary theory.

Didem Havlioğlu is a literary historian specialising in women and gender in Ottoman Turkish intellectual history, particularly in the early modern period. She has focused on how women writers subvert the traditional literary discourses from within and insert their voices in intellectual circles. She is the author of *Mihri Hatun: Performance, Gender-Bending and Subversion in Early Modern Intellectual History* and teaches in the Department of Asian and Middle East Studies at Duke University.

David Hernández de la Fuente is Professor of Greek Philology at Complutense University of Madrid. His main research interests are Literature and Society in Late Antiquity (especially Nonnus and Late Antique Religious Change), Greek Religion and Mythology and the History of Platonism (especially *Laws* and Neoplatonism). He has authored several books on Classics such as *Bakkhos Anax. Un estudio sobre Nono de Panópolis* (2008), *Oráculos griegos* (2008), *Vidas de Pitágoras* (2011), *Breve historia de Bizancio* (2014) or *El despertar del alma. Dioniso y Ariadna. Mito y misterio* (2017) among others. He has translated Greek authors, including Nonnus and Plutarch, into Spanish.

Mehmet Kalpaklı is chair of the Department of Turkish Literature and acting Chair of the Department of History at Bilkent University. He specialises in Ottoman literature, modern Turkish literature, theory of literature, cultural history of the Ottoman Empire, and digital humanities. He is co-founder and an active participant in the Ottoman Text Editing Project at the University of Washington and Bilkent University. Some of his publications are: *Ottoman Lyric Poetry: An Anthology* (with Walter Andrews and Najaat Black, University of Texas Press, 1997) and an expanded edition (University of Washington Press, 2006); *Osmanlı Divan Şiiri Üzerine Metinler* (Texts on Ottoman Divan Poetry) (Yapı Kredi Press,

1999); *Binbir Gece'ye Bakışlar*, (Edited Essays on the 1001 Nights – with Neslihan Demirkol) (Turkuaz Press, 2010); *The Complete Works of Halide Edib Adıvar* (18 books) (Özgür Press/Can Press, 1996–2011). His documentary script on the life of Fatih Sultan Mehmed as a 'Renaissance Emperor' has been shown on TRT (Turkish National Television) and published as a DVD in 2013.

Ahmad Karimi-Hakkak is Professor Emeritus of Persian language, literature and culture at the University of Maryland. He has studied in Iran and the United States and received his Ph.D. in comparative literature from Rutgers University in 1979. He writes in English and Persian and is the author, editor or translator of over 25 books, mostly analysing and interpreting Persian poetry and literary culture to Westerners. The study of ancient and medieval ideas as conceptualised and reinterpreted by modern thinkers within the intellectual currents of Iranian Islam, is an area of his scholarly focus. His most recent publication, *A Fire of Lilies*, was published by Leiden University Press in 2019.

Alexander M. Key is Associate Professor of Arabic and Comparative Literature at Stanford University. His 2018 monograph, *Language Between God and the Poets* (open access with UC Press) deals with the detailed theories of 11th-century scholars about how poetry works through syntax to create affect and how language, mind and reality interact in theology, lexicography and philosophy. He is currently working on a translation of al-Jurjānī's work on the poetics of syntax, *Dalā'il al-I'jāz*, for the Library of Arabic Literature (New York University Press).

Kazuyo Murata is Lecturer in Islamic Studies at King's College London. She is the author of *Beauty in Sufism: The Teachings of Rūzbihān Baqlī* (SUNY Press, 2017), which investigates the significance of beauty in the theology, cosmology, anthropology and prophetology of Rūzbihān Baqlī (d. 1209), a major Sufi thinker from Shiraz, Persia. She is also the co-editor of *In Search of the Lost Heart: Explorations in Islamic Thought* (SUNY Press, 2012).

Terence O'Reilly is Professor Emeritus in the Department of Spanish, Portuguese and Latin American Studies, University College, Cork. His principal field of research is 16th- and 17th-century Spain, especially its history and the influence on its literature and art of religious thought. He has written extensively on spiritual writings composed in late medieval and Golden Age Spain.

Robin Ostle is Emeritus Research Fellow in Modern Arabic at St. John's College, University of Oxford. Most of his work has been devoted to modern Arabic literature, with a particular emphasis on poetry, and the principal focus of his current research is on literature and the fine arts in Egypt in the 20th century. His recent publications include the edited volumes *Studying Modern Arabic Literature* (with Roger Allen), (Edinburgh University Press, 2015) and *Modern Literature in the Near and Middle East 1850–1970* (2nd edition, Routledge, 2017).

David Ricks is Professor Emeritus of Modern Greek and Comparative Literature at King's College London and Honorary Senior Research Fellow at the University of Birmingham. He studied classics and philosophy at Oxford before writing a University of London Ph.D. on the presence of Homer in modern Greek poetry. His publications include 'Modern Greek literature and Orthodoxy' in Augustine Casaday (ed.), *The Orthodox Christian World* (Routledge, 2012) and 'Lucretian moments in modern Greek poetry' in Dimitris Tziovas (ed.), *Re-imagining the Past* (Oxford University Press, 2014), and he has written on a number of modern Greek authors with an interest in Neoplatonism, among them Alexandros Papadiamantis, C.P. Cavafy and Angelos Sikelianos.

Peter Robinson is Professor of English and American Literature at the University of Reading and poetry editor for Two Rivers Press. He has published volumes of aphorisms, fiction and literary criticism, and been awarded the Cheltenham Prize, the John Florio Prize and two Poetry Book Society Recommendations for translation (mainly from the Italian) and for his own poetry. Recent publications include *September in the Rain: A Novel* (2016), *Collected Poems 1976–2016* (2017), *The Sound Sense of Poetry* (2018), and both *Ravishing Europa*, new poems, and *The Constitutionals: A Fiction* in 2019.

Claudio Rodríguez Fer is director of the Valente Chair of Poetry and Aesthetics and co-director of the journal *Moenia* of the University of Santiago de Compostela (Spain). He has taught at the City University of New York, Paris Est, South Brittany and Upper Brittany, where he was awarded the Doctor Honoris Causa. As a Galician poet, narrator, playwright and essayist, he has published, spoken and read his work in numerous parts of Europe, America and Africa. He coordinates the publication *Unión Libre*, and his critical work includes books and editions on Dostoevsky, Machado, Borges, Neruda, Cernuda, Goytisolo, Valente and numerous Galician writers.

Stefan Sperl, a graduate of Oxford (Arabic) and SOAS (Ph.D. 1977), and former staff member of UNHCR (1978–88), is now Professor Emeritus of Arabic and Middle Eastern Studies at SOAS. His publications include articles on Arabic, Islamic and Refugee Studies, as well as *Mannerism in Arabic Poetry: A Structural Analysis of Selected Texts* (1989), *The Kurds: A Contemporary Overview* (with Philip Kreyenbroek, 1991), *Qasida Poetry in Islamic Africa and Asia* (with Christopher Shackle, 1996) and *The Cosmic Script: Sacred Geometry and the Science of Arabic Penmanship* (with Ahmed Moustafa, 2014), which won the Iran Book of the Year Award (2016). His most recent publication is 'The Qur'an and Arabic Poetry' (*The Oxford Handbook of Qur'anic Studies*, 2020).

Suzanne Stern-Gillet studied Philosophy at the University of Liège (Lic. Phil. and D.Phil.) and Classics at the University of Manchester (M.Phil.). Having taught in universities in continental Europe and the United States, she is now Professor Emerita of Ancient Philosophy at the University of Bolton and Honorary Research

Fellow in the Department of Classics and Ancient History at the University of Manchester. Having early in her career translated Gilbert Ryle's *The Concept of Mind* into French and published in the tradition of analytical philosophy, she now concentrates her research on ancient Greek philosophy, from Plato to Plotinus. She is the author of *Aristotle's Philosophy of Friendship* (Ithaca, 1995). She has edited (with K. Corrigan) *Reading Ancient Texts: Essays in Honour of Denis O'Brien* (vol. I: *Presocratics and Plato*, vol. II: *Aristotle and Neoplatonism*) (Brill, 2007); (with Gary Gurtler SJ) *Ancient and Medieval Concepts of Friendship* (Ithaca, 2014). The author of some 60 articles, mostly on the epistemology, moral psychology and aesthetics of ancient Greek thinkers, she is currently preparing a translation and commentary of Plotinus' tractate *On the Virtues* (I.2 [19]) for Parmenides Publishing. With K. Corrigan and J.C. Baracat, she has recently completed *A Text Worthy of Plotinus: The Lives and Correspondence of P. Henry SJ, H-R. Schwyzer, A.H. Armstrong, J. Trouillard and J. Igal SJ* (Leuven University Press, 2021).

Adena Tanenbaum, Ph.D. Harvard University (1993), is Associate Professor of Near Eastern Languages and Cultures at Ohio State University. Her book, *The Contemplative Soul: Hebrew Poetry and Philosophical Theory in Medieval Spain* (Leiden, 2002), was a finalist for the Koret Foundation Jewish Book Award, Philosophy/Thought category in 2003. She has published articles on various aspects of medieval Hebrew poetry from Spain, including its translation, as well as on Zechariah Alḍāhirī's *maqāma*, *Sefer hamusar* (Yemen, 16th century) which is the subject of her forthcoming monograph. Her latest publication is 'Hidden Gems: The Hebrew Maqāma from Yemen' which has appeared online ahead of print in 2021 (doi: https://doi.org/10.1163/2212943X-20201022). It is due to be published in 2022 as part of a special issue of *Intellectual History of the Islamicate World* (vol. 10.1–2).

Colin P. Thompson is an Emeritus Fellow of St Catherine's College, Oxford, having been its Fellow and Tutor in Spanish from 1989–2011. He has written widely on the poetry and prose of the Spanish Golden Age and has published three books, each also translated into Spanish: *The Poet and the Mystic: A Study of the Cántico espiritual of San Juan de la Cruz* (Oxford University Press, 1977); *The Strife of Tongues: Fray Luis de León and the Golden Age of Spain* (Cambridge University Press, 1988); and *St John of the Cross: Songs in the Night* (SPCK and Catholic University of Washington, 2002). He has also been an ordained minister of the United Reformed Church for over 40 years.

Julian Weiss is Professor of Medieval and Early Modern Spanish Studies at King's College London. His research interests include medieval and Renaissance poetics, literary theory, court lyric and clerical narrative, as well as early modern censorship. He is a member of the international research group Seminario de Poética Europea del Renacimiento (Universitat Autònoma de Barcelona, http://spr.uab.cat/) and a co-investigator on the AHRC flagship project *Language Acts and Worldmaking* (https://languageacts.org/). His current research traces the early modern reception of the Jewish historian Flavius Josephus (1st century CE) as he travelled in Spanish translation from Iberia in 1492 to the Sephardic communities of Amsterdam in the late 17th century.

Joachim Yeshaya (Ph.D. [2009] University of Groningen) is a postdoctoral researcher at KU Leuven, Belgium, where he teaches courses on biblical and post-biblical Hebrew language and literature, Judaism and Islam. He is Medieval Judaism editor for the multi-volume *Encyclopedia of the Bible and its Reception* (EBR; De Gruyter). Dr Yeshaya has authored two books on the oeuvre of Moses Darʿī, a 12th-century Egyptian Karaite-Jewish poet (*Medieval Hebrew Poetry in Muslim Egypt*, Brill, 2011; *Poetry and Memory in Karaite Prayer*, Brill, 2014). He has co-edited, with Elisabeth Hollender (Goethe University Frankfurt), the volume *Exegesis and Poetry in Medieval Karaite and Rabbanite Texts* (Brill, 2017), and, with Elisabeth Hollender and Naoya Katsumata (Kyoto University), the volume *The Poet and the World* (De Gruyter, 2019).

Acknowledgements

When my late wife Savitri expressed interest in comparing the notions of the purification of the soul in the writings of the medieval Sufi Ḥārith al-Muḥāsibī and the texts set to music by Johann Sebastian Bach, little did I realise what consequences this intriguing idea would bring about. As we began searching for a common ancestor whom Bach and al-Muḥāsibī might possibly share, a name came into view which has not ceased to captivate me since: Plotinus, the Egyptian philosopher and founding father of Neoplatonism, whose legacy has permeated the spiritual and artistic traditions of East and West.

The significance of his role was thrown into relief yet more when I encountered him again while working on a research project with the artist and scholar Ahmed Moustafa. Our focus was the 'proportioned script', a seminal Arabic writing system dating back to the 10th century which we found to be grounded in philosophical views about geometry as a bridge between the material and the intelligible realms. Among the sources for the privileged status of geometry in the literature of the time is the Arabic adaptation of Plotinus's writings, which thus appeared to underpin the changing aesthetics of Arabic calligraphy and the Islamic visual arts with which we were concerned. As a result, I began to wonder whether a comparable link with Neoplatonism could also be found in the verbal arts, including the subject which had for long been my prime interest, poetry.

A perusal of the secondary literature on the classical poetic traditions of Europe and the Middle East revealed sundry references to Plato, Plotinus or Neoplatonism in virtually every publication, but they had not been made the subject of a wider, comparative study. One book captured my attention above all others: Adena Tanenbaum's *The Contemplative Soul* (2002), which documents the propagation throughout the Mediterranean of a type of Hebrew devotional poetry born out of the encounter between Judaism, Islam and Neoplatonism. The grand, cross-cultural panorama developed by Tanenbaum inspired the idea to bring the multi-lingual poetic traditions of the Mediterranean together by approaching them from the perspective of Neoplatonism as a shared heritage common to them all.

Ahmad Karimi-Hakkak was the first academic colleague whom I consulted on the topic. I am grateful for his enthusiastic response and sound advice which were instrumental in encouraging me to pursue the project in earnest and try to convene a conference on the topic. In order to organise it I was fortunate to obtain the invaluable support of two co-convenors without whom neither the conference nor the ensuing publication would have seen the light of day: the late Trevor Dadson, Professor Emeritus of Hispanic Studies at Queen Mary University, and my SOAS colleague Yorgos Dedes, Senior Lecturer in Turkish. I am greatly indebted to them both.

On Trevor Dadson's advice we approached the British Academy with a request to host the conference and were delighted and grateful to receive their approval. A vote of thanks must go to James Binns of York University and James Montgomery of Cambridge University for supporting our application to the Academy. Preparations for the conference began with two exploratory workshops funded by SOAS and held in the summer of 2017. The discussion helped to set the agenda for a three-day international colloquium which took place from 9 to 11 November 2017. The British Academy hosted the first two days in optimal fashion. The third day was held at SOAS with the help of a sponsorship generously provided by a former SOAS student.

The conference included a concert organised with the help of Leili Anvar (INALCO, Paris) and supported by the Iran Heritage Foundation and the Language Acts and Worldmaking Project of King's College London. The programme featured a selection of poetry from the biblical Song of Songs, the Odes to Mystical Love by Jalāl al-Dīn Rūmī and the Spiritual Canticles by St John of the Cross. The rendering of Hebrew, Persian and Spanish verses set to music by Renaud Garcia-Fons proved to be a memorable complement to the academic papers and was felt by many to encapsulate the spirit of the occasion.

The notable parallels between the conference papers, as well as the frequent appearance of comparable themes in poems of seemingly unrelated origin, engaged the participants' interest and stimulated discussions between scholars working on languages, cultures and periods seldom represented together at the same venue. The consensus arose that the conference had confirmed the significance of Neoplatonism as a cross-cultural phenomenon which links the literary traditions of Judaism, Christianity and Islam and that the publication of the papers was likely to produce a coherent volume. As a result, the speakers were invited to revise their presentations in the light of the discussions, and a number of additional papers were commissioned to ensure a wider coverage of the field. With the kind support of Charles Burnett of the Warburg Institute, an application was submitted to the British Academy to have the book published in its Proceedings Series. We are grateful for the approval we were granted, as well as for the timely help and advice provided to us throughout by the staff of the British Academy, in particular James Rivington, Geetha Nair and Portia Taylor. In the final stages of preparing the manuscript for publication we benefited greatly from the proactive and responsive support given to us by Helen Flitton of Newgen Publishing.

As editors we owe the greatest debt of gratitude to the colleagues who devoted their time, effort and expertise in order to contribute a chapter to this volume, as well as to the anonymous reviewers who agreed to comment on their drafts. A particular word of thanks must go to the late Walter Andrews, Professor Emeritus of Turkish and Ottoman Literature at the University of Washington. Though unable to attend the conference, his paper, which he was the first to submit, seemed to us emblematic of what we were trying to achieve. We are greatly saddened that he will not be with us to see it published.

In editing the papers and finalising the Introduction we have greatly benefited from the advice and support given to us by Vivian Brown, Charles Burnett, Tony Chappa, Cristina D'Ancona, Ferial Ghazoul, Nels Johnson, Alexander Key, Caroline Maldonado, Terence O'Reilly, Peter Phillips, Christine Roe, Suzanne Stern-Gillet, Julian Weiss and Joachim Yeshaya.

A special vote of thanks must go to Ahmed Moustafa for supplying us with the cover illustration of this book which shows a detail of his triptych 'Night Journey and Ascension' (2008–2011 CE/1429–1432 AH). The composition is based upon Qur'anic verses referring to the Prophet Muḥammad's heavenly journey and hence evokes a theme much attested in these pages, the ascent of the soul. Dr Moustafa's design also appears on the home page of the Online Anthology lyrics-of-ascent.net which accompanies this volume. The website has been developed thanks to the skill and expertise of Nick Awde to whom we hereby express our abiding gratitude.

In early 2020, when much of the editorial work on the papers had been completed, our project suffered two painful reversals of fortune. While working on our volume on a dark January afternoon, Yorgos and I were shocked and saddened to receive the news of the sudden death of our friend and co-editor Trevor Dadson. Soon thereafter, on 15 February, my wife Savitri died in tragic circumstances after a long illness. These events, compounded by the lockdown imposed in response of the Covid-19 crisis, brought our work to a standstill and called its completion into question. During this difficult time, I was fortunate to receive numerous tokens of friendship and support which helped me to cope and persevere despite the losses we had suffered. I am particularly grateful to Maria Calivis, Tony Chappa, Ann Marie Gibbs, Christine Roe, Julian Weiss and Owen Wright. Abebech Mimi Girma was a source of solace and new inspiration, and my remaining co-editor and friend Yorgos provided the kindest possible moral support, not to mention hours of painstaking labour on the screen.

Until his untimely death, Trevor Dadson supported our work with his trademark good humour, indefatigable energy and consummate editorial skill. In gratitude for all that he has done to help, inspire and guide us, Yorgos and I hereby dedicate this publication to his memory.

Stefan Sperl

Note to the Reader

The Online Anthology *Lyrics of Ascent*

Readers are invited to consult the website *Lyrics of Ascent: Poetry and the Platonic Tradition – An Anthology* which accompanies this volume and is accessible free of charge at www.lyrics-of-ascent.net. The hieroglyph placed next to the mention or citation of a poem in this volume indicates that the Anthology contains the relevant text in the original language with facing English translation. The website is searchable by languages and names of poets. Individual poems can be found by entering a word or phrase from the corresponding English translation cited in this volume. The Anthology also includes a number of additional poems relevant to the subject matter here discussed.

References to the *Enneads* of Plotinus

Subject to the preference of the contributors to this volume, translations of the *Enneads* are cited according to one of the following editions:

Plotinus (1966–89), *Porphyry on Plotinus, Enneads I – VI*, translated by A.H. Armstrong, 7 vols (Cambridge MA/London, Harvard University Press).
Plotinus (1991), *The Enneads*, translated by S. MacKenna, abridged and introduced by J.M. Dillon (London, Penguin Books).
Plotinus (2018), *The Enneads*, edited by L.P. Gerson, translated by G. Boys-Stones, J.M. Dillon, L.P. Gerson, R.A.H. King, A. Smith & J. Wilberding (Cambridge, Cambridge University Press).

In the references to the *Enneads* these translations are identified as A (for Armstrong), M (for MacKenna) and G (for Gerson) respectively.

References to citations from the *Enneads* appear as illustrated and explained below:

… 'the arts do not simply imitate what they see, but they run back to the forming principles from which nature derives' … (V 8 [31] 1.35–7, A: V 239).

V = *Ennead* number
8 = treatise number
[31] = number of treatise in chronological order
1 = paragraph number
35–7 = line number of the Greek text
A: = Armstrong translation [for MacKenna and Gerson this would be M: or G:]
V = volume of Armstrong translation [not relevant for MacKenna and Gerson]
239 = page number of the English translation

Introduction: ‘A Thing All Living Faces’

STEFAN SPERL AND YORGOS DEDES

> The soul, then, in her natural state is in love with God
> and wants to be united with him.
>
> Plotinus[1]

> Whether we are drunk or sober, each one of us is making
> For the street of the Friend. The temple, the synagogue,
> The church and the mosque are all houses of love.
>
> Hafez[2]

ON SEVERAL OCCASIONS, while this book was being edited, people who had gathered in what Hafez once deemed to be ‘houses of love’, met with deadly hate. A synagogue in the United States, mosques in New Zealand, and churches in Sri Lanka and France became scenes of carnage and hundreds of lives were lost. These are not isolated events. They reflect the widespread rise of centrifugal forces in the early decades of this century which are trying to drive communities apart by whatever means. It is no coincidence that they are gaining in appeal at a time of worldwide migration movements when countries are confronted with the need to integrate newcomers of different culture, ethnicity and religion into their social fabric. The resulting challenge demands concessions from all concerned and a sense of common purpose. Much has been achieved but the potential for conflict is undiminished.

Competing notions of identity are at stake. At one extreme we find those who cling to identity as a static preserve which must be guarded from alteration and to which outsiders are admitted, if at all, only at the expense of denying their former selves. Opposed to them are those who see identity as inherently multi-layered, always subject to change and enriched by accommodating difference. Both notions have ethnic, religious, cultural, class-based or gender-based manifestations. Their competing claims have led to fierce political debate and continue to spark acts of violence. On the outcome of these disputes depends the future well-being of the

[1] *Ennead* VI 9 [9] 9.33–34, A: VII 337.

[2] Cited in Lewisohn (2015: 179, [illegible]).

new, pluralist societies which are in the process of formation. How to nurture their growth and foster the rise of a collective and inclusive sense of belonging is one of the greatest challenges of our time.

The task at hand demands not only wise political leadership but constructive involvement at all levels of society. Here the Social Sciences and the Humanities have a pivotal role to play. Comparative Literature is particularly well placed to make a contribution because its prime objective is to bring different cultural and linguistic traditions into relation with one another, to stake out the common ground between them and to produce an informed understanding of their differences. It therefore offers, in the words of Mary Louise Pratt (1995: 62):

> an especially hospitable place for … the arts of cultural mediation, deep intercultural understanding, and genuine global consciousness.

The collaborative research project which led to this publication was conceived in this spirit. Its geographic focus is an intercultural and multi-lingual space second to none: the greater Mediterranean, the meeting place of three continents and the birthplace of three monotheist religions. The maritime expanse in its midst has been a bridge, but also a separation barrier, between the peoples and cultures along its rim. In recent years tens of thousands of displaced people have attempted to cross it at their peril and many continue to lose their lives at sea. Their fate is inseparable from the conflictive charge inherent in the volatile amalgam of creeds, languages and traditions which this uniquely fertile space has brought about and the effect of which has become tangible well beyond its confines.

Taking account of the richness of its heritage and the divisiveness it can entail, this publication invites the reader to reflect on ways to transcend the conundrums of the present by recourse to a dimension of the past which the region shares. This is the philosophical heritage of antiquity and of Plato in particular, as reconceived by the Egyptian philosopher Plotinus (d. 270) and his followers. First formulated in the *Enneads*,[3] it has come to be known as Neoplatonism[4] and will be introduced in more detail in the following pages. Its founding father's august vision of the human soul as endowed with a divine spark and hence able to rise above the limitations of existence and ascend towards union with the supreme principle has, through a complex process of mediation, permeated the three monotheist faiths and left a lasting imprint on their devotional practice and cultural self-expression. In the high Middle

[3] Plotinus's pupil Porphyry (d. 305) divided his master's writings into six books of nine treatises each, hence their name the *Enneads* ('The Niners'). He prefaced them with a life of Plotinus and an explanation of his editorial method (Porphyry 1989). The reference system used here for the *Enneads* and their translations is explained in the bibliography. On Plotinus and his philosophy, see *inter alia* D'Ancona (2012) and Gerson (1999; 2018).

[4] The term Neoplatonism was coined in the 18th century as a pejorative label to distinguish 'genuine Platonism' from later, supposedly deviant interpretations. For the origin and history of the term see Remes & Slaveva-Griffin (2014: 3–5). Since Plato was generally read through the lens of his Neoplatonic commentators from Late Antiquity to the end of the Early Modern period, the term Neoplatonism is used in the following to refer to the post-Plotinian Platonic tradition in general. The term Platonism only appears in order to distinguish it specifically.

Ages and the Renaissance, its resonance became pervasive throughout Europe and the Muslim world. Its significance has since receded, but it never vanished. In Europe it has continued to spawn diverse trends of literature and philosophy up to our time, while in the Middle East its spirit lives on in the theosophical writings of Islamic mysticism and Ismāʿīlism. With its longevity, its wide geographical spread and its many forms of acculturation and transmission, Neoplatonism offers a uniquely productive pathway into the intercultural ties that link this vast region.

If Neoplatonism lends itself particularly well to such an inquiry this is because its impact went far beyond the realm of theory. In both East and West its ideas had a major bearing on artistic practice and left their mark on music, painting, architecture, calligraphy as well as on poetry, the art form to which this volume is dedicated. Studies of the great poetic traditions of Europe and Western Asia rarely omit a reference to its conceptual legacy as one of the factors that has shaped their growth. Hitherto, however, no attempt has been made to gain a comparative understanding of the manner in which Neoplatonism could have affected poetry composed over centuries in such very different languages and cultures. The chapters collected in this volume provide a first overview of this rich subject. Though selective and by no means comprehensive, the material they cover is sufficient to underscore the outstanding significance of Neoplatonism as a cross-cultural phenomenon and to suggest that the poetic traditions at the confluence of Africa, Asia and Europe share elements of what may, with the benefit of hindsight, be described as a 'Neoplatonic poetics'.

Certain common features notwithstanding, the chapters do much to reveal the remarkably distinct and idiosyncratic way in which Neoplatonism makes its presence felt in the poems they discuss. This is due to the fact that its philosophical ideas were selectively transmitted and creatively acculturated until they became expressive means for ideologies which reflect the distinct provenance and personal inclination of the authors, whether they be pagan, Christian, Jewish, Muslim, Zoroastrian or, in the modern poems, humanist, agnostic or even atheist. Very few of these authors would have considered their writings indebted to Greek philosophy. It would therefore be quite misleading to label the poems here discussed as 'Neoplatonic'. This is not what is intended here, nor do the chapters in this volume seek to establish conclusive proof of Neoplatonic 'influence' in the works they discuss. The aim is rather to show how themes, images and concepts that can be associated with the Neoplatonic heritage have left comparable marks on poetic language used to achieve expressive ends that are so different as to defy any common label. By bringing their underlying kinship to awareness, this volume hopes to generate a new way of reading these works which sees them as mutually enlightening and in dialogue with each other, notwithstanding the profound cultural differences which separate them. This may in turn pave the way towards enhanced cross-cultural understanding and the discovery of a joint sense of purpose hitherto ignored.

In geographical terms, the interface between Neoplatonism and poetry covers a vast tapestry of languages, stretching from the Americas via Europe and Middle

East to Africa and South Asia. By focusing on the greater Mediterranean, this publication aims to bridge the most fundamental cultural and linguistic rift which dissects this entire tapestry: 'that between languages written from left to right and languages written from right to left' (Mallette 2013: 255). The latter are associated with the Semitic Ancient Near East, Judaism, Eastern Christianity and the Islamic realm, the former with the Greco-Roman world and Christian Europe. Of the many languages involved in the two groups, the editors have selected seven as representative of the geographical and cultural spread of the region. Among the languages customarily written from right to left, Arabic, Persian and Turkish were, on account of the outstanding richness of their poetry, chosen to represent the Islamic tradition, while the Jewish tradition is principally represented by Hebrew. Persian also features as the language of a Zoroastrian poem. Turkish is a special case. Written from right to left in Arabic characters in Ottoman times, it has come to be written from left to right in Latin characters since the language reform of 1929. Turkish thus exemplifies the above-mentioned rift in its own history. How far-reaching the cultural implications of this transformation are is discussed below in the chapter on modern Turkish poetry.

Of the languages customarily written from left to right, there was significant number of candidates: Catalan, French, Greek, Italian, Latin, Portuguese and Spanish. In order to balance the three languages chosen to represent the Muslim Middle East with an equal number associated with the Christian realm we selected the following three: Greek, as the language of Neoplatonic philosophy and the earliest poetry in the Neoplatonic vein; Italian, on account of the importance of Dante and the pan-European influence of Italian Renaissance Neoplatonism; and Spanish, on account of its outstanding Golden Age poetry and the key role played by the Iberian Peninsula in cross-cultural interaction.

The first part of the book, dedicated to the Eastern Mediterranean and the Islamic World, begins with two longer survey chapters which are intended to supplement the introduction. The first situates the Greek poetry of Late Antiquity in the milieu of Neoplatonic philosophy, before tracing its development as a Christian poetic medium up to the fall of Byzantium. The second covers Arabic poetry from pre-Islamic times to the 13th century and finds the Arabic poetic form, manifest also in several Hebrew, Persian and Turkish poems here discussed, remarkably well predisposed to convey the tenets of Neoplatonic philosophy. Then follow a chapter on Neoplatonic poetics in the light of Classical Arabic criticism, and a comparison between Plotinus and the Persian poet-philosopher Rūzbihān Baqlī (d. 1209). The golden age of Ottoman verse is represented by two chapters, one of which throws a rare light on women poets, notably Mihrî Hatun (d. *c.* 1512). The section ends with a Persian verse epic composed by the Zoroastrian visionary Āẕar Kayvān (d. *c.* 1618) in the intercultural setting of Mughal India.

The second part concerns Jewish Neoplatonism as reflected in a form of Hebrew devotional verse which began in medieval Spain and spread far and wide in the ensuing centuries. There are two chapters: one traces the tradition from the Andalusian philosopher Solomon Ibn Gabirol (d. *c.* 1058) to 16th-century Yemen, the second from the Egyptian Karaite Moses Darʿī (mid-12th century) via Byzantium to 17th-century Poland. The editors had intended to secure a third Hebrew contribution to cover the poetry of the Kabbalah and the modern period. Much to their regret, this could not be arranged.

Part 3 focuses on the Western Mediterranean and, with it, Italy and Spain. It begins with a chapter on Dante (d. 1321) and his indebtedness to Neoplatonism as mediated by the Latin authors of Late Antiquity and the Middle Ages. Ficino (d. 1499), undoubtedly the single most important figure in the transmission history of Western Neoplatonism, appears next, introduced by way of his theory of love and beauty. It was to inspire a flowering of poetry, including the verses by Michelangelo (d. 1564) and his muse Vittoria Colonna (d. 1547) discussed in the third Italian chapter. This is followed by three chapters on Spanish poetry from the Golden Age. The first traces key Neoplatonic themes in works by the most prominent authors. An in-depth study of one of the finest Spanish poems of the time, Francisco de Aldana's (d. 1578) *Carta para Arias Montano*, comes next. The section ends with a chapter on issues of gender and the critical stance adopted by women poets, which takes us as far as Mexico and the verses of Sor Juana Inés de la Cruz (d. 1695).

The texts discussed in the three sections on pre-modern poetry range from Late Antiquity and the Middle Ages up to the 17th century. Notwithstanding the religious, cultural and historical differences between them, they share a distinct cosmological orientation and a recognisable set of themes which surface throughout in a range of culture-specific guises, as outlined below under the heading 'Neoplatonic Poetics'. Much in evidence is the power of love and beauty to uplift the soul to a transcendent unitary state conceived of as the supreme goal of human existence.

The afterlife of this great vision is the subject of the seven chapters on 20th- and 21st-century poetry grouped in the final section of the book. Three of them are case studies of major Italian, Spanish and Egyptian poets whose works were found to be of special relevance: Eugenio Montale (d. 1981), José Ángel Valente (d. 2000) and Muḥammad ʿAfīfī Maṭar (d. 2010). The other four are survey chapters which examine the persistence of Neoplatonic themes in works by several contemporary poets writing in Arabic, Greek, Turkish and Persian.

More background on the subject matter of the book and the scope of its chapters is provided in the remainder of this introduction. It addresses in more detail why Neoplatonism, and the philosophy of the *Enneads* in particular, should have been singled out for such a comparative endeavour and introduces key Plotinian concepts with a view to their poetic elaboration in the literatures represented here. Next, the chapters on pre-modern poetry are located in the strikingly diverse transmission history of Neoplatonism. A comparison of the poems they discuss raises the question to what extent they can be said to share a recognisably 'Neoplatonic poetics' and how it could be defined. The concept is put to the test in the following section which compares the seven chapters on modern poetry and finds in the texts cited by their authors kindred forms of identity creation which draw on, or indeed revive, Neoplatonic roots variously mediated across the ages. Viewed together, the sense of selfhood these poems convey would appear to hold a message relevant to our current circumstances, as well as an echo, in modern garb, of the verses cited at the head of this chapter.

Considering the large number of texts discussed in all the chapters, and taking account of the size of the volume, it was decided that citations of poetry should appear in English translation only, unless the argument requires the presence of the original. Most of the works discussed or referred to in the following pages can be consulted in the original languages with facing English translation by accessing the website *Lyrics of Ascent: Poetry and the Platonic Tradition – An Anthology* which accompanies this publication (www.lyrics-of-ascent.net). As stated in the Note to Readers (p. xx), the Ancient Egyptian hieroglyph for 'writing' 𓏞 has been used to identify the poems which can be found in the Anthology.[5] The choice was inspired by Plotinus's praise for the 'wise men of Egypt' who 'manifested the non-discursiveness of the intelligible world' by the images they devised (*Ennead* V 8 [31] 6.1–9, A: V 257). His reasoning remains relevant for an enterprise dealing with poetic renderings of his philosophical legacy, for poems, like hieroglyphs, enfold in unitary form what discursive analysis prefers to segment.

In her reflections 'Towards a Literary Theory of the Mediterranean', Karla Mallette asserts that the literary traditions brought about by the cultures along its rim 'have tirelessly demonstrated the insufficiency of literary systems bounded by monolingualism'. What she observes instead is 'a parallel linguistic universe in which parallel literary traditions evolve in parallel languages' (Mallette 2013: 265–6). By drawing on the example of Neoplatonism, our findings reveal the proliferation of just such parallels. The pages of this volume, read in conjunction with the texts in the Anthology, demonstrate how languages written from right to left and left to right complement each other to generate a plurilingual poetic universe of astounding abundance and beauty.

1. Why Plotinus?

Why should Neoplatonism and its poetic echoes offer a vision which leads the gaze beyond the internecine fractures of an increasingly divided world? Expressed in the briefest terms it is because the metaphysics devised by Plotinus is inherently resistant to the categorical affirmation of any ultimate truth while at the same seeing all existing phenomena, even inanimate matter, as harbouring an aspect of that truth. The indeterminacy at the heart of his philosophy, combined with the validation it grants to all phenomena in their own right, leads to a way of thinking which does not admit of rigid boundaries and sees all meaning as necessarily multidimensional

[5] The editors are grateful to Dr Hany Rashwan for his help and advice in selecting the hieroglyph. It represents a pen tied to a bowl of water and a palette with two colours, and designates the act of writing.

and contingent. Through the all-pervasiveness of a truth, in itself unknowable, everything is connected to everything else and nothing can mean only one thing. As the late Werner Beierwaltes remarks in his 'Reflections on Neoplatonic Thought with Respect to its Place Today' (1981): 'even the language of Neoplatonic philosophy shows a fundamental anti-dogmatic trait' (1981: 245).

While the more elaborate permutations of Neoplatonic metaphysics and the cosmology it entails have long been superseded, its sense of vision as summarised in the paragraph above remains of abiding relevance. Once such a perspective is adopted there can be no radical exclusion of otherness and no justification for the violent, wholesale imposition of a single order. There will instead be a ceaseless collective quest for answers born of the awareness of a latent kinship beneath all apparent difference. It is for this reason that the Plotinian model can offer, even today, what Julian Weiss in the pages of this volume describes as 'a malleable conceptual frame for thinking across binaries in search of the place where seemingly incommensurable elements meet' (p. 349).

1.1. The One and the Many

The question how and why Plotinus achieved this, leads into the concept at the heart of his philosophy: the One as fountainhead of the many. How oneness could give rise to multiplicity had been debated in Greek metaphysics ever since the so-called Presocratics and Plato. The innovation Plotinus introduced is an 'an extreme radical monism' (Gatti 1999: 24) which led him to conclude that the One in absolute terms is beyond the purview of discursive thought: it is 'truly ineffable' and 'we can say nothing of it: we only try, as far as possible to make signs to ourselves about it' (V 3 [49] 13.1–6, A: V 117).[6] The 'signs' Plotinus felt able to make about it were sufficient for him to envisage 'a more lofty supreme principle than any of those postulated by previous philosophers' (Sheppard 1994: 5). Its supremacy resides in the attribute of perfection, which paradoxically causes the absolute One to overflow with plenitude: 'And all things when they come to perfection produce; the One is always perfect and therefore produces everlastingly; and its product is less than itself' (V 1 [10] 6.38–40, A: V 33). From the axiom of the necessary productivity of perfection in the One, Plotinus derives two consequences of fundamental importance for his thinking. First, the One, on account of its everlasting power of giving, must be synonymous with the Good and hence the source of all Beauty, as well as the source and true object of all Love. Second, through this power it forms the origin of what came to be known as the Great Chain of Being:[7] a cascade of hierarchical emanations through which the One passes ever diminishing shares of itself down to the lowest manifestations of existence.

[6] Bussanich (2005) provides a concise discussion of Plotinus's metaphysics of the One.

[7] On the Plotinian origin of the concept see Lovejoy (1960: 61–6).

The agency through which the One transmits itself are two underlying substances termed 'hypostases' to which its perfection gives rise in timeless succession. The first is the Universal Intellect which, by way of contemplating the One, transfers its life-giving force into the multiplicity of archetypal Forms which constitute the intelligible realm and from which all sensible[8] existents derive. The second is the Universal Soul, which, by contemplating the Intellect, transmits these Forms to the physical universe and hence brings about and ensouls the whole of material existence.[9] It follows that the cosmos is a 'complete living being' (*zoon panteles*)[10] all of whose diverse manifestations carry, to different degrees, traces of their progenitors: the Soul, the Intellect and the One. While the Goodness of the One is thus mediated in diminishing form by the chain of intermediaries, it is nevertheless transmitted in and of itself to all manifestations of existence, and hence immanent and 'always present to anyone who is able to touch it' (VI 9 [9] 7.4–5, A: VII 327).

Throughout this chain, oneness is the precondition for the existence of any entity no matter how insignificant or elevated its status may be in the chain. As Plotinus maintains, 'it is by the one that beings are beings ... for what could anything be if it was not one?' (VI 9 [9] 1.1–3, A: VII 303). As examples he cites an army, a chorus, a ship or a house, all of which would cease to exist if they lost their oneness. The same applies to any other conglomerations, including social structures. The degree to which they are one determines their identity. Their oneness is, however, not in any way absolute but merely a transitory and evanescent image of the archetypal One omnipresent throughout the chain of being. Nothing, in other words, owns the One. All existents have it only by 'sharing and participation' (VI 9 [9] 2.23–4, A: VII 309). It follows that all identity is necessarily derivative and contingent.

1.2. The Journey of the Soul

In the hierarchy of being, the Universal Soul, and with it by analogy the individual human soul, occupies an intermediary position, equidistant between the pinnacle and the base of the pyramid and hence able to relate in equal measure to either end. Plotinus puts it thus:

> For the soul is many things, and all things, both the things above and the things below to the limits of all life, and we are each of us an intelligible universe, making contact with this lower world by the powers of the soul below, but with the intelligible world

[8] Here and in the following the term 'sensible' denotes 'perceptible to the senses', as opposed to 'intelligible', i.e. 'capable of being understood by the mind'.

[9] Plotinus is at pains to stress that both the Universal Intellect and the Universal Soul are 'filled full of life, and, we may say, boiling with life' (VI 7 [38] 12.20–4, A: VII 127). The task of the Universal Soul is to set life in order according rational principles, just as 'the formative rational principles in seeds mould and form living beings like little ordered universes' (IV 3 [27] 10.10–14, A: IV 67).

[10] VI 7 [38] 8.15–33, A: VII 111. The concept of *zoon panteles* appears in Plato's *Timaeus* (31B1), a prime source text for Plotinus's cosmology.

> by its powers above and the powers of the universe; and we remain with all the rest of our intelligible part above, but by its ultimate fringe we are tied to the world below.
> (III 4 [15] 3.21–7, A: III 149–51)

The passage strikingly affirms the universal interconnectedness of the individual human soul. Its linkages transcend all boundaries and encompass all manifestations of being. They are grounded in the common origin from which everything in the sensible universe emanates. This is the Universal Soul[11] whose act of bringing forth Plotinus explains in an image which the Neoplatonic tradition was to resort to for centuries to come and which is also much attested in this volume. That Soul can be imagined, he declares, as 'making living creatures, not of itself and body, but abiding itself and giving images of itself, like a face seen in many mirrors' (I 1 [53] 8.15–18, A: I 111–13). In keeping with the Plotinian hierarchy, these images convey not only the Soul itself but hold an imprint of its own origin, the Universal Intellect and the One. Hence through these mirror images every individual soul harbours within itself a 'trace' (*ichnos*) of the source of all existence. The Platonic notion of 'memory', also much in evidence in the following pages, expresses the same concept by asserting that souls have the capacity to remember the divine source from which they sprang.

In order for the image to be perceived, the soul's mirror must be polished; similarly, if the soul wishes to know whence it came, its memory must be revived. For imprisonment in the body entails forgetfulness and a rusting of the mirror. Oblivious of their true origin, souls in such a state wish only 'to belong to themselves' and become prey to 'the body's raging sea'. Herein lies for Plotinus 'the beginning of evil'.[12] Losing awareness of its true self, the soul will of necessity lose awareness also of its universal connectivity, for it will no longer be able to recognise the immanence of the creative forces – the One, the Intellect and the Soul – throughout existence. The result is self-alienation, dispersal in the manifold materiality of the sensible world and, we might add, the erection of boundaries and separation barriers, the loss of a sense of kinship and the demise of empathy.

For Plotinus and the Neoplatonic tradition in general, the purpose of philosophy is to preserve the soul from this sorry fate by rekindling its primordial memory and teaching it to purify itself and 'polish its mirror'. To this effect the *Enneads* develop a cosmology of stupendous sophistication, complexity and visionary power. Two concepts of crucial relevance not only for the soul's salutary journey but also for the poems here discussed need to be singled out: beauty and love. Extensively explored

[11] Underlying Plotinus's concept of the soul is his interpretation of Plato's creation myth in the *Timaeus* (35a) which describes the Universal Soul as derived from elements that are changeless and undivided and others that are subject to change and division. This combination enables the individual soul to be 'all things', and to operate in the 'lower world' as much as in the world above and yet to remain in essence the same. As Armstrong points out, Plotinus's approach was criticised by later Neoplatonists intent on assigning the individual soul a lower status in the hierarchy of being (A: III 150–1).

[12] *Enn.* V 1 [10] 1–2, A: V 11–15. On memory loss and the complexity of the concept in Plotinus see Aubry (2014: 312–13).

in two treatises of the *Enneads* (I 6 [1] and V 8 [31]), beauty is shown to be manifest in numerous guises which the soul needs to understand in its search for itself. To summarise in briefest terms, all corporeal beauty is but an inferior manifestation of the immaterial, intelligible beauty emanating from the goodness of the One. Having originated in that sublime source, every soul latently also possesses a share of that intelligible beauty.[13] Only if it is capable of awakening that latent share and become beautiful itself – for this is what 'polishing the mirror' means – will it be able to recognise beauty in others and perceive the intelligible shining behind the corporeal shell. As Corrigan noticed, this has major ethical implications for the self and its relations with the Other. Since intelligible beauty is in essence one and the same throughout, 'to recognize the beauty of another person is … not to see an object somehow external or different to oneself but to recognize another in and of oneself … Such beauty overflows a subject/object relation or even the physical divide of two selves seeing each other' (Corrigan 2005: 212).

Understanding the true nature of beauty leads perforce to an understanding also of love. Just as all beauty is in truth a manifestation of the Goodness of the One and hence theophany, so all love is in truth the soul's innate longing for union with the One from whence it came. And since the One is the source of all beauty and love,[14] beauty cannot but stir the soul to love. First developed by Plato, this set of ideas is woven into a coherent, multi-layered cosmology in the *Enneads*. At its heart is the dialectic between two forms of love: earthly or mortal love, which the soul is captivated by when 'it has come into the world of becoming and is deceived' (VI 9 [9] 9.35–6, A: VII 337), and true or heavenly love which strives for union with the source of all love, the One. The dichotomy between the two is not absolute, however, because love as such 'has from everlasting come into existence from the soul's aspiration towards the higher and the good' (III 5 [50] 9.40–1, A: III 203). Earthly love therefore also springs from the same drive, hence to the knowing gaze every earthly beloved also harbours an image, however remote, of the heavenly ideal. The result is a subtle duality of referents between the spiritual and the corporeal, the sacred and the profane, which pervades the Neoplatonic concept of love and reverberates throughout much of the poetry featured in the following pages.

For Plotinus, as also for all mystical poetry, the true goal of love's aspiration must lead away from the earthly realm, and aim for the soul's ascent towards a sublime state of union with the One, where the soul can see itself 'glorified, full

[13] Stern-Gillet (2020a) makes an important distinction between Plato's and Plotinus's approaches to beauty. As she points out, 'the Plotinian soul "recognises" beauty in the world of sense, not so much as a reminder of a sight enjoyed in the pre-incarnation state, as Plato held, but, more significantly, as a trace of something that is "συγγενής" (akin) to her' (2020a: 69); therefore, 'it is her true self that the Plotinian soul "remembers", not a vision of realities descried in an elsewhere that Plato located in "the region beyond the heavens"' (2020a: 70).

[14] Commenting on *Enn.* VI 8 [39] 15.1–8, Bussanich declares 'that the One, or Good, is described not only as object of love but also as the lover and as love itself – all united into one reality' (1999: 61).

of intelligible light—but rather itself pure light—weightless, floating free, having become—but rather, being—a god' (VI 9 [9] 9.57–9, A: VII 339).[15]

1.3. The Faces of the Infinite

While Plotinus likens the Universal Soul to 'a face seen in many mirrors', he describes the Intellect in an arresting phrase as though it were itself endowed with more than one countenance, for he likens it to a wondrous 'thing all faces, shining with living faces' (παμπρόσωπόν τι χρῆμα λάμπον ζῶσι προσώποις, VI 7 [38] 15.26, A VII: 137).[16] The difference draws attention to the fact that the Intellect in Plotinus's scheme is the first progenitor of multiplicity out of the bounty emanating from the One. Building on Plotinus's image, the archetypal plurality generated by the Intellect may therefore be conceived of as the knowable and finite 'Faces of the Infinite', a phrase which has given rise to the title of this volume.

Why should the One be equated with the infinite and what bearing does this title have on poetry in particular? Plotinus declares that the One must be understood as infinite 'because its power cannot be comprehended' (VI 9 [9] 6.11–12, A: VII 323). The term 'One' itself, he maintains, is nothing but an inadequate image for an entity which lies entirely beyond the scope of language. Even its manifestations granted by the Intellect can only be circumscribed by 'apophasis', statements that require to be qualified and 'unsaid' by further statements none of which can lay claim to the full truth.[17] In Plotinus's writing these frequently take the form of myths, allegories and metaphors which he interprets or devises himself with consummate imaginative skill.[18] His writing therefore demonstrates that the ineffability at the heart of his metaphysics privileges poetic invention as the most effective means to convey what discursive language cannot apprehend.

That poetic language – and with it the arts in general – can go some way towards reflecting the 'Faces of the Infinite' is implied by an aspect of Plotinian metaphysics which proved to be extraordinarily influential and distinguishes it markedly from that of Plato. As if hinting at the latter's assertion that a work of art is but a copy of a copy and thus twice removed from the perfection of the intelligible Forms, Plotinus declares that

> the arts do not simply imitate what they see, but they run back to the forming principles from which nature derives; then also they do a great deal by themselves, and, since they possess beauty, they make up what is defective in things. For Pheidias too did

[15] Plotinus describes his own experience of ascent in *Enn.* IV 8 [6] 1.1–11, a famous passage referred to by several contributors to this volume (see pp. 103, 203, 261, 311 and 416).

[16] Armstrong finds Plotinus's imagery here 'strangely reminiscent of Indian many-faced representations of the gods' (Plotinus 1966–89, VII: 137).

[17] For a study of Plotinus's apophatic discourse see Sells (1994: 14–33).

[18] Brisson describes Plotinus as a 'virtuoso' in the use of 'colourful language' (2014: 140), while Slaveva-Griffin notes 'the deep poetic quality of his philosophical prose' (2012: 195–6). In comparable vein, Kalligas declares that 'Plotinus' style at its best can be deemed sublime' (Stern-Gillet 2020b: 111).

> not make his Zeus from any model perceived by the senses, but understood what Zeus would look like if he wanted to make himself visible.
>
> (V 8 [31] 1.38–41; A: V 239–41)

What enables the arts 'to run back to the forming principles' and 'to make up what is defective in things' is the fact that these principles and the beauty and perfection inherent in them are accessible to the soul of the artist without the mediation of the sensible world. Since it is rooted in the Intellect and ultimately in the One, the human soul is able to envisage them directly and to bring them to fruition in the work of art, which thereby acquires the capacity to awaken in the onlooker's soul awareness of these same principles. This Plotinian understanding of aesthetic experience 'gives the work of art a privileged status as the only sensible object deliberately and exclusively made for the soul itself' (Vassilopoulou 2014: 498). Hence art and philosophy are engaged in the same task: to rekindle the soul's primordial memory, to 'polish its mirror' and promote its ascent back towards the One.

As has often been discussed, Plotinus's deliberations on beauty, art and the soul, and their consequent validation of the arts, marked a new departure which proved extraordinarily influential.[19] Corrigan among others traces their impact from Late Antiquity and medieval Christendom via the Renaissance and the Romantic movement up to the American transcendentalism of the 19th century (Corrigan 2005: 202–3). Their relevance also for artistic production in the Muslim world will touched upon below. The common idea, interpreted and acculturated in ever new ways, is that all art 'has a natural anagogical function' (Corrigan 2005: 210) by pointing beyond itself towards 'the forming principles' emanating from the One and bringing them to experiential awareness. From this Plotinian perspective all works of art, including the poems discussed in this volume, may be validly seen as giving voice to the tangible, perceptible 'Faces of the Infinite'.

1.4. The Faces of the Other

There is yet a further, perhaps even more pertinent, aspect to the image of the face. It comes to the fore in the publication which inspired the title of this volume, Kevin Corrigan's reflections on the philosophical ethics of Emmanuel Levinas (d. 1995) and their anticipation by Plotinus and the Platonic tradition. As Corrigan explains, for Levinas an ethical imperative emerges from the face-to-face encounter with the Other. This is because 'the immediate otherness of the human face is not some "thing" to be reduced to the categories of being or systematic thought … the face bespeaks an infinity beyond my control in which I already find myself situated' (Corrigan 2007: 231). For Levinas the encounter with the face of the Other represents 'the very birth of signification beyond being' and brings about a 'responsibility without prior commitment of the "one for the other".' (Corrigan 2007: 231).

[19] For a discussion with particular reference to the Greek tradition see pp. 53–62.

By analogy, Corrigan points out that in *Ennead* VI 7 [38] 14 Plotinus argues that the human face is

> not a lump or single bulk for it has a structure and something articulated in it. What is articulated is the infinite (*to apeiron*), just as in the intelligible world the infinite is not a lump, but a multiple discourse (*logos polus*) which possesses an infinite variety of content, 'not of things confused' but of things distinctly themselves by being related in love (*philia*).
>
> (Corrigan 2007: 233)

For both Levinas and Plotinus there would seem to be, in the words of Corrigan, 'an infinity in every "I" as a primordial origin of its substantial nature' (2007: 226). Seeing the infinite not relegated only to the transcendent but immanent in the very face of the Other is perhaps the most salutary perspective for an enterprise such as this volume which aims to bring into dialogue a multitude of voices from different languages and cultures. For in each of these voices the face of an Other is manifest, each with its 'infinite variety of content' which can only be circumscribed but never exhaustively defined. Recognising the infinite in the 'I' of every voice means recognising therein an aspect of oneself and hence being impelled towards lending it an ear and seeking to cross the divide towards it.

Awareness of, and care for, the Other is not just a theoretical consequence of Plotinian thinking. It has practical consequences, as best illustrated by Plotinus's own example. While the ultimate goal of his aspirations was to leave all earthliness behind and 'escape in solitude to the solitary' (VI 9 [9] 11.51, A: VII 345), he was, in his daily conduct, eminently solicitous about the well-being of others. His integrity was such that many, upon the approach of death, chose him as 'holy and god-like guardian' for their children and their property (Porphyry 1989: 31–3). Altruism is firmly grounded in his philosophical thinking for he saw what he called the 'lower virtues' – namely those pertaining to social interaction – as an inescapable precondition for the attainment of the 'higher virtues' through which the goal of the soul's detachment from earthly concerns is to be attained.[20]

Of particular relevance to our project is that Plotinus's approach to ethics both in his writings and in his personal conduct has been found by some to anticipate modern feminist theory and pedagogy. Not only were there many women among his students, but in his interactive, conversational approach to his teaching, his avoidance of an authoritative, patriarchal stance and his desire to empower his students and encourage their critical thinking he anticipated feminist educational principles (Vassilopoulou 2003: 131–5). His writings are devoid of the disparaging comments about women frequently found among his predecessors, including Plato (Cooper 2007: 85) and his conception of the One 'coincides with feminist conceptions of the divine' in being gender-free and lacking in 'authoritarian and totalising features' (Cooper 2007: 77–8). The implications of this stance for gender

[20] For a survey of the debate over ethics in the philosophy of Plotinus see Stern-Gillet (2014).

relations and the role of women poets in a patriarchal environment are addressed in several chapters in this volume as outlined below.

The convergences between Plotinus's thinking and feminist theory is further evidence of the inclusive nature of his metaphysics. As we have seen, at the root of it is Plotinus's understanding of divinity, for it opens 'a perspective beyond all determinate being that cannot be manipulated into derivative categories or into the divisions of race, religious denomination, fraternity or otherwise' (Corrigan 2005: 231). This gives his legacy an abiding relevance and makes it singularly appropriate for an enterprise which seeks to highlight the interconnectedness of cultural traditions.

2. The Pre-Modern Poems (4th to 17th Centuries)

The transmission history of Neoplatonism is in itself an extraordinary example of multi-lingual interconnectedness operative over centuries between East and West.[21] The following pages aim to introduce the pre-modern poems by situating them in the intricate web of multi-layered currents which led to the acculturation of Neoplatonism by the monotheist religions and its consequent dissemination in new, distinct and yet inter-related forms of spirituality. To give a more complete picture, mention is made of aspects relevant to poetry which could not be covered by contributions to this volume.

We must begin with an issue of cultural politics. It centres on the question of where to situate Plotinian philosophy along the East–West divide. Is it a pure outcrop of the classical Greek tradition and hence to be readily viewed as Occidental or European as some would claim, or does it carry a substantial imprint of Oriental sources? As clarified by Majumdar, the long scholarly debate over this issue 'cannot be isolated from its colonial and postcolonial backdrop' (Majumdar 2012: 213). It arouses potentially controversial associations that may have a bearing on the reception of this volume and therefore have to be addressed. Are we, in using Neoplatonism as a framework for our inquiry, reading Eastern literatures through an inappropriate Occidental lens? Are we thereby implicitly portraying them as somehow derivative from the 'Western tradition'? What does the Plotinian heritage signify in this context?

A brief glance at Plotinus's biography would seem to suggest that he is very much a product of what today would be called the Orient:[22]

> Plotinus was born in Lycopolis, Egypt in 204 or 205 C.E. When he was 28, a growing interest in philosophy led him to the feet of one Ammonius Saccas in Alexandria. After

[21] As Wallis notes, 'a survey of Neoplatonism's influence threatens to become little more than a cultural history of Europe and the Near East down to the Renaissance, and on some points far beyond' (1995: 160).

[22] For a more detailed account of Plotinus's life see Pradeau (2019: 18–26).

> ten or eleven years with this obscure though evidently dominating figure, Plotinus was moved to study Persian and Indian philosophy. In order to do so, he attached himself to the military expedition of Emperor Gordian III to Persia in 243. The expedition was aborted when Gordian was assassinated by his troops. Plotinus thereupon seems to have abandoned his plans, making his way to Rome in 245. There he remained until his death in 270 or 271.
>
> (Gerson 2018)

Did Plotinus's interest in the East leave a mark on his thinking? Scholarship has for long observed an intriguing number of similarities between his writings and classical Indian philosophical and religious texts. Among the more recent studies is Majumdar's (2012) comparison between the *Enneads* and the *Bhagavadgītā* which identified a large number of parallels, including the notion of the supreme principle as One, the approach to ethics and the concept of a 'higher love' bestowed by the divine. Regnier (2012) and Mehta (2017) both observed a remarkable degree of convergence between the *Enneads* and Indian Advaita (non-dualist) philosophy. Adluri strikingly reveals the cultural prejudice at work in the debate over Plotinus's 'Orientalism' (2014: 85) and identifies a text in the *Mahābhārata* which he deems to bear 'the closest resemblance to Plotinian thought' (2014: 77).

Taken together, the parallels observed by these and other comparative studies are such as to preclude a simplistic identification of Plotinus's thought as 'Western'. Though composed in Greek and steeped in the legacy of Plato and Aristotle, his philosophy 'is congenial to many Eastern forms of thought' (Corrigan 2005: 231). What enabled it to be so influential and become a fountainhead of mysticism in the monotheist religions are precisely the features that it shares with Eastern thought: the conception of the human soul as inherently divine and liable to merge, propelled by a higher form of love, with a supreme, non-dualist principle inaccessible to reason in its oneness, but immanent throughout the multiple gradients of existence. For the purpose of this volume, Neoplatonism should be seen as a philosophy not unlike the blessed olive tree whose oil nurtures the light of God in the famous Qur'anic parable: it is 'neither of the East nor of the West' (*lā sharqiyyatin wa lā gharbiyyatin*, 24:35). Using it as a tool for an inter-cultural inquiry should not therefore be viewed per se as in any way prejudicial or 'pro-Occidental.'

2.1. From Late Antiquity to Eastern Christianity and Early Islam

The chapter by David Hernández de la Fuente charts the resonance of Neoplatonism with Greek poetry, from the Delphic hymn in honour of Plotinus, and the Nonnian school of Late Antiquity, to the fall of Byzantium. In doing so, it takes account of the role played by major thinkers who built on Plotinus's work and developed his ideas into a philosophical school, notably Porphyry, Iamblichus (d. 325), Syrianus (d. 437), Proclus (d. 485) and Damascius (d. 550). It is to be noted that all hailed from the Mediterranean's Eastern or Southern shores: Porphyry came from Tyre in what is today Lebanon, Iamblichus and Damascius from Syria, Syrianus from Egypt and Proclus from Lycia in Anatolia. The same applies to the early Christian writers whose adoption of Neoplatonic principles is also in evidence in the verses discussed by Hernández de a Fuente. They include the Cappadocian Fathers Gregory of Nyssa (d. 395) and Gregory of Nazianzus (d. 389), as well as the unknown Syrian author who under the pseudonym Dionysius the Areopagite (5th/6th century) decisively marked mystical theory and practice throughout Christendom.[23] It follows that the origin and early development of Neoplatonism, as well as its earliest rendering in poetic form, are rooted in Eastern territories that were eventually to become part of the Muslim world.

Perhaps the most notable observation that arises from Hernández de la Fuente's survey of over 1,000 years of Greek poetry is the continuity it reveals despite the caesura between paganism and Christianity which saw philosophers persecuted, exiled or suppressed.[24] The underlying theme, which surfaces throughout the poems he cites, is the soul's desire to contemplate, revert to or comprehend a transcendental realm which is described in recognisably Neoplatonic terms. It reflects the substantial degree to which the Church Fathers had applied Plotinian metaphysics to their religious dispensation.[25] Thus the poems of Paul the Silentiary (d. *c.* 526) and John of Gaza (6th century) bear ecstatic witness to the power of art to 'run up to the forming principles' and elevate the soul, while the hymn on the ineffable nature of divinity by Symeon the New Theologian (d. 1022) reads like an accomplished paraphrase of the Plotinian One. A subtle allegorical rendering of Neoplatonic cosmology in Christian garb is to be found in the verses of Michael Psellos (d. 1081) on body, soul and intellect conceived in astral terms. Hernández de la Fuente's discussion comes full circle with the symbolic resurrection of pagan deities in the verses of Gemistus Pletho (d. 1452), the last Byzantine poet-philosopher who also happens to be a vital link in the chain of transmission of Plotinian philosophy to Renaissance Italy and with it to Western Europe.

From the 7th century onwards, the Christian dominions which had produced the Greek-speaking poets gradually diminished in size with the expansion of Islam. By the time of Pletho, practically only Constantinople was left in Byzantine control. Reflecting on the reason why many Christians in the conquered lands abandoned their former creed seemingly without undue coercion, G. Stroumsa surmises that Islam found acceptance because 'the central tenets of the new religion were already incipient in late antique patterns of thought and behaviour' (Stroumsa 2013: 4).

[23] On the seminal influence of this author who is now generally referred to as 'Pseudo-Dionysius' (5th or 6th century CE) see Pelikan (1987), Leclercq (1987), Froehlich (1987), Hankey (2019) and Treiger (2021).

[24] The Alexandrian philosopher Hypatia was killed by a Christian mob in 414 CE (Dzielska 1996, see also pp. 389, 456–60). Justinian closed the School of Athens in 529 CE, whereupon its head Damascius is said to have moved to Persia before settling in Alexandria, though there is no conclusive evidence to prove this.

[25] For sources on this widely researched field see O'Meara (1982), Moran (2014), Dimitrov (2014), Stang (2012: 143–52) and the papers on Neoplatonism in Vinzent (2013) and Pavlos *et al.* (2019).

There had been what he called a *praeparatio islamica*[26] for which he found, in his view, a major and hitherto undervalued, testimony in Patristic literature, as exemplified in its anticipation of the Qur'anic portrayal of Abraham.[27]

This is the same literature whose reliance on Neoplatonic metaphysics left its mark on the Greek poetry illustrated by Hernández de la Fuente. It follows that the *praeparatio islamica* provided, according to Stroumsa, by Patristic literature will have included a substantial Neoplatonic component. The point serves as a reminder that the Qur'an came into being at a time when Neoplatonic thinking had already permeated the intellectual climate of the Levant for centuries. This may help to explain why later Islamic thinkers, and in particular the authors of Sufi compendia, could find in the Qur'an ample evidence to substantiate tenets which in themselves appear closely analogous to Neoplatonic principles. While an in-depth study of this question remains to be undertaken, there is no doubt that, with the advent of Islam, Arabic poetry gradually begins to exhibit an increasing degree of convergence between Qur'anic and seemingly Neoplatonic features. It culminates in the Sufi poets of the 13th century and also holds sway over Islamic mystical poetry composed in a range of languages virtually throughout the Muslim world.[28] In addition, the Classical Arabic critical tradition read the Qur'an as an allegorical source text in Neoplatonic fashion, as noted by Alexander Key in this volume. It follows that Neoplatonism in the context of Islamic culture cannot be discussed without regard to the authoritative role played by the Qur'an.

Taking account of this, Sperl's chapter in this volume approaches the Qur'an from the perspective of the *Enneads* in order to identify parallel themes and concepts which poetry was to draw upon and elaborate. These include the simultaneous transcendence and immanence of the deity, the trajectory of the soul and, most importantly, the Neoplatonic contrast between the sensible and intelligible realms and its Qur'anic equivalent, the mirroring contrast between this world and the Hereafter. The resulting conception of the cosmos as comprising two mirroring components, one material and ephemeral, the other transcendent, abiding and real, would substantially enrich the allusive range of figurative language not only in Arabic but also in Persian and Ottoman poetry. As shown by Walter Andrews, a 'doubleness' came to reign in the poetic realm in which material reality is contextualised in a Neoplatonic hierarchy of being and 'everything stands for something greater'.[29]

[26] The term alludes to the early Christian concept of *praeparatio evangelica* according to which pagan wisdom included elements designed by God to prepare the ground for the revelation of the Gospel. The term is also the title of a book by Eusebius of Caesarea (d. *c.* 340) who argued that Greek philosophy had biblical roots.

[27] Stroumsa (2013: 167–8). On this see also Stroumsa (2015: 189–98) where he introduces the term *praeparatio coranica* in the same context.

[28] From the 10th century onward poetry based on Arabic poetic forms began to be composed in a gradually expanding number of vernacular languages of the Muslim world, from West Africa to South East Asia. For details see Sperl & Shackle (1996), Bauer & Neuwirth (2005) and Neuwirth (2006).

[29] See p. 183. On this point see also Morewedge (1992: 63–4). Chittik (2019) places the double meaning of this type of figurative language into the wider context of Sufi cosmology.

2.2. Neoplatonism and Poetry in the Islamic World (9th to 17th Centuries)

The question whether the Islamic tradition bears the mark of Neoplatonic metaphysics from its very inception is certainly subject to debate. With the appearance of the Arabic adaptations of the *Enneads*, supervised by the first major Islamic philosopher al-Kindī (d. 866), we are on firmer ground. Strangely enough this body of texts, commonly known as *Plotiniana Arabica*, was not credited to Plotinus but to other authors, notably Aristotle who was deemed to have penned the most important of them, the so-called *Theology* which bears his name (Zimmermann 1986; Adamson 2002; 2017; D'Ancona 2017). The *Plotiniana* comprise substantial portions of *Enneads IV–VI* recast in conformity with Aristotelian notions of the prime mover and the Qur'anic concept of God as Creator. The result was an Arabic paraphrase in which 'the God of monotheist theology … was bound to find an unexpected confirmation and anticipation in the philosophical theology of ancient Greece' (D'Ancona 2003: 224).

The impact of the *Plotiniana* on subsequent Islamic intellectual discourse cannot be overstated. Creatively adapted and combined with kindred elements from a range of other sources, they helped to bring about a multifaceted philosophical theology which flourished over centuries from Southern Spain to the Indian subcontinent.[30] Perhaps its most influential exponent was Ibn Sīnā (Avicenna, d. 1037), whose discursive and allegorical writings, allegedly including also the famous *Ode to the Soul*,[31] were instrumental in forging a 'new religious-philosophical-mystical language' (Heath 1992: 182) in which Neoplatonism is thoroughly acculturated.[32] As a result, the latter became, in the words of Carl Ernst, 'a pervasive substratum in the post-Ibn Sīnā philosophical milieu of the Islamicate East' (see pp. 210–11) which is no longer identifiable with the type of Greek philosophy from which the Islamic tradition has repeatedly distanced itself. The thought structures and spiritual outlook of Neoplatonism had been so transformed and merged with the Qur'anic message that far from being alien adjuncts they came to represent the heart of the tradition and dictate an entire way of life. How vibrant the latter remains to this day has been noted by Van Ess with the example of the intellectual circles of modern Iran, though he is at pains to point out that no one there would call it 'Neoplatonic' (2004: 116), an unknown term in the Islamic traditions. An equally seamless and enduring convergence with Neoplatonic principles also characterises the cosmology, theology and devotional practice of the Ismāʿīlī Shīʿa (Walker 2005), the poetic renderings of which could regrettably not be covered in this volume.[33]

[30] For surveys see Fakhry (1997: 38–62), Van Ess (2004), Pessin (2014) and Adamson (2016, see index 'Neoplatonism').

[31] On the *Ode to the Soul* see p. 115 and p. 393.

[32] The acculturation intended here is concisely captured in the transition from 'philosophy' (*falsafa*) to 'Islamic wisdom' (*ḥikma/ḥekmat*) described by Sajjādī and cited by Karimi-Hakkak (see p. 420). On these terms see also Akhtar (2017: 17–18).

[33] Several attempts to secure a paper on Shīʿī and Ismāʿīlī poetry came to no fruition. The editors are all the more grateful to Tahera and Aziz Qutbuddin for agreeing at short notice to contribute a major poem

The appearance of the *Plotiniana* in 9th-century Baghdad not only affected the future direction of intellectual discourse. It also coincided with marked changes in artistic practice which may well have been encouraged by their stance towards the arts. The rise of an abstract, geometrical style has, in particular, been associated with the Neoplatonic notion of geometry as a form of wisdom reflective of the intelligible realm, which was shared by contemporary Muslim thinkers (pp. 110–11). In this context it is worth pointing out that in Late Antiquity and the early Christian period Neoplatonism gave rise to the belief, discussed in the chapter by Hernández de la Fuente, that the intelligible realm could be brought to expression by means of images and cultic statues (pp. 56–8). That Plotinian thought could have served to underpin two completely different types of visual aesthetics, one representational, the other abstract, illustrates the remarkable cross-cultural malleability of its intellectual heritage. What counted on both sides of the divide is that his metaphysics could be seen to grant a credible transcendent function to artistic expression by making it into a gateway to the intelligible realm in either form.

The impact of the *Plotiniana* on the verbal arts in Islamic lands cannot be dissociated from Sufism, whose relationship to Neoplatonism has long been the subject of debate. The two traditions share what D'Ancona called 'one of the most influential topics' of the *Plotiniana*, the 'double journey of the soul' from its origin in the divine sphere to its earthly sojourn in the body and its ascent back to its ancestral home (2017: 24). On account of these and other compelling similarities, Sufism has already, since the 19th century, been associated in part with Neoplatonism (Nicholson 1989: 12–13).[34] Recent studies have thrown more light on the degree to which Neoplatonic metaphysics may have contributed to the elaboration of Sufi theosophy whose beginnings are contemporaneous with the appearance of the *Plotiniana*.[35]

Detailed comparisons between specific aspects of the two traditions have consistently revealed quintessential differences in outlook which rule out any straightforward derivation of one from the other.[36] The examples of Sufi poetry discussed in the pages of this volume serve to confirm this impression. Far from revealing any overt traces of outside influence, the Neoplatonic associations identifiable in these poems are wholly grounded in the Arabo-Islamic tradition: in the Qur'an, in Hadith and in the tropes and structure of a poetic medium which dates back to pre-Islamic

by the Fāṭimid-Ṭayyibī Dāʿī l-Muṭlaq, Sayyidna Taher Saifuddin (1888–1965), to the Online Anthology *Lyrics of Ascent* which accompanies this volume. The introduction and commented translation they have provided serve to illustrate this important branch of Islamic poetry with Neoplatonic associations. For a collection of papers on the Ismāʿīlī poet-philosopher Nāṣir-i Khusraw (d. 1077), with substantial attention given to his Neoplatonism, see Hunsberger (2012).

34 Gnosticism, Christianity and Indian religions have also been adduced as sources of Sufism, while Sufism itself sees its origin in the example of the Prophet Muḥammad. In discounting the essentialist search for single origins of religious phenomena Ernst draws on Wendy Doniger's rather apt image of the banyan tree 'which must have an original root but sends down so many roots from its branches … that one can no longer tell which is the original' (Ernst 2016: 304).

35 For a well documented example see Akhtar's observations on Neoplatonism in the philosophical Sufism of Ibn Masarra (d. 931) (2017: 45–76).

36 For comparisons between Plotinus and al-Ghazālī see Jabre (1956), between Plato, Plotinus and Avicenna see Morewedge (1992), between Plotinus and ʿAṭṭār see Zargar (2017: 237–41), between

times. Sperl's study of a poem by Ibn ʿArabī shows that its pivotal insight into the nature of immanence and transcendence originates in a moment of illumination the poet personally experienced in front of the Kaʿba, while his poetic rendering draws on the qasida, an Arabic poetic form which from its very inception traced a pathway from separation to union and spiritual emancipation (pp. 118–24).

The chapter on classical Persian literature by Kazuyo Murata further confirms the degree to which the Neoplatonic vision constitutes an integral part of the Islamic tradition. Focusing on the concept of beauty, Murata identifies close similarities between the writings of the poet-philosopher Rūzbihān Baqlī (d. 1209), the *Enneads*, as well as their adaptation in the *Plotiniana Arabica*, but finds little evidence of what one might consider 'influence' or direct borrowing. The points they share, such as the soul's pre-eternal encounter with beauty as theophany, Baqlī derives from the Qur'an and Hadith and explicates in a language free of philosophical jargon. Moreover, Murata shows that his ideas are in one respect closer to the *Enneads* than to the corresponding Arabic paraphrase in the *Plotiniana*, which makes it even more difficult to argue for a chain of influence. What we appear to face is a convergence of spiritual orientations expounded by recourse to distinct cultural traditions.

The Ottoman poems in this volume emerge from a cultural environment where the Neoplatonic had been so internalised as to 'dissolve into an emotional script for life', to cite the title of Walter Andrews's chapter. Its medium was a ubiquitous form of homosocial love lyric termed gazel in which the male poet's infatuation with a youth acts as an earthly (and hence inferior) mirror image of the soul's quest for the divine. Andrews illustrates the intricate symbolism and gem-like structure characteristic of the genre with the example of a poem by Ḫayālī (d. 1557). By contrast, he cites a poem by Caʿfer Çelebi (d. 1515) to show how the medium was so dominant that it was resorted to also for messages decidedly at variance with its ethos. Thus Caʿfer Çelebi's verses aim to seduce a real-life female beloved, and in the process subvert and satirise the otherworldly intimations of the genre.

An even more notable counterpoint is found in the verses of the Ottoman poetess Mihrî Hatun (d. *c.* 1512) discussed by Havlioğlu. In asserting a woman's right to independent creative agency in the domains of both poetry and love Mihrî breaks the strictures of the genre. Her poem addressed to her beloved Hâtemî skilfully refashions conventional tropes in order to end by declaring, not without irony,

---

Neoplatonism and al-Ḥallāj see El-Jaishi (2018), between Dionysius and al-Ghazālī see Treiger (2021). Cornell (2019: 179–96) identifies remarkable parallels between the figure of Diotima in Plato's *Symposium* and the mythical portrayal of the early Sufi saint Rābiʿa al-ʿAdawiyya. Slaveva-Griffin's comparison of Plotinus and Rūmī (2012) is particularly insightful. The connection she makes between Plotinus's 'dance of the soul' and the Mevlevi dance inspired by Rūmī illustrates the degree to which the transition from Neoplatonism to Sufism is not a matter of 'influence' and 'borrowing' but rather represents the continuity of a living spiritual tradition in the process of creative transformation and renewal. Seeing the 'circular dance of the soul' as trans-substantiated from the 'ontological expression of substantial number' to a 'spiritual enactment' (Slaveva-Griffin 2012: 211) establishes an evolutionary pattern which may hold true not only of the Mevlevi dance but be applicable also to other forms of religious and artistic expression, including notably Arabic calligraphy (on this see Moustafa & Sperl 2014, II: 586–8).

that she 'loves him better than any boy' would. The resulting lyric remains true to the Neoplatonic ideal of love as the mirror image of a higher order but renders it free from gender stereotypes. Havlioğlu places Mihrî's stance in the wider context of Plotinian thought which is largely gender neutral and by implication allows women an equal share in the dialogue of love. Her observations are relevant also for the other women poets represented in this volume, notably Mihrî's contemporary Vittoria Colonna (d. 1547) and, in a more critical vein, Sor Juana Inés de la Cruz (d. 1695).

Carl Ernst's paper on a poem of mystic ascent by the 17th-century Zoroastrian visionary Āẕar Kayvān brings us to an altogether different and yet familiar echo of the *Plotiniana Arabica* in the Islamicate East. The familiar element is the philosophy of Ibn Sīnā which acts as a prime mediator also here, but it is combined with a range of other specifically Iranian sources: Suhrawardī illuminationism, Zoroastrian lore and evocations of ancient Persian Kingship. Their combination is symptomatic of the increasingly complex amalgam of cultural strands into which the transmission of Neoplatonism found itself woven with the passage of time.

As Ernst's chapter shows, nothing in Āẕar Kayvān's poem indicates that the author saw himself indebted to Greek, or, for that matter, any other non-Iranian sources. On the contrary, his use of a Persian language largely 'cleansed' of Arabic words and his mystical cosmology replete with a hierarchy of Persian style monarchs are clearly intended to establish a distinct Iranian identity, one moreover rooted in the union with God which the author claims to have attained at the pinnacle of his journey. Ernst's chapter ends with describing the reverberations this vision still carries today.

For the purpose of this inquiry Āẕar Kayvān's poem is of special interest because it stands for many comparable attempts at forging religious orthodoxies and supposedly 'authentic' cultural identities whose ingredients reveal themselves upon closer inspection to be heterogenous and diverse. Approaching such works in search of the interconnectedness which the Neoplatonic vision itself entails, reveals the multiplicity of ties which link supposedly autonomous and self-standing cultural constructs to each other. To cite but one example from Āẕar Kayvān's mystical journey, here is the poet having achieved union with God (p. 207):

> There was God and no sign of me
> I had no consciousness, memory or soul.

Read in the light of the Neoplatonic tradition, a line such as this cannot fail to evoke a multitude of echoes, starting with Plotinus's surmise that in the intelligible realm there can be no individual consciousness or memory.[37] The idea has a long afterlife and surfaces once more in the opening lines of Dante's *Paradiso*, as discussed in

[37] *Enn.* IV 4 [28] 1–2, as discussed by Aubry (2014: 313) and Clark (1999: 284–5). Hankey notes 'Plotinus's enormously influential discovery that when the human touches its ultimate ground, it loses all knowledge of itself and can only turn what happens into a describable experience by falling out of union' (Hankey 2019: 497).

D'Ancona's chapter in this volume.[38] Such associations between otherwise entirely different texts bear witness to a continuity and an underlying similarity in their spiritual quests which belie their exclusivity and the validity of the boundaries they seek to erect.

2.3. Jewish Neoplatonism and the Hebrew Poems

With the Jewish tradition we encounter Neoplatonism integrated into another no less complex amalgam of cross-cultural strands. The nucleus of inspiration is once more the Arabic Plotinus adaptation which travelled Westward to North Africa and the Iberian Peninsula where it helped to bring about an extraordinary, interrelated flowering of philosophy and mysticism of both Jewish and Muslim denomination.[39] It began in the 10th century with the first Jewish Neoplatonic philosopher Isaac Israeli (d. 955) and his contemporary, the Muslim philosopher and mystic Ibn Masarra of Cordoba (d. 931). Andalusian Muslim thought would reach its peak of fame and influence in the works of the philosopher Ibn Ṭufayl (d. 1185) and the mystic Ibn ʿArabī (d. 1240). The impact of the Jewish variant would be no less wide ranging. Neoplatonism, mediated by Judeo-Arabic metaphysics and combined with rabbinic and biblical sources, would assume a singularly esoteric guise in the mystical writings of Abraham Abulafia (d. 1291) and Moses de León (d. 1305), founding fathers of the Kabbalah.[40] As for Jewish philosophy of Andalusian provenance, its luminaries ranged from Ibn Gabirol (d. 1057) and Maimonides (d. 1204) to Isaac Abarbanel (d. 1508), the last representative of the medieval school. His son Judah, better known as Leone Ebreo (d. after 1521), recast this ancient heritage into a Neoplatonic philosophy of love which found acclaim throughout Renaissance Europe. We will encounter it again in the chapters on Spanish poetry.

One rather tragic reason why Andalusian Jewish mysticism and philosophy spread far and wide beyond Iberia is the persecution the Jews suffered first under Almohad Muslim and increasingly later under Christian rule. Forced into exile, mystics and philosophers, including Leone Ebreo, brought their learning to places such as Provence, Italy, Sicily and Palestine and further afield to Eastern Europe and Southern Arabia. As a result, Jewish intellectuals found themselves cast into the role of cultural emissaries between the Muslim and the Christian worlds. The chapters by Adena Tanenbaum and

[38] D'Ancona cites the relevant passage in the *Enneads* with references on the topic of memory (see p. 261, n. 25).

[39] For an entertaining and informative survey see Adamson (2016). More detailed coverage on Jewish authors is found in Goodman (1992). Neoplatonism also had a bearing on Christian thought in medieval Iberia, as best exemplified by the works of the influential Catalan poet-philosopher and mystic Ramon Lull (d. 1316, Lull 1985). The remarkable continuity of the Neoplatonic presence in Iberian culture is illustrated in the study of Hispano-Arabic and Spanish Golden Age poetry undertaken by the late Michael Hunter (2018).

[40] For Neoplatonism in the Kabbalah see Scholem (1995) and Idel (1992).

Joachim Yeshaya in this volume portray the remarkable dissemination of one aspect of their heritage, a form of Hebrew synagogue poetry known as *piyyut* whose depiction of the soul carries the imprint of Judeo-Arabic Neoplatonism as it developed in al-Andalus. Here, too, the primacy of Scripture is fundamental and never questioned, as in the other denominational poetry discussed in this volume.

The genesis of Andalusian *piyyut* is the subject of a ground-breaking study by Tanenbaum (2002) which shows how philosophical theory, traditional Jewish devotional practice and the Arabic literary heritage came together in a new form of Hebrew poetic expression of great vitality and depth. The concomitant interaction between Neoplatonism and poetry, which she portrays, was one of the factors which helped to inspire this publication. In her chapter in this volume, Tanenbaum draws on her earlier findings to illustrate the Andalusian *piyyut* tradition with an outstanding early example, Ibn Gabirol's *Keter Malkhut* (*The Royal Crown*), a hymn which traverses the gradients of the cosmos not unlike Āẕar Kayvān's journey but whose ultimate goal is not union with God but 'the sweet fruit of the intellect' in the divine realm (p. 223). In the process the hymn effectively amalgamates Neoplatonic and biblical concepts, such as emanation and creation, and, most notably, that of the soul whose return to its original, heavenly abode carries familiar Plotinian traits.

The Neoplatonic notion of the soul in Jewish attire is central to the *piyyut* tradition as a whole and travels with it as far as Yemen where it features in the poetry of the 16th-century author Zechariah Alḍāhirī who takes centre stage in Tanenbaum's chapter. His satirical and devotional writings, cast in Arabic literary forms, abound in allusions to kabbalistic themes and the by then already centuries old Andalusian tradition. Its lasting resonance and influence also on Karaite (non-rabbinic) Judaism is illustrated in the poems discussed by Joachim Yeshaya which take us from 12th-century Cairo via Constantinople/Istanbul to 17th-century Poland. What makes the Hebrew *piyyut* tradition stand out from virtually all the other poems discussed in this volume is their liturgical function, since they were composed for inclusion in the synagogue service where a number of them remain in use to this day.[41]

2.4. Neoplatonism in the Latin West up to Dante

The *Enneads* were unknown in Western Europe until the Renaissance when Ficino (d. 1499) translated them into Latin. However, their approach to metaphysics had already permeated the region centuries earlier through a range of intermediaries.

[41] The coverage of Jewish poetry in the context of this volume is not complete without a mention of the poetry of Kabbalah which both in term of form and content appears like a bridge between the traditions here represented. It includes poems modelled on Ottoman Sufi verse, such as those by Israel Najara (d. 1625) and the followers of the visionary Sabbatai Tzvi who converted to Islam (d. 1676), and poems modelled on European forms such as the sonnets by Moshe Luzzatto (d. 1746). For an anthology with annotated English translations and original texts by these and other authors see Cole & Dykman (2012).

Three main channels can be distinguished. The first comprises a number of Latin authors of Late Antiquity who became outstanding points of reference in the nascent culture of the Christian West. The most important are St Augustine (d. 430), Martianus Capella (5th century), Macrobius (d. *c.* 400) and Boethius (d. *c.* 526).[42] To what extent they had first-hand knowledge of the writings of Plotinus has been much debated. What appears to be the case is that his ideas reached them by way of Porphyry and, in the case of Boethius, also through Proclus. Special mention must be made of Boethius's *Consolation of Philosophy*, a prosimetrum with outstanding examples of Neoplatonic poetry in Latin, such as the cosmological prayer inspired by Proclus's commentary on Plato's *Timaeus* (Boethius 1999: 66–7, ).

The second channel goes back to just one author, the Irish philosopher John Scotus Eriugena (d. *c.* 877), a contemporary of the Arab philosopher al-Kindī (d. 873) and something of a counterpart to him in the transmission history of Neoplatonism. Just as al-Kindī oversaw the Arabic rendering of the *Enneads* and hence made their ideas available to the Muslim East, so Eriugena made Neoplatonic thought available to the Christian West through his Latin translation of the writings of Pseudo-Dionysius. An original thinker in his own right, Eriugena drew on the Greek Church Fathers and the above-mentioned Latin sources of Late Antiquity 'to create a consistent, systematic Christian Neoplatonism' (Moran & Guiu 2019: 1). Meister Eckhart (d. c. 1328) and Cusanus (d. 1464) were among his readers, but he was ahead of his time and has only been truly appreciated in the modern period.[43]

The third channel consists of Latin versions of Arabic philosophical texts. The great majority were Aristotelian but some had a Neoplatonic dimension which owes its existence to al-Kindī's efforts.[44] The most significant is the *Liber de Causis*, an adaptation of Proclus's *Elements of Theology*. Its Arabic original, entitled *Discourse on the Pure Good* (*Kalām fī Maḥḍ al-Khayr*), emerged from the same intellectual milieu in 9th-century Baghdad as the *Plotiniana Arabica* and reflects their influence (Taylor 1992). Among them are also writings by major philosophers who had worked aspects of the *Plotiniana* into their thinking, including Isaac Israeli (d. 955), al-Fārābī (d. 951), Ibn Sīnā and Ibn Gabirol.

The merging of the first and second channels helped to inspire the philosophical allegories produced by the 12th-century School of Chartres, a high point in the history of Neoplatonic poetry which regrettably could not be covered here. Drawing on the cosmology of Plato's *Timaeus*, the prosimetric diction of Martianus Capella and Boethius, and Dionysian mysticism, these compositions 'serve to crystallize a number of major traditions of twelfth-century thought' (Wetherbee 1972: 6). A prime example is *De mundi universitate* ('On the Totality of the World')

[42] To these must be added a seminal Platonic source, Calcidius's (4th century) partial Latin translation of the *Timaeus* which was the only Platonic dialogue available to the Latin Middle Ages. On this see p. 265.
[43] For a study of Eriugena in the context of other apophatic authors, including Plotinus and Ibn 'Arabī, see Sells (1994).
[44] For a list of Arabic philosophical works translated into Latin before 1600 see Burnett (2005: 391–404). For a survey of the influence of Arabic and Islamic philosophy on the Latin West, see Hasse (2020).

by Bernardus Silvestris (d. 1178), an allegorical creation narrative whose cosmic panorama recalls Āẕar Keyvān's astral journey and Ibn Gabirol's *Royal Crown*. Here, too, Neoplatonism figures as one of a range of sources of heterogeneous origin combined to generate a coherent image of man's place in God's design – an image forged to underpin the dominant ideology to which the poet subscribes.

One of the most celebrated renderings of such a grand vision is the *Divine Comedy* by Dante (d. 1321) which is the subject of D'Ancona's chapter in this volume. It bears the mark of all the above-mentioned channels of transmission, including the Chartres School.[45] D'Ancona's discussion homes in on a subject central to Neoplatonic poetics as a whole, the inadequacy of language and memory to capture the supernal realm. In placing Dante's verses on the topic in the context of his forebears, she unfolds a multiplicity of layers ranging from Macrobius and Thomas Aquinas's Aristotelianism to the literary theory of William of Conches. Common to them all is the realisation that allegory, myth and metaphor are the only, imperfect recourse available to render the experience of the timeless and incorporeal tangible through language. With the possible exception of Macrobius, none of the sources D'Ancona cites would have had first-hand knowledge of Plotinus.[46] Her argument, however, shows how reflections of his thought are discernible throughout, like a light refracted by an interlacing chain of mirrors.

2.5. Renaissance Neoplatonism: The Italian and Spanish Poems

With the advent of the Florentine philosopher Ficino (d. 1499) and his Latin translations of the *Enneads* and their commentators, the Plotinian light, if we may call it that, shone for the first time unmediated over Western Europe. Plato's works had already been widely studied from the time of Petrarch (d. 1374), but Ficino translated these as well. His masterly rendering of them assumed canonical status for centuries thereafter and brought the Platonic tradition into the cultural mainstream.

As demonstrated by Stern-Gillet's chapter in this volume, Ficino excelled not only as a translator but also as a philosopher. He combined the legacy of antiquity, that had reached the Latin Middle Ages earlier, with the newly available Platonic and Plotinian originals and their commentators in order to produce an integrated form of Christian Platonism which would have the widest repercussions on European cultural life, including literature and poetry. Stern-Gillet illustrates Ficino's method with the example of his commentary on Plato's *Symposium* in which these different strands come together to produce an original and yet distinctly Neoplatonic understanding of love and beauty.

[45] For a survey of possible Judeo-Arabic sources in the *Divine Comedy* see Kremers (1990).

[46] Macrobius was in all likelihood acquainted at least with one of Plotinus' treatises, that on suicide, entitled *On Going Out of the Body* (I 9 [16]), in addition to the treatise *On Virtues* (I 2 [19]), which he knew thanks to Porphyry's abridgement (communication by Cristina D'Ancona).

Its impact is evident in the poetic correspondence between Vittoria Colonna (d. 1547) and Michelangelo (d. 1564), discussed in the chapter by Abigail Brundin. Vittoria's gender, however, adds a different dynamic. Rather like her contemporary Mihrî Hatun, she carved out a role for herself as a female poet by altering the inherited gender norms in the poetry she addressed first to her deceased husband and then to the divine beloved. In accord with Plotinus's original vision, the Neoplatonic ideal of love is thereby freed of gender stereotypes and rendered universal.

Ficino's influence also on Spanish poetry comes to the fore in Terence O'Reilly's discussion of the verse epistle which Francisco de Aldana (d. 1578) addressed to his friend Arias Montano. Raised in Florence the poet was closely acquainted with Ficino's writings and in this work forged his ideas into a transformative vision of friendship in Neoplatonic terms. At its heart is the ascent of the two friends' souls through shared contemplation of divine immanence in the beauty of nature. O'Reilly shows how Aldana's verses convert into a lived experience the following maxim by Ficino which encapsulates a core principle of Neoplatonic mysticism, East and West (p. 330):

> Happy indeed are those whom the universe's beauty, that is, the lustre of the good itself, transforms by love into the good itself.

While acknowledging the debt Spanish poetry owes to Ficino, Colin Thompson's chapter in this volume places another major source of Neoplatonic inspiration centre stage, the above-mentioned Judah Abarbanel also known as Leone Ebreo. His seminal *Dialogues of Love* represent perhaps the richest amalgam in the history of Neoplatonism for it marks a point of convergence between two ancient chains of transmission which taken together span the Mediterranean from East to West. One is the Judeo-Arabic philosophy of Andalus wherein we encounter once more the legacy of Ibn Sīnā.[47] The other is the Renaissance Neoplatonism of Florence which derived both its manuscript sources and its philosophical inspiration from Byzantium,[48] where, as detailed in Hernández de la Fuente's chapter, the tradition had been preserved since antiquity. Ebreo's *Dialogues* are therefore truly emblematic of the cross-cultural dynamism of the Neoplatonic legacy. As a 'full-blown aesthetics of Judaism' (Hughes 2012: 12), the work is also a profoundly original expression of the author's religious denomination which illustrates the bridge-making role Jewish intellectuals have so often played in the annals of cultural history.

Thompson's reading of Spanish Golden Age Poetry in the light of Ebreo's *Dialogues* and Plotinus's *Enneads* aims to illustrate what he calls 'the process of accretion' whereby Neoplatonism is reconceived through ever new layers of reinterpretation and acculturation. The guises it can assume are brought to the

[47] Pines (1983) investigates the Judeo-Arabic philosophical sources mentioned in the *Dialogues* and identifies striking parallels between Leone Ebreo's theory of love and Ibn Sīnā's *Risāla fī l-'Ishq* ('Epistle on Love').

[48] Leone Ebreo's reliance on Ficino is documented by Gershenzon (1992) with the example of the circle metaphor, an archetypal Neoplatonic symbol (see pp. 63–4, 68, 77, 122 and 319).

fore through examples including the secular love lyric of Garcilaso de la Vega (d. 1536), the philosophical poetry of Fray Luis de León (d. 1591) and the mystical yearnings of San Juan de la Cruz (d. 1591) and Teresa of Ávila (d. 1582). Though noticeable throughout, the Neoplatonic vision of the soul's transfiguration is thereby shown to serve starkly different ends, ranging from the heavenly consummation of erotic love to full scale Christian adaptation in the mode of Dionysian mysticism.

Taking Ebreo's *Dialogues* and Castiglione's (d. 1529) *Book of the Courtier* as points of departure, Julian Weiss's chapter draws attention to the gender stereotypes which beset the Neoplatonic ideology of love current at the time. Its image of the female beloved, beautiful and ever subservient to guidance by the male's superior intellect, can turn into a patriarchal construct which denies individuality and agency to real women. Weiss shows how the female poets Catalina de Guzmán (d. *c.* 1680) and Sor Inés de la Cruz (d. 1695) were driven to rebel against the manufacture of such fantasy. Their portrait poems unmask the ideal as fictitious, and suggest that the truth, and with it the substance of the Neoplatonic message, resides elsewhere, 'in a universality where man-made gender distinctions do not operate' (p. 348).

With these 17th-century sonnets our survey of the pre-modern poems comes to an end. Versified traces of the Neoplatonic tradition did not vanish thereafter in the languages here represented, but a full historical overview such as that provided for English poetry in the remarkable study by Baldwin & Hutton (1994) would go much beyond the confines of one volume. The selection made covers the most important phases in the dissemination of Neoplatonism and shows that it is a pan-Mediterranean phenomenon whose creative amalgamation with other belief systems has left a significant mark on the classical poetry of the languages concerned. It will be seen in due course that the modern poems represented in this volume draw on these same classical roots and thereby inherit and further transform the Neoplatonic heritage of old.

3. A Neoplatonic Poetics?

Viewing the pre-modern poems side by side within the framework adopted by this volume raises the question whether they share, despite the cultural, linguistic and historical differences that separate them, a recognisable 'Neoplatonic poetics'. Two contributors have given thought to the concept. Aiming to define it with reference to the Greek tradition, Hernández de la Fuente identified three 'leitmotifs' (p. 62) termed gnoseology, metaphysics and aesthetics. Alexander Key's reading of the Classical Arabic critical tradition produced another threesome: the 'core categories' (p. 131) allegory, figure and genre. To what extent are their approaches borne out by the other chapters? And what would be gained by such a concept?

3.1. The Limits of Language

From the chapters collected here, a certain consensus on the nature and function of the poetry which they discuss does indeed appear to emerge. Adena Tanenbaum notes that the verse of the Andalusian Jewish poets 'achieves a spiritual potency that more discursive works would be hard-pressed to match' (p. 220). According to Walter Andrews, poetry in the Ottoman world works to 'transmute philosophy (and theology) into meaningful practice' by 'saying things emotionally rather than intellectually, rationally or logically' (p. 171). Commenting on Āẕar Kayvān's Zoroastrian journey, Carl Ernst declares that its poetic rendering gives 'dramatic testimony of an extraordinary experience' (p. 205) and 'makes possible the rhetoric of intimate address' and 'the hyperbole indicating transcendence' (p. 211).

These and other similar comments highlight the difference between philosophical discourse and its manifestation as poetry. While the former tends by nature to be objective, descriptive and detached, the latter as exemplified here is subjective, experiential and emotional. Therein lies its capacity to convey 'spiritual potency', 'meaningful practice' and 'dramatic testimony'. The practical, experiential expression of philosophical principles is, moreover, singularly appropriate for Neoplatonism because the latter is itself an experiential rather than a purely speculative philosophy. The life of virtuous conduct it advocates aims at leading the mind to an encounter with the ineffable which transcends the scope of discursive language.

The inability of language to convey the substance of the experience is one of the most frequently attested themes in our poems. The Byzantine Simeon the Theologian (d. 1022) describes it thus (p. 80):

> My intellect sees what has happened
> It can see and wishes to explain
> But can find no word that suffices
> For what it sees is invisible and entirely formless ...

The Persian Rūzbihān Baqlī (d. 1209) portrays the onlooker's resulting stupefaction in a striking image (p. 154):

> O far removed from understanding, estimation and imagination,
> speaking in description of You is impossible.
> In Your Beauty the intellect is mad,
> in Your Majesty the spirit is a moth.

As though drawing the consequence from the above the Italian Vittoria Colonna (d. 1547) admits her failure to do justice to the vision (p. 299):

> Thus I inscribe upon these pages a dark shadow
> to represent the dazzling sun, and I speak to others here
> of heavenly things with broken and inadequate words.

Though emerging from different doctrinal and cultural contexts the above verses have this in common: they ascertain the veracity of an intellectual tenet, not by describing it, but by expressing the emotional consequences of experiencing it.

Presented in this form it invites the reader to empathise and make the testimony his own. Such passages are also found in the *Enneads*,[49] but they are the exception whereas in poetry the transmutation of intellectual principles into lived experience is the rule.

3.2. Allegory and Metaphysics

The encounter with transcendence leaves the poet lost for words. By contrast, the contemplation of divine immanence opens the floodgates of speech and deepens the semantic range of every utterance. For divine immanence is ubiquitous in the Neoplatonic universe, and the poet's task consists in decoding it. Not what is seen is poetry's subject matter, but the unseen hidden beneath; not sensible reality, but what gradient it occupies in the chain of being through which the soul can ascend to its highest goal, a likeness unto God.

Paradoxically, seeking the One throughout existence thus multiplies the semantic charge of every existent. It will both signify itself and point beyond itself to a higher reality of which it is but a transitory reflection. Thus Ficino declares that 'the sun can signify to you God himself in the highest degree' (p. 331). It follows that everything here is an image, a metaphor, an allegory, with multiple reverberations all along the hierarchical chain. This applies not only to nature, but also to language, to the meaning of words, to the inherited tropes of literary convention and to religious scripture. The consequences for the poetic medium cannot be overstated. A world of metaphors is best conveyed by metaphors, with the added proviso that the images they convey are not to be read as imaginary but as more real than that which they stand for.

A certain number of images or themes listed in the index of this volume occur in, or imply the existence of, binary pairings. Among the most common are darkness and light, memory and forgetfulness, goodness and evil, purification and defilement reality and its mirror image. These are universal concepts, but their specific significance resides in the multi-layered cosmological hierarchy which their usage here implies. Read in the corresponding metaphysical framework, each one of them conjures up a range of worldly and otherworldly associations which invite comparative exploration.

The poems illustrate how this analogical habit of seeing comes to fruition in cultural contexts ranging from Golden Age Spain to the Ottoman world. Terence O'Reilly's chapter dwells in some detail on the role of metaphor in revealing 'the hidden connection' between the levels of being in Aldana's poem for Arias Montano (p. 331). As the two friends contemplate the seashells along the shore, they face 'not just the beauty of the corporeal realm but the wonders of the spiritual realm that it signals' (p. 332). The same phenomenon is at the root of what Walter Andrews

[49] None more than *Enn.* IV 8 [6] 1 which describes Plotinus's personal experience of ascent (see n. 15 above).

calls the 'confluence between rhetorical doubleness and cosmic doubleness' which prevails not only in Ottoman but also in classical Persian poetry and often confounds attempts 'to categorize it as, for example, religious or secular, sincere or conventional' (p. 175, n. 9). The onset of this style in 9th-century Arabic poetry is discussed by Sperl who traces it back to the Qur'an. It is, however, to an equal extent a natural consequence of Neoplatonic metaphysics in whatever denomination it may surface. Alexander Key's core category 'allegory' and David Hernández's leitmotif 'metaphysics' converge herein as hallmarks of Neoplatonic poetics.

To decipher the signs of creation and understand their multiple layers of meaning requires an act of introspection which the poems often portray by drawing on the distinction between soul and intellect. Hovering between the sensible and intelligible realms, the soul requires the perspicacity of the intellect in order to know in which direction to turn and how to ascend to higher spheres. The theme surfaces in most of the languages here covered and carries unmistakable Plotinian echoes. Some poems lay more stress on the intellect's limitations: it can point the way but is incapacitated by the ultimate reality, as we have seen. In others it appears in its characteristic role as superior force and guide to the soul.[50]

In the Sufi and Renaissance poems two forces encountered in our discussion of the *Enneads* take centre stage and rank above all others in their potential to impel the soul's ascent: beauty and love. Like all existents, they are endowed with a panoply of meanings, and accordingly assume a range of mirroring guises: corporeal and incorporeal, erotic and spiritualised, human and divine. The diversity is only apparent, for it derives from the equations central to the Platonic and the Neoplatonic vision: all beauty in truth is theophany, and all love in truth is love of God. In her primordial existence, the soul has acquired a trace of divine beauty and hence been roused to divine love. While here on earth, she guards a hidden memory of this sublime spark which makes her receptive to earthly beauty and earthly love. Her task is to perceive the divine archetype underneath the earthly manifestations, rediscover her 'true self'[51] in the trace of divinity which she possesses and so ascend back to her otherworldly home.

This set of ideas is central to the thematic inventory of Neoplatonic poetics. Its acculturation by the intellectual traditions of Christianity, Islam and Judaism is touched upon by several chapters in this volume. Suzanne Stern-Gillet and Abigail Brundin exemplify its Christianisation in Renaissance Italy. Leone Ebreo's Jewish variant is discussed by Colin Thompson with the example of the Spanish poets. Its prominence in the Islamic tradition is evident in all the chapters on Classical Arabic, Persian and Turkish poetry. The result is in each case a distinct amalgam of images and ideas rooted in the respective literary, socio-political and religious traditions and argued in the first instance on the authority of scripture rather than philosophical discourse. Its poetic renderings are therefore anything but similar. What the poems here discussed nevertheless share is the transmutation of the underlying set

[50] See 'intellect' in Index.

[51] See note 13.

of ideas into testimonies of a unitary experience aspired to as the highest goal and celebrated in analogous terms.

To give an example we may compare the images with which San Juan de la Cruz (d. 1591) and Ḫayālī (d. 1557) seal the attainment of union in the poems discussed by Colin Thompson and Walter Andrews. As if to confirm that his love is divine, 'unmixed by any creaturely affection at all' (p. 318), San Juan ends his work by conjuring up the biblical symbolism of the lily which conveys purity and resurrection:

> ... all ended, fell away,
> My every care consigned
> Among the lilies, out of sight and mind.[52]

The Ottoman poet also invokes scripture, for the end of his poem resonates with a Qur'anic verse which invites the 'tranquil-minded soul' to return to God, 'well pleased and well pleasing' (Qur'an 89:27, p. 178):

> Become king, Ḫayālī, of the land of tranquil-mindedness ...

By aspiring to the kingship of that realm Ḫayālī not only sets the seal on his return but implicitly declares that his 'every thought, every action manifests the will of God' (p. 178). The images of the two poems thus conjure up associations that are culture-specific and worlds apart, but serve to convey strikingly similar experiences of god-likeness and heavenly tranquillity. The outward trappings differ, but the emotional substance, the unmediated human experience, would seem to be indistinguishable and no different from the state Plotinus describes in passages such as the following:

> ... there was ... no desire for anything else when he made the ascent ... he was as if carried away or possessed by a god, in a quiet solitude and state of calm, not turning away anywhere in his being and not busy about himself, altogether at rest and having become a kind of rest.
>
> (VI 9 [9] 11.10–16; A: VII 343)

What the philosopher here outlines as an observer in descriptive prose, the poet enunciates as a participant by casting it into images governed by the pattern of poetic form. Unlike prose, poetry has the merit of integrating the multiple components of the experience into a concise, rhythmically cadenced unit which enhances the emotional charge.

3.3. Poetic Form

For Plotinus, the unifying role of form is absolutely crucial because it replicates the formative power emanating from the One and hence engenders beauty, which 'rests upon the material thing when it has been brought into a unity' (I 6 [1] 2.22–3, A: I 239). In seeking to define Neoplatonic poetics, the question how poetic form acts

[52] Colin Thompson's translation ([illegible]).

to 'transmute philosophy' into a unitary experience would therefore seem to be all the more pertinent. The issue also underscores the centrality of genre and figure, the 'core categories' identified by Key, which both pertain to literary form.

Since the poems assembled here exhibit a range of different poetic forms and rhetorical styles, a detailed comparative discussion to give the issue the attention it deserves would go beyond the bounds of this chapter.[53] As examples, two genres, both well represented here and almost diametrically opposed in their formal features, shall suffice: the Italian and Spanish sonnet, and the Arabic qasida/ghazal form which is also found in the Ottoman and Hebrew poems. The former has a varied rhyme scheme and a fixed length of 14 lines, while the latter has a fixed mono-rhyme and is of varied length. The aesthetic expectations the two forms arouse and the sense of unity they generate are therefore entirely different and certainly invite comparative research.

The Neoplatonic credentials of the two genres are examined more closely in the chapters by Julian Weiss and Stefan Sperl respectively. In the Spanish sonnets he discusses, Weiss perceives a stage for multiple voices in dialogue thanks to a 'poetics of difference' which he likens to 'Neoplatonism itself' (p. 340) for it recalls the polysemy which Plotinian thinking necessarily entails. The dialogic process serves to construct 'a subjectivity that unfolds through the verbal and syntactic patterns of the poem itself' (p. 340). The unitary experience it conveys is the fruit of thinking 'between polarities' (p. 345) and beyond boundaries, notably those of gender, and thus conducive to the search for a greater, transcendental One.

Sperl perceives in the Arabic poetic form which goes back to pre-Islamic times 'a dialectic between the one and the many' (p. 97) which predisposes it remarkably well to give expression to a Neoplatonic vision. One of its cardinal manifestations, the polythematic ode termed qasida, moreover charts the path of psychic growth in a manner which was to make it readily adaptable to convey the mystical ascent of the soul.

Of particular importance for the Arabic, and by extension also the Hebrew, Persian and Turkish traditions is the prevalence of rhetorical patterning which began with the rise of a new, ornate style in the 9th century. Sperl terms it 'geometrisation by rhetoric' (p. 113) and links it to a Neoplatonic aesthetics which favours symmetrical patterns in the visual, aural and verbal arts as tangible reflections of the beauty of the intelligible realm. The tendency towards an enhanced use of figurative language, including complex images and refined onomatopoeic effects, is pronounced

[53] In the wider context of Neoplatonic poetics mention must be made of an important poetic form not represented here, the versified allegorical narrative on the soul's quest for its divine origin. Among its earliest examples is the so-called 'Hymn of the Pearl' first attested in Syriac and then translated into Arabic, Turkish, Persian and Urdu (Ernst 2016: 320–53). Of relevance here is also the narrative of Ḥayy ibn Yaqẓān as versified in Hebrew by Abraham ibn Ezra (d. 1164) under the title Ḥay ben Meqitz (Hughes 2004). The most prominent representatives of the genre are to be found among the Persian romances of Niẓāmī (d. 1209), ʿAṭṭār (d. 1221) and Jāmī (d. 1492).

also in the Spanish and Italian poems. The overall effect, which can test language to its limits, brings to mind Sarah Pessin's caveat (2014: 542):

> that in their engagement with the very essence of being, all Neoplatonists dance with language, giving voice to a range of creative and difficult metaphors and conjuring up a range of creative and difficult imageries.

As stressed above, it would be inappropriate to label all the poets who figure in this volume 'Neoplatonist'. What they do share, however, is an aesthetic which seeks to convey the infinite through the finitude of form and hence bring the transcendental into the realm of lived experience. Though concerned with painting rather than poetry, Erwin Panowsky's verdict on the Neoplatonic dimension of mannerist style would therefore seem to be remarkably appropriate for our topic, to the extent that it encapsulates a principle of Neoplatonic poetics (Panowsky 1968: 95):

> Thus the beautiful in art no longer results from mere synthesis of a scattered yet somehow 'given' multiplicity but from the intellectual grasp of an *eidos* [idea] that cannot be found in reality at all.[54]

3.4. Gnoseology and Devotional Practice

In transmuting philosophical truth into lived experience the poet demonstrates knowledge of that truth, a point which brings us to gnoseology which Hernández de la Fuente identifies as one of the leitmotifs of Neoplatonic poetics. His treatment shows the Greek poet of Late Antiquity as inspired with divine knowledge by the Muses. He has, from a Neoplatonic perspective, participated in the One and by casting his experience into poetic form enables others to participate in turn. He can therefore claim the status of guide and model to be followed on the path to ascent.

The status of the poet as dispenser of knowledge and spiritual guide in the Neoplatonic quest appears repeatedly, with the proviso that the poet himself or herself may be in need of yet superior guidance. The chain of being in the Neoplatonic universe is matched by the chain of guides. Thus we find the poet and artist Michelangelo inspired and guided by the poetry of his muse Vittoria Colonna. Dante in Paradise is guided by Beatrice, and Fray Luis submits to the heavenly music of Salinas as his guide. Sufi poets such as Ibn al-Fāriḍ and Ibn ʿArabī chart the way heavenwards in emulation of their guiding spirit, the Prophet Muḥammad. In the Ottoman context the ethos of poetry in the mystic vein pervades wider society to the extent of becoming, in the words of Walter Andrews, 'an emotional script for life'.

Hernández de la Fuente's leitmotifs, gnoseology and metaphysics, converge in one final hallmark of Neoplatonic poetics. In embodying knowledge of transcendent

[54] In this context it is of some interest to note that the theory of poetry, which the English Renaissance author Sir Philip Sidney (d. 1586) developed under the influence of Ficino's Florentine Neoplatonism, 'in many ways … resembles the Mannerist theory of painting' (Sidney 2002: 140). As though in anticipation of Panowsky's verdict, Sidney thus affirms that 'the skill of the artificer standeth in that *Idea* [*sic*] or fore-conceit of the work, and not in the work itself. And that the poet has that *Idea* is manifest, by delivering them forth in such excellency as he had imagined them' (Sidney 2002: 85). We are grateful to John Roe for this reference.

truth and directing the internal gaze to otherworldly shores, the poetry to which it gives rise frequently forms part of devotional practice. Hernández shows that Neoplatonic verse in Late Antiquity, including Proclus's hymns, was intended for use in theurgic ceremonies. The Byzantine texts he cites are likewise cast in the form of hymns and prayers which would have been recited in ceremonial settings. The performative aspect is just as relevant for the Hebrew poetry here discussed since it came to be integrated into Jewish liturgical practice from Andalusia to Yemen. Often the texts are set to music, like Vittoria Colonna's sonnets which became a source for spiritual madrigals. Echoes of ancient theurgical practice live on in the musical renderings of Sufi poetry widely performed to this day by mystic brotherhoods. A compendium of texts currently used for musical recitation by the Shādhiliyya order,[55] which includes works by poets discussed in this volume, explains the significance of the poetry as follows:

> The purpose of qasidas in the Sufi path is to convey the experiential gnosis of the forebears to subsequent generations ... A qasida first comes as an experience from Allah, which the poet afterwards tries to clothe in words ... For experience is that which apprehends the objective truth: here the ultimately and abidingly Real. (Styer 2014: ix)

There could hardly be a clearer endorsement of the experiential dimension of what we term 'Neoplatonic poetics'. Yet Alexander Key rightly reminds us that this concept does 'not really exist outside this collected volume' (p. 131), nor would the author of the above citation be inclined to think that the poetry he introduces owes much to Greek philosophy. So what is the purpose of the concept, and does it have any antecedents in the critical literatures of the time?

3.5. Critical Precedents

A number of past critical approaches of relevance to the authors discussed in this volume deserve consideration. They agree on one or more of the following three tenets: that a certain kind of poetry exists which is the fruit of divine inspiration; that it is able to convey transcendental truths in symbolic or allegorical form; and that its formal features reflect the macrocosmic order. As shown in the chapter by Hernández de la Fuente, all three were adopted by Proclus who fused Platonic and Plotinian thought to produce what may well be deemed to be the first example of a Neoplatonic poetics. The idea of poetry as allegorical representation of metaphysical truths prevailed in the Christian Middle Ages, as D'Ancona exemplifies here with the example of Dante. In the Renaissance, it received a detailed elaboration by Leone Ebreo who set out to prove that poetic allegory is 'a necessary vehicle for the conservation of the truth' and lists a host of reasons, including to keep the message from the unworthy.[56] His contemporary

[55] The Shādhiliyya, which goes back to 13th-century Morocco, is an active and influential Sufi order with numerous subgroups and global representation.

[56] Pescatori in Ebreo (2009: 74). In this context mention should also be made of San Juan de la Cruz's interpretations of his own mystic poetry illustrated here by Colin Thompson (pp. 315–16).

Ficino was moved to assert on the authority of Plato that divinely inspired poets imitate celestial harmony even more effectively than musicians by rendering 'a sense of its inner reason into verse, feet and numbers' (Ficino 1975: 46). He thereby stresses the merit of poetic form as productive of the musical cadence and sense of order which reflect the harmony of the higher realm.[57]

As for the Islamic tradition, Alexander Key's chapter shows that the bulk of Classical Arabic criticism stayed clear of Neoplatonic notions which were reserved for the Qur'an as sole text deemed to be of divine origin.[58] Two exceptions deserve to be mentioned, however. One is the Andalusian poet Ibn Shuhayd (d. 1035), whose *Treatise on Poetry* draws on no less than the *Theology of Aristotle* to define beauty as a divine emanation which the inspired poet can bring to expression in the linguistic fabric of verse.[59] The other is the great Ibn 'Arabī, who upholds all three of the above-mentioned tenets in his characteristically profound musings on poetry.[60] Like Ficino, he considers prosody reflective of the cosmos for 'God made existence like a verse of poetry in its structure and order' (McAuley 2012: 44); like Leone Ebreo he deems poetry to be an act of encoding the truth 'in veils of symbols and riddles' to shield it from prying eyes (McAuley 2012: 46); and like Proclus, he deems poets of stature, including himself, to be recipients of divine inspiration.

These parallels and connections show that ideas conforming to Neoplatonism at various times found their way into critical approaches throughout the greater Mediterranean. The resulting conceptions of artistic and poetic creativity thus form an important culture specific backdrop to the poetry discussed in this volume and lend themselves to collation and comparative study in the wider framework of a Neoplatonic poetics such as that tentatively developed here.

Reassessing the past is not the only justification for elaborating such a concept. More important is the question to what extent it may enrich our understanding of the cultural and artistic concerns of the present. With this in mind we now turn to the modern authors represented in the chapters of this volume.

[57] For Ficino's notion of poetic inspiration in the wider context of the Platonic tradition, see Stern-Gillet (2012) and, with particular reference to his above cited letter on divine frenzy, see Zintzen (2009). For his influence on the theory of poetry see above, n. 51.

[58] The Qur'an condemns the poets as misguided and misleading, except for 'those who believe, do good and remember God' (26: 227, see also p. 100). Schmid (2017: 84–91) sees a parallel between the Qur'anic and the Platonic reservations vis-à-vis poetry and situates them in the wider context of the debate over the status of poetry in Late Antiquity; she surmises, moreover, that 'Platonic thought might actually have reached the Qur'anic milieu' via John Chrysostom (d. 407). Her arguement would seem to corroborate Stroumsa's notion of Patristic literature as *praeparatio islamica*.

[59] Monroe concludes that Ibn Shuhayd 'harmonized Neoplatonic metaphysics with the Islamic doctrine of *i'jāz* [the inimitability of the Qur'an] to produce a true aesthetics and thus account for the beauty and the creative process in poetry' (Monroe 1973: 141). Of particular interest is the attention Ibn Shuhayd gives to the role of alliteration in the experience of beauty (Monroe 1973: 143). On poetic inspiration in the Arabic and Persian tradition see also Bürgel (1999).

[60] For a detailed discussion see McAuley (2012: 32–58).

4. The Modern Poems

A Persian poem by Bījan Elāhī cited here by Karimi-Hakkak begins as follows (p. 423):

> What's up? The death of a lonely world
> Its mind dormant, its beloved gone.
> Soul of all souls, where to? Beyond where?

Read in the Neoplatonic framework outlined above, these lines have a familiar ring. The 'beloved', the 'mind' of the world and the 'soul of all souls' cannot fail to evoke the Plotinian hypostases: the One, the Universal Intellect and the Universal Soul. But the message is cataclysmic. The intellect has ceased to operate, the soul has nowhere to ascend to, the divine beloved has vanished. There is no 'beyond', no transcendental realm. The chain of being has been severed, leaving loneliness and death in its wake.

These lines do not stand alone. They are emblematic of the sense of rupture found in the works of all the modern poets here discussed. Whether they bemoan the irretrievable passing of the old order as Elāhī does, or whether they seek to revive it or substitute it, as others do, all bear witness to an existential trauma of some kind. The faith in cosmic harmony no longer holds and a sense of alienation prevails, often exacerbated by the poets' confrontation with a socio-political order perceived to be flawed and, in some cases, deeply unjust. The result is a quest for refuge in new identities composed of salvaged and revalued fragments of tradition. Recognisable among them are elements of what we termed above 'Neoplatonic poetics'.

In the following we will briefly introduce the seven chapters on modern poetry by focusing on the different guises assumed by the sense of rupture in the poems they discuss. In each case, this topic is indivisible from the other key question we will touch upon: in what form did the Neoplatonic tradition of the past reach the modern writers? We will conclude with reflections on what these poems can tell us about Neoplatonism and the formation of identity in our time. The survey will take the form of a Mediterranean language tour, starting with Italian, then circling anti-clockwise via Spanish, Arabic, Persian and Turkish to end with the time-honoured Plotinian medium, Greek, now in its modern form.

In Peter Robinson's chapter on the Italian poet Eugenio Montale (d. 1981) the rupture with the past is exemplified in the poet's verdict on Dante: the coherence of the old bard's vision is no longer realisable in modern verse, and his 'era is definitively over' (p. 359). The transcendental realm has receded and is furtively tangible only as 'a flaw in Nature, the dead point of the world' (p. 362). We nevertheless encounter Montale engaging in a Dantesque experience of his own. His beloved, the Jewish scholar Irma Brandeis, is sublimated in his poetry into Clizia, a Beatrice-like figure of otherworldly intimation. The cause is another rupture: the rise of fascism and antisemitism which forces the couple to separate. Perhaps the most striking example cited by Robinson is the poem Montale wrote on the occasion of Hitler's visit to Florence. It opposes the 'hellish messenger' and his 'hooked crosses' to Clizia as emblem of eternal love. Her appearance at the end of the work recalls the ascent of the soul and its union with the One, though presented as Christian self-sacrifice (p. 356):

> Look once again
> high above, Clizia, it's your fate, you
> who, changed, the unchanged love preserves,
> until the blind sun you bear in you
> is dazzled in the Other and destroyed
> in Him, for everyone.

Robinson sees the Neoplatonic echo in poems such as these as a form of spiritual resistance against the barbarism of the time and so perhaps equivocal and not altogether real. He shows, however, that art conceived in this manner 'may go into the lived lives of others' (p. 367), such as the young poet Vittorio Sereni whom Montale's work helped to withstand the fascist trauma.

Fascism also overshadowed the life of the Spanish poet José Ángel Valente (d. 2000), who was forced into exile where he championed a cosmopolitan sense of identity radically at variance with the narrow nationalist ethos he had left behind. As Claudio Rodríguez's chapter shows, Valente developed a mystical syncretism which drew on many sources including Neoplatonism which he encountered not only as mediated by the Judeo-Arabic heritage of al-Andalus but also by way of first-hand acquaintance with the *Enneads*. However, he introduced a striking innovation. No longer is the union of lovers an inferior image of celestial union as Plotinus had declared; by means of poetry, corporeal union is itself rendered celestial, hence loves sacred and profane merge into one (p. 380–2). The result is what Rodríguez aptly calls an 'eroticism of the infinite' in which the female partner is experienced as quasi divine. The following verse, evocative of the archetypal role of circularity in Neoplatonic imagery,[61] transforms the experience into the cosmic scale (p. 381):

> Around the solar female the universe still continues to turn darkly

If pre-modern Neoplatonic poetics transformed the transcendental from a philosophical maxim into a lived experience, Valente does the opposite: a lived experience, carnal love, is transcendentalised through the alchemy of poetic expression. We shall see presently that he is not alone in this. Other modern poets represented here have similarly aimed to use their medium in order to render the sensible world into the sole repository of a divine realm that has vanished.

Among the forces Valente strove against was not only fascism but also the intolerant orthodoxy of established religions. We encounter the same adversary in Robin Ostle's chapter on the Arabic poets of the Americas, where it appears in the form of the Maronite Church as castigated by Khalīl Jibrān (d. 1931). Its oppressive stance adds to the picture of dislocation and trauma which afflicted Lebanon after the First World War and forced countless numbers to seek their fortune abroad.

[61] 'Soul runs round God and embraces him lovingly and keeps round him as far as it can; for all things depend on him; since it cannot go to him, it goes round him' (*Enn.* II 2 [14] 2.12–15, A: II 47). On circularity, see n. 48.

Faced with the social ills in their homeland, the exiled poets found solace in the Neoplatonic concept of the soul as a pure, divine substance temporarily imprisoned in a vale of tears. Ostle shows how the idea reached them through two quite different sources: the above-mentioned *Ode to the Soul* attributed to Ibn Sīnā's which so inspired Khalīl Jibrān, and Mikhail Lermontov's exquisite miniature *The Angel* which expresses the same idea and left a lasting mark on Mikhāʾīl Nuʿayma (d. 1988), as exemplified in the following verses (p. 398):

> My soul! You are a melody whose echo sounds within me
> Played by an artist's hands who is hidden, unseen.
> You are wind, breeze, wave, sea,
> Lightning, thunder, night, dawn.
> You are divine emanation.

The ecstatic address to the soul recalls more ancient examples such as the following by Joseph ben Samuel (d. 1700) cited in Joachim Yeshaya's chapter on the Karaite poets (p. 247):

> Blessed be you, O Jewish soul,
> who imagines a faith of wisdom;
> For your image is in the heaven,
> the first light, the head of the words of the Lord …

What distinguishes Nuʿayma's lines from those above is the ensoulment of the forces of nature they invoke. It recalls the stance of French and English Romanticism which Ostle cites as another notable source of inspiration for this group of poets. Herein we encounter Neoplatonism and its vision of an ensouled cosmos again, for the Romantic movement re-invigorates it, as frequently discussed and exemplified in works such as Wordsworth's 'Immortality Ode' (Price 1994). Seeing Arab poets in the Americas drawing on this ancient heritage in such varied forms of mediation illustrates how complex and far-reaching its pervasiveness is.

Nature also becomes the vehicle for a spiritual quest in the work of the Egyptian poet Muḥammad ʿAfīfi Maṭar (d. 2010) discussed by Ferial Ghazoul, though the message conveyed is surrealist rather than romantic. It bears the mark of a dual trauma. The first stems from the collapse of traditional certainties, detectable more generally in Arabic poetry from the 1940s onwards, and most tangibly expressed in the abandonment of the poetic form which had held sway for over a thousand years.[62] Still largely maintained by the Mahjar poets discussed by Ostle, it came to be replaced by free verse in the work of Maṭar and his generation. Speaking in the vein of Ficino and Ibn ʿArabī, we might say that, without faith in cosmic harmony, the inherited 'structure and order' of poetry had lost its *raison d'être*.[63]

[62] On the form of classical Arabic poetry see pp. 97–9.

[63] Significantly the first free verse poem in Arabic, *Al-Kūlīrā* by the Iraqi poetess Nāzik al-Malāʾika, depicts the death and despair brought about by a cholera epidemic. The disease can be said to stand for the cultural and political malaise that had seized the Arab world at the time. For details see Jayyusi (1977, II: 557–60).

The second trauma is more immediate, namely Egypt's humiliating defeat in the 1967 war and, with it, the disappointed hopes of the Nasser era. Maṭar's response to this was the poem *Recitation*, a dream vision of the ascent of the soul steeped in Qur'anic echoes and evocative of the Prophet Muḥammad's heavenly journey. Ghazoul shows that it was equally inspired by Plotinus whose work Maṭar knew well for he had studied philosophy under ʿAbd al-Raḥmān Badawī, the editor of the *Plotiniana Arabica*. The poem traces his ascent from the remote Egyptian village of his birth to a supernal vantage point. At the height of his vision, 'in the lodge of ultimate certitude', Maṭar sees himself in illustrious company (pp. 414–15):

> The Oriental Sages, the Hermetists and Gnostics partake of the banquet of luminous dialogue.
> Al-Suhrawardi breathes in the fullness of space, divides bread and the silvery fish of the Nile.

The imaginary conversation with Hermetists and Gnostics embodies Maṭar's attachment to a Greco-Egyptian sense of cultural identity at variance with the narrow nationalism of the Nasser era, while Suhrawardī's liberality signals the poet's allegiance to the Sufi tradition. But the poet's sublime encounter cannot endure. As Plotinus states in the report of his own *anagoge*, the soul's heavenly ascent must come to an end, and she must return to her bodily confines. For Maṭar, this means a bitter descent to the ruptures of the present, 'to the murmur of vermin, the clinging of insects, the slither of reptiles' (p. 416). In a characteristic Neoplatonic echo, it terminates with 'memory draining from the water'.

We encounter a similarly dismal view of earthly reality in Forugh Farrokhzad's *Only the Voice Remains* discussed in Ahmad Karimi-Hakkak's chapter on modern Persian poetry. The trauma tangible here is a woman's experience of social confinement and sexual predation. In response, Farrokhzad urges herself to rise above 'the spawning ground for petrifying vermin' (p. 428) and ascend to higher climes in a spiritual journey reminiscent, like Maṭar's poem, of the Prophetic paradigm. Unlike it, however, her poem is largely free of traditional Islamic associations and elevated instead by a vision which seems lifted straight from the *Enneads* (p. 429):

> The end of all forces is union, union
> with the sun's luminous essence
> flowing into the intellect of light.

Yet there are no grounds for a direct association. As Karimi-Hakkak makes clear, the prime referent of the modern works he discusses is not Greek philosophy but the gnostic and mystical heritage of classical Persian poetry which had long ago acculturated Neoplatonism beyond recognition. It is in Plotinus as refashioned by Rūmī that Farrokhzad finds momentary refuge from her plight.

The engagement with the classical heritage across the chasms of modernity, secularism and nationalism is equally prominent in the other writers cited by Karimi-Hakkak. For Bījan Elāhī it takes the form of outright mourning over a world for ever lost, as in the excerpt cited at the beginning of this section. Sepehri's poem is cast in the form of prayer, like earlier examples of Neoplatonic poetics, but in making nature his sanctum he 'points to a metaphysical space beyond all organised religion and faith-based practice' (p. 426), in a manner reminiscent of the devotional stances adopted by Valente and Montale. Kiarostami's haiku-like vignettes reveal 'the structure of the ineffable' (p. 431) in the most ordinary of natural phenomena and appear to give voice to a secular mysticism found also in modern Turkish poetry, the next stage in our Mediterranean tour.

As clarified in the chapter by Neslihan Demirkol and Mehmet Kalpaklı, nowhere is the rupture between modernity and tradition more dramatic than in Turkey. Conceived in deliberate opposition to its Ottoman past, modern Turkish statehood brought in its wake a 'cataclysmic discontinuity' in all fields of cultural expression, including poetry. The authors show how some poets have nevertheless sought to engage with the spiritual mode of Ottoman verse such as that exemplified here by Andrews and Havlioğlu. Responses range from perfunctory gestures to the past and attempts to recruit it for modernist Islam to casting it into the moulds of non-denominational mysticism or profane spirituality. Common to them all is the search for a coherent sense of selfhood able to bridge, heal or transcend an historical severance experienced as deeply troubling.

In the process, Demirkol and Kalpaklı show how poets draw on the multiple associations of time-honoured images to give expression to a dislocated state of consciousness. A poignant example is the following verse by Hilmi Yavuz (b. 1936) where we encounter once more the classic Neoplatonic mirror metaphor. Unlike before though, there is no higher realm for it to reflect (p. 444):

> my identity has died, i renounced my name long before
> alas, now i am my mirrors and nothing more …

The orphaned self is all that remains and in this very manner reasserts itself 'in a new poetic universe' (p. 444). The most striking example of such internalisation is the poetry of Birhan Keskin (b. 1963), in whose verses the Neoplatonic ideal – the ineffable One that is unknowable and beyond all grasp and which, as Dante and Āẕar Kayvān declare, no memory can contain – morphs into the human psyche experiencing itself as total negativity (p. 450):

> I met with absolute desolation
> I was the absolute detachment from memory.
> I'm nothing, me
> pass on.

The human element effaces the divine also in much of the modern Greek poetry cited in the chapter by David Ricks, though the perspective is quite different. Instead of seeking to humanise the infinite, the focus is on what Ricks pointedly calls 'the faces of the finite: the flawed individuals drawn into contact with the current of Neoplatonism', both historical and imagined (p. 467). Among the latter is an unnamed pupil of Plotinus's revered teacher, the Alexandrian philosopher Ammonius Saccas, who appears in a world-weary satire by Cavafy (p. 461):

> He spent two years as a student of Ammonius Saccas
> but philosophy became a bore and so did Saccas. [64]

The lofty aspirations of the Neoplatonic vision could hardly be more effectively cut down to size. But the failure of its ideals to carry conviction in the modern age is not the only form of rupture to be found in the Greek poems. More ancient and of greater consequence is the fact that the Christian Orthodox identity of Greece has for long been 'founded on a confrontation with Platonism', as Ricks observes (p. 454).[65] As an example to bridge the divide, he cites an epic by Kostis Palamas (d. 1943) which acknowledges Proclus as philosopher and poet but shows him having to witness his Goddess Athena banished by the Virgin Mary.

Generally, Ricks finds in modern Greek poetry little inclination to engage with the substance of Neoplatonism, whether as transmitted by the philosophical texts or as mediated by the long tradition of Byzantine poetry adduced by Hernández de la Fuente. Its prime intellectual referents are elsewhere, unlike the modern poetry in Arabic, Persian and Turkish here discussed which draws on a classical tradition imbued with the 'neoplatonising' spirituality of Sufism. In this respect it is somewhat ironic that the sole poem cited by Ricks, which seeks to probe the mystery of transcendence, figures as its protagonist not a Greek philosopher but Ibn ʿArabī. Composed by Lorenzatos (d. 2004), it subtly seeks to reconcile Greek Orthodoxy and Sufism. The Neoplatonic backdrop is unmistakable.

If we cast our glance back over the seven chapters on modern poetry a number of similarities come into view. In all of them we find a distancing from, a repudiation of or, indeed, a flight from, totalitarianism of every kind, whether in the form of fascism, chauvinism, religious intolerance or social stricture. Thinking of Cavafy's above-cited poem, we might even add philosophy to this list, for it, too, can become constrictive and hence turn into 'a bore'. Instead, an alternative sense of identity is sought after, which is individualist, heterogeneous, syncretistic, pluralist and, most importantly, open-ended and receptive to the infinite, even if experienced as 'the death of a lonely world'. For nothingness is as limitless as utter plenitude.

Why these similarities? There was no prior agenda to specify the types of texts to be selected by the contributors. The only criterion was that the poems of their choice should be deemed to engage with the Neoplatonic tradition in the widest sense

[64] Cavafy's imaginary student should not be confused with Plotinus who spent 11 years at the feet of his master.

[65] Thus Saint Gregory Palamas, one of the luminaries of the Greek orthodox school of mysticism known as hesychasm, never ceases to inveigh against the 'love of vain philosophy' and 'the false wisdom of the Hellenists' (Palamas 2002: 25–47). This is all the more remarkable considering the fact that hesychasm is steeped in the legacy of Dionysius the Areopagite (Rossi 2002) and hence, by extension, Proclus, Plotinus and Plato.

of the term. Yet a distinct political stance with important bearings on identity formation is clearly in evidence. Its 'anti-dogmatic trait' brings to mind Beierwaltes's above-cited observation on the language of Neoplatonic philosophy, which would seem to apply in equal measure also to the modern poetry here discussed. What does this say about 'Neoplatonic poetics'? A tentative answer to this question will bring our introductory remarks to a close.

5. The Birth of Love

'When it comes to "Neoplatonism", the only critic who reads the genre across all contexts is us' (p. 145). In reaching this conclusion about our endeavour, Alexander Key reminds us that Neoplatonic poetics is in the first instance the outcome of a certain act of reading. To explain it in a musical image, we can compare the Neoplatonic framework to the soundboard of a piano the size of the Mediterranean, and the different poems in their geographical and historical spread to a panoply of strings strung within the instrument, with separate strings for each word and each image. As in a real piano, each string that is struck will cause numerous others to vibrate, from bass to treble, more or less loudly, subject to their harmonic relationship. In the same way, each poem that is read can be found to relate to others in ways that we have attempted to summarise under the heading 'Neoplatonic poetics'. We have only identified the most salient features, for the range of relationships is unquantifiable. Read within such a soundboard, key words such as 'mirror' or 'memory' will arouse millenary associations and encourage us to 'dance' in or out of tune with the languages of Neoplatonism.

The objective of the approach is not to claim that all these relationships are directly attributable to the philosophy of Plotinus and its legacy. Transmission and cross-fertilisation have certainly taken place, as outlined above, but the tracing of influence has not been our prime concern. Nor is it of relevance to what extent the poets were aware of these relationships when composing their works. In a soundboard of such unaccustomed size, harmonies arise that have not been heard before. We perceive them only with hindsight, and herein lies our objective: by showing how tenets broadly identifiable as Neoplatonic have, over a long period of time, come to expression in poetic language, we hope this publication will help to elucidate a shared dimension in the formation of cultural identities in this large region. And if comparable patterns arise, what can they tell us about the struggle over identity which is unfolding around us at the present time?

Perhaps the single most important Neoplatonic tenet is the belief that the individual human being has the capacity to emancipate him or herself to the highest rank by engaging in a loving union with the ineffable. As conceived by Plotinus, the experience is open to everyone and does not depend on social hierarchies or the mediation of priestly institutions; it is therefore inherently resistant to collective regimentation. The individual's subjectivity is given free rein to conceive the inconceivable and infinite, subject only to the ability to purify and elevate the soul.[66] Once acculturated by monotheist religions, that tenet became part of closed systems of orthodox devotional practice and is encountered in this form in the pre-modern poems here discussed. However, it never lost its individualistic flavour and gives expression to types of spirituality on the margins of doctrinal rectitude, if they do not transcend it altogether. A pursuit of the infinite cannot but break all boundaries, for in this realm none can prevail. It is therefore not surprising that adepts of this path, including poets such as al-Ḥallāj and San Juan de la Cruz, have been subject to condemnation and persecution in all the creeds here represented. The trend continues with the violent repression of Sufism seen today in different parts of the Muslim world.

In the modern poems, the transcendent realm as conceived in the past recedes, leaving nostalgia and a void behind. What remains unchanged is love and, with it, the need for, if not the perception of, the infinite. These are universal human traits and not in themselves Neoplatonic, but in our geographical region the modern poets encounter them via traditions infused with Neoplatonism and draw on its legacy to give new forms to the inherently formless. No longer coterminous with the God of established religion, the infinite now assumes a range of guises: the 'lemons' of Montale, the 'solar female' of Valente, the 'luminous dialogue' of Maṭar, the 'sycamore leaf' of Kiarostami and even the 'absolute desolation' of Keskin. Transcendence as such has vanished but its omnipresent immanence is strikingly reaffirmed.

Concomitant with this are the two features we have noticed in the modern authors and their works: a rejection of totalitarianism of any kind and an openness to the other. The homogeneity which totalitarianism seeks to impose – whether in statehood, creed or social order – is deadening in its exclusion of the other. From a Plotinian perspective it is fatally flawed because it seeks to appropriate oneness for itself by constricting it to its own image. For Plotinus, oneness is only borrowed from the absolute One, which is in itself ineffable and boundless. Everything participates in oneness but no one owns it. Any attempt to impose it in absolute terms speaks of ignorance and is doomed to failure. By contrast, any search for it must be open to all voices on that quest, whether near or far. Here is the root of the propensity of Neoplatonic thought to go beyond the strictures of race, religion and gender and to grant ensoulment also to nature, for it, too, participates in the ineffable. In the modern poems, this inclusive vision is not only undiminished, it even outshines the pain of realising that we might only be our 'own mirrors and nothing more'. It shows that the Neoplatonic spirit lives on in a new guise and points the way to a sense of human selfhood which is by its very nature inclusive, dynamic and commensurate with a rapidly changing, pluralist world.

The continuity between the old and the new is perhaps best encapsulated by juxtaposing a Plotinian metaphor with the same image in modern guise. In *Ennead*

[66] Stern-Gillet (2020a: 74–5) notes that 'unlike Plato, Plotinus held ἀνάμνεσις [recollection of the soul's divine origin] to be a capability present in all human souls, although not to the same extent or at the same depth'.

V 3 [49], one of his last works, Plotinus is at pains to prove that beyond Intellect, self-sufficiency and existence there must be the One, as the ineffable presence to which the soul aspires. As the long argument draws to its close, he realises that he has not achieved his goal and exclaims:

> Is that enough? Can we end the discussion by saying this? No, my soul is still in even stronger labour. Perhaps she is now at the point where she must bring forth, having reached the fulness of her birth-pangs in her eager longing for the One. But we must sing another charm for her, if we can find one anywhere to allay her pangs.
> (V 3 [49] 17.15–19; A: V 133)

In the following he reveals the reason for his failure: the One as object of longing can never be described in discursive terms but only experienced. It is the moment when lover and beloved, seer and the seen, fuse into one. As Plotinus puts it, the soul then 'sees by the light which is also its means of seeing'. In longing for this instant, the loving soul is as though pregnant with her own beloved, and in giving birth she gives life to her own sublimated self. For those we love become part of us. There is no us without them.

To convey the experience of such a moment, philosophy must turn into a charm to be sung for the soul in labour. The appeal to the magic of music in this image recalls the anagogical function of art in Plotinian thought and hence also of the poems discussed in this volume. Irrespective of the creed, time or place from which they stem, and irrespective of the different languages in which they were composed, the most striking impression they leave when read together in succession is that of an overwhelming longing for a unitary experience. Love and the hope for, or joy in, fulfilment pulsate throughout these verses. In 'flowing into the lives of others' the experience they convey is passed on and engenders it in turn.

Plotinus's passage must be read against the background of the harmonious, all-encompassing cosmology of the *Enneads* with its hierarchical levels ranging from the intelligible to the sensible world. In the modern poems, the assurance given by an ordered cosmic framework recedes and, with it, faith in the reality of a transcendental counterpart. The resulting discomfiture is palpable in the following verses by Birhan Keskin. Consciousness is now the sole source of being, of meaning and of love. Yet the individual creative act remains unchanged (p. 448):

> I gave birth to you…
> from my inner spring, my bitter flow
> I gave birth to you, for a dream
> from a season on loan

References

Adamson, P. (2002), *The Arabic Plotinus: A Philosophical Study of the 'Theology of Aristotle'* (London, Duckworth).

Adamson, P. (2016), *Philosophy in the Islamic World* (Oxford, Oxford University Press).

Adamson, P. (2017), 'The Theology of Aristotle', in E.N. Zalta (ed.), *The Stanford Encyclopedia of Philosophy* (Summer 2017 Edition), accessed 3 October 2020, https://plato.stanford.edu/archives/sum2017/entries/theology-aristotle/

Adamson, P. & Taylor, R.C. (eds) (2005), *The Cambridge Companion to Arabic Philosophy* (Cambridge, Cambridge University Press).

Adluri, V. (2014), 'Plotinus and the Orient: *Aoristos Dias*', in Remes & Slaveva-Griffin (2014), 77–99.

Akhtar, A.H. (2017), *Philosophers, Sufis and Caliphs: Politics and Authority from Cordoba to Cairo and Baghdad* (Cambridge, Cambridge University Press).

Aubry, G. (2014), 'Metaphysics of Soul and Self in Plotinus', in Remes & Slaveva Griffin (2014), 310–22.

Baldwin, A. & Hutton, S. (eds) (1994), *Platonism and the English Imagination* (Cambridge, Cambridge University Press).

Bauer, T. & Neuwirth, A. (eds) (2005), *Ghazal as World Literature I: Transformations of a Literary Genre* (Würzburg, Ergon).

Beierwaltes, W. (1981), 'Image and Counterimage? Reflections on Neoplatonic Thought with Respect to its Place Today', in H.J. Blumenthal & R.A. Markus (eds), *Neoplatonism and Early Christian Thought: Essays in Honour of A.H. Armstrong* (London, Variorum Publications), 236–48.

Boethius (1999), *The Consolation of Philosophy*, trans. V. Watts (London, Penguin Classics).

Brisson, L. (2014), 'Plotinus' Style and Argument', in Remes & Slaveva Griffin (2014), 126–43.

Bürgel, J.C. (1999), 'The Poet and his Demon', in A. Neuwirth (ed.), *Myths, Historical Archetypes and Symbolic Figures in Arabic Literature: Towards a New Hermeneutic Approach; Proceedings of the International Symposium in Beirut, June 25th – June 30th, 1996* (Beirut, Franz Steiner Verlag).

Burnett, C. (2005), 'Arabic into Latin', in Adamson & Taylor (2005), 370–404.

Bussanich, J. (1999), 'Plotinus's Metaphysics of the One', in Gerson (1999), 38–65.

Chittik, W. (2019), 'Jāmī on Divine Love and the Image of Wine', accessed 21 September 2020, https://ibnarabisociety.org/jami-on-divine-love-and-the-image-of-wine-william-chittick/

Clark, S.R.L. (1999), 'Body and Soul', in Gerson (1999), 275–91.

Cole, P. (trans.) & Dykman, A. (ed.) (2012), *The Poetry of the Kabbalah, Mystical Verse from the Jewish Tradition* (New Haven, Yale University Press).

Cooper, E.J. (2007), 'Escapism or Engagement? Plotinus and Feminism', *Journal of Feminist Studies in Religion*, 23.1: 73–93.

Cornell, R.E. (2019), *Rabi'a from Narrative to Myth: The Many Faces of Islam's Most Famous Woman Saint Rabi'a al-'Adawiyya* (London, One World Academic).

Corrigan, K. (2005), *Reading Plotinus: A Practical Introduction to Neoplatonism* (West Lafayette, Purdue University Press).

Corrigan, K. (2007), 'The Face of the Other: A Comparison between the Thought of Emmanuel Levinas, Plato and Plotinus', in K. Corrigan (ed.), *Platonism Ancient, Modern and Postmodern* (Brill, Leiden), 219–35.

Corrigan, K., Turner, J.D. & Wakefield, P. (eds) (2012), *Religion and Philosophy in the Platonic and Neoplatonic Traditions: From Antiquity to the Early Modern Period* (Sankt Augustin, Academia).

D'Ancona, C. (2003), 'The *Timaeus'* Model for Creation and Providence: An Example of Continuity and Adaptation in Early Arabic Philosophical Literature', in G.J. Reydams-Schils (ed.), *Plato's Timaeus as Cultural Icon* (Notre Dame, University of Notre Dame Press), 206–37.

D'Ancona, C. (2012), 'Plotin', in R. Goulet (ed.), *Dictionnaire des Philosophes Antiques, Volume 2* (Paris, Editions du CNRS), 817–1000.

D'Ancona, C. (2017), 'The *Theology* attributed to Aristotle', in K. El-Rouayheb & S. Schmidtke (eds), *The Oxford Handbook of Islamic Philosophy* (Oxford, Oxford University Press), 8–19.

Dimitrov, D.Y. (2014), 'Neoplatonism and Christianity in the East: Philosophical and Theological Challenges for Bishops', in Remes & Slaveva-Griffin (2014), 525–40.

Dzielska, M. (1996), *Hypatia of Alexandria*, trans. F. Lyra (Cambridge MA/London, Harvard University Press).

Ebreo, L. (2009), *Dialogues of Love*, trans. C. Damian and R. Pescatori, Introduction R. Pescatori (Toronto, University of Toronto Press).

El-Jaishi, S. (2018), *Early Philosophical Sufism: The Neoplatonic Thought of Ḥusayn Ibn Manṣūr al-Ḥallāj* (Piscataway, Georgias Press).

Ernst, C. (2016), *Refractions of Islam in India, Situating Sufism and Yoga* (Los Angeles/New Delhi, Sage Yoda Press).

Fakhry, M. (1997), *Islamic Philosophy, Theology and Mysticism: A Short Introduction* (Oxford, Oneworld Publications).

Ficino, M. (1975), *The Letters of Marsilio Ficino, Volume I*, Preface P.O. Kristeller (London, Shepheard-Walwyn).

Froelich, K. (1987), 'Pseudo-Dionysius and the Reformation of the Sixteenth Century', in Pseudo-Dionysius (1987), 33–46.

Gatti, M.L. (1999), 'The Platonic Tradition', in Gerson (1999), 10–37.

Gershenzon, S. (1992), 'The Circle Metaphor in Leone Ebreo's "Dialoghi d'Amore"', *Daat: A Journal of Jewish Philosophy & Kabbalah*, 29: 5–17.

Gerson, L. (ed.) (1999), *The Cambridge Companion to Plotinus* (Cambridge, Cambridge University Press).

Gerson, L. (2018), 'Plotinus', in E. Zalta (ed.), *The Stanford Encyclopedia of Philosophy* (Fall 2018 Edition), accessed 5 January 2020, https://plato.stanford.edu/archives/fall2018/entries/plotinus/

Goodman, L.E. (1992), *Neoplatonism and Jewish Thought* (Albany, New York University Press).

Hankey, W. (2019), 'Denys and later Platonic Traditions', in L. Ayres, T.L. Humphries Jr. & M.A. Volpe (eds), *The Oxford Handbook of Catholic Theology* (Oxford, Oxford University Press), 496–510.

Hasse, D.N. (2020), 'Influence of Arabic and Islamic Philosophy on the Latin West', in E. Zalta (ed.), *The Stanford Encyclopedia of Philosophy* (Spring 2020 Edition), accessed 3 October 2020, https://plato.stanford.edu/archives/spr2020/entries/arabic-islamic-influence/

Heath, P. (1992), *Allegory and Philosophy in Avicenna (Ibn Sīnā)* (Philadelphia, University of Pennsylvania Press).

Hughes, A. (2004), *The Texture of the Divine: Imagination in Medieval Islamic and Jewish Thought* (Bloomington/Indianapolis, Indiana University Press).

Hughes, A. (2012), 'Judah Abrabanel', in E. Zalta (ed.), *The Stanford Encyclopedia of Philosophy* (Fall 2018 Edition), accessed 6 October 2020, https://plato.stanford.edu/archives/fall2018/entries/abrabanel/

Hunsberger, A.C. (ed.) (2012), *Pearls of Persia: The Philosophical Poetry of Nāṣir-i Khrusraw* (London/New York, I.B. Tauris).

Hunter, M.L. (2018), *A Poetic of Analogy in the Works of Poets from the Iberian Peninsula* (unpublished Ph.D. thesis, SOAS).

Idel, M. (1992), 'Jewish Kabbalah and Platonism in the Middle Ages and the Renaissance', in Goodman (1992), 319–51.

Jabre, F. (1956), 'L'Extase de Plotin et le Fanā' de Ghazali', *Studia Islamica*, 6: 101–24.

Jayyusi, S.K. (1977), *Trends and Movements in Modern Arabic Poetry*, 2 vols (Leiden, Brill).

Kremers, D. (1990), 'Islamische Einflüsse auf Dantes "Göttliche Komödie"', in W. Heinrichs (ed.), *Orientalisches Mittelalter* (Wiesbaden, Aula Verlag), 202–15.

Leclercq, J. (1987), 'Influence and noninfluence of Dionysius in the Western Middle Ages', in Pseudo-Dionysius (1987), 25–32.

Lewisohn, L. (2015), 'Sufism's Religion of Love, from Rābiʿa to Ibn ʿArabī', in L. Ridgeon (ed.), *The Cambridge Companion to Sufism* (Cambridge, Cambridge University Press), 150–80.

Lovejoy, A.O. (1960), *The Great Chain of Being: A Study of the History of an Idea* (New York, Harper & Brothers).

Lull, R. (1985), *Doctor Illuminatus, A Ramon Lull Reader*, ed. & trans. A. Bonner (Princeton, Princeton University Press).

McAuley, D.E. (2012), *Ibn ʿArabī's Mystical Poetics* (Oxford, Oxford University Press).

Majumdar, D. (2012), 'The Enneads of Plotinus and the Bhagavadgītā: Harmony amidst Differences', in Corrigan *et al.* (2012), 213–34.

Mallette, K. (2013), 'Boustrophedon: Towards a Literary Theory of the Mediterranean', in S.C. Akbari & K. Malletta (eds), *A Sea of Languages: Rethinking the Arabic Role in Medieval Literary History* (Toronto, University of Toronto Press), 254–66.

Mehta, B. (2017), 'Self-Knowledge as Non-Dual Awareness: A Comparative Study of Plotinus and Indian Advaita Philosophy', *The International Journal of the Platonic Tradition*, 11.2: 117–47.

Monroe, J.T. (1973), 'Hispano-Arabic Poetry During the Caliphate of Cordoba, Theory and Practice', in G.E. von Grunebaum (ed.), *Arabic Poetry, Theory and Development* (Wiesbaden, Harrasowitz), 125–53.

Moran, D. & Guiu, A. (2019), 'John Scottus Eriugena', in E.N. Zalta (ed.), *The Stanford Encyclopedia of Philosophy* (Winter 2019 Edition), accessed 3 October 2020, https://plato.stanford.edu/archives/win2019/entries/scottus-eriugena/

Morewedge, P. (1992), 'The Neoplatonic Structure of Some Islamic Mystical Doctrines', in P. Morewedge (ed.), *Neoplatonism and Islamic Thought* (New York, New York University Press), 51–75.

Moustafa, M. & Sperl, S. (2014), *The Cosmic Script, Sacred Geometry and the Science of Arabic Penmanship*, 2 vols (London, Thames & Hudson).

Neuwirth, A. (ed.) (2006), *Ghazal as World Literature II: From a Literary Genre to a Great Tradition, the Ottoman Gazel in Context* (Würzburg, Ergon).

Nicholson, R.A. (1989), *The Mystics of Islam* (London, Arkana).

O'Meara, D.J. (ed.) (1982), *Neoplatonism and Christian Thought* (Albany, University of New York Press).

Palamas, G. (2002), *Holy Hesychia, The Stillness that Knows God: In Defense of the Holy Hesychasts, Book One*, trans. & commentary R. Amis (Southover, Pleroma Publishing).

Panowsky, E. (1968), *Idea: A Concept in Art Theory*, trans. J.S.J. Speake (New York, Harper & Row).

Pelikan, J. (1987), 'The Odyssey of Dionysian Spirituality', in Pseudo-Dionysius (1987), 11–24.

Pessin, S. (2014), 'Islamic and Jewish Neoplatonisms', in Remes & Slaveva-Griffin (2014), 541–58.

Pines, S. (1983), 'Medieval Doctrines in Renaissance Garb? Some Jewish and Arab Source of Leone Ebreo's Doctrines', in B.D. Cooperman (ed.), *Jewish Thought in the Sixteenth Century* (Cambridge MA/London, Harvard University Press).

Plotinus (1966–89), *Porphyry on Plotinus, Enneads I – VI*, trans. A.H. Armstrong, 7 vols (Cambridge MA/London, Harvard University Press).

Plotinus (1991), *The Enneads*, trans. S. MacKenna, abridged & introduced by J.M. Dillon (London, Penguin Books).

Plotinus (2018), *The Enneads*, ed. L.P. Gerson, trans. G. Boys-Stones, J.M. Dillon, L.P. Gerson, R.A.H. King, A. Smith & J. Wilberding (Cambridge, Cambridge University Press).

Porphyry (1989), 'On the Life of Plotinus and the Order of his Books', in Plotinus (1966–89), vol. 1, 2–87.

Pradeau, J-F. (2019), *Plotin: qui es-tu?* (Paris, Les éditions du Cerf).

Pratt, M.L. (1995), 'Comparative Literature and Global Citizenship', in C. Bernheimer (ed.), *Comparative Literature in the Age of Multiculturalism* (Baltimore/London, Johns Hopkins University Press), 68–73.

Price, A.W. (1994), 'Wordsworth's *Ode on the Intimations of Immortality*', in Baldwin & Hutton (1994), 217–28.

Pseudo-Dionysius (1987), *The Complete Works*, trans. C. Luibheid (New York, Paulist Press).

Regnier, D. (2012), 'The Simple Soul: Plotinus and Śaṅkara on Self and Soul as Partless', in Corrigan *et al.* (2012), 257–76.

Remes, P. & Slaveva-Griffin, S. (eds) (2014), *The Routledge Handbook of Neoplatonism* (London/New York, Routledge).

Rossi, V. (2002), 'Presence, Participation, Performance: The Remembrance of God in the Early Hesychast Fathers', in J.S. Cutsinger (ed.), *Paths to the Heart: Sufism and the Christian East* (Bloomington, World Wisdom), 64–111.

Schmid, N.K. (2017), *The Word Innermost: Late Antique Ascetic Knowledge and its Poetics in the Qur'an and Kharijite Thought* (doctoral dissertation, Department of History and Cultural Studies, Freie Universität Berlin).

Scholem, G. (1995), *Major Trends in Jewish Mysticism* (New York, Schocken Books).

Sells, M. (1994), *Mystical Languages of Unsaying* (Chicago, University of Chicago Press).

Sheppard, A. (1994), 'Plato and the Neoplatonists', in Baldwin & Hutton (1994), 3–18.

Sidney, P. (2002), *An Apology for Poetry or The Defence of Poesy*, ed. G. Shepherd & R.W. Maslen (Manchester/New York, Manchester University Press).

Slaveva-Griffin, S. (2012), 'Contemplative Ascent and Dance in Plotinus and Rūmī', in Corrigan *et al.* (2012), 195–212.

Sperl, S. & Shackle, C. (eds) (1996), *Qasida Poetry in Islamic Asia and Africa*, 2 vols, *I. Classical Traditions and Modern Meanings, II. Eulogy's Bounty, Meaning's Abundance: An Anthology* (Leiden, Brill).

Stang, C.M. (2012), *Apophasis and Pseudonymity in Dionysius the Areopagite: 'No Longer I'* (Oxford, Oxford University Press).

Stern-Gillet, S. (2012), 'Divine Inspiration Transformed: From Hesiod to Ficino', in Corrigan *et al.* (2012), 1–18.

Stern-Gillet, S. (2014), 'Plotinus on Metaphysics and Morality', in Remes & Slaveva-Griffin (2014), 369–420.

Stern-Gillet, S. (2020a), 'Interview with Professor Paul Kalligas', *The International Journal of the Platonic Tradition*, 14.1: 109–14.

Stern-Gillet, S. (2020b), 'Beauty and Recollection: From the Phaedrus to the Enneads', in S. Delcomminette, M.-A. Gavray & P. d'Hoine (eds), *The Reception of Plato's Phaedrus from Antiquity to the Renaissance* (Berlin/Boston, De Gruyter), 61–87.

Stroumsa, G.G. (2013), 'Athens, Jerusalem and Mecca: The Patristic Crucible of Abrahamic Religions', *Studia Patristica* 62.10: 153–68.

Stroumsa, G.G. (2015), *The Making of the Abrahamic Religions in Late Antiquity* (Oxford, Oxford University Press).

Styer, M. (ed.) (2014), *Songs of Presence, Qasidas of the Shadhili Path* (Istanbul, Ihsan Press).

Tanenbaum, A. (2002), *The Contemplative Soul: Hebrew Poetry and Philosophical Theory in Medieval Spain* (Leiden, Brill).

Taylor, R.C. (1992), 'A Critical Analysis of the Structure of the *Kalām fī mahd al-khair (Liber de causis)*', in P. Morewedge (ed.), *Neoplatonism and Islamic Thought* (New York, New York University Press), 11–40.

Treiger, A. (2021), 'From Dionysius to al-Ġazālī: Patristic Influences on Arabic Neoplatonism' [Pre-publication version of an article forthcoming in *Intellectual History of the Islamicate World* 8.2/3 (2021)], accessed 9 September 2021, www.academia.edu/42075837/From_Dionysius_to_al_%C4%A0az%C4%81l%C4%AB_Patristic_Influences_on_Arabic_Neoplatonism?email_work_card=view-paper

Van Ess, J. (2004), 'Arabischer Neuplatonismus und islamische Theologie – Eine Skizze', in R.G. Khoury & J. Halfwassen (eds) with F. Musall, *Platonismus im Orient und Okzident: Neuplatonische Denkstrukturen im Judentum, Christentum und Islam* (Heidelberg, Universitätsverlag Winter), 103–17.

Vassilopoulou, P. (2003), 'From a Feminist Perspective: Plotinus on Teaching and Learning Philosophy', *Women: A Cultural Review*, 14.2: 130–43.

Vassilopoulou, P. (2014), 'Plotinus' Aesthetics: In Defence of the Life-like', in Remes & Slaveva-Griffin (2014), 484–501.

Vinzent, M. (2013), 'Neoplatonism and Patristics, Papers presented at the Sixteenth International Conference on Patristic Studies held in Oxford 2011', *Studia Patristica*, 68.6.

Walker, P.E. (2005), 'The Ismāʿīlīs', in Adamson & Taylor (2005), 72–91.

Wallis, R.T. (1995), *Neoplatonism*, Foreword L.P. Gerson (London, Duckworth).

Wetherbee, W. (1972), *Platonism and Poetry in the Twelfth Century: The Literary Influence of the School of Chartres* (Princeton, Princeton University Press).

Zargar, C.A. (2017), *The Polished Mirror: Storytelling and the Pursuit of Virtue in Islamic Philosophy and Sufism* (London, Oneworld).

Zimmermann, F.W. (1986), 'The Origins of the So-called *Theology of Aristotle*', in J. Kraye, W. Ryan & C. Schmitt (eds), *Pseudo-Aristotle in the Middle Ages* (London, Warburg Institute), 110–240.

Zintzen, C. (2009), 'Ficino über die Inspiration des Dichters', in M.C. Leitgeb, S. Toussaint & H. Bannert (eds), *Platon, Plotin und Marsilio Ficino: Studien zu den Vorläufern und zur Rezeption des Florentiner Neuplatonismus: internationales Symposium in Wien, 25.-27. Oktober 2007* (Wien, Verlag der Österreichischen Akademie der Wissenschaften), 189–203.

Part I

From Paganism and Eastern Christianity to the Islamic World (4th to 17th Centuries CE)

1

Neoplatonism and Poetics in Ancient Greek and Byzantine Literature

DAVID HERNÁNDEZ DE LA FUENTE

1. From Aesthetics to Poetics

THE AESTHETIC IMPLICATIONS stemming from the so-called Neoplatonic School played a very important role in Greek poetry from the 4th and 5th centuries onwards. Plotinus (3rd century), generally regarded as the 'founder' of Neoplatonism, opened up the way for superseding the classical canons by considering art as a mimesis in direct contact with the world of ideas. Art was capable not only of reflecting Unity, but also of giving us a preliminary taste of the very contemplation of the One. Plotinus thought that imitation, beyond Platonic mimesis, is not only present both in the intellectual and sensible realities, but it can also take us to the principles underlying nature through the enhancement of its beauty.[1] Art gradually becomes a symbolic element and a real source of knowledge for the world of ideas. Plotinus compares the soul, in its search for reversion to the One, to that of the artist trying to represent ideal beauty in a block of stone.[2] Craft metaphors on artistic perception and representation, like that of the mirror,[3] abound in the *Enneads*.[4] Later on, Porphyry deepens these sketches of a general theory on aesthetics when he points out that the contemplation of an artistic representation of divinity – preferably with circular elements – can lead the soul to a higher level of understanding.[5] Proclus also reconsiders the Platonic views on poetics in his *Commentary on the Republic*

[1] *Enn.* IV 3 [27] 11. English translations are by the author unless otherwise indicated.

[2] *Enn.* I 6 [1] 9.

[3] *Enn.* I 1 [53] 8, I 4 [46] 10.

[4] In fact, the mirror is one of Plotinus's favourite images not only for perception but also for matter, a merely receptive substrate of illusions, not real entities (see, for example, *Enn.* I 6 [1] 8 and IV 3 [27] 12). Cf. Pépin (1970) and our discussion of the passages below.

[5] On Porphyry's lost treatise, *On statues*, see Eusebius of Caesarea, *Praeparatio Evangelica* 3.7.4 (Gifford 1981). See some previous considerations in Hernández de la Fuente (2011).

Proceedings of the British Academy, **240**, 53–92, © The British Academy 2022.

(V–VI) thereby establishing a new category of 'inspired poetry', which is a way of perceiving upper realities through art.[6]

Certainly, in Greek literature and thought, there was a long tradition of using craft metaphors in order to describe the poet's profession: the poet as a builder, sculptor or carpenter, as in the poetry by Bacchylides or Pindar and, especially, as a painter, in Simonides's definition of poetry as 'painting with a voice'.[7] Although Plato did not write a systematic treatise on poetics like his pupil Aristotle, his dialogues in dramatic form include extensive discussions of poetry and its function. There is a special emphasis upon the 'old quarrel between philosophy and poetry' (*Rep.* 607b5) and upon the perception and reflection of what we consider 'reality' as opposed to the true Reality (see in general Griswold 2016). In several dialogues, such as the *Symposium*, *Ion* or *Phaedrus*, Plato presents us with the image of a poet whose inspiration is not technical but comes as an inexplicable gift from the gods (*Phaedr.* 245a, *Laws* 719c) and thereby brings us mortals a glimpse of divine wisdom. In one of the key passages in the *Republic* (596a–597e), by contrast, poetry occupies the lowest rank of three types of 'making'[8] – the other two being that of God and that of the craftsman – since the poet makes nothing but images of appearances, like a man holding up a mirror (Halliwell 2002: 136; Murray 2015: 168). From this point onwards, metaphors of poetry as a craft and ideas of it as divinely inspired coexist in the Platonic tradition with rather more negative metaphors such as the mirror and the wax model which relegate poetry to a mere mimesis of inferior quality, a not so faithful reproduction of the world of Forms.

Another approach is found in Book III of the *Republic* where the argument centres on the function of poetry in an ethical system and its ability to encourage the soul to virtuous action. Plato seems to favour narrative poetry – *diegesis*, with the example of dithyramb, that is, lyric poetry – rather than dramatic poetry with its pure mimesis of the passions of men and gods, or mixed poetry such as epic which combines narration and imitation of mythical deeds (396c–d), since neither of these are suitable for the education of the soul. From this discussion onwards, the Platonic tradition will underline the importance of the appropriateness of poetry in its system of ethics and education. Any consideration of the mimetic beauty of, and the inspiration for, the 'images' of poetry goes beyond their relations with the models and poses complex problems regarding the purpose of mimesis, as summarised in the *Laws* (668e–669b). Any judgement of poetic imitation should, then, take three criteria into account: (1) the identity of the object; (2) how faithfully it is shown; (3) how well it is represented (Halliwell 2002: 131). The Platonic debate on the ethics of aesthetics was to become the foundation of later discussions on representation in the philosophy of art.

[6] As studied in the pioneering book by Sheppard (1980).

[7] Plutarch, *Quaestiones Convivales* 748a; Murray (2015: 159–60); Halliwell (2002: 118).

[8] Recalling naturally the Greek etymology of 'poetry' and the verb *poiein*, 'to make'.

This is especially relevant for the understanding of the Neoplatonic reworking of such theories which is no doubt related, in our view, with the strong 'visual turn' of the arts in Late Antiquity, as shown in the imposing buildings and exquisite miniatures of the period (Elsner 2006: 287). Certainly, in Late Antiquity, Classical views on aesthetics were evolving swiftly in all spheres during this time of change. The function of art was used as a propagandistic motor of power as well as a mirror of cultural principles. The Early Empire used art to highlight the dualism between naturalism and anti-naturalism, but the new Late Antique aesthetic tendencies dwelled on the transformation of philosophical and religious currents. This was a kind of 'visual' or 'phenomenological' turn, which places the idea of the image and the relation between reality and representation at the centre of the artistic debate. At the same time, aesthetics started to incorporate the dialectics between the Graeco-Roman tradition and the new Christian *Weltanschauung*, prefiguring what would subsequently become medieval art.[9] From the point of view of the representation of power, the focus switched to intellectual reflection on form and the symbolic value of images. We can see this very clearly in the evolution of the imperial portrait. The naturalistic models of the Augustan and Hadrianic age turned into sculptures whose main aim was to show the expressive force and depth of the Emperor's gaze. During the crisis of the 3rd century, instability on the throne made the short-lived emperors represent themselves with abstract values that would reinforce their weak stability as rulers (Bergmann 1977).

Artists concentrated on the task of simplifying techniques and classical expressions traditionally attributed to the emperors – serenity, nobility, majesty – and turned them into expressions of almost metaphysical strength and fearless stubbornness. The search for a representation of a unique personality with a special connection with divinity replaced the search for the classical forms that pretended to show the emperor as the pinnacle of Graeco-Roman culture (Bianchi Bandinelli 1971). This tendency appears in the famous portrait of Caracalla, fiercely expressive because he may be addressing the army, and continues in a broad range of works of art, like the portraits of the short-lived emperors of the 3rd century. Plotinus was probably acquainted with the portraits of Gordian and Gallienus – even personally with the emperor himself and his wife Salonina – which show abstraction as well as a clear debt to the Hellenistic world (Iozzia 2015: 3–9). A good example of non-naturalistic and very expressive sculptures is the famous statue of the Tetrarchs (L'Orange 1933).

[9] But let us take into account how Elsner advises 'to abandon not only the teleologies of a classical art heading for medieval decline or a Christian art rising out of the ashes of Antiquity, but also any attempt to brand different aspects of late antique art as more "Christian" or more "pagan", in a time of multiple artistic choices and interpretative possibilities' (2006: 227). As a precursor of Plotinian Neoplatonic Aesthetics we should mention here the work of Numenius of Apamea (2nd century), some of whose fragments (Des Places 1973: Fr. 2, 4b, 14, 18, 46c) could be considered as influential on Late Antique Aesthetics, especially regarding the issues of contemplation, perception, and the relation between the viewer of an image and Reality.

During Late Antiquity, Roman portraits and sculptures were enriched by art that was made in the provinces and in the areas most distant from the Roman cultural epicentre. The forms, expressions, attitudes and tastes of the different imperial regions influenced mainstream art. The movement of cultural creation was not just centrifugal from the capital but also sensitive to external influences. For example, in the decoration and buildings of Leptis Magna during the Severian age or in the statues from Hispania, Britannia, Germania, Gaul or Northern Africa. At this time, a peculiar portrait tradition was starting in Egypt, as the famous portraits of El Fayum show. Plotinus lived in Egypt, Asia Minor and Rome during this time of aesthetic transformations and he could well have been acquainted with the Graeco-Egyptian portraits from Fayum (Keyser 1955: 16; Puigarnau 1998: 237–9). The realistic intentions of the figures and the deep personalities showed in the eyes of these portraits are remarkable. But we know from Porphyry's *Life of Plotinus* (1.7–10) that the philosopher himself resisted the idea of sitting for a portrait, arguing that it was nonsense to have 'a more enduring simulacrum of a simulacrum' (εἴδωλον εἰδώλου), since our countenances and the sensible world were already unreal and a pale reflection of higher realities (Edwards 1993). We do have a group of busts identified as Plotinus from Gallienus's time; one is at the Museo Ostiense and is, perhaps, a reproduction of his real portrait (L'Orange 1951).

In parallel to the development of new tendencies in Imperial portraits, there is also a new approach to the image of the philosopher based on Caracalla's portrait (Zanker 1996). The new 'wise man' withdraws from the world and his gaze stares at eternity as a *theios aner*,[10] a divine man with charisma and extraordinary spiritual powers, as the figure of Apollonius of Tyana shows. As in the case of the emperors, the expressive turn in the portraits of intellectuals is remarkable. The emphasis is now on the philosopher as a miracle worker or a divine man, capable of prophesying and of accessing salvation. The eyes are the central elements both for emperors and philosophers, showing a connection with the divine sphere and inner enlightenment. This ideological transformation includes a striking interaction with symbols and portraits of early Christian iconography (Elsner 1998: 211–21). The new religion had an ambivalent attitude towards sacred images and their worship, and Neoplatonism will be essential for its immediate evolution. Portraits of Christian Emperors and early images of the Evangelists or Saint Paul, probably based on Plotinus's portraits, are good instances of these developments (Walter 2006; Bardill 2012).

The question of sculptures reflecting a higher power (divine, cultic or imperial) is relevant for understanding the Neoplatonic endeavour regarding aesthetics. In addition to the ancient cultic background on beliefs of the presence of the gods in statues (Mylonopoulos 2010; Eich 2011), there was a Platonic reworking of the matter in light of the relation between the intelligible and the sensitive worlds. Apart from the general term *eikon* ('image, representation'), Greek had diverse terms associated with cult images: above all *agalma* ('cult representation, statue'), but

[10] For this concept see Bieler (1967), Du Toit (1997) and an update in Alviz Fernández (2016).

also *xoanon*, *hedos* or *bretas*. This linguistic variety occasioned a Platonic debate concerning metaphors of artistic representation in statues, wax models or mirrors and the extent to which they could provide a glimpse of true realities. There were other terms such as *phasma*, *eidolon* or *phantasma*, which pointed out distorted or deceptive imitations (Steiner 2001: 63ff.; cf. v.gr. Plato, *Phaedo* 81d). This is the distinction developed by Plotinus when speaking of the mirroring of beauty in art. With *agalma* he emphasises the continuity between the material and the intelligible world through aesthetics:

> But how are you to see into a virtuous soul and know its loveliness? Withdraw into yourself and look. And if you do not find yourself beautiful yet, act as does the creator of a statue (οἷα ποιητὴς ἀγάλματος) that is to be made beautiful … and never cease chiselling your statue (καὶ μὴ παύσῃ τεκταίνων τὸ σὸν ἄγαλμα), until there shall shine out on you from it the god-like splendour of virtue.
>
> (I 6 [1] 9, M: 54)[11]

Eidolon, on the other hand, was the key term for 'false imitation', in the negative connotation of the mirroring, that of Narcissus's lost soul (I 6 [1] 8), not that of Dionysos's fragmented divinity (IV 3 [27] 12; cf. Pépin 1970). Plotinus discredits these 'phantasms within a phantasm' (εἴδωλα ἐν εἰδώλῳ); it is like a mirror showing things as in itself when they are really elsewhere, filled in appearance but actually empty, containing nothing, and pretending everything. Into it and out of it move mimicries of the Authentic Existents, images playing upon an image (εἴδωλα εἰς εἴδωλον) devoid of Form, visible against it by its very formlessness (III 6 [26] 7).

Neoplatonic interpretation of divine images placed special emphasis on the use of statues or *agalmata* where, as Porphyry or Proclus believed, were reflected or referred the powers of godly entities within the material world. This was a reinforcement of old pagan cults, conveniently updated by philosophy to face the Christian threat. It is understandable that Emperor Julian followed this belief; for example, when he speaks of a cult image of the Mother of the Gods as endowed with divinity (Or. V 161). Be it in a philosophical or ritual approach, as Porphyry's *On statues* (*Peri agalmaton*) and Proclus's theurgy respectively show, the basic Plotinian pattern of the mirroring of divine beauty and power was underlying these ideas on divine or cultic statues. As Viltanioti (2017) has proven, Porphyry's ideas on cult statues were key to understanding both his ontology and his ideas on mystic reversion. They were related to the Neoplatonic doctrine of the twofold power – every ontological level has an internal or essential power as well as an external power which constitutes the level below – and of spiritual ascent of the soul. The sculptor, through a statue of a god – or the philosopher on his mystic path of forming a meditative statue of himself – can communicate higher truths through these *agalmata*. The poet is also capable of illuminating this world through allegorical images. Another of Porphyry's works, *On the cave of the nymphs*, offers an

[11] For this passage see also the chapters by Brundin and Stern-Gillet in this volume. On the beauty of the soul, see also *Enn.* V 8 [31] 13.

allegorical key to Homer's poetry with evident references to Neoplatonic aesthetics as when he says, for example, (36) that 'he [*scil.* Homer] has concealed images of more divine things in moulding his little story' (ἐν μυθαρίου πλάσματι εἰκόνας τῶν θειοτέρων ᾐνίσσετο).

Back to visual arts, Grabar's famous essay (1945) on the origins of medieval aesthetics demonstrated Plotinus's importance as a clear forerunner of Byzantine and medieval Western art. Plotinus explained his views on what works of art should do in the following passage of the *Enneads*:

> I think, therefore, that those ancient sages, who sought to secure the presence of divine beings by the erection of shrines and statues, showed insight into the nature of the All; they perceived that, though this Soul is everywhere tractable, its presence will be secured all the more readily when an appropriate receptacle is elaborated, a place especially capable of receiving some portion or phase of it, something reproducing it, or representing it, and serving like a mirror to catch an image of it.
>
> (IV 3 [27] 11, M: 264)

In this passage the image is like a mirror representing matter that participates in its model of virtue in the Plotinian hypostatic ontology and of the principle of universal sympathy, of Stoic origin, and adopted here by the philosopher for his own purpose. Plotinian Neoplatonism put forward an ontology formed by multiple levels where the inferior ones are strictly and ontologically dependent on the former in succession, according to their greater or lesser degree of participation (*methexis*) in the Being. The One (*to hen*) beyond Being is the foundation of the whole reality but not the origin of every level, which is produced by emanation (*aporrhoe*) from the immediately superior one.[12] In Plotinus, the Intellect is produced from the One and the Soul emerges from the Intellect in a system of metaphysical, not space-temporal, causality. These three higher principles or *hypostaseis* lie behind the surface phenomena that present themselves to our senses.

This mirror of art not only reflects the appearance of material things, it is also able to somehow reproduce a glimpse of the world soul and of the spiritual essence of the intelligible world. That is why Plotinus declares that the arts, far from simply reproducing nature, go 'back to the Reason-principles from which nature itself derives' (V 8 [31] 1, M: 411). The rest of the Neoplatonists will develop a theory based on the steps of initiation through the contemplation of beauty, or 'ladder of love', already present in Plato's *Symposium* (210a–212b). Following Plato's *Republic* (518c–d), contemplation from an especial organ is required to see the highest beauty and abandon the darkness of the material world. For Plotinus, contemplation is a purely intellectual act without participation of the senses:

> When you know that you have become this perfect work, when you are self-gathered in the purity of your being, nothing now remaining that can shatter that inner unity … when you perceive that you have grown to this, you are now become very vision: now

[12] A good summary in Wallis (1995: 1–15) and Remes (2008: 35–76).

> call up all your confidence, strike forward yet a step – you need a guide no longer – strain, and see. This is the only eye that sees the mighty Beauty.
>
> (I 6 [1] 6, M: 55)

The Plotinian notion that there is a union of all the cosmic realities through the soul, that the entire universe is animated and participated in by the soul, is the basis of the metaphysical role of art as a way for us to contemplate and ascend through reflections of the real entity in our sensitive world. One must become pure vision in order to contemplate the First Beauty. Two ways in a dialectic tension then lead to aesthetic contemplation: first, elevation, since we start from the inferior strata and proceed to the superior; second, ecstasy, when contemplation of the intelligible world is finally achieved, in a kind of mystical reintegration of the soul to its origin. 'But what must we do?' Ascent is a mystic path of meditation and Plotinus put forward a metaphorical guide for this 'homecoming' of the soul. He moves away from the 'copies, vestiges, shadows' of this world, as a 'beautiful shape playing over water' in this famous passage with an allusion to the myth of Narcissus:

> ... is there not a myth telling in symbol of such a dupe, how he sank into the depths of the current and was swept away to nothingness? So too, one that is held by material beauty and will not break free shall be precipitated, not in body but in Soul, down to the dark depths loathed of the Intellective-Being, where, blind even in the Lower-World, he shall have commerce only with shadows, there as here. 'Let us flee then to the beloved Fatherland' [Hom., *Il.* 2.140]: this is the soundest counsel.
>
> (I 6 [1] 8, M: 53–4)

The notion of participation is a key aspect of Plotinian aesthetics. Art and poetry are able to provide this foretaste of the other reality, for whose contemplation we need to develop a kind of mental eye and to become similar to the That which we must see (I 6 [1] 9). Christian iconography will inherit Plotinus's development of the role of participation from an aesthetic and metaphysic-moral point of view. As late as the 8th century, the role of participation was a supportive argument for the worship of holy images during the iconoclast controversy and, in this sense, the icons 'participate' in Christ (Alexandrakis 2002: 77). In fact, John of Damascus used the notion of participation in his *On images* 1 19 when he states that 'just as iron plunged in fire does not become fire by nature, but by union and burning and participation, so what is deified does not become God by nature, but by participation (τῇ μεθέξει θεὸς γίνεται)' (Louth 2003: 33). The very consideration of sacred images, icons and statues in Christianity is related to this lively debate on cult images and mystic aesthetics that can be traced back to Plotinus. He states,

> Still the arts are not to be slighted on the ground that they create by imitation of natural objects; for, to begin with, these natural objects are themselves imitations; then, we must recognise that they give no bare reproduction of the thing seen but go back to the Ideas from which Nature itself derives, and, furthermore, that much of their work is all their own; they are holders of beauty and add where nature is lacking. Thus,

> Pheidias wrought the Zeus upon no model among things of sense but by apprehending what form Zeus must take if he chose to become manifest to sight.
>
> (V 8 [31] 1, M: 411)

Aesthetics have a key role in the ascent of the soul in Plotinus, since beauty means completeness and unity in the sensible world as a foretaste of the upper realities. The analogy with the visual arts appears again in *Enn.* VI 7 3 with the example of the beauty of wholeness: 'but something is so left if anything belonging to the shape be missing; eye, or other part' (VI 7 [38] 3, M: 472), as if a sculptor would leave something out and diminish the beauty of his/her work (Noel Hubler 2002: 195).

The transition from Plotinian aesthetics to poetics, although less studied (lately only by Iozzia 2015, and only partially), is easily understandable. These Neoplatonic ideas regarding plastic arts can be applied to poetry, or rather to a special kind of poetry with emphasis on visual elements. The understanding of the uses of metaphor in Plotinus is indispensable for his philosophical discourse regarding, the issue of the ascent to the One, in all the semantic fields related to the light, sun or heaven, and the issue of vision, contemplation, eyes, visual perception, reflections, etc. (Ferwerda 1965: 46–61 and 112–29). The literary culture of Late Antiquity had an evident fascination for the visual. This could be labelled under the modern categories of iconic or the visual turn, in line with studies of philosophy and art history from Warburg and Panofsky, to the pictorial turn of Mitchell, regarding images in mediology. Indeed, it is possible to speak of this turn in late antique literature, when visual metaphors and the emphasis on *enargeia* or poetic vividness that causes visual images through words[13] was especially felt (Francis 2012). Rethoric developed also the wide concept of *ekphrasis* – which is especially present, but not only, in descriptions of works of art – as a literary device aiming at bringing any scene or object to life (Webb 2009). Thus, this literary and rhetoric tradition is to be read together with the philosophical debate on images and the ideas on the material universe as a representation. Likewise, literary images put in words could have the same evocative power and energy upon the human faculty of *phantasia* or 'imagination' (Sheppard 2014), a philosophical concept that will be expanded in the third section of this chapter.

But what about poetics? Has Neoplatonism proven to be so influential as in the case of general views on art? The Platonic traditional categories were also in a process of revision for poetry. According to Plato's *Republic*, the inferior mimetic poetry produced false appearances and the mythic themes of traditional hexameter and Attic tragedy were not a suitable art for Plato's ideal state and should be curtailed.[14] With the possible exception of lyric poetry under the sign of Dionysus in the *Laws* (Hernández de la Fuente 2013), the Platonic State repudiated traditional poetry and poetic myths, as an inferior mimesis, and put forward a strict censorship of poetic productions. Perhaps Plotinus turned to poetry in order to amend this

[13] For this quality of language see Aristotle, *Rhetoric* 1410b–1411b and, especially, Longinus, *On the Sublime* 15.1–2.

[14] V.gr. Plato, *Resp.* 377 e 6–7, 598b6–599a7, 600 e 4–6, etc.

old dispute between philosophy and poetry present in Plato. This is especially true when we think of how the Athenian philosopher takes us to that level of allusion characteristic of his mythical discourse, either when reusing old myths or inventing new ones (Barfield 2011: 54). Although Plotinus cites a few poets, in particular Homer (V 1 [10] 2 and V 5 [32] 8), it is significant that his philosophical writing can be *a priori* described as poetic. This is demonstrated in Plotinus's abundant use of metaphor and in the explicit recognition that art originates from the same source as nature as well as complementing it by adding information where nature fails (V 8 [31] 1). That is why art and poetry seem to him valid means for exploring the true reality in a much more complete way than nature itself.

As far as metaphor is concerned, Plotinus's poetics have an anamnestic and anagogic role, like art in general. Metaphors allow the poet to represent the active role of the intelligible world in our world, turning the literary or artistic creator not into a trickster but a guide who points to the natural order of things (Iozzia 2015: 21). In *Ennead* V 9 [5] 11, Plotinus clarifies that mimetic arts that make use of symmetries 'have their principles in the intelligible world' – an extremely important passage for later arts both in the Christian and Islamic perspectives.[15] Even if Plotinus was aware that all art is imperfect without the ontological self-sufficiency that characterises the intelligible world, it can offer some functional images and metaphors that help us to understand his philosophical system. At the same time, art indicates the difference between the intelligible world and the sensible world.

We can add the instrument of poetics to our intellect to try to access superior knowledge. If at the top of the road we find contemplation of the One and Good and at the bottom is matter, the ascending path is flanked by art and poetry and is the guide we can follow. If we understand that the beauty of material things is a loan from the higher and that authentic poetry can give voice to that hidden beauty (*Enn.* V 9 [5] 2, Barfield 2011: 59–62), then the concept of 'poetic man' (*aner mousikos*) in Plotinus, one of the key expressions for Plato (*Soph.* 253b, *Phaedr.* 248d, etc.), gives the wider sense of a person versed in all the arts. This expression points to the fact that a certain type of man, not only a rational philosopher but rather a man inspired by the Muses – a musician or a poet, not just the visual artist, who has this virtue in his soul – is able to perceive beauty, respond to its presence and go in its search. Here is the transition from Plotinian aesthetics to poetics. The 'poetic men', men of the muses, are seized immediately by beauty and respond to it quickly as poets and artists (*Enn.* I 3 [20] 1), following the path of ascension in the contemplation of beauty that is found in Plato's *Symposium*.

Apart from the general and theoretical basis of Plotinus, there were other strategies for this Neoplatonic 'rehabilitation' of poetry in line with the visual turn. Allegory and symbolism were other ways of rescuing traditional poetry[16] for philosophical use as a source of allegories or even inspired knowledge in the old sense

[15] On the Arabic adaptation of this passage, see Stefan Sperl's contribution to this volume, pp. 110–11.
[16] As studied by Dillon (1976) and Lamberton (1986: 22–31). See more recently a good summary in Domaradzki (2014).

of enthusiasm (Sheppard 2014: 71–4). A Neoplatonic reading of the four kinds of *mania* in Plato[17] implies the mystic revelation of metaphysical truths in art through the poet's imagination. In this sense, Proclus developed an intelligent method to defend archaic poetry and its allegorical interpretation since the traditional hexametric poetry of Homer and Hesiod, with mythical arguments, was the basis of Greek education and Pagan religion, two legacies questioned in Proclus's time. In a Christian Empire that legislated against traditional religion and in a context of strong controversy on education with Christian men of letters and bishops, Neoplatonism provided new tools for a heritage in transformation during an 'age of anxiety' mostly for Pagans, as E.R. Dodds (1965) put it in the title of a well-known book.

2. Neoplatonic Poetry and Poetics: Some Propositions

What can we understand as 'Neoplatonic poetry' and 'Neoplatonic poetics'? Surely, Neoplatonic poetry is the one produced and used in the Neoplatonic Schools, be it hymnic, eulogistic, theurgic or oracular – but also the one composed following the main philosophical themes and using the vocabulary of this movement. In a wider sense, Neoplatonic poetics is the theory of literary forms and discourse related to this philosophical school and stemming from the aforementioned passages on poetry – and art in general – as a possible way of getting a glimpse of the eternal and intelligible world. There was a Neoplatonic theory of poetry, which can extend our concept of 'Neoplatonic poetry' to a greater number of authors of Late Antique Greek and Early Byzantine Literature, with whom we will deal in the following pages.

Prior to that, a short guide of key terms will be introduced as a methodological proposal to examine the brief selection of texts presented here, as well as to provide scope for further research. This will allow us to read the following texts without further explanation, as a first approach to 'Neoplatonic poetics'. A fundamental tenet which configures this poetics as a whole would seem to be the possibility of knowing – or not – the divine world, a key issue for the Neoplatonists, and one related to Proclus's own concept of inspired poetry. It could be said that there is a certain Neoplatonic 'phenomenology' of art here, that is, the perception of works of inspired art in particular as a possible way for the human soul to approach the vision and the understanding of the One, with its possible reflection in the descriptions of works of art, so dear to Late Antique and Byzantine poetry. As already mentioned, a list of specific topics – with their related vocabulary – could be drawn up in brief, as a sort of guide in order to perform lexical and conceptual searches in poets with possible Neoplatonic inspiration. The following classification in three large areas or leitmotifs allows a specific search for concrete themes:

1 Gnoseology: possibility of knowing and superior means of perception, especially prophecy and poetry in oracular style, so dear to Neoplatonists.

[17] Plato's *Phaedrus* 244a–245c.

2 Metaphysics: immortality of the soul, emanation and reversion to the One, relationship and ways of contact between soul, cosmos and intelligible world. Also, the idea of holiness of the philosopher-poet as a *theios aner* with inspired knowledge.
3 Aesthetics: representation of the divine and its emanations in the visual and poetic domains; for the purpose of poetry, the most important elements here are the type of poetic form (metre, rhyme, etc.) and figurative language (principally metaphor). These offer a possible way of alluding to metaphysical truths which are beyond the grasp of discursive thought and language. Special attention must be paid to poetic descriptions of works of art, spectacles and landscapes conceived as ways for the elevation of the soul towards the divine.

To these issues, it would be necessary to add more concrete observations. An interesting example is metaphors which link poetic form to the content of these three areas of research. A first instance is the metaphor of the mirror, which can be applied as follows:

1 Gnoseology: the mirror is a metaphor for cognition already in Plato's *Theaetetus* (152c) and Aristotle's *On Soul* (III 3), and is further developed by Neoplatonists from Plotinus onwards (Pépin 1970: 316).
2 Metaphysics: the mirror in Plotinus (IV 3 12) or Proclus (*In Tim.* II 80 20) is a favourite way of referring to the process of differentiation of matter, emanation, transition to matter or to the production of the individual souls.
3 Aesthetics: the reflections of the intelligible world upon the mirror are a way of expressing the imitations of art, which are always imperfect, as our notions of the world of ideas. Here the mirror is to be considered together with the wax model and other metaphors regarding arts or crafts, from painting and sculpture to weaving. Plato conceived the mirror as a false reflection of true entities (*Resp.* 596 d–e); regarding arts and crafts, there are abundant references to sculpture (*Enn.* I 6 [1] 9, II 9 [33] 4), and to weaving as a metaphor for sensation (IV 3 [27] 26).

Circularity and circular motion are another key issue to be aware of in Neoplatonic poetry. The representation of the universe as a sphere and the explanation of its motion – also related to that of the Soul and the Soul of the World – is also a Platonic idea with enormous *Nachleben* in the history of the Academy. The very act of contemplation is described by Plato as a circular motion,[18] and Plotinus deals with this in more detail in the *Enneads* with the circular movements of heaven and soul.[19] From his treatment of circularity onwards, it becomes a useful and omnipresent

[18] See Plato, *Phaedo* 111e–112e *Phaedrus* 247 b–d, *Republic* 616b–617d, *Timaeus*, 40a, among other passages.
[19] Cf. v.gr. *Enn.* II 2 [14] 2.16–27, in the section devoted to circular rotation of heavens and soul, or IV 8 [6] 1, with the circular movement of the Soul.

topos for other Neoplatonists such as Porphyry and Proclus. Following the terminology of Lakoff and Johnson (2003: 23ff.), the brief survey of the Neoplatonic orientational or ontological metaphors will make us aware of the dissemination in later poetry of such ideas. First, spatial orientations like 'down-up' in the ascent of the soul, 'circularity' in the ever-returning cycles of the cosmos, or, second, ontological analogies like that of 'the mirror or the wax model' for the perception of the soul, 'light' or 'awakening' for metaphysical knowledge, 'darkness' and 'the cave' for the world of the senses, 'colour dye' for different levels of knowledge and many others, will be emphasised whether they are present in Plato or not.

Of course, this is not an exhaustive list of themes, motifs and forms of Neoplatonism in poetry but these examples can be a first step for further research. Thus, an in-depth reading of those poets who may be considered Neoplatonic could be undertaken by recourse to these categories. Another key issue to be taken into account thereby concerns the literal and metaphorical meaning of the terminology used, with particular attention to (a) the philosophical vocabulary with poetic use (see below, the case of *noeros* ['noetic'], a crucial epithet of Proclian metaphysics); (b) the semantic, poetic and ideological scope and function of each work and poet studied; and (c) the categories extracted from the three leitmotifs proposed above in order to apply them to a selection of other works and passages.

In this context, the first Neoplatonic poems are those related to the historical Neoplatonic schools. They are linked to the traditional 'Pagan' religion, of which these philosophers were so fond. The preservation of the core of Pagan religion in the ritual, mantic and mystery traditions was one of the main concerns of many Neoplatonists (especially from Porphyry onwards) in an age when Christianity began to be favoured by the political authorities. Neoplatonism could be seen as a kind of *aggiornamento* of Paganism – they used oracles, mysticism, initiations, etc. – conceived to face the new times of depreciation of their beliefs.

There was a time when the Neoplatonists had a direct political influence on the emperors of the period, which was far from the mystical image that this philosophy had. As O'Meara (2003) has shown, these thinkers had a penchant for political philosophy and their late antique legacy prolonged well into the Middle Ages. Plotinus followed Emperor Gordian in his campaign against Persia and suggested to his successor Gallienus that he build a 'Platonopolis' or 'city of philosophers'.[20] Some authors tend to identify his disciple Porphyry as an active intellectual supporter of the Tetrarchy of Emperor Diocletian and even as an instigator of the persecution of Christians under his rule.[21] The 4th century was a turning point, an age of 'the final pagan generation' (Watts 2015: 220). After the ascension to the throne of Theodosius and his legislative measures of the 380s against Paganism, Pagans could no longer think that the religious order of the past would last forever.

[20] Porph. *Vita Plotini* 12, in Plotinus (1991: cxi–cxii).

[21] It is disputed whether Porphyry was the pagan 'priest of the philosophers' of the Diocletian government referred to by Lactantius in his Divine Institutions (V 2; Wilken 2003: 156–7). See also Goulet (2004: 61–109). and Wlosok (2005: 1–28), who shows that this identification is not convincing. Cf. also Chiaradonna (2014: 39, n. 4).

Things were changing rapidly for the worst, beginning with the closure of the School of Athens by Justinian's anti-pagan edict of 529 reported by the historian John Malalas (*Chr.* 18.47) (Cameron 1969; Watts 2004), and the subsequent exile of the philosophers to Sassanid Persia. According to the historian Agathias (II 30 3–31 4), the last director of the Academy, Damascius, and his disciples went to the court of Chosroes, returned to the Eastern Roman Empire again in 532, and founded a new School, probably in Harran.[22] It is remarkable that every Neoplatonic School had a separate fate, especially the two main seats of the Neoplatonists. From Plutarch onwards, the School of Athens was keen on Iamblichean Neoplatonism and practiced theurgy and ritual paganism (Watts 2008: 259), so that the conflict with Christianity was unavoidable. In Alexandria, however, the head of the School, Ammonius Hermeiou, and the patriarch Peter Mongus were able to reach an agreement so that Neoplatonic teaching was able to coexist with the Christian religion for more than a century after the end of the School of Athens in 529.

The link between the last Paganism and Neoplatonic poetry is evident in the case of oracular poetry. This poetic subgenre had many variations and enjoyed great success between the 4th and the 5th centuries. It contained residues of a still active Pagan religious tradition during the Late Roman imperial period from the 3rd century onwards. Indeed, poetry was of great interest for Neoplatonists, not only theoretically but also for its practical application to theurgy. Theurgy can be etymologically defined both as to 'act as a god' and 'to exercise an action upon the gods'. According to the *Suda*, the invention of theurgy is attributed to a certain Julian the Theurgist (2nd century), son of Julian the Chaldean, who was the author of several religious books. Julian the Theurgist,[23] a contemporary of Marcus Aurelius, was allegedly a miracle-worker who saved the Roman army from dying of thirst. Legend claims that he was responsible for the miracle of a torrential rainfall that terrorised the Marcomanni, whose troops were far superior to those of the Romans. He managed to save the emperor's army in 172 from almost certain disaster.[24] This episode is seen as the origin of this type of Neoplatonic magical ritual that tried to influence the gods or control the natural elements. In contrast to vulgar magic, Neoplatonic theurgy stood out for its eminently religious motivation and, most interesting for us, it was accompanied by ritual poetry for its execution.

Although in its origin theurgy and Platonism were separate,[25] they were later incorporated into the Neoplatonic conglomerate. The appearance of theurgical practice presupposes an important split between two 'schools' or tendencies among Neoplatonists, as a passage from Olympiodorus (*In Phaed.*, Norvin 1913: 123, l. 3–5) points out. This divergence can be seen between the school of Plotinus and his pupil

[22] See Tardieu (1990), and against this view Watts (2005).

[23] The legends about Julian are discussed by Athanassiadi (2010).

[24] Interestingly, Christian sources, such as a false letter from Marcus Aurelius himself, have argued that the prayers of Christians among the Roman ranks caused this prodigy.

[25] Dodds (1951: 285–6), in a classical chapter on theurgy.

Porphyry, who were more philosophical, and that of Iamblichus, Syrianus, Proclus and other 'hieratics', who had other religious derivations (*hieratike*). Iamblichus's controversial work *On the Mysteries* is traditionally configured as his answer to his teacher Porphyry on his doubts about theurgy as a way to achieve true knowledge. Porphyry preferred meditation to this practice of 'forcing' the powers of nature, but Iamblichus advocated theurgy as a valid means of contacting the divine. Much has been discussed about the nature of theurgy, trying to delimit it as a concept that lies between magic, oracle and prayer. In contrast to theology, which assumes doctrines about divinity, theurgy implies an 'action' on the divine. However, the main question is what kind of action it was (Van den Berg 2001: 67). Its core was probably summoning the gods in different ways, be it through cultic statues (*agalmata*) or through a medium, in order to fulfil epiphanies, reveal secrets or perform certain services.

This mystical practice of the later Neoplatonists was related to the *Chaldean Oracles*,[26] allegedly composed by Julian the Theurgist. These oracles combined Platonic elements with traditional pagan beliefs and their cosmological wisdom was held by some Neoplatonists such as Iamblichus to be divine revelation. Their doctrine provided a 'Father' on the summit of a hierarchical universe with a heavenly trinity of hypostases (Intellect, Hecate and World-Soul), which acted as a pseudo-religious basis for Neoplatonic metaphysics. Although only a few texts have survived, we know for certain that the *Chaldean Oracles* were very influential for Neoplatonist philosophers. From the 4th century onwards, this 'Bible of the Neoplatonists' (Busine 2005: 196–7, 317) was used not only for philosophical discourse, but also for theurgy.[27]

I will not discuss the complex cosmogony, cosmology and theology contained in the fragments of these oracles, which reflect their Middle Platonic origin. Nor will I explore their ontological scale of transcendence, with their apophatic approach to divinity and hierarchies of intermediate beings.[28] It is more interesting for our purpose to note the role of poetry in theurgy. In Van den Berg's interpretation of the hymns of Proclus, hymnic poetry was used for 'conjunctions', i.e. conjuration and animation of statues, which is a kind of ritual similar to kinetic magic but implies summoning and mystic knowledge. It is interesting that all these ritualised processes are combined with the idea of the ascent to the good, the *anagoge* of the Plotinian tradition. Whether through meditation and asceticism or through rituals with poetry and magic, the same philosophical background is evident, in spite of the distinction between theurgy and that of contemplation.[29]

[26] The bibliography on the Chaldean Oracles is vast. Cf. v.gr. Des Places (1971), Majercik (1989), Athanassiadi (1999), Lewy (2011), and a more recent and updated overview in Seng (2016).

[27] An overview in Des Places (1971: 18–52). Cf. also Saffrey (1981), Lewy (2011: 67–71), Majercik (1989: 21–5) and Tanaseanu-Döbler (2013).

[28] Such as the Iunges, Teletarchs, connectors, angels and demons, Aion or Eros. See in general Majercik (1989), Van den Berg (2001) and Seng (2016).

[29] As Majercik says (1989: 36), the late Neoplatonists tried to maintain this distinction.

These texts were a kind of battlefield for religious and ideological currents. If the *Chaldean Oracles*, for example, were soon labelled as 'pagan', and most Neoplatonists commented on them, the *Sibylline Oracles* were a favourite prophetic source for Christian writers. Thus, Neoplatonic oracular poetry can be read also in the light of previous Hellenistic and Jewish prophetic traditions. The pagan polemist Celsus declared that the *Oracula Sybillina*, a hexametrical collection of oracles on mythology, history and apocalyptic prophecies[30] which were attributed to the legendary Sibyls, were polluted by Judeo-Christian lore.[31] The ideological relevance of oracles as sources for Neoplatonic paganism and their controversy with Christianity is remarkable if we consider Porphyry's work *On Philosophy from Oracles*, written, according to Eusebius (V 36 5), explicitly against Christianity.[32] In fact, it was considered so anti-Christian that is was burned in 448 by Imperial decree, almost a century and a half after the author's death.[33] Oracles and poetry were closely related in the Neoplatonic Schools, ranging from works by Plotinus and Porphyry, to the Syrian of Iamblichus and the Athenian of Proclus.

In this context, let us consider what is perhaps the oldest extant testimony of Neoplatonic poetry: the oracular verses on the destiny of Plotinus's soul quoted by Porphyry, as a result of Amelius's consultation of the Oracle of Delphi.[34] The parallel to the consultation of Chaeremon on Socrates's wisdom is evident, as Porphyry underlines, but in this case we do have the response of the Pythia. It is worth quoting some excerpts in order to bear in mind some of the key issues of Neoplatonic poetics in the following centuries (Plotinus 1991: cxx–cxxi, [illegible]):

> I raise an undying song, to the memory of a gentle friend, a hymn of praise woven to the honey-sweet tones of my lyre under the touch of the golden plectrum ... Celestial! Man at first but now nearing the diviner ranks! the bonds of human necessity are loosed for you and, strong of heart, you beat your eager way from out the roaring tumult of the fleshly life to the shores of that wave-washed coast free from the thronging of the guilty, thence to take the grateful path of the sinless soul: where glows the splendour of God, where Right is throned in the stainless place, far from the wrong that mocks at law. Oft-times as you strove to rise above the bitter waves of this blood-drenched life, above the sickening whirl, toiling in the mid-most of the rushing flood and the unimaginable turmoil, oft-times, from the Ever-Blessed, there was shown to you the Term still close at hand: Oft-times, when your mind thrust out awry and was like to be rapt down unsanctioned paths, the Immortals themselves prevented, guiding you on the straightgoing way to the celestial spheres, pouring down before you a dense shaft of light that your eyes might see from amid the mournful gloom. Sleep never closed those eyes: high above the heavy murk of the mist you held them; tossed in the welter, you still had vision; still you saw sights many and fair not granted to all

[30] Parke (1988), Hooker (2008), Monaca (2008), and Gauger (2011).

[31] Origen, *Contra Celsum* 7, 53, 19; see Potter (1994: 87).

[32] Wilken (2003: 126–63), who deals with the role of oracles in Christian-pagan controversies *à propos* the case of Porphyry's *De philosophia ex oraculis haurienda*.

[33] For the anti-Christian activities of Porphyry, see in general Berchman (2005: 1–6).

[34] Porph. *Vit. Plot.* 22, in Plotinus (1991: cxx–cxxi). See in general Brisson & Flamand (1992).

> that labour in wisdom's quest … Rejoicing Muses, let us stay our song and the subtle windings of our dance; thus much I could but tell, to my golden lyre, of Plotinus, the hallowed soul.

This oracle is a poem on the ascent – or rather reversion (*anagoge*) – of the soul to the One. The use of circular metaphors, when the soul 'strove to rise above the bitter waves of this blood-drenched life, above the sickening whirl' (vv. 23–60) is relevant and has been related to the Plotinian idea of 'god-inspired dance' of the soul around the One (*Enn.* VI 9 [9] 8) in the process of mystical ascent.[35] In the end, in a *Ringkomposition*, the closing invocation to the Muses alludes again to circularity and to 'the subtle windings of our dance'. The text describes the philosophical salvation of the soul with its gradual ascent towards the mystical union with the God: the philosopher's soul is 'pure' and belongs to the intelligible world.[36] His experience is described as a joyful one, in the company of blessed daemons and souls of divine men who ascended to this realm before. Interestingly, both the oracle and Porphyry's oracular verses remark (23.3–4) that Plotinus was 'sleepless' even in this world of ours, using the metaphor of dying as a true awakening of the soul to the upper realities. There is a close textual relation between this Neoplatonic oracular poem and Plato's *Phaedrus* (250c).

Whether it is an authentic or embellished oracle, a theurgic Neoplatonic poem, a composition by Amelius or by Porphyry himself,[37] the important fact is to consider it as another key piece of evidence of the role of poetry in the Neoplatonic School (Agosti 2009: 35). It is obvious that Proclus's strongly Pagan approach to poetry applied in the Platonic School did not emerge out of nothing: there was a deeply rooted tradition of oracular and hymnic poetry in the Neoplatonic School and even some epigrams and dedications, of which only a few remain. Syrianus composed a hymn to Achilles, and his tomb, contemporary with that of Proclus, had an epigram by the latter. Other Neoplatonists such as Asclepiodotus, Asclepiades and Isidorus also wrote hymns, according to Damascius.[38] Damascius himself composed a lost funeral eulogy in verse to the philosopher Aedesia,[39] the wife of Hermias, and an epigram to Zosime.[40] There is another epigram dedicated to Syrianus in an inscription[41] and the *Suda* mentions that the poet Christodorus of Coptus composed a versified memorabilia of the School of Proclus, to whom some epigrams are also attributed (Gelzer 1966). This lost work entitled 'On the pupils of the great Proclus',[42] could be ascribed to a tradition of poetic paraphrases of biographies of

[35] Slaveva-Griffin (2012: 203). On circle metaphors from Plato to Plotinus, cf. Hernández de la Fuente (2011: 307–10).

[36] As Slaveva-Griffin (2013: 327–9) has noticed.

[37] On the oracle and the diverse theories regarding authorship, cf. Goulet (1982).

[38] Damascius, *Vit. Isid*, F209, F164, F112–3 (Zintzen 1967).

[39] Damascius, *apud Photium* Cod. 242, p. 341b (Bekker 1824).

[40] *Anthologia Palatina* 7.553 (Paton 1917: 299).

[41] *Supplementum Epigraphicum Graecum* LI 298 (Chaniotis *et al.* 2005).

[42] John of Lydia, *De Mag.* III 26.

Neoplatonic sages, starting with Proclus himself, which were versified in order to spread their philosophical doctrine to a wider audience (Agosti 2009).

3. From Metaphysics to Poetry: Proclus's Turn

We cannot understand the aesthetic revolution of the Neoplatonists without a glimpse into their metaphysics. The main implication of poetry in their system is to point the way to ontological truths. Human imagination (*phantasia*) and poetic inspiration were the bridge between the worlds of sensory perception (*aisthesis*) and discursive reason (*dianoia*), which possesses a character both intelligible and sensitive.[43] Plotinian Neoplatonism developed the notion of *phantasia* as imagination able to draw inspiration from the intelligible world and allow the human soul to visualise eternal principles from the supreme realities (Sheppard 2014: 47–70).[44] Among the Neoplatonic vocabulary in poetry we will find some key words related to the basics of Plotinian-Proclian metaphysics, namely, 'imitation', 'emanation', 'participation', 'reversion' and other important concepts.

Plotinian hypostatic ontology of the One, the Soul and the Intellect was further developed by Proclus[45] so that each hypostasis transmits a sort of 'power' to the inferior one, in a cause-effect relation, giving birth to it or causing its qualities. There is a form of the triad made out of Cause (*aition*), Power (*dynamis*) and Effect (*aitiaton*). The last ontological level is our sensible world, which exists in time and space and where unity disappears and the derivative process of emanation ends. The material world is an imperfect imitation of the intelligible world achieved through the impression of the divine model upon Matter. However, Proclus specifies the relationship and hierarchy of these entities in a system of triads (or Forms of the basic triads). He distinguishes the Intelligible Being (*noeton*) and the Intellective subject (*noeron*) and an intermediate level (*noeton-noeron*), object and subject at the same time. He embraces a further hierarchy of different levels corresponding to Being, Life and Intellect, filled with triads of the Intelligible, Intelligible-intellective and Intellective in a hierarchy of intermediate entities.

We can speak, in the case of Proclus and his immediate followers, of a kind of noetic-noetic poetry, allowing the reader/hearer to comprehend higher realities.

[43] Τὸ μὲν γὰρ νόημα ἀμερὲς καὶ οὔπω οἷον προεληλυθὸς εἰς τὸ ἔξω ἔνδον ὂν λανθάνει, ὁ δὲ λόγος ἀναπτύξας καὶ ἐπάγων ἐκ τοῦ νοήματος εἰς τὸ φανταστικὸν ἔδειξε τὸ νόημα οἷον ἐν κατόπτρῳ, καὶ ἡ ἀντίληψις αὐτοῦ οὕτω καὶ ἡ μονὴ καὶ ἡ μνήμη: 'The verbal formula – the revealer, the bridge between the concept and the image-taking faculty – exhibits the concept as in a mirror; the apprehension by the image-taking faculty would thus constitute the enduring presence of the concept, would be our memory of it' (*Enn.* IV 3 [27] 30, M: 284).

[44] The equation of *phantasia*, perception of a mental image, with the creative imagination to be found in philosophers such as Proclus (v.gr. *In Remp.*, Kroll 1899–1901, II: 107, 14–18) was the product of the theoretical developments with which the Neoplatonists tried to harmonise their eclectic views between Plato's theory of inspiration and the Aristotelian and Stoic ideas.

[45] See in general, for this section on Proclian ontology, Helmig & Steel (2015).

Poetry is intermediary as an object and subject, as a mediation for the understanding of the metaphysical process of emanation/reversion. The idea of a kind of poetry which can awaken a superior part of the Intellect is key in his thought and is related to his speculation, found in the *Elements of Theology* (Section 35), of the second hypostasis and the process of emanation. Here, we have another basic form of triad fundamental for causation and for the ontological structure, that of Remaining, Emanation and Reversion (*mone*, *prohodos*, *epistrophe*).[46]

Proclus is the key Neoplatonic thinker for poetry. He tried to reconcile Plato's condemnation of Homer with his traditional role as poet-theologian and master of the Hellenic *paideia.*[47] Proclus seems to base his proposal on Plato's view of the somewhat 'higher' lyric choral poetry appearing in the *Laws*, where three choruses allow differentiated education of youths, adults and seniors in the ideal state.[48] Of interest is the senior choral association under the patronage of Dionysus in the *Laws* where Plato already appeared to equate the dithyramb, a Dionysiac non-mimetic subgenre, with a more 'philosophical' poetry.[49] Proclus is then ready to rework the Platonic views on traditional poetry, putting forward an allegorical reading and stating that it is much more than just a bad imitation, since it is able to disclose philosophical teaching if appropriately read. That is to say, there is a higher sort of poetry, non-mimetic, which 'explains the divine things through symbols' (διὰ συμβόλων τὰ θεῖα ἀφερμηνεύουσα *In Remp.* ed. Kroll 1899–1901, I: 198, 14). Proclus's classification of poetry therefore consists of three types of poetry – inspired, didactic and mimetic – of which, following Plato's *Phaedrus* (245a), the first is the highest and inspires the poet to a supra-rational cognition, allowing him an understanding of metaphysical truths. At the lowest level is mimetic poetry which produces no more than images and phantasms of no philosophical value.[50] Next comes didactic poetry, which opens a path to philosophical knowledge, since 'it offers participation (*metousian*) in prudence and the other virtues to those so inclined by nature'.[51] As Domaradzki (2014: 124) notes, this type of poetry deals primarily with physics and ethics, rather than with theology, i.e. metaphysical wisdom of the One. Only 'inspired' poetry can provide this poetic wisdom allowing the soul a sort of 'connexion with the divine' (συνάπτεται τοῖς θεοῖς, *In Remp.* ed. Kroll 1899–1901, I: 177, 16) not open to everyone, but concealed in allegory and representation. Poetry is then equated to the language of the mysteries and metaphysically contains a reflection of the structure of the whole cosmos. The reader who is capable of disentangling the allegory in such poems will also have a path open to real knowledge (Sheppard 1980: 172).

[46] On this structure, see Siorvanes (1996: 48–86).
[47] Proclus, *In Remp.* I.177.7–196.13.
[48] Plato, *Leges* 664b–665c. Hernández de la Fuente (2013: 13–17).
[49] Plato, *Resp.* 394c.
[50] Procl., *In Remp.* ed. Kroll 1899–1901, I: 179, 29–32.
[51] Procl., *In Remp.* ed. Kroll 1899–1901, I: 179, 6. Lamberton (1986: 191).

This triadic taxonomy of poetry follows a general pattern in Proclus's thought and is developed with emphasis on participation. Following his teacher in the theorisation about the emanation of the intelligible world from the One, Proclus aimed at clarifying the differences between the One and the Intellect, a concern shared also by previous Neoplatonists such as Iamblichus or Porphyry. The notion of participation is another key feature of all Platonic philosophy, consisting of the way in which the supra-sensible entities, the changeless and perfect Ideas, originate the particular sensible equal things of our world as imperfect and partial reflections.[52] Thus, the Forms are essence and principle of our multiple and sensible realities. The Proclian system of *Elements of Theology* (5, 11), where unity is logically and causally prior to all pluralities, dwells especially on the necessity of understanding the One as the ultimate limit to participation. This is seen in the first statement: 'Every plurality partakes in some way of unity'. Participation has also a main metaphysical role as connexion between the hypostases, since the relationship between soul, intellect and divine henad is defined by *methexis* (Sweeny 1982). The notion of participation refers to another fundamental operation in the Proclian system: the triad composed by Unparticipated, Participated and Participating (*amethekton*, *metechomenon*, *metechon*), aimed at responding to traditional criticism of the theory of Forms in Plato's *Parmenides* and Aristotle. Other Forms of the triad are Substance (*ousia*), Power (*dynamis*), Activity (*energeia*) – a division stemming from Aristotle – and Limit (*peras*), Infinity (*apeiria*), Mixture (*mikton*) – probably of Pythagorean origin. Proclus ontology had an enormous philosophical influence both in Byzantium and in the West (De Garay Suárez-Llanos 2017).

Through art and poetry allegorically understood according to Neoplatonism, we can comprehend the unveiled connections of all the stages of our world, both sensible and intellectual, and realise the monistic hierarchy of all, from the top of perfection to our sadly lost soul *in hac lacrimarum valle*. Proclus's thought, like modern structuralism, finds the same underlying pattern in the mysteries, in theurgy, in philosophy, in language, in myth and in the world as a whole (Sheppard 1980: 161). This interpretation of poetic myths, from Homer and company, is hard to underestimate. Proclus, apart from commentaries on Plato's key dialogues, was quite a good poet. A convinced Pagan in a Christian environment, he wrote hymns to the Greek deities where he exemplifies his views on this type of superior poetry and allegorical language. Let us see, for example, the following *Hymn to the Muses* (Van den Berg 2001: 209, [illegible]):

> We hymn, we hymn the light that raises man aloft,
> of the nine daughters of great Zeus with splendid voices,
> who have rescued from the agony of this world, so hard to bear,
> the souls who were wandering in the depth of life
> through immaculate rites from intellect-awaking books,
> and have taught them to strive eagerly to follow the track leading

[52] Plato, *Phaedo* 74a–75d, 100e.

beyond the deep gulf of forgetfulness, and to go pure to their kindred star
from which they strayed away, when once they fell
into the headland of birth, mad about material lots.
But, Goddesses, put an end to my much-agitated desire too
and throw me into ecstasy through the noetic words of the wise.
That the race of men without fear for the Gods may not lead me
astray from the most divine and brilliant path with its splendid fruit;
always draw my all-roving soul towards the holy light,
away from the hubbub of the much wandering race
heavy laden from Your intellect-strengthening beehives,
and everlasting glory from its mind-charming eloquence.

Proclus sings about a sacred 'light that raises aloft' (ἀναγώγιον φῶς), the nine muses, who are a favourite group for Neoplatonists since the *Enneads*, and alludes to the possibility of ascent of our souls, who are struggling in our world, through 'mystic rites' taken 'from intellect-awakening books' (ἐγερσινόων ἀπὸ βίβλων), that is to say, from old poetry. Proclus prays to be taken by the Muses far from the region of matter (ὑλοτραφέσσι περὶ κλήροισι), to have his intellect, a kind of 'mental eye', filled with divine light until the mists of the senses are dissipated. 'Draw my all-roving soul – says Proclus – towards the holy light' (ἕλκετ' ἐμὴν ψυχὴν παναλήμονα πρὸς φάος ἁγνόν). The way to achieve this union alludes to the allegorical knowledge provided by the poetry of the Muses. The whole scheme of ascent to the light of the Good is evidently following the same mystic paths of Plotinus's oracle in *Vit.Plot.* 22, but applying the Proclian reworking of the triads, as we see in the ecstatic Bacchanalian dance of 'noetic words' (νοεροῖς με σοφῶν βακχεύσατε μύθοις).

In the Proclian system, art and poetry are a possible way of moving from the sensible to the intelligible world. The utmost importance of Proclus is hard to underestimate for later approaches to identify the traces of Neoplatonism in poetry. A great variety of images, leitmotivs, and allusions both to his ontological system and to his views on aesthetics abound in Greek poetry, both in the last Pagan poets – for instance, in Proclus's circle – and in the incipient Christian poetry, with a remarkable influence in the Byzantine world. Let us remember that Neoplatonism was a common philosophical language for both Pagans and Christians. Paradoxically, a Pagan philosopher like Proclus was followed – and of course discussed and often contested – in the theological debates of the following centuries. Much has been said about the influence of Neoplatonism on Christology and Christian theology in general.[53] It influenced strongly the early Christian thinkers, such as the so-called Cappadocian Fathers and also, especially in the late 5th or early 6th centuries, others like Pseudo-Dionysius the Areopagite. Nevertheless, this eclectic philosophy of Late Antiquity, with its triads, mysticism and soteriological doctrines, served also as a basis for Christian Poetry on theological themes such as the paradoxical Unity

[53] Cf. Wallis (1995: 160–1) and Remes (2008: 199–207).

of the Trinity, the Nature of Christ, the idea of Christ-Logos as saviour or the eternity of the world.

Neoplatonic poetics will allude to some key issues, both in the Pagan and in the Christian world, such as the representation of the supra-sensible world, especially of the heavens, time and eternity itself. Be it a hymn dedicated to the divinity or a description of a work of art with special emphasis on the circle and circular things, in poetic *ekphraseis* (written descriptions of a work of art), a very popular subgenre of poetry in Late Antiquity and Byzantium, we will find themes such as the reflection of unity in multiplicity, the contrast between the sensible and intellectual worlds or the possibility of contacting or reaching the One in a mystical way. No wonder the influence of Neoplatonism upon Christian authors is especially attested in descriptions of works of art or metaphors dealing with the perception of the divine world related to arts and crafts. Let us recall Plotinus's image of the sculptor representing ideal beauty in a block of stone as the soul seeks to model herself in search of the assimilation to the One (*Enn.* I 6 [1] 9), or the very idea that an artist can have access to the beauty of the intelligible world (V 8 [31] 1). Neoplatonic aesthetics were inspiring for Christian authors such as Gregory of Nyssa in his *Commentary on Songs of Songs*, where the Plotinian images of the sculptor and the mirror have left a deep trace (Iozzia 2015: 41–3; Karfíková 2018).[54]

The most interesting thing about Proclus is his double condition as metaphysical-aesthetic theorist and composer of hymnic poetry for ritual use. Proclus's *Hymns* contain many expressions both from religious traditions and from the *Chaldean Oracles*, which had been incorporated from the Platonic vulgate, especially since Iamblichus's *On the Mysteries*. Iamblichus redefined theurgy as a means to elevate human souls to enlightenment and unification with the Demiurge and with Beauty, which could be achieved through symbolic invocations. These invocations, called *synthemata*, are symbolic images, names, musical compositions, numbers, and also material representations such as animals, plants or stones.[55]

Proclus's passion for theurgy was manifested not only in his writings, but also in his biography as written by Marinus, which contains an entire chapter (28) dedicated to the excellence of his master in this art.[56] Among his signs as a 'divine man' (*theios aner*), Proclus the Theurgist could prevent earthquakes and foretell the future in verse, including his own destiny. Van den Berg (2001) has studied his hymns as an example of theurgy in practice, in opposition to the Iamblichean theory about the power and perfection of the prayers to the gods. Theurgy was, as stated in Proclus's *Platonic Theology*, 'a power higher than all human wisdom, embracing the blessings of divination, the purifying powers of initiation and, in

[54] V.gr. *Homily* IV (Ct 1.15–2.7), 101,17–104,15, where the soul has to choose whether to look to vice or to virtue, as in a mirror.

[55] *Synthemata* found in Proclus's *Hymns* (Van den Berg 2001: 91) are, for example, innate symbols, myths as symbols, symbolic names and material symbols.

[56] Proclus devoted an extensive commentary to the *Chaldean Oracles*.

a word, all the operations of divine possession'.[57] But in his view the deities obey the instructions of the 'divine' philosopher because of his special virtue, his ascetic way of life, and both his philosophical and poetic mastery. Finally, it is interesting to note that Proclus the philosopher was well known among his contemporaries and later admirers as a keen theurgist who 'fell in love' with oracular and ritual poems in hexameters.[58]

4. A Neoplatonic 'School' of Poets

Let us now put our taxonomy to use to examine a number of Greek poets who probably resorted to this sort of Neoplatonic poetics. Their written works may be more revealing for our purpose than poetry composed by Neoplatonic philosophers described above, since they show to what extent these philosophical views on aesthetics and poetics permeated the entire intellectual milieu of the Greek-speaking world.[59]

In the context of the 5th century, a decisive time of change and confrontation between paganism and Christianity, we encounter the curious case of the poet Nonnus of Panopolis (fl. 450), who became the head of a poetic school which bears his name. He authored the *Paraphrase of the Gospel of St. John*, a Christian epic with deep theological and philosophical implications, and the *Dionysiaca*, a long mythological epic on the pagan god Dionysus. Both were composed in Homeric style and there are so many nuances of Neoplatonic poetry that they may represent a practical application of Proclus's poetic principles.[60] Nonnus is generally considered an innovator, whose changes in hexametrical poetry and style greatly influenced several generations of poets. Some authors like Miguélez Cavero (2008) have pointed out his indebtedness to previous Rhetorical Schools. But the debt that not only Nonnus but also his followers owe to the poetics of Neoplatonism in general has been somewhat neglected.[61] If we are right, then just as Plotinus re-founded Platonic philosophy, so Nonnus can be seen as doing the same with traditional Greek Epic poetry.

Already at the beginning of the *Paraphrase*, we find a hymn to the Logos which is no mere versification of the Gospel, but rather a philosophical reading with Neoplatonic resonances which reflect the influence of the theological debates of the time (Gelzer 1993: 45). This is evident if we compare the two texts as shown below (John 1.1–8, New International Version, Biblica, and Nonnus *Par.* I 1–23; Prost, 2003: 59, [illegible]):

[57] Proclus, *Theologia Platonica* 1.113.6 (Saffrey & Westerink 1968–97).

[58] See Marinus, *Vita Procli*, 26 and Michael Psellus, *Scripta Minora* 1.241.25.

[59] See, for example, Cameron (1965) and Miguélez Cavero (2008).

[60] As pointed out already by the pioneering work of Gigli Piccardi (1985: 211–45), regarding oracular Neoplatonic poetry.

[61] I have attempted an interpretation in Hernández de la Fuente (2014).

> In the beginning was the Word, and the Word was with God, and the Word was God. He was with God in the beginning. Through him all things were made; without him nothing was made that has been made. In him was life, and that life was the light of all mankind. The light shines in the darkness, and the darkness has not overcome it.

> Ere time, ere space, ere speech dwelt the archaic Word,[62]
> God's like in age and nature, motherless, this Son,
> The Word, the spawn of self-born God, light come from light,
> Inseparate, interminable and enthroned
> With God, conseated on God's sempiternal chair:
> The Word was God's first offspring. Who from the beginning
> Compiled with God, the universal architect,
> (Himself far older than the world); and all that is,
> Inert and breathing, all through him arose. And naught
> Which is, but through this workman's word was made. In him,
> Innate, was every life; his light was nourishment
> For short-lived men. The earth-sustaining light of glory
> Flamed bolts into the murk from heav'n above, and lo,
> The dark could not enfold it.
>
> (English Translation, Prost 2003)

Nonnus's vision of the Logos and its 'intelligible light' (νοερὸν φάος, I 20) differs markedly from an Orthodox paraphrase, a fashionable genre in Christian poetry of that time. Issues such as eternal time or the emanation of the second hypostasis are expressed with phrases derived from the pagan mystery tradition (ἀρρήτῳ ἀρχῇ).[63] This is used as a way to discover the Neoplatonic return to the light of the One after a dualistic contraposition of the dark and evil material world (ἐν ἀχλυόεντι δὲ κόσμῳ) with the splendour of the intelligible One (φῶς / αἴγλη, etc.). Needless to say, such a poetic reading enhances the philosophical nuances of John's Gospel.[64] It also allows us to find traces of Neoplatonism in the Christian message[65] as exemplified not only by the hymn to the Logos, but also in the speeches of Jesus in the *Paraphrase.*

[62] The original is Ἄχρονος ἦν, ἀκίχητος, ἐν ἀρρήτῳ λόγος ἀρχῇ, literally 'Without time he was, intangible in the ineffable beginning' (Prost's translation is somewhat literary). The Greek text of the beginning of the paraphrase is: 'Ἄχρονος ἦν, ἀκίχητος, ἐν ἀρρήτῳ λόγος ἀρχῇ, / ἰσοφυὴς γενετῆρος ὁμήλικος υἱὸς ἀμήτωρ, / καὶ λόγος αὐτοφύτοιο θεοῦ γόνος, ἐκ φάεος φῶς˙ / πατρὸς ἔην ἀμέριστος, ἀτέρμονι σύνθρονος ἕδρῃ˙ / καὶ θεὸς ὑψιγένεθλος ἔην λόγος. οὗτος ἀπ᾽ ἀρχῆς / ἀενάῳ συνέλαμπε θεῷ, τεχνήμονι κόσμου, / πρεσβύτερος κόσμοιο˙ καὶ ἔπλετο πάντα δι᾽ αὐτοῦ, / ἄπνοα καὶ πνείοντα˙ καὶ ἐργοπόνου δίχα μύθου / οὐδὲν ἔφυ, τόπερ ἔσκε˙ καὶ ἔμφυτος ἦεν ἐν αὐτῷ / ζωὴ πασιμέλουσα, καὶ ὠκυμόρων φάος ἀνδρῶν / ζωὴ πάντροφος ἦεν. ἐν ἀχλυόεντι δὲ κόσμῳ / οὐρανίαις σελάγιζε βολαῖς γαιήοχος αἴγλη, / καὶ ζόφος οὔ μιν ἔμαρψε.' Let us remember, in parallel, the text of John 1.1–5: Ἐν ἀρχῇ ἦν ὁ λόγος, καὶ ὁ λόγος ἦν πρὸς τὸν θεόν, καὶ θεὸς ἦν ὁ λόγος. οὗτος ἦν ἐν ἀρχῇ πρὸς τὸν θεόν. πάντα δι᾽ αὐτοῦ ἐγένετο, καὶ χωρὶς αὐτοῦ ἐγένετο οὐδὲ ἕν. ὃ γέγονεν ἐν αὐτῷ ζωὴ ἦν, καὶ ἡ ζωὴ ἦν τὸ φῶς τῶν ἀνθρώπων· καὶ τὸ φῶς ἐν τῇ σκοτίᾳ φαίνει, καὶ ἡ σκοτία αὐτὸ οὐ κατέλαβεν.

[63] Cf. Doroszewski (2016: 29ff.).

[64] It is worth noting that Amelius, the favourite disciple of Plotinus, also viewed the beginning of St John's Gospel as referring to the World of the Soul, as reported by Eusebius of Caesarea (*Praeparatio Evangelica* 11.19); see Gifford (1981).

[65] For example, in the scene of the foot-washing of the disciples, see Greco (2004: 20).

In the *Dionysiaca*, Nonnos's mythological epic, many Platonic references can be found.[66] But most strikingly, there are many relics of pagan Neoplatonic hymns, such as the following example devoted to Selene-Hecate, queen of the sublunar cosmos where our soul dwells (44.191–199; Rouse 1940–2: III, 311–13,):

> O daughter of Helios, Moon of many turnings, nurse of all!
> O Selene, driver of the silver car! If thou art Hecate of many names,
> if in the night thou dost shake thy mystic torch in brandcarrying hand,
> come night wanderer, nurse of puppies
> because the nightly sound of the hurrying dogs is thy delight with their mournful whimpering.
> If thou art staghunter Artemis, if on the hills thou dost
> eagerly hunt with fawnkilling Dionysos, be thy brother's helper now!

A comparison of this hymn with Proclus's hymn to Hecate and Janus, the Orphic hymn to Hecate, the invocation of this divinity in the *Papyri Graecae Magicae*, and the oracles related to Hecate in Late Antique oracular poetry, shows Nonnus's deeply Neoplatonic context. In the theology of the *Chaldean Oracles*, very influential for Proclus, Hecate has a double role as a traditional goddess to whom sacrifices and ritual can be performed and as a cosmic principle identified with the Platonic World of the Soul (Majercik 2001). As goddess of a metaphysical threshold, she was a key divinity in the theurgy and theology of the *Oracles* (Johnston 1990). Similarly, the Orphic hymn invokes 'Hecate of the roads and threeways' (Εἰνοδίην Ἑκάτην κλῄιζω, τριοδῖτιν) with a continuous accumulation of epithets which dwell on her role as goddess of transition from one world to the other and as 'sovereign and key-holder of the whole universe' (παντὸς κόσμου κληιδοῦχον ἄνασσαν). Proclus accordingly writes about Hecate as the 'many-named mother of the gods' (θεῶν μῆτερ, πολυώνυμε) and guardian of the gate (προθύραιε). The magical invocations in the Greek papyri (PGM IV. 2746–55) also show the deep ritual significance of the 'Hecate of many names' (Ἑκάτη, πολυώνυμε), the 'threeheaded' goddess (τρικάρανε). It follows that Nonnus here is fully in keeping with the traditional pagan and Neoplatonic interpretations of Hecate. In the context of our previous discussion of cult images and theurgy, the philosophical and religious associations of his poetic hymn are hard to underestimate. Both of his poems deal with the godly world and its phenomena from the One to the Many. The poetic reflection of the Plotinian ontological pattern present in the pioneering work of nature has later Christian and Islamic echoes, like Pseudo-Dionysius's treatise *On the Divine Names, De los nombres de Cristo* by Fray Luis de León[67] or the one God with 99 names, a crucial theme later on in Sufism. But this goes beyond the scope of this study.

This is just an example, but there are many other passages that demonstrate Nonnus's debt to Neoplatonism. This philosophy is also a key to understanding

[66] See, for example, the allusions to metempsychosis of 'the soul returning whence it came, back to the starting-place in the circling course' in 37.3 6, or the Platonic theory of the soul's tripartition in 10.25.
[67] On this author see the chapter by Colin Thompson in this volume, pp. 310–12.

the so-called 'Nonnian' poets[68] from Cyrus[69] (d. 441) and Pamprepius of Panopolis (d. 484), almost contemporaries of Nonnus, until at least the 7th century. Nonnus's treatment of myths, and specially the cosmic allegories using the rhetorical and poetic device of *ekphrasis*, enjoyed great success in the first Byzantine School of hexametric poetry,[70] before iambic verses and dodecasyllables became predominant. Let us now briefly mention some of these Nonnian poets, most of whom wrote allegorical descriptions in their epics even though only a few poems have survived.

Christodorus of Coptus (fl. 500) wrote a poetic description of the statues in the gymnasium of the Zeuxippus, in Constantinople, and the text has been preserved in the second book of the *Palatine Anthology*. In spite of his name, Christodorus was an admirer of the pagan Neoplatonism of Proclus, as discussed above, as demonstrated by a now lost poetic work attributed to him that was a collection of memorabilia from the School of Athens in Late Antiquity. His descriptions of statues of poets, orators and philosophers, a sort of intelligible 'wise men' or *noeroi sophoi*, are full of references to Neoplatonic themes. The passage on Pythagoras (*Ant.Pal.* 2.1.120–122), for example, can be compared to the idea of 'intelligible inspiration' of the *Hymn to the Muses* by Proclus (10–11).

Paul the Silentiary, a member of the imperial bureaucracy living under Justinian, wrote among other poems two *ekphraseis* devoted to the church of Hagia Sophia in Constantinople.[71] Paul enriches Christian allegories with Neoplatonic themes dwelling precisely on ideas of circularity. Paul's descriptions of the sacred space of Hagia Sophia show abundant circular metaphors and adjectives parallel to the cosmological *ekphraseis* of Nonnus. The opening of the gates of Hagia Sophia, leading to the narthex (320–5), recalls the transition from the material to the intelligible world in the path of reversion to divinity. Other passages include the Neoplatonic idea that contemplation of such beauty in Hagia Sophia leads the mortal soul to a higher or 'noetic' knowledge of metaphysical truths. The poet is seized into an ecstatic state of contemplation (444–7, [illegible]):

> Where am I taken? (Πῆι φέρομαι;) What whirlwind drags my wandering word
> as in an ocean? I went already through the centre of the temple,
> its highest place. But come back now, my song,
> up there where is the most incredible wonder (θάμβος) to see, the most incredible to hear.

As the *ekphrasis* proceeds, the poet/viewer, as a divine philosopher, experiences illumination and knowledge of the One through the contemplation of the work of art leading to θάμβος, 'wonder'. He is allowed to have a taste of the ultimate

[68] A category coined by Keydell (1930) in a section called 'Nonnos und die Nonnianer'.
[69] According to Cameron (1982: 239), but this is still *sub iudice*.
[70] A summary in Keydell (1959: 35–42).
[71] See the classic edition of Paul's poems by Friedländer (1912).

encounter with the divine light, a paradoxical 'sun in the night', a well-known symbol in mystical visions (806–9,):[72]

> Thus is everything clothed in beauty; everything you will perceive
> with eyes full of wonder (θάμβος). But no words are sufficient
> to describe the illumination in the evening: you might say that some
> nocturnal sun filled the majestic temple with light.

John of Gaza (fl. 535) also lived in the age of Justinian, in a cultural centre of Late Antiquity which flourished especially due to its School of Rhetoric (and philosophy).[73] As Aeneas of Gaza would put it, John's hometown was the 'new Attica'.[74] John of Gaza composed the *Tabula Mundi*, a poetical description of the frescoes on the ceiling of the baths of Gaza, which presented a mixture of mythological and Christian leitmotifs. As in the case of Paul the Silentiary (fl. 562), the viewer of the work of art experiences a form of Neoplatonic enlightenment, a feeling of elevation and ascent to the Good and to Knowledge. The poet declares himself to be seized by the ecstasy of such contemplation (*Tab. Mund.* 26–30,):

> Where am I taken? (Πῆ φέρομαι;) The Sirens take me through the air
> on the crystalline murmur of their winged voice that bursts with meaning (ἔμφρονι ῥοίζῳ); The Muses fan my desire using their plectrum as a spur
> and I tread the foreign paths of the sky, a traveller on foot (πεζὸς ὁδίτης),
> raised by a creative transport. As for Apollo …

John shows a clear preference for Neoplatonic vocabulary, epithets and formulas such as *noeron phaos* (2.235) or *autotelestos*, in the allegorical interpretation of the cosmos, appearing as a wise and noetic poet, as Gigli Piccardi has pointed out in a pioneering study (Gigli Piccardi 2014). We can see some hexametric verses in his *Tabula mundi* regarding the God Oceanus and including noetic, Pagan and mystic vocabulary. In addition, John also wrote iambic *Anacreontics* where he shows clear Platonic echoes and words denoting the intelligible world (*Tabula mundi* 1.307–10; *Anacreontics* 6. 76–80). We can consider this aesthetic experience close to the mystical way leading to the contemplation of the One, as underlined by Plotinus (Gigli Piccardi 2014: 410).

Our last Nonnian poet of this brief survey is George of Pisidia (fl. 630), deacon at the church of Hagia Sophia, and official poet at the court of Emperor Heraclius, in the 7th century. This time period was not only turbulent due to civil strife and wars against the Persians and Arabs, but it was also characterised by an abrupt change in Byzantine poetry. The latter developed a preference for sacred themes at the expense of secular verse, with iambic poems gaining acceptance while the by then decadent hexameter would be reserved only for scholarly compositions (De Stefani 2014: 377–8). The Byzantine schools of rhetoric and philosophy were

[72] English translation adapted from Mango (1986: 89).
[73] Bitton-Ashkelony & Kofsky (2004), and Saliou (2005).
[74] Aeneas of Gaza, *Ep.* 18 in Massa Positano (1962).

naturally affected by the fall of the learned regions of Syria, Palestine or Egypt – let us think of Gaza or Alexandria – first to the Persians and later to the Muslims. George still wrote some hexameter poetry[75] in the Nonnian fashion (90 verses on human existence), although most of his surviving poems – some theological works and most of them eulogies of the emperor's deeds – are written in iambic trimeters. In spite of the change of metre, Neoplatonic aesthetics and ontology were kept alive in poems like the *Persian Expedition* or the *Hexaemeron*, an account of the creation of the universe which shows a very remarkable influence of Christian Neoplatonism, especially that of Pseudo-Dionysius and of negative theology. George addresses directly the alleged head of Pagan Neoplatonism, Proclus himself, in a very interesting passage (*Hex.* verses 60–5, 77–8) on the eternity of the world against the Christian idea of divine creation. Proclus appears as excessively confident in 'worldly reasons' (Ἀλλ' ὦ σοφιστὰ Πρόκλε τῶν κάτω λόγων), such as pagan science (61–70). As Blowers put it, 'George thrashes the Neoplatonist Proclus as a symbol of the pretensions of Greek cosmology, contrasting his "thunderous" sophistry which dares to view creation as eternal, with "the great power of a few syllables" [ἄκουε μικρῶν συλλαβῶν κράτος μέγα, v. 65] (referring to the opening phrase of the Genesis, "in the beginning")' (Blowers 2012: 134). Let us see the beginning of the poem, addressed to the patriarch Sergius of Constantinople, with noetic vocabulary and allusions to the light of knowledge (*Hex.* 1–17, [illegible]):[76]

> O thou who art language, mind, nourishment and heart of every work and word that speaks of God! Thou that pourest in my arid heart the currents of your speech running through the spaces of heavens! The darkness of which I was a prey constrained my mouth to silence, because it was blocked by the whirlwind that breathes the word: nothing more in the cloud of discouragement generates storm and tornados in thoughts, obscuring the sun of eloquence.

5. Some Byzantine Neoplatonic Poets

After this turning point in the history of literature, which is also very relevant in history with the entrance onto the scene of Islam, one could think that the fondness for Neoplatonic aesthetics in Greek poetry of the Byzantine period was gone for good. Perhaps the bizarre mixture of Pagan and Christian Neoplatonism represented by the School of Nonnus came to an end, but only on the surface. In my opinion, Neoplatonic poetics survived on two levels: in the official discourse of orthodox theology, where mysticism played an important role especially from the 11th century onwards; and in the poems with Neoplatonic nuances composed from the very beginnings of Byzantium, in Late Antiquity, as the remarkable hymns of Gregory of Nazianzus (329–90 CE) go to show. Gregory, as Simelidis (2009: 38) has

[75] *Patrologia Graeca* 92.1195–1754. Cf. Pertusi (1959), Ludwig (1991) and Gonnelli (1998).

[76] Translation adapted from Tartaglia (1998: 310ff.).

shown, is well aware of Neoplatonic mysticism and poetry. This can be seen in the following excerpt from a prayer to Christ, where he quotes the aforementioned oracle of Plotinus's soul,[77] the first Neoplatonic poem attested (II.1.1. 279–82; ed. Tuilier & Bady 2004,):

> Prayers and dear laments, and sleepless nights,
> angelic choirs, and those who raise psalms to God,
> They stand and send the souls to God through hymns,
> So that they sing joining the sound of many voices (ξυνὴν ὄπα γηρύοντες).

Perhaps the most conspicuous example of later Christian Neoplatonism in Byzantium is the mystical oeuvre of Symeon the New Theologian (949–1022), an heir of Gregory the Theologian, whose debt to the Platonic tradition is all-pervading. Author of a remarkable theological work written in treatises and discourses, Symeon also wrote *Hymns of Divine Love*, 58 poems in approximately 11,000 verses telling of his mystic visions of God. The poet describes his experience with this divine luminosity in a sort of ascent of the soul to the union with God as he tried to express the ineffable mysteries of the Holy Trinity, God the Father and the Nature of Christ. Let us see some excerpts of his first *Hymn* (1–4, 21–9; McGuckin 2005: 191–2,):

> What is this awesome mystery that is taking place within me?
> I can find no words to express it:
> My poor hand is unable to capture it,
> In describing the praise and glory that belong
> To the One who is above all praise,
> And who transcends every word …
> Here my tongue does not find any words.
> My intellect sees what has happened,
> But it cannot explain it;
> It can see, and wishes to explain,
> But can find no word that suffices,
> For what it sees is invisible and entirely formless,
> Simple, completely uncompounded,
> Unbounded in its awesome greatness.
> What I have seen is the totality recapitulated as One,
> Received not in essence but by participation.
> It is just as if you lit a flame from a live flame:
> It is the entire flame you receive.

Symeon contains typically Neoplatonic mystic features, such as the ascent to the One 'above all praise … and who transcends every word' (ὑπέρ ἔπαινον … ὑπέρ λόγον) and the comparison with the Greek mysteries. The human language is not enough to describe Symeon's mystic experience and although the 'intellect sees what has

[77] In 'So that they sing joining the sound of many voices' (ξυνὴν ὄπα γηρύοντες) he echoes the invocation of the oracle in Porph. *Vit. Plot.* 22.16: κλήζω καὶ Μούσας ξυνὴν ὄπα γηρύσασθαι.

happened', he is not able to interpret it (καί τά τελούμενα ὁ νοῦς ὁρᾷ, οὐχ ἑρμηνεύει). The mystic light and the Platonic participation in the One are other recurrent issues in his poetry. There are plenty of other examples whose analysis would go beyond the scope of this chapter, but which show evident familiarity with the mystic discourse of the Platonic tradition.[78] Some scholars have seen striking parallels between Symeon and the description of the One and the light in Plotinus, ultimately referring to Plato's *Republic* (507d) (Hladký 2010). In *Hymn* 50 (335–40) Symeon speaks about the ascent to the Good using the Platonic allegory of the chariot (Baranov 2015: 188–9, [illegible]):

> The saints, as we have said,
> each rising on the wings of their virtues, (τῶν ἀρετῶν ἕκαστος πτεροῖς ἀρθέντες)
> will go out to meet the Lord,
> each according to his merit how
> he prepared himself, of course,
> closer or farther from the Creator.

Let us finish by quoting the most striking parallel between Symeon and the Neoplatonic tradition. The *Enneads* conclude with Plotinus opening the way for the ultimate journey of the soul freed from the bonds of the body, towards the intelligible world, the reversion to its godly status:

> This is the life of gods and of the god-like and blessed among men (ἀνθρώπων θείων καὶ εὐδαιμόνων), liberation from the alien that besets us here, a life taking no pleasure in the things of earth, the passing of solitary to solitary (φυγὴ μόνου πρὸς μόνον).
> (VI 9 [9] 11, M: 549)

The Plotinian idea of solitary mysticism (μόνου πρὸς μόνον) and silence was also influential on Christian writers such as Basil of Cesarea and Gregory of Nyssa (Iozzia 2015: 48). As Baranov has noticed, Symeon the New Theologian often uses modifications of this Plotinian idea of 'the passing of solitary to solitary'.[79] At the very beginning of the prose introduction to his *Hymns*, Symeon consciously links his poetic endeavour with the end of Plotinus's *Enneads* in the idea of the path of solitary mysticism (Koder 1969: 150–1; Baranov 2015: 191):

> Come, truthful light! Come, eternal life! Come hidden mystery! Come, indescribable treasure! Come, ineffable thing! Come, inconceivable person! Come, endless delight! Come, unsetting light! ... Come, you for whom my poor soul longed and still longs. Come, the Alone to the alone (ὁ μόνος πρὸς μόνον), for I am alone, as You see! Come,

[78] For example, in *Hymn* 12 Symeon sings 'the One in the three hypostases of divinity' with astonishing use of Neoplatonic vocabulary regarding the mystical vision with 'noetic eyes' (τοῖς νοεροῖς ὄμμασί). Another theological hymn displaying abundant Neoplatonic vocabulary is *Hymn* 23 'On the exact theology of the imperceptible and indescribable divinity', in whose verses 177–90 Symeon speaks of the creator not with the usual word in the rest of his poems (*ktistis*) but as a Platonic Demiurge, who owns the universe as a whole, and claims that 'if you see the sensible, you'll not see the noetic sun'. *Hymn* 25 deals specifically with the 'divine light' and *Hymn* 28 bears as title 'On the noetic revelation of the energies of the divine light, etc.' Finally, let us just mention the astonishing reworking of the Platonic allegory of the Cave in *Hymn* 30 (206–20; 240–3), as studied by Baranov (2015: 183–5).

[79] Baranov (2015: 191, n. 32). *Hymn* 15.136; 23.426; 27.73; 28.1–2; 35.38; 29.260–65; 30.166.

> the One Who separated me from everything and made me alone on Earth! ... I thank you because you have become One spirit with mine ...

Christian reuse of Neoplatonism would need a separate treatment and, in fact, there are several books already trying to deal with it.[80] Nevertheless, by way of conclusion of this succinct survey, let us add that there was an underground current of Platonism deeply related to the literal meaning of the Athenian philosopher in his original pagan context, and heavily dependent on the Late Antique pagan interpretation of Neoplatonists like Proclus or Damascius. It was a current that never disappeared and one can trace it in several Byzantine philosophers often accused of being 'ideologically' pagan (*hellenes*) by their rivals. We follow here the view of Siniossoglou (2011) who argues that some pagan Platonism was maintained from the end of the Academy until the fall of Constantinople. This happened because Neoplatonic authors such as Proclus and others were continuously copied in 'scriptoria' in spite of their bad reputations and used in universities such as the one established in the palace of Magnaura, in the capital, in the 9th century by order of Caesar Bardas. A proof of this antiquarian passion for Neoplatonic lore is the fondness for oracular poetry in Byzantium. Although the *Chaldean Oracles* were regarded as deeply pagan, two key examples of learned men of letters in Byzantium commented on them: Psellos and Plethon,[81] two Byzantine Neoplatonists who, as their admired precursor Proclus did, also indulged in poetry.

The first one is the prolific writer Michael Psellos (*c.* 1018–81), appointed 'Consul of the Philosophers' by the emperor. Apart from his commentaries on Aristotelian treatises, Psellos was a devotee of Platonic and Neoplatonic traditions. In his work he discusses all kinds of philosophical issues such as the Platonic Forms, the unity of the soul and the body, or the problem of matter and evil. Psellos admired Proclus, whom he considered one of the greatest authorities of all times and the heir of the ancient wisdom. Besides Proclus, he edited and commented the aforementioned *Chaldean Oracles*, among other texts considered far from orthodox Christianity. As in the case of Proclus, this philosopher also wrote an important collection of poems, among which we can quote several reminiscent of Neoplatonic aesthetics and leitmotifs, edited by Westerink in 1992. In his *Poem* 13 the movements of the soul are compared to the movements of heaven in the tradition of Plato's *Timaeus* and *Republic* and Plotinus's *Enneads*. In this text we can see a good example of his combination of poetry and philosophy ():

> You will find in us a hidden image of the primordial movements of heaven
> and of the inherent passions in it.
> Our intellect, as a shining light-bearer,
> represents in some way the very wise sun.
> The soul is an imitation of the moon.

[80] V.gr. Iozzia (2015) or Mariev (2017).

[81] A detailed explanation goes beyond our scope, but see Seng (2012) for Psellos's political and rhetorical reutilisation of the *Chaldean Oracles* in his time. For Pletho's work on these oracles, see Tambrun (2006: 92–4 and chapter 4) and Siniossoglou (2011: chapters 1 and 2).

As the most beautiful and greatest light
the intellect is all luminous and bright.
But the soul, after falling in the nature of the body,
only shines in half.
Whatever is brought aptly to the intellect
has a participation in the light as in the first one.
But if something falls down to perception,
it will be deprived of light and full of darkness.
While the intellect hears the sublime words
and refers them wisely with splendid bright,
the soul, sitting amid shadows,
is darkened there in her nature.
In the dark somehow, surrounded by obscurity
and running out of the intelligible light,
embraces its shining rays.
And here is the earth, moon, light-bearer,
soul and flesh and mind accordingly.
One against another they oppose somehow, except in good reason,
intellect with the sun, body with the earth,
animated substance with the moon.
For the intellect is naturally the substance of the light,
the body is devoid of light,
and the soul, which happens to be between both of them,
participates of the light when close to the intellect,
and does not participate, when near the body.

The allegorical method of Proclus and Damascius is applied in this poem to the stars and the primordial movements of heaven as they are equated to those of the intellect, the soul and the body. Following the typical metaphor, the intellect is the sun of wisdom and the soul falls into the lunar influence as an imitation of the moon. The fall of the soul, its enslavement in the body and the way in which it perceives only a distant light of the *nous* also recall the Neoplatonic system. In our dark and sensible world, the soul is far from the noetic light, but whenever it gets closer to the sun of the intellect it participates in this illumination.

Another interesting poem of the corpus of Psellos includes an allegory of the three parts of the soul, according to Plato's *Republic* and evoking also the myth of the Charioteer in *Phaedrus* (poem n.10, verse 8): θυμός, λόγος πόθος τε, κρειττόνων ἔρως. Much richer and complex are the Platonic echoes of the longer *Hexaemeron*, a poem on the Creation (n.55), or the rich interaction between Platonism and Biblical poetry in his commentary on the Psalms, dedicated to Emperor Michael. *Poem* 63, normally known as *De anima sua*, seems a Christianised Neoplatonic testament regarding the circular voyages of the soul on its way to reversion (31–5, [illegible]):

Intellect, with the wings of the heart ...,
Go up most swiftly to heavens,
Cross the angelic multitudes,
Advance through the triachies of archangels,
Arrive before the divine throne of Trinity ...

Last but not least, we have the Pagan Neoplatonic revival of George Gemistus (1355–1452), on the eve of the end of Byzantium as a political entity. George Gemistus called himself Pletho, paying homage to Plato thanks to a synonym of his surname. It is very remarkable that Pletho went beyond the long-term dissimulation of pagan Platonism and challenged the orthodoxy of his turbulent time by proposing a new utopia heavily based on Plato, especially on the Laws, and on the renewal of the old pagan religion. His treatise *On the Laws* contains a utopian constitution for a perfect state, in the Platonic tradition, including a religion based on ancient Hellenism. As Mariev states,

> he was convinced that the salvation of the Byzantines depended on a political and spiritual renewal ... The pantheon that he developed in the *Laws* shows clear analogies with Proclian theology. And yet, his attitude towards Neoplatonism and especially the Neoplatonic doctrines of Proclus is not merely receptive. On the one hand, Plethon did adopt and reformulate within his own theoretical framework a number of important elements of Proclus' metaphysics. On the other hand, the theoretical distance between him and Proclus is difficult to overlook.
>
> (2017: 18–19)

But in addition to being inspired by Proclian theology and ontology Pletho also composed poems in the Proclian manner to honour the ancient gods as new gods of his utopian state (Alexandre & Pellissier 1858: 203–5,):

> *First annual hymn, to Zeus*:
>
> Father Zeus, self-father, most ancient creator,
> O King, Maker of everything, most excellent and possessor of all things,
> Omnipotent, you who are the Being, the One, and the Good in yourself,
> you who from eternity generated everything,
> the greatest from yourself, the other things from these,
> bestowing upon them the greatest excellence possible,
> be favourable and save us leading us with the rest of nature
> through your always illustrious children, to whom you commended
> the destiny fixed by you, as it is suitable, which is destined to us too.
>
> *Second hymn, also annual, to the gods*:
>
> Illustrious children of Zeus, Being in himself and Maker of everything,
> O commanders who lead us with justice,
> Let us not cease to have you for our guides
> and to obey the correct laws you love,
> as far as we can, for they are the only ones capable of putting us in the good way.
> But you, O Gods, lead the intellect our charioteer,
> that you made of similar nature to yourselves,
> allow us to lead our lifetime well in all aspects
> and above all let us chant with you the supreme Zeus.

The *First hymn*, to Zeus, speaks of an abstract deity that is named Neoplatonically the demiurge, the essence of every ontology and absolute Unity (αὐτοεόν τε, καὶ αὐτοὲν). In the *Second hymn*, to the gods, the philosopher-poet addresses the whole polytheistic pantheon hoping to obtain illumination for the mind (*nous*). These hymns are contained in Book III of the *Laws*, with three sections explaining morning, afternoon and evening 'invocations to the gods', following very detailed instructions and the liturgy to follow (Woodhouse 1986: 344–53). These poetic and philosophical prayers portray a world ruled by Zeus as 'first cause, existing by himself, one in himself, good in himself, exceedingly great' (346), with intermediate deities and entities (Hera, Pluto, Kronos, the Titans ...); for Zeus created the second order of gods and gave them power to create a third one, so that deity is 'multiplied into a trinity' and granted us participation in the Good through imitation of this hierarchical ontology.

The debt to Proclus's triadic theology and hymnic poetry is evident, but some authors have compared Pletho's hymns and rites to a mystic and even magic path of self-improvement through *phantasia*, in the Neoplatonic tradition. Pletho's purported Neopagan approach was highly controversial already in his lifetime and he was soon read by both Renaissance and Ottoman intellectuals. His views on invocations and theurgic poetry have been compared, for example, to that of Ficino and to the Islamic tradition. For Walker (2000: 61), Pletho's invocations, 'like Ficino's, do not aim at an objective effect of the deity addressed, but only at a subjective transformation of the worshipper, particularly his imagination'. On the other side, the Arabic translator of Pletho viewed his philosophy as similar to Sufism, which he disapproved of (Mavroudi 2013: 202), and was fully aware of its theurgical background. In any case, it is certainly surprising to find, as late as the 15th century, such a vindication of Neoplatonic paganism, symbolizing both the *rentrée* of Hellenism to Renaissance Europe and its long-term survival in the Islamic tradition. Like other Greek masters and emigrés, Pletho had a great influence on Italian soil through his pupil, Cardinal Bessarion (Woodhouse 1986: 32–3), and was himself in Italy in the famous council of Florence of 1438, where the Great Schism between the Eastern and Western churches took place.

Hladký (2014) has also recently studied Pletho and, contrary to Siniossoglou (2011), believes that Pletho was a mere philosopher devoted to Platonism and rather unorthodox, but not a pagan. In fact, he argues that Pletho supported orthodoxy at the Synod of Ferrara-Florence (1438–9) as a true Christian (2014: 280) and that his *Laws* were a personal and literary exercise of stylisation of himself as a 'second Plato', creating a classicising alter ego. In any case the radical Neoplatonic poetics of Pletho, who died in 1452, opened the way for new utopian and humanistic thought in Western Europe and constitutes in my view the last example of Greek Neoplatonic poetry, symbolically coinciding with the fall of Constantinople to the Ottoman Turks and the inauguration of a new epoch. In a parallel manner to that first Neoplatonic poem about the destiny of the soul of Plotinus, Cardinal Bessarion, the most outstanding disciple of Pletho, paid a poetic homage to his master in a eulogistic epigram, which can well be a *coda* to this contribution (Siniossoglou 2011: 7; Centanni 2019: 377–8,):

Cardinal Bessarion to the wise Pletho

Earth for his body, but George's soul rules among the stars
There, in that most sacred place, all learning has its home.
Greece has inspired many god-like men

> both in the field of learning and in other virtues.
> but all of them by Plethon are eclipsed
> as morning stars are dimmed by Phaeton's gleam.

If Pletho seemed at first a new Proclus, for his combination of philosophical theory and poetic praxis, here the journey of Pletho's soul reminds us of that of Plotinus, which also 'entered at once the heavenly consort' and 'crowned with unfading life', dwells now 'with the Ever-Holy'. Bessarion cheats a bit in the metre,[82] as if the end of Neoplatonic verse was also marked by a certain decay of classical poetry precisely in the age of the tragic Fall of the New Rome. He was also apparently inspired by Proclus's epigram: when the Athenian philosopher died, 'in the 124th year from Julian's accession to the empire … on the seventeenth of April' (485 CE), his disciple and biographer Marinus (*Vit. Procl.* 36) records an epigram, which Proclus himself had composed to be engraved on the double funerary monument he shared with his master Syrianus (Edwards 2000: 113, [illegible]):

> Proclus I am, by race a man of Lycia, whom Syrianus
> fostered here to become the successor to his own school.
> This is the common tomb which received the bodies of both men.
> Oh may a single Place be a portion of both their souls.

Pletho died in Mistra in 1452, or most probably in 1454, according to George of Trebizond (Monfasani 1976: 170). If the second date is correct, he lived to know of the Fall of Constantinople in 1453. He was buried there, although some years later, in 1466, some of his disciples from Italy, headed by the Neo-Pagan Sigismundo Malatesta, took his remains from Constantinople to the 'Tempio Malatestiano' in Rimini, so that he could rest 'among free men'.[83] His epitaph reads 'prince among the philosophers of his time' (IEMISTII BIZANTII PHILOSOPHOR. SVA TEMP. PRINCIPIS RELIQVVM, Peritore 1977: 169; Centanni 2019: 379). He was no doubt both the last Neoplatonist and the last Neoplatonic poet of the Greek Pagan tradition.

References

Agosti, G. (2009), 'La Vita di Proclo di Marino nella sua redazione in versi. Biografia e poesia nella scuola Neoplatonica', *Cento Pagine*, 3: 30–46.

Alexandrakis, A. (2002), 'Neoplatonic Influences on Greek Iconography', in A. Alexandrakis & N.J. Moutafakis (eds), *Neoplatonism and Western Aesthetics* (Albany, SUNY Press), 75–87.

Alexandre, C. & Pellissier, A. (1858), *Pléthon. Traité des Lois* (Paris, Firmin Didot).

Alviz Fernández, M. (2016), 'El concepto de θεῖος ἀνήρ en la antigüedad tardía. Hacia un nuevo marco definitorio', *Espacio, Tiempo y Forma. Serie II. Historia antigua*, 29: 11–25.

[82] Ebbesens (2013: 9, n. 13): unless τῇ τε ἄλλῃ is changed to τῇ τ 'ἄλλῃ the metre does not work and in παραλλάσσει there is no possible correction.

[83] Siniossoglou (2011: 9); Paganelli (2013: 44, n. 9); Hladký (2014: 230).

Athanassiadi, P. (1999), 'The Chaldean Oracles: Theology and Theurgy', in P. Athanassiadi & M. Frede (eds), *Pagan Monotheism in Late Antiquity* (Oxford, Oxford University Press), 149–83.

Athanassiadi, P. (2010), 'Julian the Theurgist: Man or Myth?', in H. Seng & M. Tardieu (eds), *Die Chaldaeischen Orakel: Kontext, Interpretation, Rezeption* (Heidelberg, Universitätsverlag Winter), 193–208.

Baranov, V. (2015), 'Escaping Plato's Cave: Some Platonic Metaphors in Symeon the New Theologian', *Scrinium: Journal of Patrology and Critical Hagiography*, 11: 181–96.

Bardill, J. (2012), *Constantine, Divine Emperor of the Christian Golden Age* (New York, Cambridge University Press).

Barfield, R. (2011), *The Ancient Quarrel between Philosophy and Poetry* (Cambridge/ New York, University of Cambridge Press).

Bekker, I. (ed.) (1824), *Photii bibliotheca* (Berlin, G. Reimeri).

Berchman, R.M. (2005), *Porphyry Against the Christians* (Leiden, Brill).

Bergmann, M. (1977), *Studien zum römische Porträt des 3. Jahrhunderts n. Chr*, vol. 3 (Bonn, Habelt).

Bianchi Bandinelli, R. (1971), *Rome, the Late Empire: Roman Art, A.D. 200–400* (London, Thames & Hudson).

Bieler, L. (1967), *Theîos Anér: das Bild des Göttlichen Menschen in Spätantike und Frühchristentum* (Darmstadt, Wissenschaftliche Buchgesellschaft).

Bitton-Ashkelony, B. & Kofsky, A. (eds) (2004), *Christian Gaza in Late Antiquity* (Leiden/ Boston, Brill).

Blowers, P.M. (2012), *Drama of the Divine Economy: Creator and Creation in Early Christian Theology and Piety* (Oxford, Oxford University Press).

Brisson, L. & Flamand, J.-M. (1992), 'Structure, contenu et intentions de L'Oracle d'Apollon (Porphyre, VP 22)', in L. Brisson *et al.* (eds), *Porphyre. La Vie de Plotin*, vol. 2 (Paris, J. Vrin), 565–602.

Busine, A. (2005), *Paroles d'Apollon. Pratiques et traditions oraculaires dans l'antiquité tardive (IIe–VIe siècles)* (Leiden/Boston, Brill).

Cameron, A. (1965), 'Wandering Poets: A Literary Movement in Byzantine Egypt', *Historia*, 14: 470–509.

Cameron, A. (1969), 'The Last Days of the Academy at Athens', *Proceedings of the Cambridge Philological Society*, 195: 7–29.

Cameron, A. (1982), 'The Empress and the Poet: Paganism and Politics at the Court of Theodosius II', *Yale Classical Studies*, 27: 217–89.

Centanni, M. (2019), 'Bessarione e Gemisto Pletone: Lettere dall'esilio', in F. Furlan, G. Siemoneit & H. Wulfram (eds), *Exil und Heimatferne in der Literatur des Humanismus von Petrarca bis zum Anfang des 16. Jahrhunderts* (Tübingen, Narr), 361–83.

Chaniotis, A., Corsten, T., Stroud, R.S. & Tybout, R.A. (eds) (2005), *Supplementum Epigraphicum Graecum LI (2001)* (Amsterdam, J.C. Gieben).

Chiaradonna, R. (2014), 'Tolleranza religiosa e Neoplatonismo politico tra III e IV secolo', in A. Marcone, U. Roberto & I. Tantillo (eds), *Tolleranza religiosa in età tardoantica. III–IV secolo*: *Atti delle giornate di studio sull'età tardoantica, Roma, 26–27 maggio 2013* (Cassino, Edizioni Università di Cassino), 37–80.

De Garay Suárez-Llanos, J. (2017), 'The Reception of Proclus: From Byzantium to the West (an Overview)', in S. Mariev (ed.), *Byzantine Perspectives on Neoplatonism* (Berlin/ Boston, Walter de Gruyter), 153–73.

De Stefani, C. (2014), 'The End of the "Nonnian School"', in Spanoudakis (2014), 375–402.

Des Places, E. (1971), *Oracles Chaldaïques. Avec un choix de commentaires anciens* (Paris, Les Belles Lettres).

Des Places, E. (1973), *Numénius, Fragments* (Paris, Les Belles Lettres).

Dillon, J. (1976), 'Image, Symbol and Analogy: Three Basic Concepts of Neoplatonic Allegorical Exegesis', in H. Baine (ed.), *The Significance of Neoplatonism* (Norfolk, SUNY Press), 247–62.

Dodds, E.R. (1951), *The Greeks and the Irrational* (Berkeley, University of California Press).

Dodds, E.R. (1965), *Pagan and Christian in an Age of Anxiety* (Cambridge, Cambridge University Press).

Domaradzki, M. (2014), 'Symbolic Poetry, Inspired Myths and Salvific Function of Allegoresis in Proclus' Commentary on the Republic', *Peitho. Examina antiqua*, 5: 119–37.

Doroszewski, F. (2016), *Orgie słów. Terminologia misteriów w 'Parafrazie Ewangelii wg św. Jana' Nonnosa z Panopolis* (Toruń, UMK).

Du Toit, D.S. (1997), *THEIOS ANTHROPOS. Zur Verwendung von θεῖος ἄνθρωπος und sinnverwandten Ausdrücken in der Literatur der Kaiserzeit* (Tübingen, Mohr).

Ebbesens, S. (2013), 'Georgios Gemistos, også kaldet Plethon: Memorandum til kejser Manuel Palæologos om forholdene på Peloponnes', *Aigis*, 113.1: 1–15.

Edwards, M.J. (1993), 'A Portrait of Plotinus', *The Classical Quarterly*, 43.2: 480–90.

Edwards, M.J. (ed.) (2000), *Neoplatonic Saints: The Lives of Plotinus and Proclus by their Students, Translated with an Introduction by M. Edwards* (Liverpool, Liverpool University Press).

Eich, P. (2011), *Gottesbild und Wahrnehmung: Studien zu Ambivalenzen früher griechischer Götterdarstellungen (ca. 800 v.Chr. - ca. 400 v.Chr.)* (Stuttgart, Franz Steiner Verlag).

Elsner, J. (1998), *Imperial Rome and Christian Triumph* (Oxford, Oxford University Press).

Elsner, J. (2006), 'Late Antique Art: The Problem of the Concept and the Cumulative Aesthetic', in S. Swain & M.J. Edwards (eds), *Approaching Late Antiquity: The Transformation from Early to Late Empire* (Oxford, Oxford University Press), 271–309.

Ferwerda, R. (1965), *La signification des images et des méthaphores dans le pensée de Plotin* (Groningen, J.B. Wolters).

Francis, J.A. (2012), 'Late Antique Visuality: Blurring the Boundaries Between Word and Image, Pagan and Christian', in D. Brakke, D. Deliyannis & E. Watts (eds), *Shifting Cultural Frontiers in Late Antiquity* (Farnham/Burlington, Ashgate), 139–49.

Friedländer, P. (1912), *Johannes von Gaza und Paulus Silentiarius: Kunstbeschreibungen Justinianischer Zeit* (Leipzig, Teubner).

Gauger, J.D. (2011), *Sibyllinische Weissagungen. Griechisch-Deutsch* (Düsseldorf/Zürich, Tusculum).

Gelzer, T. (1966), 'Die Epigramme des Neuplatonikers Proklos', *Museum Helveticum*, 23.1: 1–36.

Gelzer, T. (1993), 'Heidnisches und Christliches im Platonismus der Kaiserzeit und der Spätantike', in D. Willers *et al.* (eds), *Riggisberger Berichte I: Begegnungen von Heidentum und Christentum in spätantiken Ägypten* (Riggisberg, Abegg Stiftung), 33–48.

Gifford, H.E. (ed.) (1981), Eusebius, *Preparation for the Gospel*, II (Grand Rapids, Baker Book House).

Gigli Piccardi, D. (1985), *Metafora e poetica in Nonno di Panopoli* (Florence, La Nuova Italia).

Gigli Piccardi, D. (2014), 'Poetic Inspiration in John of Gaza: Emotional Upheaval and Ecstasy in a Neoplatonic Poet', in Spanoudakis (2014), 403–20.

Gonnelli, F. (1998), *Giorgio di Pisidia, Hexaemeron* (Pisa, Edizioni ETF).

Goulet, R. (1982), 'L'Oracle d'Apollon', in L. Brisson, M.-O. Goulet Cazé & D. O'Brien (eds), *Porphyre, La Vie de Plotin*, vol. 1 (Paris, J. Vrin), 371–412.

Goulet, R. (2004), 'Hypothèses récentes sur le traité de Porphyre *Contre les chrétiens*', in M.Narcy & E. Rebillard (eds), *Hellénisme et Christianisme* (Villeneuve d'Ascq, Presses Universitaires du Septentrion), 61–109.

Grabar, A. (1945), 'Plotin et les origines de l'esthétique médiévale', *Cahiers Archéologiques de la fin de l'antiquité et du Moyen Age*, 1: 15–34.

Greco, C. (2004), *Nonno di Panopoli, Parafrasi del Vangelo di S. Giovanni. Canto tredicesimo* (Alessandria, Edizioni dell'Orso).

Griswold, C.L. (2016), 'Plato on Rhetoric and Poetry', in E.N. Zalta (ed.), *The Stanford Encyclopedia of Philosophy* (Fall 2016 Edition), accessed 9 February 2019, https://plato.stanford.edu/archives/fall2016/entries/plato-rhetoric/

Halliwell, S. (2002), *The Aesthetics of Mimesis: Ancient Texts and Modern Problems* (Princeton, Princeton University Press).

Helmig, C. & Steel, C. (2015), 'Proclus', in E.N. Zalta (ed.), *The Stanford Encyclopedia of Philosophy* (Summer 2015 Edition), accessed 9 February 2019, https://plato.stanford.edu/archives/sum2015/entries/proclus/

Hernández de la Fuente, D. (2011), 'The One and the Many and the Circular Movement: Neo-Platonism and Poetics in Nonnus of Panopolis', in D. Hernández de la Fuente (ed.), *New Perspectives on Late Antiquity* (Newcastle upon Tyne, Cambridge Scholars Publishing), 305–26.

Hernández de la Fuente, D. (2013), 'Der Chor des Dionysos: Religion und Erziehung in Platons Nomoi', *Zeitschrift für Religions- und Geistesgeschichte*, 65.1: 1–17.

Hernández de la Fuente, D. (2014), 'Neoplatonic Form and Content in Nonnus', in Spanoudakis (2014), 229–50.

Hladký, V. (2010), 'Světelná metaforika v Hymnech Symeóna Nového Theologa a její role v Plótínově filosofii', *Parrésia*, 4: 11–32.

Hladký, V. (2014), *The Philosophy of Gemistos Plethon: Platonism in Late Byzantium, between Hellenism and Orthodoxy* (Farnham/Burlington, Ashgate).

Hooker, M.A. (2008), *The Use of Sibyls and Sibylline Oracles in Early Christian Writers* (Cincinnati, University of Cincinnati).

Iozzia, D. (2015), *Aesthetic Themes in Pagan and Christian Neoplatonism: From Plotinus to Gregory of Nyssa* (London/New York, Bloomsbury Academic).

Johnston, S.I. (1990), *Hekate Soteira: A Study of Hekate's Roles in the Chaldean Oracles and Related Literature* (Atlanta, GA, Scholar's Press).

Karfíková, L. (2018), 'The Metaphor of the Mirror in Platonic Tradition and Gregory's Homilies on the Song of Songs', in G. Maspero, M. Brugarolas & I. Vigorelli (eds), *Gregory of Nyssa: In Canticum Canticorum. Analytical and Supporting Studies* (Leiden, Brill), 265–87.

Keydell, R. (1930), 'Die griechische Poesie der Kaiserzeit (bis 1929)', *Bursians*, 231: 41–161.

Keydell, R. (1959), *Dionysiaca I* (Berlin, Wiedmann).

Keyser, E. (1955), *La signification de l'Art dans les Ennéades de Plotin* (Louvain, Bibliothèque de l'Université).

Koder, J. (1969), *St. Syméon le Nouveau Théologien: Hymnes I: I–XV* (Paris, Éditions du Cerf).

Kroll, G. (ed.) (1899–1901), *Procli Diadochi in Platonis Rem Publicam Commentarii*, 2 vols (Leipzig, Teubner).

L'Orange, P. (1933), *Studien zur Geschichte des spätantiken Porträts* (Oslo, Aschehoug).

L'Orange, P. (1951), 'The Portrait of Plotin', *Cahiers Archéologiques de la fin de l'antiquité et du Moyen Age*, 5: 15–30.

Lakoff, G. & Johnson, M. (2003), *Metaphors We Live By* (London, The University of Chicago Press).

Lamberton, R. (1986), *Homer the Theologian: Neoplatonist Allegorical Reading and the Growth of the Epic Tradition* (Berkeley, University of California Press).

Lewy, H. (2011), *Chaldaean Oracles and Theurgy Mysticism, Magic and Platonism in the later Roman Empire*. Troisième édition par Michel Tardieu, avec un supplément 'Les Oracles chaldaïques 1891–2011' (Paris, Institut des Etudes Augustiniennes).

Louth, A. (ed.) (2003), *St John of Damascus: Three Treatises on the Divine Images* (Crestwood, St Vladimir's Seminary Press).

Ludwig, C. (1991), 'Kaiser Herakleios, Georgios Pisides und die Perserkriege', in P. Speck (ed.), *Varia III, Poikila Byzantina 11* (Bonn, Habelt), 73–128.

Majercik, R. (1989), *The Chaldean Oracles* (Leiden, Brill).

Majercik, R. (2001), 'Chaldean Triads in Neoplatonic Exegesis: Some Reconsiderations', *The Classical Quarterly*, 51.1: 265–96.

Mango, C.A. (1986), *The Art of the Byzantine Empire 312–1453: Sources and Documents* (Toronto, University of Toronto Press).

Mariev, S. (2017), 'Neoplatonic Philosophy in Byzantium', in S. Mariev (ed.), *Byzantine Perspectives on Neoplatonism* (Berlin/Boston, Walter de Gruyter), 1–30.

Massa Positano, L. (1962), *Enea di Gaza: Epistole*, 2nd edn (Naples, Libreria Scientifica Editrice).

Mavroudi, M. (2013), 'Plethon as a Subversive and His Reception in the Islamic World', in D. Angelov & M. Saxby (eds), *Power and Subversion in Byzantium: Papers from the 43rd Spring Symposium of Byzantine Studies, University of Birmingham, March 2010* (Farnham/Burlington, Ashgate Variorum), 177–204.

McGuckin, J.A. (2005), 'Symeon the New Theologian's Hymns of Divine Eros: A Neglected Masterpiece of the Christian Mystical Tradition', *Spiritus. A Journal of Christian Spirituality*, 5.2: 182–202.

Miguélez Cavero, L. (2008), *Poems in Context: Greek Poetry in the Egyptian Thebaid 200–600 AD* (Berlin/New York, Walter de Gruyter).

Monaca, M. (2008), *Oracoli Sibillini* (Rome, Città Nuova).

Monfasani, J. (1976), *George of Trebizond: A Biography and a Study of His Rhetoric and Logic* (Leiden, Brill).

Murray, P. (2015), 'Poetic Inspiration', in P. Destrée & P. Murray (eds), *A Companion to Ancient Aesthetics* (Hoboken, Wiley-Blackwell), 158–74.

Mylonopoulos, J. (2010), 'Divine Images versus Cult Images: An Endless Story about Theories, Methods, and Terminologies', in J. Mylonopoulos (ed.), *Divine Images and Human Imaginations in Ancient Greece and Rome* (Leiden, Brill), 1–19.

Noel Hubler, J. (2002), 'The Role of Aesthetics in Plotinus' Ascent of the Soul', in A. Alexandrakis & N.J. Moutafakis (eds), *Neoplatonism and Western Aesthetics* (Albany, SUNY Press), 193–205.

Norvin, W. (ed.) (1913), *Olympiodorus in Platonis Phaedonem commentaria* (Leipzig, Teubner).

O'Meara, D. (2003), *Platonopolis: Platonic Political Philosophy in Late Antiquity* (Oxford, Clarendon Press).

Paganelli, L. (2013), 'Ezra Pound in Rimini', *Linguistics and Literature Studies*, 1.1: 43–5.

Parke, H.W. (1988), *Sibyls and Sibylline Prophecy in Classical Antiquity* (London/New York, Routledge).

Paton, W.R. (1917). *The Greek Anthology, Volume 2: Books 7–8* (Cambridge MA, Harvard University Press).

Pavlos, P.G., Janby, L.F., Emilsson, E.K. & Tollefsen, T.T. (eds) (2019), *Platonism and Christian Thought in Late Antiquity* (London & New York, Routledge).

Pépin, J. (1970), 'Plotin et le Miroir de Dionysos (Enn. IV, 3 [27], 12, 1–2)', *Revue Internationale de Philosophie*, 24/92.2: 304–20.

Peritore, N.P. (1977), 'The Political Thought of Gemistos Plethon: A Renaissance Byzantine Reformer', *Polity*, 10.2: 168–91.

Pertusi, A. (1959), *Giorgio di Pisidia. Poemi, Panegirici epici* (Ettal, Buch-Kunstverlag).

Plotinus (1991), *Plotinus's Enneads*, ed. J. Dillon, trans. S. Mackenna (Harmondsworth, Penguin).

Potter, D.S. (1994), *Prophets and Emperors: Human and Divine Authority from Augustus to Theodosius* (Cambridge MA/London, Harvard University Press).

Prost, M.A. (ed.) (2003), *Nonnos of Panopolis: The Paraphrase of the Gospel of John* (Ventura, CA, The Writing Shop Press).

Puigarnau, A. (1998), 'Plotino, filósofo y teológo de la luz: antecedentes para una teología medieval de la imagen', *Ars Brevis: anuario de la Càtedra Ramon Llull Blanquerna*, 4: 223–46

Remes, P. (2008), *Neoplatonism* (Stocksfield Hall, Acumen).

Rouse, W.H.D. (ed.) (1940–2), *Nonnus, Dionysiaca*, 3 vols (Cambridge MA, Loeb Classical Library).

Saffrey, H.D. (1981), 'Les NéoPlatoniciens et les Oracles Chaldaïques', *Revue des Études Augustiniennes*, 27: 209–25.

Saffrey, H.D. & Westerink, L.G. (eds) (1968–97), *Proclus, Théologie Platonicienne. Texte établi et traduit. Livres I–VI* (Paris, Les Belles Lettres).

Saliou, C. (ed.) (2005), *Gaza dans l'Antiquité tardive. Archéologie, rhétorique et histoire* (Salerno, Helios).

Seng, H. (2012), 'Chaldaeerrhetorik bei Michael Psellos', in U. Criscuolo (ed.), *La retorica greca fra tardo antico ed età bizantina: idee e forme; convegno internazionale, Napoli 27–29 ottobre 2011* (Naples, D'Auria), 355–69.

Seng, H. (2016), *Un livre sacré de l'Antiquité tardive: Les Oracles Chaldaïques* (Turnhout, Brepols).

Sheppard, A.D.R. (1980), *Studies on the 5th and 6th Essays of Proclus' Commentary on the Republic* (Göttingen, Vandenhoeck & Ruprecht).

Sheppard, A.D.R. (2014), *The Poetics of Phantasia: Imagination in Ancient Aesthetics* (New York, Bloomsbury Academic).

Simelidis, C. (2009), *Selected Poems of Gregory of Nazianzus: I.2.17; II.1.10, 19, 32: Critical Edition with Introduction and Commentary* (Göttingen, Vandenhoeck & Ruprecht).

Siniossoglou, N. (2011), *Radical Platonism in Byzantium* (Oxford, Oxford University Press).

Siorvanes, L. (1996), *Proclus: Neo-Platonic Philosophy and Science* (Edinburgh, Edinburgh University Press).

Slaveva-Griffin, S.E. (2012), 'Contemplative Ascent in Plotinus and Rūmī', in K. Corrigan, J.D. Turner & P. Wakefield (eds), *Philosophy and Religion in Late Antiquity* (Sankt Augustin, Akademie Verlag), 195–212.

Slaveva-Griffin, S.E. (2013), 'Between the Two Realms: Plotinus' Pure Soul', in V. Adluri (ed.), *Greek Religion: Philosophy and Salvation* (Boston/Berlin, Walter de Gruyter), 313–42.

Spanoudakis, K. (ed.) (2014), *Nonnus of Panopolis in Context: Poetry and Cultural Milieu in Late Antiquity with a Section on Nonnus and the Modern World* (Berlin/Boston, Walter De Gruyter).

Steiner, D. (2001), *Images in Mind: Statues in Archaic and Classical Greek Literature and Thought* (Princeton, Princeton University Press).

Sweeny, L. (1982), 'Participation and the Structure of Being in Proclus' *Elements of Theology*', in R. Baine Harris (ed.), *The Structure of Being: A Neoplatonic Approach* (Albany, State University of New York Press), 140–55.
Tambrun, B. (2006), *Pléthon. Le retour de Platon* (Paris, Vrin).
Tanaseanu-Döbler, I. (2013), *Theurgy in Late Antiquity: The Invention of a Ritual Tradition* (Göttingen, Vandenhoeck & Ruprecht).
Tardieu, M. (1990), *Les paysages reliques. Routes et haltes syriennes d'Isidore à Simplicius* (Louvain/Paris, Peeters).
Tartaglia, L. (ed.) (1998), *Giorgio di Pisidia. Carmi* (Turin, Utet).
Tuilier, A. & Bady, G. (eds) (2004), *Saint Grégoire de Nazianze, Oeuvres poétiques Tome I. 1re partie. Poèmes personnels II, 1, 1–11. Texte établi par André Tuilier et Guillaume Bady. Traduit et annoté par Jean Bernardi* (Paris, Les Belles Lettres).
Van den Berg, R.M. (2001), *The Hymns of Proclus* (Leiden, Brill).
Viltanioti I.-F. (2017), 'Divine Powers and Cult Statues in Porphyry of Tyre', in A. Marmodoro & I.-F. Viltanioti (eds), *Divine Powers in Late Antiquity* (Oxford, Oxford University Press), 61–74.
Walker, D.P. (2000), *Spiritual and Demonic Magic: From Ficino to Campanella* (University Park, Pennsylvania State University Press).
Wallis, R.T. (1995), *Neoplatonism*, 2nd edn (London, Hackett).
Walter, C. (2006), *The Iconography of Constantine the Great, Emperor and Saint: With Associated Studies* (Leiden, Alexandros Press).
Watts, E.J. (2004), 'Justinian, Malalas, and the End of Athenian Philosophical Teaching in A.D. 529', *Journal of Roman Studies*, 94: 168–82.
Watts, E.J. (2005), 'Where to Live the Philosophical Life in the Sixth Century? Damascius, Simplicius, and the Return from Persia', *Greek, Roman and Byzantine Studies*, 45: 369–85.
Watts, E.J. (2008), *City and School in Late Antique Athens and Alexandria*, 2nd edn (Berkeley/London, University of California Press).
Watts, E.J. (2015), *The Final Pagan Generation* (Oakland, University of California Press).
Webb, R. (2009), *Ekphrasis, Imagination and Persuasion in Ancient Rhetorical Theory and Practice* (Ashgate, Surrey).
Westerink, L.G. (ed.) (1992), *Michaelis Pselli Poemata* (Teubner, Stuttgart-Leipzig).
Wilken, R.L. (2003), *The Christians as the Romans Saw Them*, 2nd edn (New Haven/London, Yale University Press).
Wlosok, A. (2005), 'Die christliche Apologetik griechischer und lateinischer Sprache bis zur konstantinischen Epoche. Fragen. Probleme, Kontroversen', in *Entretiens sur l'antiquité classique LI: L'apologétique chrétienne gréco-latine à l'époque prénicénienne* (Vandœuvres – Genève, Fondation. Hardt), 1–28.
Woodhouse, C.M. (1986), *George Gemistos Plethon, the Last of the Hellenes* (Oxford, Clarendon Press).
Zanker, P. (1996), *The Mask of Socrates: The Image of the Intellectual in Antiquity*, trans. A. Shapiro (Berkeley, University of California Press).
Zintzen, C. (ed.) (1967), *Damascii vitae Isidori reliquiae* (Hildesheim, Olms).

2

Stages of Ascent: Neoplatonic Affinities in Classical Arabic Poetry

STEFAN SPERL

THE AIM OF this chapter is to resolve a paradox.[1] Among the types of Classical Arabic verse where Neoplatonic concepts are most clearly in evidence is that of Sufism. But Sufi poetry makes little overt reference to philosophy. Its form, structure and conventional themes derive from a poetic tradition that came into being centuries before Greek philosophical texts were translated into Arabic. The question then arises whether Sufi poetry is tantamount to a Neoplatonic recasting of that earlier heritage or whether that heritage itself contains certain seeds of a Neoplatonic vision.

With the term 'seeds' I mean thematic, structural, prosodic or stylistic features of early Arabic poetry which would subsequently become significant expressive means to convey a recognisably Neoplatonic message. The case I would like to argue is that such features do exist and that identifying them can deepen our understanding of the development of Classical Arabic poetry. In addition, they may help to explain how for centuries in Islamic lands poetry that evolved out of Arabic models gave expression to man's relationship to the divine through principles which may appear Neoplatonic but which poets and audiences alike never perceived to be anything other than authentically Islamic. The chapters on Persian and Turkish poetry in this volume provide ample evidence for this, none more so than that of Walter Andrews which shows the Neoplatonic so internalised in the fabric of Ottoman society that it became 'an emotional script for life' (see pp. 169–87).

The argument proceeds by approaching a selected number of Arabic sources from the perspective of the *Enneads* in order to determine what affinities, analogies and differences come into view. We must begin with samples from pre-Islamic poetry and the Qur'an (6th to early 7th centuries CE) because together they provide

[1] I am greatly indebted to the late Emil Homerin and Mohammad Salama for their comments on this chapter.

Proceedings of the British Academy, **240**, 93–130, © The British Academy 2022.

the foundational point of reference for all Arabic poetry composed in subsequent times. Next, we turn to panegyric poetry produced in Iraq during the early Abbasid period (late 8th to 9th centuries) when a new, ornate and metaphorical style known as *al-badīʿ* ('the unprecedented') came into being which would dominate Arabic literary expression until the modern era. Lastly, we turn to the 13th century in order to show how the 'Plotinian seeds' identified in the earlier periods came to full flowering in the structure, style and themes of Sufi poetry and its most outstanding practitioners. Special attention is given throughout to the wider significance this development has had for poetry in other languages, notably Hebrew, Persian and Turkish as illustrated in the pages of this volume.

1. Pre-Islamic Poetry: The Path to Civic Virtue

From a Plotinian perspective the validity of any human endeavour must depend on the degree to which it promotes the soul's advance towards its highest goal: detachment from the sensible world and assimilation to the One. *Ennead* I 2 [19] reflects on the role of the Platonic virtues in this process and sees them operating at two distinct levels. At the lower level, wisdom, courage, self-control and justice function as 'civic virtues' by subjecting social interaction to order and measure. At the higher level, they turn into 'purificatory virtues' which serve to assist the individual soul in transcending the sensible world, in contemplating the intelligible realm and seeking union with the One.

The treatise concludes with the example of self-control. As a civic virtue, it enables the observance of limits to bring about the life of a good human being. As a purificatory virtue, it enables the isolation and detachment required of the life of a god (I 2 [19] 7, G: 62):

> For assimilation is to gods, not to good human beings. Assimilation to good human beings is making an image of an image, one from another. But the other assimilation is like making an image from a paradigm.[2]

If these criteria are applied to pre-Islamic poetry, certain similarities and differences become apparent. The notion of 'purificatory virtues', so important for Plotinus, would seem to be absent. What reigns supreme instead is an amalgam of 'civic virtues', known as *muruwwa* to which man is expected to aspire in order to become a 'good human being'. Indeed, the principal literary form of pre-Islamic poetry, the polythematic ode or 'qasida', has the purpose of charting the path towards the attainment of these virtues.[3]

[2] For the philosophical background of Plotinus's notion of god-likeness, see Stern-Gillet (2019).

[3] The centrality of virtues in pre-Islamic poetry has been recognised already by Classical Arabic critics, including notably Qudāma ibn Jaʿfar (d. 948) whose approach seems to have been inspired by Greek philosophical ethics as observed by Bonebakker (1956: 29–31). In modern times, the pre-Islamic canon of virtues has been extensively studied by a range of scholars, notably Izutsu (2002) and Montgomery (1986: 20) who deemed *muruwwa* as celebrated by poetry to be a form of 'transient transcendence' in the face of death.

What Plotinus and the ethos of pre-Islamic poetry nevertheless have in common is that they both perceive the objective of man's existence as the ascent from an inferior to a superior mental state. Both give equal weight to the perennial quest for assimilation to a higher ideal. With the qasida, pre-Islamic poetry brought about an influential and powerful artistic medium designed to give expression to this quest and to urge the listener to engage in it. This form constitutes the first 'Plotinian seed' I wish to identify, though by using this term I do not intend to imply that it is Plotinian in origin. Rather, it became Plotinian in effect, for it would, at a much later stage, turn out to be a supremely suitable medium to convey the mystic quest for assimilation to the divine.

1.1. The Qasida as 'Transcended Function'

Generally, qasidas are composed of three distinct thematic units. In the first the poet gives vent to his attachment to a former beloved whose memory is rekindled as he comes across the remains of a desert encampment where they had met in former times. Often the separation is relived and copious tears are shed. In the second part nostalgia is left behind as the poet engages in a journey through the wilderness with his camel as sole companion. In the third and final part the civic virtues take centre stage through fulsome eulogy of those who are declared to embody them: the poet's tribe or its leader, or, indeed, the poet himself.

In pre-Islamic poems this tripartite structure comes to the fore in many different permutations, but one characteristic is common to them all: the sequence of the parts is not presented in the form of a narrative nor is it explained in the form of an argument. Instead the parts are juxtaposed as seemingly separate entities, sometimes without any transition. This way of composition has in the past given rise to much questioning among critics. Why should poems begin with a lover's complaint and end with eulogy, and what is the link between them?

An explanation provided by Suzanne Stetkevych has gained much traction since she first proposed it in a seminal article (1983). She noticed a parallel between the tripartite qasida structure and the three stages of the rite of passage which Arnold van Gennep and Victor Turner had famously defined as separation, liminality and reaggregation. The lover's complaint could then be seen as equivalent to the ritual subject's separation from a former state of being, the desert journey as representing the initiatory trial he undergoes in the liminal realm, and the concluding eulogy as celebrating his 'reaggregation' into the social fold. While this interpretation shows that the qasida's thematic sequence follows a familiar ritualistic pattern, the process of growth it conveys would seem to be in the first instance psychic, with any ritualistic parallels of secondary import.

This psychic dimension is addressed in Nadia Jamil's *Ethics & Poetry in Sixth-Century Arabia* (2017) which engages in a close reading of many works by the celebrated pre-Islamic poet Imru' al-Qays (6th-century CE). Rather than the rite of passage she resorts to 'the Jungian theory of psychological growth and transformation' as an analytical paradigm because it 'offers a better adjusted *form-sensitive* lens' through which to view the poetry (2017: 347). From this perspective the qasida can be understood as a poetic manifestation of the 'transcendent function', a pivotal concept in Jungian psychology which denotes the transition to a new mental state through the integration of opposing conscious and unconscious factors. Ethics, or the acquisition of 'civic virtues' through a process of psychic growth, therefore emerges as the central concern of the pre-Islamic poetic corpus she has studied.

The Jungian dimension of the qasida structure gives added credence to its proposed status as a 'Plotinian seed' in view of the established parallels between Neoplatonism and analytical psychology.[4] As observed among others by the philosopher Hazel Barnes, both 'hold that the individual soul or conscious psyche is but a small part, isolated only superficially from a greater psychic world' (1945: 576). The process of individuation or psychic growth brought about through the 'transcendent function' results in renewed and salutary contact with this greater world of belonging. As Barnes (1945: 576) notes:

> Plotinus refers to this process as an ascent to higher spheres; Jung speaks of it as a descent to deeper realms of consciousness. Each expression is of course metaphorical and is, I think, substantially the same in meaning.

To illustrate how this process is manifest in the qasida we can turn to an ode by the 6th-century poet al-Musayyab which Jacobi chose as a succinct example of the tripartite form (1996: 29–30). As convention dictates, it begins with the separation of lovers and ends with the eulogy of a tribal chief to whom the poem is dedicated. The transformation to which it gives expression is best symbolised in the water imagery which links beginning and end. In the first part it conveys the inebriating delight of the beloved's kiss (al-Musayyab 1996: 69):

> … if you taste thereof,
> It is like wine from ʿĀna, mixed with water running through reeds,
>
> Or like rain from a morning cloud, milked by the East wind,
> with wine freshly drawn from a shining cask sealed by clay.

Brusquely, however, the poet resolves to turn away from these captivating charms by renouncing what he calls *ṣibā*, youthful passion, or, as Jamil aptly translates the term, 'juvenile folly' (2017: 13–14):

> But then I decided to shun youthful passion (*ṣibā*)
> and awoke from longing and bewilderment.

This moment of awakening sets in motion the 'ascent' to a new and superior state of consciousness. The means of transition is the poet's 'mighty camel', a detailed description of which leads on to the concluding eulogy where the water imagery is encountered once more. Here it conveys a civic virtue central to the pre-Islamic canon: the generosity (*jūd*) with which the tribal chief al-Qaʿqāʿ cares for communal welfare in times of need:

[4] For a recent study of the parallels between them, see MacLennan (2006).

You are more generous than a canal brimming with waves
that surge upon one another and batter the banks,

As if its piebald steeds on either side
were charging the water-wheels of the farmers.

The contrast between the two occurrences of the water image encapsulates the 'transcendent function' accomplished by the poem's progression. It is a movement from physical pleasure to civic virtue, from individual gratification to communal welfare. At the beginning, the mixture of water and wine conveys the transitory delight of a liaison that remains without offspring; at the end the bountiful irrigation canal charging the farmer's water wheels conveys the promise of fertility for the benefit of all. The lesson is that the individual psyche can only truly prosper by amalgamation into 'a greater psychic world', which in the pre-Islamic qasida is constituted by the tribe and the civic virtues represented by their leader.

Viewed from the perspective of the Plotinian dialectic between the one and the many, this development can be summarised succinctly as a movement 'from the one of many to the many as one'. The 'one of many' denotes the lone individual detached from his tribe whose search for individual gratification remains fruitless, while the 'many as one' denotes the tribal collective unified by a shared sense of values from which salvation and survival spring.[5]

1.2. One and Many in the Arabic Poetic Form

A comparable type of dialectic between unity and multiplicity characterises the second 'Plotinian seed' to be found in pre-Islamic poetry. If the first is a matter of content as manifest in the thematic sequence of the qasida, the second concerns the form in which these as well as all shorter, monothematic poems are composed. In keeping with its nomadic origin, the relationship between the one and the many, which this form of composition exhibits, can be usefully compared to that between individual and tribe. The single verse, termed *bayt* ('house or tent') in Arabic, should be an independent, self-sufficient syntactic unit and hence can be deemed to represent the individual. The poem composed of an indefinite number of such independent verses stands for the tribe. What holds the verses together and gives them their 'tribal identity' is that all must be composed in the same, unchanging metre and all share the same unchanging end-rhyme.[6] The predictability of the monorhyme generates a sense of expectation which is enhanced by the fact that each verse is divided by the metre into two hemistichs of roughly equal length.

The resulting effect produces what Scheindlin called the 'anticipation – resolution pattern' within the single verse (1974: 31–59). It means that each verse is

[5] Izutsu (2002: 62) describes the pre-Islamic tribal ethos as 'the only possible principle of unity by which to preserve a balance and good order among the people'. Hence 'all the noble qualities were considered to reside not so much in the individual members of the tribe as in the tribe itself'.

[6] For a detailed discussion of rhyme and metre in classical Arabic poetry, see Gelder (2012).

like a new beginning that ends on a note of harmonious completion as the listener is brought back home to the familiar, already anticipated rhyme. Hence every verse is tantamount to an expectation fulfilled, a tension resolved, a question answered or, metaphorically speaking, an individual soul reintegrated into the folds of a 'greater psychic world'. In that sense every verse of an Arabic poem performs a Jungian 'transcendent function' in miniature.[7]

The mono-rhyme governs more than just the sound structure of the poem. By limiting the choice of rhyme words to a single pattern, its influence pervades the entire linguistic fabric (Gelder 2012: 183–91). The choice of rhyme is therefore of great importance for it determines, in more than one sense, the oneness which holds the poem together. The mono-rhyme *āʿī* of the above-cited ode, for instance, is not chosen at random but is derived from the name of its dedicatee al-Qaʿqāʿ which sonorously begins the eulogy:

> I'm resolved to send a qasida with the wind
> penetrating everywhere on its way to al-Qaʿqāʿī.

It goes to the core of the poem's message that the tribal leader, as the one who conjoins the many, should supply the sound pattern which forges it into a unity.

This form of composition has been extraordinarily influential for not only has it prevailed in Arabic poetry until the modern period but it has also been adopted and adapted by poetic traditions in numerous other languages of the Muslim world, including Hebrew, classical Persian and Ottoman, as illustrated by several of the poems discussed in this volume. In every case the rhyme has a unifying function directly relevant to the core message of the poem. The Hebrew poem on the soul by al-Darʿī for instance rhymes on the feminine singular ending of verbal forms many of which have the soul – which is feminine in Hebrew – as their subject. The entire poem is therefore well and truly 'ensouled' by the rhyme.[8]

In classical Persian and Ottoman poetry the rhyme scheme is supplemented by the *radīf* (*redîf* in Turkish), a word which is repeated after the mono-rhyme throughout the poem and which both strengthens and diversifies the semantic cohesion. The two poems discussed by Walter Andrews have *redif*s which are central to their message: *ṭaġıt*, which conveys the sense of 'achieving spiritual nakedness', and *ʿiṣḳ/ʿaşḳ* glossed as '(Neo)Platonic love'.[9] In poems such as these, a single concept is illuminated anew by every verse to generate a composite picture from a multiplicity of angles, like an object reflected in a sequence of different mirrors. While clearly not Neoplatonic in origin, this form of composition is an expressive medium uniquely predisposed to reflect in poetic terms the manifold self-disclosure of the One, a notion of absolute centrality in both Neoplatonism and Islam.[10]

7 On this see also Arberry as cited in Gelder (2012: 193).

8 See Joachim Yeshaya's chapter, pp. 240–4. On the soul as feminine, see also Adena Tanenbaum's chapter, p. 219.

9 See Walter Andrew's chapter in this volume, p. 174 (*ṭaġıt*) and p. 181 (*ʿaşḳ*).

10 Bürgel (1992: 66) describes the mono-rhyme as 'particularly apt for expressing ideas within a monotheistic culture' before discussing the aesthetic impact of the *radīf* in the Persian ghazal (1992: 67–72).

There is yet one more factor which qualifies this form to be deemed a Plotinian seed. Oneness, or formal unity, functions in it at two contrasting levels which relate in a manner reminiscent of the immanence and transcendence of the One in Plotinian thought. In the poem, oneness in its immanent form results from the prosodic rules we have discussed: it must be composed in *one* rhyme and *one* metre and consist of separate verses making *one* statement each. What governs the oneness of the poem as whole or, in other words, its organic unity as a single coherent statement, is not subject to the same strictures. As noted above, the thematic sequence is neither narrative nor discursive but consists of a juxtaposition of individual verses or groups of verses of varying number, a characteristic also found in much later Persian and Ottoman verse. It has given rise to the famous verdict that such poems are 'Orient pearls at random strung'.[11]

What gives these poems their 'oneness' is that which is left unsaid: the gap between the juxtaposed verses and segments which the listener is called upon to fill with meaning in order to forge them into a unity. Oneness at the level of the poem as a whole can therefore rightly be called 'transcendent'. Grasping it requires an act of creative emotional participation which is experiential, subjective, and goes beyond the verbal domain. It is in that very experience that the 'transcendent function' of the poem, its ability to uplift and integrate, is carried out.

The dialectic between the one and the many, the immanent and the transcendent, the verbal and the non-verbal, inherent in this form from the outset predisposes it singularly well to bring to experiential awareness the message of mystical poetry: the elusiveness and polysemousness of ultimate truth and the myriad faces of the One.

2. The Qur'an: Pathway to the One God

If pre-Islamic poetry generally aims to rouse the listener to civic virtues, the Qur'an marks a giant step towards the 'higher virtues' in the Plotinian sense. At the centre of its new code of ethics is *taqwā*, pious awareness of the absolute supremacy of God, 'the best provision' for the wayfarer of life (Qur'an 2:197).[12] To promulgate this message the Qur'an resorts to a rhetoric so captivating and powerful that its inimitability as a literary text came to be enshrined in religious doctrine. By venting its teaching in such supreme artistic form it confronted not only pre-Islamic but all subsequent Arabic poetry with a radical challenge in the domain of both ethics and aesthetics. The resulting rivalry over moral authority and verbal excellence has been a constant in Arabic letters which has taken many forms and subsists to this day (Sperl 2020).

[11] For a survey on this debate, see Gelder (1982: 14–22). Gruendler (2008) shows to what extent individual poems have been disassembled and reassembled in performance and how fluctuating their unity consequently is.

[12] Neuwirth (2014: 53) describes *taqwā* as a 'concept equivalent to the Greek notion of *eusebia* that was central to late antique Christian thought'. For a study of the transition from pre-Islamic virtues to Qur'anic ethics, see Izutsu (2002).

The Qur'an challenges the poets head-on in the famous passage which declares that they 'say what they do not do' and are followed by 'those who are lost in error', though it exempts from censure those 'who believe, do good deeds and often remember God'.[13] Poetry is thus not condemned wholesale but circumscribed and made subservient to the Qur'anic message. It cannot rival prophecy which holds the sole monopoly of truth. This has had major consequences for the status of poetry in the Classical Arabic tradition. As detailed by Kermani (2014: 269–74), it may be the reason why Islamic philosophers such as Ibn Sīnā and al-Farābī saw it fit to apply Platonic and Neoplatonic theories of divine inspiration to prophecy but never to poetry. Similarly, the Classical Arabic critical tradition remained resolutely Aristotelian and failed to develop a Neoplatonic poetics, as noted in Alexander Key's contribution to this volume (pp. 143–5).

If poetic theory stayed clear of the Neoplatonic legacy the same cannot be said with equal certainty of poetic practice, and this not only with respect to the mystical poets. Undoubtedly, however, a major conduit for whatever may appear Neoplatonic in classical Arabic poetry must be traced back to what I would call the Plotinian seeds to be found in the Qur'an. For viewed from the perspective of the *Enneads* the Qur'an is a veritable repository of significant parallels. Some of them are central to the Qur'anic message, others appear in the form of allusions and images which later exegesis expanded upon to bring them into a Neoplatonic framework. They are so numerous that only a detailed comparative study can do them justice.[14] In the following I will briefly touch on three topics which have had the greatest bearing on the poetic tradition and on mystical poetry in particular: the analogy between this world and the next, the trajectory of the soul, and the immanence and transcendence of God

2.1. This World and the Next

The first topic brings us to the Plotinian seed of Qur'anic provenance which arguably had the greatest impact on Arabic poetry. It involves a tenet which has been considered 'fundamental to Platonism in virtually any guise' (Louth 1994: 54), namely the polarity between the sensible and the intelligible realms. The former, comprising material existence as perceived by the senses, is nothing but a transitory, imperfect and unreal reflection of immutable archetypes which reside in the latter and constitute the sole true reality. The entire Qur'anic message is structured around an equivalent polarity, that between this world, termed *al-dunyā*, and the

[13] Qur'an 26:224–7 on which there is an extensive literature, including Bauer (2010) and Kermani (2014: 277–86).

[14] As Oliver Leaman notes, 'there is no reason why Neoplatonic ideas should not be expressed in Qur'anic ways, and often they were'. However, he attributes any semblance between such ideas and the Qur'an as resulting from an 'intellectual inquiry' which proceeds by 'examining the resources of a religion via some theoretical machinery and seeing what happens' (2016: 34). The point being made here is that there are certain intrinsic similarities in the religious visions of both texts.

Hereafter, termed *al-ākhira*. One is 'mere play, illusory pleasure and passing delight' (6:32), the other is the 'abode of permanence' (40:39), in the form of eternal bliss in Paradise or eternal damnation in the caverns of hell (e.g. 57: 20–1).

While the Plotinian and the Qur'anic understandings of these polarities are by no means identical, they converge on a principle of fundamental importance for both: namely that all manifestations of the lower realm harbour within themselves pointers to their origins in the higher realm. Thus, Plotinus asserts that 'all things are filled full of signs' (II 3 [52] 7, A: II 69) and detects even in stones and mountains a trace of the 'ensouled forming principle' which fashioned their archetype in the intelligible realm (VI 7 [38] 10, A: VII 121). The comprehensive significatory power of the lower realm is emphatically asserted also in the Qur'an where it appears in a range of different guises. The most important centres on the concept of *āya* (pl. *āyāt*) which denotes both a 'verse of revealed scripture' and 'any element of the lower realm in its capacity as signifier of the higher realm', the common denominator being that both Scripture and creation are to be read as mutually corroborating compendia of signs that emanate from, and affirm the existence of, God. All manifestations of nature have this significatory charge (Abrahamov 2006).

It is this 'Qur'anic way of seeing', as it might be termed, which would seamlessly merge with a Neoplatonic worldview and decisively influence and amplify the semantic range of poetic language. The process began in the early Islamic period when the conventional tropes inherited from pre-Islamic times came to be recast into this new, allegorical mould. This applies most prominently to the themes of love and wine, as scenes of earthly revelry were portrayed in language whose Qur'anic allusions transposed them metaphorically into a paradisiacal setting, a technique which sublimated their earthly allure but also made them appear all the more ephemeral by contrast with the heavenly ideal.[15]

At what point in the history of Arabic poetry this type of ambivalence between this world and the next, between microcosm and macrocosm, begins to carry the actual imprint of Neoplatonic philosophy is probably impossible to determine. As will be shown below, by the 9th century such a merger seems to have taken place. It also flowed into classical Persian and Ottoman verse where it lent all images of the poetic inventory an air of ambiguity and transcendence which reflects what Walter Andrews in this volume describes as 'the doubleness of a cosmos in which every perceptible thing has an analogue in another, more real reality' (see p. 175).

2.2. The Trajectory of the Soul

If we scan the Qur'an for traces of the Plotinian conception of the soul, the result is rather perplexing. The most important difference, one that would seem to annul all

[15] For an insightful example see the poem by Abū Nuwās (d. 814) discussed by Montgomery (1994). Fowden (2007) develops the latter's findings with particular reference to imagery associated with Christian monasticism in early Arabic love and wine poetry.

equivalence from the outset, is the fact that the concept of the soul in the Plotinian sense does not seem to exist in the Qur'an. As noted by Homerin, a close study of Qur'anic usage shows that the term *nafs*, which is usually translated as 'soul', designates a whole person or aspects of a person's character, but not a distinct spiritual substance. Indeed, 'the Qur'an never states that the *nafs* is a soul that joins or enters a body' (2006: 4).[16] The belief in the existence of the soul generally upheld by Muslim theology since its inception in the 8th century is, according to Homerin, 'indebted more to Aristotle, Neoplatonism and Christianity than to the Qur'an, with its holistic view of the human being' (2006: 1).[17]

Remarkably, however, if we follow the exegetical tradition and read the Qur'anic term *nafs* as designating 'soul', we discover key elements of its Plotinian itinerary dispersed throughout the text, as though the original narrative had been broken up and its fragments built into a new edifice, rather like the Byzantine columns in the mosque of Kairouan. We recognise, each woven into a different context, the 'soul' captivated by earthly temptation and commanding evil (12:53), engaged in self-reproach (75:2), being purified (91:9), finding peace (89:27–8) and returning to its divine source of origin upon death (29:57). The notions of forgetting and remembering, no less crucial in the Qur'an than in the *Enneads*, are made part of the reciprocal mirroring relationship between man and God, between the lower and the higher realm, as in the following examples:

> Remember me, so that I may remember you.
>
> (2:152)

> Today we shall forget you as you forgot your encounter with this day.
>
> (45:34)

Even the Plotinian urge to seek salvation through contemplation would seem to have a counterpart in the stress the Qur'an so often places on the need for mankind to resort to thought, reflection and intellection in order to comprehend the message of divine immanence conveyed by the 'signs' inherent throughout the lower realm.

Two crucial aspects of the Plotinian narrative, however, do not have an explicit Qur'anic equivalent: the pre-existence of the soul and the concept of its ascent. The exegetical tradition extrapolated them from brief, allusive passages which would become the subject of mystical speculation and poetic elaboration. In the first of these God causes mankind to bear witness about themselves by asking them before

[16] The same applies to the Hebrew Bible. According to Robert Alter, author of a new Bible translation, the Hebrew word *nefesh* which like the Arabic *nafs* has often been translated as 'soul', 'can mean many things ... But it's not quite "soul"' (Steinberg 2018). As noted by Adena Tanenbaum in this volume (p. 219), this did not prevent the Andalusian Hebrew poets from investing the term with a philosophical conception derived from Neoplatonic sources.

[17] The Qur'an's lack of specificity on the nature and existence of the soul has given rise to a considerable range of diverging views on the matter in Muslim theology which have been aptly summarised by Calverley & Netton (1993).

their birth 'am I not your Lord?' (*a-lastu bi-rabbikum*, 7:172). 'Yes, we testify' is the affirmative response, which later exegesis interpreted as a covenant sealed between God and the souls at the dawn of creation.[18] Both the Neoplatonic and substantial components of the Islamic tradition would concur that every soul carries a dormant memory of this primordial encounter which it is urged to re-awaken by acts of devotion and purification. Known in Islam as the Day of *Alast*, the event became a cornerstone of mystical psychology, as exemplified in some detail in the chapter by Kazuyo Murata (pp. 154–7). The theme is also attested in a modern Persian poem discussed by Ahmad Karimi-Hakkak (p. 424).

The ascension topos concerns the soul's capacity to attain, already during a person's lifetime, a temporary form of encounter with the ultimate reality, such as that experienced by Plotinus when he found himself 'above all else in the realm of the intellect' and 'came to identity with the divine' (IV 8 [6] 1; A: IV 397). Qur'anic evidence for the notion of the soul's ascent was found in the following verse which the exegetical tradition took as a reference to the Prophet Muḥammad's night journey and ascension to heaven. A segment of this text (Qur'an 17:1) appears on the cover of this volume: 'Glory be to Him who made His servant travel by night from the sacred place of worship to the furthest place of worship, whose surroundings we have blessed, to show him some of our Signs.' As recorded by the Prophet's biographer Ibn Isḥāq (2001: 181–6) and subsequently expanded upon in numerous accounts,[19] the narratives depicting the Prophet's ascent came to map out the spiritual geography of the Sufi tradition, 'both in the forms of paradigms of Sufi experience and in Sufi accounts of their own personal ascents' (Sells 2001: 4). Their long-lasting impact on poetic diction is illustrated in modern Arabic and Persian poems discussed by Ferial Ghazoul and Ahmad Karimi-Hakkak in this volume (see below, pp. 413, 427–8).

2.3. Immanence and Transcendence

The dialectic between divine immanence and transcendence is as central to the Qur'an as it is to the *Enneads*, with the proviso that the latter seeks to systematise it theoretically while the former expresses it in axiomatic declarations. A striking example of their difference is found in the manner in which the two texts assert the immanence of the One by way of His omnipresence. Plotinus seeks to prove the point in *Enneads* VI 4 [22] and VI 5 [23] whose title 'On the presence of Being, one and the same, everywhere as a whole' gives a foretaste of the staggeringly subtle investigation which is to follow. It concludes: 'To that god the cities turn, and all the earth and all the sky, who everywhere abides by himself and in himself and has from himself being ... moving to an unbounded unity through his sizeless unboundedness' (VI 5 [23] 12; A: VI 359). In the Qur'an an analogous idea of

[18] For details see Böwering (2001: 5–6).
[19] For details, see Amir-Moezzi (1996) and Colby (2008).

equally universal import takes the form of brief, forceful utterances such as the following:

> To God belong the East and the West; wherever you turn there is the face of God. (2:115)

> Abiding is the face of your Lord, the glorious and beneficent. (55:27)

We shall encounter one of the many echoes of these statements in due course when discussing a poem by Ibn ʿArabī.

While the *Enneads* uphold the categorical oneness of the source of all existence no less emphatically than the Qur'an, they also assert that 'this one, proceeding to [the sensible world] as far as … it can, would appear to be many and even, in a sense, be many' (VI 5 [23] 1; A: VI 327–9). In the Qur'an this apparent diversity of the One also exists, but it is not subject to theoretical cogitation. It comes directly to the fore in the numerous 'beautiful names'[20] with which God is invoked and which reverberate throughout the text. Later codified to 99, they became the subject of an extensive literature on the divine attributes. A major issue raised thereby was the question to what extent man could acquire a share of these attributes in order to render himself godlike and thus attain to the supreme goal also aspired to by Plotinus.[21]

Notwithstanding His immanence and status as supreme exemplar, the Qur'anic God is as transcendent and ineffable as the One of Plotinus: 'not a thing is like Him', the Qur'an declares (*laysa ka-mithlihi shay*ʾ, 42:11), a statement which recalls Plotinus' repeated assertions that the One 'transcends all things', 'for if it is one thing it would not be the absolute One' (V 3 [49] 13; A: V 117). However, for Plotinus this means that the One is also radically beyond the reach of language 'for whatever you say about it you will always be speaking about a "something"' – and the One is no 'thing' (V 3 [49] 13; A: V 117). Indeed, the *Enneads* as a whole are a testimony of the author's struggle with the ontological incapacity of language to grasp the subject matter he wishes to convey. By comparison the Qur'an is an astounding innovation, for here this utterly remote and ineffable creative power has chosen to reveal itself in the form of language – language, moreover, which tradition has invested with the supreme goodness and beauty reserved for the One in the Enneadic vision. In these words the transcendent One is most supremely, permanently and tangibly perceived to be immanent.[22]

[20] On this term, see Qur'an 7:180, 17:110, 20:8 and 59:24 and Böwering (2002).

[21] For an example see the chapter by Kazuyo Murata (p. 160). Al-Ghazālī's treatise on the divine names (1992) provides a methodical reflection on achieving god-likeness (*taʾalluh*) by acquiring the share of the divine attributes accessible to man. For his definition of *taʾalluh*, see (1992: 52).

[22] For the aesthetic dimension of the Qur'an and its impact on the arts, culture and mystical spirituality of Islam, see notably Kermani (2014).

3. The Abbasid Panegyric: Civic Virtue Sublimated

By the time of the early Abbasid period (750–900 CE) the message of the Qur'an had spread from the Atlantic to the borders of China and inspired the foundation of an empire which encompassed this vast region. At its centre was Baghdad which had become a vibrant meeting point of Arabic, Hellenic and Indo-Iranian culture. Under a state-sponsored enterprise, numerous works of philosophy, statecraft, science and medicine were translated into Arabic and helped to spawn one of the most creative periods in the gestation of Islamic civilisation (Gutas 1998). Among the works which attracted the attention of the intellectual milieu of the Abbasid court were the *Enneads*, though strangely the name of their author was not transmitted. Substantial extracts of *Enneads* IV, V and VI were adapted, rearranged and expanded upon in Arabic treatises, the most important of which became known as the *Theology of Aristotle*.

Considering that centuries had gone by since the pre-Islamic period we might well have expected the Arabic panegyric to have changed beyond all recognition in the intervening years. Surprisingly, it looks much the same as before: the two-hemistich mono-rhymed qasida still charts the path towards a very similar set of civic virtues, though its addressees are no longer tribal chiefs but state officials, including the reigning caliphs.[23]

This conservatism is deceptive. The inherited themes, including the catalogue of virtues, have acquired a wider range of meaning. Most importantly, a new style of expression has taken hold. How unprecedented it was felt to be at the time is evident in its name, for it was termed *al-badīʿ*, the 'newly originated and wonderful'.[24] Not everyone favoured it, however, and it became the subject of much controversy which centred on the work of Abū Tammām (d. 845), the Abbasid court poet who championed it above all others. In a major study of his work Stetkevych defined the style as 'the intentional, conscious encoding of abstract meaning into metaphor' (1991: 8) and explained it as the product of a new intellectual climate dominated by the Muʿtazila, a school of speculative theology which had been adopted as the official doctrine of state by several Abbasid Caliphs. From a Plotinian perspective this is not without interest, because Muʿtazilite thinking centres upon a topic familiar from the *Enneads*: the categorical oneness of God.[25]

[23] For seminal studies on the panegyric qasida, see Stetkevych (2002) and Gruendler (2003).

[24] For a recent survey of literature on the *badīʿ* style, see Fakhreddine (2015: 57–92).

[25] Since God is the absolute One, so its proponents argued, He cannot have attributes for that would render Him into a multiplicity. It follows that the divine names which feature in the Qur'an (e.g. 'the Merciful') should not be taken as designating a quality distinct from the divine essence, and that any anthropomorphic descriptions of God (i.e. his hands or throne) should not be taken literally but read as metaphors. It is this privileging of metaphorical speech, combined with 'a mentality that was conceptual, analytical and analogical' which Stetkevych sees reflected in the *badīʿ* style of the poets (1991: 9).

That Muʿtazilism and Neoplatonism are in some way related seems assured, though the exact nature of that relationship need not concern us here.[26] What matters is whether the phenomenon of *al-badīʿ* exhibits features that might justify it being deemed to be one more Plotinian seed in our trajectory of classical Arabic poetry. The long-lasting resonance the new style had not only with Arabic but also with classical Persian and Ottoman verse gives this question all the more importance. As an illustration, there is perhaps no better candidate than the panegyric Abū Tammām composed for the son of the reigning Caliph al-Muʿtaṣim (d. 842), Aḥmad ibn al-Muʿtaṣim, who also happened to be the dedicatee of the *Theology of Aristotle*. The poem was, moreover, recited in the presence of the man who had supervised the production of the *Theology* and issued the dedication, the illustrious philosopher al-Kindī (d. 873) (Adamson 2018). As we shall see presently, one of the verses of the panegyric gave rise to a brief but revealing altercation between poet and philosopher.

3.1. In Praise of God's Shadow

The poem is a traditional qasida in terms of form and structure. In time-honoured vein, it begins with the mention of the abandoned campsite and a tearful lover's complaint. The ensuing section of praise centres on generosity (*jūd*), the same virtue which occasioned the laudation of the tribal chief in the pre-Islamic poem cited above. There it had a concrete, material signification: it meant giving hospitality and sustenance to the needy, and was compared to the water that brings fertility to the land. In Abū Tammām's poem, both generosity and the irrigating water to which it is compared become metaphorical concepts that operate at a range of different, hierarchically stratified levels.

The beginning of the section of praise introduces the pinnacle of the hierarchy: just as God grants 'nourishment' to creation, so the sky grants the water of hospitality to the earth and the Abbasid dynasty fulfils the hopes placed in it by the people. Significantly, it is also here that the source of the poem's mono-rhyme *āsī* is revealed, since it derives from the name of the ruling house (Abū Tammām 1969: 246,):

11 The One who created all creatures nourishes them
with nutriments to counter the vagaries of Time,

12 Likewise the earth is a gift of the sky's bounty,
and the needy are granted the sons of ʿAbbās (*Bānū ʿAbbāsī*)

The Arabic word for 'nutriments' in line 11 above, *aqwāt*, evokes a Qur'anic passage on creation in which God is described as having measured out the 'nutriments' of

[26] As observed by D'Ancona (2000) and Adamson (2002: 165–70), several passages in the *Theology of Aristotle* bear the imprint of the Muʿtazilite debate over the divine attributes.

the earth (*qaddara fīhā aqwātahā*, 41:10), an association which anchors the analogy between God, the sky, and the ruling dynasty in Qur'anic cosmology. A further manifestation of the same analogy focuses on the dedicatee of the poem and the succour he provides for the one unable 'to ride the saddle of misfortune' (Abū Tammām 1969: 251,):

> 29 In penury – and penury is disease! – you supplied him
> with generosity – and generosity is the healing physician.

Here, too, a Qur'anic echo renders the act of generosity into an emulation of the divine exemplar, for the phrase *amdadtahu* ('you supplied him') evokes numerous Qur'anic usages of the same verb with reference to the bounties that God grants to mankind. These associations elevate the virtue of generosity into a manifestation of God's goodness and, by extension, every act of generosity into an approximation of the divine paradigm. The higher the individual's status is in the social hierarchy, the closer the approximation. And as 'shadows of God and harbingers of his religion', as Abū Tammām terms it (line 13), the Abbasids occupy the highest rank. We are reminded here of the above cited statement by Plotinus that 'assimilation is to gods, not to good human beings'. By rendering the civic virtues into reflections of divine attributes, the analogical universe of *al-badīʿ* enacts the same principle.

In portraying penury as disease and generosity as the healing physician the above line poignantly illustrates the 'encoding of abstract concepts into metaphor' which Stetkevych (1991) sees as the hallmark of the *badīʿ* style. As so often, the phrasing evokes multiple layers of meaning. Thus, the word *ʿudm*, translated above as 'penury', also means 'categorical absence, non-existence' while the word *jawā*, translated as 'disease', also denotes the 'pain of ardent love'. These cannot but bring to mind the beginning of the ode where the poet himself appears as the victim of both *ʿudm* and *jawā*, since he grieves over the absence of his beloved. It is also in the opening lines where we first encounter the theme of giving and watering at the lowest rank of the hierarchy, that of the abandoned lover offering tears to the soil which once gave him joy (Abū Tammām 1969: 242,):

> 1 There is no harm in halting for an hour
> to discharge our debt to the effaced abodes of spring.
>
> 2 Perhaps your eye will give help with its water;
> some tears don't soothe and some do comfort bring.

The ensuing lines assert that these tears must be honest and deeply felt because they commemorate a precious encounter which his beloved urges him to remember for evermore (Abū Tammām 1969: 245,):

> 10 Don't ever forget these engagements! Note, your name
> is 'human' (*insān*) because you forget (*nāsī*)!

Characteristically for Abū Tammām, the wordplay here serves for him to extract a multifaceted truth from the fabric of language. Overtly speaking, the poet is being urged by his beloved not to forget his debt of allegiance. Covertly speaking and by analogy, however, the patron is with these same words indirectly urged not to forget his debt of gratitude for the poem, a debt through which he will cure the poet from the 'disease of penury'.

But the line also has far wider reverberations because the term *ʿuhūd*, translated above as engagements, also means covenants and as such conjures up a pivotal moment in the Qur'anic creation story, when Adam forgot the covenant that God had made with him (20:115). By association and fully in keeping with the conceptual edifice of the poem, the line thus shows the particular as a mirror image of the archetypal. Man's forgetfulness, enshrined in his very name, derives from that of the first man.

Al-Kindī, when listening to this, might have approved of Abū Tammām's statement for a different reason if his editorial work on the *Theology of Aristotle* had by that time reached the Arabic rendering of *Ennead* IV 4 [28] 5. It dwells extensively on the forgetfulness of the human soul and asserts that her downward motion into the body 'causes her not to remember anything at all' of her august origins (Plotinus 1959: 77).[27] Might Abū Tammām himself have been aware of this text? All we can say is that his verse, recited to this audience at this particular instance in the intellectual history of Islam, reads like a meeting point of two separate and yet curiously intertwined worlds – Neoplatonism and the Qur'an.

What we do know is that al-Kindī did not approve when some lines later Abū Tammām declared his patron to possess an amalgam of virtues proverbially associated with certain legendary figures of the past (line 23). At this point al-Kindī is said to have interrupted the recitation with the words 'the prince is greater in all respects than those with whom you have compared him'.[28] Coming from a philosopher of his stature these words cannot be taken as mere flattery. We can surmise that Abū Tammām's invocation of ancient paragons infringed the Neoplatonic hierarchy being espoused by al-Kindī, whereby merit must flow from the higher to the lower ranks and never the other way.[29] As 'God's shadow on earth' the prince's virtues reflect the supernal realms and cannot be compared to those of ordinary mortals. *Ennead* V 5 [32] – which al-Kindī will have known since extracts of it figure in the *Theology* – says as much when it compares the hierarchy of the intelligible realm to a royal procession. It ends with the king, the symbol of the One, who is cardinally different from the rest. As Plotinus is at pains to stress, he 'is other than those who precede him, who are other than him' (V 5 [32] 3, G: 586). In the same way the Caliph's offspring must be other than the heroes of old.

[27] As shown by Endress (1994: 201), *Ennead* IV 4 clearly left its mark on al-Kindī for it is one of the sources for his treatise on the soul's capacity of remembrance. The text has been translated into English by Pormann & Adamson (2012: 99–106). I am grateful to Peter Adamson for these references.

[28] The anecdote is cited in Abū Tammām (1969: 250) and al-Ṣūlī (2015: 260–1), and discussed in Gruendler (2008: 384).

[29] As explained by Suzanne Stern-Gillet in this volume, 'no emanated entity … can initiate changes in the reality from which it is emanated' (p. 284); see also Cristina D'Ancona's comments in her chapter (p. 257, n. 12).

Abū Tammām's response to this critique is no less revealing. After a brief period of reflection, he recited the following lines which were subsequently incorporated into the poem at this point (Abū Tammām 1969: 250,):

> 24 Don't reject my choosing those beneath him
> as wayward image for his munificence and courage.
>
> 25 For God chose an image of yet lower kind –
> the niche and lamp! – for His own light.

The celebrated light verse of the Qur'an[30] here serves the poet as a defence against al-Kindī's insistence that the qualities of the prince are beyond compare. In the image of 'niche and lamp' there is proof that all objects of the sensible world can be signs of divine immanence and therefore legitimate vehicles of comparison with the higher realm. He thereby posits a striking analogy between his image-making faculty and that of God. It justifies the disputed verse, elevates the status of his craft and gives the poet himself an exalted place in the hierarchical universe of the poem. Like the prince he acts in analogous emulation of the Lord.

Abū Tammām's defence was well received and earned him double the reward. In the appropriately confident ending of the poem the image of the fertile earth returns once more and thereby binds the levels of the poem together. The motif harks back to the beginning, to the earth the poet moistened with his tears and from which his beloved's smile emerged like 'camomile flowers in sandy soil' (line 7), a memory then superseded by the prince likened to fragrant blooms rising from the 'fertile soil' of his ancestry (lines 18–21). In its final appearance the image symbolises the divinely sanctioned beneficence of the realm and marks the poet's reception into the 'greater psychic world' (Abū Tammām 1969: 252,):

> 34 Now is the time for me to plant my hopes
> in bounty's soil and build on true foundations.

What does this poem tell us about Neoplatonism and *al-badīʿ*? The work is neither mystical nor philosophical: there is no mention of the soul's ascent or of purificatory virtues. But there is a hierarchical order of analogies which the poetic art aims to elucidate by means of metaphor. This marks the beginning in Islamic literature of what Meisami (1987) called 'the poetics of analogy', a style of writing which would go on to dominate Persian and Ottoman court poetry, but whose root may be traced back to Arabic *badīʿ* poetry of the early 9th century such as this ode of Abū Tammām.[31] Its underlying cosmology results from a perception of the universe as a harmoniously structured hierarchy composed of analogous gradients in which

[30] See also the chapter by Alexander Key in this volume, pp. 137–8.

[31] Referring to Meisami's argument in the context of Ottoman literature Walter Andrews in this volume rightly stresses that 'analogy is not the same as metaphor, that human interactions are not *similar to* or *like* cosmic interactions, they are directly comparable to them' (p. 175, n. 9). Terence O'Reilly in this volume (pp. 331–2) makes the same point about Ficino's understanding of metaphor as substantive rather than rhetorical.

man figures as a microcosmic mirror image of the macrocosmic order. Meisami notes that a similar analogical cosmology also arose in medieval Europe[32] and sees its poetic impact as incorporating 'a number of essentially Pythagorean elements' (1987: 32). That this cosmology may also owe something to Neoplatonism we may surmise from the fact that its most comprehensive exposition in medieval Islam, the 10th-century encyclopaedia known as the *Epistles of the Brethren of Purity*,[33] exhibits such close parallels to Plotinian emanationist thinking that it has been deemed to be the work of 'Muslim Neoplatonists' (Netton 1982). As shown by Nokso-Koivisto, an integral part of the *Epistles*'s analogical vision was that 'Man imitates God as creator, while the work of art that man produces imitates the creation of God' (2011: 265) – the very idea that Abū Tammām resorted to in his defence against al-Kindī.

3.2. The Arts and 'the Beauty of Symmetry'

How did this vision develop and what significance does it have? It has ancient roots and may derive from the fusion between Neopythagoreanism, Aristotelianism and Neoplatonism which became part of a widely shared undercurrent of popular philosophy in the Hellenistic Near East.[34] In the early Abbasid period these inherited notions received a new intellectual stimulus with the translation of Greek philosophical and scientific texts. The impact was profound. Not only poetry, but also the visual arts underwent a decisive change at this particular time. Samarra, the new capital founded by Abū Tammām's patron, the Caliph al-Muʿtaṣim, saw the beginnings of the '*girih* mode', an abstract, geometrical style of visual expression which Necipoğlu considers 'a radical innovation' (1995: 95) and whose legacy for Islamic art would be no less significant than that of the *badīʿ* style for poetry and prose. In a detailed investigation, which covers also poetry and music, she attributes the rationale behind this new visual aesthetic to the impact of Neoplatonic philosophy as documented in the writings of al-Kindī, al-Fārābī and the *Epistles of the Brethren of Purity* (Necipoğlu 1995: 185–215).

If we ask ourselves which quality might have been seen as enabling poetry, music and the visual arts to reflect the macrocosmic order notwithstanding the different media in which they operate, there is no better place to find the answer than the Arabic adaptation of *Ennead* V 9 [5] 11 which appears in the *Epistle on Divine Science*. It declares that none of the accidental qualities of the sensible world exist in the eternal Forms of the 'world of mind', except for one which

[32] For European parallels see the sources given in Meisami (1987: 32), as well as Eco (2002: 52–64) and Tymieniecka (2006).

[33] For a concise introduction to this remarkable compendium, see Baffioni (2016).

[34] As observed by Jamil, certain types of analogy between microcosm and macrocosm are already found in pre-Islamic poetry. Thus 'early Arabic representations of corporate cohesion, virtue, and ritual, ultimately appear to be a conscious reflection of the patterns and perceived properties of the celestial sphere' (Jamil 2017: 335).

happens to be outstandingly relevant for the arts. This is the 'condition which arises from the symmetry (*iʿtidāl*) of the living things' (Plotinus 1959: 425). Its exalted status is due to the fact that it:

> comes from the intellectual faculty, and therefore the art of music becomes a pattern of what is in that world. Music derives this from that intellectual world and is intellectual, not sensible ... The arts that are sensible and intellectual, such as building and carpentry, insofar as they employ symmetric principles, and produce a beautiful order and arrangement (*ḥusn al-naẓm wa l-tarkīb*), are also a pattern of what is in the intellectual world. For they achieve the beauty of symmetry (*ḥusn al-iʿtidāl*) from the dominion that springs from there ... As for the art of geometry, since it is intellectual it is indubitably there. And from there it attains to this science here, because it is a lofty wisdom, concerned with the knowledge of the first essence, the first being.
>
> (Plotinus 1959: 425)

We can infer from the above that the quality which enables material objects to appear analogous to the intellectual realm is their being composed in accordance with principles which come from the intellectual faculty. These are the principles of 'symmetry', a term whose Arabic equivalent *iʿtidāl* also conveys the notions of harmony, balance and proportion.[35] It is from these, in themselves incorporeal, principles that works of art derive their beauty. Music and geometry are the intellectual disciplines which encapsulate them in their purest form.

The impact which this thinking had on musical theory and practice was profound. Here al-Kindī once again takes centre stage on account of the influential musical treatises composed by him and his disciples which build on this approach and went on to become a major source for Sufi theories on the salutary role of musical harmony in the search for spiritual ascent (Montgomery 2008: 152).[36] The 'lofty wisdom' of geometry was granted an equivalent status. According to the *Epistles of the Brethren of Purity*, it permits the soul to 'separate itself from this [corporeal] world in order to join, thanks to its celestial ascension, the world of the spirits and eternal life' (Necipoğlu 1995: 191). Applied to the visual arts, it is readily apparent how the edificatory power detected in geometry could give rise to an aesthetic 'that privileged the imagination's abstracting capacities over naturalistic representation' (1995: 209).

To what extent is the *badīʿ* style a poetic response to an aesthetic that privileges the abstract over the concrete? And how does it convey such principles of 'symmetry'? To return once more to Abū Tammām's poem, like the Arabic panegyric mode in general, it makes no attempt to portray what we would call the 'real', historical Aḥmad ibn al-Muʿtaṣim. Instead it resorts to tropes that were already then centuries old in order to convey what this individual represents in the wider, cosmic scheme of things. 'Symmetry' is thereby manifest at two quite different

[35] For *iʿtidāl* as a philosophical concept and its relevance for the arts, see Moustafa & Sperl (2014, I: 115–18, 148–9, 157).

[36] For a Spanish golden age equivalent, see the role of music in the ode by Fray Luis discussed by Colin Thompson in this volume, pp. 310–11.

but complementary levels which can be succinctly illustrated by the following two lines (Abū Tammām 1969: 247,):

15 My high endeavour rests on hope in Aḥmad,
my hold on tradition and my allegories' daring circulate around him,

16 The one chosen, selected and primed for praise,
adorned by it and in it draped.

In the poem these lines take the place of the pre-Islamic desert journey which Abū Tammām here as elsewhere has shortened into a brief, metaphorical evocation of movement, though it is not a movement towards the patron as would have been expected. Rather it is a circumambulation around him, which elevates him to the status of a sanctuary, as though he were the Kaʿba. Furthermore, it is not the poet that moves, but his intellectual faculties, notably his allegorical reasoning (*qiyās*)[37] – the very reasoning which has produced the cascade of allegories of which the entire poem is composed as we have seen.[38] It is these allegories that portray 'symmetry', namely that between the mirroring levels of the cosmic hierarchy.

At the second level, 'symmetry' is manifest not by portraying it but by embodying it in the verbal fabric of the poem, as suitably illustrated in the sound pattern of line 16. The word for praise, *ḥamd*, is placed at the centre of two identically patterned groups of participles: *mujtabā*, *muṣṭafā* and *mustarā* for 'selected, chosen and primed'; and *ḥālī* and *kāsī* for adorned and vested:[39]

bi-'l- mujtabā wa-'l- muṣṭafā wa-'l-mustarā
lil-ḥamdi wa 'l-ḥālī bihi wa 'l-kāsī

The play of alliterations occasions a two-fold 'symmetry', one through harmony within each group, the other through opposition between them due to their contrasting morphological patterns. This use of grammatical patterns for the sake of creating symmetries of sound, morphology, and syntax is absolutely characteristic of the *badīʿ* style and may be taken as equivalent to the role played by geometric patterns in the visual arts. That the rules of geometry and grammar have parallel functions as tools of artistic expression has been observed by Jakobson whose reflections on the subject may be deemed highly pertinent for an understanding of the *badīʿ* style in its historical context (Jakobson 1981: 95):

> The abstractive power of human thought underlying … both geometrical relations and grammar, superimposes simple geometrical and grammatical figures upon the pictorial world of particular objects and upon the concrete lexical 'wherewithal' of verbal arts.

[37] On the significance of this term in this context, see Meisami (1987: 32, n. 65).

[38] Fakhreddine (2015: 138) fittingly describes the Abbasid poet's treatment of the desert journey as 'a metaphor for the very act of composing poetry'.

[39] In combination with the evocation of the Kaʿba in the previous line, the associations of *muṣṭafā* (a sobriquet of the Prophet) and *kāsī* (from the same root as *kiswa*, the drape of the Kaʿba) lend the word *ḥamd* a distinct religious echo and hence forge yet one more 'symmetry', that between praise of God (termed *ḥamd* in the Qur'an) and praise of the dynasty which is his shadow.

In the *badīʿ* style, this 'superimposition of grammatical figures' has often been described as merely 'ornamental' and 'artificial', though it is, in its original intent, no ornament at all. The grammatical fabric of the language serves not merely to embellish but to reveal, in abstract terms, the 'beautiful symmetries' hidden underneath the trappings of the sensible world, in order to let the macrocosmic whole shine through every microcosmic part and thereby to astonish, delight and elevate the soul.

In conclusion we might say that the twin components of the *badīʿ* style may be described as 'allegorisation' by metaphor at the level of content and 'geometrisation' by rhetoric at the level of form. Both are, to varying extents, in evidence in the panegyric odes which dominate the poetic legacy of the Abbasid period. Composed by celebrated authors such as Abū Tammām, al-Buḥturī (d. 897) and al-Mutanabbī (d. 965), it is not recognisably Neoplatonic in content nor has it ever been deemed as such by the Arabic critical tradition, as clarified in Alexander Key's contribution to this volume. But it springs from a cosmology and an aesthetic in which Qur'anic and Neoplatonic features imperceptibly converge, and its place in literary history cannot be fully grasped without them. This is all the more important considering its flourishing afterlife in the Ottoman and Persian tradition where the panegyric qasida in *badīʿ* style reached the apogee of refinement.[40]

4. Arabic Sufi Poetry: Love the Virtue Supreme

The lifetime of al-Kindī (*c.* 801–74) saw not only the birth of a new poetic style but also the rise of a new type of theosophy which would become the intellectual foundation of Sufism. The beginnings of this movement are generally traced back to a group of early devotees, including Ḥasan al-Baṣrī (d. 728) and Rābiʿa al-ʿAdawiyya (d. 801), but it received its distinctly mystical flavour only in the writings of 9th- and 10th-century thinkers such as Bayazid al-Bisṭāmī (d. 874), Sahl al-Tustarī (d. 896) and al-Junayd (835–910), the founder of the Baghdad school of Sufism (Melchert 2015). What makes it mystical is their belief that the purpose of human existence is to enter into communion with God and, in so doing, to seek approximation to the source from which the human soul derived and whose imprint it still carries.[41] That this emanationist thinking arose at the very time when the circle of al-Kindī produced the Arabic Plotinus adaptations is certainly remarkable[42] and led Sedgwick among others to conclude that 'Neoplatonism ... gave Sufism its main analytical framework' (2017: 31).

[40] For the Ottoman panegyric, see Andrews (1996) and Dedes & Sperl (2013); for the Persian panegyric in Mughal India, see Shackle (1996).

[41] For a comprehensive study of approximation to the divine and the concept of god-likeness in classical Sufi sources, see Gramlich (1998).

[42] That al-Kindī himself upheld the notion of approximation to the divine as supreme goal is evident in his *Epistle on the Soul* which declares that purification may grant the soul a power of insight 'closely similar to that of the Lord Most High' (al-Kindī 1950: 276). For a study of this text, see Jolivet (1996).

4.1. The Sufi Ghazal

Returning once more to the topic of virtue with which our discussion began, we find it prominently represented in Sufi writings, though clad in a new attire which looks distinctly familiar when viewed from a Plotinian perspective. For much of the voluminous theoretical literature of Sufism produced from the 9th century onwards can be read as increasingly sophisticated attempts to recast inherited concepts of civic and religious virtue into purificatory virtues in the Plotinian sense. Notions such as generosity (*jūd*) and steadfastness (*ṣabr*), familiar from the ancient qasida's code of honour, are transformed into 'waystations' (*maqāmāt*) on the soul's ascent towards the encounter with the divine, where they function alongside Islamic notions such as piety (*taqwā*) and prayer (*du'ā'*).[43]

The most exalted of these waystations is not a traditional virtue, but love (*maḥabba*). Into it all the others 'are dissolved', as declared by Ansari (2010: 140) who deemed it to be the highest of the 'one hundred fields' leading the servant up to his Lord.[44] The supremacy of love is of course not alien to Plotinian thinking. It found its way into the *Theology of Aristotle* where love (*maḥabba*) in the intellectual realm 'unites all things ... and makes them one so as never to be severed, because the whole of that entire world is pure love'.[45] For Sufism, though, not Plotinus but verse 5:54 of the Qur'an serves as the point of reference. Speaking of a people whom God loves and who love Him, it provides the foundation stone for an extensive Sufi literature on the supreme status of love. As detailed in Lewisohn's recent survey (2015), the notion is thereby integrated into a hierarchical cosmology of the type we encountered in Abū Tammām's poem. At its pinnacle is the divine essence, itself perceived as love by the poet and mystic al-Ḥallāj (d. 920), who also proclaimed 'the doctrine of essential union (*ittiḥād*) between lover and beloved', a daring vision which helped to give grounds for his execution (Lewisohn 2015: 162). Building on al-Ḥallāj, Aḥmad al-Ghazālī (d. 1126) saw love as 'a single reality composed of various analogical graduations', with human love serving as a bridge to the divine (166–7). His thinking culminates in the notion of a veritable 'religion of love' (Ilahi-Ghomshei 2010) which we shall encounter presently.

The comprehensive revaluation of ethics undertaken by Sufism left a lasting mark on poetry in Islamic lands. As we saw both in the pre-Islamic ode by al-Musayyab and in Abū Tammām's eulogy, for all its beauty and bliss, love in the traditional qasida is an inferior state of being, a kind of 'juvenile folly', which the hero must transcend on the path to virtue. By elevating love to such supreme status Sufism turned this ideology on its head and transformed poetry in the process. Since all human love is but a sign of the soul's primordial longing, traditional love poetry as a whole was invested with a

[43] See the definition of virtues in the widely disseminated *Principles of Sufism* by al-Qushayrī (d. 1072); generosity, for example, is here tantamount to complete self-abnegation for the sake of proximity to God (al-Qushayrī 2002: 299–305).
[44] The *One Hundred Fields* by Ansari (d. 1089) is one of the earliest Persian treatises on the Sufi path.
[45] Plotinus 1959: 473, adapted from *Ennead* VI 7 [38] 14. For the Arabic text, see Badawī (1977: 99).

deeper meaning.[46] Out of these more ancient roots a new type of verse arose, the Sufi ghazal, described by the 10th-century author al-Kharrāz as (Lewisohn 2015: 156):

> composed in the language of the lovers which the mystic never ceases to intone whether during the darkness of the night or the radiance of the day.

Among its precursors was a certain kind of verse termed ʿUdhrī, according to the tribe who practised it. Dating back to the early Islamic period (7th century), it anticipates the Sufi stance in that it, too, renders love into a supreme, all-consuming force. Its most famous proponent Qays ibn al-Muwallaḥ (d. 688) became known as al-Majnūn ('the madman') on account of his unhappy love for Laylā from which he refused to desist and to which he ultimately succumbed.[47] Between the 8th and 10th centuries the legacy of ʿUdhrī poetry, combined with other earlier strands of the poetic tradition such as bacchic and ascetic verse, developed into an ever-broadening flow of mystical poetry composed by the early Sufis.[48] In the process the inherited tropes were transformed into metaphors for divine love and fused with new theosophical concepts, as exemplified in the ode by al-Ḥallāj cited by Alexander Key in this volume (pp. 131–2). Most of them were short, monothematic poems which anticipate the far more voluminous corpus of mystical ghazals later composed in Persian and Turkish. The longer polythematic qasida only appeared in mystic garb from the 12th century onwards. Though always less popular than the ghazal, it led Arabic mystical poetry to its greatest exploits. In the following, four examples are intended to illustrate the ingenuity with which the pre-Islamic ternary pattern was adapted to convey a new message.

4.2. The Qasidas

There is, first, the ode by the Iraqi poet Ibn al-Shahrazūrī (d. 1037), deemed to be earliest full-length Sufi qasida.[49] As shown by Homerin (2015: 43), it is a 'dramatic mystic allegory' forged out of the ancient poetic themes and suffused with Sufi

[46] For a discussion of this process in Hispano-Arabic love poetry with particular reference to Neoplatonism, see Monroe (2004: 16–21).

[47] Like the tropes of classical love poetry so Majnūn's legend, too, was reinterpreted until it became a veritable paradigm of the mystic lover's fate and appeared as such in the celebrated romances by the Persian poets Niẓāmī (d. 1209) and Jāmī (d. 1492). For the Arabic sources on the Majnūn legend, see Beck (2018), for its later development Watson (2013).

[48] For the rise of Arabic mystical poetry, see Schimmel (1982: 11–48) and Ernst (2018: 10–24), the latter with particular focus on al-Ḥallāj. A survey of traditional amatory tropes and the Sufi charge they were made to carry is given by Sells (1996: 56–74).

[49] Mention must also be made of the Ode to the Soul attributed to Ibn Sīnā (d. 1037, [illegible]), though it is more a philosophical allegory than a Sufi poem in the strict sense of the term. The authenticity of this much discussed work has for long been subject to dispute (Gutas 2014: 454, Madelung & Mayer 2016: 31–56). As shown by Homerin (2011: 107–8), it charts the trajectory of the soul in Neoplatonic terms by recourse to the traditional imagery of the qasida. Significantly, it rhymes on the letter *ʿayn*, a phoneme whose Arabic name also means 'source, essence' and as such is often used to denote the ultimate reality in a mystical sense. Hence every line of the poem ends with a metaphorical hint, in audial form, at the subject matter of the work as a whole: the primal origin and ultimate destination of the soul. As discussed in the chapter by Robin Ostle in this volume (pp. 393–4), the poem became a major source of inspiration for the modern Arab writer Khalīl Jubrān..

terms and Qur'anic associations. The abandoned campsite is transformed into a meeting place of lovers desperate to reach the fire of Laylā which gleams on the horizons. Her name, by that time synonymous with the ultimate beloved, suitably provides the rhyme letter 'l' of the poem. As they search for her, the lovers find themselves confronted by guardian spirits who seek to ward off the unworthy. In the ensuing combat, the war imagery and the martial virtues championed by the qasidas of old are transformed into metaphors of inner, spiritual struggle on the path to union. Though the adepts are vanquished, their hearts live 'for a second chance' (Homerin 2015: 34) and they will not give up.

Our second example is certainly the most remarkable poetic exploration of the mystic quest undertaken in Arabic, the great poem rhyming in 't' (*al-Tāʾiyya al-Kubrā*) by the master of the Sufi qasida, the Egyptian Ibn al-Fārīḍ (d. 1234). In Arabic grammar, the consonant 't' is the grammatical marker of the feminine for nouns and for verbs in third person perfect, so it offers a sheer unlimited scope for making mono-rhymes, as required for a poem of 761 lines. The resulting dominance of the feminine gender places the femininity of the archetypal beloved resolutely centre stage.[50] If the mono-rhyme is a Plotinian seed, then its potential as pointer to the multiple permutations of the One in female guise certainly comes to full flowering in this poem.[51] She appears in the very first line, endowed with a 'beauty surpassing all forms of beauty', to speak with St Teresa of Ávila as cited in this volume[52] (Ibn al-Fāriḍ 2004: 66):

> *Saqatnī* ***ḥu****m**ayya l-**ḥu**bbi rā**h**atu mu**qlatī***
> *Wa-kaʾsī* ***muḥ****ayya* ***m****an ʿani l-**ḥu**sni ja**llatī***
> The hand of my sight gave me the fire of love to drink
> and my cup was the face of Her who exceeds (*jallatī*) all beauty.

The metaphorical diction and the interlacing sound pattern of the line (note the alliterations and the inverted symmetry between *ḥumayya*, 'fire', and *muḥayya*, 'face') bear witness to Ibn al-Fāriḍ's consummate command of the *badīʿ* style. The unparalleled exploration of Sufi concepts in the ensuing verses has been much commented upon.[53] Suffice it to point out that the poem's core subject, love, displays its power in progressive stages, in keeping with the qasida's ternary structure (Sperl 1996: 74–81). The first part shows it captivating the hearts of all bygone lovers, notably also al-Majnūn, while in the central section the poet himself is so entirely seized by it as to be elevated to a moment of well-nigh pantheistic

[50] As noted by Lewisohn, women are of 'central spiritual significance' for the Sufi since, in the words of Ibn ʿArabī, 'the contemplation of God in women' is 'the best and most perfect kind' (2015: 175).

[51] It is worth noting that the feminine ending on 't' also acts as a marker of singularity in collective nouns. Thus, *bayḍ* means 'eggs' whereas *bayḍat*^{un} means 'one egg'. Many rhyme words of this poem are of this kind, and hence engender a ceaseless interplay between the one and the many.

[52] See Colin Thompson's chapter in this volume, p. 315.

[53] For commented translations of the poem, see Arberry (1952) and Homerin (2001). For an analysis of the poem, see Homerin (2011), and for the circumstances of the poem's composition and the controversies it aroused, see Homerin (1994).

ecstasy. The effect is such as to lend him the voice of the divine presence which declaims the final section of the poem. Here love itself is elevated to a unitary force which equally inspires all forms of human worship. Not only Muslims, Jews and Christians, but idol worshippers and Magians too are shown to be driven by desire for the same ultimate goal, 'for the eyes do not swerve in any faith'.

Our third example is the *Nūniyya* (poem rhyming in 'n') by the Hispano-Arabic Sufi al-Shushtarī (d. 1296) who is known for short strophic poems of great lyricism and humour. As a fully-fledged philosophical qasida, the *Nūniyya* stands out from the rest and reads like a personal confession of faith. It begins by outlining the goal of the mystic which transcends paradise in its endeavour for union and the extinction of the self. The middle section illustrates the arduous nature of this quest through the image of the pre-Islamic desert journey with its strife, toil and hardship. The obstacle to be confronted, however, is not a physical wilderness, but the human intellect whose discursive bent bars the way, while paradoxically being the sole available guide.

As Alvarez notes,[54] the poem's final section is tantamount to the panegyric part of the classical ode. Remarkably, however, the poet's eulogy is not directed at an earthly patron but at his spiritual forbears: an array of philosophers and mystics, ranging from Socrates, Plato and Aristotle via Ibn Sīnā and Ibn al-Fāriḍ, up to his own mentor, the mystical thinker Ibn Sabʿīn (d. 1271). The poet thus sees the theosophical tradition to which he belongs as stretching back to classical antiquity in an uninterrupted chain of transmission. True guidance is to be found by joining their fold, as affirmed by the last line (Alvarez 2009: 135,):

> Those who desire to go to the side of
> holiness, let them accept it from us.

The words 'from us' (*ʿannā*) coincide with the poem's mono-rhyme *nā*, a syllable which designates the first-person plural ending and recurs in this sense frequently throughout the work. It variously stands for the poet, his mystic travellers and his spiritual forebears, while its occurrence in the above-cited final verse cannot fail to evoke also the *plurale majestatis* with which the divine subject often refers to Himself so frequently in the Qur'an.[55] In thus implicitly identifying the many with the One, the final rhyme affirms that integration into a 'greater psychic world' has been attained and that the journey's ultimate goal is within reach.[56]

[54] See Alvarez (2009: 128).

[55] A famous Hispano-Arabic love poem, the *nūniyya* of Ibn Zaydūn, uses the same rhyme *nā* to similar multi-layered effect in order to convey what Monroe (2004: 20) described as 'the Neoplatonic fusion of souls'.

[56] In view of the poem's theosophical content its rhyme letter 'n' (*nūn*) calls for more comment. Not only is the *nūn* given special status in Sura 68 of the Qur'an where it figures as an oath, but in Sufi esoteric thinking it also figures as cosmic symbol on account of its semi-circular shape: ن. According to Ibn ʿArabī (1997: 113) the semi-circle of *nūn* symbolises the lower, material realm which perennially points to the existence of the superior, invisible realm symbolised by the unseen upper half of the semi-circle. The question how to use the seen as springboard towards the unseen, the verbal as key to the unutterable is at the heart of this poem, hence the esoteric symbolism of the rhyme-letter truly sums up its contents.

The offer of guidance in the closing verse acts also as a reminder that what Plotinus called 'assimilation to good human beings' remains highly relevant for the Sufi tradition, provided such goodness derives from the progress they have made on the path towards that supreme goal. Sufism knows many such guiding spirits, the most exalted being the Prophet conceived as the Perfect Man,[57] followed by the saints and the founding fathers of Sufi brotherhoods. The poets, too, are exemplars, for works such as those discussed above bear witness to their personal quest and point the way for others to follow. This certainly applies to Ibn al-Fāriḍ who came to be venerated as a saint, and, above all, to the 'Greatest Master' (*al-Shaykh al-Akbar*), Ibn ʿArabī (d. 1240).

Despite their difference all three poems convey a process of psychic growth in which divergent and seemingly contradictory forces are brought together to engender a state of consciousness closer to the goal they share: assimilation to the ultimate reality. The Jungian 'transcendent function', identified by Jamil in the pre-Islamic qasida, is therefore in evidence also here – if anything to an even greater extent since all three poems are descriptive of mental states. Thus, Ibn al-Shahrazūrī forges hope out of defeat in a psychic battle, while the search for union leads both Ibn al-Fāriḍ and al-Shūshtarī to an integrative, from a modern perspective transcultural, consciousness in which Greek and Arabic thinkers and the followers of all religions are understood as equally oriented towards the same goal.

This remarkable, unitary vision characterises the inclusive spirituality of classical Sufism[58] and brings to mind the following oft-cited verses by Ibn ʿArabī (1961: 43, [illegible]):

> My heart has come to adopt every form:
> a grazing ground for gazelles and a cloister for monks,
> A temple for idols and a Kaʿba for the circling pilgrim,
> tablets for a Torah and scrolls for a Qur'an.

The message here conveyed would seem to be singularly appropriate for a publication such as this which straddles the confluence of cultures and religions. But what exactly does it state and what insight does it emanate from? And how does it relate to Neoplatonism? These questions are of such topical relevance that a closer look at the poem from which the lines derive is warranted. It will bring our survey to conclusion.

5. Ibn ʿArabī and the Heart of Many Forms

The verses feature in *The Interpreter of Desires* (*Tarjumān al-Ashwāq*), a collection of love poems inspired by Ibn ʿArabī's encounter with Niẓām, a beautiful and erudite

[57] According to Ibn ʿArabī, the Perfect Man (*al-insān al-kāmil*) represents the highest degree of assimilation to God a human being can attain. For details see Takeshita (1983). As though in anticipation of the Sufi notion, the *Theology of Aristotle* describes man in the upper world as 'complete and perfect' (*tāmm kāmil*) (Plotinus 1959: 441; Badawī 1977: 139).

[58] For a fine example, see Lewisohn's work on al-Shabistārī (1995).

Persian lady whom he met in Mecca. But she is not the only addressee. The other is God, manifest in 'divine inspirations, spiritual revelations and sublime intimations' (Ibn ʿArabī 1961: 9) which the author explains in an extensive commentary. Taken together, poems and commentary provide an object lesson on the convergence of love sacred and profane, a tenet equally shared by Sufism and Neoplatonism.

While the above cited verses are widely known, their place in the context of the poem and their significance in the context of Ibn ʿArabī's theoretical writings was not discussed in detail until the appearance of two remarkable studies by Sells (1991; 1994: 90–115). In the following we intend to show that his findings can be corroborated and further developed if the poem in question is viewed in the light of the pre-Islamic qasida and its movement 'from the one of many to the many as one' which we identified in al-Musayyab's poem.

That the poem does indeed map out a qasida-like trajectory is evident in the radical change of mood to which it gives expression. At the beginning we find the poet in a state of inner torment occasioned by a hidden agony of love which he is desperate not to reveal. At the end, by contrast, he proclaims love as his religion and happily joins the fellowship of legendary poet lovers. In this movement from separation to triumphant integration into a greater collective we can recognise the characteristic outer movements of the qasida. The desert journey which traditionally links the two also has an equivalent, for it resides at the centre of the poem, in a form already encountered in Abū Tammām's ode: the pilgrimage journey to Mecca and the circumambulation of the Kaʿba. The poem can therefore be read as one more recasting of this time-honoured pattern. Let us examine more closely how it leads up to its unitary vision.

A plea for mercy sets the scene (Ibn ʿArabī 1961: 40, [illegible]):

> 1. 'O doves of the Arāk and Bān trees
>   be gentle, don't double my sorrows with your sorrow!
>
> 2. Be gentle, don't disclose by crying and lamenting
>   my covert longings and concealed torments!'

By the time this poem was composed, the doves whose cooing deepens the lone sorrow of the lover had been a well-known poetic image already for centuries. As shown by Sells (1991: 2–3), the Arāk and Bān trees also have ancient associations with the tropes of early Arabic love poetry. This conventional setting is not to be taken at face value for it harbours a deeper layer of meaning, which is the subject of Ibn ʿArabī's commentary. He explains the doves as *wāridāt*, a technical term of Sufism which denotes 'that which arrives in the heart from any divine name … It may arrive with sobriety or intoxication, contraction or expansion, awe or intimacy or innumerable other affairs' (Chittick 1998: 148).

Ibn ʿArabī's mystical revaluation of the doves does not stand alone. As his commentary makes clear, all the inherited tropes of classical Arabic love poetry are to be understood as bearers of an ulterior message. They have been comprehensively 'metaphorised', in keeping with the principle of *badīʿ* poetry we encountered in the ode of Abū Tammām. For Ibn ʿArabī such metaphorisation means reading the tropes as *āyāt*, as 'signs' in the Qur'anic sense, a term which he explains as (Chittick 1998: 4): 'signifiers that He is the Real who is manifest within the loci of manifestation that are the entities of the cosmos'. As the poem progresses the sorrowful longing evoked by the doves drives the lover to virtual extinction through 'agonising heart-ache, pangs of passion and every kind of rare affliction' till he utters the following cry (Ibn ʿArabī 1961: 41,):

> 6. Who will give me Jamʿ and al-Muḥaṣṣab of Minā,
> who will take me to Dhāt al-Athl and Nuʿmān?

These place names conjure up the environs of Mecca and the stations of the pilgrimage, while their metaphorical meanings as explained by Ibn ʿArabī all hint at the bliss brought about by the sacred union of lover and beloved. At this point a sudden exchange of roles takes place. Instead of the poet being the hapless lover, he is now himself the target of no less ardent longing. For the forces which first aroused his love through the cooing of the doves are now seized by desire for him. Why this exchange of roles? As stated in a famous hadith much cited by Ibn ʿArabī, the human heart is the sole recipient in the sensible realm with the capacity of containing the divine essence. Thus, the mention of the pilgrimage stations has aroused in the detached spirits of the divine names with which the poem began the hope and desire for reunion with the divine essence in the very heart of the lover (Ibn ʿArabī 1961: 42,):

> 7. They circle round my heart hour after hour
> in distress and passionate love and kiss the veil of my pillars,
>
> 8. Like the Best of Prophets circled around the Kaʿba,
> which proof of reason declares to be deficient,
>
> 9. And kissed stones therein, though he has speech.
> Where ranks that House compared to a human?

Not only do these verses occupy the exact centre of the poem, but their significance is much enhanced by the seminal role played by the Kaʿba in Ibn ʿArabī's personal journey. As he narrates in the introduction to his *Meccan Openings*, when he first saw it he wondered why a dead object made of stones should be the subject of veneration.[59] In declaring the Kaʿba to be deficient to the eye of reason and questioning its status compared to that of a living being the above lines allude to this moment of bewilderment. The solution to the mystery was revealed to him by a divine emissary whom he encountered at the black stone and who was to grant him the insights expounded in the *Meccan Openings*. Ibn ʿArabī paraphrased his advice in the following verses (Ibn ʿArabī 1972: 215):

> Look at the house: its lights shine,
> openly displayed to those pure of heart

To the eyes of the heart, the humble status of the signifier is elevated beyond measure by the sublimity of the signified. As they continued to converse Ibn ʿArabī

[59] For a detailed discussion of Ibn ʿArabī's personal account of these events, see Chodkiewicz (2015).

found himself initiated into the mystery of divine self-disclosure. It is encapsulated in the following statement spoken by the stranger (Ibn ʿArabī 1972: 223):

> The one who chains Me to one form to the exclusion of another, it is his fantasy image that he worships.

At the root of the matter is the paradox between the simultaneous transcendence and immanence of the deity, the very issue which Sells identified as the reason why the lover's heart should be open to all forms of worship. In its transcendence, the deity is 'unmanifest, undifferentiated, absolute unity' (Sells 1994: 93), and hence entirely beyond the range of human perception. By contrast, in its immanence it 'manifests itself through innumerable forms or images but is confined to none' (Sells 1994: 91). Hence chaining it to one form only is tantamount to self-delusion.

If the mind seeks to comprehend this conundrum by means of discursive reasoning alone it is bound to fail, as asserted also in al-Shushtarī's abovementioned qasida. The intellect (*ʿaql*) will by nature seek to reduce the deity to what Ibn ʿArabī called 'the God of belief' (*ilāh al-iʿtiqād*), a truncated vision which seeks to limit the inherently limitless. Where the intellect fails, the heart as seat of spiritual apperception comes to the rescue. It is 'dynamically integrative' as Sells puts it, and therefore able to comprehend 'the perpetually changing forms in which the real appears' (Sells 1994: 92).

Plotinus and the Sufi tradition converge in upholding both the paradox between the transcendence and immanence of the deity and the incapacity of the intellect to comprehend it. Both also feature in the Arabic Plotinus adaptation commissioned by al-Kindī. The *Epistle on Divine Science*, based in part on *Ennead* V 5, includes a long reflection on divine transcendence which puts the contradiction very bluntly: 'the first of first principles exists in the things and does not exist in them' (Plotinus 1959: 353). The passage also leaves no doubt about the deficiency of the human intellect, for it 'will never be capable of comprehending or describing the [Almighty Creator] ... When it strives after knowledge of him it does but increase in remoteness of him' (Plotinus 1959: 355).[60]

Despite this convergence of views, it would be rash to conclude that Ibn ʿArabī's understanding of divinity reflects the influence of his philosophical forebear. While he may have read the Arabic Plotinus adaptations, he makes no overt reference to them[61] and instead derives his argument from Prophetic sayings and the Qurʾan. As evidence for the superiority of the heart over the intellect he cites the Qurʾanic verse 'In that [God's supremacy] is a reminder (*dhikr*) for one who has a heart (*qalb*)' (50:37). He then points out that the text did not state 'for one who has an intellect (*ʿaql*)', because only the heart can grasp the 'constant transformation in forms and attributes' of the ultimate reality while the mind binds and limits it to one description (Sells 1994: 99).

[60] For a more detailed critique of human reason which parallels Ibn ʿArabī, see *Ennead* VI 7 [38] 33.

[61] Notable similarities between Ibn ʿArabī's cosmology and ideas expounded in the tenth chapter of the *Theology of Aristotle* have been detected by Bashīr (2017: 400–26).

It follows that the motifs in the central lines of the poem – the circumambulation, the wonder at the status of the Kaʿba, the kissing of the stones and the references to heart and intellect – allude to a truly transformative moment in Ibn ʿArabī's life. In the same way, they mark a transformative moment in the development of the poem and pave the ground for the ensuing verses on the unitary vision of the heart capable of assuming every form. Thanks to the encounter at the Meccan sanctuary, the heart learned how to recognise the lost Beloved in a multiplicity of guises – or, in other words, to perceive the many as One.

The two concluding verses of the poem reveal the fruit of this inner journey, as faith and fortitude are reborn and the horizon falls wide open (Ibn ʿArabī 1961: 44, [illegible]):

15. I profess the creed of love wherever its caravans their faces turn,
for love is my doctrine and my faith.

16. We have exemplars in Hind of Bishr and her sister,
in Qays and Laylā, Mayy and Ghaylān.

From having visited the centre the poet has himself become a centre whence he looks out in all directions, in emulation of the legendary lovers of the past. The operative word is *tawajjaha*, which means 'to turn one's face towards', and in this context cannot fail to evoke the above-cited Qurʾānic verse (2:115):

To God belong the East and the West; wherever you turn there is the face of God.

In 'turning his face' with the caravans the poet thus turns towards the divine countenance which is to be found wherever he directs his gaze. The full depth of this image becomes apparent if it is read in the light of Ibn ʿArabī's doctrine of the 'specific face' (*wajh khāṣṣ*) with which each created thing is endowed by God and through which it obtains its knowledge of God. In his meditations on the symbolism of the circle[62] he explains the genesis of this concept as follows (Chittick 1998: 229): 'The line that emerges from the centre point toward one point on the encompassing circumference is the specific face that every existent thing has from its Creator.' It follows that the circumference is, so to say, lined with the numberless 'specific faces belonging to each possible thing that has proceeded from him' (Chittick 1998: 143). In this image we encounter once more the conjunction between absolute unicity and the multiplicity to which it gives rise and through which it gains immanence and makes itself known. It has a remarkable parallel in *Ennead* VI 7 15 where Plotinus likens the multiplicity generated out of the One through the agency of the Intellect to a 'richly varied sphere' or a 'thing all faces, shining with living faces'. He adds the proviso, however, that (VI 7 [38] 15, A: VII 137): 'if one imagined it like this one would be seeing it somehow as one sees another from outside; but one must become that and make oneself the

[62] Circularity and circular movement have an equally important and in many ways analogous function in the cosmologies of Plotinus and Ibn ʿArabī. This is evident when comparing passages such as *Ennead* II 2 [14] 2 or VI 8 [39] 18 with the *Futuḥāt* citations on circularity assembled by Chittick (1998: 223–33).

contemplation'. Subject and object, seer and the seen, lover and beloved must fuse into one entity and thereby vicariously restore the unity from which this multiplicity derives. Ibn ʿArabī expresses this notion explicitly in other poems,[63] but it is relevant here too. For the true journey of the caravan of love must be a journey inwards, into the inner self, in search of the God-given 'special face' we carry in us and through which we may reconnect to the centre.

The closing line of the poem holds up the example of the legendary lovers of the past. As Ibn ʿArabī notes in his commentary, 'love is a single reality for them and us, despite the fact that they pined for a [created] being (*kawn*) and we for an [uncreated] essence (*ʿayn*)' (1961: 44). The analogy between human and divine love, illustrated by the whole of *The Interpreter of Desires*, brings us to a final parallel with Plotinus for he asserts precisely the same link. Speaking about the soul propelled by love to seek union with 'the first nature of beauty', he declares that 'lovers and their beloveds here below imitate this in their will to be united' (VI 7 [38] 34, A: VII 193).

With respect to the pre-Islamic qasida we noted Jamil's view of it as a poetic manifestation of the Jungian 'transcendent function'. To what extent could this hold true also of this Sufi qasida? If we cast our glance back at the structure of this poem a striking analogy emerges between the sequence of themes we have discussed and the three stages of Jungian individuation which MacLennan defined as 'call, crisis and cure'.[64] The *call* is the result of awakened psychic forces calling for integration which destabilise and trouble the mind unprepared to respond to this challenge. In our poem, the call of the doves in the initial verses and the perturbation it brings about would seem to perform precisely this function. As for the *crisis*, it may lead to a 'dissolution of ordinary personality' and the appearance of spiritual guides and 'symbols of centrality such as the cosmic axis' (MacLennan 2006: 4). This can be seen to correspond to the poet's near self-annihilation followed by the vision of the Prophet as spiritual guide and his circumambulation of the Kaʿba, the ultimate symbol of centrality in Islam. Lastly, the third stage, *cure*, is no less reminiscent of our poem for it involves a 'reintegration of the psyche' and a renewed 'communication and cooperation with the archetypal forces of the universe'. Reintegration is signalled by the heart's ability 'to adopt every form' in its quest for the deity, while love, elevated here to a religion, assumes the status of ultimate archetypal force for it leads to the highest goal – assimilation to God.

As a result, the poem may be viewed as retracing the steps of a process of individuation in a combined Jungian, Neoplatonic and Sufi sense. The time-honoured form and the ancient images still perform the same psychic function but at a different, radically internalised and spiritual level. Another traditional feature, the expressive function of the mono-rhyme which we have touched upon throughout

[63] See, for instance, the poems in the 'Treatise of Unification' (Ibn ʿArabī 2006).

[64] The ensuing discussion is based on MacLennan (2006: 3–4) whose terminology derives from Ryan's study of Shamanism and Jungian psychology (2002).

this chapter, is no less tangible here. The poem rhymes on the sound pattern *ānī*, which seems singularly appropriate to convey the personal experience of individuation because both the long vowel *ī* and the syllable *nī* can act as grammatical markers for the first person singular and appear as such repeatedly in the rhyme. The resulting sound pattern means that every line ends with an explicit or implicit return to the poetic self and hence highlights the immediacy of the personal experience expressed. Both in terms of sound and meaning, the development culminates in the following, penultimate line (Ibn ʿArabī 1961: 44,):

> 15. I profess the religion of love wherever its caravans
> their faces turn, for love is my religion and my faith.
>
> *Adīnu bi-dīni ʾl-ḥubbi annā tawajjahat*
> *rakāʾibuhu fa ʾl-ḥubbu dīnī wa īmānī*

The line is a fine example of the 'geometric' sound patterning encountered with Abū Tammām as a hallmark of the *badīʿ* style. The word *ḥubb*, twice repeated, is symmetrically framed on either side by the close assonance between two phrases, *adīnu bi-dīni* ('I profess the religion') and *dīnī wa-īmānī* ('my religion and my faith'). In combination with the mono-rhyme, the resulting sound pattern emphatically conveys that this new creed is the poet's own: **my** religion and **my** faith.

The nature of this faith is contextualised by the other rhyme words, notably *insānī* (human being, line 9) and *Qurʾānī* (line 14). The associations of sound and meaning the rhyme thereby establishes between the Qur'an, mankind and faith serve to confirm that the creed which is the fruit of the poet's inner transformation is not a distancing from Islam, but quite the reverse. As we have seen, it is born out of the encounter with the divine presence at the Meccan sanctuary which is relived at the centre of the work. It follows that the famous lines on the heart should not be read as an expression of religious relativism or tolerance in the modern sense, as has often been asserted. Rather, the poem is, in Schimmel's words, 'a glowing tribute to Islam' (1982: 38), a point of view argued more recently and in great detail also by Lipton (2017: 1–54).

What distinguishes Islam from the other creeds in the experiential world of this poem and its wider associations in Ibn ʿArabī's work is the privileged insight it grants into the intellectual premise which opens the heart and gives rise to the religion of love. This is the absolute transcendence of God as the One, and His consequent immanence in the forms of the Many. Seen from a wider historical perspective this secret, revealed in front of the Kaʿba, appears rooted in a negative theology with distinct Plotinian parallels.

6. Conclusions

Our reflections on points of convergence between Neoplatonism and Classical Arabic poetry began with Plotinus's distinction between civic and purificatory virtues, coupled with his assertion that 'assimilation is to gods, not to good human beings'. In the pre-Islamic qasida we encountered a poetic form which charts the path towards the acquisition of a body of civic virtues manifest in the tribal leader as primordial 'good human being'. In the Abbasid qasida by Abū Tammām, we encountered that same poetic form charting the path towards civic virtue sublimated as a reflection of divine attributes and manifest in an individual conceived as the representative of divine authority. This vision and its expression through the *badī'* style mark a step closer towards the Plotinian ideal. In the process the inherited poetic themes are transubstantiated into polyvalent metaphors reflective of a hierarchical cosmic order in which micro and macrocosm mirror each other. Rhetorical devices serve as tools to forge language into quasi-geometric patterns of sound and meaning whose 'beautiful order and arrangement' aim to reflect the timeless symmetries of the intelligible realm. The style therefore appears designed to convey a cosmology and an aesthetic which carry recognisably Neoplatonic traits. Lastly the Sufi qasida retraces the ascending steps of its earlier forbears, but similar to the Plotinian ideal its ultimate goal is 'assimilation to God'. In the process, the virtues are reconfigured as purificatory waystations on the soul's ascent and made subordinate to Love as the single most powerful force which propels it towards union.

If in conclusion we were to ask whether Ibn 'Arabī's qasida on the doves of the Arāk tree can justifiably be deemed to be Neoplatonic, the answer may well depend on the perspective adopted by the viewer. For our findings would seem to suggest that Neoplatonism both exists and does not exist in this poem. It does not exist as a separate extraneous element, because all the poem's constituents, its form, themes, structure, style and religious vision are derived from the combined resources of Arabic poetry and the Qur'an. In this sense Ibn 'Arabī's qasida is an entirely authentic product of the Islamic tradition. At the same time, if it is viewed in the light of the *Enneads*, these same constituents, and with them the intellectual foundation upon which their message rests, display a range of significant parallels. The dialectic between the one and the many and the intellect's incapacity to comprehend it, the ubiquitous significatory charge of all existents, love as a single all-embracing force conjoining the sacred and profane – these and other parallels – show that the work exhibits a profound kinship with the Neoplatonic tradition. This kinship is not an alien element, an influence recognisably derived from an outside source. It is intrinsically organic and begins at the very roots, with what we called the Plotinian seeds – the pre-Islamic qasida and the mono-rhyme, which already encapsulate the quest for ascent and the paradigmatic interplay between the many and the one.

References

Abrahamov, B. (2006), 'Signs', in J.D. McAuliffe (ed.), *Encyclopaedia of the Qur'ān* (Washington DC, Georgetown University), accessed 27 June 2019, http://dx.doi.org/10.1163/1875-3922_q3_EQCOM_00182

Abū Tammām, Ḥabīb b. Aus (1969), *Dīwān Abī Tammām bi-Sharḥ al-Tabrīzī*, ed. M.'A.'Azzām, vol. 2 (Cairo, Dār al-Ma'ārif).

Adamson, P. (2002), *The Arabic Plotinus: A Philosophical Study of the 'Theology of Aristotle'* (London, Duckworth).

Adamson, P. (2018), 'Al-Kindi', in E.N. Zalta (ed.), *The Stanford Encyclopedia of Philosophy* (Summer 2018 Edition), accessed 27 June 2019, https://plato.stanford.edu/archives/sum2018/entries/al-kindi/

Alvarez, L.M. (2009), *Abū al-Ḥasan al-Shushtarī: Songs of Love and Devotion*, Foreword M.A. Sells (New York, Paulist Press).

Amir-Moezzi, M.A. (ed.) (1996), *Le voyage initiatique en terre d'Islam, ascensions celestes et itinéraires spirituels* (Louvain/Paris, Peters).

Andrews, W. (1996), 'Speaking of Power: The "Ottoman Kaside"', in Sperl & Shackle (1996), vol. 1, 281–300.

Ansari, A. (2010), *Stations of the Sufi Path: The One Hundred Fields Sad Maydān by ʿAbdu'llāh Ansārī of Herat*, trans. & introduction N. Angha (Cambridge, Archetype).

Arberry, A.J. (1952), *The Poem of the Way Translated into English from the Arabic of Ibn al-Fāriḍ* (London, Emery Walker).

Badawī, A. (ed.) (1977), *Aflūṭīn ʿinda 'l-ʿArab, Theologia Aristotelis et fragmenta quae supersunt* (Kuwait, Wakālat al-Maṭbūʿāt).

Baffioni, C. (2016), 'Ikhwân al-Safâ'', in E.N. Zalta (ed.) *The Stanford Encyclopedia of Philosophy* (Fall 2016 Edition), accessed 21 June 2019, https://plato.stanford.edu/archives/fall2016/entries/ikhwan-al-safa/

Barnes, H. (1945), 'Neoplatonism and Analytical Psychology', *The Philosophical Review*, 54.6: 558–77.

Bashīr, S. (2017), *Nāfidha ʿalā 'l-Ghayb bayna Ibn al-ʿArabī wa Ibn Rushd fī 'l-Khayāl wa 'l-Ittiṣāl wa Maʿrifat 'l-Nafs* (Freiberg, Al-Kamel Verlag).

Bauer, T. (2010), 'The Relevance of Early Arabic Poetry for Qur'anic Studies, including Observations on *kull* and on Qur'an 22:27, 26:225 and 52:31', in A. Neuwirth, N. Sinai & M. Marx (eds), *The Qur'an in Context: Historical and Literary Investigations into the Qur'anic Milieu* (Leiden, Brill), 699–732.

Beck, K. (2018), 'Iṣbahānī's Invitation to Madness: Introduction to the Majnūn-Laylā Story', *Journal of Arabic Literature*, 49.4: 330–54.

Bonebakker, S.A. (1956), *The Kitāb Naqd al-Shiʿr by Qudāma b. Jaʿfar al-Kātib al-Baghdādī* (Leiden, Brill).

Böwering, G. (2001), 'Covenant', in J.D. McAuliffe (ed.), *Encyclopaedia of the Qurʾān* (Washington DC, Georgetown University), accessed 27 June 2019, http://dx.doi.org/10.1163/1875-3922_q3_EQSIM_00098

Böwering, G. (2002), 'God and his Attributes', in J.D. McAuliffe (ed.), *Encyclopaedia of the Qurʾān* (Washington DC, Georgetown University), accessed 27 June 2019, http://dx.doi.org/10.1163/1875-3922_q3_EQCOM_00075

Bürgel, J.C. (1992), 'Ecstasy and Order: Two Structural Principles in the Ghazal Poetry of Jalāl al-Dīn Rūmī', in L. Lewisohn (ed.), *The Legacy of Medieval Persian Sufism* (London/New York, Khaniqahi Nimatullahi Publications).

Calverley, E.E. & Netton, I.R. (1993), 'Nafs', in P. Bearman, Th. Bianquis, C.E. Bosworth, E. van Donzel & W.P. Heinrichs (eds), *Encyclopaedia of Islam, Second Edition*, accessed 27 June 2019, http://dx.doi.org/10.1163/1573-3912_islam_COM_0833

Chittick, W.C. (1998), *The Self-Disclosure of God: Principles of Ibn ʿArabī's Cosmology* (New York, State University of New York Press).

Chodkiewicz, M. (2015), 'The Paradox of the Kaʿba', *Journal of the Muhyiddin Ibn ʿArabī Society*, 57: 57–83.

Colby, F.S. (2008), *Narrating Muḥammad's Night Journey: Tracing the Development of the Ibn ʿAbbās Ascension Discourse* (Albany, State University of New York Press).

D'Ancona, C. (2000), 'L'influence du vocabulaire arabe: "causa prima est esse tantum"', in J. Hamesse & C. Steel (eds), *L'élaboration du vocabulaire philosophique au Moyen Âge: Actes du colloque international de Louvain-la-Neuve et Leuven, 12–14 septembre 1998* (Turnhout, Brepols), 51–97.

Dedes, Y. & Sperl, S. (2013), '"In the Rosebower every Leaf is a Page of Delicate Meaning": An Arabic Perspective on Three Ottoman Kasides', in H. Aynur, M. Çakır, H. Koncu, S. Kuru & A.E. Özyıldırım (eds), *Kasîdeye Medhiye: Biçime, İşleve ve Muhtavaya Dair Tespitler, Eski Türk Edebiyatı Çalişmaları VIII* (Istanbul, Klasik), 240–313.

Eco, U. (2002), *Art and Beauty in the Middle Ages* (New Haven/London, Yale University Press).

Endress, G. (1994), 'Al-Kindī über die Wiedererinnerung der Seele: arabischer Platonismus und die Legitimation der Wissenschaften im Islam', *Oriens*, 34: 174–221.

Ernst, C. (2018), *Hallaj: Poems of a Sufi Martyr* (Evanston, Northwestern University Press).

Fakhreddine, H.J. (2015), *Metapoesis in the Arabic Literary Tradition: From Modernists to Muḥdathūn* (Leiden, Brill).

Fowden, G. (2007), 'Greek Myth and Arabic Poetry at Quṣayr Amra', in A. Akasoy, J.E. Montgomery & P.E. Pormann (eds), *Islamic Crosspollinations: Interactions in the Medieval Middle East* (Exeter, Gibb Memorial Trust), 29–45.

Gelder, G.J. van (1982), *Beyond the Line: Classical Arabic Literary Critics on the Coherence and Unity of the Poem* (Leiden, Brill).

Gelder, G.J. van (2012), *Sound and Sense in Classical Arabic Poetry* (Wiesbaden, Harrassowitz).

Ghazālī, Abū Ḥāmid al- (1992), *The Ninety-Nine Beautiful Names of God. Al-Maqṣad al-Asnā fī Sharḥ Maʿānī Asmāʾ Allāh al-Ḥusnā*, trans. D.B. Burrell & N. Daher (Cambridge, Islamic Texts Society).

Gramlich, R. (1998), *Der eine Gott. Grundzüge der Mystik des islamischen Monotheismus* (Wiesbaden, Harrassowitz).

Gruendler, B. (2003), *Medieval Arabic Praise Poetry: Ibn al-Rūmī and the Patron's Redemption* (London/New York, RoutledgeCurzon).

Gruendler, B. (2008), '*Qaṣīda*, Its Reconstruction in Performance', in B. Gruendler (ed.) with M. Cooperson, *Classical Arabic Humanities in Their Own Terms, Festschrift for Wolfhart Heinrichs* (Leiden, Brill), 325–89.

Gutas, D. (1998), *Greek Thought, Arabic Culture: The Greco-Arabic Translation Movement in Baghdad and Early ʿAbbāsid Society (2nd-4th / 8th – 10th Centuries)* (London/New York, Routledge).

Gutas, D. (2014), *Avicenna and the Aristotelian Tradition: Introduction to Reading Avicenna's Philosophical Works* (Leiden, Brill).

Homerin, Th.E. (1994), *From Arab Poet to Muslim Saint: Ibn al-Fāriḍ, His Verse and His Shrine* (Columbia, University of South Caroline Press).

Homerin, Th.E. (2001), *ʿUmar Ibn al-Fāriḍ: Sufi Verse, Saintly Life* (New York: Paulist Press).

Homerin, Th.E. (2006), 'Soul', in J.D. McAuliffe (ed.), *Encyclopaedia of the Qurʾān* (Washington DC, Georgetown University), accessed 27 June 2019, http://dx.doi.org/10.1163/1875-3922_q3_EQSIM_00398

Homerin, Th.E. (2011), *Passion Before Me, My Fate Behind: Ibn al-Fāriḍ and the Poetry of Recollection* (Albany, State University of New York Press).

Homerin, Th.E. (2015), 'A Distant Fire: Ibn al-Shahrazūrī's Mystical Ode and Arabic Sufi Verse', *Journal of Sufi Studies*, 4: 27–58.

Ibn al-Fāriḍ, ʿUmar (2004), *Dīwān*, ed. G. Scattolin (Cairo, Institut Français d'Archéologie Orientale).

Ibn ʿArabī, Muḥyī al-Dīn (1961), *Tarjumān al-Ashwāq* (Beirut, Dār Ṣādir).

Ibn ʿArabī, Muḥyī al-Dīn (1972), *Al-Futuḥāt al-Makkiyya*, ed. ʿU. Yaḥyā, vol. 1 (Cairo, Wizārat al-Thaqāfa wa ʿl-Iʿlām).

Ibn ʿArabī, Muḥyī al-Dīn (1997), 'Kitāb al-Mīm wa 'l-Wāw wa 'l-Nūn', in M.Sh. al-ʿAzabī (ed.), *Rasāʾil Ibn ʿArabī* (Beirut, Dār Ṣādir).

Ibn ʿArabī, Muḥyī al-Dīn (2006), *The Universal Tree and the Four Birds, Treatise on Unification (al-Ittihād al-Kawnī)*, trans. A. Jaffery (Oxford, Anqa Publishing).

Ibn Isḥāq (2001), *The Life of Muḥammad: A Translation of Isḥāq's Sīrat Rasūl Allāh*, trans. A. Guillaume (Karachi, Oxford University Press).

Ilahi-Ghomshei, H. (2010), 'The Principles of the Religion of Love in Classical Persian Poetry', in L. Lewisohn (ed.), *Hafez and the Religion of Love in Classical Persian Poetry* (London, I.B. Tauris), 77–106.

Izutsu, T. (2002), *Ethico-religious Concepts in the Qurʾān* (Montreal/Kingston, McGill-Queen's University Press).

Jacobi, R. (1996), 'The Origins of the Qasida Form', in Sperl & Shackle (1996), vol. 1, 21–34.

Jakobson, R. (1981), 'Poetry of Grammar and Grammar of Poetry', in S. Rudy (ed.) *Selected Writings*, vol. 3 (The Hague/Paris/New York, Mouton).

Jamil, N. (2017), *Ethics & Poetry in Sixth-Century Arabia* (Exeter, Gibb Memorial Trust).

Jolivet, J. (1996), 'La topographie du salut d'après le discours sur l'âme d'al-Kindī', in Amir-Moezzi (1996), 149–58.

Kermani, N. (2014), *God is Beautiful: The Aesthetic Experience of the Quran*, trans. T. Crawford (Malden MA, Polity Press).

al-Kindī, Abū Yaʿqūb (1950), *Rasāʾil al-Kindī al-Falsafiyya*, ed. M.A. Rīdah (Cairo, Maktabat al-Khānjī).

Leaman, O. (2016), *The Qur'an: A Philosophical Guide* (London/New York, Bloomsbury Academic).

Lewisohn, L. (1995), *Beyond Faith and Infidelity: The Sufi Poetry and Teachings of Maḥmūd Shabistarī* (Richmond, Curzon Press).

Lewisohn, L. (2015), 'Sufism's Religion of Love, from Rābiʿa to Ibn ʿArabī', in Ridgeon (2015), 150–80.

Lipton, G.A. (2017), *Rethinking Ibn ʿArabi* (Oxford, Oxford University Press).

Louth, A. (1994), 'Platonism and the Middle English Mystics', in A. Baldwin & S. Hutton (eds), *Platonism and the English Imagination* (Cambridge, Cambridge University Press), 52–64.

MacLennan, B.J. (2006), 'Individual Soul and World Soul: The Process of Individuation in Neoplatonism & Jung', accessed 2 May 2019, www.researchgate.net/publication/242238106_Individual_Soul_and_World_Soul_The_Process_of_Individuation_in_Neoplatonism_Jung

Madelung, W. & Mayer, T. (2016), *Avicenna's Allegory on the Soul: An Ismaili Interpretation*, Arabic edition by W. Madelung, trans. & introduction T. Mayer (London, I.B. Tauris).

Meisami, J.S. (1987), *Medieval Persian Court Poetry* (Princeton, Princeton University Press).

Melchert, C. (2015), 'Origins and Early Sufism', in Ridgeon (2015), 3–23.

Monroe, J.T. (2004), *Hispano-Arabic Poetry: A Student Anthology* (Piscataway, Gorgias Press).

Montgomery, J.E. (1986), 'Dichotomy in *Jāhili* Poetry', *Journal of Arabic Literature*, 17: 1–20.

Montgomery, J.E. (1994), 'Revelry and Remorse: A Poem by Abū Nuwās', *Journal of Arabic Literature*, 25: 116–34.

Montgomery, J.E. (2008), 'Convention as Cognition: On the Cultivation of Emotion', in G.J. van Gelder & M. Hammond (eds), *Takhyīl: The Imaginary in Classical Arabic Poetics* (Exeter, Gibb Memorial Trust).

Moustafa, M. & Sperl, S. (2014), *The Cosmic Script: Sacred Geometry and the Science of Arabic Penmanship*, 2 vols (London, Thames & Hudson).

Musayyab ibn ʿAlas, al- (1996), 'Qasida in Praise of al-Qaʿqāʿ', trans. R. Jacobi, in Sperl & Shackle (1996), vol. 2, 68–71.

Necipoğlu, G. (1995), *The Topkapı Scroll: Geometry and Ornament in Islamic Architecture: Topkapı Palace Library MS H. 1956*, with an essay on the geometry of the muqarnas by M. al-Asad (Santa Monica, Paul Getty Center for the Arts and Humanities).

Netton, I. (1982), *Muslim Neoplatonists: An Introduction to the Thought of the Brethren of Purity (Ikhwān al-Ṣafāʾ)* (London, Allen & Unwin).

Neuwirth, A. (2014), *Scripture, Poetry and the Making of a Community: Reading the Qur'an as a Literary Text* (Oxford, Oxford University Press).

Nokso-Koivisto, I. (2011), 'Summarized Beauty: The Microcosm-macrocosm Analogy and Islamic Aesthetic', *Studia Orientalia*, 111: 251–69.

Plotinus (1959), *Plotini Opera*, vol. 2, ed. P. Henry & H.-R. Schwyzer, with English translation of the 'Plotiniana Arabica' by G. Lewis (Paris, Desclée de Brouwer & Bruxelles, L'Édition Universelle).

Pormann, P. & Adamson, P. (eds) (2012), *The Philosophical Works of al-Kindī* (Oxford, Oxford University Press).

al-Qushayrī, Abū-l-Qāsim (2002), *The Risālah: Principles of Sufism*, trans. R. Harris, ed. L. Bakhtiar (Chicago, Kazi).

Ridgeon, L. (ed.) (2015), *The Cambridge Companion to Sufism* (Cambridge, Cambridge University Press).

Ryan, R.E. (2002), *Shamanism and the Psychology of C.G. Jung, The Great Circle* (London, Vega).

Scheindlin, R.P. (1974), *Form and Structure in the Poetry of al-Muʿtamid ibn ʿAbbād* (Leiden, Brill).

Schimmel, A. (1982), *As through a Veil: Mystical Poetry in Islam* (New York, Columbia University Press).

Sedgwick, M. (2017), *Western Sufism from the Abbasids to the New Age* (Oxford, Oxford University Press).

Sells, M. (1991), 'Ibn ʿArabi's "Gentle Now, Doves of the Thornbury and Moringa Thicket" (The Eleventh Poem of the *tarjumān al-ashwāq*)', *Journal of the Muhyiddin Ibn ʿArabī Society*, 10: 1–11.

Sells, M. (1994), *Mystical Languages of Unsaying* (Chicago, Chicago University Press).

Sells, M. (1996), *Early Islamic Mysticism: Sufi, Qur'an, Miʿraj, Poetic and Theological Writings* (New York, Paulist Press).

Sells, M. (2001), 'Ascension', in J.D. McAuliffe (ed), *Encyclopaedia of the Qurʾān* (Washington DC, Georgetown University), accessed 27 June 2019, http://dx.doi.org/10.1163/1875-3922_q3_EQCOM_00019

Shackle, C. (1996), 'Setting of Panegyric: The Secular Qasida in Mughal and British India', in Sperl & Shackle (1996), vol. 1, 205–52.

Sperl, S. (1996), 'Qasida Form and Mystic Path in Thirteenth Century Egypt: A Poem by Ibn al-Fāriḍ', in Sperl & Shackle (1996), vol. 1, 65–81.

Sperl, S. (2020), 'The Qur'an and Arabic Poetry', in *The Oxford Handbook of Qurʾanic Studies* (Oxford, Oxford University Press), 401–15.

Sperl, S. & Shackle, C. (eds) (1996), *Qasida Poetry in Islamic Asia and Africa*, vol. 1, *Classical Traditions & Modern Meanings*, vol. 2, *Eulogy's Bounty, Meaning's Abundance: An Anthology* (Brill, Leiden).

Steinberg, A. (2018), 'After More than Two Decades of Work, a New Hebrew Bible to Rival the King James: The Pre-eminent Scholar Robert Alter Has Finally Finished His Own Translation', *The New York Times Magazine*, 20 December, accessed 13 February 2019, www.nytimes.com/2018/12/20/magazine/hebrew-bible-translation.html

Stetkevych, S.P. (1983), 'Structuralist Analyses of Pre-Islamic Poetry: Critique and New Directions', *Journal of Near Eastern Studies*, 43: 85–107.

Stetkevych, S.P. (1991), *Abū Tammām and the Poetics of the Abbasid Age* (Leiden, Brill).

Stetkevych, S.P. (2002), *The Poetics of Islamic Legitimacy: Myth, Gender and Ceremony in the Classical Arabic Ode* (Bloomington/Indianapolis, Indiana University Press).

Stern-Gillet, S. (2019), '*Homoiōsis theōi* in the *Theaetetus* and in Plotinus', *Ancient Philosophy*, 39: 89–117.

al-Ṣūlī, Abū Bakr (2015), *The Life and Times of Abū Tammām*, ed. & trans. B. Gruendler (New York/London, Library of Arabic Literature).

Takeshita, M. (1983), 'Ibn ʿArabī's Theory of the Perfect Man and its Place in the History of Islamic Thought', *Orient*, 19: 97–102.

Tymieniecka, A. (ed.) (2006), *Islamic Philosophy and Occidental Phenomenology on the Perennial Issue of Microcosm and Macrocosm* (Dordrecht, Springer).

Watson, A. (2013), 'From Qays to Majnun: The Evolution of a Legend from ʿUdhri Roots to Sufi Allegory', *The La Trobe Journal*, 91: 36–45, accessed 29 May 2019, www.slv.vic.gov.au/sites/default/files/La-Trobe-Journal-91-Alasdair-Watson.pdf

3

What are Neoplatonic Poetics? Allegory; Figure; Genre

ALEXANDER M. KEY

POETRY AND THOUGHT moved between Greek Neoplatonism and Arabic Neoplatonism. In this chapter I use genre differences between the two literary cultures (and some references to English poetry) to help answer a question that has arisen from the collective endeavour of the conference from which this volume is drawn: 'what *is* Neoplatonic poetics?' I argue for the relevance of three core categories: allegory, figure and genre. They are found in every literary culture. But is Neoplatonism also found in every literary culture? Neither in Ancient Greek nor in Classical Arabic was poetry composed or criticism written under such a label. It is only 21st-century critics or scholars who choose to identify and then trace a 'Neoplatonic poetics'.

Today we can turn to the classical handbooks for help with the task of identifying allegories, figures or genres, but when it comes to Neoplatonism there is no such assistance to be had. I would therefore like to start to trace a Neoplatonic poetics with the help of three short snatches of poetry from different times and places. This will frame some of the central dynamics for our conversation, not least the concern that unlike allegory or figures, Neoplatonic poetics do not really exist outside this collected volume or similar endeavours. My quotations come from Manṣūr al-Ḥallāj's early 10th-century *al-ʿishqu fī azali -l-āzāli*, Robert Lowell's 1946 *The Quaker Graveyard in Nantucket* and Robert Duncan's 1960 *Often I Am Permitted to Return to a Meadow*. Here is my somewhat free translation of al-Ḥallāj's poem ():[1]

> Love has always been. In the eternity of eternities.
> There with God. From God. A beginning appears.
>
> Love is not an event. Love is a quality.
> Of a God whose slain are alive.

[1] For a more literal translation see Ernst (2018: 128), with references to the sources of the Arabic text and relevant secondary literature.

Qualities from him. In him. Not created.
Created things don't create anything else.

In the beginning God made his love appear. As a quality.
There. A fire glittered.

The 'f' and 'r' of 'fire' connect. Composed.
Each is one. But they reach the mind together.

We can separate them into two. And when we do.
They become a slave and a lord.

This is how truth works: the fire of longing flares
up out of ontological reality. Whether or not they stay or go.

They are weak beyond measure when they light up.
The very strongest are weak when they desire.

The beginning of this short poem sets the scene and fixes its conceptual orientation: God's love, at the moment of the creation of the universe, is already there. The God who can raise humans to a real afterlife, 'whose slain are alive', has love even before he starts to create. The act of divine creation does not create love, it just makes it appear. With that cosmology and theology in place, al-Ḥallāj then introduces the metaphor: God's love is a fire, kindled in the space of the beginning of the world. And then he slips out of the oracular mode into hermeneutics: the source of his metaphor, the word 'fire', acts on the mind as a single unit, but also has letters that can be separated. That separation leads to an allegory of slave and lord, and 'this is how truth works'. The final couplet reaches into the spiritual lives of the audience with an ascetic inversion of strength and weakness.

The first three couplets present a static divine cosmology, and then at the end of the fourth couplet we meet the spark that animates and drives action in this cosmological space. The fire is knowledge, it is love, and it is longing. Catalysed by a hierarchy, it is witnessed and experienced by humanity. The combination of cosmology and desire is an old one; in the penultimate couplet al-Ḥallāj uses an Arabic word for 'longing' (*shawq*) that also appeared at the beginning of the Arabic *Theology of Aristotle* when the author of that work was explaining the principle that drove action and motion in the Plotinian cosmological space. When immaterial intellect descended into the world of corporeal reality it acquired this longing, a desire to construct the world in accordance with the Intellect.[2] As Cristina D'Ancona (2017) has noted, that was a moment when Aristotle's *Metaphysics* shows through in Plotinus: it is desire, together with thought, that moves the unmoved mover of *Lambada*.

A millennium after al-Ḥallāj, Robert Lowell 'looked out at the turbulent Atlantic where his cousin died during World War II [with] the classical elegy in mind' (Hass 2017: 165). His poem 'The Quaker Graveyard in Nantucket' ends (Lowell 1961: 14):

[2] The passages in question are: *Enn.* IV 7 [2] 13, A: IV 389 and Badawī (1955: 18.13f.). They are analysed here: D'Ancona (1999: 70–6). The Greek word for desire, *orexis*, is that used by Aristotle in *De Anima* for the appetite of the soul for what is pleasant (Arist. *De an.* 414b6, cf. *Metaph.* 1048a.10).

... It's well;
Atlantic, you are fouled with the blue sailors,
Sea-monsters, upward angel, downward fish:
Unmarried and corroding, spare of flesh
Mart once of supercilious, wing'd clippers,
Atlantic, where your bell-trap guts its spoil
You could cut the brackish winds with a knife
Here in Nantucket, and cast up the time
When the Lord God formed man from the sea's slime
And breathed into his face the breath of life,
And blue-lung'd combers lumbered to the kill.
The Lord survives the rainbow of His will.

In the stormy Atlantic Ocean, angels move up while monsters move down. Earlier in the poem, the ocean has been divine: 'in the hand of the great God, where time's contritions blue ...'. But now there is a Lord God who 'survives the rainbow of his will'. I am following Robert Hass's reading of the poem here quite closely; Hass identifies two gods: 'as in a lot of cosmologies, he [Lowell]'s had to split off the good God from the bad one. Here the Creator Spirit is one thing and the blue killer of the Atlantic another' (Hass 2017: 180). Another approach to the cosmological stance of the final line is to read it as reflecting the tension between a God on whom cosmology depends as the first cause, and a God who is involved with 'the rainbow of His will'; the business of ruling and controlling the created world. D'Ancona (2017), again, has noted that the question of the deity's dual role goes back to, again, Aristotle's *Metaphysics*. In the final line of *Lambada*, Aristotle gave a political valence to his Prime Mover's role ('the rule of many is not good; let one be the king') that would prove problematic for subsequent Neoplatonists and catalyse the distinction between the One and the Intellect.[3] In a reaffirmation of the human tendency to trace such connections across languages, genres and centuries, Aristotle was with that phrase quoting some old poetry: Odysseus rallying the Greeks to Agamemnon's leadership in Homer's *Iliad*.[4]

The last of my opening three poetry quotations comes from Robert Duncan in San Francisco at the beginning of the 1960s (Duncan 1973: 7, [illegible]):

Often I am Permitted to Return to a Meadow
as if it were a scene made-up by the mind,
that is not mine, but is a made place,
that is mine, it is so near to the heart,
an eternal pasture folded in all thought
so that there is a hall therein
that is a made place, created by light
wherefrom the shadows that are forms fall.
Wherefrom fall all architectures I am
I say are likenesses of the First Beloved

[3] Arist. *Metaph*, 1076a.
[4] Hom. *Il.*, ii:204.

> whose flowers are flames lit to the Lady.
> She it is Queen Under The Hill
> whose hosts are a disturbance of words within words
> that is a field folded.

This is an internal scene of creation, a personal mental cosmology. But just like al-Ḥallāj's creation scene it is eternal, and there is a fire representing a driving force. Language is here too, but in place of al-Ḥallāj's letters that reach the mind together we have an enfolded disturbance of overlapping words. And there are shadows here that fall from the light, creating an architecture of forms that are 'likenesses of the First Beloved'. Just as with al-Ḥallāj, there is love at this cosmological starting point, and the force of the copula in 'shadows that *are* forms' lends the predicate 'forms' a status equivalent to the use of a Platonic uppercase 'F'.

The juxtaposition of these three snatches of poetry, selected almost at random from vastly disparate historical contexts, forces us to ask: who chooses to connect poetry to something called Neoplatonism, and how do they do it? With al-Ḥallāj, Lowell and Duncan it does not take a particularly close reading to draw out the cosmological scenes, their metaphysical stakes and the shared dynamics: God, fire and language in al-Ḥallāj and Duncan, vertical hierarchies in Duncan and Lowell. The same is true of the differences between their visions: al-Ḥallāj's deity is prior and static with a love that flares and connects, Lowell's God rises untrammelled above the test of his own creation, and Duncan's God may only exist in the poet's hidden mind – 'Under The Hill'. All this can be usefully called 'Neoplatonism'; poetics and theology of a certain sort. But there is much more in the poems beside this, and al-Ḥallāj would not have known what 'Neoplatonism' meant. Lowell too may well have been thinking of Dante more than Plotinus, and Duncan of the medieval and Renaissance literature he studied at Berkeley.

The scale of the historical disparity defeats any attempt to trace influence (Cristina D'Ancona faces the same question with Dante and Plotinus in her contribution to this volume). When we choose to give the dynamics that these poems share the label of 'Neoplatonism', our choice exerts a centripetal force on the subsequent analysis. Duncan's poem ends with dreams, secrets and 'a given property of the mind that certain bounds hold against chaos' (Duncan 1973: 7). While Lowell's poem is all about the relationship between God and man (it is introduced by a quote from the Bible, 'Let man have dominion over the fishes of the sea…' Gen. 1:26), the two gods problem that Hass identified is arguably not its central concern. And al-Ḥallāj was speaking to his audience about their God, not to Plotinus's audience about his. The 'Neoplatonism' label pulls diversity into conversation, and it does so as a deliberate critical act, one that has an ethical salience in the moment that it is made. To give up on the label would be to give up on that *critique*.

If we are therefore determined to continue the experimental practice of locating something called Neoplatonism in poems (and I am), we need to develop a framework within which to do so. I would like to propose a tripartite analytical structure here – allegory, figure, genre – in the hope of giving us a better sense of the variety of ways in which poems can be Neoplatonist. While it is self-evidentially not the case that allegory, figure and genre comprise a toolbox sufficient to describe all poetry (even if one wanted to do such a thing), I think that there is a strong case to be made that all the vectors and dynamics that one can read as Neoplatonist fall into one or more of these three categories. They therefore constitute our Neoplatonist poetics.

1. Allegory

I will start with allegory, which I understand here as a set of words that target and sustain a nonverbal realm (the word in classical Arabic theory is *mathal*: proverb, analogy, example). In Neoplatonic poetry, the nonverbal realm sustained is almost always divine. This fits well with allegory, which 'designates primarily a distance in relation to its own origin' (de Man 1983: 207). Allegory has therefore always been a good way for human language to deal with the ineffable; it refers 'to a meaning that it does not itself constitute', and to a cosmological realm that must have been there before the words of the allegory itself were put together.[5] This separation of the target from the source lends itself to the development of hierarchies within the audience, as well as to exegetical performances of expertise. As al-Rāghib al-Iṣfahānī (litterateur and exegete, fl. in or before 1018) understood it, the allegory (*mathal*) pairs a universally accessible surface with a depth that needs the investment of recovery (al-Rāghib 1988: 181.11–183.16; Key 2011). There is an irony here, for in order for someone to have enough knowledge to recover the details of the target realm, they must necessarily be without need of the allegory itself. Allegories are therefore fundamentally pedagogical. Allegory exists in a symbiotic relationship with its own explication, and it needs someone to be in charge. In al-Rāghib's Islamic context God was in charge and said so: 'God uses allegories for human beings; perhaps they will understand' (Qur'an 24:35). And al-Rāghib (1988: 182.8–9) said that God uses allegory for a reason; he is not just telling stories. For in allegory there is always something else at stake, and in Neoplatonic allegory that something else is both true and divine; it is what al-Rāghib called *al-ḥaqāʾiq* (the truths, the accurate accounts) (1988: 182.10, 183.13).

The same allegorical mechanism that al-Rāghib identified in the 11th century can be found in the Greek *Enneads*, that foundational 3rd-century text by Plotinus. Plotinus uses poetry in the *Enneads* to help him describe the relationship between the realms of human beings and the gods. Homer's 'dread and dank house which even the gods loath' is a description of the underworld, referenced by Plotinus ('what the gods hate, as a poet says') to explain how heaven was lifeless and dark before soul entered it.[6] Homer's Odysseus drew a distinction between the ghost of

[5] de Man (1979: 208–10); see also de Man (1983: 222).
[6] *Il.*, 20.65, *Enn.* V 2 [11] 2.28, A: V 15, Plotinus (1964: 2:264.5).

Hercules and the ghosts of Agamemnon and Achilles: Hercules was immortal and, unlike dead men, actually present on Olympus rather than being down in Hades. For Plotinus, this distinction is useful because it helps him explain how the soul can be divine but also descend and inhere in the body.[7] Homer's Odysseus also wanted to leave Circe's magical pleasures and go back to his real home with Penelope in Ithaca, a desire for true beauty that Plotinus uses to explain how inner sight works. When invoking Odysseus in this last example, Plotinus hinted at the allegorical function of Homer's poetry: 'We shall put out to sea, as Odysseus did, from the witch Circe or Calypso – as the poet says (I think with a hidden meaning).'[8] In all three of these examples, Greek poetry provides illustrative imagery for Plotinus's philosophy, and in that last example imagery is understood as useful because it contains meaning that is both hidden and recoverable. None of these passages or quotations of poetry became part of the Arabic *Theology of Aristotle*.

But one Plotinian reference to poetry did become part of the Arabic. It was Plotinus's remark that Pythagoras was 'unclear because he writes poetry', made because Plotinus thought we should stick to Plato.[9] The Greek phrase (*tō de parēn kai dia poiēsin ou safei einai*) was translated as: *innamā kallama l-nāsa bi-l-amthāli wa-l-awābid* (Badawī 1955: 23.12–13). The Greek word for 'poetry' (*poiēsin*) has become the Arabic word for 'allegories' (*amthāl*), and the Greek phrase for 'unclear' (*ou safei*) has become the Arabic word for 'wild' or 'bizarre' (*awābid*). Allegory might seem to be a mistranslation, but this is not the case. We will see how the Arabic translator/author of *The Theology of Aristotle*, which was a detailed Aristotelian engagement with Plotinus, made an accurate assessment of what poetry was to Greek Neoplatonists.

Poetry for Greek Neoplatonists was of course still Homer. The *Odyssey* and *Iliad* were, as we have just seen, a reliable source of imagery and meaning, but Homer was nearly a millennium old when Plotinus taught. There was more recent poetry available, and it was used primarily as a source of myth accessed via allegory. Luc Brisson (2017: 214–20) has shown how Proclus and his 5th-century contemporaries used the *Orphic Rhapsodies* and the *Chaldean Oracles* to develop their Platonic philosophies. Both works were in verse, and allegory was how the School of Athens could preserve myth within a Platonic system: 'the Chaldean Oracles and the Orphic Rhapsodies were supplanting Homer's and Hesiod's poems as sources of myths, though these last two were not totally neglected'.[10] David Hernandez, in his contribution to this collaboration, has demonstrated the impact this had on Greek poetry itself from the 5th century onwards. The Arabic translator of the *Enneads* was right: Greek poetry in Plotinus's world was read as allegory.

We therefore have in Greek two familiar and connected ways to deal with poetry: one can use it to convey truth, and one can read it to divine truth. Both paths

[7] *Od.* 11.601-602, *Enn.* I 1 [53] 12.32f, A: I 121, Plotinus (1964: 1.121).

[8] *Il.*, 2.140, *Enn.* I 6 [1] 8.17–20, A: I 257, cf. *Od.* 9.29f and 10.483–484 via note in Plotinus (1964: 1.257).

[9] *Enn.* IV 8 [6] 1.21f, A: IV 397, Plotinus (1964: 4:399).

[10] Brisson (2008: 88); see also Brisson (2012: 128–30).

are allegory, connections to a nonverbal realm. But in Classical Arabic, the situation was slightly different. Poetry was certainly used to convey truth, but often through force of style rather than reference to otherworldly realms like Homer's Aeaea, Olympus or Hades. For example, in al-Rāghib's book of ethics, *al-Dharīʿah*, just as in almost all Arabic prose of this period, there is a substantial amount of poetry quoted in the service of the work's goals. The famous poet al-Mutanabbī (d. 965) is quoted to make the following point about wealth and glory:[11]

> There is no glory in this world for the poor
> There is no money in this world for the weak

Poetry here was used as a source of apposite phrasing; al-Rāghib knew what he wanted to say and he turned to al-Mutanabbī's Arabic in exactly the same way as Plotinus turned to Homer's Greek (al-Rāghib intended the exact opposite of the Gospel allegory that it is harder for a camel to pass through the eye of a needle than for a rich man to enter heaven).[12] Poetry is marshalled in support of a truth already laid out in the prose text. This is not allegory; truth does not lie in the text, waiting for hermeneutic explanation, and no separate world is invoked.

Al-Rāghib did not read poetry as allegory. He read the Qur'an as allegory. Revealed scripture played the same role in his Arabic Neoplatonism that the *Rhapsodies* and *Odes* did in Greek. And while the Qur'an self-identifies as not being poetry,[13] it is unquestionably literature:

> God is the light of the heavens and the earth; the likeness of his light is as a niche wherein is a lamp (the lamp in a glass, the glass as it were a glittering star) kindled from a blessed tree, an olive that is neither of the East nor of the West whose oil well-nigh would shine, even if no fire touched it; light upon light; (God guides to his light whom he will.)

This is A.J. Arberry's translation of Qur'an 24:35 (al-Nūr), known as 'the light verse'. Al-Rāghib identified the light as 'reason' (*al-ʿaql*), an elevation of the intellect that was characteristic of his contexts and oeuvre[14] but by no means inevitable.[15] He then connects this light of reason to a specific concept: the 'acquired intellect' (*al-ʿaql al-mustafād*), which was one of the two types of reason that structured his epistemology (the other was the innate intellect: *al-ʿaql al-gharīzī*). Without acquired intellect, human reason is only potential, like a child or a seed (al-Rāghib 2007: 33.9–16). Acquired intellect is the reason that enables you to put two things

[11] *Fa-lā majda fī l-dunyā li-man qalla māluhu | wa-lā māla fī l-dunyā li-man qalla majduhū*. al-Mutanabbī (2002: 1:413.3), al-Rāghib (2007: 111.1–2).

[12] Matthew 19:24, Mark 10:25, Luke 18:25.

[13] See statements at Qur'an 21:5 (al-Anbiyāʾ), 26:224 (al-Shuʿarāʾ), 36:69 (Yā Sīn), 37:36 (al-Ṣāffāt), 52:30 (a-Ṭūr), and 69:41 (al-Ḥāqqah).

[14] *Mathalu nūrihī yaʿnī mathalu nūri l-maʿrifati fī qalbi l-muʾmini ... wa l-māʾu lladhī fī l-qindīli shubbiha bi-l-ʿilmi wa-dhihn*. Abū Layth al-Samarqandī (1993: 2:440.12–14). See also, Böwering (2001: 134, 137).

[15] al-Rāghib (2007: 69.10–12, 134.3–5). Cf. two exegetes for whom the light was just the Qur'an itself: al-Ṭabarī (1994: 5:426.6) and Ibn Fūrak (2009: 144).

together, to say not just X but that X is Y. Al-Rāghib says it is reason that is grammatically transitive (*yataʿaddā ilā mafʿūlayn*). He also says that the phrase 'acquired intellect' is found in both revelation and in the works of the philosophers (*fī-l-sharʿi wa-fī kalāmi l-ḥukamāʾ*) (al-Rāghib 2007: 140.13–18).[16] By revelation he means the light verse in the Qur'an, and in philosophy he may have been aware of the force of light that illuminates reason in the Arabic (and Greek) Plotinus (*al-quwwah al-nūrīyah ... tansaḥu ʿalā l-ʿaql*).[17] Al-Rāghib's engagement with the Qur'anic text is hermeneutic and allegorical; he finds Neoplatonic cosmology and epistemology in Islamic revelation.

Avicenna's (Ibn Sīnā, d. 1037) exegesis does the same thing with more detail: the niche for Avicenna was 'material intellect' (al-Rāghib had 'chest of the believer') and the glass containing the lamp was 'intellect *in habitu*' (al-Rāghib had 'heart of the believer'). The intellect *in habitu* used either 'thought' (the olive tree, which for al-Rāghib was 'religion') or the oil of 'guessing correctly' to acquire secondary intelligibles. When these intelligibles were in the soul as 'light upon light', the lamp became the 'actual intellect', perfected in the 'acquired intellect' (the intellect al-Rāghib chose to include). Avicenna then went on to say that the agent which moves the intellect through these three stages is the 'active intellect'.[18]

In both cases, Arabic scholars were using the Qur'an to elevate and explain human reason, and they were doing so in a philhellenic philosophical tradition. We can call it Neoplatonic, and we can identify the process as allegory: just as in Greek Neoplatonism, so Arabic Neoplatonism used literature to access a realm of divine truth. The difference is simply that while the texts in Greek were the poetry of the *Rhapsodies* and *Odes*, Arabic Neoplatonists could read the language of the monotheist god himself.

2. Figure

A second form that poetics can take is the taxonomy of rhetorical figures. This was perhaps the dominant form of literary criticism in Classical Arabic in the long millennium from the 800s to the 20th century. Taxonomy of rhetorical figures is also found in Late Antiquity and European scholasticism. However, this congruence in genre across centuries and literary cultures does not mean that the figures themselves are ever exactly equivalent. Even within Arabic critical texts of the same period, different scholars give different examples and explanations for the same figure. This is no evidence of incoherence, but rather of a critical landscape in which scholars

[16] Cf. al-Rāghib (1992: 560/1.19-561/2.1). And, for example, *Enn.* VI 7 [38] 35.24–25, A: VI 197, Plotinus (1964: 6:143–5).

[17] Badawī (1955: 6.9).

[18] *ʿAqlan hayūlānīyan* ('material intellect') ... *ʿaqlan bi-l-malakati* ('intellect *in habitu*') ... *ʿaqlan mustafādan* ('acquired intellect') ... *al-ʿaql al-faʿʿāl* ('active intellect'). al-Rāghib (2007: 69.10f, 134.3–5), Ibn Sīnā & al-Ṭūsī (1983–94: 2:390–2). Translations from Gutas (1988: 186).

seeking to understand poetry through the enumeration of its techniques were each happy to reinvent the wheel. It is tempting to imagine that they did so because they felt that writing and reading taxonomies of rhetorical figures was itself a way to read poetry, an act of criticism rather than a claim on some realm of fact in which single stable conceptions of each figure applied universally. But here we are speculating.

Let us examine a paradigmatic example of this taxonomical process, a not particularly famous work edited by Geert Jan van Gelder in 1987: *Kitāb al-Maḥāsin fi-l-Naẓm wa-l-Nathr* by Abū al-Ḥasan Naṣr b. Ibn al-Ḥasan al-Marghīnānī (fl. 5th/11th century).[19] After a brief one-page introduction that justifies study of the arts of poetic innovation as necessary to understand their miraculously inimitable use in the Qur'an, al-Marghīnānī launches straight into a taxonomy of figures designed to enable readers to find the beauty in the Qur'an's language, and to argue successfully with their opponents (al-Marghīnānī & Ibn Aflaḥ 1987: 67). The nature of the projected debates is left unsaid, but the understanding of literary criticism as being connected to the literary beauty of the Qur'an (a text nearly 300 years old when al-Marghīnānī was writing) as well as the performance space of interpersonal debate is common in Classical Arabic. The first figure al-Marghīnānī addresses is the rhyming pattern within a single line (*tarṣī'*), and his first set of examples come from expressions in ordinary language: *kullu lis**ānin** yadh**ummuhā** wa-kullu ins**ānin** ya**ḍummuhā*** ('every tongue criticizes it and every person embraces it') (al-Marghīnānī & Ibn Aflaḥ 1987: 67.19). Then comes a definition of *tarṣī'* as 'speech with balanced sections and a consistent structure, like the examples we have just seen'.[20] Then come a couple more examples from more ornate speech with religious content praising God, then three quotations from the Qur'an itself (al-An'ām 6:70/Yūnus 10:4, al-Infiṭār 82:13–14, al-Ghāshiya 88:25–6). After the Qur'anic quotations are two prophetic Hadith. The language of the prophet and the language of God display the same internal rhyme as the speech of ordinary humans: ***innā ilayna** iy**ābahum** thumma **inna ilaynā** ḥis**ābahum*** (Qur'an 88:25–6 'we have their resurrection; then we have their reckoning') and *irfa'hu fa-innahu **atqā li-**rab**bika** wa-**anqā li-**thaw**bika*** ('[the prophet said to someone dragging their robe in the dirt:] lift it up; it will be more pious for your lord and cleaner for your robe') (al-Marghīnānī & Ibn Aflaḥ 1987: 67.27–28, 68.1).

Al-Marghīnānī next returns to a more general literary critical evaluation of the figure of *tarṣī'*: it has the highest status among all the figures of eloquence because, while it is the hardest to achieve with success and clarity, it is most beloved by the audience and most subtle in its impact. It is innovative in prose, but even more so in poetry.[21] Only then, with the figure described, analysed and explained via divine

[19] al-Marghīnānī & Ibn Aflaḥ (1987: 4–5).

[20] *Wa-ma'nā l-tarṣī'i an ta'iya bil-kalāmi mu'tadili l-aqsāmi muttafiqi l-niẓāmi 'alā l-ṣīghati llatī qasamnāhā wa-l-ṣan'ati llatī rasamnāhā* (al-Marghīnānī & Ibn Aflaḥ 1987: 67.23–25).

[21] *Wa-hādha l-naw'i min l-kalāmi arfa'u manzilatan wa-a'lā ratbatan min sā'irihi 'inda l-bulaghā'i li-kawnihi ab'ada marāman wa-aṣ'aba niẓāman ... idhā ... khalā min l-iltibāsi wa-l-ishtibāhi ... fa-huwa aḥabbu l-kalāmi ilā l-sam'i wa-akhaffuhu 'alā l-ṭab'i qāla l-tarṣī'u fī l-kalami l-manthūri badī'un wa-fī l-manẓūmi abda'u* (al-Marghīnānī & Ibn Aflaḥ 1987: 68.2–7).

and human examples, does al-Marghīnānī provide a set of examples that are poetry. Among the poets he cites are the famous Abū Ṭayyib al-Mutanabbbī (d. 965), Ibn Fāris (d. 1004) and al-Buḥturī (d. 897) whose couplet (I have altered the lineation) reads:[22]

> The rain flows when it beats down
> The lion protects its cubs' den
> But the flow and protection of Musta'īn?
> Complete blessing: overflow.

These are the opening two lines of al-Buḥturī's poem in praise of the caliph al-Musta'īn (reg. 862–6), whose name literally means 'someone *asking* for help', a double reference in Arabic, lost in my translation, that extends the dynamic of assistance sought and granted. Al-Marghīnānī cites both lines but says he is interested in the *tarṣī'* only in the first line: *mā l-gh**aythu yahmī** 'inda as**bālihi*** | *wa-l-**laythu yaḥmī** khīsa ash**bālihī***.

Al-Marghīnānī is not attempting to describe how this poem locates its subject as a force of nature, nor is he concerned with the hierarchy set up in the opening couplet between caliph, rain and lion, nor with the social and political meaning of the caliph's subjects as lion cubs. Rather, he is writing literary criticism designed to answer questions about poetic technique. He uses God's own language in the Qur'an and the ordinary language of the humans (including the prophet) whom he believed were created by God to establish an analytical frame. Qur'an, Hadith and people's commonplace rhyming expressions all help establish a category – the figure of *tarṣī'* – that then helps the reader of poetry understand what is going on in particularly well-constructed lines. The genre of poetics, thus created, equips its readers to read poetry and connect poetic techniques to both God and their fellow citizens. They would then be able, one might assume, better to enjoy the canonical poetry they knew and better explain it in literary salons.[23]

Al-Marghīnānī is himself not the most famous exponent of this genre; one might name Ibn al-Mu'tazz (d. 908), Abū Hilāl al-'Askarī (d. 1005) and others, but he is without question representative of an approach to poetry that flourished in Classical Arabic and then in the madrasa centuries provided the methodological basis for the great textbooks of al-Sakkākī (d. 1229), al-Qazwīnī (d. 1338) and their commentators. The taxonomy in this genre is relentless, there is no let-up in the proliferation of rhetorical figures, the development of larger categories into which they are placed, and the overwhelming sense of inconsistency: one scholar's *tarṣī'* is not necessarily the same as another's (this is not unique to Arabic) (Vinson 2003: 13).

[22] *Mā l-ghaythu yahmī 'inda asbālihi* | *wa-l-laythu yaḥmī khīsa ashbālihī* || *ka-l-musta'īni l-musta'āni lladhī* | *tammat lanā l-nu'mā bi-ifḍālihī*. al-Buḥturī (1963: 1636, #638), al-Marghīnānī & Ibn Aflaḥ (1987: 69.4–5). The Dīwān has *ṣawba* for *'inda* in the first hemistich and *lahu* for *lanā* in the final hemistich.

[23] On these salons, see Ali (2010) and England (2017).

While some scholars may in the past have understood this as a critical failure,[24] I rather feel that the lively and original complexity with which each critic, including al-Marghīnānī, sets up a complete taxonomy, fully equipped with quotations of great poetry, should lead us to see this genre as composed of deliberate conversation starters. If Classical Arabic literary critical taxonomies of rhetorical figures were intended to give readers of Classical Arabic poetry something to think about and talk about, and a way to read poetry outside and alongside the collected works of poets or recitations, then they succeeded.

Was there Neoplatonism in this conversation? It seems not, for two reasons. First, that mystic poets such as al-Ḥallāj were not included in literary critical works like that of al-Marghīnānī. Second, if poetry with Neoplatonic import did appear in a work of literary criticism, its Neoplatonic aspects were not addressed. The ideas that we identified in al-Ḥallāj, Lowell and Duncan were not al-Marghīnānī's concern, and neither were the hierarchies of power probed by al-Buḥturī. It takes a critic to create Neoplatonic poetry, and in Classical Arabic the critics were busy doing something else.

3. Genre

Classical Arabic might have identified different concerns if its taxonomies were accountings of subject matter rather than technique. We can see what this might have looked like with the example of Menander Rhetor (3rd century BC, and popular in Greek for over a millennium thereafter). Menander wrote pedagogical works designed to enable readers to write better compositions on a variety of enumerated topics. He was 'a practical professor of rhetoric', and, 'too good a teacher to confine himself to [a taxonomical] skeleton' (Bremer 1995: 263–4). His text walks the reader through a taxonomy designed to enable them to write. This is different from Classical Arabic literary criticism, where we might characterise the criticism as designed to empower poetry's audience rather than the poets themselves.[25] But Menander could still have chosen to teach young authors a taxonomy of rhetorical figures. He did not; his taxonomy enumerates the subject matters of literary composition in 3rd-century Greek: it is therefore an account of genre. Whether he is describing the appropriate ways to praise a city, or the best way to write to someone from whom one is separated, Menander is eminently practical: 'If you are inviting a governor to a city which has no very grand or historic features …' (1981: 193).

Menander classifies literature as a teacher of rhetoric: according to the purpose of each piece. His structuring epistemology is genre, not technique. The first

[24] G.E. von Grunebaum in al-Bāqillānī (1950: xxi).

[25] While this characterisation certainly works for al-Marghīnānī, we must note Ibn Rashīq's (d. *c.* 1070) *al-'Umda*, written in the Western Mediterranean for aspiring poets and containing a survey of themes and genres). And for a detailed review of generic statements in Classical Arabic, see Schoeler (2010–11).

treatise starts with the statement: 'Rhetoric as a whole is divided into three parts.' These are legal, private and epideictic. That third category is then split into two headings: praise and blame. Praise is then divided according to its target: hymns to gods (sub-divided by god) and praise of mortal objects (sub-divided into cities, countries and living creatures). Living creatures is sub-divided into rational and non-rational. Non-rational is sub-divided into land animals and water animals, and land animals are sub-divided into flying or walking. 'These then are all the divisions of the epideictic part of rhetoric taken as a whole' (Menander 1981: 4–5).

Menander's taxonomy makes it clear to us that Classical Arabic works such as al-Marghīnānī's were by no means the first in the region to organise literary knowledge through systematic enumeration.[26] But Menander makes claims on genre, not on technique (the same is true of the redactors of Classical Arabic *dīwāns* studied by Gregor Schoeler [2010–11: 24–39]). If allegory is a moment in a text that is created by hermeneutics, and figure is a technique located by criticism, genre is a structuring claim about how people and institutions treat literature. This may help us locate Neoplatonic poetics. Neither al-Marghīnānī nor Menander practice criticism that could be called Neoplatonic; they do not identify content to which we could give that label. Is this because they were not talking about poetry that was itself Neoplatonic? Or is it because their criticism was itself unconcerned with Neoplatonism? In both cases the answer is to be found in genre.

The poetry of religious and political figures such as al-Ḥallāj, whether we call them Sufis, mystics, ascetics or another label less complicated than the reality of their lives, was not a formal genre in the way that the Classical Arabic qasida was a formal genre with attendant reception, documentation and criticism. Carl Ernst remarked in the course of our conference that Sufi poetry might best be regarded as an informal genre, existing on the equivalent of the back of envelopes, but no less meaningful because of that form. Sufi poetry had religious meaning, literary impact and sometimes political salience, but it did not have a contemporaneous scholarly tradition of edited collections and commentary on technique.

In his contribution to this volume, Stefan Sperl makes a successful argument for shared conceptual frameworks that exist between Sufi poetry, Plotinian cosmology and the Qur'an. We can usefully give these shared frameworks the label 'Neoplatonic', and Sperl reads them as evidence of a 'wider spiritual tradition' rather than any evidence of an intertextuality that could be recovered by philology. This is persuasive, and yet when we consider the role genre plays in this system there are some interesting conclusions to be drawn. We have already seen that Plotinus, writing Platonic philosophy, had a suspicion of the epistemological accuracy of poetry that echoed Plato's own famous remarks in the *Republic*. The Qur'an itself, self-presenting as a divine work of perfect Arabic, had a parallel suspicion of poets and their rival claims on truth and persuasion. The Qur'an expressed

[26] For a survey of Ancient Greek scholars dealing with figures (*skhēmata*) and technique, see Novokhatko (2013).

confidence that those who doubted the prophetic mission would be unable to replicate its language: 'Bring a *sūra* like this! And call whomever you can, apart from God!'[27] These attitudes in both Greek and Arabic served to create genre boundaries between poetry on the one hand and philosophy/revelation on the other. In Arabic, this created a productive critical tension between responses to the beautiful words of God and to the beautiful words of his creation. This tension is worked through in the scholarly genre of works on the inimitability of the Qur'an, and also in the defences of poetry advanced by both Ibn Rashīq and ʿAbd al-Qāhir al-Jurjānī (d. 1078).[28] But the poem by al-Ḥallāj with which we began sits between poetry and the Qur'an, negotiating its own religious status without access to the legitimating critical discourse of works such as al-Marghīnānī's.

Genres therefore serve to divide the shared spiritual tradition that Sperl identifies, whether genres of literary production (both human and divine) or genres of scholarly analysis. This is true even without consideration of the religious gap between Islam (or indeed Christianity) and Platonism. And yet genre is the only framework within which we can make the claim that Neoplatonism exists. We have seen that Neoplatonism does not exist within any enumeration of rhetorical figures, and that while Neoplatonic ideas are often accessed through the mechanism of allegory, Neoplatonism itself is by no means the same thing as allegory. Neoplatonism is a genre, and as such it is created by those who bring a genre into existence. In this case, it is us, in this volume, who do this work.

Genre is a set of constraints, functioning as a conversation, that people set up within institutions to negotiate any number of demands, be they rival truth claims, social dynamics or politics itself. Like any discourse, genre then exerts its own force on those who use it: the force of generic convention (in the form of his contemporaries) may have explicitly prevented al-Marghīnānī from engaging al-Ḥallāj's use of rhetorical figure, or genre may simply have silently guided him to the canon of al-Buḥturī and al-Mutanabbī instead. Neoplatonism as it exists today in our critical and scholarly practice is a genre that exerts the same kind of forces: bringing certain texts and ideas into the foreground and smoothing away others – all the while serving to make a persuasive argument rooted in our own 21st-century context for shared cosmological commitments across literary cultures. These observations should not be taken as criticism of either al-Marghīnānī, or ourselves.

I would like to end this section with a brief philological focus on one word that does different things in different Classical Arabic genres. All literary criticism, whether based on allegory, figure or genre, includes a perspective on the functioning of language. This is how Brisson (2008: 101) describes the assumptions made by Plotinus:

> Human language … is grounded in the unifying and generating power of the divinity, that is, at the level of the intellect. But between the [intellect] and matter are several levels of perception, each having a corresponding mode of discourse (*logos*) …

[27] Qur'an 10:37–8 (Yūnis). See also Qur'an 2:23 (al-Baqara), Qur'an 11:13 (Hūd), Qur'an 52:33–4 (al-Ṭūr).

[28] al-Jurjānī (1992: 7f); Ibn Rashīq al-Qayrawānī (2009: 1:74–80).

> the *logoi* … are creative emanations of the Intellect that structure the universe. This conception of language has two consequences. The divinity cannot express himself directly in human language … even though the Chaldean Oracles can at times be considered as direct revelation. Each level of the *logos* can be viewed in relation to the level below it, as a 'metalanguage' capable of explaining it, of providing its meaning. Thence, each level of language must be interpreted with the help of the language level immediately above it.[29]

The ontological assumptions made about language in Classical Arabic were quite different. There, a level of proto-linguistic content (*maʿnā*) was shared between God and man. God used the Qur'an to communicate this content to humanity through patterns of language in which audible or written expressions (*alfāẓ*) each pointed at different mental contents (*maʿānī*). In this process, the accuracy of that pointing and the extent of human access to divine truth were central. The word used to denote moments when an expression in language pointed directly at the correct mental content was *ḥaqīqa* (I expand on this analysis elsewhere: Key 2018).

The word *ḥaqīqa* appeared in the poem by al-Ḥallāj that I translated above. There it became 'truth' and 'ontological reality' in English. Both choices reflect the fact that I read it as a word for accuracy. But accuracy is not a substance or a fixed referent, it is a quality, a judgement made about something, a decision that a connection is accurate. The word *ḥaqīqa* in Classical Arabic works in exactly this way; scholars use it to claim that a certain connection between a *maʿnā* (a mental content) and either the world, or God, or a linguistic expression (*lafẓ*), is accurate. For the philologist, the word *ḥaqīqa* is therefore an index: from its usage in a text we can divine genre. When *ḥaqīqa* appears in Classical Arabic literary criticism, it is always an accurate connection between mind and words, between mental contents and vocal forms, between *maʿānī* and *alfāẓ*. Truth is a mind-to-language connection.

For example, when Ibn Rashīq said that all language which goes beyond *ḥaqīqa* but can still be meaningfully said is *majāz*,[30] he was talking about a set of accurate connections between ideas and words that are accurate (*ḥaqīqa*). When people use words outside those connections, it is *majāz* (a concept roughly equivalent to 'non-literal' or 'metaphorical'). For example, in this line by the Abbasid court poet al-ʿAttābī (d. *c.* 835), it is not accurate to say that birds speak in the morning, or that the night itself is sleepless; an accurate account of either act would restrict it to humans. But these statements are still made, and they are *majāz*:[31]

[29] See also Cristina D'Ancona's contribution to this volume, which focuses on how language in Dante (via Plotinus, Aquinas and others) is unable to express divine reality.

[30] *Wa mā ʿadā l-ḥaqāʾiqa min jamīʿi l-alfāẓi thumma lam yakun muḥālan maḥḍan fa-huwa majāz*. Ibn Rashīq (2009: 1:421.16–17).

[31] *Yā laylatan lī bi-jawwārīna sāhiratan | ḥattā takallama fī l-ṣubḥi l-ʿāṣāfīru || fa-jaʿala l-laylata sāhiratan ʿalā l-majāzi wa-innamā yusharu fīhā wa-jaʿala li-l-ʿaṣāfīri kalāman wa-lā kalāma lahā ʿalā l-ḥaqīqati*. Ibn Rashīq (2009: 1:422.6–8). My translation follows Yāqūt, who gives Ḥuwwārīn (a fortress near Homs in Syria) instead of Ibn Rashīq's *jawwārīn* (the farmers one works alongside). Al-Ḥamawī (1977: 2:315).

Sleepless night in Ḥuwwārīn
Until in the morning
The birds speak.

Al-Ḥallāj's *ḥaqīqa* is very different. His accurate connections are not made between ideas and words, but rather between human minds and a divine, emanationist cosmology. This ontology is not unlike that described by Brisson in the quotation above. Al-Ḥallāj's accuracy is truth, not the sort of truth we get by checking accurate words in the dictionary or being 'literal' about word meanings, but the truth we get when we interact with the flame of love and light that abides in and flows down through levels of divinity emanating from the one truth: 'This is how truth works: the fire of longing flares / up out of ontological reality.'

This brief excursion into the meaning and usage of the Classical Arabic word for 'accuracy' reinforces our conclusions about genre. There are two kinds of accuracy in Classical Arabic poetry, two kinds of truth. Whether one finds a truth in which birds cannot speak, or a truth in which God's fire emanates down, the answer depends on the kind of question being asked. Both answers can be found in al-ʿAttābī and al-Ḥallāj, but actual critics have tended to choose to look for one or the other. When we look for Neoplatonism in Arabic poetry, we can find it just as we find it in English. The themes are the same despite the intervening millennium, and they are recovered – when they are recovered – in the same way: by allegory. This happens across genre: whether it is the Qur'an, or the poetry of al-Ḥallāj, or the poetry of Robert Lowell and Robert Duncan, there is a truth in the literature that is extricable as meaning by a critic. But the critic is us. Or rather, when it comes to 'Neoplatonism', the only critic who reads the genre across all contexts is us.

No one puts 3rd-century Platonists together with 11th-century Qur'anic exegetes and 20th-century English poets except us. No one calls the themes we find 'Neoplatonism' except us. Our brief investigation of Classical Arabic literary criticism reminded us of this fact. Al-Ḥallāj's poetry could easily have been read allegorically by Neoplatonists, but genre boundaries prevented Classical Arabic critics from reading him. In the poetry they did examine, their genre-specific practice led them to focus on technique rather than content; they looked for figure not allegory. And those scholars who did use allegory read the Qur'an not poetry. Avicenna and al-Rāghib worked on the Qur'an in the same allegorical mode as Greek exegetes reading the *Rhapsodies* and *Oracles*. Finally, while all this was happening, Classical Arabic poets still spoke of love, power and imagination just like Lowell and Duncan. For poetry grows in a relationship with its criticism, but can always do more than criticism explains. And after the relationship has ended, criticism is free to create new genres with old material. There is no shame in the newness of the critical endeavour, whether we are parsing the figures of poetic technique, identifying shared concerns about love and power between 9th-century Iraq and 20th-century Northern California, or looking across a millennium of tangentially connected literary genres at certain allegories we call Neoplatonic.

References

Abū Layth al-Samarqandī, Naṣr B. Muḥammad (1993), *Tafsīr al-Samarqandī al-Musammā Baḥr al-ʿUlūm* (Beirut, Dār Abū al-Kutub al-ʿIlmīyah).

Ali, Samer M. (2010), *Arabic Literary Salons in the Islamic Middle Ages: Poetry, Public Performance, and the Presentation of the Past* (Notre Dame, University of Notre Dame Press).

Arberry, A.J. (1955), *The Koran Interpreted* (London, Allen & Unwin).

Badawī, ʿA. (1955), *Aflūṭīn ʿinda al-ʿArab* (Cairo, Maktabat al-Nahḍa al-Miṣriyya).

Bāqillānī, Abū Bakr Muḥammad b. Al-Ṭayyib al- (1950), *A Tenth-Century Document of Arabic Literary Theory and Criticism: The Sections on Poetry of al-Bāqillānī's Iʿjāz al-Qurʾān Translated and Annotated* (Chicago, University of Chicago Press).

Böwering, G. (2001), 'The Light Verse: Qurʾānic Text and Ṣūfī Interpretation', *Oriens*, 36: 113–44.

Bremer, J.M. (1995), 'Menander Rhetor on Hymns', in D.M. Schenkeveld, J.G.J. Abbenes, S.R. Slings & I. Sluiter (eds), *Greek Literary Theory after Aristotle: A Collection of Papers in Honour of D.M. Schenkeveld* (Amsterdam, VU University Press), 259–75.

Brisson, L. (2008), *How Philosophers Saved Myths: Allegorical Interpretation and Classical Mythology* (Chicago, University of Chicago Press).

Brisson, L. (2012), 'Allegory as Used by the Later Neoplatonic Philosophers', in K. Corrigan, J.D. Turner & P. Wakefield (eds), *Religion and Philosophy in the Platonic and Neoplatonic Traditions: From Antiquity to the Early Medieval Period* (Sankt Augustin, Academia), 121–30.

Brisson, L. (2017), 'Proclus' Theology', in P.D. Hoine & M. Martijn (eds), *All From One: A Guide to Proclus* (Oxford, Oxford University Press), 207–22.

Buḥturī, Abū ʿUbādah al-Walīd al- (1963), *Dīwān* (Cairo, Dār al-Maʿārif).

D'Ancona, C. (1999), 'Porphyry, Universal Soul and the Arabic Plotinus', *Arabic Sciences and Philosophy*, 9: 47–88.

D'Ancona, C. (2017), 'The Impact of Greek Neoplatonism on Arabic Philosophy: Plotinus' Concept of the Universal Intellect and Soul', lecture delivered on 8 November 2007 at the Institute of Ismaili Studies, London, United Kingdom.

de Man, P. (1979), *Allegories of Reading: Figural Language in Rousseau, Nietzsche, Rilke, and Proust* (New Haven, Yale University Press).

de Man, P. (1983), 'The Rhetoric of Temporality', in P. de Man (ed.), *Blindness and Insight: Essays in the Rhetoric of Contemporary Criticism* (Minneapolis, University of Minnesota Press), 187–228.

Duncan, R. (1973), 'Often I Am Permitted to Return to a Meadow', in *The Opening of the Field* (New York, New Directions Publishing Corporation), 7.

England, S. (2017), *Medieval Empires and the Culture of Competition: Literary Duels at Islamic and Christian Courts* (Edinburgh, Edinburgh University Press).

Ernst, C.W. (2018), *Al-Hallaj, Poems of a Sufi Martyr Translated from the Arabic by C.W. Ernst* (Evanston, North Western University Press).

Gutas, D. (1988), *Avicenna and the Aristotelian Tradition: Introduction to Reading Avicenna's Philosophical Works* (Leiden, Brill).

Ḥamawī, Yāqūt al- (1977), *Muʿjam al-Buldān* (Beirut, Dār Ṣādir).

Hass, R. (2017), *A Little Book on Form: An Exploration into the Formal Imagination of Poetry* (New York, Ecco/HarperCollins Publishers).

Ibn Fūrak, Abū Bakr Muḥammad (2009), *Tafsīr al-Qurʾān al-ʿAẓīm [Qurʾan 23:1 to 32:73]* (Mecca, Jāmiʿat Umm al-Qurā).

Ibn Rashīq al-Qayrawānī (2009), *Al-'Umdah fī Maḥāsin al-Shi'r wa-Ādābihī* (Tunis, al-Majma' al-Tūnisī li-l-'Ulūm wa-l-Ādāb wa-l-Funūn).

Ibn Sīnā, Abū 'Alī Al-Ḥusayn & Al-Ṭūsī, Naṣīr al-Dīn (1983–94), *Al-Ishārāt wa-l-Tanbīhāt* (Cairo, Dār al-Ma'ārif).

Jurjānī, 'Abd al-Qāhir b. 'Abd al-Raḥmān al- (1992), *Dalā'il al-I'jāz* (Cairo, Dār al-Madanī).

Key, A. (2011), 'Al-Rāghib al-Iṣfahānī', in M. St. Germain & T. DeYoung (eds), *Essays in Arabic Literary Biography* (Wiesbaden, Harrassowitz Verlag), 925–1350.

Key, A. (2018), *Language Between God and the Poets: Ma'nā in the Eleventh Century* (Oakland, University of California Press).

Lowell, R. (1961), 'The Quaker Graveyard in Nantucket', in R. Lowell, *Lord Weary's Castle* (New York, Meridian Books), 8–14.

Marghīnānī, Naṣr Ibn al-Ḥasan al- & Ibn Aflaḥ, 'Alī (1987), *Two Arabic Treatises on Stylistics*, ed. G.J. van Gelder (Istanbul, Nederlands Historisch-Archaeologisch Instituut te Istanbul).

Menander (1981), *Menander Rhetor*, ed. with translation & commentary by D.A. Russell & N.G. Wilson (Oxford, Oxford University Press).

Mutanabbī, Abū al-Ṭayyib al- (2002), *Sharḥ Dīwān al-Mutanabbī* (Beirut, Dār al-Fikr).

Novokhatko, A. (2013), 'Figures (*skhemata*), Ancient Theories of', in G.K. Giannakis (ed.), *Encyclopedia of Ancient Greek Language and Linguistics* Online Edition, 589–92, accessed 25 July 2021, http://dx.doi.org.stanford.idm.oclc.org/10.1163/2214-448X_eagll_COM_00000131.

Plotinus (1964), *Plotini Opera [Enneads]* (Oxford, E Typographeo Clarendoniano).

Rāghib, Abū al-Qāsim al-Ḥusayn b. Muḥammad al-Iṣfahānī al- (1988), *Al-I'tiqādāt* (Beirut, Mu'assasat al-Ashrāf).

Rāghib, Abū al-Qāsim al-Ḥusayn b. Muḥammad al-Iṣfahānī al- (1992), *Mufradāt Alfāẓ al-Qur'ān al-Karīm* (Beirut/Damascus, Dār al-Qalam/Dār al-Shāmīyah).

Rāghib, Abū al-Qāsim al-Ḥusayn b. Muḥammad al-Iṣfahānī al- (2007), *Kitāb al-Dharī'ah ilā Makārim al-Sharī'ah* (Cairo, Dār al-Salām).

Schoeler, G. (2010–11), 'The Genres of Classical Arabic Poetry: Classifications of Poetic Themes and Poems by Pre-modern Critics and Redactors of Dīwāns', *Quaderni di Studi Arabi*, 5/6: 1–48.

Ṭabarī, Muḥammad b. Jarīr al- (1994), *Tafsīr al-Ṭabarī: Jāmi' al-Bayān 'an Ta'wīl Āy al-Qur'ān* (Beirut, Mu'assasat al-Risālah).

Vinson, M. (2003), 'Rhetoric and Writing Strategies in the Ninth Century', in E. Jeffreys (ed.), *Rhetoric in Byzantium: Papers from the Thirty-Fifth Spring Symposium of Byzantine Studies*, Exeter College, University of Oxford, March 2001 (Aldershot, Ashgate), 9–22.

4

Beauty Stings: Plotinus and Rūzbihān Baqlī on Beauty

KAZUYO MURATA

Readers of Sufi literature often remark how 'Neoplatonic' 'Sufism' can appear, because of various similarities found in 'Neoplatonic' and 'Sufi' texts. The impression of 'Neoplatonic influence' on 'Sufism' also seems reinforced by the fact that Plotinus's *Enneads* IV, V and VI have been available to Muslims in partial Arabic translation or paraphrase since the 9th century. Such an impression may even become stronger if one looks at Sufi theorists of beauty like Rūzbihān Baqlī (d. 1209), whose understanding of beauty has some striking parallels to that of Plotinus (d. 270).

Rūzbihān Baqlī was a major Sufi master active in 12th-century Shiraz in southwest Persia, famous for his love of beauty, which he expressed in prose and verse in Arabic and Persian. Among the many Sufis who have spoken on beauty, Rūzbihān stands out for the sheer amount and sophistication of his discussion on beauty. His writings were widely circulated, particularly 'among a select group of readers in Iran, India, Central Asia, Ottoman Turkey, and Africa' (Ernst 1996: 10). He came to be known as an important Sufi exegete through the composition of a multi-volume Qur'an commentary in Arabic, *The Brides of Elucidation on the Realities of the Qur'an* (*ʿArāʾis al-Bayān fī Ḥaqāʾiq al-Qurʾān*), while his Persian masterpiece in defence of passionate love (*ʿishq*), *The Jasmine of Passionate Lovers* (*ʿAbhar al-ʿĀshiqīn*), has established his standing as a major theoretician of love in Islam.

The present study compares Rūzbihān and Plotinus on several key questions on beauty, including: Where does beauty come from? Why are human beings attracted to beauty, and why do they take pleasure in it? Is bodily beauty an impediment to spiritual ascent and therefore to be shunned by human beings? What is the difference between the good and the beautiful? Finally, why did beauty matter to Plotinus and Rūzbihān?

It must be stated at the outset that it is not the purpose of the present study to compare 'Neoplatonism' and 'Sufism' on questions of beauty, as if these two are fixed, easily definable entities, which they are not.[1] In fact, both terms are inventions of Western historians in the 18th and 19th centuries (Ernst 1997: 9; Gerson 2014). Instead of comparing abstract entities marked by 'isms', the present study focuses on and compares two specific individuals, namely Plotinus and Rūzbihān.

Further, the present study does not aim at tracing possible lines of knowledge transmission from Plotinus to Rūzbihān or showing how Rūzbihān's understanding of beauty in particular may have been informed by Plotinus's work, which is virtually impossible to prove. This is because, first, Rūzbihān was not the kind of Muslim philosopher to make direct quotations of Greek philosophical texts in Arabic translation or even of Muslim philosophical writings. Second, by Rūzbihān's time in the 12th century, elements of Greek thought had been 'naturalised' in Muslim thought and elaborated upon by several generations of Muslim thinkers as part of their own intellectual tradition. Moreover, while Rūzbihān incorporated technical terms of Sufism and Muslim theology (*kalām*) in his writings, he came to develop a unique poetic language with limited presence of the technical terms of Muslim philosophy (*falsafa*). Whatever the reason may have been, his preference for non-philosophical language makes the task of tracing any transmission of ideas from Greek through Arabic to his writings extremely difficult.[2]

[1] In this way the present study endeavours to avoid what Michael L. Satlow calls 'a historiographical model of static encounters between easily defined cultures' (2008: 40), which fails to recognise 'the inherent weakness of explanatory models that turn culture into static binary encounters, characterised by "conflict", "resistance", "influence", "assimilation", "acculturation", or "appropriation"' (2008: 38).

[2] One text with substantial philosophical content that Rūzbihān is known to have been familiar with is *The Book of the Inclination of the Familiar* Alif *toward the Inclined* Lām (*Kitāb 'Aṭf al-Alif al-Ma'lūf 'alā al-Lām al-Ma'ṭūf*) by Abū al-Ḥasan al-Daylamī (fl. *c.* 950), the biographer and disciple of Ibn Khafīf (d. 982) – see al-Daylamī (1363sh/1984; 2005). This book is one of the earliest Arabic compendia on passionate love (*'ishq*) containing a wide range of sayings on love by Muslim philosophers, theologians, Sufis, historians, litterateurs, Bedouin Arabs and Greeks including Heraclitus, Empedocles, Hippocrates, Plato, Aristotle and Galen (but not Plotinus). Al-Daylamī was an older contemporary of Ibn Sīnā (c. 980–1037), so the latter's ideas did not enter *The Book of the Inclination*, though al-Daylamī (2005: 159) mentions al-Kindī (d. 873) by name, among others. Al-Daylamī and Ibn Sīnā may have drunk from a similar pool of philosophical knowledge available in Arabic from the 10th to 11th centuries. For a study on the Greek philosophical material al-Daylamī may have had access to, see Walzer (1962). Takeshita (1987: 128) has examined the extent to which Rūzbihān adapted al-Daylamī's work in composing *The Jasmine of Passionate Lovers* and argues, 'While Daylamī tries to blend Ḥallāj into philosophy and support his views with many quotations of *ḥadīth* and other authorities, Rūzbihān hides Ḥallajian thought with highly poetical and sometimes enigmatic prose and sophisticated terminology. According to Massignon, Daylamī probably received Ḥallajian theory of love, not from Ibn Khafīf, but from Abū Ḥayyān Tawḥīdī, who, in turn, received it from Abū Sulaymān Manṭiqī Sijistānī. Therefore it can be said that Daylamī represents the philosophical Ḥallajism, which tries to interprete [*sic*] Ḥallāji's [*sic*] thought in terms of Hellenistic philosophy. On the other hand, in Rūzbihān, we see a representative of experiential Sufism. He is not interested in philosophy nor metaphysics; he is a "practicing" Sufi full of mystical visions. However, in spite of these differences, we can still notice in them a continuation of the Ḥallajian tradition of love mysticism in Shiraz, the tradition which is distinct from that of Aḥmad Ghazzālī and that of Ibn 'Arabī.' Ascertaining the immediate source for elements of philosophy in Rūzbihān's thought – whether it is exclusively al-Daylamī or includes the works of later authors such as Ibn Sīnā and al-Ghazālī (d. 1111) – is beyond the scope of the present study, as there is no definite indication in Rūzbihān's works that he utilised the latter two authors, for instance.

The main sources for analysis in this study are Rūzbihān's writings in Arabic and Persian, including one Persian poem serving as a central text for analysis, and Plotinus's *Enneads*. Since the focus of this study is a content comparison of the two thinkers' ideas, the *Enneads* I, II and III are included as sources for the following comparative analysis, even though these three *Enneads* were most probably not available to Muslims in Arabic during Rūzbihān's time. In addition, occasional reference will be made to the Arabic Plotinus corpus, that is, the Arabic paraphrases of the *Enneads* IV, V and VI produced in the 9th century that are extant in the form of three Arabic texts: *The Theology of Aristotle* (*Uthūlūgiyā Arisṭāṭālīs*), *[Sayings of] the Greek Sage* (*[Qawl] al-Shaykh al-Yūnānī*), and *Epistle on the Divine Science* (*Risāla fī-l-ʿIlm al-Ilāhī*).[3] The Arabic Plotinus corpus is included as a source for the present study because a three-directional comparison of Plotinus, Rūzbihān, and the Arabic Plotinus reveals curious combinations of divergent opinions among the three. Naturally there are points on which all three agree, but there are also points where only two of them – which could be any combination of Plotinus and the Arabic Plotinus, the Arabic Plotinus and Rūzbihān, and most curiously, Plotinus and Rūzbihān – agree, while leaving one out. Their similarities and divergences offer much food for thought.

1. Cosmogony: Out of the Unknown into the Known and Beautiful

Islamic intellectual discourse on beauty begins with the idea of God as 'beautiful', *jamīl* and *ḥasan* in Arabic. These two terms have roots in the Qur'an and Hadith, the former representing the word of God and the latter being Muhammad's sayings. There are various Qur'anic verses that describe God as beautiful (*ḥasan*), among which is 'Blessed is God, the most beautiful (*aḥsan*) of creators' (Q 23:14). The most important hadith on beauty is the one in which Muhammad proclaims, 'Indeed, God is beautiful (*jamīl*), and He loves beauty (*jamāl*)'.[4] While the Qur'an and the Hadith positively describe God as beautiful in this manner, God is at the same time considered ultimately unknowable, just as the Qur'an says, 'There is nothing like Him' (Q 42:11), which has led to the development of negative theology in Muslim intellectual discourse.

Rūzbihān engages in both positive and negative theology in his writings. The following Persian poem recorded in Rūzbihān's hagiography written by his great-grandson, ʿAbd al-Laṭīf Shams b. Ṣadr al-Dīn Rūzbihān Thānī (d. 705/1305), is a good example of Rūzbihān's exploration of the knowable and unknowable aspects of God while highlighting the significant role that beauty plays in this theological

[3] For textual and historical details on the Arabic Plotinus corpus, see Adamson (2002: 5–26). For the manuscript tradition of the Arabic Plotinus corpus, see Gutas (2007).

[4] This hadith is found in major Muslim collections such as those by Muslim and Ibn Ḥanbal.

polarity. The present section is devoted to analysing this poem in detail in comparison with relevant aspects of Plotinus's thought. This poem has been chosen as a central text for analysis in the present study because it encapsulates Rūzbihān's understanding of divine beauty while touching on important subthemes that are evocative of Plotinus's ideas.

The poem begins with Rūzbihān emphasising divine transcendence and human incapacity to comprehend God (ʿAbd al-Laṭīf 1347sh/1969: 340, [illegible]):

> The recognisers at the house of the seven climes
> have all surrendered because of incapacity.
> In His path incapacity is perception.
> If you claim [to perceive Him], that would be associationism.
> His Essence is not encompassed by intellects.
> Witnessing It is not described as incarnationism.

The first hemistich of the third verse expresses a well-known dictum in Muslim theology: God as He is in Himself – or the divine essence – is unknowable to everything other than God. Rūzbihān continues on this theme of the unknowability of God's essence for another couple of verses:

> Temporal origination hangs from Eternity,
> or rather it flees from eternal Severity.
> Though the universal intellect knows guidance,
> when it comes to His Essence, it falls short.

Thereafter the main theme of the poem shifts from the fact of God's ultimate unknowability to the resulting human reaction of perplexity and rapture:

> Spirits are enraptured in this battlefield,
> perplexed at the threshold of Majesty.
> When they saw the glories of His Majesty,
> they cut off coveting the Essence Itself.[5]
> The secret of Eternity was never perceived by anyone,
> for Eternity is not described by nonexistence.
> The holiness of His Essence accepts no imagination.
> How could He who created the creatures die?
> Until you see His Essence through the spirit of the spirit,
> how will you recognise His signs through your secret core?
> The prophets are enraptured in Him.
> The saints are the dust of His road and His servants.

In Sufi literature, the theological dictum of the unknowability of God's essence is sometimes expressed more poetically as the 'hidden treasure' (*kanz makhfī*). This

[5] This is Rūzbihān's oblique reference to Moses on the mount asking God, 'Show me so that I may look upon you', to which God replies, 'Thou shalt not see Me' (Q 7:143), which echoes the biblical verse, 'No one shall see me and live' (Exodus 33:20). Rūzbihān extensively discusses the manifold implications of Moses's encounter with God on the mount in various works, including his Qur'an commentary (Baqlī 2008).

expression comes from a creation myth often discussed by Sufis. Some present it as a dialogue between God and the prophet David,[6] who asks God why He created the world. To this God replies, 'I was a hidden treasure, so I loved to be recognised. So I created the creatures so that I may be recognised'. Sufis including Rūzbihān take this saying to imply creation as God's self-manifestation.

The myth of the hidden treasure and the aforementioned hadith, 'God is beautiful and He loves beauty', together form the basis for the common Sufi understanding that the driving force for creation is God's love for His own beauty to be manifest and recognised by something other than Himself. In an Arabic prose work, *The Journey of the Spirits* (*Sayr al-Arwāḥ*), Rūzbihān makes precisely this point:

> In eternity [God] became the lover of His own beauty (*jamāl*). Inevitably love, lover, and beloved were one. Since they are attributes, they do not have the defect of temporal origination. When He became His own lover, He wanted to create a creation so that it would become the place of His love and gaze, without alienation or intimacy. In His eternity He created the spirits of the lovers and made their eyes see His beauty. He taught them that He was their lover before they came to be: 'I was a Hidden Treasure, so I loved to be recognised.'[7]
>
> (Baqlī 1998b: 6)

If creation is God's means of making His beauty known, the implication of this is that He would have remained forever hidden and unknown except to Himself, had He not created anything, for then there would have been nothing but God.

Let us now turn to Plotinus, as he makes a number of points similar to Rūzbihān's. The origin of all in Plotinus's system of thought is 'the One', which is ineffable like the divine essence presented in Rūzbihān's poem. The One is the first of the three hypostases in Plotinus's thought, from which emanates the second hypostasis, Intellect, from which in turn emanates the third hypostasis, Soul. Plotinus emphasises the ultimately inconceivable and ineffable nature of the One, as 'it would be absurd to seek to comprehend that boundless nature' (V 5 [32] 6, A: 173). Hence, no positive description of the One is possible, and all that can be said about the One is 'not this' (V 5 [32] 6, A: 173), according to Plotinus.

It is only through the emanation of the second hypostasis, *Nous* or Intellect, that any intelligibility in positive terms becomes possible. In other words, without this emanation from the One, everything would have remained hidden. Plotinus writes, 'there must not be just one alone – for then all things would have been hidden, shapeless within that one, and not a single real being would have existed if that one had stayed still in itself, nor would there have been the multiplicity of these

[6] For example, Kubrawī Sufi, Najm al-Dīn Dāya al-Rāzī (d. 1256) ascribes this saying to David (Rāzī 1980: 26). Chittick (2013: 18) writes, 'Early authors do not suggest that it came from the Prophet's mouth, but attribute it rather to the corpus of stories handed down about the prophet David.' Chittick (2013: 439, n. 6) also notes that while an early attribution of this saying to 'one of God's prophets' can be found in the *Rasā'il* of Ikhwān al-Ṣafā' (fl. 10th century), he has 'not found an explicit attribution of this saying to the Prophet before Ibn al-'Arabī' (d. 1240).

[7] For an extensive analysis of this passage, see Murata (2017: 76–7).

real beings which are generated from the One' (IV 8 [6] 6, A: 415). One key difference between Plotinus's discussion here and Rūzbihān's cosmogony is the lack of intention on the part of the One in Plotinus's account, as emanation is a logical, impersonal process,[8] whereas in Rūzbihān's account there is the divine intention of *wanting* to make Himself known. The mythic nature of Rūzbihān's language is typical of Sufi literature in general, as it follows the language of the Qur'an and Hadith.

It is a curious fact that an Arabic translation of the above passage (IV 8 [6] 6) found in chapter 7 of the *Theology of Aristotle* contains two additional words that were not part of the Greek original. These are the words 'beauty' (*ḥusn*) and 'splendour' (*bahā'*): 'If the creator did not originate things and were simply alone, the things would have been hidden and their beauty and splendour would not have been manifest and clear' (Badawī 1955: 84–5).[9] With the addition of the words 'beauty' and 'splendour', the Arabic version of this passage puts an emphasis on the emergence of beauty through creation, which comes close to Rūzbihān's discussion above (Baqlī 1998b: 6).

Let us return to Rūzbihān's poem and examine its final four verses. There he first says that without the manifestation of God's beauty, there would not have been any love, for it is the manifestation of beauty that gives rise to love ('Abd al-Laṭīf 1347sh/1969: 340, [illegible]):

> Were there no unveiling of His Beauty,
> how could there be love in people's spirits?
> He made Himself recognised in the signs;
> then He gave out the descriptions of the attributes.

The word 'signs' (*āyāt*) in the latter verse is a classic reference to creation in Muslim literature, as creation is understood to reveal the Creator's existence and qualities as His sign. Underlying Rūzbihān's reference to the attributes (*ṣifāt*) in the same verse is the idea that while the essence of God cannot be directly known by creatures, God can be known indirectly by way of His attributes. If one were to link this discussion to the title of the present volume, one could say that it is the attributes that are the *faces* of the infinite. The very reason why the divine essence is unknowable is that it is limitless therefore unspecifiable. Attributes are the knowable faces or aspects of the unknowable, infinite being. Further, one can say that the infinite is therefore hidden – or the hidden treasure. The multitude of divine attributes and acts (i.e. all created beings) are the knowable faces or signs of that hidden treasure.

[8] Adamson (2002: 164) argues that this is an aspect of Plotinus's thought that the 9th-century Arabic adaptor preserved faithfully in his translation of the *Enneads*, even though there are a number of changes that he has introduced to the text: 'The [Arabic] Adaptor … agrees with Plotinus in rejecting all desire on the part of the One: "intellectual and sensible things desire to know Him, but He does not desire to know anything" (*DS* 166 [B 179]).'

[9] The English translation of the Arabic Plotinus corpus in this study generally follows that by Geoffrey Lewis in Plotinus (1977) with occasional modifications. Lewis's translation of this passage can be found in Plotinus (1977: 243).

Rūzbihān ends his poem by pointing out how divine beauty makes the intellect *mad*, in the sense that it both incapacitates the intellect and makes it fall madly in love. He writes ('Abd al-Laṭīf 1347sh/1969: 341, [illegible]):

> O far removed from understanding, estimation, and imagination,
> speaking in description of You is impossible.
> In Your Beauty the intellect is mad,
> in Your Majesty the spirit is a moth.

The 'moth' is an allusion to the famous imagery in Sufi literature, where the moth represents the human lover and the fire the divine beloved. Because the moth loves and seeks union with the fire, it eventually enters the fire, only to be consumed and annihilated by it, thereby achieving union.

The idea that beauty instils love in its perceiver is common to Rūzbihān and Plotinus. Plotinus writes: 'If anyone sees [the highest beauty], what passion will he feel, what longing in his desire to be united with it, what a shock of delight!' (I 6 [1] 7, A: 253). For both thinkers the story of existence begins with the single unnameable source of all, the unfolding of which reveals multiple qualities entailed by it, key among which is beauty.

2. Mechanism of Aesthetic Experience

There are several key questions on beauty that both Rūzbihān and Plotinus address. One is the origin of beauty, which they both find in that single source of all being, as seen in the previous section. Another important question concerns how human experience of beauty works. In particular, why are human beings attracted to beauty, and why do they find aesthetic experience to be pleasurable?

According to Rūzbihān, human attraction to beauty originates in a primordial encounter between God and humanity, which is a Qur'anic event often referred to as the Covenant of 'Am I not' (*Alast*). In the Qur'an 7:172, God asks the children of Adam, 'Am I not your Lord?', to which they reply, 'Yea, we testify'. A basic Muslim understanding of this Qur'anic event is that it was human beings' covenant of servanthood to God. Rūzbihān points out that this event signifies much more than a covenant of servanthood: it was also the first occasion on which God displayed His *beauty* to human beings, thereby turning them into His lovers.[10] He writes, 'The Real unveiled His beauty (*jamāl*) to the spirits of the passionate lovers in His first appearance after introducing Himself to them by saying, "Am I not your Lord?"' (Baqlī 1974: 10). Hence, in his view this event also signified humanity's covenant of *love* to God. The

[10] It must be noted that Rūzbihān is not the only thinker to hold this view. For example, 'Ayn al-Quḍāt (d. 1131) writes, 'Remember that day on which the beauty (*jamāl*) of "Am I not your Lord" was unveiled to you' (Hamadānī 1380sh/2001: 106).

test of human life, therefore, lies in whether one can keep serving and loving that beautiful God throughout one's life as one's only Lord and only object of love.

Rūzbihān maintains that the primordial memory of that Lord is retained by the innate human nature (*fiṭra*) that lies within each person. He writes, 'God captured within the nature of the souls a luminous, intellective, and holy innate nature that testifies to its bringer-of-existence' (Baqlī 1998a: 174). The idea of the innate human nature comes from a well-known hadith, 'Every child is born according to the innate human nature'. Rūzbihān points out that this innate nature itself is beautiful too, because the recognition of that beautiful Lord is ingrained in it, which idea Rūzbihān expresses by the phrase 'the innate human nature of beauty' (*fiṭrat al-ḥusn*) (Baqlī 1974: 133). The innate human nature functions as an indelible link between the soul – or spirit (*rūḥ, jān*) in Rūzbihān's terminology – leading an embodied life and its higher origin.[11] Thus the primordial encounter with the beautiful Lord has manifold implications for human life on earth.

The idea that human beings' longing for beauty predates their bodily existence is also present in Plotinus's thought. In the *Ennead* III 5 [50] 1, A: 167–9 – which is one of the first three *Enneads* and therefore did not form part of the Arabic Plotinus corpus – he writes, 'And if someone assumed that the origin of love was the longing for beauty itself which was there before in men's souls, and their recognition of it and kinship with it and unreasoned awareness that it is something of their own, he would hit, I think, on the truth about its cause.'

Moreover, Plotinus discusses the idea that the human soul, even after entry into the body, remains connected to its higher origin. He writes, 'even our soul does not altogether come down, but there is always something of it in the intelligible' (IV 8 [6] 8, A: 421). This passage exists in a slightly expanded Arabic paraphrase in chapter 7 of the *Theology of Aristotle* (Badawī 1955: 90; cf. Plotinus 1977: 249), though the main content remains unaltered:

> the soul does not descend in its entirety to this lower, sensible world – nor does the universal soul nor our souls – but something of it remains in the intelligible world, not departing from it, since it is not possible that a thing should depart from its world completely except by its corruption or by deviation from its essence. So even if the soul descended to this world it would remain attached to its own world, for it is possible for it to be there without withdrawing from this world.

Thus Plotinus, Rūzbihān and the Arabic Plotinus all maintain that the individual soul remains connected to its higher origin even while leading an embodied life.

So why are human beings attracted to beauty, and why do they find aesthetic experience to be pleasurable? In Rūzbihān's view, aesthetic experience is like déjà vu, an occasion for the remembrance (*dhikr*) of the primordial vision of the

[11] See Stern-Gillet's chapter in the present volume for a striking parallel to Rūzbihān's ideas in Ficino's discussion of 'the treasure hidden in the deepest part of [the soul]' that can be forgotten but can be rediscovered through a process of self-purification by turning inward (pp. 286–7).

beautiful God. In the following passage, he discusses the divine 'address of eternity' – referring to 'Am I not your Lord?' (Q 7:172) – and explains how the spiritually advanced keep hearing this 'eternal speech' of God every time they encounter something beautiful in this world:

> In every witness [of the Unseen], there remains the sweetness of the address of eternity. When [those who have reached the station of audition] hear any goodly (*ṭayyib*) sound, see and witness anything comely (*malīḥ*) and deemed beautiful (*mustaḥsan*), or smell any goodly fragrance in this world, they will hear it as an intermediary between the [divine] attribute and the [divine] essence through the quality of being prior to any act that emerges from the Real. It is as if one hears from the Real through the Real. Hence, every speck of engendered being has a specific tongue that speaks to him with the eternal speech.
>
> (Baqlī 1974: 85)

What Rūzbihān describes here is certainly not the everyday experience of people in general but an advanced psychological state of those who travel on the path to God. For these people, an encounter with any beautiful thing or person constitutes a re-enactment of the primordial covenant. Those who actively remember what they saw on the day of the covenant can see and hear that beautiful Lord every time they perceive something beautiful in this world. Thus, every beautiful thing functions as a sign and reminder of that beautiful Lord.

If in Rūzbihān's language aesthetic pleasure comes from finding something *familiar* due to a primordial encounter, in Plotinus's language aesthetic pleasure comes from finding something *akin* to oneself, though ultimately there is no significant difference in meaning between these two formulations. In *Ennead* I 6 [1] 2, A: 237–9 – another part not included in the Arabic Plotinus corpus – Plotinus writes:

> the primary beauty in bodies ... is something which we become aware of even at the first glance; the soul speaks of it as if it understood it, recognizes and welcomes it and as it were adapts itself to it. But when it encounters the ugly it shrinks back and rejects it and turns away from it and is out of tune and alienated from it. Our explanation of this is that the soul, since it is by nature what it is and is related to the higher kind of reality in the realm of being, when it sees something akin to it or a trace of its kindred reality, is delighted and thrilled and returns to itself and remembers itself and its own possessions. What likeness, then, is there between beautiful things here and There? If there is a likeness, let us agree that they are alike.

The distinction that Plotinus makes between beauty as akin and ugliness as alien to oneself presupposes that one's nature is beautiful. This resonates with Rūzbihān's aforementioned notion of the beautiful innate human nature. Moreover, Plotinus maintains that the soul derives its aesthetic delight from finding something akin to itself, which in turn causes the soul to return to itself and remember its true nature. Kuisma (2003: 184) calls this experience 'anamnetic "déjà-vu"' and explains, 'Perceptible beauty may turn the subject's attention to intelligible Beauty, which is then experienced as an anamnetic return to one's true home' (2003: 190). This idea is congruent with Rūzbihān's view that an encounter with beautiful things prompts recollection of one's beautiful innate nature and origin – God.

Plotinus and Rūzbihān thus agree that every instance of beauty in the world is a pointer to its source that lies on a higher order of being, which is why they regard aesthetic experience to be an occasion for the recollection or remembrance of the source of all beauty. Moreover, both thinkers urge human beings to remember and return to it. They also agree that human beings are attracted to beauty and find its perception pleasurable because it resonates with their own nature that is beautiful. Longing to return to whence one came is another theme that figures prominently in the writings of Rūzbihān (along with other Sufis) and Plotinus, as the latter says by way of quoting from the *Iliad*, 'Let us fly to our dear country' (I 6 [1] 8, A: 257). How one might make one's way home is another question, which will be examined next.

3. Inward Journey

It is one thing to say that for Plotinus and Rūzbihān aesthetic experience is an occasion for recollecting the source of all beauty, but it is quite another whether this is the everyday experience of each human being. While both thinkers maintain that everyone has the same capacity to see reality as they do, they admit that most people have this power only in potentiality, not exercised in actuality. Plotinus exhorts: 'Shut your eyes, and change to and wake another way of seeing, which everyone has but few use' (I 6 [1] 8, A: 259). Both Plotinus and Rūzbihān maintain that such a mode of seeing needs to be awakened through conscious effort and training. Plotinus explains that this can be accomplished by turning inward, which will awaken an inner eye that sees the interior of a thing rather than its exterior:

> How can one see the 'inconceivable beauty' which stays within the holy sanctuary and does not come out where the profane may see it? Let him who can, follow and come within, and leave outside the sight of his eyes and not turn back to the bodily splendours which he saw before.
>
> (I 6 [1] 8, A: 255–7)

In a crucial discussion on beauty in *Ennead* I 6 [1] 9, A: 259–61, Plotinus clarifies his method of awakening the inner sight:

> And what does this inner sight see? When it is just awakened it is not at all able to look at the brilliance before it. So that the soul must be trained … How then can you see the sort of beauty a good soul has? Go back into yourself and look; and if you do not yet see yourself beautiful, then, just as someone making a statue which has to be beautiful cuts away here and polishes there … so you too must cut away excess and straighten the crooked and clear the dark and make it bright, and never stop 'working on your statue' till the divine glory of virtue shines out on you, till you see 'self-mastery enthroned upon its holy seat.' If you have become this, and see it, and are at

> home with yourself in purity … then you have become sight; you can trust yourself then; you have already ascended and need no one to show you; concentrate your gaze and see. This alone is the eye that sees the great beauty.[12]

For Plotinus, turning inward entails self-reflection and self-rediscovery. It is important to note that Plotinus regards this as a process of *purification*, rather than acquisition of new qualities. At the end of this process of purification – that is, elimination of all that is alien to the true nature of the soul such as vices and engrossment in the body – what remains and is rediscovered within oneself is beauty. As Plotinus writes, 'his ugliness has come from an addition of alien matter, and his business, if he is to be beautiful again, is to wash and clean himself and so be again what he was before' (I 6 [1] 5, A: 249). This again parallels Rūzbihān's notion of the beautiful innate human nature, which only needs unearthing.

Plotinus explains the beautiful nature of human beings in this manner: 'For when we ourselves are beautiful, it is by belonging to ourselves, but we are ugly when we change to another nature: when we know ourselves we are beautiful, but ugly when we are ignorant of ourselves. Beauty therefore is in that higher world and comes from there' (V 8 [31] 13, A: 281). Chapter 8 of the *Theology of Aristotle* provides a close paraphrase of this passage: 'Thus we are beautiful (*ḥisān*) and complete as long as we see and recognize ourselves and subsist in our nature (*ṭabīʿa*). If we did not see or recognize ourselves but were carried away to the nature of senses, we would become ugly' (Badawī 1955: 120; cf. Plotinus 1977: 409). Though the 9th-century Arabic translator used the word *ṭabīʿa* to refer to the nature (*phusis*) of the human being, Plotinus's implied sense here seems even closer to Rūzbihān's usage of *fiṭra* ('innate human nature').

Rūzbihān also has his own expressions to refer to an ability similar to what Plotinus calls the 'inner sight'. One is 'the eye of gathering' (*ʿayn al-jamʿ*), about which Rūzbihān writes: 'the Real discloses Himself in beauty (*ḥusn*) and what is deemed beautiful[13] to those who seek to witness Him … This is an allusion to the eye of gathering, which none knows but passionate lovers' (Baqlī [no date A]: I.328, para. 137). It is called the eye of 'gathering' because it is a mode of perception that sees both the Creator and the created in a single vision as if gathering them together. An example of this mode of perception would be to see a beautiful flower and recognise its beautiful Creator through it simultaneously.

[12] Corrigan explains how Plotinus turns around two passages from Plato's *Phaedrus* (252 d 7 and 254 b 7, respectively) to give a new emphasis on the importance of self-improvement: 'In the *Phaedrus*, it is the lover who works upon the soul of the beloved, making him "like a statue for himself as though the beloved were a god…" (252d). Plotinus has adapted the image to express the quality of one's own self-relatedness', by which Corrigan means 'his or her concern for goodness, nobility, and justice' (2005: 212).

[13] 'What is deemed beautiful' (*mustaḥsan*) is a technical term in Rūzbihān's writings that refers to beautiful objects in the world – which can also be deemed ugly (*mustaqbaḥ*) depending on one's perspective, as they belong to the realm of relative or possible being – in contrast to *ḥusn*, which is beauty itself or absolute beauty, belonging to God. For a detailed discussion of *mustaḥsan*, see Murata (2017: 37–40, 43–4).

Such usage of 'gathering' is part of standard Sufi terminology, in which 'gathering' (*jam'*) is contrasted with 'separation' (*tafriqa* or *farq*).[14] Naturally Rūzbihān adopts this contrast and posits 'the eye of separation' as the opposite mode of perception. If the eye of gathering is an 'intoxicated' mode of perception that only some attain after much spiritual exercise, the eye of separation represents the 'sober' mode of perception that people use on a daily basis, in which they draw a clear line between the Creator and the created while looking at the world, as if emphatically separating the two. An example of this mode of perception would be to see a beautiful flower only as a flower, without immediate association with its Creator. Put differently, the eye of separation emphasises the distinction between the Creator and the created thereby highlighting the transcendence of God, whereas the eye of gathering focuses on the immanence of God. The eye of gathering can turn every aesthetic experience into recollection of God because it highlights the beautiful God's presence – rather than absence – in each of His creations.

Another expression that Rūzbihān uses is 'the eye of contentment' (*'ayn al-riḍā*). He writes, 'When the eye of contentment is opened … one will see the quiddity of being and the beauty (*ḥusn*) of God's artisanry (*iṣṭinā'*) that becomes manifest from [that quiddity] in every atom … and will deem all things decreed by the Unseen as beautiful' (Baqlī 1974: 72–3). Elsewhere he explains the eye of contentment by quoting some lines of poetry (Baqlī 2008: II, 29):

> The eye of contentment sees the ugly as beautiful (*ḥasan*) among all, just as it was said:
>
> The eye of contentment is dim toward every shortcoming
> but the eye of evil makes appear evil traits.
>
> It was said:
>
> The eye of enmity is responsible for evil traits
> while the eye of contentment is dim toward shortcomings.

The eye of contentment allows the human being to find beauty everywhere by foregoing the distinction between the beautiful and the ugly among objects of perception and by letting one focus on the mere fact of their existing. This is to see all things equally as good-and-beautiful (*ḥasan*) insofar as they exist (cf. Murata 2017: 42–3, 119), without regard for their relative perfection or imperfection. In this way one becomes *content* with and comes to appreciate all that exists, which is an ideal human state that the prophets have attained and the rest of humanity should strive to achieve, according to Rūzbihān.

There seems to be another parallel between Rūzbihān and Plotinus in connection to 'the eye of evil' in the above poem, which Rūzbihān has contrasted with the eye of contentment. Plotinus (I 6 [1] 9, A: 261) writes,

> But if anyone comes to the sight blear-eyed with wickedness, and unpurified, or weak and by his cowardice unable to look at what is very bright, he sees nothing, even if someone shows him what is there and possible to see. For one must come to the

[14] See for instance Qushayrī's contrast of *jam'* with *farq* (2007: 87–8).

> sight with a seeing power made akin and like to what is seen. No eye ever saw the sun without becoming sun-like, nor can a soul see beauty without becoming beautiful. You must become first all godlike and all beautiful if you intend to see God and beauty.

Here Plotinus shows how those who are 'blear-eyed with wickedness' fail to see beauty, just as Rūzbihān's 'eye of evil makes appear evil traits' (Baqlī 2008: II, 29). An important point that Plotinus makes in the above passage is that in order to see anything, one needs to make oneself akin to it. This implies that if one is ugly inside, one sees ugliness outside; if one is beautiful inside, one sees beauty outside. This is a point on which again Plotinus and Rūzbihān seem to agree.

Earlier in this section we saw Plotinus urging human beings to polish their inner self and 'never stop "working on your statue" till the divine glory of virtue shines out on you' (I 6 [1] 9, A: 259). Muslims refer to a similar process of inner purification-cum-perfection as 'assuming the character traits of God' (*takhalluq bi-akhlāq Allāh*), a state of human perfection that people should endeavour to attain. Rūzbihān describes this state in various ways, for example:

> When all the [divine] names, qualities, and attributes are attributed to the recogniser (*ʿārif*) while he is unified with the lights of the [divine] essence, has become God's bride in the beauty (*jamāl*) of intimacy, and has become holy in God's holiness, the Real names him with His most tremendous name just as He named Himself with His most tremendous name.
>
> (Baqlī 1974: 232)

In fact, in Rūzbihān's major Arabic prose work that outlines the 1,001 stations that human spirits traverse in their journey to God, he presents the above state, namely the embodiment of all the divine names and attributes, as the last and highest, 1,001st station (Baqlī 1974: 317). Like Plotinus, Rūzbihān argues that reaching this station requires a process of purification and self-rediscovery rather than acquisition of new qualities that one never had. The basis for his argument is the Qur'anic verse, 'He taught Adam the names, all of them' (Q 2:31), which he understands as God bestowing all of the divine names and attributes upon the human being (Baqlī 1974: 156; cf. Murata 2017: 102–4).

4. Attitude to Beauty in Bodies

One of the remaining questions concerns the attitude of Plotinus and Rūzbihān towards beauty in bodies. If they emphasise the importance of the inner eye over the outer, physical eye, does that mean that they consider bodily beauty only as a hindrance to one's spiritual ascent that needs to be avoided by human beings? On this question, there seem to be some important differences among Rūzbihān, Plotinus and the Arabic Plotinus.

Let us examine Rūzbihān first. In his Hadith commentary, he discusses Muhammad's saying, 'Gazing at a beautiful (*ḥasan*) face increases sight', which can be taken as prophetic endorsement of sensory pursuit and appreciation of beauty. Rūzbihān's interpretation does not contradict this, but he emphasises the point that pursuit of beauty or 'seeking intimacy' with beautiful things is rather an inevitable consequence of one's inborn love for the beautiful God. He writes:

> Whoever seeks intimacy with the beauty (*jamāl*) of the Beginninglessness seeks intimacy with the beauty of the forms of temporal origination by yearning for the quarry of holiness, because no one knows the degrees of intimacy with the Real except those who recognise the saying of the master of humanity: 'Gazing at a beautiful face increases sight.'
>
> (Baqlī [no date B]: 57, para. 112; cf. Baqlī 1974: 133)

In fact, Rūzbihān considers 'seeking intimacy with beautiful things' (*isti'nās bi-l-mustaḥsanāt*) as an important and commendable practice. Of course, he is aware of its potential danger in leading its practitioner to become absorbed in the physicality of beautiful things. However, Rūzbihān seems to trust his audience – which he does not always explicitly identify but are usually those in the Sufi path rather than the general public – as capable of seeing bodily beauty as a ladder leading to the source of beauty rather than as an end in itself, a trap to fall into, or a hindrance in the path to God.[15]

In contrast, Plotinus seems to be more cautious about, as well as explicit in, warning people against the danger of being stuck in the physicality of beautiful things. He writes, 'When he sees the beauty in bodies he must not run after them; we must know that they are images, traces, shadows, and hurry away to that which they image' (I 6 [1] 8, A: 257). To Plotinus, the power of beauty is so strong and obvious that in his treatise *Against the Gnostics* he disparages those who fail even to have a sense of wonder:

> But if someone who sees beauty excellently represented in a face is carried to that higher world, will anyone be so sluggish in mind and so immovable that, when he sees all the beauties in the world of sense, all its good proportion and the mighty excellence of its order, and the splendour of form which is manifested in the stars, for all their remoteness, he will not thereupon think, seized with reverence, 'What wonders, and from what a source?' If he did not, he would neither have understood this world here nor seen that higher world.
>
> (II 9 [33] 16, A: 291)

Plotinus also rebukes those who fail to differentiate between beauty and ugliness, and goes so far as to say they have no contemplation and therefore no God:

> They do not look any differently at ugly or beautiful ways of life, or beautiful subjects of study; they have no contemplation, then, and hence no God. For the beauties here exist because of the first beauties. If, then, these here do not exist, neither do those; so these are beautiful in their order after those. But when they say they despise the beauty here, they would do well if they despised the beauty in boys and women, to avoid

[15] In fact, Rūzbihān repeatedly defends the appreciation of beauty in creatures, particularly in people (cf. Baqlī 1380sh/2001: 42; Murata 2017: 93).

> being overcome by it to the point of abandoned wickedness. But one should notice that they would not give themselves airs if they despised something ugly.
>
> (*Ennead* II 9 [33] 17, A: 293)

If lack of discernment between beauty and ugliness is despicable yet despising beauty in bodies is not ideal, what does Plotinus consider to be the correct attitude to beauty and ugliness in bodies? He explains that the correct attitude is not to cling to beauty in this world but to admire its maker 'without insulting these beauties here' (II 9 [33] 17, A: 295). Plotinus's critical stance on the gnostic denial of the material world including what is beautiful, which in his view is likely to create a problematic sense of ascetic superiority, is clear here. Kuisma (2003: 79) summarises his view thus: 'Indifference to beauty would be acceptable in restraining human sexuality, but as a general attitude it would lead to barbarism and atheism.' Appreciation of the relative value of beauty in contrast to ugliness even in the material world seems crucial to Plotinus.

There is one passage where the Arabic Plotinus seems to depart slightly from Plotinus in discussing bodily beauty. The Arabic paraphrase of *Ennead* V 8 [31] 2 found in chapter 4 of the *Theology of Aristotle* reads:

> The beauty of nature (*ḥusn al-ṭabīʿa*) is hidden from us because we are not capable of seeing with eyesight the interior of a thing nor do we seek that. However, we see with eyesight the outside and exterior of a thing and are amazed by its beauty. If we coveted seeing the interior of a thing, we would abandon (*rafaḍa*) and despise (*iḥtaqara*) the outer beauty and would not be amazed by it.
>
> (Badawī 1955: 60; cf. Plotinus 1977: 379–81)

Such harsh tone in rejecting outer beauty, in particular the recommendation for *despising* it, is not found in the original *Ennead* V 8 [31] 2, A: 243–5:

> But certainly nature which produces such beautiful works is far before them in beauty, but we, because we are not accustomed to see any of the things within and do not know them, pursue the external and do not know that it is that within which moves us: as if someone looking at his image and not knowing where it came from should pursue it. But the beauty also in studies and ways of life and generally in souls makes clear that what is pursued is something else and that beauty does not lie in magnitude: it is truly a greater beauty than that when you see moral sense in someone and delight in it, not looking at his face – which might be ugly – but putting aside all shape and pursuing his inner beauty.

Plotinus's point here that in order to focus on inner beauty, one should, if necessary, *ignore* the *ugliness* of its possessor's face, turns into the idea that in order to see inner beauty, one should *despise* outer *beauty* in the Arabic version.[16] It is a curious fact that

[16] This is not to say that Plotinus entirely dismisses the idea of 'despising' outer beauty, as seen earlier in *Ennead* II 9 [33] 17, A: 293. However, Miles raises a question about the word 'despise'. In connection to *Ennead* I 6 [1] 6, A: 251 – 'Again, greatness of soul is despising the things here: and wisdom is an intellectual activity which turns away from the things below and leads the soul to those above' – Miles (1999: 41) writes, 'Indeed, the translation distorts: Plotinus's word for "despise" is literally "look over" – a differently toned word than "despise". To "look over" objects of sense is conceptually to see

as far as this discussion is concerned, Rūzbihān and Plotinus agree in commending the appreciation of beauty in bodies, while the Arabic Plotinus diverges from them both by being more disparaging of bodily beauty. Could it be that the Arabic adaptor was more dismissive of the material world than Plotinus and Rūzbihān were? Adamson (2002: 173) suggests the possibility that the Arabic adaptor failed to grasp one important aspect of Plotinus's thought, namely that

> Plotinus himself rejected the gnostic conception of the sensible world as evil, even though he counseled us to raise our attention from material to immaterial things. This comes out most clearly in *Enn.* II.9 against the gnostics, a treatise the Adaptor may not have read. But whatever his knowledge of Plotinus's stance on this issue, the Adaptor chose to exaggerate the *Enneads*' negative statements about the physical world, as well as the peril that this world presents to our souls ... The ethical dimension of the Adaptor's thought, then, is decidedly scornful regarding things of the lower world.

5. Good versus Beauty

The final point for contrast is how Rūzbihān and Plotinus differentiate between goodness and beauty. Arabic has two main terms denoting 'beauty'. One is *jamāl*, which is ascribed to God in the Hadith literature, and the other is *ḥusn*, which is used in the Qur'an to describe God, as seen above (pp. 150–4). While many Muslim writers use *jamāl* and *ḥusn* indistinguishably to denote beauty, Rūzbihān notes that from one perspective it is possible to differentiate the two in the following manner: *ḥusn* is a wider concept than *jamāl* in that it simultaneously denotes beauty and goodness, while encompassing *jamāl* along with its conceptual counterpart, *jalāl* (majesty).

Put in the language of Muslim theology, Rūzbihān considers *ḥusn* to be an attribute of God's essence, which by definition has no counterpart (i.e. a complementary quality of contrasting nature), while he regards *jamāl* as an attribute of God's act – i.e. an attribute that describes God's dynamic interaction with creation accompanied by a counterpart, which would be *jalāl* in the case of *jamāl*. Furthermore, it is important to note that the totality of the divine names[17] (i.e. both the names of the essence and those of the act) is referred to in the Qur'an as 'the most beautiful names' (*al-asmā' al-ḥusnā*) (Q 7:180; 17:110; 20:8; 59:24). The fact that this Qur'anic expression uses the superlative of *ḥasan* ('good-and-beautiful') to describe the totality of the divine names again points to the all-embracing nature of *ḥusnā*/*ḥusn* over *jamāl* (cf. Murata 2017: 72, 146, n. 6).

Rūzbihān argues that because *jamāl* is accompanied by *jalāl*, it is a kind of beauty that can cause awe and fear. In contrast, *ḥusn*, being a stand-alone concept

---

their essential form.' The word used by the Arabic adaptor above, *iḥtaqara*, is a strong word clearly denoting despite and disdain, certainly not the gentle 'looking over' of Plotinus.

[17] Grammatically speaking, divine 'names' are the adjectival forms of divine attributes. For example, 'the Merciful' is a divine name, while 'mercy' is a divine attribute.

connoting all-encompassing goodness and beauty, is presented as gentle and not fear-inducing: 'The difference between *ḥusn* and *jamāl* is [only] in words, and there is no difference in the realities of the meanings of the[se] attributes. However ... *jamāl* makes emerge in the passionate lover passionate love along with fear and recognising majesty, while His *ḥusn* makes hope and expansiveness emerge' (Baqlī 1974: 133). As Rūzbihān himself points out, such distinction between *ḥusn* and *jamāl* is only implicit and not emphasised in the rest of his writings. However, the fact that he uses *nīkū'ī* – which has a combined sense of 'goodness' and 'beauty' – as a Persian equivalent of *ḥusn* (Baqlī 1380sh/2001: 42; cf. Murata 2017: 30, 92–3, 136, n. 9) does highlight the connotation of overall goodness in his usage of *ḥusn*.

In contrast, the distinction between the good and the beautiful is more pronounced in Plotinus's thought, due to the clear demarcation of the first hypostasis, the One (or the Good), from the second hypostasis, Intellect, which is referred to as 'the beautiful', as it represents intelligible beauty, being the totality of the Forms.[18] Plotinus writes,

> That which is beyond this [i.e., Intellect] we call the nature of the Good, which holds beauty as a screen before it. So in a loose and general way of speaking the Good is the primary beauty; but if one distinguishes the intelligibles [from the Good] one will say that the place of the Forms is the intelligible beauty, but the Good is That which is beyond, the 'spring and origin' of beauty; or one will place the Good and the primal beauty on the same level.
>
> (I 6 [1] 9, A: 261–3)

Just as the unknowable divine essence can come to be known by human beings indirectly through the intermediary of the knowable divine attributes, Plotinus's indescribable One holds intelligible beauty 'as a screen before it'.

[18] Scholars still point out the vagueness that remains in Plotinus's presentation of beauty in relation to the Good. While it is clear that 'the beautiful' may only refer to Intellect but not to the One, they wonder if the One may be called 'beauty'. Inge (1918: 126) writes, 'Plotinus insists that the Absolute [i.e., the One] cannot be "the Beautiful", but Beauty, or the source of the Beautiful.' Rist (1967: 54–5) writes, 'The distinction of the Good and the Beautiful is clear, and Plotinus makes the inferiority of the Beautiful still clearer in 11. 32–3 [*sic.*; [V 5] 12. 32–3] when he declares that "yonder" in the supra-sensible world the Good has no need of the Beautiful but the Beautiful stands in need of the Good. Yet this sentence in fact also complicates matters, for Plotinus has, in the first part of it, remarked that both the Good and the Beautiful participate in the One which is prior to them. This seems to confuse the previous arguments, which are based on the idea of the Good as the ground of Being for all things and thus as identified with the One.' It is also worth noting that Plotinus's presentation of intelligible beauty differs from Plato's. Corrigan (2005: 217) notes, 'For Plotinus, by contrast [to Plato], there is no individual "Form of the Beautiful" in V, 8. The whole of intellect is beauty. Why should this be so? Plato, of course, distinguishes the beautiful from the good, at least in terms of individual things, though the line between *kalon* and *agathon*, beautiful and good, as we saw above, is not easy to draw (cf. *Republic* 506 a; *Symposium* 201 b 10–c 2). The "Form of the Good" is the highest form beyond being and intellect in the *Republic*. The "Form of the Beautiful" is the highest form in the *Symposium*, though the question of the good is very much a part of Socrates-Diotima's speech (see 204 e ff.). Plotinus seems to hold a rather nuanced view of all this.' All this vagueness in Plotinus's language with regard to the One only seems to highlight its ineffable, unspecifiable nature, which defies all naming, as Plotinus repeatedly points out.

The ontological priority of the Good over beauty is therefore clear: 'The Good itself does not need beauty, though beauty needs it. The Good is gentle and kindly and gracious, and present to anyone when he wishes. Beauty brings wonder and shock and pleasure mingled with pain' (V 5 [32] 12, A: 193). An Arabic paraphrase of this passage is found only in a truncated form in the *Epistle on Divine Science*, with the last two sentences missing: 'The Good (*al-khayr*) is prior to the beautiful (*al-ḥasan*), prior not in time but in truth and reality. In the Good is all power. The power of the Good originated the power of the beautiful, being the cause of all things' (Badawī 1955: 182; cf. Plotinus 1977: 357). Thus the Arabic version reveals a divergence in terminology between Plotinus, the Arabic Plotinus, and Rūzbihān. Plotinus's contrast between the Good (*agathon*) and the beautiful (*kalon*) is presented by the Arabic Plotinus as a contrast between *khayr* (good) and *ḥasan* (good-and-beautiful), while Rūzbihān's contrast presented above is between *ḥasan* and *jamīl* (beautiful).[19]

While there are certain commonalities between Plotinus and Rūzbihān in their contrast of *agathon* and *kalon* on the one hand and *ḥasan* and *jamīl* on the other, ultimately these seem to constitute two different discussions. Plotinus's contrast between *agathon* and *kalon* seems to be primarily about the distinction between the two hypostases, the One and Intellect, the Good and the beautiful, or the indescribable and the intelligible. This particular contrast by Plotinus seems analogous to the distinction made between the unknowable essence of God and the knowable attributes of God in Muslim theological discourse. As for Rūzbihān's contrast between *ḥusn* and *jamāl*, both terms pertain to the intelligible realm, that is, the divine attributes – which may be compared to the intelligible Forms of Plotinus – rather than to the unknowable realm, namely the divine essence. *Ḥusn* and *jamāl*, however, belong to two different levels of divine attributes: *ḥusn* is an attribute of God's essence, while *jamāl* is an attribute of His act, as discussed earlier.

[19] *Khayr* has been the most common translation for *agathon* in Arabic philosophical texts (cf. Endress *et al.* 2018, s.v. *agathon*). As for *kalon*, the two equally common translations for it have been *ḥasan* and *jamīl* (Endress *et al.* 2018, s.v. *kalon, kallos, kalos*). In Muslim philosophical texts in Arabic, *al-khayr al-maḥḍ* ('the sheer good') is often used in reference to God, while non-philosophers rarely use this expression as it is an imported term originating in the translation movement from Greek into Arabic. The Qur'an does not call God *al-khayr* (cf. Gimaret 1988: 395), while it presents God to be the source of all goodness, e.g. 'In Your hand is the good (*al-khayr*)' (Q 3:26). In fact, the Qur'anic usage of *khayr* is more often in reference to a good deed of human beings or fortune befalling them, which is contrasted with *sharr* ('evil'), which can refer to an evil human deed or misfortune (cf. Izutsu 2002: 217–21). The fact that *kalon* signifies both moral and aesthetic beauty seems to indicate its greater proximity to *ḥusn* than to *khayr*. As Kuisma (2003: 44) points out, 'Depending on context, *to kalon* (and *kalos*) in Greek could denote divine or human beauty as well as ethical or aesthetic beauty … Modern readers should consider carefully which of these senses, or of their possible combinations, is at issue in particular classical texts. In particular, the ethical sense of *to kalon* is more fundamental than the aesthetic sense since ethical beauty (i.e., moral virtue) is good simpliciter, while aesthetic beauty is good on the condition that it is not against moral value.' If the three Arabic words, *khayr*, *ḥusn* and *jamāl*, were to be put on scales of the strongest to the weakest connotations of goodness and beauty, they would appear in the same order of *khayr*, *ḥusn* and *jamāl*, with the word on the far left having the strongest connotation of goodness specifically and the word on the far right having the strongest connotation of beauty specifically, with the word in the middle having both connotations equally.

If beauty is secondary to and derivative of the ultimate source of all, why did Plotinus and Rūzbihān spend so much time discussing beauty, urging people to turn their attention to it? Indeed, as Rist (1967: 64) points out, 'to choose Beauty over Goodness would thus be to choose something lacking the universality of Goodness and thus, relatively speaking, to choose the bad'. The key to this conundrum seems to lie in Plotinus's recognition of the different psychological effect that the Good and the beautiful have on human beings. He writes,

> But the Good, since it was there long before to arouse an innate desire, is present even to those asleep and does not astonish those who at any time see it, because it is always there and there is never recollection of it; but people do not see it, because it is present to them in their sleep. But the passionate love of beauty, when it comes, causes pain, because one must have seen it to desire it.
>
> (V 5 [32] 12, A: 191)

Corrigan in his study of this passage uses the expression 'the quiet presence of the Good' (2005: 30) to highlight the unperturbed nature of the Good, due to which it may remain 'unperceived' by human beings, in contrast to beauty, which is unmissable due to the astonishment and pain it causes to its perceiver.

Thus, Plotinus notices unique power of beauty. It is the very specificity of beauty compared to the all-pervasiveness of the Good that gives beauty the special ability to wake people up and pull them towards itself. Plotinus seems to be pointing out that everyone knows that goodness is good, but it is beauty that makes people take an action because it wakes them up by attracting them, causing in them passionate love, desire, pleasure and pain, unlike the gentle goodness, which often requires the full exercise of rationality for human beings to find it more appealing than beauty. Moreover, it must be noted that while goodness is primarily intelligible, beauty can be both sensory and moral (therefore intelligible), which implies its wider appeal.[20] Goodness quietly invites those with awakened intelligence to itself without perturbation, whereas beauty – while giving pleasure to its onlooker – *stings*, just like the rose. Rūzbihān too recognises the power of beauty (*jamāl*) in causing awe and fear along with passionate love, as we have seen already. There seems to be a 'sting' accompanying pleasure where there is beauty.

Perhaps it is the recognition of this power in beauty to bring both pleasure and pain to its perceivers that has led both Rūzbihān and Plotinus to talk so much about beauty – despite its ontological inferiority to goodness – in the hope that beauty will sting and awaken as many souls as possible to help initiate their movement, even just towards beauty in bodies, because both thinkers believed that if human beings truly sought beauty, they would eventually turn their gaze upwards.

[20] See Kuisma (2003: 162–3), who notes, 'In Plato's *Phaedrus* (246a–256d) beauty's unique position is praised in poetically exalted words, partly because its powerful influence can be captured through perception, i.e., through the sense of sight. Beauty can instantly arouse passionate love in human beings, whereas truth and goodness do not have a comparable magical power to affect people in their everyday lives. Human beings react to perceptible beauty and ugliness without volitional effort, but in the case of truth and goodness the situation seems to be different.'

References

ʿAbd al-Laṭīf, Shams b. Ṣadr al-Dīn Rūzbihān Thānī (1347sh/1969), *Rawḥ al-Jinān fī Sīrat al-Shaykh Rūzbihān*, in M. Dānishpazhūh (ed.), *Rūzbihān-nāma* (Tehran, Intishārāt-i Anjuman-i Āthār-i Millī), 151–371.

Adamson, P. (2002), *Arabic Plotinus: A Philosophical Study of the 'Theology of Aristotle'* (London, Duckworth).

Badawī, ʿAbd al-Raḥmān (ed.) (1955), *Aflūṭīn ʿind al-ʿArab* (Cairo, Maktabat al-Nahḍa al-Miṣriyya).

Baqlī, Rūzbihān [no date A], *al-Maknūn fī Ḥaqāʾiq al-Kalim al-Nabawiyya*, ed. ʿAlī Ṣadrāʾī Khuʾī, in *Kitābkhāna-yi Madrasa-yi Fiqāhat*, 2 vols (n.p.), accessed 31 January 2018, http://lib.eshia.ir/27484/1/255

Baqlī, Rūzbihān [no date B], *Manṭiq al-Asrār*, ed. M. Shahsavari (unpublished critical edition).

Baqlī, Rūzbihān (1974), *Kitāb Maṣrab al-Arvāḥ va huva'l-Maşhūr bi-Hazār u Yak Maḳām (bi-Alfi Maḳāmin va Maḳāmin)*, ed. N.N.M. Hoca (Istanbul, Edebiyat Fakültesi Matbaası).

Baqlī, Rūzbihān (1998a), *Kitāb Masālik al-Tawḥīd*, in P. Ballanfat (ed.), *Quatre traits inédits de Rûzbehân Baqlî Shîrâzî* (Tehran, Institut français de recherche en Iran), 167–90.

Baqlī, Rūzbihān (1998b), *Kitāb Sayr al-Arwāḥ*, in P. Ballanfat (ed.), *Quatre traits inédits de Rûzbehân Baqlî Shîrâzî* (Tehran, Institut français de recherche en Iran), 1–62.

Baqlī, Rūzbihān (1380sh/2001), *ʿAbhar al-ʿĀshiqīn*, ed. J. Nūrbakhsh (Tehran, Intishārāt-i Yaldā-Qalam).

Baqlī, Rūzbihān (2008), *ʿArāʾis al-Bayān fī Ḥaqāʾiq al-Qurʾān*, ed. A.F. al-Mizyadī, 3 vols (Beirut, Dār al-Kutub al-ʿIlmiyya).

Chittick, W.C. (2013), *Divine Love: Islamic Literature and the Path to God* (New Haven, Yale University Press).

Corrigan, K. (2005), *Reading Plotinus: A Practical Introduction to Neoplatonism* (West Lafayette, Purdue University Press).

Daylamī, Abū al-Ḥasan al- (1363sh/1984), *Sīrat al-Shaykh al-Kabīr Abū ʿAbd Allāh Muḥammad b. al-Khafīf al-Shīrāzī: Tarjama-yi Fārsī, Rukn al-Dīn Yaḥyā b. Junayd Shīrāzī*, ed. A. Schimmel-Tari (Tehran, Intishārāt-i Bābak).

Daylamī, Abū al-Ḥasan al- (2005), *A Treatise on Mystical Love*, trans. J.N. Bell & H.M. al-Shāfiʿī (Edinburgh, Edinburgh University Press).

Endress, G., Arnzen, R. & Arzhanov, Y. (2018), *Glossarium Græco-Arabicum*, accessed 9 May 2018, http://telota.bbaw.de/glossga

Ernst, C. (1996), *Rūzbihān Baqlī: Mysticism and the Rhetoric of Sainthood in Persian Sufism* (Richmond, Curzon).

Ernst, C. (1997), *The Shambhala Guide to Sufism* (Boston, Shambhala).

Gerson, L. (2014), 'Plotinus', in E.N. Zalta (ed.), *The Stanford Encyclopedia of Philosophy* (Summer 2014 Edition), accessed 31 January 2018, https://plato.stanford.edu/archives/sum2014/entries/plotinus

Gimaret, D. (1988), *Les noms divins en Islam: Exégèse lexicographique et théologique* (Paris, Editions du Cerf).

Gutas, D. (2007), 'The Text of the Arabic Plotinus, Prolegomena to a Critical Edition', in C. D'Ancona (ed.), *The Libraries of the Neoplatonists* (Leiden, Brill), 371–84.

Hamadānī, ʿAyn al-Quḍāt (1380sh/2001), *Tamhīdāt*, ed. ʿA. ʿUsayrān (Tehran, Manūchihrī).

Inge, W.R. (1918), *The Philosophy of Plotinus: The Gifford Lectures at St. Andrews, 1917–18*, vol. 2 (London, Longmans, Green and Co.).

Izutsu, T. (2002), *Ethico-Religious Concepts in the Qur'an* (Montreal, McGill-Queen's University Press).

Kuisma, O. (2003), *Art or Experience: A Study on Plotinus' Aesthetics* (Helsinki, Societas Scientiarum Fennica).

Miles, M.R. (1999), *Plotinus on Body and Beauty: Society, Philosophy, and Religion in Third-century Rome* (Oxford, Blackwell).

Murata, K. (2017), *Beauty in Sufism: The Teachings of Rūzbihān Baqlī* (Albany, SUNY Press).

Plotinus (1977), *Plotini Opera Tomus II: Enneades IV–V*, ed. P. Henry & H.-R. Schwyzer (Oxford, Clarendon Press).

Qushayrī, Abū al-Qāsim al- (2007), *Epistle on Sufism: Al-Risala al-Qushayriyya fi 'Ilm al-Tasawwuf*, trans. A.D. Knysh (Reading, Garnet).

Rāzī, Najm al-Dīn Dāya al- (1980), *The Path of God's Bondsmen*, trans. H. Algar (North Haledon, Islamic Publications International).

Rist, J.M. (1967), *Plotinus: The Road to Reality* (Cambridge, Cambridge University Press).

Satlow, M.L. (2008), 'Beyond Influence: Toward a New Historiographical Paradigm', in A. Norich & Y.Z. Eliav (eds), *Jewish Literatures and Cultures: Context and Intertext* (Providence, Brown Judaic Studies), 37–53.

Takeshita, M. (1987), 'Continuity and Change in the Tradition of Shirazi Love Mysticism: A Comparison between Daylamī's *'Atf al-Alif* and Rūzbihān Baqlī's *'Abhar al-'Āshiqīn*', *Orient*, 23: 111–31.

Walzer, R. (1962), 'Aristotle, Galen, and Palladius on Love', in *Greek into Arabic: Essays on Islamic Philosophy* (Cambridge MA, Harvard University Press), 48–59.

5

Ottoman Poetry: Where the Neoplatonic Dissolves into an Emotional Script for Life

WALTER G. ANDREWS

For reasons both topographical and temporal, the Ottoman Empire lies at a nexus where not only global East–West trade routes but major currents of thought, art and literary culture intersect. From at least the 15th century on, Ottoman poetry, as the dominant and central representative of Ottoman literary art, built upon the developed foundations of Arabic and Persian literatures in concert and contact with the burgeoning of Azeri and Chagatai Turkic literatures to the East. Its practitioners came not only from Anatolia but from Eastern and Central Europe, from Venice and Genoa, from Greece, from Iraq, the Levant, Egypt, the Persian-speaking East, the Crimea, the Caucasus and other reaches of an extensive empire, including those places that functioned as semi-permeable cultural membranes, where they lived in direct contact with Western and Asian enemies, friends and trading partners. Faced with a daunting cultural, social, ethnic, moral and spiritual multiplicity, the residents of the Empire at all levels found comfort and meaning in certain basic philosophical concepts naturalised in literary form.

1. Gathering the Threads

A significant amount of new work has appeared in recent years highlighting the impact of Neoplatonic-like mystical thought, practices and institutions on the development of pre- and early Ottoman Anatolian cities, governing organisations and social structures. In a tumultuous era beginning approximately in the mid-13th century, the decline in Selcukid rule over Anatolia and conditions in Central Asia and the Middle East created space for local powers to dominate city states that attracted populations fleeing disease, war and political upheavals elsewhere. Among these refugees was a significant group of wandering dervishes and mystical sages, who established religious, educational, health and social welfare institutions in parallel to and in competition with the traditional institutions of mosque and medrese.[1]

[1] See, for example: Wolper (2003), Goshgarian (2013).

Proceedings of the British Academy, **240**, 169–187, © The British Academy 2022.

Amid the welter of conversions, conquests, alliances, heterodoxies and syncretism that roiled Anatolia in the late 13th and early 14th centuries, the descendants of the warlord Osman set out on a path that would eventually lead to the establishment of a mighty empire. In an atmosphere influenced, if not dominated, by mystical thought with a Neoplatonic flavour, seemingly antagonistic confessional communities had begun to reflect each other and spiritual boundaries seemed less and less to resemble barriers. For example, Christian hesychasm, with its focus on the heart and inner peace melted into the mysticism of Ibn ʿArabī in a kind of Neoplatonic philosophical union, which, among other strands, interpreted on a popular level, helped usher former Christians and new Muslims into a rather syncretistic Muslim spiritual order.[2] This coalescence of spiritualities was supported and, indeed, driven by influential, primarily poetic literary developments in Persian, primary among them the work of Celâlettin Rûmî which had a powerful influence on the growth of Turkish as a literary language (Johanson 1993). As Selim Kuru (2013; 2016: 176) points out, the rise of Turkish as a literary medium occurred in a milieu in which there already existed:

> a strong tradition of sacred literature that reconfigured prevalent mystical ideas. The dream of a world beyond the grim living conditions appears to have had a strong grip on the authors' imaginations; in this context, the author acting as a seer re-evaluated older sources in order to reveal descriptions of a world beyond that otherwise remains hidden.

As Ottoman hegemony spread and Ottoman Turkish began to spread its wings as a literary language, the relation between this world and that (other world) took on added significance for both rulers and ruled.

2. Sultan and Poet

Sometime in the years 1481–2, immediately prior to his death (in 1482), Sultan Mehmed II, the Conqueror of Constantinople, sent envoys with lavish gifts to the famed Persian poet, scholar and mystic Câmî (al-Jâmî, al-Djâmî) in Herat in present-day Afghanistan, where he was one of the most brilliant stars in the firmament of the Turkic ruler Hüseyin Baykara's court. Over the years, Câmî had been patronised by Mehmed with gifts and invitations to visit Istanbul but had, perhaps wisely, declined – it being easier to visit a ruler's court than to leave it at will. This time, however, the Sultan had a specific request. He wanted Câmî, in his role as scholar and Sufi, to write for him a treatise comparing and critiquing the positions of the theologians, the philosophers and the Sufis on the Sciences of Reality (*ʿulūmu'l-ḥaḳīḳa*). In response to this request, Câmî complied with a treatise known as *ad-Dürretü'l-Fâḫirah*, *The Precious Pearl*, a concise adjudication addressing several issues from 'the nature of God's existence and its relation to His essence' to 'the emanation of the universe from God …'.[3]

[2] See, for example, Dedes (2016: 334–5) on the roles of mystical thought in the conversion of non-Muslim inhabitants of Anatolia and the influences of Ibn ʿArabî.

[3] For the English translation of this work, from which we have borrowed the story of Mehmed and Câmî, see Heer (1979: 3, 6–7).

This little vignette depicting an Ottoman monarch, at a foundational, transitional, imperial moment, seeking the counsel of a famed Persian poet, author and intellectual bound to the court of a Central Asian Turkic ruler, summarises the breadth, if not the total complexity, of influences on the culture of the Ottoman Empire in the early years of its rapid growth and maturation. We can imagine a host of questions at the core of the ruler's plea: how are we to ground spiritually our governing of a multiplicity of multiplicities? What does our present understanding of the nature of the cosmos and the relation of the Primal Intelligence to the actual observable material universe tell us about how to act in a complex and confusing world? How are we – both ruler and ruled – going to live and interact successfully in a large, growing and extremely diverse empire? What emerged from the turmoil of the time and place of its birth was an empire whose pragmatic answers to such questions allowed its inhabitants to live in relative peace and security within borders aggressively defended against powerful rivals. It is often difficult to perceive, through a haze of wars and political conflicts and uprisings, how philosophy and poetry (and music and art) contribute to the construction of a functioning state and to providing a grounding of beliefs about the self and the world that make that construction possible. But this difficulty does not mean that we cannot catch suggestive glimpses of how poetry works in the Ottoman world to transmute philosophy (and theology) into meaningful practice.

3. The World of Ottoman Poetry

By the latter decades of the 15th century and increasingly thereafter, the vast majority of Ottoman subjects – from high-level courtiers, officials and scholars to artisans, soldiers, bazaar workers and even villagers and common labourers – shared some level of awareness of a, to some extent, Neoplatonic set of general principles that inform and, in a sense, 'theorise' a personal relationship to the Divine, constructed, in large part, through the medium of poetry and the practices of Sufism as experienced in many settings, in many ways, by people in all walks of life. The ascendancy of poetry and its proliferation as both a passive activity (listening, reading, reciting) and a creative activity (composing, extemporising, writing), can be seen as, in part, the consequences of a dynamic tripartite relation – subsumed in Ottoman Sufism – among Neoplatonism as a theory of the origins and nature of material existence, Neoplatonism as a theory of human emotions, and poetry as Neoplatonic medium or language for saying things emotionally, rather than intellectually, rationally or logically.

The general principles or grounding philosophy of an enduring popular Ottoman Neoplatonism might be summarised as follows:

- The material, physical, visible, tangible universe/cosmos is the last (and most degenerate) of a series of emanations descending from a Primal Unity loosely signified by notions of 'God' or 'God as the (ultimate) Truth' (*el-Ḥaḳ*).

- Things of this world are imperfect, varied and varying analogues of ideal Forms existing in a 'higher' non-material and invisible world.
- Human beings are material receptacles for a spiritual (immaterial) essence (spirit/soul?) commonly understood as a detached/alienated 'fragment' of the Primal (and Eternal) Unity.
- Human beings can, through spiritual discipline, move in stages back up the path of emanation towards re-union with the Primal Unity, on the way discarding the individual and the material, including the very properties (the 'physics') of the material world, which also includes properties such as time, location, gravity (weight) and even vulnerability to physical ailments or injury.[4]

From these principles follow certain beliefs/truths about the nature and significance of emotions, including:

- The notion that what we *feel* is 'truer' or more accurate in relation to the higher planes of reality and the hierarchy of being than what we *believe we know* on the basis of our rationally constructed (visual, aural, tangible) experience of the material world.
- Feeling is prior to reason. Human beings apprehend the perfection of the ideal Forms by glimpsing and reacting emotionally to the reflection of the ideal in its material analogues perceived in this world.
- Our notion of physical beauty is a consequence of our (unconscious) perception of the spiritual perfection of the ideal Forms. Thus, what we experience as love, or desire, or longing for attachment inspired by beauty is, in reality (the real reality), longing for union (or re-union) with the spiritual perfection of the ideal Forms. Consequently, the path to union is open only to those who can achieve 'spiritual nakedness' by casting off all attachments to the material world, as Câmî says,

> Moreover the basis (*mustanad*) of the position taken by the Ṣūfīs is mystical revelation and insight (*al-kashf wa-al-ʿiyān*) rather than reason and demonstration (*al-naẓar wa-al-burhān*). For indeed since they have turned towards God in complete spiritual nudity (*al-taʿriyah al-kāmilah*) by wholly emptying their hearts of all worldly attachments (*al-taʿalluqāt al-kawnīyah*) and the rules of rational thought (*al-qawānīn al-ʿilmīyah*).
>
> (Heer 1979: 37)

[4] The tales of Sufi masters are filled with examples of adepts who overcame the bonds of time, place and physical limitation. Adepts fly on carpets, emerge unscathed from raging fires, and are even able to be in two places at once, for which see, for example, the story of Hajji Bektash (Ḫacı Bektaş) being present in Anatolia while saying his prayers in Mecca (Duran 2007: 470–8). On this see also the poem by Lorenzatos discussed by David Ricks in this volume (pp. 464–6).

4. A Dervish Poet: Ḫayâlî

Just how these general principles both philosophical and psychological, are enacted, rehearsed and constructed through the medium of love poetry is best demonstrated by looking closely at the poetry itself, to some extent, through Ottoman eyes. We will begin with a poem by a recognised 'dervish' poet to demonstrate overtly that even the popular understanding of a perceived 'essential' meaning of love and love poetry is constructed (however loosely) about terminologies, metaphors and practices of a generic (and 'genetic') Sufism as the Ottoman representation of a mystical perspective evolved over centuries in the religions and cultures of several languages. A quite famous court poet, during the reign (1520–66) of Sultan Süleyman, known by the penname Ḫayâlî ('the Imaginative', d. 1557), is an interesting and instructive case.[5]

The story of Ḫayâlî's life begins (*c.* 1500) with him living in the Macedonian town of Vardar Yenicesi as an emancipated (or orphaned) youth in his teens, with an educated interest in literature.[6] He became attached to a band of wandering Kalenderi or, more accurately perhaps, Hayderi dervishes in the role of 'the beautiful boy beloved' (*köçek*) who acts ritually as the focus of erotic desire and analogue of the ideal (Divine) Beloved.[7] When the band reached Istanbul, the dervishes' blatant public display of mystical eroticism and socially deviant antinomianism offended the authorities and Ḫayâlî was 'rescued' from the clutches of the dervishes and settled as the ward of a pious official, under whose guidance he was educated and launched on a social and literary career that would in time bring him – still identified as a dervish – into the circle of the Sultan and eventually procure him an administrative retirement position as a provincial governor.

Whether or not this little narrative is entirely 'true' or 'accurate', it does bring to the surface some aspects of the complex matrix of apparent contradictions that underlie the amalgam of Ottoman social, political and spiritual practices during the influential 'golden age' of the 16th century. For example, the fate of a youth, without family ties and attachments other than to a band of rejectionist, antinomian dervishes, who rises to prominence and influence at the court of the sultan, coexists with the power, in the same setting, of established ulema (educated elite) individuals and families and palace educated 'slave' (*ḳul*) bureaucrats. On a broader scale, this reflects the relatively unstructured (and often unsupervised), multiplicity of dervish groups, orders, lodges, retreats and shrines operating privately (or semi-privately) in parallel to the overarching institutions of public piety: mosque,

[5] For a brief introduction to the Antinomian Sufi groups to one of which Ḫayâlî was an adherent, see Karamustafa (2014).

[6] Andrews *et al.* (1997: 233–5); Owens (1971: f. 270b, l. 14ff.); Tarlan (1945: vii–xvii); Karamustafa (1994: 70 and 93).

[7] On the subject of the beloved in Ḫayâlî's poetry, see Andrews & Kalpaklı (2005: 138–40, 295–8, 324–8, 345–50).

medrese and judicial institutions. The interactions of these institutions are material, tangible manifestations of the uneasy coexistence of a social contract that, on one hand, enforces extreme modesty of dress, separation of the sexes and avoidance of behaviours that subvert public order while, at the same time, taking an ill-defined permissive stance towards socially deviant and often eroticised behaviours and practices grounded in mystical spirituality. The position of the sultan as Defender of the Faith requires walking a fine (and often shifting) line between the faith that grounds and supports order in the material world and faith in a spiritual perspective that rejects the ultimate reality of this world. The result is a widespread acceptance of the principle that 'being in the world' implies an essential 'doubleness', which naturalises an apparently contradictory (or, at times, even seemingly hypocritical) situation in which the defender of orthodoxy patronises a socially deviant rejectionist dervish with material rewards and the socially deviant, anti-materialist mystic accepts them.

4.1. Ḫayâlî's Poem

We will begin our exploration of this situation by 'unpacking' some of the condensed general understanding contained in a five-couplet gazel also called a *penc-beyt* (five-coupleter) by Ḫayâlî. The poem is centred thematically about the *redîf* (refrain word or phrase) *ṭaġıt* (following the complex rhyme '—*āmeyi*'). The poem[8] begins ()

> Oh decree of the beloved's young beard, broadcast the message everywhere
> 'The lovers are dead and gone', broadcast this tumultuous cry

Ṭaġıt is an imperative verb from a root that means, 'scatter, strew, cast off/out', which, by repetition, reflects a pervasive theme of 'achieving spiritual nakedness' by discarding – perhaps in an ecstatic, disorganised way – the objects, attitudes, perspectives, rules and roles of this material world. The first image in the couplet – the beloved's youthful ('peach-fuzz') beard – foregrounds a commonplace play on the word *ḫaṭṭ*, which means not only 'the young beard' but, more usually, 'writing in the Arabic script or something written in that script (a message, note, or royal decree)'. Thus, the boy's young beard (or decree) is the vehicle for broadcasting a message (*nâme*) saying, 'the lovers are dead and gone'. This may seem strange to us but the meaning would have been obvious to Ottoman subjects across the social spectrum.

A 'beardless' man, especially a handsome young man whose face sports a dusting of 'peach fuzz' – the youthful Ḫayâlî for example – was considered an appropriate object of sexual/erotic desire. An adult male, whose beard grows dark and full, was not. The message given by the beard/script and repeated/spread by the clamouring of disappointed lovers is that this beloved has started growing a man's beard and is no longer a permissible target for love/erotic desire – alas! The commonplace notion

[8] Tarlan (1945: 113–14); Çavuşoğlu (1987: 100–1).

of the lovers 'dying' for love and especially because of the unavailability of the cruel beloved, is given a new dimension, in the context of the beloved growing too old to be a legitimate love object, by a device, popular among the best poets, of letting an idiom be meaningfully read literally. Here the idiom 'işi bitti' (he died) which reads literally 'his business is finished' gives the reading 'the lovers' business is finished' or 'now that he's grown a beard there will be no more lover business with him'.

In our worldview, equivoques of the types 'writing/script, decree, peach-fuzz beard' and 'the lovers are dead/their business is finished' are often understood and described as 'word play' which is to say, less-than-serious rhetorical trickery.

In the Ottomans' generally Neoplatonic/mystical worldview, however, the 'slipperiness' of words, which can have two or more quite different meanings, is significant evidence or confirmation of the 'doubleness' of a cosmos in which every perceptible thing in this world has an analogue in another, more real, reality.[9] In Ḫayâlî's couplet, the confluence of rhetorical doubleness and cosmic doubleness produces a reading in which the 'decree' is the expression of a dominant social code which determines the erotic availability of a young man in this material world and the 'beard's transformation' points to a higher, spiritual plane on which 'love' (or erotic attraction) has matured to the point at which the 'actual' (less really real, this worldly) beloved is no longer necessary and must be discarded (cast off) in order for the lovers to attain the next stage in their spiritual journeys. In the first sense, the cries of the lovers are agonised wails of sorrow and disappointment, in the second, they are cries of ecstasy and joy. For those with esoteric knowledge, the greatest pain is the greatest joy. Loss and sorrow in this world are a token converted to gain and ultimate joy in the world of ideal types. Although each major feature of this couplet – the beard, beloved, message, lovers, outcry – is imbued with rhetorical doubleness, this is a doubleness that by the 16th century has been naturalised and assimilated to the extent that it is in no way as complex and puzzling to its audiences as it might appear to those outside the tradition.

> The mountain trees reached out branches to me and said
> 'Become naked for love, come to us and cast your garments away'

The second couplet, is, for Ottoman verse, rather straightforward. Yet, what an Ottoman would recognise immediately may still seem opaque to us. The poet/

[9] Julie Meisami, in her seminal study of Neo-Persian court poetry (1987: 30–9), includes a foundational exposition of what she calls 'the analogical habit of thought' (31), a perspective from which the structures of the universe can be visualised and understood as a pattern that repeats itself in its various parts and processes including the structures of human interaction. She makes the point that analogy is not the same as metaphor, that human interactions are not *similar to* or *like* cosmic interactions, they are directly parallel or comparable to them. In the end she points out (237–98) that the rift separating the analogical from the metaphoric makes lyric love poetry – ghazal – 'the most opaque and elusive of Persian poetic genres' (239), a description that could apply mutatis mutandis to the Ottoman gazel as well. The slipperiness of Ottoman (and Persian) gazel/ghazal poetry, the way it confounds attempts to categorise it as, for example, religious or secular, sincere or conventional, is one result of the analogical character of relations among hierarchical levels of cosmic individuation resulting in the material/sensible universe with which human beings interact.

dervish (or the one addressed by the trees) is in the mountains, which implies he is alone and secluded (he has cast off social connections in favour of solitary contemplation). It is autumn or winter because the trees are bare of branch, having already cast off the garments (the leaves) of spring and summer. In speaking to the poet/dervish they use the unmistakable terminology of Sufism, evoking 'naked for love' (*ʿuryân-ı ʿaşḳ*), which is Câmî's '(perfect/complete) spiritual nudity' (*al-taʿriyah al-kāmilah*) (Heer 1979: 37). We are to understand that the trees in autumn and the dervish achieving spiritual nudity are both pointing to the same underlying (or overarching) ideal. Here the material world is represented by the leaves on the trees, the garments that a person wears, and – in the context of the first couplet – the need for a physical beloved as the focus of love. Only by casting these off (throwing them away) can the ideal object of desire be approached.

> When the ideal alphabet[10] of worldly existence is but the truth of a dot
> O learned one, be wise and cast away both leaves and reed

In the third and middle couplet, the development finds an axis on which the whole poem turns. The language of the first hemistich evokes a host of potential references without absolutely fixing on any of them. There is a popular aphorism attributed to the Prophet's son-in-law Ali that goes something like this: 'All truth is in the Qur'an, the Qur'an in the "Opening" (*Fātiḥa*) Sura, the Opening Sura in the "*Bismillah*" ("in the name of God" which begins the sura), and the *Bismillah* in the "B" (of *Bismillah*), and the "B" in the dot under the (Arabic) letter "B" (ب)'.[11] This is surely a reference that would be widely familiar to Ottoman audiences. However, elite Ottoman poets seldom intended only the commonplace. So we must also keep in mind that the letters (*ḥarf*, pl. *ḥurūf*) of the Arabic (and Persian) alphabet(s) are considered to have magical properties, that the occult properties of letters can be used to reinterpret certain letter combinations and can be used for divination, and that the emanations which eventually resulted in the material cosmos were initiated by a word – 'be' (the Arabic imperative *kun*) of which the nominal is *kevn* (existence, being). Moreover, the notion that there is an ideal alphabet behind the letters of this world – the doubleness again – is reflected in the cabalistic aspect of mystical beliefs based on the understanding that God, the Hidden Treasure, revealed himself through the initiating Word, which consists of 'letters' (*ḥurūf*), each letter of the alphabet having a numerical value that can be used to calculate hidden interpretations of other writings or combinations of letters including those in the Qur'an. Hurufism ('Letterism'), the interpretation offered by the 14th-century mystic, Fażlullāh Astarābādī, suggested that this revelation was ongoing and embodied in human beings who, at a certain stage of 'casting off' attachments to this world, could say, with the martyr al-Ḥallâc, 'I am God'. Hurufism itself never developed into a major religious movement but its ideas still ran deep in popular Ottoman

[10] For 'hurufism', see Bashir (2005: 45–60, 69–74, 112–13 [dots], 116–17 [faces]).
[11] Ceyhan (2006: 402–98) and Çavuşoğlu (1987: 100–1).

mysticism and Ottoman poetry. Thus, the 'letters' of the Arabic script in this world are proportioned calligraphically on a metric based on the size of a 'dot' made by the broad-tipped pen used – for example, a letter will be so many dots high or long – and letters themselves are often distinguished from one another by a dot or dots above or below them.[12] However, in the world of ideal/real Forms the letter shapes that we can see written all over nature and, in the case of the Hurufis, especially on human faces disappear into the 'dot' or 'point' that is the source and Unity – the Truth – behind writing, language, and indeed all creation.

When one is an *'ârif*, a truly wise person or a gnostic who perceives the Divine intuitively, one ceases to need the 'letters'. One can discard the 'leaf' (*varaḳ* = both a sheet of paper, and the leaf of a tree, which connects this couplet to the leaf-divesting theme of the previous couplet) and the 'reed' (*ḳalem* = a reed and reed pen). Studying the truth in books or writing about it with the pen can be 'cast off/thrown away/scattered' in favour of experiencing the concealed Truth (el-Ḥaḳ or God the Truth) in one's own being.

Yet again, this seeming complexity is reducible to a few widely understood principles that integrate Neoplatonic (neoplatonistic?) and popular Hurufi perspectives:

- The double or multiple nature of language – that a word can point to quite different things – is not an accident but represents or points to a truth about the analogical nature of material reality.
- There is a 'truer' meaning to my life, my behaviour, and my feelings than is apparent on the surface (or absent interpretation).

The fourth couplet conforms to the concentric structure that we often see in Ottoman poems, where the first and last couplets, second and penultimate, and so on, match thematically around a transitional central couplet (here the third of five).[13] The lush, flower-filled springtime of wine-intoxicated conviviality of couplet 4 is matched and contrasted with the bare-branched spare, anchorite autumn of couplet 2:

> In the season of flowers, if the people beg a fatwa permitting wine
> Let a host of the greatest scholars scatter to every corner of this earth

Yet there is a progression in this poem that reverses the apparent contrast to reveal an overlay of congruence. The Ottoman would not miss the point, hinted at in the third couplet, that giving up or casting off the things of this world also means giving up, or reinterpreting on a higher spiritual plane, the rules of canon law and the social covenant. For example, drinking alcohol, including wine, is forbidden to Muslims by God. This is a prohibition that defines a God-given boundary (*ḥadd*) that no believer should cross. Yet, at one extreme of the quest for 'spiritual nudity', the Kalenderi-Hayderi and other socially deviant dervishes, including the band that brought the young Ḫayâlî to Istanbul, renounced the religious and social rules that

[12] Babayan (2002: 57–117) on the Nuktavi ['Dot-ist'] Sufis.

[13] On ring composition in Ottoman poetry and its Arabic antecedents, see Dedes & Sperl (2013: 249–50, 270–93).

manage life in this world and sought affirmation of their beliefs in being censured by the well-behaved and pious. For example, among other things, they shaved their beards, moustaches, heads and eyebrows, dressed immodestly in rough and skimpy garments. They intentionally avoided ritual ablutions and cleanliness in general. They did not fast, did not observe the times of prayer, worshiped beautiful boys, and drank wine. These behaviours are a material, this-worldly analogue of the spiritual station of those who are the 'greatest scholars', the 'wisest of the wise', the *'allâme* who have gone beyond or cast away learning, theology, and philosophy to experience directly the reality behind the appearances of this world. In such a state, these 'super-muftis' (wandering dervishes?) can scatter around the world to answer the people's call for springtime wine – the wine of spiritual intoxication (*sükr*) – by making it lawful according to the canon of the heart.

> Become king, Ḫayâlî, of the land of tranquil-mindedness
> With the sword of (holy) patronage, scatter the soldiers of blame

The final couplet, evoking the terminology of Sufism and the stations of the soul or self (*nefs*), closes part of a circle implied by the notions of *mebde'* and *me'ād* (مبدأ ومعاد), 'origin and return'. Simply put, the 'origin' is the site of the first emanation at which *ta'ayyun* or individuation from the Primal Unity of all being (God/Allah) occurs. The 'return' is the journey of the soul/self from physical embodiment back along the path of emanations towards dissolution in the longed-for unity. In its 'lowest' form the 'inciting' soul/spirit/self (*nefs-i 'ammâre*), driven by bodily urges, desires (or lusts after) evil destructive gratifications (forbidden food, intoxicating drink or drugs, sexual activity, cruelty, injustice ...). In the imagery of this poem, at this stage, the soul/self is crazed by desire for the beardless boy (the boy with *ḫaṭṭ* instead of beard) and some simply remain at this stage, looking for another object of sexual desire. Others recognise the lowliness and unprofitability of this kind of desire and seek a higher ideal object. At this stage, the soul/self is transmuted into the 'blaming, censuring' soul/self (*nefs-i levvâme*) which both desires and resists or blames those desires. This is the stage of the gnostic who becomes intuitively aware of the 'world beyond the world' and the need to divest oneself of all the 'covering' of this world. At this stage, the dervish will withdraw from the world to remove himself from its taint.

The final stage, that of 'tranquillity of mind' (*muṭma'inne*) is reached when the desires of the self and the desires of the Divine are so perfectly in accord that every thought, every action manifests the will of God. There is no more struggle, no more choosing, no anxiety of possibilities. This stage is reached through the aid of 'holy patronage, or concern, or gifts' granted by a mystical master.

At the surface level, this is all elementary Sufism – very nearly 'what every Ottoman subject knows about the progress of the soul'. What is easier to miss or ignore is how neatly what seems to be a pretty but minor poetic discourse on the mystical spirituality of desire aligns with some very this-worldly desires. Consider the story of Ḫayâlî's life-journey from dervish 'beloved' (*köçek*) to court poet and high-level administrator. The beautiful boy casts away his (remunerative?) role of love-object by growing up (growing a beard). He can only make his way by casting off worldly love, accepting his poverty and embracing the role of dervish. What turns his fortunes around is being discovered by the truly wise, those who have gone beyond book learning and appearances to recognise the spiritual beauty and God-given talent of the poet-dervish. The final stage of this worldly journey will be the patronage of the sultan, who can make a poet contented or tranquil-minded in a very material sense. The earthly journey is a distorted mirror of the spiritual journey and Ḫayâlî positions himself rhetorically as master of both.

5. A Scholar Poet: Caʿfer Çelebi

If Ḫayâlî could be considered a 'court dervish', Caʿfer Çelebi, whose poem we will take as our next example, appears to stand in stark contrast. Caʿfer was the son of Taci Bey, an Amasya notable and boon companion of the Prince Bayezit during his long governorship of the province prior to his accession to the throne as Bayezit II following the death of his father Mehmet II, the Conqueror, in 1481. Young Caʿfer received an excellent medrese education with notable professors and became a medrese professor in the provinces himself, until, aided by the patronage of Çandarlı İbrahim Paşa, an Amasya connection and former tutor to Prince Bayezit, he was appointed to a prestigious Istanbul medrese (1493–4) and subsequently to the powerful position of *nişancı* or Inscriber of the Royal Signature (*tuğra*) in the court of Sultan Bayezit. In his heyday Caʿfer was a noted poet and patron of poets, whose *meclises* (salons) were a stepping stone to popularity for many younger poets.

5.1. Caʿfer's Poetry

Far from being a dervish, Caʿfer was known (and censured) for being a 'lover of women', which implied an unredeemed carnality to his affections and love poetry that the typical homoerotic and 'platonic' love poetry of the educated elites and mystics supposedly transcended. The biographer of poets, ʿÂşıḳ Çelebi, in his 1566 biographical dictionary of poets, tells a revealing story about Caʿfer and Sultan Selim I, who himself composed a collection of mystical poetry in Persian. The anecdote translates freely as follows:

During a conversation with the late Sultan Selim, he (Caʿfer) even reportedly said: 'I am a denier of *ʿışḳ* (spiritual/(neo)platonic love); *ʿışḳ* is a fantasy and it is ignorant for people of intelligence to assert (the existence of) *ʿışḳ*'. The late monarch deigned to reply, saying, 'Don't swear (to that because it isn't necessary). Your denial of *ʿışḳ* and your not knowing what *ʿışḳ* is are obvious from your poetry, because in your poetry the flavour of *ʿışḳ* is non-existent' (Owens 1971: 61b, l. 18).

Some eight years after the appearance of ʿÂşıḳ's *tezkere*, the poet-biographer Laṭîfî issued a major rewriting of his 1546 biography of poets which included a greatly expanded Conclusion (*ḫâtime*) section containing a sustained critique of the Ottoman Turkish poetry of the day. He points out that, in all fairness, there are some Turkish-language poets who can be counted among the greats in the art of poetry like the noble ancestral poets (i.e. the Arab and Persian poets). But, nonetheless

> their verses, like those of the masters among the ancients, should (have) double meanings (should be *ẕū'l-vecheyn* = two-sided) and the union of opposites (*müştemilü 'ż-żıddeyn*), and their intent and wish and heart's desire (when speaking of) wine and tavern, the grape and the glass should be the attraction of their intoxication with divine love and their wine-worship of the glass of holy desire.
>
> (Canım 2000: 581)

He goes on to point out that it is clear that the poetry of many moderns lacks this doubleness and so cannot be read in a spiritually authentic way.

What is striking about both ʿÂşıḳ's anecdote and Laṭîfî's critique is the assumption that 'true' poetry has a recognisable mystical character with Neoplatonistic overtones and interpretations. Laṭîfî even suggests that the technical vocabulary of traditional rhetorical analysis is based to some extent on a mystical/Neoplatonic theory of the spiritual grounding of poetic language. Moreover, the fact that there is a discourse that asserts an expert ability to recognise when a love poem is spiritual and when it is not suggests that this is often a non-obvious distinction. That the distinction is understood to imply a value judgement – general in Laṭîfî's case, specific in Selim's critique of Caʿfer – says something about what the poetry is supposed to be when it is good or serious poetry. That these comments do not identify any particular features of the poetry that mark it as non-spiritual suggests that every poem ought to be read as a spiritual poem (as a Neoplatonic poem). The critique also implies that it is customary to read every love poem, however addressed, as a 'spiritual/mystical' poem.

5.2. A Love Poem by Caʿfer

Returning to Caʿfer's poetry, let us consider the following poem. In the light of ʿÂşıḳ's anecdote about Sultan Selim's critique and what we know about the context of this poem, it raises some interesting issues including its relation to the ubiquitousness of the Neoplatonic in Ottoman poetry.

Sometime around 1493, Caʿfer wrote his famous verse romance, the *Hevesnâme* (*Book of Desire*) in rhyming couplets liberally strewn with romantic lyrics (gazels).[14] Unlike the vast majority of romantic narrative poems in the Ottoman and Persian tradition, the *Hevesnâme* is clearly not a mystical (and, hence, Neoplatonistic) allegory. Rather, it is a tale set in contemporary Istanbul, ostensibly describing a young

[14] Sungur (2006). For a brief description and some translated excerpts from the *Hevesnâme*, see Andrews & Kalpaklı (2005: 180–7).

poetically inclined man (unsuccessfully) pursuing a love affair with an attractive married woman whom he encounters while picnicking in the popular nature park on the river at Kağıthane. In the course of his impassioned pursuit, the young man conveys and recites to his beloved a number of love poems, among them the following gazel, which we will examine in some detail.

First, we must be aware that when ʿÂşıḳ's anecdote appears in the second half of the 15th century some 50 years after Caʿfer's death, it adds a layer of some (retrospective) irony to this poem. Its *redîf* (post-rhyme refrain) is the very *ʿışḳ*/*ʿaşḳ* or '(Neo)Platonic love' that the Caʿfer of the anecdote denies and the sultan finds (sadly) lacking in his verses. In Caʿfer's narrative, the poet is young, callow and an object of mild derision on the part of some of his beloved's (female) companions. So, it is certainly possible, read in the light of ʿÂşıḳ's anecdote, that Caʿfer is poking fun at the poets of his day who have, perhaps naively or insincerely, become devotees of mystical/Neoplatonic love. This raises the question of why dwell on this poem out of the hundreds of thousands of indubitably sincere Neoplatonic-like poems that dominate the Ottoman tradition? The reason is to illustrate how Caʿfer wields the vocabulary and imagery of Neoplatonic love with great skill in a context intended to evoke a romanticised (and possibly satirical) verisimilitude. Moreover, this is a strikingly non-traditional, even non-spiritual verisimilitude in which the erotic element is sexualised rather than spiritualised by being aggressively hetero-erotic instead of reflecting the 'normal' homoerotic setting of Ottoman lyrics.[15] In Caʿfer's tale the only male character is the hapless lover. All the rest are women: the beloved, her attendants, protectors and companions. That the poet could mobilise the central discourse of Ottoman poetry in the service of subtle satire, is a vivid indication of how deeply naturalised the Neoplatonic psychology is in the 16th-century Ottoman Empire.

Caʿfer's gazel[16] begins with a typical evocation of love ([illegible]):

1 *ʿÂlem-i dilde ʿalemler ḳaldurup ṣulṭân-ı ʿışḳ*
Pâdişāh-ı ʿaḳl olupdur bende-i fermân-ı ʿışḳ
In the world of the heart
Banners were raised by the Sultan of love
The Monarch of reason
became a slave to the royal decree of love

The opening line (*maṭlaʿ*) is the restatement of a commonplace. Love is always a power. It is never gentle or kind except to vanquish. It is a warrior, a ruler, an unstoppable army, a lion, a flood, storm, catastrophe. As ʿĀşıḳ's contemporary Bāḳī says in his own ʿışḳ/ʿaşḳ poem:

Degme naḫcîrin şikâr itmez bu deştüñ şîr-i ʿaşḳ
Şîr-merdân-ı dil-âverdür yine naḫcîr-i ʿaşḳ[17]

[15] Heterosexual romances do occur in traditional Perso-Ottoman narrative poems, but these are overwhelmingly stories about rulers and dynastic concerns. For the sexuality of Ottoman poetry, see Andrews & Kalpaklı (2005: *passim*) and, more generally, of the Persian tradition, see Meisami (1987: 180–7).
[16] Sungur (2006: 255–6); Erünsal (1983: 287–8).
[17] Küçük (1994: 246).

The lion of love in this desert
    hunts no trifling prey
It is brave lion-like men
    who are the prey of love

Neoplatonic love is not for the weak or faint of heart. Those who believe that they are controlled by reason have never encountered 'real' love. Love defeats reason every time. Real (metaphysical) love is cataclysmic because it brings with it the realisation that it is grounded in something not accessible to the sense perceptions we are accustomed to relying on to build a rational world. It exceeds the beloved of the moment and this immediate experience. It is bewildering and terrifying. It is worth noting that in the context of the narrative, there is nothing dangerous or frightening in the fictional poet's situation beyond his own emotional hyperboles.

2 If union and separation
    are the same to me, no wonder,
How can he tell day from night,
    one bewildered and confused by love?

Union (*vaṣl*) and separation (*hecr*, *hicrân*) are key terms in the poetic vocabulary of Ottoman mystical love. 'Union', even in an erotic context, evokes the primal union for which the union of actual physical love is only a metaphor. Thus, for the poet 'metaphoric (*mecâzî*) love' is what we would call 'real' or 'earthly' love. In (Ottoman) reality, being human in this world means being fundamentally separated from what is ultimately real and true. Basic emotional needs for affection, for attachment, for belonging and seemingly unmotivated anxieties, for example, feelings of loneliness and alienation even when among friends or family, stem from the primal separation. In the context of this poem, it is impossible to say whether the poet marshals the discourse of metaphysical love to elevate the passions of a besmitten young man and the object of his affections, or to deride, from a materialist perspective, the absurdity of believing at all in the 'metaphysicality' of love, as ʿÂşıḳ's anecdote suggests.

3 At its table, the green vault of the heavens
    took the place of vegetables
When the feast of love was set for the lover
    in the gathering of eternity

In the world of Ottoman poetry, the social locus of love is a gathering: a (literary) salon, a party (*meclis/bezm*), picnic or feast.[18] Many or even most of the communal practices of Ottoman Sufism were analogues of the typal party including abstract rehearsals of love conversation, of experiencing overmastering emotional connection, of (spiritual) intoxication, ecstatic dance and (chaste) gazing at

[18] Andrews (1985: 143–74); Andrews & Kalpaklı (2005: 36, 63–84). For the history of the party/gathering in the Middle East, see Ali (2010).

beautiful boys.[19] Ottoman poetry revels intentionally in extravagant hyperbole, so even the most effusive imagery is practically impervious to being read as satire. Love always has its grounding in a cosmic connection and so is always, in some sense, above reproach. Nonetheless, this poem, unlike most others, is set in a narrative context that connects it also to a particular place and activities in the material world. In this case, the poet sublimates the activities of pleasure-seekers in the park by placing them in the context of 'love', which reinterprets seemingly 'normal' entertainment activities as spiritual experiences. In the following two couplets, the activity of boating on the river – which is how the picnickers travel to the park, is evoked by representing the heart as a helpless coracle drawn into the whirlpool of the beloved's dimple when battered by the turbulent ocean of love. Here we see basic themes mounting up: the overwhelming power of love, the helplessness of the lover, the connection between, say, a picnic and the endless sky, or between love and a limitless sea, or between the verdant meadow of the pleasure park with its sweet-smelling herbs and the beloved's captivating black and scented hair. Where love is in play the limits of the material world are no longer meaningful and a doubleness reigns, in which everything stands for something greater.

4. The ship of the heart fell into
 the whirlpool of the beloved's dimple
 When it began to be battered
 with waves by the endless ocean of love

5. Oh my beloved, this (world) is a meadow, where the heart,
 in a black passion for your locks,
 Blooms in every corner with hyacinths
 and the fragrant herbs of love

However, the lover's state is always fraught with danger and the promise of suffering. The true beloved is always a coquette, always aloof, always demanding sacrifice. The lover is always poised on the balance of heart and soul/life. To tilt the balance in favour of the heart's inaccessible desire is to sacrifice one's life, to cling to life (in the material world) is to sacrifice the true beloved and (re)union with cosmic, oceanic Primal Unity.

6. What they suffer, at every moment,
 is melancholy passion for stony-hearted loves
 The heart and soul have come to resemble
 scales on the balance of love

The true Ottoman lover, throughout centuries, celebrated the anguish of love by scratching bloody strands (resembling the beloved's hair) on the breast and branding it with a little roll of burning felt, scarring it with small circles or semi-circles (like the beloved's eyes and eyebrows). And those who see the lover's chest thus scarred might think that this is the image of the battlefield of love inhabited by the tents of

[19] 'Boy-gazing' is a long-standing and well attested feature of Sufism in the Islamic world; see, for example, El-Rouayheb (2005: 95–9 and 111–18).

rebels, because the lover in the throes of passion is a rebel against the propriety and modesty expected by polite society.

7. Those who see my breast say —
  imagining your lovelock and brows—
Filled with the tents of insurgents
  is the battlefield of love

So, perhaps those eyebrow semi-circles are not the tents of rebels. Perhaps they are polo mallets offered to those whose hearts are hardened by fear of public censure until they are like polo balls and impervious to love, so that they might drive this imperviousness from their lives and open themselves to love.

8. To drive the polo-ball of reproach
  from the soul, with the hand of desire,
Your eyebrows offered to the heart-less ones
  the mallet of love

At this point, if the preceding simple metaphors were not enough to imply a certain naivete, the poet's rather straightforward attempt to calm a skittish beloved seems to border on the risible.

9. I am a lover, do me a favour,
  as it is with the rest of my virtues,
Don't make a cause for anxiety
  and disappointment of the gnostic wisdom of love

He can be understood to be saying: 'You are not frightened or repulsed by the fact that I'm educated and a poet (and young and good-looking to boot) so don't be put off by the intense passion of my expressed desire. This is just the way that the Neoplatonic/mystical (non-sexual, unthreatening) love your beauty has aroused in me commonly comes out in poetic language. It's the way we poets talk about love.' And then he follows with an example.

10. See my heart, passionate for your cheeks,
  in the night of your lovelocks
Adorned with lamps
  of divine light is the shop of love

In this (spiritual) passion for the glow of her cheeks in the dark night of her locks, the poet's heart – the place where the business of love is transacted – is filled with the light of divine love the way that shops are adorned with lamps especially during the great religious festivals celebrating the Prophet and his message. In a sense, this is, on the surface – on the level of the jejune poet of the story – not an unusually complex or opaque metaphor. However, the way in which it 'Islamicises' the Neoplatonic cosmology and 'Neoplatonises' fundamental Muslim lore says much about the influence of Neoplatonic ideas on Ottoman poetry in a far from obvious way. From an Ottoman 'Neoplatonistic' perspective, the Ottoman poets and their audiences know that divine light, *nûr*, was the first material emanation of the Primal Unity. On the four 'Lamp Nights' (*ḳandīl geceleri*), this light and its emanation is made manifest in the Prophet, his conception, his birth, his night-time ascension and his recitation of Allah's decree (the Qur'an), all of which are represented metaphorically by the lighting with lamps of mosques and shops. The Prophet becomes the embodiment of the One, a living ideal form whose words (the Qur'an) and actions (the Hadith) represent the unmediated will of the Divine. In this sense, Caʿfer – the 'fictionalised' Caʿfer of ʿÂşıḳ Çelebi's anecdote at least – embeds a critique of pure Neoplatonistic thinking in which the material beloved acts as a bridge to the ideal of beauty when, in fact, love of the Prophet directs itself to the ideal without any need of a bridge.

11. Oh Caʿfer, this poem of mine
    Is a declaration of affection
For that rose-cheeked cypress,
    Whose rubric is the word 'love'

Caʿfer's poem – or the poem of the poet-hero of Caʿfer's narrative – concludes in what for an Ottoman poem is a decidedly straightforward, non-mystical statement about the purpose of *this particular* poem. It is a declaration of affection for a beloved entitled 'love' (recalling that titles are often written in red ink) and not much more, which fits the narrative context in which it is a poem composed as part of a planned seduction. One conclusion that might be drawn from this is that it is not possible for an author, at the turn of the 15th century, to create a believably realistic but fictional Ottoman poem that is not densely interpretable as Neoplatonistically spiritual.

6. Conclusions

It is difficult to be comfortable with reducing a discussion of Neoplatonism in Ottoman poetry to the analysis of two poems about love, one by a highly placed dervish poet and the other a poem ostensibly extemporised by a fictional lover in a rather humorous 'realistic' romance in rhyming couplets. This is especially difficult when considering that, in the early-modern Ottoman Empire, love poetry in various forms and genres was a major literary endeavour at all levels of society and that the output of this endeavour was prodigious for almost six centuries. Mystical spirituality, in the many guises of elite and popular Sufism, weathered the assaults of fundamentalist preachers and their adherents and endured right up to the great Turkish cultural revolution of the 20th century. When the sheer volume of Ottoman poetry brimming with Sufi or Sufistic tropes is combined with the widespread social practice of Sufi rituals and behaviours, it becomes easier to imagine how it is possible and productive to think of Ottoman life as being to a significant degree scripted by a mystical narrative influenced by or analogous to Neoplatonism.[20] The result was an attitude towards the world and an 'emotional ecology' that grounded the lives of individuals in Ottoman society.[21]

In the end, however, it would be misleading to say that Ottoman poetry can be generally interpreted in the context of 'Neoplatonism' without pointing out that the Ottoman Empire arose in an area long permeated not only by Hellenistic influences but by pre-existing layers of ancient Asian and Middle Eastern spiritual and mystical thought that constituted the soil in which the Hellenistic and Neoplatonic as well as the Judaic, Christian and Islamic grew.[22] In the early years of Western scholarship on the Islamic World, scholars in the West were drawn to seeing Neoplatonism writ large on the Islamic literatures because this perspective privileged a narrative based on the Hellenic roots of a dominant 'Western Civilisation'.[23] In the context of this publication, however, the term 'Neoplatonism' is used as a shorthand for a point at which a host of spiritual perspectives, both Eastern and Western, coalesce, confounding our drive to seek origins, to assert primacy, and perhaps even our post-modern reluctance to talk about universals.

References

Ali, S.M. (2010), *Arabic Literary Salons in the Islamic Middle Ages* (Notre Dame, University of Notre Dame Press).

Andrews, W.G. (1985), *Poetry's Voice, Society's Song* (Seattle/London, University of Washington Press).

Andrews, W.G. (2012), 'Ottoman Love: Preface to a Theory of Emotional Ecology', in J. Liliequist (ed.), *A History of Emotions, 1200–1800* (London, Pickering and Chatto), 21–47.

Andrews, W.G. & Kalpaklı, M. (2005), *The Age of Beloveds* (Durham NC/London, Duke University Press).

Andrews, W.G., Black, N. & Kalpaklı, M. (1997), *Ottoman Lyric Poetry* (Austin, University of Texas Press).

Babayan, K. (2002), *Mystics, Monarchs, and Messiahs* (Cambridge MA, Harvard University Press).

Bashir, S. (2005), *Fazlallah Astarabadi and the Hurufis* (Oxford, Oneworld).

Canım, R. (ed.) (2000), *Latīfī Tezkiretü'ş-Şu'arā ve Tabsiratü'n-Nuzamā* (Ankara, Atatürk Kültür Dil ve Tarih Yüksek Kurumu, Atatürk Kültür Merkezi).

Çavuşoğlu M. (1987), *Hayālī Bey ve Divānından Örnekler* (Ankara, Kültür ve Turizm Bakanlığı Yayınları 708).

Ceyhan, A. (2006), *Turk Edebiyati'nda Hazret-i Ali Vecizeleri* (Istanbul, Öncü Kitapevi).

[20] For a more detailed outline of how this scripting might be visualised, see Andrews (2012: 21–47).

[21] In this context, it is not surprising that, when Turkey turned away from the Ottoman Empire and Ottomanism, the new Turkish Republic outlawed the dervish orders and closed their lodges.

[22] An interesting example of this confluence of ancient Middle Eastern, Hellenistic and Islamic practices can be found in the first chapter of Ali (2010: 13–32).

[23] See, for example, Schimmel (1975: 3–22, and especially 8–12).

Dedes, Y. (2016), 'Bursa', in D. Wallace (ed.), *Europe: A Literary History, 1348–1418*, vol. 2 (Oxford, Oxford University Press), 331–46.

Dedes, Y. & Sperl, S. (2013), 'In the Rose Bower Every Leaf Is a Page of Delicate Meaning: An Arabic Perspective on Three Ottoman Kasides', in H. Aynur *et al.*, *Kasîdeye Medhiyye: Biçime, İşleve ve Muhtevaya Dair* (Edebiyat, Istanbul, Klasik), 240–313.

Duran, H. (ed.) (2007), *Hacı Bektaş-ı Veli: Vilayetname* (Ankara, Türkiye Diyanet Vakfı).

El-Rouayheb, K. (2005), *Before Homosexuality in the Arab-Islamic World, 1500–1800* (Chicago, University of Chicago Press).

Erünsal, İ.E. (ed. & introduction) (1983), *The Life and Works of Tācī-zāde Ca'fer Çelebi, with a Critical Edition of his Dīvān* (Istanbul, Edebiyat Fakültesi Basımevi).

Goshgarian, R. (2013), 'Opening and Closing: Coexistence and Competition in Associations Based on Futuwwa in Late Medieval Anatolian Cities', *British Journal of Middle Eastern Studies*, 40: 36–52.

Heer, N. (trans.) (1979), *The Precious Pearl: Al-Jāmī's Al-Durrah Al-Fakhirah Together with His Glosses and the Commentary of 'Abd al-Ghafūr al-Lārī* (Albany, State University of New York Press).

Johanson, L. (1993), 'Rumi and the Birth of Turkish Poetry', *Journal of Turkology*, 1.1: 23–37.

Karamustafa, A.T. (1994), *God's Unruly Friends: Dervish Groups in the Islamic Later Middle Period 1200–1550* (Salt Lake City, University of Utah Press).

Karamustafa, A.T. (2014), 'Antinomian Sufis', in L. Ridgeon (ed.), *The Cambridge Companion to Sufism* (Cambridge, Cambridge University Press), 101–24.

Küçük, S. (ed.) (1994), *Bāḳī Dīvānı* (Ankara, Atatürk Kültür Dil ve Tarih Yüksek Kurumu, Atatürk Kültür Merkezi).

Kuru, S.S. (2013), 'The Literature of Rum: The Making of a Literary Tradition (1450–1600)', in S. Faroqhi & K. Fleet (eds), *The Cambridge History of Turkey*, vol. 2 (Cambridge, Cambridge University Press), 548–92.

Kuru, S.S. (2016), 'Portrait of a Shaykh as Author in Fourteenth Century Anatolia: Gülşehri and his *Falaknāma*', in A.C.S. Peacock & S.N. Yıldız (eds), *Islamic Literature and Intellectual Life in Fourteenth- and Fifteenth-Century Anatolia* (Würzburg, Ergon Verlag in Kommission), 173–96.

Meisami, J.S. (1987), *Medieval Persian Court Poetry* (Princeton, Princeton University Press).

Owens, G.M. (ed.) (1971), *Mesa'ir üs-Şu'ara or Tezkere of 'Asik Celebi. Edited in Facsimile from the Manuscript Or. 6434 in the British Museum with Introduction and Variants from the Istanbul and Upsala Manuscripts* (London, E.J.W. Gibb Memorial Series 24).

Schimmel, A. (1975) *Mystical Dimensions of Islam* (Chapel Hill, University of North Carolina Press).

Sungur, N. (ed.) (2006), *Tācī-zāde Cafer Çelebi: Heves-nāme* (Ankara, Türk Dil Kurumu Yayınları).

Tarlan, A.N. (ed.) (1945), *Hayâlî Beg Dîvânı* (Istanbul, İstanbul Üniversitesi Yayınları).

Wolper, E.S. (2003), *Cities and Saints: Sufism and the Transformation of Urban Space in Medieval Anatolia* (University Park, Pennsylvania State University Press).

6

Mihrî Hatun and Neoplatonic Discourse: Legitimation of Women's Writing in Early Modern Ottoman Poetry

DIDEM HAVLIOĞLU

PLATO'S *SYMPOSIUM* IS set at a festive banquet during which exclusively male figures debate the meaning of love. After each of the notables has expostulated on love, Socrates explains that he himself learned the true meaning of love from a woman, Diotima, whom he defines as a wise woman 'about this [Love] and many other things', adding, 'she is also the one who taught me the ways of Love' (Plato 1999: 37). He relates that, for Diotima, Love is neither mortal nor immortal, but a spirit that falls between gods and humans. She teaches Socrates that the function of Love is 'giving birth in beauty both in body and in mind' (Plato 1999: 43). Furthermore, she adds that 'all human beings are pregnant in body and in mind, and when we reach a degree of adulthood, we naturally desire to give birth ... Yes, sexual intercourse between men and women is a kind of birth. There is something divine in this process, and this is how mortal creatures achieve immortality, in pregnancy and giving birth' (Plato 1999: 43). Diotima proposes reproduction as the human desire for immortality – the same applies to animals – and gives biological birth as an example of the desire to maintain one's existence. She then explains that maintaining knowledge, or studying, can also be a form of a desire for immortality. She compares the two types of pregnancy in human beings: 'Men who are pregnant in body are drawn more towards women ... Men who are pregnant in mind ... are pregnant with what it is suitable for a mind to bear and bring to birth. So what is suitable? Wisdom and other kinds of virtue' (Plato 1999: 46). She offers poets and craftsmen as examples of such men who search for beauty in other men, as women were not assumed to have such beauties, i.e. beautiful minds.

Feminist scholarship has taken issue with this point that Plato makes via Socrates and Diotima, which proposes that Love is the desire to reproduce beauty and that, although reproduction (a union of man and woman) and wisdom (a union of men) are both manners of reproducing beauty, the latter is ultimately superior. Some acknowledge the social context of Plato's proposition, which corresponds with the exclusively homosocial intellectual space of his time (Okin 1979: 15–70). Others, such as Keller, suggest that Plato's model can equally be applied to homosocial desire among women (1985: 21–32). Switching focus from Plato to the Neoplatonists, such as Plotinus, allows us to see that there are various interpretations of Love. Cooper discusses Plotinus' position on the human desire for regeneration, suggesting that, for Plotinus, pure beauty cannot be regenerated at all (2007: 87). Therefore, neither reproduction nor the homosocial desire for immortal wisdom can be achieved. Furthermore, as Cooper suggests, for Plotinus, 'the separateness of individuals is relatively superficial, arising at the level of bodies but disappearing at the level of the soul' (2007: 91). Cooper's understanding of Plotinus, whose commentary adopts a non-binary and gender-neutral thought, is the basis of my reading of Plato's representation of Diotima. Diotima's entrance into the conversation in *The Symposium*, even in the third person as a character in Socrates' story, is a crucial choice on Plato's part. First, it complicates the exclusivity of the male party. Second, she enters as a superior and a source of wisdom, hence a wise woman. Finally, although she seems to suggest that wisdom is something learned from men only, in reality she is the teacher of the wisest of men, Socrates. Thus, Plato implies the possibility of women's participation in the quest for wisdom.

Diotima's subject position as a woman points to a puzzle about Neoplatonism's development throughout history. A school of thought that evolved from Plato's dialogues and that spread around the world, Neoplatonism influenced a wide range of cultures, religions and literary practices. It appealed to many for its inclusive understanding of human existence: it introduced the idea of a unitary cause of reality and postulates that everything originates from a single cause, the One. Although some feminists suggest that such unity undermines individual differences, such as being a woman, recent studies of gender have shown that gender is a matrix and a social construct. Focusing on the difference of the binary category of 'woman' only reproduces the patriarchal system, which established the difference of woman based on her 'lack' of intellectual skills and her tendency towards the emotional. Time and time again, in every language and culture, these misconceptions have been challenged by women writers, poets and intellectuals as they have shown that intellectual capacities – or any other positive values exclusively attributed to men – are not innate qualities but could be acquired by anyone, men or women alike. Neoplatonic thought offers the possibility of steering away from this kind of difference between the binary categories of man and woman, as the One transcends categories. However, as we move into early modern times and examine the literary appropriations of Neoplatonism in different languages and cultures, there is a clear tendency towards a male-dominated literary discourse that systematically excluded women.

Here, I discuss the paradoxical theory and practice of Neoplatonism in early modern court literature, primarily the Ottoman Islamicate case, in terms of its construction of gender.[1] Merging with either Judeo-Christian or Islamic courtly

[1] I use the term Islamicate to indicate the influence of Islam in diverse literary and cultural expressions, rather than religious practice.

traditions, Neoplatonism was appropriated according to historical and local sensitivities. With this in mind, the best place to trace this divergence is in the works of women poets. While mystical women were accepted and celebrated, women who composed in the courtly tradition[2] were either excluded, discouraged or at most idealised as beloveds[3] in this prestigious literary discourse.[4] Although women might enjoy some limited agency and a temporary reversal of hierarchy in courtship as beloveds in European literatures (Dawson 2002), there are very few examples in which they took the role of the speaking subject/poet and composed poetry. The few cases that we have, however, imply the possibility of their participation.[5] To highlight their nuanced but ultimately subversive voices – subversive in that they summon the ideals rather than the practice of Neoplatonism – I will focus on the early modern woman poet Mihrî Hatun (d. *c.* 1512) and trace her ways of existing and surviving as a poet in a male-dominated literary world.[6] A close reading of her poetry reveals her awareness of the limitations imposed on a woman poet and the techniques that she used in her writing to demonstrate that these limitations should never have existed. The acceptance of her voice in the homosocial intimate literary spaces of the early modern Ottoman era (which were not usually open to privileged women) is evidence of the gender-neutral ideal of poetry.

In this volume, Julian Weiss discusses two Spanish women poets, Catalina Clara Ramírez de Guzmán (1611–*c.* 1680) and the Mexican nun Sor Juana de la Cruz (1651–95), alongside some of their male contemporaries, arguing that women poets refuse the 'masculine lyric discourse' and that they show 'the desire to escape the patriarchal constraints of femininity' that trap them in a silent and subservient role

[2] In this volume, Abigail Brundin discusses an early modern Italian woman poet, Vittoria Colonna, as the first published secular woman poet in Italy, highlighting the difference between religious and secular love poetry, in terms of women's access and production.

[3] Although the Neoplatonic discourse is ideally gender neutral, as Ann Rosalind Jones (1990: 1) explains, poetic discourses were constructed by and for male writers, and in their works women appear as silent objects of desire.

[4] Neoplatonic ideas were embraced in various Islamic traditions and evolved into mystical renditions of Islam that allowed everybody, including women, to participate in literary production. For instance, women poets like Rābiʿa al-ʿAdawiyya (d. 801) or ʿĀ'ishah al-Bāʿūniyyah (d. 1517) remained in the spiritual realm and sought agency through Neoplatonic ideals, such as sexual abstinence. They were not only allowed into intellectual circles but also celebrated. For a further discussion, see Yaghoobi (2017: 45–71) and Schimmel (1997).

[5] The reasons that so few women poets are found in both European and Ottoman literary history is addressed in Jones (1990), Andrews & Kalpaklı (2005) and Havlioğlu (2017). Courtiers, courtesans and concubines were always part of court entertainments. However, privileged women were not supposed to participate in these gatherings. If they did, they risked their reputation. By the 19th century, however, these unwritten rules had changed considerably, and women patrons held regular salons, for example Nigâr Hanım (1856–1918) or Leylâ Hanım (1850–1936) in Ottoman Turkey, and many other European women.

[6] I have written about Mihrî Hatun on many occasions, including in my recently published book (2017). Therefore, I will refer back to those earlier publications when necessary. However, I have not discussed her poetry in relation to Neoplatonism in detail, as I do here. The first poem I discuss has never been analysed and the second has never before been published in English.

(p. 345). Weiss focuses on portrait sonnets, a popular genre of the time, to examine women's criticism of the gendered inequality of poetic language. He demonstrates that women poets resisted and rose above the language that assigns women particular values and turns them into objects of desire.

Ottoman women poets followed a similar path to that of Ramírez de Guzmán and de la Cruz. They also resisted preassigned gender roles or the negative qualities associated with femininity, such as the lack of intellectual capacity or natural wickedness. Being aware of these conceptual obstacles in their way to becoming poets, these Ottoman women poets not only consciously attacked femininity as defined by male poets but also redefined it in their own terms.

We know of three women poets from the early modern Ottoman period, each of whom touched on the issue of femininity. Zeynep Hatun (d. *c.* 1450) is the earliest woman poet to appear in Ottoman biographical dictionaries. Although her poetry collection has not survived, a poem attributed to her contains the following couplet about the association of beauties of this world with femininity:

> Zeyneb, stop yearning for the frills of this world, like a woman,
> In the manner of men be plain-speaking, abandon all décor.

A poet should resist the beauties of this world, such as beautiful human beings or the illusory pleasures that distract the poet from their spiritual path. These temptations are associated with the female gender, considered to be beautiful on the outside but dangerous on the inside. Poets are expected not to fall into the traps of feminine beauty in order to prove their masculine resistance. This performative act is conceived of as courageous and is thus associated with the male gender. Zeynep playfully challenges this (mis)conception and asserts that leaving the beauties of the world behind is actually womanly. She attempts to prove that she is as good a poet as any of her male colleagues. To do so, she must redefine the feminine. Even though she is a woman, she is capable of leaving behind worldly temptations, and the fact that she could compose this couplet is proof of her claim. Like Diotima, she is the realisation of her own argument. This is a conventional technique among women poets: pointing to a gendered misconception and setting an example by doing the opposite of the gendered expectations.

Zeynep, Catalina Clara Ramírez de Guzmán and Sor Juana de la Cruz were all aware of the issues of gender disparity in poetic language. However, one clear difference between the European and Ottoman literary traditions is the lack of a clear gender for the beloved in Ottoman poetry. This lack of distinction means that said gender disparity is not immediately evident in the poetic language. However, Andrews and Kalpaklı have demonstrated that the beloved was accepted to be androgynous: a boy with no clear gender signs.[7] This is evident from the familiar trope of the beloved's growing of a beard – disqualifying him as a beloved and thus

[7] See Andrews & Kalpaklı (2005: 37) for a detailed discussion of the gender of the beloved in the Ottoman tradition.

causing agony for the poet.[8] Although the gender-neutral third person in Turkish, as in Persian, allows this ambiguity around the beloved's gender, the poet is almost always expected to be male. He proves his masculinity in his poems with a series of performative acts, such as resisting the feminine world. In short, the poetic tradition is constructed for two male characters: the poet as the speaker and the beloved as the silent object of desire. Therefore, it seems as though this poetic tradition had no place for women. Seen in this light, Ottoman women poets' resistance to femininity is understandable due to its negative associations, such as vanity, temporality and wickedness. Yet, interestingly, these women poets did not defy femininity by hiding their gender; instead, they challenged the negative meanings of femininity, redefining them by setting different examples.

1. Neoplatonic Influences in Islamicate Aesthetics

Before analysing the poems, a brief discussion of the major ideas of Neoplatonism and their reflection in Islamicate aesthetics will help situate my discussion of Mihrî's poetry. As mentioned in the introduction, the idea of the One as the origin of everything, rather than binary constructions, is the centre of my discussion of women poets and their appeal to this ideal. The influence of Neoplatonism on Islamic Sufism and its literary renditions and visual arts has been discussed by various scholars (Behrens-Abouseif 1999; Elias 2012; Gonzalez 2001). Going into detail about their historical interaction is beyond the scope of this chapter. It will suffice, here, to offer a few examples that highlight key concepts in my discussion.

Slaveva-Griffin (2012: 195) discusses Neoplatonic concepts of contemplation and ascent in her comparison of Plotinus and Rûmî. She suggests that the conceptual foundation of the dervishes' whirling dance is contemplative and that it leads to transcendence. This is similar to Plotinus' idea of the ascent, as he presents music and dance as contemplative practices in the *Enneads*. The ascending journey, according to Plotinus, is a process of returning home after a period of wandering. Slaveva-Griffin brilliantly explains the whirling motion of the dervishes' dance as 'coming home', ultimately a metaphor for arriving at the One. The dance of the polarities, the heaven, and earth, the intellectual and spiritual all return to one another in the circular movement. She also suggests that, during his Sufi training, Rûmî would likely have been introduced to al-Ghazâlî, who attacked al-Farâbî and Ibn Sînâ for their affiliation with Greek rationalism but still adopted some ideas of Neoplatonism.

Rûmî's poems are the guiding force of Islamic mysticism, which was also the backbone of Ottoman poetry. Walter Andrews explains what he calls the 'Perso-Ottoman poetic tradition' as a reflection of the mystical Islamic 'understanding [of]

[8] In this volume, Walter Andrews (pp. 174–5) also explains the significance of the beloved's beard or lack thereof. He treats the beard as a script of love which dictates the permissible limits.

the role of human beings in a cosmic context'.[9] Poetry is the place where the negotiation between polarities – such as this world and that world, religious and profane, or self and other – occurs, and where the difference between them becomes less clear. As Andrews discusses in this volume (p. 175), the poet intends to construct a 'doubleness' to reveal what is hidden in the physical (this) world that is directly related to the spiritual (that) world. Therefore the poet's purpose – like that of the mystic – 'is to penetrate the veil of illusion woven by the inability of the senses and human reason to perceive beyond the physical world, and thus to experience the truth, the essence of existence, which is, in turn, the experienceable aspect of God' (Andrews 1985: 67).

Similarly, Sperl and Dedes (2013: 198) note that, according to the Qur'an, every created object is a 'sign', an *āya* (Turkish *âyet*), that points to the Creator. It follows that the poet or mystic intends to point out the 'sign' and take the audience to the real/hidden meaning of every created object. Sperl and Dedes further compare Islamic mysticism to Neoplatonism and argue that 'what they have in common is the notion that all manifestations of material reality carry within themselves the imprint of the heavenly power which brought them into existence' (2013: 190). Therefore, poetry can shed light on the true meaning of material objects. Furthermore, in the language of love, the beloved is the embodiment of all that is beautiful and is thus able to guide the poet in an illuminating path to the truth, to the One.

The idea of illumination appears both in Islamic mysticism and Neoplatonism. As Gonzalez explains, Islamic philosophers like Ibn Sînâ emphasise the principle of emanation in search of beauty and understand beauty as an ideal that can only be perceived with the spiritual light (2001: 12). God is the source of light, and beauty owes its existence to this divine source. As the widely known hadith reminds us, 'God is beautiful and loves beauty'. Similarly, al-Ghazâlî explains that beauty (*jamāl*) or ugliness (*qubḥ*) cannot be confined to sight but can be experienced by the heart (*qalb*) (Hillenbrand 1994: 225).

Behrens-Abouseif (1999: 26) suggests that, for al-Ghazâlî, 'pleasure is a form of cognition' and 'to enjoy is to know'. In other words, it is only possible to grasp true beauty with the eye of the heart. The intention of poetry is to lead the audience to this understanding. For this reason, early modern Ottoman poets do not set out to describe the material world, including the physical details of the beloved. Poetry thus encourages the audience to imagine a form of beauty that is ideal, known by each in their hearts alone. In fact, the depiction of the beloved is almost always in the realm of abstraction. Their appearance is described in terms of their moon faces or cypress-like swaying postures. This kind of ambiguity not only allows an unlimited imagination but also makes the boundaries between genders fluid.

In summary, the Neoplatonic influences on Islamicate aesthetics created an ideal environment for women poets. Poets were expected to achieve ambiguity in

[9] See Andrews (1985: 63). He refers to a wide range of sources, including Annemarie Schimmel's understanding of Islamic mysticism and its place in poetry.

their conceptualisation of male and female genders as fluid parts of a whole, or the One, rather than binary opposites. Because of the ambiguity of the material world, including the body and its gender, there was nothing theoretically wrong with a woman composing poetry. The idea that the beloved is ultimately God and that the love is Platonic presented an opportunity for women to be part of this poetic tradition.

However, when it came to courtly love, practice took precedence over theory. This is partly because poetry was not only a written art but also a performance that necessarily took place within a specific space. In the case of Islamicate poetry, this space was the *meclis*, while in the case of European poetry, it was the court or salon. Early modern poetry was not composed to be read silently or individually; rather, it was intended for performance in a semi-public space, in which myriad socio-economic dynamics were at play. An aspiring poet needed an invitation to prominent courts to prove himself or herself as a poet as well as to find patrons. This performative aspect of poetry is significant and was much more decisive in a poet's career than, for instance, education or family background, although these factors could be helpful. In other words, to become an Ottoman poet in the early modern times, one had to find a way to be included in the existing artistic, intellectual and social circles.

When we consider women in this milieu, it is evident that they faced social restrictions beyond the aesthetics of poetry. First, we must consider whether these circles were exclusively male or if they included both genders. According to Halil İnalcık (2011: 184), Ottoman entertainment courts sometimes included women who were slaves, but it was not considered acceptable for Muslim women to be part of any courtly gatherings. Although this restriction explains the lack of women in literary history, it does not help us to understand why we do have at least some women poets. Their existence hints at questions that are hard to answer: did some of these courtly gatherings include women? Did women have their own gatherings? We do not know for sure. However, we do know that some women were exceptional enough to become poets. Somehow, they managed to join the intellectual circles of their day, therefore causing both a spatial and conceptual rupture.

When Ottoman women took on the role of the speaker, they did something they might not have intended: they caused a transgressive intervention in the discourse of love. Although ideally, the beloved had no gender marks in Turkish, the conventions of love had been constructed for a male speaker. This was because male poets were overwhelmingly dominant in number and Ottoman poetry was primarily a homosocial male intellectual culture practised in the literary spaces. Therefore, a woman speaker/poet fundamentally challenged this system, as her gender was not expected to be included. If they had hidden their gender and taken male pseudonyms (like some women in the European tradition), they might not have mounted any challenge. However, Ottoman women poets kept their feminine names and, moreover, they engaged with gender issues in their poetry. In so doing, they challenged the meanings of both femininity and manliness and its association with the male poet.[10] On an aesthetic level, the reception of Ottoman women poets may have been related to the fact that manliness, although historically used to refer to men, was performative. As this was a male-dominated world, the language reflected its rulers. Consequently, all positive human attributes, such as courage and reason, were attributed to men. However, this did not mean that all men, simply because they were physically male, could be manly. Thus, a woman poet could make the argument in her poetry that she was more manly than those who did not have her courage and reason. Moreover, as Mihrî shows, a woman could fulfil the role of the lover or beloved as well as a man.

2. Actors of Love

Mihrî Hatun is the earliest Ottoman woman poet whose poetry collection (*divân*) survives to this day. She lived in Amasya, in Turkey, near the Black Sea. At the time, the city of Amasya was considered to be an intellectual hub of the Ottoman Empire. Additionally, it was a significant eastern province governed by crown princes, most of whom ascended to the throne. In Mihrî's lifetime, Amasya was governed by Bayezid II (1447–1512), who had strong ties with the heterodox religious communities of the city. Mihrî's own family were the founders of the Amasya branch of the Halvetiyye Sufi order. Her father was a poet as well, although his poems have not survived. Mihrî's poetry specifically reflects her ties to the influential circles in the city. Although information about her education is unknown, the biographical dictionaries are clear that she was never married. Other than the monetary awards she received from the palace for her poetry, we do not know how she sustained herself. We can assume that her privileged background allowed her to remain single, i.e. independent, and consequently, she could compose poetry and continue being part of the intellectual circles.

Mihrî's poetry gives a glimpse into the life of an early modern Ottoman woman poet. A close reading of her lines reveals her techniques for building a career in a male-dominated profession. Some of the strategies she used to intervene and insert herself as a woman actor were carefully calculated to allow her to remain as a marginal and subversive voice. The first poem I discuss here is a wonderful example of her poetic mastery in challenging one of the most distinguished poets of her time. The poem is in the form of a gazel, or lyric/love song, dedicated to Hâtemî. Hâtemî was the pen name of Mü'eyyedzâde Abdurrahman Çelebi, the boon companion to Bayezid II in Amasya, as well as Mihrî's good friend. According to the biographical dictionaries, Mihrî studied 'love' with Mü'eyyedzâde.[11] This suggests that she studied poetry with him, as he

[10] For a detailed discussion of the performative nature of manliness in Ottoman poetry, see Havlioğlu (2017: 116–27).

[11] For a detailed discussion of the way their relationship is depicted in the sources, see Havlioğlu (2017: 81–2).

was one of the most prominent poets and patrons of the time, although it might also mean that their relationship was romantic. Either way, it is clear that they knew one another and most probably both attended the *meclises* of Bayezid II when he was the governor of Amasya.

From Mihrî's poem, which is present in her poetry collection, we can assume that Müʿeyyedzâde had composed a poem for her (there is no record of it) to which she responded with her own poem. This was a common practice among early modern Ottoman poets, called writing a parallel poem [*nazire*], done either to honour or challenge one another. Even when poets did not specifically note the name of the poet in their parallel poem, they left obvious hints for the audience, such as using the same rhyme scheme or refrain word or working on similar themes. In this case, Mihrî specifically mentions Hâtemî's name, leaving no doubt that this poem was dedicated to him. It was not unusual for Mihrî to mention a man's name in her poems: she mentions many of her colleagues' names, doing so each time for a specific reason. She either claims a connection with a celebrity poet such as Hâtemî or Necatî or challenges a fellow poet like Makamî. As she performed her poetry, though, her existence challenged the core structure of the tradition of love. The following poem exemplifies Mihrî's intentional challenge to the homosocial aesthetics of poetry and her presentation of an alternative love between man and woman. The opening line declares that her beloved has sent her some verses that she treasures (Havlioğlu, 2017: 178,):

> As brilliant lyrics reached us from that beloved,
> so, Jesus-like, a breath of life reached my dead body.

Although she does not identify him as Hâtemî (until later in the poem), it is clear she knows this beloved, as she uses the demonstrative 'that' to refer to him. She considers receiving the poem from him so refreshing that it felt like Jesus's breath – the beloved's breath as the resurrection or new life is a common metaphor in Ottoman poetry – for her dead body. In this first couplet, Mihrî constructs the doubleness of the poem: the paradox of life and death or that of the seeming reality and truth. Although she is alive, she used to feel like a dead person. Similarly, words are not supposed to give life like breath, but in this case, they do as they come from the beloved. Moreover, the beloved's breathing life into Mihrî points to the ultimate source of breath as the divine essence which is vicariously present in the soul, *cân*, or the beloved. With these lines, she prepares us to be surprised at her play with juxtapositions.

In the second couplet, Mihrî introduces her unusual kind of love in Ottoman poetry. She makes a move common in Ottoman poetry, alluding to a classic love story: Ferhad (male) and Şirin (female):

> Your sweet (*şîrîn*) lip's Ferhad became crazy at heart for it
> He would give up life and this world but never give it up

As a poet/lover, she understandably compares her longing for the beloved's sweet lips to Ferhad's longing for Şirin. However, Mihrî's positioning herself as Ferhad complicates these lines when we later learn that the beloved is Hâtemî, an adult man. According to the traditional love story and its binary gender roles, Mihrî's role as Ferhad places Hâtemî, as the beloved, in the female role of Şirin. She depicts his lips as '*şîrî n la'lin*', 'your Şirin (sweet) lips', an apparent reference to Şirin. This is an excellent example of Mihri's reversal of gender roles in her poetry, and she continues with similar manoeuvres throughout the poem:

Parted from you, I bent my body like a signet
I was hit on the head by a stone of reproach made of coral

Here, she begins to leave hints that this beloved is Hâtemî by referring to the meaning of his pen name: '*ḫâtem*' means signet. She compares her body, consumed by the agony of separation, to a signet's round shape. This kind of dedication to love depletes the body and takes its liveliness away. Yet, as it loses its life and decays, it becomes truly beautiful. Her bent body is like a ring with a precious stone on its top, as his reproaches – precious stones – have hit her head many times. In other words, her body is now precious as it is wasted with love.

When the morning breeze comes to the rose-bed of your cheek, beloved,
The whole world smells sweet of hyacinth and sweet herbs

The fourth couplet is a classic courtship line in its reference to his cheek as a rose bed. The morning breeze – like the refreshing breath of Jesus – touches the beloved's cheek, making the whole world smell of the sweet aroma of roses and herbs. The hyperbole brings the micro- and macrocosm together, as the beloved's cheek means the entire world for her. This couplet also prepares us for the next line, in which she declares her love:

My dear, since I saw you, o lord of beauties, in your street
I have had no desire for Paradise and have given up beautiful boys

Since the day she saw the beloved in his neighbourhood, she has had no desire for Rıdvan, the angel waiting at the heaven's door, let alone beautiful boys. The themes of life and death continue in this couplet as she finally comes to her point: she has no desire for '*ġilmān*', the youths of heaven, anymore. These *ġilmān* represent ideal beauty in the Neoplatonic sense and refer to spiritual or otherworldly love. Poets yearn for boys because they want to unite with the primal unitary, the One. In this couplet, Mihrî clearly makes the distinction between the boys and the specific beloved of this poem, Hâtemî, who is a real person, a grown man:

He is ignorant, vastly clownish and clueless
Who does not consider you superior to Selmân-ı Sâvecî

Even as he provokes her to forget the spiritual love of the poetic world, the beloved is noted to be a great poet who is much better than the legendary Persian poet

Selmân-ı Sâvecî (d. 1376). Ironically, the beloved's poetic abilities are not enough to make her forget material reality, and she reminds him and her audience of her passion for him. The play between this world and that intensifies in this couplet as she prepares to finish the poem with this statement:

> O Hatemî, you pose as a lover to Mihrî
> But, by God, she loves you better than any boy [would]

In the final couplet, which also includes the signature line – she leaves her pen-name here too – she clearly pronounces his name. It is a statement of worldly love, and she invites him to consider her as a real lover. With both of their pennames appearing in the same couplet, she suggests a union between this unconventional lover and beloved. She playfully accuses him of being pretentious in his poetic love for her in the poem to which she is responding. If he remained within the traditional poetic language in this missing poem, i.e. without any reference to her gender or name, she might have been understood by an audience to be a boy, as is expected from a traditional beloved. This kind of poetic love can be pretentious, but, she claims, her love, which is unconventional, is better and real. Therefore, she says, she loves him better than a boy would. She implies that a woman's love, even though it is conceived of as unworthy in this poetic practice, can be stronger and valuable. Furthermore, by taking a grown man as a beloved in her poetry, she also challenges the traditional conception of the beloved.

It is significant that Mihrî selected Hâtemî as a beloved for a poem in which she criticises the tradition of love and its exclusion of women. As we know that Mihrî and Hâtemî actually knew each other and were likely part of the same court, they are an excellent example of a man and a woman who could engage in the tradition of Neoplatonic love. She constantly twists the polarity between this life and that to prove the point that they are not separate from one another. The doubleness of this poem is evidence of her insistence that reality and imagination, this world and that, man and woman are part of a whole. Overall, with a basis on Neoplatonic ideals, she challenged not only the all-male culture of the poetic circles but also the aesthetics of poetry by reflecting a real-life relationship between a man and a woman.

As a lover, Mihrî also challenged conventional ideas about womanhood and femininity. She presented a new kind of woman who encompassed positive values associated with both the feminine and the masculine. This might seem revolutionary; however, she was not doing anything new. In the framework of Neoplatonism, she was only harking back to the ideal that opposites are part of the One. Perhaps for this reason, her poetry and presence were accepted and celebrated, not rejected.

3. The Last Word

The second poem I discuss appears in Mihrî's 461-couplet-long narrative (*mesnevî*) titled 'Tazarrû'nâme' ('A Humble Petition'). The narrative is an explanation of the reasons behind her engagement in poetry and a request for God's forgiveness. It was a common practice among poets to compose such appeals (*sebeb-i te'lîf*) to explain their involvement in seemingly questionable activities. One example of this is Enderunlu Fazıl's (1757–1810) appeal in his poem 'Zenânnâme' ('The Book of Women'), which classifies female beauties according to their race and ethnicity. As discussed above (p. 194) and by Walter Andrews in this volume, in the Neoplatonic love tradition, beloveds were expected to be male.[12] Because of this, Fazıl felt the need to explain the reasons behind composing such a book dedicated to women. As he writes there, it was not his choice to talk about women, but that he wrote the poem to please his patron (Fazıl 1839). While Mihrî does not seem to have crossed red lines in her poetry like Fazıl, her being a woman would in itself have been considered transgressive, meriting an explanation. However, a closer look at the poem reveals that this is another example of Mihrî's use of double meaning to deliver her message. Although the poem masquerades as a traditional appeal, Mihrî used this conventional tool to bring to the forefront specific topics that would not usually be addressed in such poems. In this poem, she calls attention to gender discrimination in the poetic world.

The poem remains true to the traditional aspects of a *mesnevî* narrative poem. There are sections with separate titles in which Mihrî discusses different subjects, such as a dedication to the Prophet and his four successors. The section I discuss here is titled 'Ḫâtime-yi Risâle' ('The Last Word').[13] In the first six couplets, she presents a prayer expressing her gratitude for being able to finish her poetry collection. She mentions that it was God's blessing that allowed her to complete this massive undertaking. It is evident from her writing that she not only refers to this specific poem but the collection as a whole, which must have taken years to finish. Then she adds that, with the help of God who 'put off [her] end', she was able to finish it while her mind was still working well. This and the next line (as well as the overall tone of this poem) hint that Mihrî may have been older while composing these lines. This is easily confirmed by a brief study of her life story.[14] Next, she states her intention for composing these lines and, most probably, all of her poems: expiating her sins as well as those of the readers and listeners. To accomplish her goal, she writes, she kept her poetry precise and clear. She asks that the reader be merciful as to its deficiencies.

After the opening lines, in the seventh and eighth couplets, Mihrî turns directly to the reader, to whom she refers as 'the excellent one', and leaves a clear message: she surmises that poetry, a human artefact, is inherently deficient.

[12] Walter Andrews (pp. 179–85) discusses another poet, Tacizâde Ca'fer Çelebi, who was known to be interested in women rather than young men. This was an issue that merited being addressed in biographical dictionaries.

[13] I have published the transcribed version of this poem elsewhere, see Havlioğlu (2007).

[14] According to the gift registry in Topkapı Palace she was granted monetary awards on five occasions between 1508 and 1512. I assume that one of these occasions was for the presentation of her poetry collection and it coincides with the end of her career. For more information about her life story, see Havlioğlu (2017).

Therefore, she asks her readers to show sympathy and reminds them that they have all the skills and power needed to understand her. It is not clear why she addresses her readers in this manner; however, it can be assumed that a reader who spent money on a copy of a woman poet's collection and spent the time to read it must have been considered exceptional. Knowing this well, Mihrî expresses her gratitude and bonds with her readers. She asks them to protect her from the ignorant ones who cannot understand a woman poet. Also, she leaves her mark on history from the ninth to twelfth lines (Havlioğlu, 2017: 95,):

> Since they say women lack reason
> All their words should be excused
> But your well-wisher Mihrî's notion is that
> He who is perfectly wise has this to say
> A capable woman is much better than
> A thousand incapable men
> A clear-headed woman is much better than
> A thousand muddle-headed men

These lines almost always appear in those biographical dictionaries that mention Mihrî Hatun. Their significance lies in Mihrî's attempt to undo or redefine a misconception about women: their lack of reason. As I have argued elsewhere (Havlioğlu 2017: 96), this statement is based on a hadith that appears in al-Bukhārī's *Ṣaḥīḥ*, which asserts that 'women are deficient in reason and religion'. This hadith was especially popular among those who wanted to prevent the education of women and their presence in the intellectual fields. The significance of this hadith for Mihrî is clear: as a poet, she had to deny it to be a legitimate member of the intellectual world. By composing these lines, she proves that she does not lack reason. Like Zeynep's lines, discussed earlier in this chapter (p. 191), Mihrî presents a problematic belief – even one based on a hadith – and proves by example that it is incorrect. In this way, she not only resists the negative associations with femininity that were tied to women, but she also redefines femininity through her actions. By completing her poetry collection and receiving monetary awards, she proves that this misconception is incorrect.

The comparison between men and women in the poem is carefully constructed. Mihrî does not compare just any men and women, but she deliberately contrasts an intelligent or clear-minded ('*ehl*' or '*zihn-i pâk*') woman with unintelligent or muddle-headed ('*nâ-ehl*' or '*bî-idrâk*') men. In other words, it is a matter of intelligence, not of gender, that makes a person worthy in the world of poetry. Ultimately, not all men are intelligent and thus accepted in the intellectual realm by their gender. As Diotima notes (via Socrates) in *The Symposium*, an intellectual has the desire for wisdom, and this manifests itself in expressions of love – in Mihrî's case, poetry. Being a poet means being a lover, and this has nothing to do with one's gender. However, it does relate to one's aspirations to wisdom.

From the thirteenth couplet to the end, Mihrî asks her readers to commemorate her with blessings as they read her lines. She writes that she makes this request because one can only be saved by the prayers of another human. Only then can a human find peace in the two worlds, earth and heaven. She predicts that, since she has now collected her poetry in written form, people will read her poems after her lifetime. In this, she was not wrong: for over 500 years, with these exact lines, she has had a place in Ottoman literary history. Her legacy, along with other Ottoman women poets, proved the legitimate place a woman could hold in the poetic world.

4. Conclusion

Plato's presentation of Diotima as a wise character and the source of Socrates's knowledge of love allows a gender-neutral reading of *The Symposium* in terms of the ideals of beauty and love. Furthermore, Diotima's existence in one of the major sources of Neoplatonism opens opportunities for women to be part of this prestigious literary discourse. Along the same lines, Mihrî's entrance into the Ottoman poetic world harked back to the gender-neutral ideals of the discourse of love, which had been practised only among men. Her poetry transformed the courtly codes as she took on the role of the traditionally male poet/lover. At the same time, she also played with the idea of the female beloved as an alternative to the idealised boy. Apart from the gender of the lover and the beloved, i.e. the main actors of the Platonic love structure, Mihrî brought another fundamental trait into the picture: wisdom or intelligence, suggesting the desire of wisdom as the source of Love in Diotima's discussion. Mihrî managed to twist this discourse in such a brilliant way as to be indisputable either in the poetic or intellectual world at large.

Later in history, women writers in the Islamicate world would develop similar strategies to make arguments for their inclusion based on the Islamic tradition. Mihrî's clear contribution to the Ottoman poetic world was her challenge to the gendered structure of the discourse of love and the attributes of femininity and masculinity. For this chapter, however, it is imperative to highlight the similar boundaries women poets faced in different cultures and with which they dealt using similar strategies, such as summoning the gender-neutral ideals of the Neoplatonic discourse. As I demonstrate in my readings of Mihrî's poems, this discourse gave women poets a rhetorical tool to challenge the prevailing gender roles in early modern court literature. Thus, one main reason for women poets' acceptance in early modern literary history was their ability to remain true to the Neoplatonic ideals of love, which could be used to generate a space for women's voices and agency.

References

Andrews, W. (1985), *Poetry's Voice, Society's Song: Ottoman Lyric Poetry* (Seattle, University of Washington Press).

Andrews, W. & Kalpaklı, M. (2005), *The Age of Beloveds: Love and the Beloved in Early-Modern Ottoman Culture and Society* (Durham NC, Duke University Press).

Aşık Çelebi (2010), *Meşa'ir'üş-Şu'ara*, ed. F. Kılıç (Istanbul, İstanbul Araştırmaları Enstütüsü).
Behrens-Abouseif, D. (1999), *Beauty in Arabic Culture* (Princeton, Princeton University Press).
Cooper, E.J. (2007), 'Escapism or Engagement? Plotinus and Feminism', *Journal of Feminist Studies in Religion*, 23.1: 73–93.
Dawson, L. (2002), '"New Sects of Love": Neoplatonism and Constructions of Gender in Davenant's *The Temple of Love* and *The Platonick Lovers*', *Early Modern Literary Studies*, 8.1, 4: 1–36, accessed 4 April 2019, http://purl.oclc.org/emls/08-1/dawsnew.htm
Elias, J. (2012), *Aisha's Cushion: Religious Art, Perception and Practice in Islam* (Cambridge MA, Harvard University Press).
Fazıl, E. (1286/1839), *Defter-i Aşk, Hubannâme, Zenânnâme* (Istanbul, Ali Rıza Efendi Matbaası).
Gonzalez, V. (2001), *Beauty and Islam: Aesthetics in Arts and Architecture* (London, I.B. Tauris).
Havlioğlu, D. (2007), 'Osmanlı Şiirinde Kadının Sesi. Mihri Hatun'un Hatime-yi Risale'si ve Necati'ye bir naziresi', *Journal of Turkish Studies* [In Memoriam Şinasi Tekin I], 31.1: 37–46.
Havlioğlu, D. (2017), *Mihri Hatun: Performance, Gender-Bending and Subversion in Ottoman Intellectual History* (Syracuse, Syracuse University Press).
Hillenbrand, C. (1994), 'Some Aspects of al-Ghazali's View on Beauty', in A. Giese & J.C. Bürgel (eds), *Gott ist schön und er liebt die Schönheit: Festschrift für Annemarie Schimmel* (Bern, Peter Lang), 249–65.
İnalcık, H. (2011), *Has-bağçede 'Ayş u Tarab: Nedimler, Şairler, Mutribler* (Istanbul, Türkiye İş Bankası Yayınları).
Jones, A.R. (1990), *Currency of Eros: Women's Love Lyric in Europe 1540–1620* (Bloomington, Indiana University Press).
Keller, E.F. (1985), 'Love and Sex in Plato's Epistemology', in E.F. Keller (ed.), *Reflections on Gender and Science* (New Haven, Yale University Press).
Okin, S.M. (1979), *Women in Western Political Thought* (Princeton, Princeton University Press).
Plato (1999), *The Symposium*, trans. C. Gill (London, Penguin Books).
Schimmel, A. (1996), *My Soul is a Woman: The Feminine in Islam*, trans. S. Ray (New York, Continuum, 1997).
Slaveva-Griffin, S. (2012), 'Contemplative Ascent as Dance in Plotinus and Rumi', in K. Corrigan, J.D. Turner & P. Wakefield (eds), *Religion and Philosophy in the Platonic and Neoplatonic Traditions: From Antiquity to the Early Medieval Period* (Sankt Augustin, Academia Verlag), 195–213.
Sperl, S. & Dedes, Y. (2013), 'Her Varak Bir Nüktedir Gülşende: Üç Osmanlı Kasidesine Bir Arap Bakışaçısı' ['In the Rose Bower Every Leaf Is a Page of Delicate Meaning: An Arabic Perspective on Three Ottoman Kasides'], in H. Aynur *et al.*, *Kasîdeye Medhiyye: biçime, işleve ve muhtevaya dair* (Edebiyat, Istanbul, Klasik), 188–314.
Yaghoobi, C. (2017), *Subjectivity in Attar, Persian Sufism, and European Mysticism* (Bloomington, Purdue University Press).

7

Poetry and Ishraqi Illuminationism among the Esoteric Zoroastrians of Mughal India

CARL W. ERNST

1. Plotinus on the Ascent and Descent of the Soul

> Many times it has happened: Lifted out of the body into myself; becoming external to all other things and self-encentered; beholding a marvellous beauty; then, more than ever, assured of community with the loftiest order; enacting the noblest life, acquiring identity with the divine; stationing within It by having attained that activity; poised above whatsoever within the Intellectual is less than the Supreme: yet, there comes the moment of descent from intellection to reasoning, and after that sojourn in the divine, I ask myself how it happens that I can now be descending, and how did the soul ever enter into my body, the soul which, even within the body, is the high thing it has shown itself to be.
> (*Ennead* IV 8 [6] 1, M: 334)

So begins the memorable treatise of Plotinus on the descent of the soul, experienced as a fall from its previous ascent, the classic formulation of a theme that is widespread in the history of philosophy and religion. To call it a Neoplatonic theme is perhaps a truism, but there are numerous other examples of similar narrations in the ancient world, ranging from the Hekhalot mysticism of early Judaism to the ascension of the Prophet Muḥammad into Paradise.

2. The *Unveilings* of Āẕar Kayvān

Here I would like to introduce a little-known text on the theme of ascension from a later period, the *Unveilings* of the Zoroastrian[1] mystic, Āẕar Kayvān (d. between

[1] The term 'Zoroastrian' here does not imply the ritual orthopraxy of modern Parsis, and indeed the followers of Āẕar Kayvān use the equivalent term *zardushtī* to describe a very limited part of the vast panorama of Persian mytho-history described in their texts; the main example is in Āẕar Sāsānī (1983: I, 72–118). I use it only as a shorthand to distinguish these non-Muslim Persianate loyalists, for whom Zoroaster was an exemplar, from other religious groups found in the Safavid and Mughal realms.

1609 and 1618), in order to interrogate its possible relationship to Neoplatonism. Born in Shiraz, Āẕar Kayvān inspired a remarkable intellectual and religious movement of the Mughal era, notable for its nostalgic imagination of the ancient Persian kings, depicted as ascetic philosophers who practised yoga; this vision was portrayed through the lens of the Ishraqi Illuminationism of the martyred Persian philosopher Suhrawardī (d. 1191), with attention to Ibn Sīnā's writings as well. Āẕar Kayvān's followers also engaged eclectically with Hinduism and Sufism, with frequent quotations from the great Persian poets by way of illustration.

2.1. The Style of the *Unveilings*

Positivist historians have rejected the Āẕar Kayvānī writings as fraudulent, condemning their imaginative reconstruction of supposedly ancient esoteric texts in an invented pure Persian language, but recent scholarship has begun to investigate the significance of this movement in its own right (Corbin 1987; Sheffield 2015). The poetic expression of this late Persianate mysticism is the *Unveilings*, in which Āẕar Kayvān recorded his ascensions through the heavens to attain union with God.[2] This is a poem of some 325 rhyming *masnavi* couplets, divided into four cantos entitled Splendours (*gashasp*), in keeping with the light imagery of Illuminationism. Each canto in turn has from two to 14 subsections called Brilliances (*furūgh*). The vocabulary of the poem is almost entirely in an archaic style of Persian, creating a notable aesthetic texture for a language that normally has a high proportion of Arabic terms. An exception is made for the Arabic titles of the four Splendours (possibly supplied by the commentator), which deal with the states of dream (*ru'ya*), absence (*ghayba*), sobriety (*saḥw*) and disrobing (*khal'*). The poetic text is accompanied by a prose commentary by a little-known author named Khudājūy ibn Nāmdār (literally, 'God-seeker son of Famous'), entitled, 'The Cup of Kaykhusraw', an allusion to the world-seeing vessel of an ancient Persian king.[3] This commentary provides helpful glosses on obscure Persian terms that are not to be found in ordinary texts, along with extensive explanations of the psychology and cosmology of the post-Ibn Sīnā schools of philosophy.

There are several formal aspects of the poetry which are not discussed in the commentary but which deserve recognition. First is the unmistakable use of rhyming couplets in the sonorous Persian poetic metre (*mutaqārib*) associated with the epic *Book of Kings* by Firdawsī (d. 1030), lending the poem an aura of seriousness and antiquity, not to mention Persian authenticity. References to Zoroastrian priests

[2] All references are to the *Mukāshafāt* of Āẕar Kayvān, the text embedded in the commentary of Khudājūy ibn Nāmdār & Qazvīnī (2012), cited by canto ('Splendour'), section ('Brilliance') and verse. Translations are mine unless otherwise noted.

[3] The commentator on the first page of his preface also refers to Āẕar Kayvān as 'the Kaykhusraw of heaven' and 'the Kaykhusraw of the spiritual world', adding that it was his son Kaykhusraw ibn Kayvān who gave the book its title.

and other Iranian themes enhance this identification. Second, the poem is narrated throughout in the first person, relating a series of cosmic and psychic voyages with remarkable imagery. Yet this account is relieved of monotony by frequent remarks addressed to a listener or listeners, who are invoked over 30 times in the course of the poem, mostly in the singular but sometimes in the plural. These formulas ('oh fame-seeker', etc.) have the effect of giving dramatic testimony of an extraordinary experience for which this audience will be the witnesses. Third, the language of the poem is cast in a highly experiential mode, with frequent statements that 'I saw …', and regular descriptions of 'face-to-face' encounters (*rū bi-rū*, I.3.7; an alternative expression is 'even with my (eye)brow', *barābar bi-pīshānī-am*, I.4.9, or *barābar bi-abrū*, I.6.3). In spite of the abstract and allegorical language of the commentary, the poem itself can be read as a complex expression of the dynamics of the ascent and descent of the soul. Fourth, the poem draws upon the language of hyperbole, uncountable numbers and the inadequacy of words to heighten the sense of transcendence that is apparent throughout the poem. Finally, it should be added that the couplets are not always complete units of thought, for there are many cases where the sense runs on into two or more verses.

2.2. Summary of the *Unveilings*

The trajectory of the *Unveilings* may be summarised as follows. The first canto begins by depicting the narrator in an ascetic retreat, which leads to visions of light (I.1.5–11, I.2), at first appearing before his face, and then going into his body and emerging from his chest. These visions are described in detail (I.3–I.11) as a sequence of colours: multicolour, blue, red, white, yellow, black and green. That list of colours, with some variations, is repeated in reverse order in the planetary ascensions of cantos II and III. Sometimes described as swimming or flying, the narrator moves from one level to another, encountering towns, people and fields. At each stage of this scenario, the narrator encounters ten thousand veils that radiate light of the appropriate colour. He is given untaught knowledge, his self disappears, and he becomes God.

In the next phase, canto II consists almost entirely of an account of ascension through the spheres, following the colour sequence: green, multicolour, white, yellow, red, blue, black. The commentary identifies these colours with the moon, Mercury, Venus, the sun, Mars, Jupiter and Saturn. In the narrator's account, each of these stages is a world in which the dominant colour is found everywhere, particularly in clothing. In each case, there is a monarch referred to by the Persian title Khusraw, enthroned in a palace. His attendants proclaim that he is God (*īzad*). Then, in a scene reminiscent of the Hymn of the Pearl, the narrator becomes the double of the King's minister and unites with him; then the two become separate. The sequence of union and division is repeated 100,000 times on the first level, the level of the moon. A similar story plays out at each planetary sphere, except that the number of unions and separations is increased by 100,000 at every stage, until at the sphere of the fixed stars, it reaches 800,000 embraces. The traveller continues to the starless heaven, encountering a black light that signals union with God; at that point, the narrator returns to his body.

The third canto proclaims at the start an allegory of the intellect portrayed as a city with a king, continuing on to describe the faculties of the soul and the internal and external senses according to the psychology of Ibn Sīnā (III.1–III.5). This account shows similarities to some of the philosophical allegories of Ibn Sīnā, such as the narrative of Ḥayy ibn Yaqẓān (Corbin 1990). Inevitably the descriptions of each level focus on kings enthroned in palaces. The narrator proceeds to visit a series of worlds with the same colour sequence as in canto II. Each of these worlds is populated by people having professions appropriate for the planet in question (e.g. soldiers are in the red world, which the commentary again identifies as the world of Mars). Again, the narrator is regularly led to the throne and placed upon it. At the end, he reaches the black world beyond the throne, disappears in God, and then returns whence he came.

Canto IV delivers once more the message of escape from the body, in a narrative that the commentary locates in the 'imaginal world'. After reaching the 'world of worlds', he makes a rapid ascent through the spheres in only a few verses (IV.3.1–8). At this point the text takes on a didactic tone as the narrator surveys the heavenly intellects and heavenly souls that drive the planets through the celestial realms. After closing this account on a note of esoteric secrecy, with further advice about escaping from the body, the narrator ascends once more to the heights where the souls, intellects and God may be encountered. Yet after becoming God himself, the narrator returns once more to his body, which he can exit easily when he wishes. Indeed, the narrator speaks like a prophet as he describes his disciples. At this point seeming to recall a sudden need for modesty, the narrator concludes by proclaiming the transcendence of God over all other things, for only God can praise himself adequately.

2.3. An Excerpt from the *Unveilings*

The style and tone of the poem can be grasped from the following excerpt, the fifth and concluding Brilliance section of the fourth canto ():[4]

I drew my soul running from the souls,
  I was running to angels and intellects,
I saw them increase beyond counting —
  for every thirteen one was produced.
In every sphere and star I saw
  A separate guard standing at attention,
Upon each element separately,
  but count that one as also connected.

[4] Āẕar Kayvān, *Mukāshafāt* IV.5.1–29, in Khudājūy & Qazvīnī (2012: 100–1, 103). Translation by the author.

For each thirteen there was a lord
  that I saw, and I told you something.
In them I became powerful like them,
  I became wise, aware, and knowing.
I knew all things in existence,
  I reached the angel of the great host.
When I found in him such sublimity,
  I blazed with glory from God.
When the spark increased, my ego left,
  neither angel nor demon remained.
From that I became God, and I was he —
  I was not I then, I was God.
There was God, and no sign of me.
  I had no consciousness, memory, or soul,
I found everything was my shadow.
  I radiated with the intellects of angels,
I was shining from the intellects on the soul —
  Read it so — even as far as bodies.
I so became everything as far as the earth,
  I saw nothing, great or small, but myself.
I was so powerful, wise, and sublime,
  until I came down from that station.
By the way I came, I went to the body
  with a hundred godlike glories of that company.
Now I am powerful in this world,
  adorning it and sometimes destroying it.
My body is no more than a garment for the soul,
  I have no companion or fellow in faith.
From the body I happily go to God
  and I return to the body, oh messenger.
When some of my happy upright disciples
  I sent to the transcendent world,
My disciples brought me the news —
  who possesses the royal glory like me?
But the lord has a station so high that
  a servant's nature should not deserve it.
Wisdom is by his light, as the earth to the sun,
  far higher than the nature of servants.
If the soul is illuminated by him,
  it leaves itself, unconsciously saying, 'I am!'
The world is a drop from the ocean of his existence —
  tell the droplets what their being is!
'You are not droplets of those drops, you are an even smaller drop!
  I don't know how to tell you that you are even smaller than that'.
From mercy he is generous to his servants,
  for the abject should be raised up.
He spoke to me freely and empowered me,
  placing the divine glory in me.
None is able to praise him save him,
  for he is not contained by any expression.

This text richly demonstrates the constellation of themes that this Zoroastrian sage invoked. The separation of the soul from the body is a recurrent and powerful emphasis, and it is depicted in terms of the cosmological theories of the post-Ibn Sīnā era, in which angelic intelligences are the sources of celestial movement. Characteristically, the author does not fail to conclude his text with a potent Iranian symbol, the 'divine glory' (*farr-i īzadī*) that forms the basis for the iconography of the halo.

3. Are the *Unveilings* Neoplatonic?

To what extent could we describe the *Unveilings* of Āẕar Kayvān as a Neoplatonic text? While the theme of ascent of the soul and descent into the body clearly resonates with the ideas of Plotinus, there is no overt engagement with Neoplatonic writings in this poem. To the contrary, the principal filiation that the author seeks to establish is entirely focused on Iranian sources, whether real or imagined. Indeed, the choice of poetry as the literary form for this text, emulating the rhyme and metre of the Persian *Book of Kings*, was in part doubtless inspired by the air of Iranian authenticity that would be projected by its recitation in the same majestic style, not to mention the archaic diction and use of arcane pure Persian words.

3.1. Philosophy According to the Dabistān

To consider more fully the possible relation of this text to philosophical antecedents, the most important evidence aside from the commentary consists of reader responses to the *Unveilings* in the remarkable comparative treatise on religious teachings, the *Dabistān-i maẕāhib*. This highly eclectic work was composed in the middle of the 17th century in northern India by a member of the Āẕar Kayvān group named Mīr Ẕūl-fiqār Āẕar Sāsānī, who also composed highly ornate Persian verses under the penname Mobad (meaning a Zoroastrian priest). As I have discussed elsewhere (Ernst 2017), the *Dabistān* used the language of universalism to advance a programme that drew heavily on traditions of Iranian revivalism, that for centuries nourished a series of anti-Arab revolts (sometimes connected to Shiʿism, as in the case of the Safavids). There were several examples of Persianate charismatic movements at this time in India, which received detailed treatment in separate chapters of the *Dabistān* (the Rawshaniyya followers of the 'Enlightened Master' Bāyazīd Anṣārī among the Afghans, the messianic Nuqṭawiyya with their message of occult-inflected materialism, and the Mughal Emperor Akbar and his millennial dispensation). But by the time the *Dabistān* was written, all of these movements had run their courses unsuccessfully, so Āẕar Sāsānī was left to contemplate the apparent frustration of their prospects. It is in this context that he gives us his own version of the history of philosophy.

The description of the philosophers is the eleventh out of 12 chapters in the *Dabistān*. It has three sections: (1) an account of the beliefs of the philosophers;

(2) the relationship of philosophy to prophecy; and (3) accounts of contemporary philosophers and sages.[5] The universalism espoused by the followers of Āẕar Kayvān was based on the premise of complete translatability, and the *Dabistān* frequently supplies ingenious equivalents of particular concepts in Persian, Arabic and Hindi. Thus, in the first of the three sections, on the beliefs of the philosophers, we are informed as follows:

> The great ones of this group are of two types, one the Illuminationists and the other the Peripatetics. The Illuminationists are also called Stoics, and in Persian 'the Splendid' and 'Lightning' and 'Enlightened Heart', and in Hindi 'Pure Mind' (*nirmal man*) and 'Master of Yoga' (*jogishar*); their path is asceticism. The Peripatetics are called in Persian 'Leader' and 'Seeker', and in Hindi 'Dialectician' (*tarkik*), and their path is thought and reflection.
>
> (Āẕar Sāsānī 1983: 316)

The teachings of the Illuminationists are held to be identical with the philosophy of the ancient Persian predecessors of Āẕar Kayvān. The *Dabistān* further stipulates that up to Plato, all of the wise men of ancient Greece were Illuminationists, but that with Aristotle and the Peripatetics the emphasis shifted to reason and logical proof. Nevertheless, we are told that both schools were in theological agreement about the transcendence of God and the nature of the divine attributes, and furthermore, that this inevitably leads to the emanation of the first intellect, the universal soul, and all of the technical details of cosmology normally associated with the philosophy of Ibn Sīnā. After this brief synopsis, the rest of this first section comprises a series of allegorical explanations of scriptural passages from the Qur'an in philosophical terms.

The second section of the chapter on philosophers consists of a presentation of the philosophical explanation of religion according to al-Fārābī and Ibn Sīnā, as a necessary fiction that will sustain public morality among the masses. It also includes the text of Ibn Sīnā's Persian commentary on the ascension of the Prophet Muḥammad (Heath 2010). The third section of the chapter introduces a series of individual philosophers known personally by the author of the *Dabistān*, who display a degree of eclecticism that it would be hard to find the equal of elsewhere.

3.2. Persianate One-Upmanship

With these preliminary remarks on the distinctive outlook of the followers of Āẕar Kayvān, it should come as no surprise to find that they were not particularly inclined to consider themselves as followers of Plato. From the patriotic Iranian position, they viewed the Greek philosophers as obviously derivative from the teachings of the Persian prophet, Zoroaster. The central scripture of the school of Āẕar Kayvān, the *Dasātīr*, in fact relates that it was none other than the great Greek philosopher

[5] Āẕar Sāsānī (1983: I, 315). For the authorship of this text, see now Āẕar Sāsānī (1393/2015).

Ṭūṭiyānūsh (Titianus) who sought out Zoroaster and imbibed his teachings directly, thus setting the stage for the rest of Greek philosophy. This was confirmed and approved by Alexander the Great himself (Āẕar Sāsānī 1983: 154–68). Those who might be sceptical of this account should also be aware that, in a very similar manner, a leading Indian philosopher whose name sounds very much like Shankaracharya likewise came to the feet of Zoroaster to receive his teachings. These reports of philosophical one-upmanship fall into the same category as the remark of al-Bīrūnī and Shahrastanī, that the philosophers of India had learned everything from Pythagoras; this claim was so annoying that Hindu intellectuals writing in Persian in the 17th century reversed this account and argued that it was Pythagoras who had gone to India to become a disciple of Vyasa, author of the Mahabharata. All this of course makes one think of the quixotic journey of Plotinus in the company of the Roman Emperor Gordian's expedition to Persia, in the hopes of learning Persian and Indian wisdom. And likewise there is the unfortunate event of Justinian's closing of the Platonic Academy in Athens, which led the resident philosophers to seek refuge in Persia; alas, they were disappointed by their reception and returned within a year. While those Greek gestures to Persia were not particularly fruitful, Suhrawardī insisted on a dual lineage for Illuminationism, going back to the Athenian philosophers and Hermes on one hand, and to the royal Iranian sages on the other. Āẕar Kayvān and his followers simply took the Persianisation of philosophy one step further. Henry Corbin has referred to this process as 'the repatriation of the Hellenized Magi to Persia' (Corbin 1971: 354).

3.3. Plotinus in Mughal India

Any description of Neoplatonism in India at this time would have to be considered somewhat attenuated, except insofar as the Illuminationism of Suhrawardī invoked prominent Neoplatonic themes. In Persian poetry, Plato was sometimes confused with the Cynic, Diogenes, and was described as living in a barrel; he was also viewed as a physician, to be mentioned in the same breath as Galen. While libraries in Persia contained numerous Arabic manuscripts of the writings of Plotinus known as the *Theology of Aristotle*, they were not as widely distributed in India.[6] Nevertheless, the author of the *Dabistān* refers to it (misspelling its title *Uthūlijiya* as *Usūlujiya* according to its Persian pronunciation) when he mentions that it was the deathbed choice of reading for the philosopher Kāmrān of Shiraz, along with the section on theology from Ibn Sīnā's *Healing* (Āẕar Sāsānī 1983: 338). Beyond Āẕar Kayvānī circles, Illuminationism was a focus of interest at the Mughal court, as seen in the Persian translation of Shahrazūrī's Illuminationist history of philosophy, commissioned by the emperor Jahangir, and in several commentaries on the works of Suhrawardī. It probably makes sense to speak of Neoplatonism as a

[6] The Iranian manuscript database Aghabozorg.ir lists 50 copies of the *Theology of Aristotle*, including copies of Ibn Sīnā's commentary on the text. Eight copies of the *Theology of Aristotle* in Indian libraries are described by Daiber (1986).

pervasive substratum of the post-Ibn Sīnā philosophical milieu of the Islamicate East, rather than as an orientation that one might choose or reject.

4. Other Poetic Texts of the Āẕar Kayvānīs

While the *Unveilings* of Āẕar Kayvān were quoted at length in the *Dabistān*, they were not the only venture into poetry by members of this group. Suhrawardī himself had composed a series of litanies in Arabic, addressed to the planetary intelligences, and these were still in circulation among the Āẕar Kayvānīs (Suhrawardī 1976: 483–92). Āẕar Sāsānī, author of the *Dabistān*, also composed a fair amount of verse in his *Dīvān*, found in a unique manuscript preserved in Patna (Askari 1977). While it has historical interest, much of it is very convoluted and idiosyncratic. Nevertheless, it may be worth quoting the author's favourite poem, a very bookish verse that occurs twice in his *Dīvān*, and which is also prominently quoted at the beginning of the *Dabistān* (Āẕar Sāsānī 1983: 3):

> Your name is the title page for children of the school,
> Your memory is night's candle for wise elders.
> Without your name, Persia has no taste for language,
> However much it knows the speech of Arabia.
> With your name, the bodily heart of devotee and mystic
> Is the peaceful ruler of the throne of the kingdom of delight.
> Every road I took connects to your address —
> You are the desire of existence, and you are the realm of desire.
> Mobad knows the knowledge, no other's known than this:
> God is your professor, and the world is your academy.

I will leave to others the task of rescuing this poetry from its well-deserved obscurity.

But a fundamental question remains regarding the *Unveilings* of Āẕar Kayvān. Why did he choose poetry as the medium for these revelations? And should the poem be regarded more as a record of his experiences, or rather as a programmatic mapping of concepts in an allegorical fashion? My feeling is that the poetry is important. The poetic medium in the style of the *Book of Kings* makes possible the rhetoric of intimate address, the hyperbole indicating transcendence, and the mystique of Persian kingship as a vehicle to finding the true self. Āẕar Kayvān's embrace of this poetic form to express his teachings moves in the opposite direction from allegory, which establishes a distance from a canonical text in order to read it in terms of an external reference. Of course, the poem was immediately subjected to an allegorical and systematic commentary, but that was perhaps inevitable.

5. Āẕar Kayvān, Ascension and Neoplatonism

And is there any point in calling the poem Neoplatonic? We have seen how remote this identification seems from the Āẕar Kayvānī project, despite the fact that

Plotinus was smuggled into the Aristotelian curriculum, and was therefore invisibly present in the basic architecture of knowledge.[7] The opening line of the poem (*Unveilings*, I.1.1) arguably refers to the realms of the intellect, the soul and the body, in terms that any Neoplatonist would understand, even if they are obscured by their archaic Persian vocabulary:

> In the name of the God who inscribed the intellect (*bahman*),
> created the soul (*ravān*), and raised up the body (*tana*) —

So the term Neoplatonic does not identify anything particularly typical about Āẕar Kayvān and his *Unveilings*. A brief comparison with another ascension text from Mughal India helps to clarify what actually makes Āẕar Kayvān distinctive. The example I have in mind is a meditative practice of an important Sufi master of the 16th century, Muḥammad Ghawth Gwāliyārī (1500–63), called the Nine Lodges.[8] This is a visualisation of a journey through nine planetary and astral realms, with obvious formal similarities to the accounts of Āẕar Kayvān. Yet the goals of the two texts are quite different. In the case of the Sufi formulation, the purpose is initiatic; at every level, the wayfarer meets the reigning angelic presence, and various prophets inform him that he is accepted by God and that his name is recorded in the Preserved Tablet of destiny. This experience in effect brings the individual into the full cosmic connections of a Sufi order. In contrast, the experiences of the Āẕar Kayvān journey present a vision of the self, expressed in royal archetypes, depicted as a series of unions with angelic intelligences or with God directly. While a number of the same basic ideas here are also found in Neoplatonism, introducing the term does not provide any particular analytical help towards understanding the text.

6. Contemporary Appeal of the *Unveilings*

What about the current status of the text? After the Persianate restoration failed to occur in Mughal India, the texts of the Āẕar Kayvān movement found unexpected supporters in British Orientalists like Sir William Jones, who saw the universalism of the *Dabistān* as the key to understanding Asia. This culminated in the 1843 publication of an English translation of the *Dabistān*, which was of such stupendously bad quality as to amount to malpractice.[9] Leaders of the Parsi community in the 19th century sponsored publication of the Persian texts of the *Dasātīr*, the *Dabistān* and the *Unveilings* of Āẕar Kayvān, and had them translated into Gujarati as well.

[7] The text from Plotinus (*Ennead* IV 8 1) quoted at the beginning of this chapter was prominently cited in the Arabic *Talwīḥāt* by the philosopher Suhrawardī (1993: 112), though it only describes the first part on ascension, and not the later descent. See also the same passage in the *Theology of Aristotle*, in Badawī (1977: 22).

[8] Ernst (1999: 72–5). While in that publication I attributed the text to a later author, Ismāʿīl ibn Maḥmūd Sindhī Shaṭṭārī, it turns out to have been borrowed from *Jawāhir- khamsa*, the popular meditation manual of Muḥammad Ghawth. See Anooshahr (2017).

[9] Ernst (2019).

This enthusiasm evaporated, however, when Parsi leaders realised that Europeans were beginning to view the texts as bogus. Inward-looking Zoroastrian priests rejected mysticism and focused on restoring definitive rituals. Any dreams of restoring Persian kingship in India seemed ridiculous. Nevertheless, the last Shah of Iran succumbed to that fantasy and attempted to cast himself as the champion of 2,500 years of Persian kingship. The film *Flame of Persia* (hubristically entitled 'Forūgh-i Javīdānī' or 'Eternal Splendour' in Persian), which recorded the ceremonies held in Persepolis in 1974 to celebrate this royalist achievement, is thick with irony in view of the revolution that would explode a few years later (Gulistan 1972). So, it might seem that the *Unveilings* of Āẕar Kayvān are just a historical curiosity at this point.

But the striking thing about archetypes is that they never go away. The text of the *Unveilings* upon which my translation is based is a publication printed in New Delhi in 2012 as a collaboration between two Iranian writers, Mas'ūd Riżā Mudarrisī Chahārdihī and 'Abbās Kayvān Qazvīnī. This critical edition is a considerable improvement on the 1849 Bombay lithograph, and it has been carefully collated with several manuscripts of the Persian text. Not only that, one of the editors is the son of a prominent writer on alternative religious movements (Nūr al-Dīn Chahārdihī, d. 1997), and both father and son plus co-editor Qazvīnī (d. 1979) claimed to be authentic living representatives of the teachings of Āẕar Kayvān. Qazvīnī, a former member of the Gunābādī Sufi order, had become a critic of institutional Sufism; he named himself Kayvān in honour of the Zoroastrian sage, and has written his own ascension treatise. All this information, including the text of the *Unveilings* and much more, is available in books advertised on their website razdar.com, the name of which means 'keeping the secret' in Persian.[10] In short, things seem to be looking up for this particular variety of ascension narrative, which is thriving more because of its Persian credentials than because of any overt Neoplatonic gestures.

References

Aghabozorg.ir. Accessed 8 January 2018, www.aghabozorg.ir/search.aspx

Anooshahr, A. (2017), 'The Shaykh and the Shah: On the Five Jewels of Muhammad Ghaws Gwaliori', in A. Patel & T. Daryaee (eds), *India and Iran in the Longue Durée*, Ancient Iran Series, vol. 3 (Irvine CA, UCI Jordan Center for Persian Studies), 91–102.

Askari, S.H. (1977), 'Dabistān-i Madhahib and Diwan-i Mubad', in F. Mujtabai (ed.), *Indo-Iranian Studies Presented for the Golden Jubilee of the Pahlavi Dynasty of Iran* (New Delhi, Indo-Iran Society), 85–104.

Āẕar Sāsānī, M.Z. [K. Isfandiyār, attr.] (1983), *Dabistān-i Maẕāhib*, ed. R. Riżāzāda Malik, vol. 1 (Tehran, Tāhūrī).

[10] Razdar.

Āẕar Sāsānī, M.Z. (1393/2015), *Dabistān-i Maẕāhib: Chāp-i ʿAksī-yi Nuskha-yi Khaṭṭī-yi Sāl 1060/1659*, ed. K.N. Barzigar (Tehran, Sāzmān-i Asnād va Kitāb-khāna-yi Millī-yi Jumhūrī-yi Islāmī-yi Īrān).

Badawī, ʿA. (ed.) (1977), *Aflūṭīn ʿinda al-ʿArab* (Kuwait, Wikālat al-Maṭbuʿāt).

Corbin, H. (1971), *En Islam iranien, aspects spirituels et philosphiques*, vol. 2, *Sohrawardi et les platoniciens de Perse* (Paris, Gallimard).

Corbin, H. (1987), 'Āẕar Kayvān', in *Encyclopaedia Iranica*, vol. 3, 183–7, accessed 8 January 2018, www.iranicaonline.org/articles/Āẕar-Kayvān-priest

Corbin, H. (1990), *Avicenna and the Visionary Recital*, trans. W.R. Trask (Princeton, Princeton University Press).

Daiber, H. (1986), 'New Manuscript Findings from Indian Libraries', *Manuscripts of the Middle East*, 1: 26–48.

Ernst, C.W. (1999), *Teachings of Sufism* (Boston, Shambhala).

Ernst, C.W. (2017), 'Concepts of Religion in the *Dabistān*', in C.W. Ernst, *It's Not Just Academic! Essays on Sufism and Islamic Studies* (Thousand Oaks, SAGE Publications), 437–62.

Ernst, C.W. (2019), 'The *Dabistān* and Orientalist Views of Sufism', in J. Malik & S. Zarrabi-Zadeh (eds), *Sufism East and West: Mystical Islam and Cross-Cultural Exchange in the Modern World*, Studies on Sufism, vol. 2 (Leiden, Brill), 33–52.

Gulistan, S. (1972), *Flame of Persia* (Tehran, Ministry of Culture and Arts, National Film Board).

Heath, P. (2010), *Allegory and Philosophy in Avicenna (Ibn Sīnā) With a Translation of the Book of the Prophet Muhammad's Ascent to Heaven* (Philadelphia, University of Pennsylvania Press).

Khudājūy ibn Nāmdār & Qazvīnī, ʿAbbās Kayvān (2012), *Nāma-i Jām-i Kaykhusraw, Sharḥ-i Mukāshafāt-i Āẕar Kayvān bar asās-i nuskha-yi khaṭṭī, wa Risāla-i Miʿrājiyya va Mavāʿiẓ*, ed. M.R. Mudarrisī Chahārdihī (New Delhi, Alpha Art).

Razdar. Accessed 3 September 2017, http://razdar.com/

Sheffield, D.J. (2015), 'Primary Sources: New Persian', in M. Stausberg & Y.S.-D. Vevaina (eds), *The Wiley Blackwell Companion to Zoroastrianism* (London, Wiley Blackwell), 529–42.

Suhrawardī, Shihāboddīn Yaḥyā (1976), *L'Archange empourpré: quinze traités et récits mystiques*, trans. H. Corbin (Paris, Fayard).

Suhrawardī, Shihāb al-Dīn (1993), *Majmūʿa-i Muṣannafāt-i Shaykh Ishrāq*, ed. H. Corbin, vol. 1 (Tehran, Mu'assasa-i Muṭālaʿāt va Taḥqīqāt-i Farhangī [Pizhuhishgāh]).

Part II

Jewish Neoplatonism and Hebrew Poetry in Muslim and Christian Realms (11th to 17th Centuries CE)

8

Andalusian Hebrew Poems on the Soul and their Afterlife

ADENA TANENBAUM

DURING THE 11TH and 12th centuries, Hebrew poets in Islamic Spain sought to capture the individual's quest for God in an intimate tone, using innovative imagery and potent new symbols. Spurred by a heightened interest in spirituality in the surrounding Islamic milieu, they infused the ancient, native Jewish tradition of synagogue poetry, or *piyyut*, with novel contemplative themes drawn from the Arabic philosophical canon. To accommodate these unprecedented ideas and motifs, they developed new genres which straddled the realms of the liturgical and the non-liturgical and which were conducive to individual reflection and private prayer, as well as to more traditional liturgical uses. Alongside this corpus, these members of the Andalusian Jewish intelligentsia produced philosophically informed Bible commentaries, ethical tracts and metaphysical treatises in Judeo-Arabic. They drew on Arabic-language works that had already filtered Greek philosophy and science through the monotheistic lens of Islam and thus helped to pave the way for the integration of the secular sciences into Judaism. In its exploration of inner experience, the Andalusians' contemplative poetry reflects a conviction that Greco-Arabic philosophy meshed comfortably with time-honoured Jewish approaches to prayer, spirituality and introspection. In particular, the poets adapted the cosmology and metaphysics of the late antique strain of thought that came to be known as Neoplatonism.[1]

The Neoplatonic idea of the soul and its odyssey captured the poets' imagination to such a degree that it came to occupy a place of paramount importance in their new type of verse.[2] It was a commonplace among medieval authors – Muslim, Jewish and Christian – that the human body is a temporary residence for the soul, whose real home is in the celestial realms. Often the body was portrayed not as a benign

[1] On the question of nomenclature, see Gerson (2011: 3): 'the term "Neoplatonism" … is an artefact of 18th-century German scholarship … intended mostly as a pejorative … It was assumed that "Neoplatonism" represented a muddying of the purest Hellenic stream.' Gerson favours the 'less tendentious' 'Platonism' or 'late Platonism'. See also Remes & Slaveva-Griffin (2014).

[2] For an example see the poem by Judah ha-Levi in [illegible].

Proceedings of the British Academy, **240**, 217–236, © The British Academy 2022.

inn, but as a sinister prison. The duality of soul and body was closely associated with a belief that the cosmos is divided into an upper world of unchanging realities and a lower world of unstable, ephemeral phenomena. Originating in the supernal realm, the soul was incorporeal and immortal. Its union with a mortal body was a result of its descent to the sub-lunar world of generation and decay. Human beings, then, were composites, containing elements of the physical and the spiritual worlds. Their bodily passions, if unchecked, might lower them into beastlike behaviour and the pursuit of meaningless, transient goals. But if disciplined, the soul could soar above the material world to regain the world of intellect and attain its absolute truths. Grasp of these truths represented the summit of human perfection.[3]

These ideas had their origin in the dialogues of Plato, whose theory of the soul was joined with elements of Aristotle's psychology in the writings of Plotinus, a 3rd-century Graeco-Egyptian philosopher (205–270 CE).[4] Although they did not know him by name, it was largely via his synthesis that the medieval writers acquired their views of body and soul and the duality of the upper and lower worlds. Plotinus was not an adherent of an established monotheistic religion, but with its quest for a unique transcendent entity his scheme lent itself to adaptation by monotheistic scholars. Indeed, Paul Fenton has noted that the Arabic text corresponding to the Greek Plotinus, particularly in its Longer Version, contains doctrinal interpolations more congenial to monotheistic sensibilities.[5] As a result, Neoplatonism penetrated Islamic, Jewish and Christian thought in the Middle Ages, partly by way of *The Theology of Aristotle*, an expansive 9th-century Arabic paraphrase of portions of the *Enneads*, pseudepigraphically attributed to Aristotle.[6] Following Plotinus, *The Theology of Aristotle* envisions the upper world as a triad of hierarchically arranged hypostases or fundamental realities. At the pinnacle stands the transcendent One, from which all existence and multiplicity emerge in stages. According to this theory of emanation, each successive order of being issues forth from one more perfect

[3] On the contrast between these two worlds in Greek thought, see Lovejoy (1964: 24–66).

[4] For Plato see especially the excerpts from *Alcibiades I*, *Republic*, *Meno*, *Phaedo* and *Phaedrus* in Flew (1964: 34–71). See also: *Timaeus*, 41D–42E, 69C–72D, 90A–D, and Lovibond (1991). For Aristotle see the selections from *De Anima* in Flew (1964: 72–81). See also: Jaeger (1962: 39–53, 331–4); Lloyd (1968: 181–201); Frede (1992); and Sorabji (1979). For Plotinus see: Armstrong (1940); Pistorius (1952); Rist (1967); Gerson (1994: esp. 127–63); and Blumenthal (1976).

[5] Fenton (1986) put forward the tantalising hypothesis that the Longer Version represents 'a recension of the work created by a circle of Jewish Neoplatonists' active in Egypt during the Fatimid period.

[6] One of the principal mediators of Neoplatonic thought to the Arabic-speaking world, the *Theology* was a product of the 9th-century translation movement that rendered Greek works of philosophy and science into Arabic. Although ascribed to Aristotle, the *Theology* is actually an expansive Arabic paraphrase of portions of Plotinus' *Enneads*, in which the order of the original Greek text is significantly altered. It is one of three collections that rework parts of the *Enneads* in Arabic; the other two are the text ascribed to 'The Greek Sage' and the *Epistle on Divine Science*. Taken together, these texts are apparently the remainder of what was at one time a complete Arabic version of *Enneads* IV–VI. See: Badawī (1955); Zimmermann (1986); Morewedge (1992); Goodman (1992); O'Meara (1982); and Armstrong (1979). Note that the *Theology* was unknown in the Latin West until the 16th century but a similar work, the *Liber de causis*, was influential already in the 13th century; see Kraye (1986: esp. 265, 275).

than itself, and all being flows ultimately from one perfect Source. From the One, the Universal Intellect (Gr. *nous*, Ar. *ʿaql*) and Universal Soul (Gr. *psukhé*, Ar. *nafs*) emanate in descending order. The Universal Soul is generally portrayed as the source of all individual souls, but sometimes human souls are said to originate in the Intellect. Either alternative implies that man's soul derives from the world of eternal and quasi-divine realities, and is therefore immortal itself. The lowest rungs of this hierarchically structured cosmos represent the material world of generation and decay. Though lodged there temporarily, the embodied soul, by means of profound reflection and purification from the defilements of this world, can shed its bodily frame and return to its supernal abode. Implicit in this gradated scheme of descent is the analogy between different levels of existence which allows lower and more mundane aspects of creation to mirror or parallel in their symmetries those higher and more perfect.[7] The notion that the universe is an organism underlies the Neoplatonic belief that man is a microcosm whose harmoniously ordered body corresponds to the physical world and whose sublime soul mirrors the spiritual realm. By knowing one's soul, therefore, one could come to know God. This idea reflected the metaphysical ideal of mimesis or assimilation, via contemplation, to a higher level of being.

The poets found many Scriptural passages suggestive of their philosophical conception of the soul. Even where the surface sense seemed to be in tension with their readings, they believed they were eliciting its deeper meanings and potentialities. They focused especially on verses in which the terms *ruaḥ*, *nefesh* or *neshamah* occurred. Connected etymologically with the notion of breath or wind, these terms overlap semantically. The most common among them, *nefesh*, bears a range of meanings: soul; a living being; life; the self; a person; the seat of the desires, appetites, emotions or passions.[8] Like *neshamah*, *nefesh* is grammatically feminine, and the Andalusians resorted to the feminine gender in personifying this abstract principle, often drawing on biblical love imagery to evoke the yearnings of the earth-bound soul for her celestial Source.[9] Post-biblical literature yielded brief, often anecdotal discussions of the soul, interspersed throughout the two Talmuds and a vast array of midrashic compilations. These rabbinic opinions are remarkably varied and lack all pretense to systematic exposition. Their heterogeneity reflects internal developments, some of which were the result of an earlier contact with Hellenistic thought.[10] In formulating their own views of the soul, the medieval Andalusians carefully took these sources into account. For more theoretical models, the Arabic philosophical sources available to them included not only

[7] See Sperl (2009: 461), regarding '(t)he analogical cosmology of the time which held that all parts of existence are mirror-images of each other on different scales'.

[8] See Brown *et al.* (1955: 659–61). For an extensive philological treatment, see Murtonen (1958).

[9] The noun *ruaḥ* could be either feminine or masculine.

[10] On changes in the attitudes towards body and soul in rabbinic literature, see Rubin (1989). On rabbinic treatments of psychology and eschatology see also: Hirsch (1947); Kohler (1918: 206–309 *passim*); Moore (1927: I, 445–59 and II, 279–395); and Urbach (1979: 214–54 and 436–44).

the *Theology of Aristotle* and related Arabic texts based on Plotinus, but also the *Epistles of the Brethren of Purity* (*Rasāʾil Ikhwān al-Ṣafāʾ*), the writings of Ibn Sīnā, and the work of the earlier North African Jewish thinker, Isaac Israeli (*c.* 850–*c.* 950). In addition, they drew on Islamic pietistic ideas, particularly as articulated in *zuhd* asceticism and its ramified corpus of sermonic *zuhdiyyāt* poems (Scheindlin 1993a; 1993b; 1994).

This convergence of biblical, rabbinic and Neoplatonic ideas allowed the poets discreetly to redefine some of the fundamental assumptions and symbols of classical Judaism. Their poems are preoccupied with the individual in a way that earlier Hebrew poetry was not, even though they do not emphasise subjectivity, and intentionally omit unique biographical details. But rather than an exclusive concern with the collectivity and its historical relationship with God, the new poems reflect an unprecedented awareness of the individual's spiritual quest and eschatological expectations. They convey startling new interpretations of what it means to serve and praise God, exploring the act of prayer as an expression of the soul's affinity with God. And they reveal a novel understanding of what is meant by ultimate recompense for living a life of piety. At times they betray unorthodox layers of meaning, equating the return and illumination of the soul with Paradise and ultimate reward (Altmann & Stern 1958: 192–3). Yet, even the poets' most daring innovations are couched in familiar, Scriptural language, and are successfully naturalised in their literary setting. Their verse achieves a spiritual potency that more discursive works would be hard-pressed to match.

1. *Keter Malkhut*

This new approach was pioneered by Solomon Ibn Gabirol (1021/2–*c.* 1057/8), a complicated, solitary, often acerbic, but acutely perceptive personality who was the first known Jewish philosopher in Spain, as well as a poet of exceptional sensitivity and range.[11] His monumental *Keter Malkhut* (*The Royal Crown*) is an unprecedented attempt to present a comprehensive, philosophically informed picture of man's place vis-à-vis God and the universe within a hymnic framework.[12] Meticulously constructed, *Keter Malkhut* correlates Neoplatonic cosmology and psychology with liturgical themes and classical Jewish dicta on the origin and nature of the soul; the relationship between the spiritual and the corporeal; and the status of the soul after death. Composed in rhymed prose and biblical diction, *Keter Malkhut* combines systematic exposition of highly technical ideas with sublime praise for God and penitential prayer. In his epigraph Ibn Gabirol describes the work as his own private

[11] For a brief, insightful portrait, see Scheindlin (2016: xi–xxv).

[12] There are several English renderings of *Keter Malkhut*. These translations are marked by notable differences of conception, form and diction. See: Zangwill & Davidson (1924 [1974]: 82–123); Lewis (1961 [2003]); Loewe (1989: 105–62); Slavitt (1998) and Cole (2001: 137–95). See also Tanenbaum (2000).

prayer, but expresses the hope that it will serve as a source of inspiration and instruction for others: 'May this my prayer aid mankind/ The path of right and worth to find.'[13] And while this profoundly moving work was eventually included in the Sephardic and Yemenite rites for the Day of Atonement, *Keter Malkhut* transcends the limits of prayer as previously conceived.[14] Its theoretical content springs from contemporary scientific investigation and philosophical speculation and can, in part, be correlated with Ibn Gabirol's Neoplatonic treatise known as *Fons Vitae*, a crucial conduit of psychological theory for the other Andalusians.[15] But unlike *Fons Vitae*, *Keter Malkhut* integrates philosophical conceptions into a devotional context, directly and deliberately translating speculative motifs into a more liturgical idiom. By means of this linguistic delicacy, *Keter Malkhut* subtly endorses the meshing of classical Judaism with elements of Neoplatonism, appealing to the philosophically sophisticated while minimising the potential for offending a non-philosophically inclined reader or worshiper.

Keter Malkhut is tripartite in structure.[16] Part One consists of nine cantos of exquisite praise for God. The first extols God's splendour, majesty and sovereignty over all His creations; acknowledges the recompense He has stored up for the righteous; and meditates on the riddles of His eternity and existence, mystery and transcendence. Marked by anaphora, each of the eight remaining cantos is devoted to one particular divine attribute: Unity, Existence, Life, Grandeur, Strength, Luminosity, Divinity, Wisdom.[17] Part Two, the most substantial of the three, is an expansive paean to God as Creator. Each of its cantos celebrates God's formation of one of the components of the universe and opens with a rhetorical question which implicitly contrasts human insignificance with God's limitless power: 'Who can tell Your mighty acts?'; 'Who can articulate Your grandeur?'; 'Who can fathom Your mysteries?' Here Ibn Gabirol traces the arc of creation by reversing the order of

[13] *Bi-tfillati yiskon gever/ki vah yilmad yosher u-zekhut*. For this translation see Zangwill & Davidson (1924 [1974]: 82).

[14] Though it is not clear that *Keter Malkhut* was originally intended for liturgical use, it was included in Sephardic *maḥzorim* from the early 16th century. According to Elbogen (1993: 294), it was incorporated into the Ashkenazi rite in the 17th century, under the influence of Lurianic mysticism. See also Langermann (2003b).

[15] This is not to imply that there is a precise or complete correspondence between *Fons Vitae* and the philosophical content of *Keter Malkhut*, but there are areas of congruence between the two. Moses Ibn Ezra's *Maqālat al-Ḥadīqa* concludes with a lengthy chapter 'On the Three Souls' (*fī 'l-nufūs al-thalāth*), which quotes liberally from *Fons Vitae*, albeit without mentioning the work or its author by name; see: Pines (1957–8), and Fenton (1976; 1992; 1997: 393–403).

[16] Part I: cantos 1–9; Part II: cantos 10–32; Part III: cantos 33–40. It is conceivable that the tripartite structure is on analogy with the recurrent motif of the triad in Neoplatonic cosmology.

[17] Alexander Altmann observes that Ibn Gabirol interprets negatively each of the affirmative attributes he ascribes to God. He notes that phrases such as 'You are wise … without having acquired knowledge from elsewhere' (canto 9) echo *kalām* formulations intended to counter the notion that God's attributes are distinct from His Essence. Ibn Gabirol's negative language is in keeping with the approach of Plotinus to the problem of describing an unknowable God (*Enn.* V 5 [32] 13); see Altmann (1966: esp. 40–6), and Sells (1994: 1–33). On the inclusion of Luminosity among God's attributes see Cantarino (1967), who argues that light occupies an elevated rank in the ontological hierarchy elaborated in *Fons Vitae*. Unlike the light of the sublunar world, this sublime light is incorporeal and 'partakes of the divine Essence' (1967: 61).

emanation, leading us straight down to earth and then ascending step by step from the sublunar world through the celestial spheres that surround it, painstakingly mapping the universe and magnifying God at each successive stage. This progression has a decided rhetorical function: by starting with the most mundane level of creation, the poet ensures that each veneration of God will be more exalted than the previous one.[18] On the surface, *Keter Malkhut* seems to reflect the accepted view of an omnipotent God who creates *ex nihilo*. Yet, upon closer inspection, it becomes apparent that the principle of emanation also plays an important role in Ibn Gabirol's cosmogony. Ever so discreetly, he subordinates the emanative process to God's will by making God the agent of the verb *aṣal*, whose meaning is 'to cause to overflow'.[19] The careful reader comes to appreciate the hybridity of this synthesis: by incorporating a volitional God who sets the creative mechanism in motion, Ibn Gabirol deviates from 'orthodox' Neoplatonism. Yet his use of the theory of emanation implies a thoroughgoing reinterpretation of creation as customarily understood.[20]

After reaching the outer limits of the physical universe, *Keter Malkhut* turns to the soul, which originates in the incorporeal sphere of the Intellect. Despite his generally negative view of embodiment, the poet here applauds the soul's divinely ordained mission to 'serve and preserve' the body (Canto 29) and to act as its moral guide (Canto 31). Continuing to ascend through the spiritual domain, we come to the Divine Throne. Here we find a striking reinterpretation of classical eschatology. In measured phrases whose regular rhymes and recognisable language belie their daring content, Ibn Gabirol explicitly identifies the rabbinic world to come (*'olam ha-ba*) with the immortality of the individual soul ():

> Who can equal Your almighty deeds?
> Beneath Your Throne of Glory You have made
> A place for all the souls of Your saints.
> Abode of pure souls,
> Bound in the bond of life.

[18] This progression is reminiscent of what Altmann & Stern (1958: 185–217) have called 'The Upward Way'.

[19] See, e.g., line 282: *ve'aṣalta 'aleha ruaḥ ḥokhmah ve-qara'ta shmah neshamah*. For similar usages of the root *'a.ṣ.l.*, see lines 78, 198–9, 204, 214 and 299. Two scriptural verses underlie Ibn Gabirol's formulation in line 282; these are Num. 11:17: *ve-aṣalti min ha-ruaḥ asher 'alekha ve-samti 'aleihem* and Num. 11:25: *va-ya'ṣel min ha-ruaḥ asher 'alav*. While the plain sense of *'a.ṣ.l.* in these verses is to 'separate out', 'set aside' or 'reserve' (a portion of something), it is clear from the context that in *Keter Malkhut* Ibn Gabirol understands the verb in the Neoplatonic sense of 'emanate' or 'cause to overflow'. (In the *nif'al* the verb means 'to be derived via emanation'; see lines 198–9). But cf. Naḥmanides' Commentary to Num. 11:17, where he criticises 'the translators' for using the root *'a.ṣ.l.* to designate emanation, citing as an example a verse from a poem about the soul by Judah ha-Levi; see Septimus (1983: 27, n. 58). For the view that *'a.ṣ.l.* does not yet signify the Neoplatonic notion of emanation in Ibn Gabirol's writings, see Liebes (1987: 87–8).

[20] According to some scholars, even in *Fons Vitae* there is an attempt to modify the naturalistic Neoplatonic scheme so that it accommodates the monotheistic principle of divine volition by interposing the Divine Will between God and the universe that comes into existence via emanation. See Schlanger (1968: 277–98 and 308–12), and Hyman (1992: 118–21). See also Wolfson (1959) and cf. Altmann (1979).

Where those weary and worn
Their strength can restore.

...

A place of endless, boundless bliss,
It is the World to Come.[21]

This bold evocation spiritualises the common view of the world to come as 'the historical period ushered in by resurrection in which the righteous receive their ultimate reward and the wicked their ultimate punishment' (Septimus 1982: 40–1). Here the disembodied souls of the righteous enjoy not material rewards, but 'the sweet fruit of the intellect' in the King's own palace.[22] 'This', says the poet, 'is the serenity and the legacy whose goodness and beauty are endless; the milk and honey of the promised land'.[23] In the third and final Part, the poet turns inward, closing the work with a personal prayer that combines a lyrical confession of sins and shortcomings with petitions for divine compassion.

2. Reception in the Oeuvre of Zechariah Alḍāhirī

Many of these characteristic motifs also figure in the Andalusians' shorter, philosophically coloured poems devoted to the soul, which do not, as a rule, aspire to a systematic exposition of technical ideas.[24] These pieces circulated widely and enjoyed an extraordinary reception history that extended well over 400 years, from Provence to the Yemen. In the centuries following the efflorescence of the Andalusian school, the poem on the soul was appropriated and transformed by Hebrew poets who fit it to new literary forms in strikingly diverse cultural milieus: mystical reworkings in 13th-century Catalonia and 16th-century Safed; Italian Hebrew 'sonetto morale' poems (13th–17th centuries); Byzantine Karaite compositions for use in a sectarian liturgy (13th–14th centuries.); and Hebrew *maqāmāt* by Judah Alḥarīzī (Toledo, 1165–Aleppo, 1225), Immanuel of Rome (*c.* 1261–1335) and Zechariah Alḍāhirī (Yemen, 16th century).[25] This extensive and remarkably varied 'afterlife' reflects the abiding fascination and appeal of the Andalusians' signal achievement.

[21] Canto 27, lines 257–62. See also lines 263–8.

[22] Line 266: *u-mit'adnot be-meteq peri ha-sekhel.*

[23] See Loewe's fine translation (1989: 140). A similarly spiritualised interpretation of *'olam ha-ba* is evident in a Hebrew prose work from roughly the same period – Abraham Bar Hiyya's *Hegyon ha-nefesh ha-'aṣuvah* – and is widespread in the writings of philosophically informed thinkers following Ibn Gabirol and Bar Hiyya; see Idel (1983). In the wake of the early 13th-century controversy sparked by Maimonides's purely spiritual view of *'olam ha-ba*, Moses Naḥmanides noted that Maimonides's controversial stance was anticipated by Ibn Gabirol in *Keter Malkhut*. See Septimus (1983, esp. 27–8; 1982: 39–60).

[24] For a fuller discussion, see Tanenbaum (2002). There are a number of poems modelled on *Keter Malkhut*, including Moses Ibn Ezra's *Be-shem 'el 'asher 'amar*, which in turn inspired an imitation by Meir Halevi Abulafia. See: Tanenbaum (1996) and Pagis (1970: 248–52). On imitations inspired by the confessional portion of *Keter Malkhut*, see Ratzaby (1961; 1991: 322–31).

[25] Note also Van Bekkum (2008), who discusses a 'soul' poem from 13th-century Baghdad.

For the remainder of this chapter, we will focus on adaptations by Zechariah Alḍāhirī, a little-known 16th-century Yemenite poet, exegete and religious scholar, who was also instrumental in transmitting Kabbalah to Yemen.[26] A product of the intellectual flowering of Yemenite Jewry, which spanned the 14th–16th centuries, Alḍāhirī revered Maimonides, and considered philosophical discourse a legitimate and desirable mode of expressing religious thought.[27] Moreover, as Tzvi Langermann has demonstrated, the Yemenite Jewish reading of Maimonides incorporated elements of Neoplatonism.[28] Yemenite Jewish thinkers read Maimonides's injunction to seek out the truth, regardless of its source, as a mandate for rational inquiry which allowed them to draw on a wide range of speculative sources. Indeed, Alḍāhirī often moves so fluidly between what we would consider philosophical and mystical modes that the boundaries between the two appear to be fairly porous.[29] His commentary on the Pentateuch, *Sefer ṣeidah la-derekh* (*Provision for the Road*), is informed by Neoplatonic and Maimonidean (Aristotelian) thought as well as by theosophical notions drawn from classical Kabbalah. Philosophical and kabbalistic themes are also evident in his *Sefer hamusar* (*Book of Moral Instruction*), the only picaresque Hebrew *maqāma* to emerge from Yemen. Over half of his 250 extant poems appear in *Sefer hamusar*; the rest are preserved in various printed and manuscript sources.

[26] Alḍāhirī's precise dates cannot be established with certainty. Yehuda Ratzaby placed his year of birth between 1516 and 1519, and his death between 1581 and 1585. But as Yehuda Amir's careful reassessment of Ratzaby's chronology makes clear, there is no firm basis for doing so. Amir (2005) suggests 1531 as a more likely date of birth.

[27] One of the key literary accomplishments of this efflorescence was philosophical midrash, the application of philosophical interpretation (*ta'wīl*) to Scripture, a genre that Tzvi Langermann has done so much to elucidate. Langermann has highlighted the striking diversity of sources considered legitimate for this exegetical enterprise, ranging from the Maimonidean corpus to the writings of al-Ghazālī, and even Hermetic works from India. See Langermann (1996).

[28] Regarding the distinction between the two, Langermann (2003a: 153–4; 2011: 21–2) notes that the Eastern philosophical tradition of Ibn Sīnā, Suhrawardī and the Ishrāqīs conceived of the rational soul as part of the divine, celestial world that inhabits a human body during an individual's lifetime, whereas what Maimonides and the Western Aristotelian tradition term the rational soul 'is a potential, or hylic intellect. It is not a substance pre-existing in some unearthly domain, but rather one of the psychic faculties that come into being along with the human body. It is the capacity to think, to test data and inspect them, and, finally, to reach sound conclusions; and the human imperative consists in this, to actualise one's potentiality, by making full and intelligent use of the ratiocinative and cognitive gifts with which one has been endowed'. For Maimonides, 'perfection is a goal to be achieved, not an initial condition to be preserved'. Langermann has highlighted the blend of Maimonidean and Neoplatonic ideas evident in the allegorical commentary on Canticles by Zechariah ha-Rofé, one of Alḍāhirī's illustrious 15th-century predecessors. Above all, this commentary emphasises the imperative to know one's soul as a means to knowing God, a motif which recurs throughout the Andalusian corpus, as well as in Alḍāhirī's work. See Langermann (2003a: 149), who writes that at 'the heart of the commentary are the disquisitions on the soul which, as a rule, have nothing to do with the verses to which they are attached'. On Maimonides and Neoplatonism, see also Ivry (1991; 1992).

[29] On the diversity of genres considered legitimate sources of sublime truth, see Langermann (1996: xvii–xxx).

As a poet, Alḍāhirī pioneered the mimetic technique known in Yemenite Jewish letters as *jawāb* (response).[30] Like the classical Arabic *muʿāraḍa*, this technique involved the deliberate matching of a new poem's formal features to those of an existing model. (Perhaps the closest Western European analogue is 'contrafaction', the medieval and Renaissance practice of setting new lyrics to the melodies of older songs.)[31] Literally, the term *muʿāraḍa* signified 'opposition' or 'confrontation', much as the verb *contrafactio* denoted 'a setting in opposition or contrast'.[32] Thus, *muʿāraḍa* entailed counter-writing, or counterfeiting the original by transforming its genre, form, structure, wording or meaning. As we shall see, a *jawāb* could signal a response to the *content* of the earlier poem, as much as to its form. This sort of rewriting or counter-writing often 'corrected' a perceived misapprehension in the original, or substituted a more orthodox content for that of the earlier poem.[33] The exemplars Alḍāhirī chose to rework were drawn largely from the corpus of the Andalusian Hebrew poets, which suggests that these texts had achieved a sort of canonic status for him, and thus the enterprise had an exegetical dimension to it.

3. *Sefer Hamusar*

Sefer hamusar centres on the adventures of two invented characters, a peripatetic narrator named Mordecai ha-Ṣidoni and a shape-shifting hero called Abner ben Helek ha-Teimani, whose escapades unfold throughout the Muslim East over 45 self-contained chapters.[34] Inspired by the Arabic *Maqāmāt* of Abū 'l-Ḥasan al-Ḥarīrī (d. 1122) and the Hebrew *Taḥkemoni* of Judah Alḥarīzī (d. 1225), the work features typical *maqāma* plots involving disguise, deception and swindling by means of brilliant rhetorical display. But it also has a sober side, written as it was against the tumultuous background of the first Ottoman occupation of Yemen and the 1568 imprisonment of Sanaʿa's Jews by the local Zaydī Muslim authorities. Alḍāhirī, who was himself incarcerated, threaded his *maqāma* with anguished poems lamenting the persecution and beseeching God to hasten the longed-for messianic advent and final redemption. Thus, *Sefer hamusar* oscillates between cavalier and grave subject matter. Rich in contemplative and theoretical themes, it draws on Andalusian Jewish philosophical thought and theosophical Kabbalah. Through his protagonists,

[30] The related technique of *ziyāda* (augmentation, addition) consisted of augmenting an earlier poem by inserting into it alternating verses of the later poet's invention and subsuming it within a composition of his own.

[31] See Alexander (2014).

[32] This sense of the term also underscored the artistic rivalry which frequently motivated an imitation in its bid to surpass its model. See Falck (1979) and Alexander (2003).

[33] See: Tanenbaum (2005); Maswari Caspi (1974: esp. 75; 1977); Tobi (1974; 1982); Tanenbaum (1996; 2002: 241–2). On the significance of the *jawāb*, see Tobi (1975: esp. 317).

[34] Alḍāhirī (1965).

Alḍāhirī champions the cultivation of Kabbalah whose broader reception in Yemen dates only to the first decades of the 16th century, concurrent with the great mystical revival centred in the Land of Israel (Tanenbaum 2009). At the same time, he makes creative use of earlier Neoplatonic texts. In what follows, he engages with the Neoplatonic scheme of *Keter Malkhut* in two very different modes.

4. Reverberations of *Keter Malkhut* in *Sefer ha-musar*

In the fourteenth *maqāma* of *Sefer hamusar*, Abner (the rogue-hero) appears late at night in the guise of a solitary pietist improvising a pre-dawn devotion. But instead of asking God for forgiveness while his fellow men sleep, he praises God's creation using an emanative cosmology framed in language distinctly reminiscent of Ibn Gabirol's *Keter Malkhut*.[35] In a highly condensed version of the Neoplatonic scheme, Abner traces the downward flow of all existence from a transcendent God, who effortlessly created the cosmic Intellect, from which He caused to emanate the Universal Soul.[36] This cosmogony takes as a given Ibn Gabirol's bold innovation of subordinating the emanative process to God's will, and thus preserves the customary view of God as volitional creator. Our pietist praises God for establishing the physical universe, which consists of the rotating spheres, at whose centre stands the earth with its diverse creatures. Of these, man is preeminent, for he alone is endowed with a divine, immortal soul that may – if it is disciplined – attain eternal repose in the world to come. Its biblical diction pregnant with philosophical meaning, Alḍāhirī's language testifies to Ibn Gabirol's remarkable success in naturalising the highly technical ideas elaborated in *Keter Malkhut*:

> Blessed be He who has chosen us from among all the nations ... He who is hidden in highest mystery, elevated above all that is exalted (*ha-ne'elam be-rum ḥevyon/ ha-na'aleh 'al kol 'elyon*), who created the First Intellect without toil or speech, and caused to emanate from it the precious Universal Soul, which is distinct from the angels (*bara' ha-sekhel ha-rishon/beli 'amal ve-lo raḥshon/ve-he'eṣil mimmenu nefesh yeqarah kollelet/min ha-mal'akhim nivdelet*).[37]

Economical and evocative, the poetic medium renders this weighty and daring synthesis accessible and acceptable to Alḍāhirī's audience in a way that a more

[35] For a philosophical approach to early morning prayer, see the excerpt from *Sirāj al-'Uqūl* by the 15th-century Yemenite Jewish author Ḥoṭer ben Shelomoh in Langermann (1996: 108–14). Note also that Ibn Gabirol's younger contemporary and fellow Saragossan, Baḥya Ibn Paquda, had recommended the performance of supererogatory nighttime devotions out of a concern that prayer be meaningful. For this purpose, he composed a poetic exhortation to the soul entitled 'Barekhi nafshi', which he appended, along with a *baqqashah*, or confessional meditation, to his *Book of Direction to the Duties of the Heart* (*Kitāb al-Hidāya ilā Farā'iḍ al-Qulūb*), including instructions for their recitation in the work's final treatise. See Mansoor (1973: 10–16).

[36] On Neoplatonic influences and the role of the Universal Soul in Yemenite Jewish cosmology, see Langermann (1995: 336–7; 1996: 21–44).

[37] On the relationship between angels and souls see Tanenbaum (2002: 62–3).

discursive form likely could not.[38] But the new, blatantly fictional literary context furnished by *Sefer hamusar* also colours the borrowing from *Keter Malkhut*. While Abner initially appears as a serious divine who expounds profound theological and cosmological doctrines, he is subsequently transformed into a suave rhymester and a sneaky swindler. Alḍāhirī thus undercuts the force and gravitas of Abner's seemingly sober address by interlacing it with a narrative thread that highlights his cunning, his disarming disregard for propriety and his deceptive use of language. The chapter as a whole conforms to a pattern found in Arabic picaresque *maqāmāt*: an individual posing as a preacher or holy man turns out to be a charlatan who, under the guise of his piety, and by dint of his way with words, manages to enrich himself by defrauding his gullible prey.[39] While the primary intention of such works was to amuse, there could also be a didactic aim, achieved through biting satires of recognisable social types and professions. The contiguity of the episode's scenes suggests Abner's rapid transformation from austere divine to outright fraud, and thereby intimates the fluidity of his persona and morals. Possibly, his appropriation of *Keter Malkhut* was intended to make his disguise more credible. But Abner's transgression of social conventions and mores also exposes the human weaknesses lurking behind the façade of excessive piety. In its larger narrative context, then, the cosmogony borrowed from Ibn Gabirol becomes part of a satire. Yet it is noteworthy that Alḍāhirī chooses to put Ibn Gabirol's language and emanative scheme in the mouth of his fictional pietist, regardless of how comically the new narrative setting undermines the sincerity of his rhetoric.[40] The assumption that pietists praise God's creation in the naturalised Neoplatonic language of *Keter Malkhut* reflects the degree to which Ibn Gabirol's synthesis had become an accepted, enshrined part of the devotional and intellectual landscape for 16th-century Yemenite Jews such as Alḍāhirī.

5. A Kabbalistic Response to *Keter Malkhut*

Alḍāhirī also composed a short and entirely serious kabbalistic poem in response to Ibn Gabirol's hymn. In the Yemenite *tiklāl*, or prayer book, it was inserted *en bloc* into *Keter Malkhut* already in the 18th century, and the two were recited together on the Day of Atonement. The opening underscores the limits of human apprehension: 'My Lord, who can reach the limits of Your wisdom? How profound

[38] Cf. Petuchowski: 'Statements and arguments which, in prose, would immediately be branded as "heretical" have become, once they were couched in poetic form, ingredients of the liturgy, and continue to be rehearsed – often with more devotion than comprehension – by multitudes of the unsuspecting pious who would be utterly shocked to discover the true intent of their authors' (1978: 5).

[39] See, e.g., al-Hamadhānī (1915: 55–8 [no. 10, 'The Maqāma of Isfahan']); al-Ḥarīrī (1867: 108–12 [no. 1, 'Of Sana'a']; 163–8 [no. 11, 'Of Saweh']; 223–8 [no. 21, 'Of Rayy']; al-Ḥarīrī (1898: 37–57 [no. 32, 'Of Taybeh']; 108–13 [no. 41, 'Of Tanīs']). See also Beaumont (1994).

[40] Were Alḍāhirī not so completely immersed in the received medieval worldview, we might even construe this as an attempt to poke fun at the perceived arcana of Ibn Gabirol's system.

are Your thoughts.'[41] The poet then praises God as the source of the ten *sefirot*, or aspects of divinity, as elaborated in classical Kabbalah. Medieval kabbalists speak in intricate symbolism and mythical language of the emanation of ten *sefirot* from *Ein sof* – the infinite, concealed and unknowable aspect of the divinity – to convey the progressive unfolding of the divine in the cosmos. Although God in Himself is inscrutable and beyond comprehension, the *sefirot* emanating in successive stages from *Ein sof* correspond to more immanent aspects of the Godhead which can be known through contemplation. Alḍāhirī accordingly delineates the descending *sefirot* from highest to lowest, tracing God's 'flowering into the cosmos' (Ginsburg 2008: 24), and thereby reversing *Keter Malkhut*'s upward progression. The poem's echoes of *Keter Malkhut* are nevertheless deliberate and unmistakable. Its incipit signals this intertextual relationship by reworking the beginning of Ibn Gabirol's Thirtieth Canto, which sets out a spiritualised conception of purgatory.[42] While the *sefirot* are differentiated from the philosophers' emanations by their dynamic qualities and unusual symbolic values,[43] it is clear that Alḍāhirī saw an affinity between the Neoplatonic scheme of *Keter Malkhut* and the kabbalistic doctrine he was attempting to convey to a wider audience.[44] Structurally, this analogy had been put in place by Catalonian and Provençal kabbalists of the late 12th century, who, as Moshe Idel has written, sought an alternative to the newly ascendant Aristotelianism of Maimonides and were eager 'to exploit the hierarchical structure of Neoplatonism in mediating between the divine and lower realms' (1992: 320).[45]

[41] *Adonai mi yagi'a 'ad takhlit ḥokhmatekha/ me'od 'amqu maḥshevotekha*. For the phrase *me'od 'amqu maḥshevotekha*, cf. Ps. 92:6. In the standard printed edition of the Yemenite prayer book, the insertion runs to just 24 lines long.

[42] Thirtieth Canto: *Adonai mi yagi'a le-ḥokhmatekha, be-titekha la-nefesh koaḥ ha-de'ah, asher bah tequ'ah?* ('My Lord, who can reach Your wisdom, in giving the soul the faculty of knowledge, which is fixed in her, so that knowledge is her glory, and decay has no rule over her … the wise soul is not subject to death'). It would seem that the choice was not random: Ibn Gabirol here sets out a philosophical conception of purgatory which complements his spiritualised interpretation of ultimate reward. He specifies that his remarks pertain to the rational soul, whose capacity for reason renders her immortal. If tainted by sin at the conclusion of her earthly sojourn, this highest of souls must undergo an ordeal 'more bitter than death'. Only so will she be purged of her impurities and made fit to 'approach the sanctuary', that is, to take her place in the world to come.

[43] Dan: 'What differentiates the Kabbalah from other systems that use emanation as the metaphor for the unfolding of Being is twofold: first, the unique symbolic values, and second, the dynamic qualities of the *sefirot*' (1986: 8).

[44] Only a handful of late 15th- to early 17th-century Yemenite works informed by Kabbalah have come to light, revealing a small core of authors committed to presenting the rudiments of classical Kabbalah to a largely uninformed reading public. This, despite the fact that in the late 16th century, Lurianic Kabbalah was already leaving its singular stamp on piety and spirituality elsewhere in the Jewish world. See: Hallamish (1984: 9) and Tobi (1997: 21 and n. 21).

[45] Idel notes (1992: 319–20) that as the 'regnant Neoplatonism of [the Andalusians] lost its dominance in favor of more Aristotelian ways of thinking like that of Maimonides', the Provençal Kabbalah emerged as the main 'speculative alternative in the environment of the Maimonidean controversy in Europe'. But see Septimus (1983), who notes that the early kabbalists' attitudes towards Maimonides are nuanced and complex.

By interweaving his kabbalistic hymn into Ibn Gabirol's capacious poem, Alḍāhirī suggests that his is an analogous attempt to evoke a cosmogony that mediates between the metaphysical and the acutely physical. Nevertheless, it is important to bear in mind that most kabbalists did not place the world of emanation *outside* the Godhead as the Neoplatonists did (Ginsburg 2008: 26). In claiming that the soul derived from the celestial sphere of the Intellect, the philosophers implied that it was a product of the created realm, whereas early kabbalists placed the soul's true origins and ultimate home far higher, in the world of the divine *sefirot*, within the Godhead itself (Septimus 1983). Perhaps not acknowledging these differences, Alḍāhirī's insertion intimates that the contemplative fabric of *Keter Malkhut* could accommodate an added theosophical dimension. Thus, as in much poetic emulation, the relationship between new and old is not unidirectional, for the very act of contrafaction forges ties of intertextuality and interdependence between the response and the original to which it reacts and pays homage. By establishing the dialogue, the later poem looks back to its model, not only to derive and define its own meaning, but inevitably to cast light on the earlier poem as well. What, then, can we say about Alḍāhirī's two uses of *Keter Malkhut*? The comic entertainments of the *maqāma* bear little resemblance to the sober, devotional content of the prayer-book, and the experience of reciting philosophical and mystical poems while fasting on Yom Kippur could not be further from reading (or hearing) a picaresque narrative with its antic escapades. The fact that Alḍāhirī could adapt *Keter Malkhut* for such widely divergent purposes suggests not only that it had achieved canonical status, but also that its refined Neoplatonic language and idealised imagery was seen to convey some essential truth about man's place in the universe, the nature of his spirituality and his relationship with God.[46]

6. Admonishing the Soul: Contrafaction as Anti-Parody

Alḍāhirī also employed contrafaction to respond to a provocative exhortation to the soul. In the sixth *maqāma* of *Sefer hamusar*, the narrator journeys via the upper Galilee to Safed, the centre of the great mystical revival of the 16th century. There he attends the *yeshivah* of the renowned mystic and legal scholar, Joseph Karo (1488–1575).[47] An unnamed yeshivah student – whom the narrator later recognises as his old crony, Abner – recites a poem chastising the soul. Full of Neoplatonic commonplaces, *Nefesh yeqarah, eikh be-tokh guf tishkeni* ('Precious soul, how can you dwell in a body?') asks rhetorically how the soul can dwell in a body when she is inherently pure and hewn from the divine splendour. It

[46] See Tobi (1997) on later poems modelled on this one. See also Amir (2015: 52, n. 7), who refers to the 'culture of additions in Yemenite poetry'.

[47] On Karo and his Safed contemporaries, see, e.g., Schechter (1945); Fine (2003: 41–77; 1984: 1–80 *passim*); Werblowsky (1977; 1987).

exhorts her to withdraw from the corrupting corporeal world, abandon sin and prepare for Judgment Day, warning that she cannot rest until she returns to her celestial abode.[48] But informed readers would know that Abner's poem is modelled on *Nefesh yeqarah, eikh be-sikhlekh tivteḥi* ('Precious soul, how can you trust in your intellect?'), a crafty admonition from the 'Dispute of the Soul with the Body and the Intellect' in Judah Alḥarīzī's 13th-century *maqāma, The Book of Taḥkemoni*.[49] The 'Dispute' showcases the mutual recriminations of soul and body, with both parties disavowing responsibility for their sins. But Alḥarīzī introduces two additional participants, the intellect and the evil inclination, who both address poetic exhortations to the soul. 'Precious soul, how can you trust in your intellect?' is in fact declaimed by the evil inclination. While it draws on the conventions of solemn contemplative and liturgical poetry as well as on serious prose sources, Alḥarīzī's 'Dispute' subtly tests the limits of sobriety and propriety by including the evil inclination's poetic reproof. In part, the 'Dispute' recalls the dialogue of personified soul and intellect in Baḥya Ibn Paquda's esteemed spiritual manual, *The Book of Direction to the Duties of the Heart*, where the intellect is cast as the soul's moral guide and adviser in an interiorised debate between conflicting human tendencies.[50] It also harks back to a well-known midrash and earlier *piyyutim* portraying the posthumous judgement of body and soul.[51] But Alḥarīzī transposes these older paradigms to the new literary context of the *maqāma*, a work of secular entertainment aimed at a broad audience.[52] In his 'Dispute', the intellect urges the soul not to succumb to the machinations of the evil inclination, but to cleanse herself of the body's defilements, repent, and look to her original home in the divine world.[53]

[48] Alḍāhirī (1965: 122–3, lines 120–34). The piece is reminiscent of the Andalusian Hebrew *tokheḥah*, or poem of reproof. On the *tokheḥah* genre see Tanenbaum (2002: 19–20). Note that the direct address to the soul yields an abundance of second person feminine endings (long *ee* sounds), which mirror the content in aural effect.

[49] For a fuller discussion of the 'Dispute', see Tanenbaum (2002: 203–17).

[50] Baḥya was a younger contemporary of Ibn Gabirol and fellow Saragossan. This dialogue occurs in the larger context of Baḥya's chapter on man's obedience to God (*ṭāʿat allāh*), where the intellect's divinely inspired admonition (*tanbīh*) is intended to complement the precepts of religious law by fostering knowledge of God and the ability to discern traces of His wisdom in the world. See: Mansoor (1973: 198–220); Vajda (1937; 1947: 33–60); and Lobel (2011). See also Lobel: 'We see this [viz. that the *Hidāya* is modelled on Sufi devotional manuals] vividly in the structure of the book itself: the reader is led through ten gates, each representing a quality to be embodied in the soul's journey toward love for God' (2000: 4).

[51] See bSan. 91a-b, translated in Urbach (1979: 223). There are additional versions of the parable of the lame and the blind in Leviticus Rabbah, Midrash Tanḥuma, and the Mekhilta. The parable also occurs in Christian and Islamic literature; see Urbach (1979: 786, n. 23); Malter (1912: 454–57); and Meisami (1991: 319–20).

[52] Devin Stewart (2016) has speculated that Alḥarīzī's personification of the intellect may have been inspired by Ibn al-Jawzī.

[53] Baḥya also personifies the rabbinic *yeṣer ha-raʿ* or evil inclination in the fifth treatise of his *Duties of the Heart*, where he warns that the temptations and wicked advice of the *yeṣer* (*waswās al-hawā wa-ishārātuhu*) spoil man's sincere devotion to God; see Tanenbaum (2002: 216).

A rabbinic construct, the evil instinct is man's worst enemy, whom the Andalusians identified with the lower souls of the Neoplatonic triad. In Alḥarīzī's 'Dispute', he insinuates himself into the proceedings and, opening his remarks in rhymed prose, reminds the noblest soul of the transience of her worldly pleasures, urging her to enjoy these fleeting delights while she can. Such *carpe diem* motifs are, of course, hallmarks of courtly verse.[54] But when voiced by the wily *yeṣer ha-ra'*, they cleverly invert the standard pious advice to the soul to look to the next world, precisely *because* the material and sensual satisfactions of this world are ephemeral. The evil *yeṣer* then issues a denial of any kind of afterlife, in words that deliberately subvert Maimonides's purely spiritual interpretation of the World to Come.[55] In *Nefesh yeqarah* – the insolent poem that follows – every nostrum proffered by the evil inclination contradicts the intellect's sage counsel. If the intellect's poem typifies the Andalusian homily to the soul, the evil inclination's is a clever spoof which slyly reverses the genre's characteristic themes.

It is this very provocation to sin that prompted Alḍāhirī's response. His *Nefesh yeqarah* adopts the rhyme scheme, metre and hortatory opening of the evil inclination's *Nefesh yeqarah, eikh be-sikhlekh tivteḥi*. What it does not duplicate, however, is the element of parody in the original. It is just possible that his predecessor's mischievous humour eluded Alḍāhirī. But from a narrative perspective, his high-minded reworking of the earlier parody may well be a calculated effort to further his rogue hero's cunning stratagem: while Abner qua seminarian makes an outward show of godliness, few readers would recognise that underlying his pietistic verse is a doctrinally subversive poem much more in line with his typical chicanery. Of course, it is one thing for your invented protagonist to exploit a poem that runs counter to spiritual ideals; but it is quite another for a well-respected poet and scholarly translator of philosophical texts like Judah Alḥarīzī to have flirted with such materialist notions. Viewed in this light, Alḍāhirī's contrafaction is an intentional *anti*-parody; a deliberate attempt to offset or make amends for the unseemly and irreverent content of his predecessor's poem. His *jawāb* would then match the original's formal features while reinterpreting and rectifying its discomfiting impieties. Such an implicit critique and doctrinal correction compels the reader to revisit, and perhaps re-evaluate, the earlier poem. Remedied and sanitised in the

[54] See Scheindlin (1986: 25–8; 39; 46–9; 54–9; 135) and Brann (1991: 9–22 *passim*).

[55] In his code of law, the *Mishneh Torah*, Maimonides had cited a well-known passage at bBerakhot 17a in support of his view that there are no bodies in the world to come, only the souls of the righteous who have attained knowledge of the divine. Echoes of his *Ha-'olam ha-ba ein bo guf u-gviyyah ... ein bo lo akhilah ve-lo shetiyyah* can be heard in the phrasing of the evil *yeṣer*'s *aḥarei ha-mavet ein simḥah ve-ein marge'ah, ve-ein yeshivah ve-ein nesi'ah*. It is even possible that Alḥarīzī's choice of *yeshivah* was intended to remind the reader of Maimonides's figurative interpretation, in the same discussion, of the talmudic statement that the righteous 'sit' in *'olam ha-ba* with their crowns on their heads, enjoying the splendour of the Shekhinah. Since sitting is a physical act, but there are no bodies in the world to come, Maimonides had explained the phrase as a metaphor for the effortless existence of the souls of the righteous after death, just as he had interpreted the 'crowns on their heads' as a metaphor for the crowning knowledge of God, through which they merit eternal life (*Mishneh Torah*, Teshuvah 8:2).

new poem, the evil inclination's excesses lose their bite. By retaining its form while displacing its words, Alḍāhirī effectively rewrites his predecessor's impish and impudent piece. If this was in fact Alḍāhirī's intent, it was certainly effective: his poem sparked a chain of no less than eight Yemenite contrafactions.[56]

7. Conclusions

In crafting *Sefer hamusar*, Alḍāhirī added his own distinctively Yemenite touches which conjure a unique world and render the work quite unlike any of its predecessors. And yet, half a millennium after the emergence of the Andalusian poem on the soul, that genre still retained its appeal for him, despite the fact that it had evolved in a dramatically different socio-political and cultural milieu. Even when Alḍāhirī – like Alḥarīzī before him – embedded the Andalusian prototype in his playful, picaresque *maqāma*, its lofty Neoplatonic themes still resonated with him and spurred him to creativity. With its array of pleasing forms and transcendent ideals, the Andalusian paradigm inspired his contrafactions, furnished language and a frame of reference for his fictional pietists, and furthered his dissemination of kabbalistic ideas. Whether his models were grave or irreverent, devotional, purely contemplative or droll, Alḍāhirī remained an avid proponent of the poetic tradition reaching back to Ibn Gabirol.

References

Alḍāhirī, Z. (1965), *Sefer hamusar: Maḥberot rabbi zekhariah al-ḍāhirī*, ed. Y Ratzaby (Jerusalem, Ben-Zvi Institute).

Alexander, G. (2003), 'The Elizabethan Lyric as Contrafactum: Robert Sidney's "French Tune" Identified', *Music and Letters*, 84: 378–402.

Alexander, G. (2014), 'On the Reuse of Poetic Form', in E. Scott-Baumann & B. Burton (eds), *The Work of Form: Poetics and Materiality in Early Modern Culture* (Oxford, Oxford University Press), 123–43.

Altmann, A. (1966), 'The Divine Attributes: An Historical Survey of the Jewish Discussion', *Judaism*, 15: 40–60.

Altmann, A. (1979), 'Creation and Emanation in Isaac Israeli: A Reappraisal', in I. Twersky (ed.), *Studies in Medieval Jewish History and Literature* (Cambridge MA, Harvard University Press), 1–15.

Altmann, A. & Stern, S.M. (eds) (1958), *Isaac Israeli* (Oxford, Oxford University Press).

Amir, Y. (2005), 'Ḥayyei Rabbi Zekhariyah Alḍāhirī', in S. Seri & I. Kessar (eds), *Halikhot qedem be-mishkenot teiman* (n.p., E'ele Betamar Association), 459–66.

Amir, Y. (2015), 'Tosafot ḥadashot le-"kheter malkhut" le-shelomo ibn gabirol me-ḥibbur r. Yiḥye ben Avraham Ḥarazi', *Tema*, 13: 51–4.

[56] The poems, from the 17th through 19th centuries, are enumerated in Tobi (1970). In keeping with the devout inclination of late medieval Yemenite Jewish society, they are all pious admonitions to the soul, though some accommodate kabbalistic ideas and others, a Judeo-Arabic idiom.

Armstrong, A.H. (1940), *The Architecture of the Intelligible Universe in the Philosophy of Plotinus* (Cambridge, Cambridge University Press).
Armstrong, A.H. (1979), *Plotinian and Christian Studies* (London, Variorum Reprints).
Badawī, A. (ed.) (1955), *Aflūṭīn ʿinda ʾl-ʿArab* (Cairo, Maktabat al-Nahḍa al-Miṣriyya).
Beaumont, D. (1994), 'The Trickster and Rhetoric in the Maqāmāt', *Edebiyât* n.s., 5: 1–14.
Blumenthal, H.J. (1976), 'Plotinus' Adaptation of Aristotle's Psychology: Sensation, Imagination and Memory', in R. Baine Harris (ed.), *The Significance of Neoplatonism* (Norfolk VA, International Society for Neoplatonic Studies), 41–58.
Brann, R. (1991), *The Compunctious Poet: Cultural Ambiguity and Hebrew Poetry in Muslim Spain* (Baltimore, Johns Hopkins University Press).
Brown, F., Driver, S.R. & Briggs, C.A. (eds) (1955), *A Hebrew and English Lexicon of the Old Testament* (Oxford, Oxford University Press).
Cantarino, V. (1967), 'Ibn Gabirol's Metaphysic of Light', *Studia Islamica*, 26: 49–71.
Cole, P. (ed. & trans.) (2001), *Selected Poems of Solomon Ibn Gabirol* (Princeton, Princeton University Press).
Dan, J. (ed. & introduction) (1986), *The Early Kabbalah*, trans. R.C. Kiener (New York/Mahwah/Toronto, Paulist Press).
Elbogen, I.M. (1993), *Jewish Liturgy: A Comprehensive History*, trans. R.P. Scheindlin (Philadelphia, Jewish Publication Society and New York, Jewish Theological Seminary).
Falck, R. (1979), 'Parody and Contrafactum: A Terminological Clarification', *The Musical Quarterly*, 65: 1–21.
Fenton, P. (1976), 'Gleanings from Moseh Ibn Ezra's *Maqālat al-Ḥadīqa*', *Sefarad*, 36: 285–98.
Fenton, P. (1986), 'The Arabic and Hebrew Versions of the Theology of Aristotle', in Kraye *et al.* (1986), 241–64.
Fenton, P. (1992), 'Shem Tov Ibn Falaquera ve-ha-Te'ologiyah shel Aristo', *Daat*, 29: 27–39.
Fenton, P. (1997), *Philosophie et exégèse dans Le Jardin de la métaphore de Moïse Ibn 'Ezra, philosophe & poète andalou du XIIe siècle* (Leiden, E.J. Brill).
Fine, L. (1984), *Safed Spirituality* (New York/Ramsey/Toronto, Paulist Press).
Fine, L. (2003), *Physician of the Soul, Healer of the Cosmos: Isaac Luria and His Kabbalistic Fellowship* (Stanford, Stanford University Press).
Flew, A. (ed.) (1964), *Body, Mind, and Death* (New York, Macmillan Publishing Co.).
Frede, M. (1992), 'On Aristotle's Conception of the Soul', in M.C. Nussbaum & A.O. Rorty (eds), *Essays on Aristotle's De Anima* (Oxford, Clarendon Press), 93–107.
Gerson, L.P. (1994), *Plotinus* (London and New York, Routledge).
Gerson, L.P. (2011), 'General Introduction', in L.P. Gerson (ed.) *The Cambridge History of Philosophy in Late Antiquity*, vol. 1 (Cambridge, Cambridge University Press), 1–10, accessed 24 April 2017, https://doi.org/10.1017/CHOL9780521764407
Ginsburg, E.K. (2008), *The Sabbath in the Classical Kabbalah* (Oxford/Portland, Littman Library of Jewish Civilization).
Goodman, L.E. (ed.) (1992), *Neoplatonism and Jewish Thought* (Albany, State University of New York Press).
Hallamish, M. (ed.) (1984), *Le-toldot ha-qabbalah be-teiman bereishit ha-me'ah ha yod-zayyin: Sefer Segulloth ve-Sefer Leḥem Shelomoh* (Ramat Gan, Bar-Ilan University Press).
Hamadhānī, al- (1915; repr. 1973), *The Maqāmāt of Badīʿ Al-Zamān al-Hamadhānī*, trans. W.J. Prendergast (London, Curzon).
Ḥarīrī, al- (1867; repr. 1969), *The Assemblies of al-Ḥarīrī*, vol. 1, trans. T. Chenery (London, Williams and Norgate; repr. Gregg International).
Ḥarīrī, al- (1898; repr. 1969), *The Assemblies of al-Ḥarīrī*, vol. 2, trans. F. Steingass (London, Royal Asiatic Society; repr. Gregg International).

Hirsch, W. (1947), *Rabbinic Psychology* (London, Edward Goldston).

Hyman, A. (1992), 'From What Is One and Simple Only What is One and Simple Can Come to Be', in Goodman (1992), 111–35.

Idel, M. (1983), 'Defusim shel pe'ilut go'elet bimei ha-beinayim', in Z. Baras (ed.), *Meshiḥiyut ve-eskhaṭologiyah: ḳovets ma'amarim* (Jerusalem, The Zalman Shazar Center), 253–79.

Idel, M. (1992), 'Jewish Kabbalah and Platonism in the Middle Ages and Renaissance', in Goodman (1992), 319–51.

Ivry, A. (1991), 'Neoplatonic Currents in Maimonides' Thought', in J.L. Kraemer (ed.), *Perspectives on Maimonides* (Oxford, Oxford University Press for The Littman Library), 115–40.

Ivry, A. (1992), 'Maimonides and Neoplatonism: Challenge and Response', in Goodman (1992), 137–56.

Jaeger, W. (1962), *Aristotle: Fundamentals of the History of His Development*, 2nd edn (London, Oxford University Press).

Kohler, K. (1918), *Jewish Theology* (New York, The Macmillan Company).

Kraye, J. (1986), 'The Pseudo-Aristotelian *Theology* in Sixteenth- and Seventeenth-Century Europe', in Kraye *et al.* (1986), 265–86.

Kraye, J., Ryan, W. & Schmitt, C. (eds) (1986), *Pseudo-Aristotle in the Middle Ages* (London, Warburg Institute).

Langermann, Y.T. (1995), 'Yemenite Philosophical Midrash as a Source for the Intellectual History of the Jews of Yemen', in D. Frank (ed.), *The Jews of Medieval Islam: Community, Society, and Identity* (Leiden, Brill), 335–47.

Langermann, Y.T. (1996), *Yemenite Midrash: Philosophical Commentaries on the Torah* (San Francisco, HarperCollins).

Langermann, Y.T. (2003a), 'Saving the Soul by Knowing the Soul: A Medieval Yemeni Interpretation of Song of Songs', *Journal of Jewish Thought and Philosophy*, 12.2: 147–66.

Langermann, Y.T. (2003b), 'A Judaeo-Arabic Paraphrase of Ibn Gabirol's *Keter Malkhut*', *Zutot*, 3: 28–33.

Langermann, Y.T. (2011), 'Maḥshevet hodu be-qerev yehudei teiman: ha-sefer "Mirʾāt al-Maʿānī"', *Alei Sefer: Studies in Bibliography and in the History of the Printed and the Digital Hebrew Book*, 22: 19–27.

Lewis, B. (trans.) (1961; repr. 2003), *The Kingly Crown* (London, Vallentine, Mitchell; repr. University of Notre Dame).

Liebes, Y. (1987), 'Sefer yetsirah etsel rabbi shelomoh ibn gvirol u-ferush ha-shir "Ahavtikha"', *Meḥqere yerushalayim be-maḥshevet yisra'el*, 6: 73–123.

Lloyd, G.E.R. (1968), *Aristotle: The Growth and Structure of His Thought* (Cambridge, Cambridge University Press).

Lobel, D. (2000), *Between Mysticism and Philosophy: Sufi Language of Religious Experience in Judah Ha-Levi's Kuzari* (Albany, SUNY Press).

Lobel, D. (2011), *A Sufi-Jewish Dialogue: Philosophy and Mysticism in Bahya ibn Paquda's 'Duties of the Heart'* (Philadelphia, University of Pennsylvania Press).

Loewe, R. (1989), *Ibn Gabirol* (London, Peter Halban).

Lovejoy, A.O. (1964), *The Great Chain of Being: A Study of the History of an Idea* (Cambridge MA, Harvard University Press).

Lovibond, S. (1991), 'Plato's Theory of the Mind', in S. Everson (ed.), *Psychology*, Companions to Ancient Thought, vol. 2 (Cambridge, Cambridge University Press), 35–55.

Malter, H. (1912), 'Personifications of Soul and Body: A Study in Judaeo-Arabic Literature', *Jewish Quarterly Review*, n.s., 2: 453–79.

Mansoor, M. (trans.) (1973), *The Book of Direction to the Duties of the Heart* (London, Routledge & Kegan Paul).

Maswari Caspi, M. (1974), 'The Jawab Poetry (Shire Ma'ane) in Jewish Yemenite Poetry', *Hebrew Abstracts*, 15: 72–6.

Maswari Caspi, M. (1977), 'Penei aryeh shelaḥ', *Afikim*, 13.64: 14–15.

Meisami, J.S. (1991), *The Sea of Precious Virtues (Baḥr al-Farā'id): A Medieval Islamic Mirror for Princes* (Salt Lake City, University of Utah Press).

Moore, G.F. (1927), *Judaism in the First Centuries of the Christian Era*, 2 vols (Cambridge MA, Harvard University Press).

Morewedge, P. (ed.) (1992), *Neoplatonism and Islamic Thought* (Albany, State University of New York Press).

Murtonen, A. (1958), 'The Living Soul: A Study of the Meaning of the Word *næfæš* in the Old Testament Hebrew Language', *Studia Orientalia* (Helsinki), 23.1: 3–105.

O'Meara, D.J. (ed.) (1982), *Neoplatonism and Christian Thought* (Albany, State University of New York Press).

Pagis, D. (1970), *Shirat ha-ḥol ve-torat ha-shir le-Mosheh Ibn 'Ezra u-vene doro* (Jerusalem, Bialik Institute).

Petuchowski, J.J. (1978), *Theology and Poetry: Studies in the Medieval Piyyut* (London, Routledge and Kegan Paul).

Pines, S. (1957–8), 'Sefer "'Arugat ha-bosem": ha-qeta'im mi-tokh sefer "Meqor ḥayyim"', *Tarbiẓ*, 27: 218–33.

Pistorius, P.V. (1952), *Plotinus and Neoplatonism* (Cambridge, Bowes and Bowes).

Ratzaby, Y. (1961), 'Millu'im le-ha-vidduy be-kheter malkhut', *Oṣar Yehudei Sefarad*, 4: 122–4.

Ratzaby, Y. (1991), *Migginzē Shirat Hakkēdem* (Jerusalem, Misgav Yerushalayim).

Remes, P. & Slaveva-Griffin, S. (2014), 'Introduction: Neoplatonism Today', in P. Remes & S. Slaveva-Griffin (eds), *The Routledge Handbook of Neoplatonism* (London/ New York, Routledge), 1–10.

Rist, J.M. (1967), *Plotinus: The Road to Reality* (Cambridge, Cambridge University Press).

Rubin, N. (1989), 'Mi-monizm le-du'alizm: ha-yaḥas guf-nefesh be-tefisat ḥakhamim', *Da'at*, 23: 33–63.

Schechter, S. (1945), 'Safed in the Sixteenth Century: A City of Legists and Mystics', in *Studies in Judaism*, Second Series (Philadelphia, The Jewish Publication Society of America), 202–85.

Scheindlin, R.P. (1986), *Wine, Women, and Death: Medieval Hebrew Poems on the Good Life* (Philadelphia, Jewish Publication Society).

Scheindlin, R.P. (1993a), 'Ibn Gabirol's Religious Poetry and Arabic *Zuhd* Poetry', *Edebiyât*, n.s., 4: 229–42.

Scheindlin, R.P. (1993b), 'Contrasting Religious Experience in the Liturgical Poems of Ibn Gabirol and Judah Halevi', *Prooftexts*, 13: 141–62.

Scheindlin, R.P. (1994), 'Ibn Gabirol's Religious Poetry and Sufi Poetry', *Sefarad*, 54: 109–41.

Scheindlin, R.P. (2016), *Vulture in a Cage: Poems by Solomon Ibn Gabirol* (New York, Archipelago Books).

Schlanger, J. (1968), *La Philosophie de Salomon Ibn Gabirol: étude d'un néoplatonisme* (Leiden, Brill).

Sells, M. (1994), *Mystical Languages of Unsaying* (Chicago, University of Chicago Press).

Septimus, B. (1982), *Hispano-Jewish Culture in Transition: The Career and Controversies of Ramah* (Cambridge MA, Harvard University Press).

Septimus, B. (1983), '"Open Rebuke and Concealed Love": Naḥmanides and the Andalusian Tradition', in I. Twersky (ed.), *Rabbi Moses Naḥmanides: Explorations in His Religious and Literary Virtuosity* (Cambridge MA, Harvard University Press), 11–34.

Slavitt, D.R. (trans.) (1998), *A Crown for the King: Solomon Ibn Gabirol* (New York/Oxford, Oxford University Press).

Sorabji, R. (1979), 'Body and Soul in Aristotle', in J. Barnes, M. Schofield & R. Sorabji (eds), *Articles on Aristotle, 4: Psychology and Aesthetics* (London, Duckworth), 42–64.

Sperl, S. (2009), 'Darkness Transformed into Light: Ibn al-Muʿtazz on the Pen', in C. Allison, A. Joisten-Pruschke & A. Wendtland (eds), *From Daēnā to Dīn: Religion, Kultur und Sprache in der iranischen Welt* (Wiesbaden, Harrassowitz), 457–63.

Stewart, D. (2016), 'Of Rhetoric, Reason, and Revelation: Ibn al-Jawzī's Maqāmāt as an Anti-Parody and Sefer Taḥkemoni of Yehudah al-Ḥarīzī', *Middle Eastern Literatures*, 19.2: 206–33.

Tanenbaum, A. (1996), 'Nine Spheres or Ten? A Medieval Gloss on Moses Ibn Ezra's "Be-shem el asher amar"', *Journal of Jewish Studies*, 47.2: 294–310.

Tanenbaum, A. (2000), 'On Translating *Keter Malkhut*', *Prooftexts*, 20.3: 349–62.

Tanenbaum, A. (2002), *The Contemplative Soul: Hebrew Poetry and Philosophical Theory in Medieval Spain* (Leiden, Brill).

Tanenbaum, A. (2005), '"Credit is Due to the One Who Completes It": Zechariah Alḍāhirī on Poetic Originality and Plagiarism', *Journal of Jewish Studies*, 56: 101–19.

Tanenbaum, A. (2009), 'Kabbalah in a Literary Key: Mystical Motifs in Zechariah Alḍāhirī's *Sefer Hamusar*', *The Journal of Jewish Thought and Philosophy*, 17.1: 47–99.

Tobi, Y. (1970), 'Shirim ʿal ha-nefesh be-shirat teman', *Afikim*, 35, 8 & 36: 8–9.

Tobi, Y. (1974), 'Shir maʿaneh la-shir mi-yein shoshan le-yiṣḥaq ha-levi', *Afikim*, 52–4: 11, 17.

Tobi, Y. (1975), 'Bein shirat teiman le-shirat sefarad', in Y. Yeshaʿyahu & Y. Tobi (eds), *Yahadut teiman: pirqei meḥqar ve-ʿiyyun* (Jerusalem, Yad Izhak Ben-Zvi), 303–32.

Tobi, Y. (1982), 'Shir nosaf mi-yeṣirato shel rabbi zekhariah alḍāhirī', *Afikim*, 77: 20–1.

Tobi, Y. (1997), 'Rabbi Yitzhaq Wannah and the Intensification of Kabbalah Learning in Yemen' [Hebrew], *Daʿat*, 38: 17–31.

Urbach, E. (1979), *The Sages: Their Concepts and Beliefs* (Cambridge MA, Harvard University Press).

Vajda, G. (1937), 'Le dialogue de l'âme et de la raison dans les Devoirs des Coeurs de Bahya Ibn Paquda', *Revue des Études Juives*, 102: 93–104.

Vajda, G. (1947), *La Théologie ascétique de Baḥya Ibn Paquda* (Paris, Imprimerie Nationale).

Van Bekkum, W. (2008), 'Pietism and Poetry in Thirteenth-Century Baghdad: A "Soul" Poem by Eleazar Ben Jacob Ha-Bavli', *Zutot*, 5.1: 43–50.

Werblowsky, R.J.Z. (1977), *Joseph Karo, Lawyer and Mystic* (Philadelphia, The Jewish Publication Society of America).

Werblowsky, R.J.Z. (1987), 'The Safed Revival and its Aftermath', in A. Green (ed.), *Jewish Spirituality*, vol. 2 (New York, The Crossroad Publishing Company), 7–33.

Wolfson, H.A. (1959), 'The Meaning of *Ex Nihilo* in Isaac Israeli', *Jewish Quarterly Review*, 50: 1–12.

Zangwill, I. (trans.) & Davidson, I. (ed.) (1924; repr. 1974), *Selected Religious Poems of Solomon Ibn Gabirol* (Philadelphia, Jewish Publication Society of America).

Zimmermann, F.W. (1986), 'The Origins of the So-called *Theology of Aristotle*', in Kraye *et al.* (1986), 110–240.

9

Karaite Poems about the Nature of the Soul from the Muslim East, Byzantium and Eastern Europe

JOACHIM YESHAYA

> Eine Seele ohne Körper ist so unmenschlich und entsetzlich, wie ein Körper ohne Seele, und übrigens ist das erstere die seltene Ausnahme und das zweite die Regel. In der Regel ist es der Körper, der überwuchert, der alle Wichtigkeit, alles Leben an sich reißt und sich aufs widerwärtigste emanzipiert. Ein Mensch, der als Kranker lebt, ist nur Körper, das ist das Widermenschliche und Erniedrigende, er ist in den meisten Fällen nichts Besseres als ein Kadaver.
>
> (Mann 1924: 139–40)

THE EPIGRAM OF this chapter is taken from the German author Thomas Mann (1875–1955), who infused his celebrated 1924 novel *Der Zauberberg* (*The Magic Mountain*) with lengthy philosophical discussions between the humanist Lodovico Settembrini, his Jesuit antagonist Leo Naphta, and two young Germans: the protagonist Hans Castorp and his tubercular cousin Joachim Ziemssen. This epigram which gratifyingly sets the stage for the intended discussion of soul/body dualism in Hebrew texts was obtained quite unexpectedly from one of Settembrini's monologues about illness and suffering. According to Settembrini:

> A soul without a body is as inhuman and horrible as a body without a soul – though the latter is the rule and the former the exception. It is the body, as a rule, which flourishes exceedingly, which draws everything to itself, which usurps the predominant place and lives repulsively emancipated from the soul. A human being who is first of all an invalid is *all* body; therein lies his inhumanity and his debasement. In most cases he is little better than a carcass.[1]

[1] Translated from the German by Lowe-Porter (1928: 100). For recent *Magic Mountain* scholarship, see the essays collected by Vaget (2008), e.g. on the topic of Jewish characters in Mann's *Magic Mountain*.

Proceedings of the British Academy, **240**, 237–252, © The British Academy 2022.

This idea is repeated by the author when the dutiful Joachim, having left Davos for some time to continue his military training, is forced to return to the sanatorium due to the deterioration of his lungs (to which he in due course would succumb):

> The body triumphs, it wants something different from the soul, and puts it through – a slap in the face of all those lofty-minded people who teach that the body is subordinate to the soul. Seems to me they don't know what they are talking about, because if they were right, a case like this would put the soul in a pretty equivocal light.
>
> (Lowe-Porter 1928: 500)

Among these 'lofty-minded people who teach that the body is subordinate to the soul' could be mentioned the Karaite-Jewish poets under discussion in this chapter. As will be illustrated below, these authors – who have often been characterised as belonging to a Jewish 'sect'[2] which rejected the authority of the Rabbinic tradition and based its customs exclusively on the Hebrew Bible – were well aware of the soul/body dualism characteristic of Jewish Neoplatonic thought, which privileged the soul (or non-corporeal realms) over the body (or corporeal world).

This chapter examines a selection of Hebrew poems dealing with this polarity between the spiritual world of the soul and the material world of the body. The Karaite-Jewish authors of these poems lived in different historical eras and widely dispersed geographical and cultural contexts, respectively in the Muslim East (Moses Darʿī, mid-12th century, Egypt), Byzantium (Aaron ben Joseph, late 13th to early 14th century, Constantinople) and Eastern Europe (Joseph ben Samuel, late 17th century, Poland).

The purpose of this investigation is threefold: first, this study gives additional evidence of the composition of philosophically charged Hebrew poetry outside the Iberian Peninsula, where Andalusia was singled out for its strong connection between poetry and philosophical theory, as discussed by Adena Tanenbaum in her groundbreaking 2002 study *The Contemplative Soul*.[3] The second purpose of

[2] On the inadequacy of the term 'sect' as applied to Karaism, see Rustow (2008: xv–xvii and xxvi–xxix). See also the volume edited by Polliack (2003) that uses the term Karaite 'Judaism' in its title in order to reject the conception of Karaism as a sect. The origin of the name *qara'im* 'Karaites' is a matter of debate and different suggestions concerning its Arabic or Hebrew origin have been suggested; however, the most obvious explanation is that it derives from the Hebrew word for Scripture – *miqra'* (note that the Arabic word *Qur'an* features the same root letters) – and that it can be translated as 'readers' or 'those who read Scripture'. In fact, an alternative name is *benei miqra'* ('sons of Scripture'), reflecting the Karaite conviction that only the Written Torah should be a source of religious law and not the Oral Torah, which according to Rabbinic belief was also given to Moses on Mount Sinai at the same time as he received the Written Torah. See Kizilov (2009: 5–6). The Karaites have sometimes been described as 'Jewish protestants' because of their insistence on *sola scriptura*, although in fact it has been widely recognised that the emergence and development of Karaism cannot be analysed without understanding its Islamic context and acknowledging that many of Karaism's driving factors lie within the intellectual world and mentality of medieval Judaism, see Polliack (2002; 2006).

[3] In the final chapter of Tanenbaum (2002: 218–43), the reception and transformation of Andalusian poems on the soul in Catalonia, Provence, Italy, Byzantium, Palestine, and Yemen is documented. Further details on their reception in Yemen are found in Adena Tanenbaum's chapter in this volume (pp. 224–32). Particularly relevant for the present chapter is Tanenbaum's discussion (2002: 226–32) of the poetic oeuvre by the Byzantine Karaite scholar Aaron ben Joseph ha-Rofe.

this study is to show that the aforementioned Karaite authors were indeed attuned to contemporary philosophical concerns, notably the soul/body dualism characteristic of Jewish Neoplatonic thought in Andalusian-Hebrew poetical garb.[4] Third, by outlining some parallels and differences between the three poems included in the anthology, this chapter considers elements of continuity and innovation in the Karaite reception of Andalusian poems on the soul.[5]

1. 'A Soul, Adorned with God's Glory'

The first poem was composed by Moses ben Abraham Darʿī, who lived in Egypt in the middle of the 12th century. His *maqāma*-style work (Davidson 1926), written in rhymed prose with interspersed verse, suggests that Darʿī, born into a family of Moroccan Jewish immigrants, was probably not born a Karaite but joined the movement in his youth, after travelling from his place of birth, Alexandria, to Fusṭāṭ-Cairo, the foremost Eastern center of Karaism after the Crusaders' conquest of Jerusalem in 1099 CE.[6] This work – entitled *Maqāma of Alexandria and Cairo* – also sheds light on the manner in which an aspiring professional poet like Darʿī went in search of patronage, and how his evident poetical talent seems to have gained him entry into the Karaite-Jewish community of Fusṭāṭ-Cairo for which he would become a sort of house poet (see Yeshaya 2014b). Indeed, while he visited Damascus and undertook a pilgrimage to Jerusalem, Darʿī spent most of his professional life as a poet and physician in the Karaite community of Fusṭāṭ-Cairo.

This community formed a distinct group with its own courts and synagogues; nonetheless, they did not consider themselves as separate from mainstream Judaism nor did the Rabbanites consider them as such. The actual differences between the two groups focused more on theoretical issues than on matters of daily life. While

[4] Leon Weinberger has written on this soul/body dualism in Karaite poetry from South-Eastern Europe, and to a lesser extent, from Egypt, see Weinberger (1991: 39–44; 1992: 150–8; 1998: 415–21; 2000: 3–42).

[5] By comparing Karaite poems written in the Muslim East, Byzantium and Eastern Europe, this paper on the one hand complements the studies by Tanenbaum and Weinberger mentioned in notes 3 and 4. On the other hand, it reflects the approach followed in the DFG-funded project 'The Introduction of Liturgical Poetry in the Karaite Prayer Book, from Moses Darʿī to Aaron ben Joseph,' which was conducted from 2010 to 2016 (first at Ruhr University Bochum then, from 2011 onward, at Goethe University Frankfurt). One of the main results of this project is the volume edited by Yeshaya & Hollender (2017).

[6] From the second half of the 10th century to the end of the 11th century, Jerusalem had been the Karaites' spiritual and intellectual centre. During this 'Golden Age' of Karaite literary activity, the Karaites produced major Judeo-Arabic works on Hebrew grammar, Bible translation, exegesis, law and philosophy. The name by which the Jerusalem Karaites are best known, 'Mourners of Zion', reflects their self-perception as a pioneering community that pursued an ascetic life of mourning, prayer and Bible study; see Erder (2003).

they did differ in dietary customs and on calendrical issues, this did not prevent intercommunal contact, as is evident from the intermarriage between Karaites and Rabbanites in 11th- and 12th-century Egypt. These marriages did not necessarily entail conversion; indeed marriage contracts contained special clauses showing how mixed marriages should be arranged so as to guarantee respect for one another's religious requirements (see Olszowy-Schlanger 1998: 252–5; Yeshaya 2011: 43–4). It should be noted that this Egyptian atmosphere of close-knit cooperation stands in contrast to the generally more troubled relations between Karaites and Rabbanites elsewhere in the Muslim East, Byzantium or Eastern Europe.

Darʿī has attained considerable fame as the exemplary Karaite poet; even in 1931 a new Karaite synagogue in Cairo's ʿAbbāsiyya quarter was named after him.[7] More than 500 of his poems have been preserved in two parts compiled by the poet himself. Darʿī is unique among Karaite poets for having written both liturgical poetry intended for synagogue service and secular (or non-liturgical) verse, as well as several poems lying between these distinct categories. Darʿī's liturgical poems, attached to the Torah readings on each Sabbath as well as the holidays, are amongst the earliest examples of inserting poetry and Andalusian poetical norms into Karaite prayer.[8] His secular collection contains panegyrics, wine and love poetry, and gnomic epigrams. Furthermore, he composed elegies, riddles, wedding songs, homonymic poems, Judeo-Arabic and bilingual verse. He also has a notable series of philosophically informed poems on the soul, inserted at the start of the first part of his poetical collection.[9] One of these poems provides evidence for regarding Judah ha-Levi (*c.* 1075–1141) as a poetic role model for Darʿī, who was active near the time that this major Andalusian philosopher and poet visited Egypt (between 1140 and 1141) and as such was one of the first Eastern-Jewish poets to bring into play Andalusian-Hebrew standards of poetry and poetics.[10]

In this chapter we will focus on the first and longest of these Hebrew soul poems,[11] which is preceded by the Judeo-Arabic heading *wa-mimmā qultu ayḍan fī*

[7] This synagogue is described in Meital (1995: 81–6).

[8] This is corroborated by the fact that Darʿī's liturgical poems (see Yeshaya 2014a) were composed well before the redaction of the Karaite prayer book by Aaron ben Joseph in the late-13th to early-14th century, see *infra* for more on this Byzantine Karaite poet.

[9] Poems no. 2, 3 and 5 in manuscript NLR Evr. I 802, fol. 5b–6b; see Yeshaya (2011: 71–2, 109–12, 152–8).

[10] The opening verse of this poem (no. 3), taken from Psalms 116:7: 'Return, my soul, to your repose for God has favored you with grace' is reminiscent of a liturgical poem by Judah ha-Levi evoking the soul's return beginning with the same Biblical quotation, see Tanenbaum (2002: 174–94, [illegible]). For other poems in Darʿī's collection that appear to have been modelled on ha-Levi's poems, see Yeshaya (2014a: 44–54).

[11] Poem no. 2 in manuscript NLR Evr. I 802: fol. 5b–6a; see Yeshaya (2011: 109–12, 152–5), where the Hebrew poem (and its Judeo-Arabic heading) was edited, translated into English, and provided with a Hebrew commentary referring to biblical quotations and allusions. In this paper, we will revise the English translation and present a fresh analysis of this remarkable Karaite poem on the nature of the soul. For more on the Judeo-Arabic poem headings in Darʿī's collection, see Yeshaya (2013). Note that this mono-rhyme poem is written in a shortened quantitative metre close to the Hebrew metre *ha-shālēm* (based on the Arabic *al-kāmil* metre).

irdāʿ al-nafs ʿan al-maʿāṣī wa-idhkārihā yawm al-qiṣāṣī ('What I also said about refraining the soul from sins and keeping in mind the Day of Reckoning') ():

A soul, adorned with God's glory,
How was she associated with the body?

Or how is it that she being enlightened by all light,
will be buried amidst all those who are preserved in their bodies?

Or how will she be defiled by menstrual blood,
a girl whose foundation is from the source of purity?

Or how did she leave divine sons and living angels,
to be tied up with the five senses?

5 Or after having been seated on the royal throne, (Esth 1:2)
will she be ready to serve the body like a loyal maidservant?

Or after having been free in heaven,
will she be tied up in a body, bound by chains?

Or after living in a high and holy dwelling,
will she be detached from it being on earth?

Or how was it that she, being created to the worship of her Creator,
betrayed her Maker and chose for her inclination?

She loved maggot and worm, and the moment of leaving [the body]
and returning upwards, she did not remember,

10 whereas she forgot the Day of Judgment and the Time of Reckoning,
with regard to every sin she gathered inside [the body];

She will receive punishment for her debt and for
her Lord's commandments which she did not keep;

Intellect will contest her in front of the Rock, at the time
of judgment, since she ignored his advice;

She will find no answer (Job 32:3) to reply him, out of great
shame for her sins, when she recollects them;

She will be ashamed and abashed for having forsaken admonitions
of moral and for having been foolish and not being careful;

15 They will take her to hell and her body will be
burnt by the burning breath of God; (Isa 30:33)

She will weep because she denied suggestions of wisdom
and because she broke the yoke from her neck; (Jer 30:8)

Who is the One who can rebuke the stubborn [soul],
who exhausted all other reproachers without being reprimanded,

who sold tomorrow by this day and whose destiny was
replaced by a void and vain beginning;

Maybe she will take heed and listen to His admonition:
that is how she will be saved from all evil;

for God has the power to evoke repentance for her,
and the right hand of her Maker is not too short to make amends;

God will grant her to do His will, and among
the souls of His adherents she will no longer rage;

And in His mercy she will slumber instead of doing
any evil, while she awakens to worship Him;

Thus she will be saved from the destruction of Time and
reach the Garden of Eden, like the man who entered Zoar;[12]

And amongst girls, there she will look like a gracious
beauty, beloved and happy;

Until amidst all the beloved ones her name will be known as:
'A soul, adorned with God's glory.'

The words of the opening hemistich of the poem, 'A soul, adorned with God's glory', are repeated in the last hemistich, a technique known as *inclusio* or the 'return'. These words contain both a Neoplatonic technical term, namely the divine *kaḇod* or glory,[13] the luminous realm from which the angels and the human soul are derived, as well as a reference to the philosophical motif of the adornment of the soul (see Tanenbaum 2002: 132–45). Then follows in the same line and in the following seven lines – all starting with the same Hebrew word ʾȯ ('or') – a whole string of questions dealing with the duality of soul and body and the agonising question as to how the pure soul became associated with the impure body. Since the Hebrew word for soul, *nefesh*, is grammatically feminine, it comes as no surprise that Darʿī – like various Andalusian-Hebrew poets before him – resorted to the feminine gender in his description of the soul as 'a girl whose foundation is from the source of purity' (in line 3); yet, the soul's portrayal in this same line as a *nidda*, a menstruating woman defiled by blood and for that reason ritually impure (cf. the discussions of menstrual laws in Leviticus 12 and 15 and in the Mishnah and Talmud tractates bearing the title *nidda*), is striking and illustrates how in Darʿī's poem one can discern a rather unfavourable perception of the soul's earthly sojourn and a relatively negative approach to the body and the senses.[14] Reference is further

[12] The reference here is to Lot, who was saved from the destruction of Sodom and Gomorrah (Gen 19:23–9).

[13] Not surprisingly, Solomon Ibn Gabirol (*c.* 1020–*c.* 1057), a pioneer of Neoplatonism in Muslim Spain, uses this term in canto no. 29 of his lengthy devotional poem based on the Neoplatonist system, *Keter Malkhut* (*Kingdom's Crown*); see Cole (2001: 137–95, esp. 172) and Tanenbaum's chapter in this volume.

[14] Such negative perceptions of the soul's embodiment are widespread in Andalusian-Hebrew poetry, but here and there, e.g. in Ibn Gabirol's *Keter malkhut*, a more positive approach to the body can be found, as has been noted by Tanenbaum (2002: 68–9). For the soul's portrayal as a menstruating woman, and more generally for feminine imagery of the soul and gender issues in medieval Hebrew literature, see chapter 4 (entitled 'Poor Soul, Pure Soul: The Soul as Woman') in Rosen (2003: 83–102, esp. 93). I thank Prof. Tova Rosen (Tel Aviv University) for directing me to her work during the XIth EAJS Congress in Kraków in 2018.

made to the conventional images of the body as the soul's grave (line 2)[15] or prison (line 6) and that of the soul as a servant of the body (line 5).[16] One can also find typical Neoplatonic light imagery (line 2), even if other metaphors suggesting emanation are missing.

Line 8 – that is, the final line starting with the Hebrew word ʾo (ʻor') – introduces a new part in the poem (lines 8–10), which shifts the emphasis onto the soul's unfaithfulness to God as a result of her union with a human body, which after death will decompose with the help of 'maggot and worm'.[17] Moreover, because of her lack of self-restraint and her pursuit of corporeal experiences, the immortal soul is unable to bear in mind on the one hand one of the crucial stages in the process of emanation – namely, the moment of leaving the physical realm of the mortal body and returning to her true source in the divine realm (line 9) – and on the other hand the punishment awaiting sinners on Judgment Day (line 10).

This idea of the punishment in the world to come is further developed in the next part of the poem (lines 11–6). Interestingly, in line with Neoplatonic theory, Darʿī differentiates between the soul and the intellect (*sekhel*),[18] which in line 12 is summoned, during the trial at the Last Judgment, to accuse the soul of turning a blind eye to good advice and of not keeping God's commandments.[19]

This allegation and the recollection of sins trigger a feeling of shame that leaves the soul speechless, as is detailed in lines 13–4. In line 15, the soul's punishment in hell, where 'her body will be burnt', is pronounced. It is unclear whether in this case 'her body' refers to the mortal world of the body in which the immortal soul dwells, or rather to the Neoplatonic theory that the soul possesses a 'vehicle' which allows her to return to the One after bodily death.[20] This part of the poem ends with the soul's expression of grief for having repeatedly ignored the warnings of the intellect.

The final part of the poem (lines 17–25) leaves little room for doubt about who might be successful in exhorting the soul to repentance, after the intellect and other

[15] This image came with a nice wordplay in Greek: soma seima, 'the body is a grave'. I thank Dr Bram Demulder (KU Leuven) for the stimulating suggestions about the three poems under discussion in this chapter.

[16] This image can also be found in canto no. 29 of *Keter Malkhut*, see Cole (2001: 172).

[17] The word combination 'maggot and worm' used by Darʿī in line 11 can be considered in the light of the following biblical source texts, Isaiah 14:11: 'Your pomp is brought down to Sheol, and the strains of your lutes! Worms are to be your bed, maggots your blanket!' and Job 25:5–6: 'Even the moon is not bright, and the stars are not bright in His sight. How much less man, a worm, the son-of-man, a maggot.'

[18] According to Tanenbaum (2002: 38–9), 'this technical distinction between soul and intellect becomes blurred in most Andalusian *piyyutim* devoted to the soul'.

[19] Cf. the trial scenes dealing with the judgement of body and soul in Andalusian poetry and rhymed prose, particularly Judah al-Ḥarīzī's (1165–1225) 'Dispute of the Soul with the Body and the Intellect', see Tanenbaum (2002: 51–4, 203ff.). Note also that the relations between the intellect – traditionally identified as male – and the soul – stereotypically conceived of as female, as we have noted before – are often explicitly gendered in medieval Hebrew literature, see Rosen (2003: 83–5). See also Adena Tanenbaum's chapter in this volume.

[20] This theory was developed by a successor to Plotinus and Porphyry, Iamblichus (245–325 CE), who brought a new religiosity to the Neoplatonist philosophical system, see Finamore (1985); Finamore & Dillon (2002).

rebukers have failed in this mission – namely, God. Furthermore, by listening to the divine admonition and performing acts of worship, the soul is able to escape the body – which will not survive the destruction of Time[21] – and reclaim her position as one of God's beloveds[22] amongst the pure souls in the divine world, where she will be known as 'A soul, adorned with God's glory', restating the words of the opening hemistich in Darʿī's poem.

2. '(O Soul), Emanated from a Holy Place'

In addition to Muslim Egypt, the centre of Karaite (literary) activities since the 12th century was Christian Byzantium, especially Constantinople, where the Karaite scholar Aaron ben Joseph ha-Rofe (*c.* 1250–1320) worked,[23] although he had probably immigrated from Crimea. Aaron was the most influential Byzantine Karaite of his time. He authored important exegetical works, including the Torah commentary *Sefer ha-mibḥar* (*The Choice Book*), which has been studied and commented upon by several Karaite authors over the centuries.[24] His biblical exegesis is proof of the reception of Andalusian Rabbanite thought and exegesis, including references to Abraham Ibn Ezra (1089–1167) and Moses Maimonides (1138–1204). Aaron also transformed the Karaite prayer ritual; in addition to his own cycle of poetic introductions to each weekly Torah reading, he included well-known liturgical compositions by Rabbanite authors, among them the Andalusians Judah ha-Levi and Abraham Ibn Ezra, creating a hybrid liturgy that has survived until today.[25]

While the linguistic purism of the Andalusian school of Hebrew poetry and the preference of its members for a biblical style might have appealed to Aaron ben Joseph, his own non-metered poems show limited participation in the aesthetics and the formal, prosodical or rhetorical preferences of that poetic school. In this

[21] In line 25, the soul is compared to Lot ('the man who entered Zoar'), who survived the destruction of Sodom and Gomorrah in Genesis 19:23–9.

[22] For more on the description of the soul as God's beloved in medieval Hebrew poetry, see Scheindlin (1991).

[23] 'The Physician;' also known as Aaron the Elder, to distinguish him from his 14th-century successor, Aaron ben Elijah of Nicomedia, also referred to as Aaron the Younger. For more on the Karaites in Byzantium, see Akhiezer (2012) and Ankori (1959).

[24] In addition to at least four supercommentaries on *Sefer ha-mibḥar*, written between the 16th and 19th centuries, a commentary on Aaron's poetic introductions to each weekly Torah reading was written in 18th-century Crimea. For the latter work, which shows how Aaron's poems were perceived as part of his exegetical work by later Karaites, see Hollender (2017). See also Yeshaya (2017) for an analysis of Aaron's oeuvre as a prime example for the interaction of poetry and exegesis, where phrases and ideas often occur parallel in his poems and in his commentary on a respective Torah portion.

[25] Due to its central importance the Karaite *Siddūr* or prayer book was the first Karaite book to be brought to press and the only one to be reprinted with any frequency. While the first edition was issued by Daniel Bomberg (d. *c.* 1549) in Venice (1528), present-day Karaites in Israel, mostly of Egyptian origin, use the Vilna edition (1891), or one of its reprints.

his poetry differs from that of Moses Darʿī, which may have contributed to the long-term acceptance of his work as opposed to that of his Eastern predecessor in Karaite poetry. Aaron ben Joseph, unlike Moses Darʿī, did not compose distinctly secular poems; yet his oeuvre does include, besides a large number of liturgical and paraliturgical poems for various occasions, a series of poems on the soul; see Weinberger (1991: 516–17, 519–20, 551–2). One of these poems, analysed in Tanenbaum (2002: 226–32), exemplifies how the language and themes used therein are strikingly similar to Andalusian precedents, reflecting a distinctive Neoplatonic notion of the soul's journey.

As the second poem in our corpus, we will now examine another example of such a soul poem by the Byzantine Karaite Aaron ben Joseph, the poem with the name acrostic *Aharon ben Yosef ḥazaq* 'Aaron ben Joseph, be strong' and the incipit *aṣula mi-meqom qadosh* 'emanated from a holy place' ():[26]

O soul, emanated from a holy place, praise Your Rock (= God);
Be unique for 'only one' (Ps 22:21) is your name, and do not be disobedient;
Observe with the eye of your heart how your charioteer [relates to] your chariot, when you look within yourself;
Get rid of immaturity, like waste, and favour whiteness over blackness;
Ask the four-fold prison, who requests your light, when it will be opened;
Withdrawn and hewn one, detest [the body brought forth] in pain from a very narrow pass;
Suppress whoredom, keep far from evil and receive knowledge;
Since the pleasure [of the body results] in grief and weakness, shun every error;
Overcome ways [of life] that are rife with pain and days spent in fear;
Turn to your Redeemer, your Glory and Splendour, associate yourself to Him;
Appeal to Him in order to encamp there and pitch your tent near Him;
[Sing] hymns and songs in praise [of Him] and look forward to your prosperity;
Conduct yourself like His holy Seraphim and draw [water] from their well:
May His mercy and His awe be your mantles and may you always put them on;
Your shoe (= body) [drives] you to sin, but the One who lifts you up to heaven deserves your praise.

Hallelujah. Praise the Lord, O my soul! (Ps 146:1)
O Lord, open my lips, and let my mouth declare Your praise. (Ps 51:17)

Aaron ben Joseph's opening of the poem with this specific epithet for the soul on the one hand puts the theory of the soul's emanation from the divine realm in sharp focus; on the other hand, it brings to mind two other poems also opening with the Hebrew word *aṣula* and composed by his eminent Spanish Rabbanite predecessor in the fields of exegesis and poetry, Abraham Ibn Ezra (see Tanenbaum 2002: 229; Tuori 2013: 234). Tuori indicates that 'the subject aroused Karaite enthusiasm, and

[26] See Weinberger (1991: 551–2). In his commentary on this poem, which he did not translate into English, Weinberger refers to a commentary by Aaron the Younger on this poem, although it is more likely that this commentary was actually written by the Polish-Lithuanian Karaite scholar Shelomo ben Aharon (1670–1745), see Bizikovich & Firkovich (1909: 5ff.); Tuori (2013: 234, 334). Unlike Darʿī's poem, this mono-rhyme poem is not written in a quantitative metre based on Arabic models.

many poems with similar titles follow the same theme'. In the second line, the soul, which Aaron ben Joseph (unlike Darʿī in his poem) has chosen as addressee, is approached with another characteristic epithet, namely *yeḥida* 'only one', based on Psalms 22:21: 'Save my soul from the sword, my only one from the clutches of a dog.' As has been noted by Tanenbaum (2002: 151), 'In his comments on Psalm 22:21–2 Ibn Ezra links this epithet to the separable quality of the human soul, which parts from the Universal Soul to sojourn with the body, and ultimately quits the body to rejoin the Universal Soul.' In the first two lines of the poem, the soul is instructed in a straightforward way to praise God and obey Him.

The third line contains an order of a more introspective nature: 'Observe with the eye of your heart how your rider [relates to] your chariot, when you look within yourself.' While 'the sight of the heart' is a typical Andalusian expression, employed as a metaphor for intellectual apprehension,[27] the rider-chariot image seems to hark back all the way to Plato's chariot allegory, used to explain his view of the human soul as a chariot pulled by two horses and ridden by a charioteer representing the intellect.[28]

So like Darʿī before him but unlike the majority of Andalusian poets, Aaron makes a distinction between the soul and the intellect. But does his use of the chariot image mean that he also accepts the notion of composite souls consisting of a lower, irrational soul and a higher, rational soul? This question becomes even more pertinent when reading the next line: 'Get rid of immaturity, like waste, and favour whiteness over blackness,' and taking into account the fact that the two horses in Plato's allegory were respectively described as white (the noble one) and black (the ignoble one). In addition to these allusions, this line includes wordplay inspired by Andalusian models – in this case, Judah ha-Levi – both in the first half of the verse (*naʿari naʿarut ki-nʿoret* 'Get rid of immaturity, like waste') and in the finding that the Hebrew word *shaḥarut* ('blackness') can also mean – like *naʿarut* – 'youth'.[29]

[27] See Tanenbaum (2002: 190): 'Ibn Gabirol and the poets following him use "the sight of the heart" and "the sight of the mind" interchangeably as metaphors for intellectual apprehension of the divine. According to Elliot Wolfson, ha-Levi uses the same metaphors, but his "vision of the heart" is a product of the imagination, rather than the intellect, and represents an experiential mode of knowing God, akin to prophetic vision.' One can find parallels for such inward vision of God – evoking the notion that the heart is capable of grasping more of the divine presence than human reason – among other Neoplatonic and/or Sufi writers. Ibn ʿArabī (1165–1240; of Spanish descent, like ha-Levi) in particular contrasts the superiority of the heart (*al-qalb*) over reason (*al-ʿaql*) as organ of perception (see Sells 1994: 90–100).

[28] *Phaedrus*, 246a–246b. In his Hebrew commentary to this line, Weinberger quotes from the commentary in Bizikovich & Firkovich (1909: 5ff.), which does equate the 'rider' with the intellect, but unlike Plato associates the 'chariot' with the body.

[29] Both hemistiches in Aaron ben Joseph's fourth line – 'Get rid of immaturity, like waste, and favour whiteness over blackness' – refer to Judah ha-Levi's poem *yeshena be-ḥeq yaldut* ('[O soul] sleeping in the bosom of youth'), an interior monologue between the speaker and his soul, which contains quasi identical words in the first lines: '*neʿurim ka-nʿoret ninʿaru*' (line 1) and '*ha-laʿad yeme ha-shaḥarut*?' (line 2); for the Hebrew text of ha-Levi's poem, see http://benyehuda.org/rihal/rihal10_4.html#26 (last accessed September 2018). I thank Dr Yonatan Vardi (Hebrew University of Jerusalem) for this reference given during the XIth EAJS Congress in Kraków in 2018.

In line 5 the body, described as a four-fold prison longing for the light of the soul, comes into play. This reflects contemporary scientific knowledge about the four elements (earth, water, air and fire) which provide the building blocks of the body, a combination of elements which could only thrive when being animated by the soul. While dealing with the duality of soul and body, the poet maintains the direct address to the soul in this line and throughout the poem; the soul is advised to ask the four-fold prison when it will be unlocked. In the following lines, the soul is urged to turn away from the pleasures of the body (lines 6–9) and instead turn towards God (lines 10–15). In line 6, we find two epithets for the soul which reflect knowledge of Ibn Gabirol's *Keter Malkhut* – namely, *neqira gezura* 'withdrawn and hewn one'[30] – as well as a reference to the pain that awaits women in labour. The instruction in line 7 to receive knowledge (apparently as a means of expediting the return to the divine realm) is followed later on in the poem with the advice to approach God through prayer, piety and good conduct.[31] The poem ends with more wordplay (*na'alekh ma'alekh u-ma'alekh be-ma'alekh haleli*) and surprising epithets for respectively the body ('your shoe'[32]) and God ('the One who lifts you up to heaven') in line 15, before it is concluded by a couple of fitting quotations from the biblical book of Psalms.

3. 'Blessed be you, O Jewish Soul'

The third poetic fragment was composed by Joseph ben Samuel (*c.* 1650–1700) in Poland, thus bearing witness to the long-lasting and far-reaching nature of the Karaite reception of Andalusian poems on the soul ( ):

> Blessed be you, O Jewish soul,
> who imagines a faith of wisdom;
> For your image is in the heaven,
> the first light, the head of the words of the Lord;
> Since your residence in the body is short,
> strive to know the works of the Lord (Ps 118:17);
> For it (i.e., the body) will return to oblivion
> whereas you will return to the hand [upon] the throne of the Lord (Exod 17:16).

[30] Cf. Isaiah 51:1: 'Look to the rock you were hewn from, to the quarry you were dug from' and canto no. 29 in Ibn Gabirol's *Keter malkhut*: 'Who could grasp Your intensity in forming the radiance of purity from the glow of Your glory, from a rock the Rock has hewn, from the hollow of a clearness withdrawn?' The Hebrew text can be found in Levin (2005: 276), whereas the English translation is taken from Cole (2001: 172).

[31] This reminds us of the different attitudes of Solomon Ibn Gabirol and Judah ha-Levi towards intellectualism, cf. Tanenbaum (2002: 180): 'Where Ibn Gabirol prescribes philosophical speculation as the means of elevating one's soul to the divine realm, ha-Levi speaks of approaching God through prayer and pious deeds.'

[32] In his Hebrew commentary on this line, Weinberger quotes from the commentary in Bizikovich & Firkovich (1909: 5ff.), which explains this epithet as follows: the body relates to the soul like the shoe relates to the foot, since feet can walk without shoes, but not vice versa.

Not much is known about the author of this poem;[33] he may have been active as a *ḥazzan* (cantor) of the Karaite community of Halicz (present-day Halych on the Dniester River in western Ukraine). The fragment contains the sixth strophe of a paraliturgical poem comprising nine eight-line strophes in total, dedicated to Shavuot, the Feast of Weeks. The strophe starts with a notable difference with the previous two poems in that it addresses the 'Jewish soul', assuming a particularistic touch quite unlike Neoplatonic theory with its attention to the human or Universal Soul. Yet in the remainder of the strophe, the parallels it shares with the previous two poems are obvious. Besides their stress on knowledge acquisition, the most striking shared themes are the return of the immortal soul to its divine source – the Throne of Glory which Neoplatonists equated with the sphere of the Intellect – and the contrast with the extinction of the mortal body in which the soul temporarily resides.

4. Conclusion

This leads us, in conclusion, to some final remarks concerning elements of continuity and innovation in Karaite adaptations of the Andalusian poem devoted to the soul. The subject of the polarity between body and soul was a constant source of inquiry in medieval philosophy, exegesis and poetry, also among Karaite Jews. How else can it be explained that Karaite poets living in Cairo, Constantinople and Halicz in different historical eras were composing philosophically charged Hebrew poems evoking popularised Neoplatonic concepts about the soul's divine origin and its imprisonment in the body? Their source of inspiration was unquestionably the Andalusian-Hebrew poetical tradition, as is evident by their adoption of typical metaphors, stock epithets for the soul and Neoplatonic technical terms first used by the Jewish pioneers of Neoplatonism in Muslim Spain, in the first place Solomon Ibn Gabirol.

Yet while the overall tradition of composing Hebrew poems on the soul was stable and highly conventionalised, it is possible nevertheless to detect a few innovative touches in the three poems discussed in this chapter. Some of these are shared between two of the authors discussed here. For example, Moses Darʿī and Aaron ben Joseph, unlike the majority of Andalusian poets, both seem to make a distinction between the soul and the intellect. Others are more personal. Living in Egypt near the time of Judah ha-Levi's visit, Moses Darʿī was most directly

[33] For more on this author, see Tuori (2013: 75–8), who edited and also partly translated the poem (including the strophe addressing the 'Jewish soul'; it should be noted that this is the only appearance of this word combination in Tuori's corpus and as such rather unusual also among Eastern European Karaite authors). See also Tuori's excellent discussion (on pp. 230–4, esp. p. 232) of Eastern European Karaite poems dealing with the polarity between body and soul. For more on the Karaites in Eastern Europe and the Crimea, see Harviainen (2003). Unlike Darʿī's poem, this mono-rhyme poem is not written in a quantitative metre based on Arabic models.

and comprehensively influenced by the aesthetics and the formal, prosodical, and rhetorical preferences of the Andalusian school of Hebrew poetry. Moreover, his hesitant use of metaphors suggesting emanation may possibly be understood against the background of ha-Levi's ambivalent attitude towards Greco-Arabic philosophy.[34]

Aaron ben Joseph was the only one of these three Karaite poets to have written important exegetical prose works incorporating theoretical discussions of philosophy in addition to his poetical compositions, and this is noticeable in his dense use of technical language, conventional or more original epithets, and wordplay.[35] Aaron seems to have drawn inspiration from contemporary philosophical, psychological and scientific knowledge and from previous Andalusian poetry and exegesis; his role model in both of the latter fields was Abraham Ibn Ezra.

In his turn, the Byzantine-Karaite scholar Aaron ben Joseph later became a paragon of a poet-exegete whose works were studied and commented upon even centuries later by Crimean and Eastern European Karaites. One of his admirers and followers in the Polish-Lithuanian Commonwealth was Joseph ben Samuel. His poem – like Aaron's – directly addresses the soul, but assumes a particularistic touch by the addition of the identifier 'Jewish' to the soul. Yet the rest of the stanza illustrates once again the soul/body dualism typical of the Karaite poets' Andalusian models, with whom they shared a fascination with the Neoplatonic myth of the immortal soul's ascent from incarceration in the mortal body to her true source in the divine realm.

References

Akhiezer, G. (2012) 'Byzantine Karaism in the 11th to 15th Century', in R. Bonfil, O. Irshai, G.G. Stroumsa & R. Talgam (eds), *Jews in Byzantium: Dialectics of Minority and Majority Cultures* (Leiden/Boston, Brill), 723–58.

Ankori, Z. (1959), *Karaites in Byzantium: The Formative Years 970–1100* (New York, Columbia University Press).

Bizikovich, J. & Firkovich, I. (1909), *Tĕhillōt yiśrā'ēl* (Berditshev, Sheftel).

Cole, P. (2001), *Selected Poems of Solomon Ibn Gabirol* (Princeton, Princeton University Press).

Davidson, I. (1926), 'The Maqāma of Alexandria and Cairo' [Hebrew], *Maddā'ē ha-Yahădūt*, 2: 296–308.

[34] Cf. Tanenbaum (2002: 181): 'The Neoplatonic drama of the soul figures prominently in Halevi's poetic corpus. Deftly crafted, his poems on the soul feature the full range of motifs which, by his time, had come to be associated with the genre. Occasionally, though, it is possible to detect an omission or slight alteration of emphasis which implies a reluctance to endorse a purely philosophical eschatology.' For more on ha-Levi as a philosopher, see Goodman (1997). For more on the soul/body dualism in Jewish thought, see Rudavsky (1997).

[35] It would be interesting to investigate to what extent Aaron's poem can be expounded against the background of his own exegetical writing, along the lines of Yeshaya (2017); such investigation is, however, beyond the scope of this chapter.

Erder, Y. (2003), 'The Mourners of Zion: The Karaites in Jerusalem in the Tenth and Eleventh Centuries', in Polliack (2003), 213–35.

Finamore, J. (1985) *Iamblichus and the Theory of the Vehicle of the Soul* (Chico, Scholars Press).

Finamore, J. & Dillon, J. (2002) *Iamblichus'* De Anima*: Text, Translation, and Commentary* (Leiden, Brill).

Frank, D. & Lehman, O. (eds) (1997), *History of Jewish Philosophy* (London/New York, Routledge).

Goodman, L. (1997), 'Judah Halevi', in Frank & Lehman (1997), 188–227.

Harviainen, T. (2003), 'The Karaites in Eastern Europe and the Crimea', in Polliack (2003), 633–55.

Hollender, E. (2017), 'Berakha ben Joseph's Commentary on the *piyyūṭīm* by Aaron ben Joseph', in Yeshaya & Hollender (2017), 292–317.

Kizilov, M. (2009), *The Karaites of Galicia: An Ethnoreligious Minority among the Ashkenazim, the Turks, and the Slavs 1772–1945* (Leiden/Boston, Brill).

Levin, I. (2005), *The Crown of Kingship ('Keter Malkhut') of Solomon Ibn Gabirol* [Hebrew] (Tel Aviv, Tel Aviv University Press).

Lowe-Porter, H.T. (1928) *Thomas Mann, The Magic Mountain*, trans. H.T. Lowe-Porter (repr. 1971: London, Secker & Warburg).

Mann, T. (1924) *Der Zauberberg* (Berlin, S. Fischer Verlag; repr. 1982: Stuttgart-Hamburg-München, Deutscher Bücherbund).

Meital, Y. (1995), *Jewish Sites in Egypt* [Hebrew] (Jerusalem, Ben-Zvi Institute).

Olszowy-Schlanger, J. (1998), *Karaite Marriage Documents from the Cairo Geniza: Legal Tradition and Community Life in Medieval Egypt and Palestine* (Leiden, Brill).

Polliack, M. (2002), 'Medieval Karaism', in M. Goodman (ed.), *The Oxford Handbook of Jewish Studies* (Oxford, Oxford University Press), 295–327.

Polliack, M. (ed.) (2003), *Karaite Judaism: A Guide to Its History and Literary Sources* (Leiden, Brill).

Polliack, M. (2006), 'Rethinking Karaism: Between Judaism and Islam', *Association for Jewish Studies Review*, 30.1: 67–93.

Rosen, T. (2003), *Unveiling Eve: Reading Gender in Medieval Hebrew Literature* (Philadelphia, University of Pennsylvania Press).

Rudavsky, T. (1997), 'Medieval Jewish Neoplatonism', in Frank & Lehman (1997), 149–87.

Rustow, M. (2008), *Heresy and the Politics of Community: The Jews of the Fatimid Caliphate* (Ithaca, Cornell University Press).

Scheindlin, R. (1991), *The Gazelle: Medieval Hebrew Poems on God, Israel and the Soul* (Oxford, Oxford University Press).

Sells, M. (1994), *Mystical Languages of Unsaying* (Chicago, Chicago University Press).

Siddūr ha-tĕfillōt kĕ-minhāg ha-yĕhūdīm ha-qārā'īm, 4 vols (Vilna, 1891; repr. Ramle, 1978; repr. Ashdod, 2010).

Tanenbaum, A. (2002), *The Contemplative Soul: Hebrew Poetry and Philosophical Theory in Medieval Spain* (Leiden, Brill).

Tuori, R. (2013), *Karaite Zĕmīrōt in Poland-Lithuania: A Study of Paraliturgical Karaite Hebrew Poems from the Seventeenth and Eighteenth Centuries* (Helsinki, Unigrafia).

Vaget, H.R. (ed.) (2008), *Thomas Mann's* The Magic Mountain*: A Casebook* (Oxford, Oxford University Press).

Weinberger, L. (1991), *Rabbanite and Karaite Liturgical Poetry in South-Eastern Europe* (Cincinnati, Hebrew Union College Press).

Weinberger, L. (1992), 'Karaite *Piyyuṭ* in Southeastern Europe', *Jewish Quarterly Review*, 83.1–2: 145–65.

Weinberger, L. (1998), *Jewish Hymnography: A Literary History* (London, The Littman Library of Jewish Civilization).

Weinberger, L. (2000), *Jewish Poet in Muslim Egypt, Moses Darʿi's Hebrew Collection* (Leiden, Brill).

Yeshaya, J. (2011), *Medieval Hebrew Poetry in Muslim Egypt: The Secular Poetry of the Karaite Poet Moses ben Abraham Darʿī* (Leiden, Brill).

Yeshaya, J. (2013), 'A Bouquet of Arabic and Hebrew Flowers: The Judaeo-Arabic Poem Headings in Moses Darʿī's *dīwān*', in U. Vermeulen *et al.* (eds), *Egypt and Syria in the Fatimid, Ayyubid and Mamluk Eras* 7 (Leuven, Peeters), 165–71.

Yeshaya, J. (2014a), *Poetry and Memory in Karaite Prayer: The Liturgical Poetry of the Karaite Poet Moses ben Abraham Darʿī* (Leiden, Brill).

Yeshaya, J. (2014b), 'Some Observations on Jewish Poets and Patrons in the Islamic East: Twelfth-Thirteenth Centuries', in E. Alfonso & J. Decter (eds), *Patronage, Production, and Transmission of Texts in Medieval and Early Modern Jewish Cultures* (Turnhout, Brepols), 79–97.

Yeshaya, J. (2017), 'Aaron ben Joseph's Poem for *Pārāshat Yitrō* Considered in Light of His Torah Commentary *Sēfer ha-miḇḥār*', in Yeshaya & Hollender (2017), 207–27.

Yeshaya, J. & Hollender, E. (eds) (2017), *Exegesis and Poetry in Medieval Karaite and Rabbanite Texts* (Leiden, Brill).

Part III

Christian and Jewish Neoplatonism in Italy and Spain (14th to 17th Centuries CE)

10

'*Nostro intelletto si profonda tanto*': The Philosophical Background of Dante's *Paradiso* I, 1–12 and IV, 22–60

CRISTINA D'ANCONA*

1. Dante and Neoplatonism: An Outline

DANTE'S PHILOSOPHICAL POSITIONS have long been debated. In the past century, the contrast between 'Thomism' and 'Averroism' as the main inspiration of his thought set the tone of scholarly discussions,[1] but the presence of Platonic and Neoplatonic ideas in addition to his fundamental Aristotelian allegiance has also been repeatedly noticed by variou scholars. Some contended that the entire *Commedia* reveals a Neoplatonic stance, with its overarching idea of the unique causality of God that is received differently by the different degrees of the creation (Dronke 1965: 389–91; see also Palgen 1955; 1974), its movement of descent from and ascent to the first

* I am deeply grateful to Trevor Dadson, Gianfranco Fioravanti, Stefan Sperl and Mirko Tavoni. They saved me from a number of errors; for those which remain I am alone responsible. My heartfelt thanks also go to Yorgos Dedes.

[1] Nardi famously advocated the second view, protesting against 'la leggenda del tomismo di Dante' (Nardi 1911, 1912; 1967: 379); Mandonnet (1935) advocated a refined version of the first view. In arguing his point, Nardi did not fail to highlight the Neoplatonic influences, mostly conveyed by Albert the Great. In the *Avvertenza* that opens the 1930 collection of his previous studies under the label *Saggi di filosofia dantesca*, he summarises his position as follows: 'Dante conosce certamente alcuni scritti tomistici e ne fa uso; ma molto piú spesso egli cita opere di Alberto Magno, che sono state per lui una ricca miniera di informazioni dottrinali e dalle quali proviene, in gran parte, quella forte tinta neoplatonica, e per niente tomistica, che colorisce tutto quanto il pensiero filosofico del poeta' (Nardi 1967: ix). For a balanced, though critical evaluation of Mandonnet (1935), see É. Gilson (1939); see also Marenbon (2000); for a comprehensive assessment, see Fioravanti (2019) and, for a more general perspective, the volume which contains Fioravanti's essay: de Libera *et al.* (2019). Towards the end of the past century, the debate verged towards Aristotelianism *vs* 'eclecticism': see Dronke (1986) and Mazzotta (1992). This 'eclecticism' is at times coupled with 'encyclopedism' (for an overview see Baranski 2000: 77–101), but if this term implies distance from academic culture, it gives room to disagreement: see the remarks by Fioravanti (2014: 9–10), who emphasises, with special reference to the *Convivio*, that the works quoted by Dante point to the university teaching of philosophy in its most technical output. For contemporary caveats on 'Neoplatonic' influences,

principle (Freccero 1959; 1962), and the climax towards intuitive vision of the circles 'of three colours and one circumference' (*di tre colori e d'una contenenza*, *Par*. XXXIII, 116–17) that represent the theophany of the ineffable One God (Pézard 1954: 174). For others, inspirations of Platonic origin like the celestial topography with the Empyrean encompassing the Aristotelian earth-centred cosmos (Nardi 1967: 167–214), the ideas of the cosmic soul (Freccero 1962: 117–18), the soul's wings (Pézard 1954: 176–8),[2] man as a microcosm and ultimate happiness as *deificatio* (Palgen 1955; McMahon 2006: 1–63)[3] are best understood as Neoplatonic concepts with which Dante became acquainted through various channels of transmission: Augustine, Dionysius the pseudo-Areopagite, Boethius and the Latin versions of Arabic works like the *Liber de Causis* (Nardi 1924).[4] All point to the *Timaeus* as the main Platonic source, directly read in Calcidius's translation,[5] or indirectly known through other authors, chiefly but not exclusively Boethius.[6]

Among the Platonic-Neoplatonic ideas that contributed to shape Dante's mindset, that of the inadequacy of human language to express the divine realities is admittedly among the most relevant. Stated at the very beginning of the *Paradiso*, limitations of language are argued for in the *Convivio*[7] and in the *Letter to Cangrande della Scala*.[8] Dante's claims have been commented upon repeatedly in the light of the influence of negative theology in all its medieval versions (Montemaggi 2010), while noting his allegiance to a theory of literary expression that has been labelled as 'symbolism' by some (Singleton 1949; Pépin 1987) and as 'semiotics' by others (Baranski 2000).[9]

In the *Convivio*, commenting upon the Canzone seconda *Amor che ne la mente mi ragiona*, Dante points to two reasons why the human intellect (*mente*)[10] cannot completely grasp the divine realities: the first *ineffabilitade* has to do with the

see Moevs (2005), Hedley (2010), Gardner (2013); for a recent survey of Dante's debt to Thomas Aquinas, see S. Gilson (2013).

[2] Although not mentioning Dante, Courcelle (1974) fills the gap indicated by Pézard (1954: 178), when the latter alluded to the 'large tradition platonicienne' transmitting the image of the winged soul to the 'courant de l'éloquence religieuse avant que Dante vint s'y abreuver'.

[3] Palgen (1955); McMahon (2006: 1–63).

[4] For an overview of the main Neoplatonic sources see Gardner (2013).

[5] Pézard (1954: 166); Palgen (1955: 283); Freccero (1962: 116–7); De Bonfils Templer (1986; 1987).

[6] For a survey of the opinions in Cristiani (1984^2 [2005]) and Gardner (2013: 115) see below n. 49. On Boethius as Dante's source see Gardner (2013: 141–44) and Lombardo (2013).

[7] *Conv*. III iv 1–4; see Fioravanti (2014: 393).

[8] The passage of the *Ep*. XIII directly refers to the beginning of the *Paradiso* quoted below, § 3, see n. 13. A survey of the main scholarly positions apropos the authorship of *Ep*. XIII is given in Villa (2014: 1565–7).

[9] Gardner (2013: 125) voices this attitude very clearly: 'the greatest importance of Neoplatonism for the poet lies not in philosophical positions which he supports against contemporary Aristotelian challengers, but in the mode by which he integrates his philosophical theology into his poetry'.

[10] On the definition of 'mente', based on Aristotle's *De Anima* reinterpreted in Neoplatonic terms, cf. *Conv*. III ii 14: 'E quella anima che tutte queste potenze comprende, [ed] è perfettissima di tutte l'altre, è l'anima umana, la quale colla nobilitade della potenza ultima, cioè ragione, partecipa della divina natura a guisa di sempiterna Intelligenza: però che l'anima è tanto in quella sovrana potenza nobilitata e dinudata da materia, che la divina luce, come in angelo, raggia in quella: e però è l'uomo divino animale dalli filosofi chiamato'. For the sources of this statement (Boethius, Avicenna, Thomas Aquinas) cf. Fioravanti (2014: 379); in particular on Boethius – the direct source – cf. Lombardo (2013: 181). Dante's

incapacity of the human mind to understand them completely; the second, with the incapacity of language adequately to express what the intellect has conceived.[11] This idea governs the opening *terzine* of the *Paradiso*, and Beatrice devotes a specific philosophical development to it in canto IV. After discussing the beginning of the *Paradiso* and surveying its Neoplatonic background, I will focus on Beatrice's argument, where Dante's philosophical assumptions about language, its limitations and its power are outlined. Finally, the connection between vv. 1–12 of the first canto of the *Paradiso* and Beatrice's philosophical excursus in the fourth will be presented against the background of Plotinus's theory of Platonic myths. This does not imply engaging in hypotheses about Dante's own position, an issue that a non-specialist simply cannot discuss. My point will only be to suggest that Plotinus should be taken into account in this context. There are two reasons for this, notwithstanding the fact that Dante obviously never read a line of the *Enneads*. First, the philosophical implications of Plotinus's interpretation of those assessments in the *Timaeus* that are expressed in mythical language go beyond the topic of the allegorical exegesis of the story of the creation of the cosmic soul and visible world. Second, and more importantly for the present purpose, the possibility exists that an echo of the characteristically Plotinian way to present the reasons why Plato decided to express some of his doctrines through myths reached Dante through Macrobius, who is arguably his source on this specific issue.

2. *Paradiso* I, 1–12: The Neoplatonic Background

As mentioned above, the beginning of the *Paradiso* is often quoted apropos Dante's hierarchical vision of the cosmos, whose Neoplatonic inspiration appears in the *Letter to Cangrande della Scala* (I, 1–3, [illegible]):[12]

---

mente of *Conv.* III ii 19 is reminiscent of the Neoplatonic *apex mentis*: 'Onde si puote omai vedere che è mente: che è quella fine e preziosissima parte dell'anima che è deitate. E questo è il luogo dove dico che Amore mi ragiona della mia donna'. On the Neoplatonic ἄνθος τοῦ νοῦ or *apex mentis* in Medieval Latin philosophy and literature cf. von Ivánka (1950) and Beierwaltes (1963).

[11] *Conv.* III iii 14–15. Fioravanti (2014: 36–7) remarks that this does not imply downgrading philosophy in favour of metaphoric language. 'Esiste infatti anche una filosofia specificamente umana … e di cui Dante intende parlare nel seguito del trattato (cfr. *Cv* III xiii 3). È una filosofia segnata dal limite: come viene ripetuto piú volte, l'intelletto umano non può conoscere l'essenza di Dio, né quella degli enti immateriali (angeli per i teologi e per "la volgare gente", intelligenze motrici dei cieli per i filosofi) né la natura dell'eternità, né quella della materia prima (cfr. *Cv* III iv 9; xv 6). Si tratta però di un limite naturale della nostra ragione … Esso non ci impedisce di raggiungere, qui su questa terra, quella beatitudine di cui aveva parlato Aristotele, esaltando nell'*Etica Nicomachea* la vita di chi, esercitando al grado massimo la razionalità, realizza pienamente le sue capacità di uomo'. See also De Bonfils Templer (1990).

[12] Here Dante explains himself about the philosophical assumptions of the *terzina* quoted above: 'Dicit ergo quod "gloria primi Motoris" qui Deus est "in omnibus partibus universi resplendet", sed ita ut "in aliqua parte magis, et in aliqua minus". Quod autem ubique resplendeat, ratio et auctoritas manifestat'. The *ratio* is construed as an argument based on Aristotle's warning against infinite regression; the *auctoritas* is Prop. 1 of the Neoplatonic *Liber de Causis*, about the priority of the first cause over the causality of every derivative principle, as universal as it might be. The cosmic hierarchy based on the different levels of

> The Glory of Him who moveth everything
> penetrates all the Universe, and shines
> more brightly in one part, and elsewhere less.[13]

But also the three subsequent *terzine* are Neoplatonic in inspiration, even though the echo of St Paul's second Letter to the Corinthians gives the prevailing tone (I, 4–12, [illegible]):[14]

> Within the Heaven which most receives His light
> I was; and saw what he who thence descends
> Neither knows how, nor hath the power, to tell;
>
> for as it draweth near to its Desire,
> our intellect so deeply skins therein,
> that recollection cannot follow it.
>
> As much, however, of the holy Realm
> as in my memory I could treasure up,
> shall now become the subject of my song.[15]

What we have here, put in philosophical terms, is the twin claim that (1) what is 'seen' in the Empyrean cannot be expressed because of the failure of memory, and (2) notwithstanding this, the vision has been in part retained in the visitor's mind and will form the subject of the third cantica.[16]

---

reception of the causality of the first principle is accounted for as follows: 'Quod autem subicit de "magis et minus" habet veritatem in manifesto; quoniam videmus in aliquo excellentiori gradu essentiam aliquam, <aliquam> vero in inferiori, ut patet de celo et elementis, quorum quidem illud incorruptibile, illa vero corruptibilia sunt' (*Ep.* XIII, 20 and 23).

[13] All translations of the Divine Comedy are from Langdon (1921). 'La gloria di colui che tutto move / per l'universo penetra, e risplende /in una parte piú e meno altrove.'

[14] Echoed in the concluding passages of the *Letter to Cangrande della Scala*: 'Et hoc insinuatur nobis per Apostolum ad Corinthios loquentem, ubi dicit: "Scio hominem, sive in corpore sive extra corpus nescio, Deus scit, raptum usque ad tertium celum, et vidit arcana Dei, que non licet hominem loqui". Ecce, postquam humanam rationem intellectus ascensione transierat, quid extra se ageretur non recordabatur' (*Ep.* XIII, 28). This forgetfulness (*non recordabatur*) is often accounted for in terms of a psychological phenomenon accompanying mysticism, with no specific philosophical import: cf. for instance Mazzotta (1992: 155), commenting upon this same passage of the Letter: 'Prophetic visions from the Old Testament, estatic raptures from the New Testament, and patristic treatises of mystical and contemplative theology are bundled together as the heterogeneous context for the poet's own visionary claims'. The Neoplatonic inspiration of Dante's ideas about the insufficiency of language is instead acknowledged by Montemaggi (2010) and Gardner (2013: 139).

[15] 'Nel ciel che piú de la sua luce prende / fu' io, e vidi cose che ridire / né sa né può chi di là sú discende, /perché appressando sé al suo disire, / nostro intelletto si profonda tanto / che dietro la memoria non può ire. / Veramente quant'io del regno santo / nella mia mente potei far tesoro / sarà ora materia del mio canto.'

[16] Dante comments as follows: 'Ad que intelligenda sciendum est quod intellectus humanus in hac vita, propter connaturalitatem et affinitatem quam habet ad substantiam intellectualem separatam, quando elevatur, in tantum elevatur, ut memoria post reditum deficiat propter transcendisse humanum modum' (*Ep.* XIII, 28).

Is this an ambiguity due to the fact that poetry is not expected to follow the rules of technical philosophy? Obviously not. The same ambiguity characterises the entire Platonic tradition when confronted with the apparently inconsistent statements that the human soul is destined to forget what it has seen in the hyperuranion[17] before descending again to the terrestrial world (*Republic*), while recollection of what had been seen in that realm can somehow be reactivated in the soul (*Meno*). Recollection is successful, and brings the soul back to the hyperuranion, if the desire caused by the soul's exposure to beauty is directed towards the true object of love, namely the intelligible (*Phaedrus*, *Symposium*). Thus, it comes as no surprise that at the end of the *Purgatorio* Beatrice mentions the Platonic immersion in the river Lethe as the cause of forgetfulness,[18] nor is it surprising that Dante, in the auto-commentary on the opening *terzine* of the *Paradiso*, has recourse to Plato.[19]

The same dual status of the human cognition of the intelligible – forgetfulness versus an innate capacity for recollection – features in Plotinus who expresses it in various ways, all highly sophisticated. Taken by itself, the soul is characterised by discursive thinking which cannot grasp the intelligible substances as they are. However, the knowledge of these must be granted to the soul in some form, unless one is ready to dismantle the most elementary assumption of Platonism: the natural affinity between the soul and the intelligible (*Phaedo*). In Plotinus's account, the intellect, the highest of the cognitive faculties of the soul, can grasp that level of being which, although inaccessible to sense-perception, is not only real, but even more real than the visible world. The real being – the intelligible – has the power to 'produce' the visible world as it is the cause of the intrinsic rationality (hence reality) of all that exists, albeit in a derivative way. The intelligible Forms that grant the visible things their rational structure can be grasped by the human soul, provided that it is ready to go outside the cave, which in Plotinus's view means that it should be prepared to learn from Plato how to recollect the Forms that are already present in it. Once instructed at Plato's feet (under the guidance of Plotinus's own heavily interpretive reading), the soul aiming at recollection realises that the intelligible Forms have to be conceived according to their own principles, not as

[17] Plato's expression ὑπερουράνιος τόπος (lit. 'the place beyond the heavens') occurs in the myth of the winged chariot at *Phaedr.* 247 C 3. It indicates in spatial terms the intelligible reality seen by gods, and also by the human souls before their fall to the earth. The same reality is called in the *Republic* νοητὸς τόπος (VI, 508 C 1).

[18] *Purg.* XXXIII, 95–6. This obviously does not imply any acquaintance with the *Republic*. On Dante's sources (chiefly Virgil, *Aen.* VI, 704–5), cf. Mazzamuto (1984, 2005).

[19] After having mentioned the Pauline ascent to the third heaven (see above n. 14), Dante continues: 'Vidit ergo, ut dicit, aliqua "que referre nescit et nequit rediens". Diligenter quippe notandum est quod dicit "nescit et nequit": nescit quia oblitus, nequit quia, si recordatur et contentum tenet, sermo tamen deficit. Multa tamen per intellectum videmus quibus signa vocalia desunt: quod satis Plato insinuat in suis libris per assumptionem metaphorismorum: multa enim per lumen intellectuale vidit que sermone proprio nequivit exprimere' (*Ep.* XIII, 29).

if they were visible items transferred to the hyperuranion. The adoption of this Aristotelian principle[20] elicits the characterisation of the intelligible Forms by a series of features that, counter-intuitive as they might be, solve some Platonic puzzles, though predictably creating new ones. Examples would go beyond the limits of this chapter, but one of these features relates to the question of human knowledge and should be mentioned. Plotinus repeatedly points out that while our discursive knowledge proceeds by taking into account the intelligibles one after another, if we were capable of seeing the intelligibles as they are, we would realise that they operate all together, ὁμοῦ πάντα,[21] something that is suggested by the status of the theorems 'in' the science of geometry, where their distinction from one another does not impede the presence of geometry as a whole in each of them (cf. Tornau 1998). Non-discursive knowledge, or intellectual intuition, grasps the simplicity and at one and the same time the co-implication of the intelligible Forms; but this is not the usual way our soul operates. Such a cognitive status can happen after prolonged concentration and is not impossible for the human soul; the intellectual intuition of the real nature of the intelligible items is in fact quite frequent for those who exercise their reasoning.[22] This is the way in which Plotinus interprets, or overstates if you so wish, the Platonic dividing line between the sensible and the intelligible realms.[23] The consequence is that intellectual intuition of the Forms and discursive reasoning about them are both contiguous (by dealing with the same object and by being faculties of one and the same soul) and irreconcilable (in their operational mode).

This sketch of Platonic and Neoplatonic doctrine sounds familiar; less familiar, and typical of Plotinus, is the refusal to allow memory to be present as a faculty of the soul when the latter is 'in' the intelligible realm. In his long and convoluted treatise *On Difficulties about the Soul*,[24] Plotinus has a discussion of memory and the intelligible and concludes that there is no room for memory 'there'. It is true that he deals here with a topic that is different from Dante's: while the *terzine* quoted above

[20] *Enn.* VI 5 [25] 2.1–9, A: VII, 329: 'Λόγος δὲ ἐπιχειρήσας ἐξέτασιν ποιεῖσθαι τοῦ λεγομένου οὐχ ἕν τι ὤν, ἀλλά τι μεμερισμένον, παραλαμβάνων τε εἰς τὴν ζήτησιν τὴν τῶν σωμάτων φύσιν καὶ ἐντεῦθεν τὰς ἀρχὰς λαμβάνων ἐμέρισέ τε τὴν οὐσίαν τοιαύτην εἶναι νομίσας, καὶ τῇ ἑνότητι ἠπίστησεν αὐτῆς ἅτε μὴ ἐξ ἀρχῶν τῶν οἰκείων τὴν ὁρμὴν τῆς ζητήσεως πεποιημένος. Ἡμῖν δὲ ληπτέον εἰς τὸν ὑπὲρ τοῦ ἑνὸς καὶ πάντη ὄντος λόγον οἰκείας εἰς πίστιν ἀρχάς· τοῦτο δ' ἐστὶ νοητὰς νοητῶν καὶ τῆς ἀληθινῆς οὐσίας ἐχομένας.' 'But the reason which tried to make the investigation of what we are talking about, since it is not one thing but something divided and brings along to its enquiry the nature of bodies and takes its principles from them, both divided substance, thinking that it was of this [bodily] kind, and disbelieved in its unity, because it did not take the starting-point of its enquiry from the principles proper to substance. But we must take for our reasoning about the one and altogether existent principles which, being proper to it, will lead to conviction: that is, intelligible principles of intelligibles and those which belong to true substance.' The Aristotelian source is *An. Post.* I 2, 71 b 23 and 72 a 6.

[21] Anaxagoras' fr. B1 is repeatedly quoted by Plotinus, obviously out of context and for the purpose of illustrating the nature of the intelligible realm.

[22] See the passage quoted below, n. 27, where the adverb πολλάκις ('often') occurs.

[23] *Resp.* VI, 509 D 6 – 511 D 5.

[24] *Enn.* IV 3–5 [27–9].

reflect the traditional Platonic account of the forgetfulness that affects the soul when it descends to the visible world, in *Difficulties about the Soul* Plotinus argues that the human soul, once back in the intelligible realm, does not retain any memory of its earthly life. However, it is admittedly the Plotinian model of intellectual intuition that forms the philosophical background of the medieval accounts of the *visio beatifica*, and this model excludes memory as a kind of knowledge for which there is no need in such a cognitive state.[25] Intellectual intuition would be reminiscent of Russell's 'knowledge by acquaintance', were it not for the fact that, at variance with this kind of non-descriptive cognition, the form of knowledge alluded to by Plotinus when he adopts the (Stoic) terminology of ἐπιβολὴ ἀθρόα[26] has nothing to do with perception.

Even more germane to the present topic is that in other passages Plotinus speaks of exactly the same thing as Dante: the incapacity of the human mind to sustain the brilliance of the intelligible world once 'ascended' to it, and the paucity of the knowledge it can recover of such an object, once 'descended' to discursive thinking.[27]

[25] *Enn.* IV 4 [28] 1.11–16, A: IV, 137: 'Εἰ δὲ καί, ὥσπερ δοκεῖ, ἄχρονος πᾶσα νόησις, ἐν αἰῶνι, ἀλλ' οὐκ ἐν χρόνῳ ὄντων τῶν ἐκεῖ, ἀδύνατον μνήμην εἶναι ἐκεῖ οὐχ ὅτι τῶν ἐνταῦθα, ἀλλὰ καὶ ὅλως ὁτουοῦν. 'Αλλὰ ἔστιν ἕκαστον παρόν· ἐπεὶ οὐδὲ διέξοδος οὐδὲ μετάβασις ἀφ' ἑτέρου ἐπ' ἄλλο.' 'But if, as we believe, every act of intelligence is timeless, since the realities there are in eternity and not in time, it is impossible that there should be a memory there, not only of the things here below, but of anything at all. But each and every thing is present there; so there is no discursive thought or transition from one to the other.' The remark that memory implies time and perception of time is of course Aristotelian: *De Mem.* 1, 449 b 24–31: 'ἔστι μὲν οὖν ἡ μνήμη οὔτε αἴσθησις οὔτε ὑπόληψις. ἀλλὰ τούτων τινὸς ἕξις ἢ πάθος, ὅταν γένηται χρόνος. Τοῦ δὲ νῦν ἐν τῷ νῦν οὐκ ἔστι μνήμη, καθάπερ εἴρηται καὶ πρότερον. ἀλλὰ τοῦ μὲν παρόντος αἴσθησις, τοῦ δὲ μέλλοντος ἐλπίς, τοῦ δὲ γενομένου μνήμη. διὸ μετὰ χρόνου πᾶσα μνήμη.' 'Memory is not perception or conception but a state or affection of one of these, conditioned by lapse of time. As already observed, there is no such thing as memory of the present while present, for the present is object only of perception, and the future, of expectation, but the object of memory is the past. All memory, therefore, implies a time elapsed' (trans. Beare [1908]). For a detailed analysis of Plotinus's reception of and reactions to Aristotle's doctrine of memory cf. King (2009); for a survey of the medieval reception of the Platonic and Aristotelian notions of memory see Coleman (1992).

[26] *Enn.* IV 4[28] 1.20, A: IV, 139, translates it as 'unified intuition'. Ficinus' rendition is *intuitus totus*. This makes memory not suitable in such a cognitive status; as King (2009: 163) has it, 'the characteristic performances of memory are propositional performances'.

[27] *Enn.* IV 8 [6] 1.1–11, A: IV, 397: 'Πολλάκις ἐγειρόμενος εἰς ἐμαυτὸν ἐκ τοῦ σώματος καὶ γινόμενος τῶν μὲν ἄλλων ἔξω, ἐμαυτοῦ δὲ εἴσω, θαυμαστὸν ἡλίκον ὁρῶν κάλλος, καὶ τῆς κρείττονος μοίρας πιστεύσας τότε μάλιστα εἶναι, ζωήν τε ἀρίστην ἐνεργήσας καὶ τῷ θείῳ εἰς ταὐτὸν γεγενημένος καὶ ἐν αὐτῷ ἱδρυθεὶς εἰς ἐνέργειαν ἐλθὼν ἐκείνην ὑπὲρ πᾶν τὸ ἄλλο νοητὸν ἐμαυτὸν ἱδρύσας, μετὰ ταύτην τὴν ἐν τῷ θείῳ στάσιν εἰς λογισμὸν ἐκ νοῦ καταβὰς ἀπορῶ, πῶς ποτε καὶ νῦν καταβαίνω, καὶ ὅπως ποτέ μοι ἔνδον ἡ ψυχὴ γεγένηται τοῦ σώματος τοῦτο οὖσα, οἷον ἐφάνη καθ' ἑαυτήν, καίπερ οὖσα ἐν σώματι.' 'Often I have woken up out of the body to myself and have entered into myself, going out from all other things; I have seen a beauty wonderfully great and felt assurance that then most of all I belonged to the better part: I have actually lived the best life and come to identity with the divine; and set firm in it I have come to that supreme actuality, setting myself above all else in the realm of Intellect. Then after that rest in the divine, when I have come down from Intellect to discursive reasoning, I am puzzled how I ever came down, and how my soul has come to be in the body when it has shown itself to be by itself, even when it is in the body.' Cf. also V 1 [10] 1.1–3, A: V, 11: 'Τί ποτε ἄρα ἐστὶ τὸ πεποιηκὸς τὰς ψυχὰς πατρὸς θεοῦ ἐπιλαθέσθαι, καὶ μοίρας ἐκεῖθεν οὔσας καὶ ὅλως ἐκείνου ἀγνοῆσαι καὶ ἑαυτὰς καὶ ἐκεῖνον.' 'What is it, then, which has made the souls forget their father, God, and be ignorant of themselves and him, even though they are parts which come from his higher world and altogether belong to it?'

That Plotinus's account, in his rephrasing of Plato's *Republic* and *Phaedrus*, echoes indirectly St Paul's II Corinthians 12: 2–5 is a fair guess,[28] and that the verse *vidi cose che ridire / né sa né può chi di là su discende* (saw what he who thence descends / neither knows how, nor hath the power, to tell) echoes the Pauline passage is said by Dante in as many words.[29] What Plotinus and Dante share with St. Paul is the reshaping of the Platonic heritage of the soul's forgetfulness in terms of ineffability.[30] A descended soul cannot *express* the nature of the things seen or heard in the 'third heaven' (St. Paul) or intelligible realm (Plotinus) or Empyrean[31] (Dante). As the latter states in the *Epistola a Cangrande della Scala*, this failure of the soul to express what it has seen and to some extent also understood – a failure that echoes the second kind of *ineffabilitade* of the *Convivio* – accounts for the fact that Plato switched to allusive language (*metaphorisma*) when speaking of realities that can be seen *per lumen intellectuale*, but do not have the corresponding *signa vocalia*, at least if one wants to express them accurately (*sermone proprio*).[32] Although keeping the poetical and scriptural allegories distinct in Dante's vein,[33] it

[28] II Corinthians, 12: 2–4. 'οἶδα ἄνθρωπον ἐν Χριστῷ πρὸ ἐτῶν δεκατεσσάρων – εἴτε ἐν σώματι οὐκ οἶδα εἴτε ἐκτὸς τοῦ σώματος οὐκ οἶδα, ὁ θεὸς οἶδεν – ἁρπαγέντα τὸν τοιοῦτον ἕως τρίτου οὐρανοῦ. καὶ οἶδα τὸν τοιοῦτον ἄνθρωπον – εἴτε ἐν σώματι εἴτε χωρὶς τοῦ σώματος οὐκ οἶδα, ὁ θεὸς οἶδεν – ὅτι ἡρπάγη εἰς τὸν παράδεισον καὶ ἤκουσεν ἄρρητα ῥήματα ἃ οὐκ ἐξὸν ἀνθρώπῳ λαλῆσαι.' English trans. (English Standard Version): 'I know a man in Christ who fourteen years ago was caught up to the third heaven – whether in the body or out of the body I do not know, but God knows – and I know that this man was caught up into paradise – whether in the body or out of the body I do not know, but God knows – and he heard things that cannot be told, which man may not utter.' See above n. 14 and n. 19.

[29] See above n. 14.

[30] According to Corti (1987: 17) 'Dante risulta il primo scrittore ad aver inserito il lessema *ineffabile* coi suoi derivati nel volgare italiano.'

[31] See Nardi (1967: 167–214).

[32] The text is quoted above, n. 19.

[33] For the distinction between the 'allegoria dei poeti' and the 'allegoria dei teologi' cf. *Conv.* II i 5: 'Veramenti li teologi questo senso prendono altrimenti che li poeti; ma però che mia intenzione è qui lo modo de li poeti seguitare, prendo lo senso allegorico secondo che per li poeti è usato.' To explain the allegorical meaning of his canzoni is the task Dante sets for himself in the *Convivio*, I i 18 – a claim to be read with the following remarks by Fioravanti (2014: 26–27): 'Ora una caratteristica rilevante della cultura filosofica del XIII secolo è proprio il rifiuto di ogni polisemia, tanto piú se programmatica: i testi di Aristotele sono certamente suscettibili di diverse interpretazioni … ma compito del commentatore è precisamente quello di ricondurli ad un significato univoco. A maggior ragione ogni ambiguità semantica sarà bandita dall'altro grande settore della vita intellettuale universitaria, quello della disputa, e verrà fatta propria l'avvertenza formulata da Aristotele nei *Topici* secondo cui è scorretto utilizzare metafore nella discussione di problemi scientifici e filosofici. Rimane certamente il vastissimo campo della teologia intesa come esegesi dei testi bibilici, ed è proprio a questa che Dante sembra voglia riallacciarsi … Ma la polisemia del testo sacro, segno di una ricchezza inesauribile di senso aperta ad una interpretazione infinita, era stata considerata fin da Agostino un caso particolare. Dante non può pretendere di mettere le sue canzoni alla stregua della parola rivelata e dunque distingue tra allegoria dei teologi e allegoria dei poeti. Ponendosi, sia come autore che come esegeta, sotto l'egida della seconda, egli si riallaccia ad una tradizione tardoantica che aveva nel commento di Macrobio al *Somnium Scipionis* il fondamento teorico e nelle interpretazioni virgiliane di Fulgenzio il primo esempio di applicazione dell'interpretazione allegorica ad un testo poetico nella sua interezza.'

is noteworthy that in the *Epistola a Cangrande della Scala* he applies to Plato the epistemic principle that if something is ineffable in the second sense, then the language adopted cannot but be inaccurate.

3. Neoplatonism and Aristotelianism in *Paradiso*, IV, 22–60

Paradiso IV is the *locus classicus* for the discussion of Dante's 'Platonism', because it is one of the two places where the *Timaeus* is mentioned, its doctrine of the descent of the souls from and return to the stars is partly rehabilitated, and the topic of the language of both Plato's *Timaeus* and Scripture is discussed.[34] Dante's encounter with Piccarda Donati in *Paradise* III – more precisely, the fact that he meets the souls of Piccarda and of Costanza d'Altavilla in the sphere of the Moon – gives rise to twin instances of doubt, which are divined by Beatrice and to whose solution *Paradise* IV is devoted. In what follows the first doubt[35] will be ignored and the focus will instead be on the second: 'where' in the intelligible realm are the blessed souls? Why do they appear distributed, so to speak, according to a hierarchy, if – as the Christian faith proclaims – they all will see God 'face to face' once in heaven?

Beatrice's theological solution is directly derived from the principle that shapes the entire treatment of the *Paradiso*, namely the first *terzina* quoted above. The diversity of glory enjoyed by the blessed souls depends upon their diverse capacity as recipients, not upon a supposedly diverse effusion of the divine light, which would imply God's 'decision' to grant only a diminished glory to some (IV, 37–9,):

> They did not here reveal themselves, because
> this special sphere had been allotted them,
> but to express the lowest heavenly state.[36]

The solution (vv. 28–39) is encapsulated between two philosophical statements: (1) the allusion to Plato's doctrine of the return of the souls each to the star it descended from, which is presented as the explanation that comes to Dante's mind (IV, 22–4,):

> Again it gives thee cause for doubt, that souls
> seem to return unto the stars again,
> according to the opinion Plato held.[37]

[34] Cf. Vanni Rovighi (1971), Prandi (2007) and Gardner (2013: 149–56). Deen Schildgen (2007) suggests reading *Paradise* IV against the background of the Islamic tradition on allegory.

[35] The question is how is it possible that blessedness is diminished because of an event that happened by force. Both Piccarda and Costanza were obliged to leave the monastic life, nonetheless their souls are located in the relatively low sphere of the Moon as if they had decided to leave of their own free will.

[36] 'Qui si mostraro, non perché sortita / sia questa spera lor, ma per far segno /della spiritual c'ha men salita.'

[37] 'Ancor di dubitar ti dà cagione / parer tornarsi l'anime alle stelle / secondo la sentenza di Platone.'

And (2) the mention of the Aristotelian principle that governs the solution. The principle is expressed as follows (IV, 40–2):

> Thus must one speak to your intelligence,
> since only from sense-objects can it learn
> what it thereafter fits for understanding.[38]

This doctrine is grounded in the *Posterior Analytics*, I 18, on which more later. For the moment, let us pause to note that in Beatrice's solution, the practice of Scripture to represent the suprasensible realities, including God, in a sensible form is based precisely on this Aristotelian principle. Because our *ingegno* operates on the grounds of sense-perception, Scripture speaks of God and the separate substances in anthropomorphic terms (IV, 43–5):

> Because of this the Scriptures condescend
> to your capacity, and feet and hands
> ascribe to God, and yet mean something else.[39]

Then Beatrice proceeds to explain a doctrine in the *Timaeus* which in her opinion is the cause of Dante's perplexity (IV, 49–51):

> That which Timaeus teaches of the soul
> is not like that which one up here beholds,
> for, as he says it, so he seems to mean.[40]

The subsequent account of the *Timaeus* (IV, 52–7) elaborates on this idea, to the effect of disavowing the face value of Plato's assertions. According to Beatrice, this passage of the *Timaeus* may not really intend to state that each soul returns to the star it descended from. From a Christian perspective, this meaning can hardly be accepted, on the one hand because it has deterministic implications that contradict the direct creation of the human soul by God, and, on the one other because it is incompatible with the principle of free will. Beatrice, however, does not charge Plato with heterodoxy;[41] instead, she declares that the passage may have a deeper meaning which deserves to be explored because the overt meaning does not make sense (IV, 52–7):

> He says that each soul to its star returns,
> because he thinks that it was severed thence,
> when Nature granted it as form; and yet

[38] 'Cosí parlar conviensi al vostro ingegno / però che solo da sensato apprende / ciò che fa poscia d'intelletto degno.'
[39] 'Per questo la Scrittura condescende / a vostra facultate, e piedi e mano / attribuisce a Dio, ed altro intende.'
[40] 'Quel che Timeo de l'anime argumenta / non è simile a ciò che qui si vede, / però che, come dice, par che senta.'
[41] This applies instead to those alluded to by William of Conches in the passage from his *Glosae super Platonem* which is cited below; see n. 53.

His doctrine is, perhaps, of other guise,
than what his words imply, and may possess
a meaning which is not to be despised.[42]

The relevant passage, *Tim.* 42 a 3 – c 1, reads:

> So, once the souls were of necessity implanted in bodies, and these bodies had things coming to them and leaving them, the first innate capacity they would of necessity come to have would be sense perception, which arises out of forceful disturbances. This they all would have. The second would be love, mingled with pleasure and pain. And they would come to have fear and spiritness as well, plus whatever goes with having these emotions, as well as their natural opposites. And if they could master these emotions, their lives will be just, whereas if they were mastered by them, they would be unjust. And if a person lived a good life throughout the due course of time, he would at the end return to his dwelling place in his companion star, to live a life of happiness that agreed with his character. But if he failed in this, he would be born a second time, now as a woman.[43]

The Latin version of the *Timaeus* was the work of the otherwise unknown late Antique scholar Calcidius,[44] who between the end of the 4th century and the beginning of the 5th authored both a translation of the dialogue until 53 c, and a commentary on part of the section he had translated.[45] The commentary covers the part from 31 c to 53 c.[46]

Calcidius's *Timaeus* – translation and commentary – was well known in the Middle Ages,[47] but neither the Latin version of the passage quoted above,[48] nor the explanation offered by Calcidius of the relationship between souls and stars,[49] contain anything apt to shed light on Dante's verses. Hence scholarship

[42] 'Dice che l'alma a la sua stella riede / credendo quella quindi esser decisa / quando natura per forma la diede; / e forse sua sentenza è d'altra guisa / che la voce non suona, ed esser puote / con intenzion da non esser derisa.'

[43] Trans. Zeyl (1997: 1245).

[44] Ed. Waszink (1975); English trans. Magee (2016).

[45] Waszink (1975: xv); see also Ratkowitsch (1995).

[46] As such, the commentary belongs to the well-established tradition of commentaries on sections of the dialogue, a literary genre on which see Ferrari (2000; 2012). The foundational study on the commentaries on the *Timaeus* is Baltes (1976–8); see also Baltes (1993: 209–10).

[47] On Calcidius's translation and commentary at Chartres see Klibansky (1939: 21–31), Gibson (1969), Wetherbee (1972: 28–36), Ratkowitsch (1996), Somfai (2002).

[48] *Timaeus a Calcidio translatus* 42 A 3 – C 1: 'Cumque necessitate decreti corporibus inserentur corporeaque supellex uarie mutabitur quibusdam labentibus et alii inuicem succedentibus membris, primo quidem sensum et uiolentis passionibus excitari, post quem mixtam ex uoluptate tristitiaque cupidinem nasci, tum uero metum atque iracundiam ceterasque pedissequas earum perturbationes diuerso affectu pro natura sua permouentes; quas quidem si frenarent ac subiugarent, iustam his lenemque uitam fore, sin uincerentur, iniustam et confragosam. Et uictricibus quidem ad comparis stellae contubernium sedemque reditum patere acturis deinceps uitam ueram et beatam, uictas porro mutare sexum atque ad infirmitatem naturae muliebris relegari secundae generationis tempore.'

[49] Calcidius, *Commentarium*, CXXXVI: 'Quasdam tamen animas quae uitam eximie per trinam incorporationem egerint uirtutis merito aereis uel etiam aethereis plagis consecrari putat a necessitate

has often questioned whether he had even been acquainted with the text itself.[50] The prevailing view is that his knowledge of the dialogue was second-hand. The best candidate as the source of Dante's information about the Platonic doctrine of the descent of the souls from and return to the stars is Albert the Great.[51] In any case, there is nothing in Calcidius's account of *Timaeus* 42 a 3 – c 1 that may have suggested the existence of a more profound philosophical meaning, *sentenza*, beyond Plato's *voce* ('His doctrine is, perhaps, of other guise, than what his words imply', trans. Langdon).[52] Rather, there is general scholarly agreement that Dante's evaluation of the Platonic metaphors as adumbrating valuable philosophical truths is rooted less in Calcidius's translation than in the medieval reception of it, chiefly in the School of Chartres. Thus, we move from the 4th or 5th century to the 12th, and from Calcidius's Middle Platonic commentary to the allegorical interpretation propounded by the Chartrian philosopher-theologians (Wetherbee 1972; Lemoine 1998), here voiced by William of Conches's *Glosae super Platonem*.[53]

> Now some, reading the letter of the text, say that here Plato taught heresy: for Holy Writ says that God creates new souls daily. But what wonder, if at times an Academic speaks Academically? If he always spoke the truth, he would not be an Academic. All the same, if one grasps not merely Plato's words but his meaning, not only will he not find heresy, he will find profoundest philosophy hidden beneath a veil of words. And as we love Plato, we will endeavor to reveal it. (trans. Gardner 2013: 117)

The commentaries upon *Paradise* IV all have recourse to William's distinction between the *littera* ('letter') that functions as *integumentum* ('surface layer'), and the philosophical truth concealed beneath it.[54] The doctrine of the

---

incorporationis immunes. CXCVI: Horum omnium praemia etiam constituit, uictricibus uitiorum animis reditum ad caelestem sedem perpetuamque immunitatem.'

[50] Whether or not Dante had direct knowledge of the *Timaeus* in Calcidius's version is a long debated question, recapitulated as follows by Cristiani (1984², 2005): 'D. lo cita solo due volte, in *Cv* III V 6 e in *Pd* IV 49, senza tuttavia dimostrare familiarità con i temi dell'opera; si è infatti discusso a lungo se egli ebbe o no conoscenza diretta del dialogo platonico. (…) Per la conoscenza diretta del T. da parte di Dante, nulla si può stabilire con certezza prendendo in esame la confutazione da parte di Beatrice (in *Pd* IV 22–5 e 49–63) di un testo ben noto del T. (41d e ss.) ov'è questione del ritorno dell'anima alla stella a cui è legata da particolari relazioni; del resto, per la dottrina dell'anima D. appare in contrasto puntuale con alcune tesi platoniche. È stato anzi osservato (…) che l'atteggiamento esitante di Beatrice (cfr. vv. 55–61) lascia piuttosto pensare a una conoscenza incerta.' As for *Convivio* III, V 6, Fioravanti (2014: 401) shows by means of textual comparisons that 'nonostante il riferimento esplicito al *Timeo*, l'esposizione delle dottrine platoniche dipende sempre da quanto ne dice Aristotele (*De caelo* II 13, 293 b 30–2), con alcune differenze'. Also for Gardner (2013: 127, n. 28) 'direct knowledge is unlikely', while Pézard (1954: 174, n. 3) and De Bonfils Templer (1986: 277) side with the idea of direct reading.

[51] Vanni Rovighi (1971: 73) points to Albert the Great's *De Natura et origine animae*, II 7, ed. Geyer (1955: 30–1); Prandi (2007: 130) quotes the same passage. See also below, n. 66.

[52] See above, n. 42.

[53] Guillelmi de Conchis *Glosae super Platonem* ed. Jeauneau (2006).

[54] On the topic of *integumentum*, with special but not exclusive reference to Guillaume of Conches, see Jeauneau (1957); for Bernardus Silvestris, see Silvestris (1978: 75); for a very useful survey see

various levels of meaning developed in the Middle Ages for Scripture is thereby extended to the *Timaeus*.[55] Hence the different locations where the blessed souls dwell – be it a star as in the *Timaeus*, or a *mansio* like in Scripture[56] – allude to the diverse degrees of vicinity to God. Thomas Aquinas elaborates further on this topic as follows:

> In addition, 'room' seems to indicate a 'place'; but the 'place' where the saints will be blessed is not a physical one, rather it is a spiritual one, namely God, and God is one. Hence there is only one 'room', and for this reason the different degrees of blessedness cannot be defined 'rooms' ... As for the second argument, the point is that even though the spiritual place is only one, there are nevertheless different degrees of vicinity with respect to that place, and in this sense different 'rooms' are set in place. [57]

This passage might well be the direct or indirect[58] source of Dante's verses 37–39: 'they did not here reveal themselves, because / this special sphere had been allotted to them, / but to express the lowest heavenly state' (trans. Langdon).

By distinguishing between *integumentum* and *sensus*, Beatrice's solution to Dante's doubt thus appears to be the result of extending to the *Timaeus* the frequently attested literary theory of the allegorical reading of the Scripture. This in itself is worthy of note, but there is still more to these verses.

As mentioned above, what is characteristic of Dante and in keeping with the philosophical culture of his time is that, following in Thomas's footsteps, he makes Beatrice justify the Chartrian distinction between *integumentum* and *sensus* on Aristotelian grounds. The relevant passage is *Posterior Analytics*, I 18, 81 a 38–40:

> It is evident too that if some perception is wanting, it is necessary for some understanding to be wanting too – which is impossible to get if we learn either by induction or by demonstration ... (trans. Barnes 1984: 132)

In the Latin version,[59] this passage runs:

> Manifestum est autem quod, si aliquis sensus deficit, necesse et scientiam defecisse, quam inpossibile sumere si discimus aut inductione aut demonstratione.[60]

Wetherbee (1972: 36–48); in relationship with Dante, Hollander (1969); with special reference to *Par.* IV, Vanni Rovighi (1971: 74), Prandi (2007: 126–8).

[55] Cf. de Lubac (1959–64).

[56] The passage commented upon by Thomas here is John 14:2: 'In my Father's house are many rooms. If it were not so, would I have told you that I go to prepare a place for you?' (English Standard Version).

[57] Thomas Aquinas, *Super Sent.*, lib. 4, d. 49, q. 1 a. 4 qc. 3 arg. 2; ad 2.

[58] Dante's acquaintance with works of Thomas Aquinas other than the *Summa contra Gentiles* (whose knowledge is unanimously acknowledged) is discussed, with reference to previous literature, by S. Gilson (2013).

[59] On the Latin versions of the *Posterior Analytics*, with special reference to the text at the disposal of Thomas Aquinas, see Minio-Paluello (1952).

[60] *Aristoteles latinus* IV, 1–4 ed. Minio-Paluello (1968: 136).

Although surely available to him on chronological grounds, this Latin version is not the direct source of Dante.[61] Rather, it is Thomas's use of the Aristotelian tenet that resonates in Beatrice's speech. Not only the saying *nihil in intellectu quod prius non fuerit in sensu* is attested in philosophical texts like the *De Veritate*, but in the *Summa theologica* Thomas offers also a comparison with Scripture that is in all likelihood Dante's source. In the second question of his *De Veritate*, Thomas says:

> In addition, there is nothing in the intellect unless first it was in sense-perception. As for the 19th argument, it should be said that this sentence is to be referred to our intellect, whose knowledge begins from the external things: little by little, intellect brings a thing from its materiality to immateriality, and this happens via the immateriality of sense-perception: this is why it is necessary that what is in our intellect was prior in sense-perception.[62]

In the *Summa theologiae*, I, q. 1 a. 9 resp., he says:

> I respond: It is appropriate for Sacred Scripture to teach about divine and spiritual things by means of likenesses drawn from corporeal things. For God provides for all things in a way that is suitable to their nature. But it is natural for man to approach intelligible things through sensible things, since all our cognition takes its origin from the senses. Hence, it is appropriate for Sacred scripture to teach us spiritual things by way of metaphors drawn from corporeal things.
>
> (trans. Freddoso)

Beatrice's exegesis of the *Timaeus* – which she likens in this respect to the metaphorical language of Scripture – rephrases Thomas Aquinas's confidence that when the latter adopts a mode of expression *sub similitudine corporalium*, it simply takes into account a natural feature of human cognition that has been singled out, as happens almost everywhere, by Aristotle.

4. A Neoplatonic Source for *Paradiso* IV

While surely prominent, the Chartrian and Aristotelian traditions are not the only ones to be echoed in *Paradiso* IV. The first book of Macrobius's commentary on the *Dream of Scipio*[63] contains an account of the use of myths to convey philosophical truths, that could justifiably be considered to be one of the sources of Beatrice's solution.

[61] First, the wording is different; second, Minio-Paluello (1980: 68) remarks that, at variance with what he does when quoting other Aristotelian works, 'With one minor exception – five words quoted from Boethius' translation of *De Sophisticis Elenchis* – Dante never mentions Aristotle's name or exact titles of works when he uses concepts or procedures coming from the Philosopher's logical and epistemological works'.

[62] Thomas Aquinas, Q.D. *De Veritate*, q. 2, a. 3, 19; ad 19.

[63] Cf. Flamant (1977) and Armisen-Marchetti (2001–2). On the reception in the Middle Ages see Caiazzo (2002); on Macrobius as a source for Dante see Prandi (2007: 119), Gardner (2013: 129–35) and Rossi (2017).

Myths and fabulous narratives, says Macrobius, can be used in philosophical discourse only subject to qualification. Only when the philosophical doctrine involved concerns the lowest degrees of the divine is one allowed to have recourse to myths. If the subject matter is the First Principle, fabulous narratives are inadequate, and for this reason Plato declared the First Principle to be beyond any linguistic expression. Indeed, the intelligible reality cannot be expressed by the human mind in a way which is adequate to its real status: beyond space and time, accessible only to intellect and in no way to imagination based on sense-perception, that reality cannot be described adequately if one has recourse to images or narratives. Now, Macrobius continues, this is precisely what the 'ancient popular tradition' does, when it represents the gods in a visible way, as having different ages or as being located in one or another place. The *philosophi* have clearly seen the insufficiency of such images and narratives, going as far as to deny any truth to the *simulacra* of the gods, and it is only when they consciously move to another mode of language in order to express features that go beyond understanding, that they have recourse to *similitudines* and *exempla*, like the Sun of the *Republic*. Here too, however, such a figurative mode of speech is apt to account only for some features of the divine, and not the highest:

> [13] We should not assume, however, that philosophers approve the use of fabulous narratives, even those of the proper sort, in all disputations. It is their custom to employ them when speaking about the Soul, or about spirits having dominion in the lower and upper air, or about gods in general. [14] But when the discussion aspires to treat of the Highest and supreme of all gods, called by the Greeks the Good (*tagathon*) and the First Cause (*proton aition*), or to treat of Mind or Intellect, which the Greeks call *nous*, born from and originating from the Supreme God and embracing the original concepts of things, which are called ideas (*ideai*), when, I repeat, philosophers speak about these, the Supreme God and Mind, they shun the use of fabulous narratives. When they wish to assign attributes to these divinities that not only pass the bounds of speech but those of human comprehension as well, they resort to similes and analogies. [15] This is why Plato, when he was moved to speak about the Good, did not dare to tell what it was, knowing only this about it, that it was impossible for the human mind to grasp what it was. In truth, of visible objects he found the sun most like it, and by using this as an illustration opened a way for his discourse to approach what was otherwise incomprehensible. [16] On this account men of old fashioned no likeness of the Good when they were carving statues of other deities, for the Supreme God and Mind sprung from it are above the Soul and therefore beyond nature. It is a sacrilege for fables to approach this sphere. [17] But in treating of the other gods and the Soul, as I have said, philosophers make use of fabulous narratives; not without a purpose, however, not merely to entertain, but because they realize that a frank, open exposition of herself is distasteful to Nature, who, just as she has withheld an understanding of herself from the uncouth senses of men by enveloping herself in variegated garments, has also desired to have her secrets handed by more prudent individuals through fabulous narratives.
>
> [20] In truth, divinities have always preferred to be known and worshiped in the fashion assigned to them by ancient popular tradition, which made images of beings that had no physical form, represented them as of different ages, though they were

> subject neither to growth nor decay, and gave them clothes and ornaments, though they had no bodies. [21] In this way Pythagoras himself, and Empedocles, Parmenides, and Heraclitus spoke of the gods, and Timaeus, their disciple, continued the tradition that had come down to him.[64]

That this account of the use of myths in philosophy, and in particular section [20] above, has a bearing on *Paradise* IV is suggested by a telling detail. Compare Macrobius's account of popular tradition 'which made images of beings that had no physical form' and 'represented them as of different ages, though they were subject neither to growth nor to decay' (*quae et imagines et simulacra formarum talium prorsus alienis, et aetates, tam incrementi quam diminutionis ignaris … adsignavit*) with the souls in *Paradise* IV, 33 whose 'being does not have more or fewer years' (*né hanno all'essere loro piú o meno anni*). This verse has been interpreted also in other ways,[65] but it seems to me that Macrobius's passage sheds light on Beatrice's comparison between the truth (there is no time in the divine realm) and the appearance (souls, or gods in the myths, feature as young or old people).

In addition to this, Macrobius's passage ends with a mention of the philosophers who made use of the same device: Pythagoras, Empedocles, Parmenides and Heraclitus. Their disciple Timaeus continued the same tradition, and it is a fair guess that this passage inspired Dante, either directly or indirectly since his key source Albert the Great also alludes to a philosophical tradition of Platonic provenance that discusses myths.[66]

But if this so, philosophical consequences arise whose relevance goes beyond the mere hunt for sources. Macrobius, here as elsewhere, is not an original thinker. He does nothing more than elaborate on Plotinus's ideas about the use of myths to give a sequential account of the intelligible realities whose mode of being is in fact one of unchangeable perfection and simultaneous omnipresence in their logical truths. This is the status of all the principles present in the intelligible realm, and this explains why memory, whose *ratio* is, by contrast, the apperception of mental contents in succession, has no place in it.

According to Plotinus, Plato can convey in one and the same work metaphysical truths that express the real nature of the intelligible, with no other shift than the inevitable alternation between intellectual intuition, discursive reasoning and also myths. To discuss Plotinus's exegesis of the *Timaeus* in depth would go beyond the scope of this chapter, but we should at least point out that when he cites this dialogue as a source for metaphysical statements apropos the nature of the divine

[64] Macrobius, *Commentary on the Dream of Scipio*, trans. Stahl (1952, reprint 1990: 85–7).

[65] Prandi (2007: 119) points to the idea that 'i beati, senza una dislocazione precisa, senza alcuna età o 'anzianità' rispetto al tempo che hanno trascorso in Paradiso, godono dell'unità in Dio, pur partecipando in gradi diversi del suo amore'.

[66] Cf. the passage that is the probable source of Dante's summary of the *Timaeus*, singled out by Vanni Rovighi (1971), above n. 51, Albert says: 'Haec igitur fuit opinio Socratis et Platonis et omnium in Academia philosophantium, et super hoc multae fundantur fabulae poetarum.' The allusion to the *fabulae poetarum* suggests that Albert was familiar with Macrobius's passage.

Intellect, or the constitution of the world-soul, or again the nature of time and eternity, he takes its wording at face value. When, on the other hand, he has to account for the fact that the dialogue presents the divine Intellect as though it were a craftsman operating in time and after deliberation, he engages in lengthy and complex explanations to persuade his readers that this is not what Plato intended. Is Plato here resorting to metaphorical language, according to Plotinus? Not exactly. The point for him is that when the intelligible reality is described in its causal relationship with that inferior degree of reality that involves time, the inadequacy of language is even more blatant. Herein lies the reason why Plato has recourse to myth when he presents us with divine intelligible principles engaged in temporal action, and this also explains the similarity between myth and discursive reason. The latter resembles myth in that it cannot grasp the intelligible contents all at once, as they are in reality. Our soul can only grasp them one by one, and for this reason the causality of the intelligible principles is expressed by us in terms of priority in time, while obviously being of logical-ontological nature. One of the best-known passages where Plotinus formulates this analogy between myth and discursive reasoning occurs in his interpretation of the myth of *Symp.* 203 b – e:

> But myths, if they are really going to be myths, must separate in time the things of which they tell, and set apart from each other many realities which are together, but distinct in rank or powers, at points where rational discussions, also, make generations of things ungenerated, and themselves, too, separate things which are together; the myths, when they have taught us as well as they can, allow the man who has understood them to put together again that which they have separated.[67]

Plotinus has sophisticated arguments both on myths in philosophical works and on rationality, time, and memory as compared to intellect, eternity, and intuition. Dante knew nothing of this. However, thanks to Macrobius an echo of the Neoplatonic epistemology reached him and contributed to shape the idea that when faced with the divine reality *nostro intelletto si profonda tanto / che dietro la memoria non può ire.*

References

Armisen-Marchetti, M. (2001–2), *Macrobe. Commentaire au Songe de Scipion*, I-II (Paris, Les Belles Lettres).

Baltes, M. (1976–8), *Die Weltentstehung des platonischen Timaios nach den antiken Interpreten*, I-II (Leiden, Brill).

[67] III 5 [50] 9.24–9, A: III 201. Wolters (1984: 248), remarks: 'A common misconception is that the introduction of temporal distinctions is the characteristic feature of mythology for Plotinus. The fact is that he is here more concerned with another feature of myths: their splitting up (quite apart from time) of an integral reality into a plurality of distinct mythical symbols. Furthermore, neither of these features is typical of myths: Plotinus explicitly states that both apply also to philosophical discourse (λόγοι). In fact, Plotinus here gives no systematic account of the nature of myths at all, though we may infer that he considers the "temporalising" and "pluralising" nature of language in general to be particulary evident in myths.'

Baltes, M. (1993), *Der Platonismus im 2. und 3. Jahrhundert nach Christus. Band 3. Bausteine 73-100: Text, Übersetzung, Kommentar* (Stuttgart–Bad Cannstatt, Frommann-Holzboog).

Baranski, Z.G. (2000), *Dante e i segni. Saggi per una storia intellettuale di Dante Alighieri* (Napoli, Liguori).

Barnes, J. (1984), *The Complete Works of Aristotle: The Revised Oxford Translation*, I (Princeton, Princeton University Press).

Beare, J.I. (1908), *Aristotle. De memoria et reminiscentia*, in J.I. Beare & G.R.T. Ross, *Aristotle The Parva naturalia* (Oxford, Clarendon Press).

Beierwaltes, W. (1963), 'Der Begriff des *unum in nobis* bei Proklos', in P. Wilpert & W.P. Eckert (eds), *Die Metaphysik im Mittelalter. Ihr Ursprung und ihre Bedeutung* (Berlin, De Gruyter), 255–66.

Caiazzo, I. (2002), *Lectures médiévales de Macrobe* (Paris, Vrin).

Coleman, J. (1992), *Ancient and Medieval Memories: Studies in the Reconstruction of the Past* (Cambridge, Cambridge University Press).

Corti, M. (1987), 'Il modello analogico nel pensiero medievale e dantesco', in M. Picone (ed.), *Dante e le forme dell'allegoresi* (Ravenna, Longo), 11–20.

Courcelle, P. (1974), 'Tradition néo-platonicienne et tradition chrétienne des ailes de l'âme', in *Plotino e il Neoplatonismo in Oriente e in Occidente. Atti del convegno internazionale Roma, 5–9 ottobre 1970* (Roma, Problemi attuali di scienza e cultura. Accademia Nazionale dei Lincei), 265–325.

Cristiani, M. (1984[2] [reprint 2005]), 'Platone', 'Platonismo', '*Timeo*', in *Enciclopedia Dantesca*, Istituto della Enciclopedia Italiana (Roma, Treccani), vol. 13, 17–30; vol. 25, 442–3.

De Bonfils Templer, M. (1986), 'La prima materia de li elementi', *Studi danteschi*, 58: 275–91.

De Bonfils Templer, M. (1987), 'Il dantesco "amoroso uso di Sapienza"', *Stanford Italian Review*, 7: 5–27.

De Bonfils Templer, M. (1990), 'Le due ineffabilitadi del *Convivio*', *Dante Studies*, 108: 67–78.

de Libera, A., Brenet, J.B. & Rosier-Catach, I. (eds) (2019), *Dante et l'averroïsme* (Docet omnia, 5) (Paris, Collège de France, Les Belles Lettres).

de Lubac, H. (1959–64), *Exégèse médiévale. Les quatre sens de l'Écriture*, I–II (Paris, Aubier).

Deen Schildgen, B. (2007), 'Philosophers, Theologians, and the Islamic Legacy in Dante: *Inferno* 4 versus *Paradiso* 4', *Dante Studies*, 125: 113–32, reprinted in J. Ziolkowski (ed.) (2015), *Dante and Islam* (New York, Fordham University Press) (same pagination).

Dronke, P. (1965), 'L'amor che move il sole e l'altre stelle', *Studi medievali*, III.6: 389–422.

Dronke, P. (1986), *Dante and Medieval Latin Traditions* (Cambridge, Cambridge University Press).

Ferrari, F. (2000), 'Commentari specialistici alle sezioni matematiche del *Timeo*', in A. Brancacci (ed.), *La filosofia in età imperiale. Le scuole e le tradizioni filosofiche* (Napoli, Bibliopolis), 169–224.

Ferrari, F. (2012), 'L'esegesi medioplatonica del *Timeo*: metodi, finalità, risultati', in F. Celia & A. Ulacco (eds), *Il Timeo. Esegesi greche, arabe, latine* (Pisa, Pisa University Press), 81–131.

Fioravanti, G. (2014), *Convivio*, in Dante Alighieri, *Opere*, edizione diretta da M. Santagata, vol. 2, *Convivio, Monarchia, Epistole, Egloge*, a cura di G. Fioravanti, C. Giunta, D. Quaglioni, C. Villa and G. Albanese (Milano, Mondadori).

Fioravanti, G. (2019), 'Dante et l'historiographie de l'averroïsme', in de Libera *et al.* (2019), 403–17.

Flamant, J. (1977), *Macrobe et le néoplatonisme latin à la fin du IVe siècle* (Leiden, Brill).

Freccero, J. (1959), 'Dante's Firm Foot and the Journey Without a Guide', *Harvard Theological Review*, 52: 245–81.

Freccero, J. (1962), 'Dante e la tradizione del *Timeo*', *Atti e memorie dell'Accademia nazionale di scienze lettere e arti di Modena*, VI.4: 107–23.

Freddoso, A.J. (trans.) *New English Translation of St. Thomas Aquinas's* Summa Theologiae, University of Notre Dame, accessed 14 October 2019, www3.nd.edu/~afreddos/summa-translation/TOC-part1.htm

Gardner, P.M. (2013), 'Plato and Platonisms in Dante's Poetry', in Honess & Treherne (2013), 111–74.

Geyer, B. (1955), *Alberti Magni De natura et origine animae primum ad fidem autographi edidit Bernhardus Geyer* (Münster, Aschendorff).

Gibson, M. (1969), 'The Study of the *Timaeus* in the Eleventh and Twelfth Centuries', *Pensamiento*, 25: 183–94.

Gilson, É. (1939), *Dante et la philosophie* (Paris, Vrin).

Gilson, S. (2013), 'Dante and Christian Aristotelianism', in Honess & Treherne (2013), 65–109.

Hedley, D. (2010), 'Neoplatonic Metaphysics and Imagination in Dante's *Commedia*', in Montemaggi & Treherne (2010), 245–66.

Hollander, R. (1969), *Allegory in Dante's Commedia* (Princeton, Princeton University Press).

Honess, C.E. & Treherne, M. (eds) (2013), *Reviewing Dante's Theology*, vol. 1 (Oxford, Peter Lang).

Jeauneau, É. (1957), 'L'usage de la notion d'*integumentum* à travers les *Gloses* de Guillaume de Conches', *Archives d'histoire doctrinale et littéraire du Moyen Age*, 24: 35–87.

Jeauneau, É. (2006) *Guillelmi de Conchis Glosae super Platonem* Editionem nouam … curauit (Brepols, Turnhout).

King, R.A.H. (2009), *Aristotle and Plotinus on Memory* (Berlin, De Gruyter).

Klibansky, R. (1939 [reprint 1982]), *The Continuity of the Platonic Tradition during the Middle Ages: Outlines of a Corpus Platonicum Medii Aevi* (London, The Warburg Institute).

Langdon, C. (1921), *The Divine Comedy of Dante Alighieri.* The Italian Text with a Translation in English Blank Verse and a Commentary (London/Oxford, Harvard University Press).

Lemoine, M. (1998), *Intorno a Chartres. Naturalismo platonico nella tradizione cristiana del XII secolo* (Milano, Jaca Book).

Lombardo, L. (2013), *Boezio in Dante. La* Consolatio philosophiae *nello scrittoio del poeta* (Venezia, Edizioni di Ca' Foscari).

Magee, J. (2016), *Calcidius. On Plato's Timaeus*, ed. & trans. J. Magee (Cambridge, MA/London, Harvard University Press).

Mandonnet, P. (1935), *Dante le théologien. Introduction à l'intelligence de la vie, des œuvres et de l'art de Dante Alighieri* (Paris, Desclée de Brouwer).

Marenbon, J. (2000), 'Dante's Averroism', in J. Marenbon (ed.), *Poetry and Philosophy in the Middle Ages: A Festschrift for Peter Dronke* (Leiden/Boston/Köln, Brill), 349–74.

Mazzamuto, P. (1984^{2} [reprint 2005]), 'Lete (Letè)', in *Enciclopedia Dantesca*, Istituto della Enciclopedia Italiana (Roma, Treccani), vol. 10, 508–9.

Mazzotta, G. (1992), *Dante's Vision and the Circle of Knowledge* (Princeton, Princeton University Press).

McMahon, R. (2006), *Understanding the Medieval Meditative Ascent: Augustine, Anselm, Boethius, & Dante* (Washington, DC, The Catholic University of America Press).

Minio-Paluello, L. (1952), 'Note sull'Aristotele latino medievale, V. L'ignota versione moerbekana dei *Secondi Analitici* usata da S. Tomaso', *Rivista di filosofia neo-scolastica*, 43: 389–97 (reprint: Id., *Opuscula. The Latin Aristotle* (Amsterdam, Hakkert, 1972), 155–63).

Minio-Paluello, L. (1968), *Aristoteles latinus IV, 1-4 Analytica Posteriora. Translationes Iacobi, Anonymi sive 'Ioannis', Gerardi et Recensio Guillelmi de Moerbeka*, ed. L. Minio-Paluello & B.G. Dod, editio altera (Leiden, Brill).

Minio-Paluello, L. (1980), 'Dante's Reading of Aristotle', in C. Grayson (ed.), *The World of Dante: Essays on Dante and His Times* (Oxford, Clarendon Press), 61–80.

Moevs, Ch. (2005), *The Metaphysics of Dante's Comedy* (Oxford, Oxford University Press).

Montemaggi, V. (2010), 'In Unknowability as Love: the Theology of Dante's *Commedia*', in Montemaggi & Treherne (2010), 60–94.

Montemaggi, V. & Treherne, M. (eds) (2010), *Dante's Commedia: Theology as Poetry* (Notre Dame, University of Notre Dame Press).

Nardi, B. (1911, 1912), 'Sigieri di Brabante nella Divina *Commedia* e le fonti della filosofia di Dante', *Rivista di Filosofia Neoscolastica*, 3: 526–45; 4: 73–90, 225–39.

Nardi, B. (1924), 'Le citazioni dantesche del *Liber de Causis*', *Giornale critico della filosofia italiana*, 5: 193–215 (reprinted in Nardi 1967: 81–109).

Nardi, B. (1967), *Saggi di filosofia dantesca* (Firenze, La Nuova Italia).

Palgen, R. (1955), 'Die Spur des Timaios in Dantes Paradiso', *Anzeiger der Österreichische Akademie der Wissenschaften. Philosophisch-historische Klasse*, 92: 272–84.

Palgen, R. (1974), 'Gli elementi plotiniani nel *Paradiso*', in *Plotino e il Neoplatonismo in Oriente e in Occidente. Atti del convegno internazionale Roma, 5–9 ottobre 1970* (Problemi attuali di scienza e cultura; Roma, Accademia Nazionale dei Lincei), 509–26.

Pépin, J. (1987), *La tradition de l'allégorie de Philon d'Alexandrie à Dante* (Paris, Études Augustiniennes).

Pézard, A. (1954), 'Regards de Dante sur Platon et ses mythes', *Archives d'histoire doctrinale et littéraire du Moyen Age*, 21: 165–81.

Prandi, S. (2007), 'Dilemma e allegoresi nel canto IV del *Paradiso*', *Studi danteschi*, 72: 103–40.

Ratkowitsch, Ch. (1995), *Die Cosmographia des Bernardus Silvestris. Eine Theodizee* (Köln/Weimar/Wien, Böhlau).

Ratkowitsch, Ch. (1996), 'Die Timaios-Übersetzung des Chalcidius. Ein Plato Christianus', *Philologus*, 140: 139–62.

Rossi, F. (2017), 'Circolazione e recezione di Macrobio nell'età di Dante: dai *Commentarii in Somnium Scipionis* alla *Commedia*', *Studi danteschi*, 82: 167–246.

Silvestris, B. (1978), *Cosmographia*, ed. with introduction and notes by P. Dronke (Leiden, Brill).

Singleton, Ch.S. (1949), 'Dante and Myth', *Journal of the History of Ideas*, 10: 482–502.

Somfai, A. (2002), 'The Eleventh-century Shift in the Reception of Plato's *Timaeus* and Calcidius's *Commentary*', *Journal of the Warburg and Courtald Institutes* 45: 1–21.

Stahl, W.H. (1952 [reprint 1990]), *Commentary on the Dream of Scipio by Macrobius*, trans. with an introduction and notes by W.H. Stahl (New York, Columbia University Press).

Tornau, Ch. (1998), 'Wissenschaft, Seele, Geist: zur Bedeutung einer Analogie bei Plotin (*Enn.* IV 9, 5 und VI, 2, 20)', *Göttinger Forum für Altertumswissenschaft*, 1: 87–111.

Vanni Rovighi, S. (1971), 'Il Canto IV del *Paradiso* visto da uno studioso di filosofia medievale', *Studi danteschi*, 48: 67–82.

Villa, C. (2014), *Epistole*, in Dante Alighieri, *Opere*, edizione diretta da M. Santagata, vol. 2, *Convivio, Monarchia, Epistole, Egloge*, a cura di G. Fioravanti, C. Giunta, D. Quaglioni, C. Villa, G. Albanese (Milano, Mondadori).

von Ivánka, E. (1950), '*Apex mentis*. Wanderung und Wandlung eines stoïschen Terminus', *Zeitschrift für katholische Theologie*, 72: 129–72.

Waszink, J.H. (1975), *Timaeus a Calcidio translatus commentarioque instructus, in societatem operis coniuncto P.J. Jensen edidit J.H. Waszink* (London/Leiden, The Warburg Institute/Brill).

Wetherbee, W. (1972), *Platonism and Poetry in the Twelfth Century: The Literary Influence of the School of Chartres* (Princeton, Princeton University Press).

Wolters, A.M. (1984), *Plotinus on Eros. A Detailed Exegetical Study of Enneads III, 5* (St. Catharine's, Ontario, Wedge Publishing Foundation).

Zeyl, D.J. (1997). *Plato. Timaeus*, reprinted in *Plato. Complete Works*, ed. with introduction and notes by J.M. Cooper, associate editor D.S. Hutchinson (Indianapolis-Cambridge, Hackett).

11

Agathon Redivivus: Love and Incorporeal Beauty in Ficino's *De Amore, Speech V*

SUZANNE STERN-GILLET

THERE CANNOT HAVE been a more powerfully syncretistic mind in the history of Western philosophy than Marsilio Ficino (1433–99), the prince of Renaissance commentators. Rather than merely combining various texts and traditions, he made them speak to each other and, in the process, evolved a system that was both *sui generis* and attuned to the new ways of thinking that were then emerging in quattrocento Florence. A man of immense literary and scientific culture, Ficino had made himself familiar with most of the philosophical texts that by his time were becoming increasingly available in the West. These included, not only Plato's dialogues and Plotinus's *Enneads*, but also several Neoplatonic commentaries – as we now call them – as well as a variety of esoteric and mystical compendia. As an ordained priest, Ficino was also well acquainted with the writings of the Church Fathers. His in-depth understanding of all these texts, together with his ability to spot similarities, analogies and correspondences between them, enabled him to fuse into a coherent system various elements which a modern historian of philosophy would regard as dissimilar if not incompatible. The result was achieved, whether deliberately or not, through a process of adjustment and, at times, alteration and transformation of the elements brought into the formation of the alloy. Ficino's syncretism stems from his ability to bind together doctrinal layers of various provenances. So much has long been recognised. What, by contrast, may not have been explored in sufficient detail is the manner in which he was led, not only to coax into compliance canonical texts of different traditions, but also, when he thought it appropriate, to improve on the views of those he regarded as his masters and to fill gaps in their arguments.

Ficino's methods of handling texts can be shown to best advantage in his most widely read treatise, a Latin commentary of Plato's *Symposium*, entitled

Proceedings of the British Academy, **240**, 276–291, © The British Academy 2022.

Commentarium in Convivium Platonis De Amore.[1] By way of an object lesson, I shall here select Speech Five of the commentary to highlight the way in which Ficino succeeded in blending Platonic, Plotinian and Christian elements in the reconstruction of an argument that Plato had meant us to regard as flawed to the core. First, however, some introductory remarks on the nature of Ficino's syncretism are in order.

1. Three Levels of Syncretism

Ficino's syncretism manifests itself at three distinct levels. Its first and most basic level stems from a conception of the Platonic corpus which profoundly differs from our own. Ficino did not regard Plato as the author of a philosophical system to be studied alongside other systems, or a set of theories that evolved over time, or indeed a world that radically differed from his own and challenged him in its otherness. Plato, to whom he likes to refer as '*Plato noster*', was for him the truth or, at least, a large part of the truth, and it was not a truth that he was inclined to question radically and openly. For him, therefore, to read and explain Plato did not require placing the text in its historical, cultural or doctrinal context, or subjecting it to methods of internal and external criticism, which, in any case, had not yet been developed by his time. From Ficino's point of view the dialogues constituted a doctrinal monolith which had remained largely unaffected by whatever intellectual evolution their author might have undergone or which the passage of time may have made alien to later ages. Accordingly, his mission, as he conceived it, was to initiate his contemporaries into the philosophy of Plato with the aim of enriching their worldview. It should come as no surprise, therefore, that with little concern for the relative chronology of the dialogues,[2] Ficino could happily hop from one dialogue to another, taking from one whatever material he thought useful for glossing another. I shall refer to Ficino's tendency to treat the dialogues synchronically, as a single solid block of doctrine, as *first-level syncretism*.

[1] Ficino wrote two versions of the commentary, one in Latin, written in 1464 and published in 1469 and another in Tuscan, which did not come out until 60 years later. The Tuscan version, addressed to a less learned audience but presenting no dramatic differences with the Latin version, was admirably translated into English by Arthur Farndell (Ficino 2016). Some of my translations of passages in the Latin version owe much to his skill as a translator. All references to, and quotations from, the Latin text are in Laurens's edition (Ficin 2002).

[2] He took the *Phaedrus* to be Plato's first dialogue, as many would in the following centuries. Be it noted, however, that there are occasions on which Ficino notes a change of mind on Plato's part. He does so, for instance, in *De amore*, VI, 13, where he notes that while in early dialogues, as he took them, reasons (*rationes*) are 'painted' in the soul at its inception, they are described in later works such as the *Republic* as gifts from our divine creator. Robichaud (2017: 78–81) notes that although 'modern developmental categories were a feature of neither ancient nor Renaissance interpretations of the corpus', Ficino was not unaware of 'certain developmental features of Plato's works'.

Plato did not come alone for Ficino. To fulfil the mission of reviving Platonic philosophy, for which, according to tradition,[3] Cosimo de' Medici had entrusted him the direction of the *Accademia Platonica* at Careggi, Ficino availed himself of whatever help he could get from the many Platonic and post-Platonic writings and commentaries that had recently become available. These included Plotinus's *Enneads* first and foremost, but also writings by Alcinous, Porphyry and Iamblichus as well as commentaries on individual Platonic dialogues by Proclus and Hermias, all of whom treated the dialogues as a seamless body of doctrines. Since Ficino studied those writings at the same time as he was translating Plato and writing introductory *argumenta* to the dialogues, it was well-nigh inevitable that he would bring post-Platonic views to bear on the interpretation of Plato's writings. This was all the more likely since the earlier commentators had themselves been of a syncretistic turn of mind, regarding themselves as '*diadochoi*' (successors), who traced their line of succession back to the 'divine Plato' himself. Ficino, who saw no reason to distrust the self-description of those he regarded as his philosophical forebears and mentors, took over their syncretism and became, so to speak, the latest of the *diadochoi*.

The crucial role played by the so-called commentators in the transmission of Platonism is worth stressing in so far as present-day philosophers are fond of drawing a distinction between, on the one hand, philosophers, whose business it is to think, and, on the other hand, exegetes, whose role it is to interpret the thoughts of others. The distinction is based on ignorance. Firstly, late antique commentators took the writing of commentaries on Plato's dialogues or Aristotle's treatises as the only form of philosophical activity available to them since they considered that the truth on all subjects had been discovered by Plato or Aristotle, depending on which of the two authors they were working on. Second, and more decisively, late antique philosophers-commentators, from Plotinus to Porphyry and Proclus, who styled themselves as 'Platonists', rarely recognised openly the extent to which they were altering the theories they claimed to be merely expounding.[4] They did not, therefore, take the measure of their own philosophical originality and creativity. So much is true even of Plotinus, the third and last towering giant of Western classical philosophy, who hardly ever explicitly disagrees with Plato, however significantly he altered – and improved – his doctrines. A minor paradox of the history of philosophy, therefore, is that most of the thinkers whom we now classify as 'Neoplatonist commentators' were unaware of being philosophers in their own right as well as followers of the vastly altered form of Platonism developed by Plotinus.[5]

Ficino's study of Plotinus was exceptionally thorough since by 1463, when he embarked on the translation of the dialogues, he not only had a copy of the

[3] Hankins (1990) has convincingly shed doubt on this traditional claim.

[4] On Proclus, see Stern-Gillet (2011).

[5] The word Neoplatonism as a classificatory term to designate the School of Plotinus was not coined until the 19th century. It was meant to signify that Platonism had entered a new phase with Plotinus. Although not incorrect, the appellation runs counter to the way in which the philosophers we now call Neoplatonists described themselves.

Enneads to hand,[6] but had also prepared for himself a manuscript in which selected passages from Plato were followed by what he took to be Plotinus's comments on them. No doubt, the time and dedication required for compiling such an aid to study accounts for the strong Plotinian flavour that pervades Ficino's writings and, more particularly, the paraphrases of Plotinian passages that found their way into his *argumenta* to, and commentaries on, Plato's dialogues.[7] Familiarity with the writings of Plotinus and his successors had made Ficino well-nigh impervious to the doctrinal gap that yawns between Platonism and what we now call Neoplatonism. Since he did not question the claims of the 'Neoplatonic' commentators to be faithful expositors of Plato, he could, without obvious qualms, help himself to the words and theories of one member of the *familia platonica* to gloss the writings of another. Rather than explaining Plato by Plato, he often tended to rely on the concepts and categories of 'Neoplatonic' metaphysics to comment on whatever Platonic dialogue he was dealing with at the time. Moreover, to the extent that the 'Neoplatonic' commentators also relied on a miscellany of mystic texts, such as the *Corpus Hermeticum* (which includes the *Asclepius* and the *Pœmandres*), the *Orphic Hymns*, the *Chaldean Oracles*, as well as some Neo-Pythagorean writings, all of which had become loosely associated with their own philosophy through the contingencies of school traditions, scholarly travel, and political upheavals, their Platonism was Platonism vastly enlarged. As a consequence, so, too, became Ficino's Platonism, although he never lost the sense that his prime responsibility was to Plato's philosophy. Together with Plato's dialogues, the 'Neoplatonic' commentaries and associated mystico-philosophical writings made up the fertile soil on which Ficino's *second-level, trans-authorial, syncretism* drew.

As if this was not syncretism enough, Ficino went further. Through his familiarity with the writings of Augustine and Pseudo-Dionysius, he had been introduced early to a Christianised version of Neoplatonism. This predisposed him to consider that Platonism in Plato's or in Plotinus's version, when he came later to encounter it, was in fundamental accord with Christianity. As a consequence, he always resisted the separation of philosophy from religion and thought it entirely appropriate to integrate Christian terminology in his commentaries on Plato's dialogues as well as in his marginalia of Plotinus's texts.[8] Furthermore, he had no qualms in switching from Neoplatonic to Christian terminology in the space of a page of *in quarto* manuscript to refer to the ultimate ontological principle, calling

[6] The ultimate provenance of the manuscript that Ficino used for his translation of the *Enneads* remains a matter of speculation. As for the proximate manuscript, it has been convincingly argued by Henry (1941: 45–52), on the basis of extensive codicological research, to have been a copy ordered for Ficino by Cosimo de' Medici. In 1441, Cosimo had purchased a manuscript of the *Enneads* from the library of Niccolò Niccoli, a well-known Florentine collector, who had himself acquired it from Aurispa, a humanist and merchant who traded in manuscripts from the east. Henry's conclusions have been endorsed by Saffrey (1996). On the contents of Ficino's library, see also Laurens in Ficin (2002: lxxvii).

[7] For a detailed description of the process, see di Dio (2016).

[8] As noted in Robichaud (2017: 64).

it now the One and now God or even God the Father while making clear that it was the God of Christianity that he was referring to. He Christianised the Plotinian Intellect by calling it the Angelic Mind and described what Plotinus had presented as the stages of emanation – from the One to Intellect to Soul to Nature – as the three faces of God.[9] Lastly, undeterred by the risk of anachronism, or perhaps unaware of it, Ficino did not scruple to rely on Christian doctrines (such as creation and providence) in his interpretation of Plato's texts. He translated the traditional Greek virtues into the terminology of Christianity, assimilating justice, for example, as Plato and Plotinus had conceived it, to the Christian virtue of charity. For these reasons, Ficino's Plato can be described as a *Plato christianus* or, in Pascal's somewhat cryptic remark, a Plato that 'disposes to Christianity'.[10] The coexistence of pagan and Christian concepts in Ficino's writings is a manifestation of an even broader, because trans-doctrinal, syncretism. I shall refer to it as his *third-level syncretism.*

All three levels of syncretism, I shall here argue, are in evidence in the fifth speech of the *De amore*. The main interest of the speech, I shall claim, lies in highlighting the exegetical problems that faced Ficino, who, for reasons of fictional coherence, found himself having to defend a thesis diametrically opposed to one put forward by Plato in the *Symposium*. The exegetical acrobatics that the exercise entailed show the extent to which his multi-levelled syncretism gave him opportunities for being philosophically innovative. Syncretism, as the example of Ficino demonstrates, need not be a symptom of a second-rate or derivative mind.

2. The Speech of Marsuppini/Agathon

The *De amore* is a fictional account of proceedings said to have taken place on 7 November 1468 at the Accademia Platonica in Careggi.[11] To honour Plato's birthday, assumed to have taken place on that day, seven notables sat down to a banquet during which Plato's *Symposium* was read. The reading was followed by speeches given by the guests in turn, each of which consisted in a commentary on one of the speeches in the original. Ficino gave himself the role of fictional amanuensis whose presence was necessary to record the proceedings. As the occasion demanded, the speeches were deferential to the standpoint of the original Platonic

[9] See *De amore*, V 4, 46 and 11, *passim*.

[10] 'Platon pour disposer au Christianisme' (Pascal 1963: 612). On the issue of Ficino's Christianised interpretation of Plato, see, e.g., Marcel (1958), Saffrey (1996) and Magnard (2001).

[11] Such, at any rate, is the information given by Ficino himself in the opening paragraph of Speech 1. However, as mentioned in n. 3 above, historians now dispute the accuracy of the claim. What is certain, *pace* Ficino, is that the tradition of celebrating Plato's assumed birthday, far from ending with Porphyry as he claimed, was still alive in Proclus's time (412–485 CE), as attested by his *In Platonis Rem Publicam Commentarii*. Since a manuscript of Proclus's commentary on the *Republic* only reached Florence in 1492, Ficino's mistake was due to lack of available evidence rather than ignorance. On this question, see Gentile (1984: 151–2).

speaker. Accordingly, Marsuppini,[12] the latter-day Agathon, began by praising the ancient Agathon for his careful (cf. *diligenter*) enumeration of the properties of Love as a deity (*Erōs*) and his description of the benefits that he bestows upon humankind. Marsuppini's approval is grounded, not, as might have been expected, in the pivotal role that Agathon's speech plays in the economy of the dialogue – it provides an opening and a foil for Diotima's own – but, more surprisingly, in the very substance of Agathon's central claim, namely that, of all the gods, *Erōs* is the happiest, most beautiful and best (*beatissimus, pulcher(r)imus et optimus*, V 8, 55).

The exegetical challenge that faced Ficino at that point was to combine the definition of love that he was putting in the mouth of Marsuppini with the opposite viewpoint that Plato had ascribed to Socrates/Diotima. In having Marsuppini re-interpret the ancient Agathon's claim that Love (*Erōs*) is perfect, Ficino ran counter to Socrates/Diotima's presentation of him as a *daimon*, whose parentage – father *poros* (inventiveness) and mother *penia* (poverty) – had made needy by nature and forced to be forever in search of what he lacks.[13] Since the daimonic character of Love is the lynchpin of the *Symposium*, Ficino's deviation from the Platonic stance cannot be over-stressed, all the more so since Agathon's initial failure to recognise the strength of Socrates's counter-arguments has led most readers of the dialogue to dismiss Agathon's speech as a vapid piece of Gorgianic rhetoric, and Agathon himself as a feather-brained belletrist. How was Ficino to proceed if he was to rehabilitate the views of the ancient Agathon while remaining true to the thesis of Socrates/Diotima, which had almost certainly been Plato's own view?

Let it first be noted that although Marsuppini presents his argument as a defence of Agathon's eulogy of Love (*Erōs*), he begins by departing from it in several ways, as he does also from Diotima's definition of beauty. The love that Marsuppini praises at the start of his speech is not the individual divine being that Agathon had made it out to be, but an impersonal force that exerts its attraction at both the worldly and the otherworldly level. As for beauty, the paradigmatic object of love, Ficino/Marsuppini presents it, not as a transcendent Form variously instantiated in the world below, as Plato had taught, but as a property. While it is reasonable to assume that Ficino modified Agathon's position to make it compatible with his own conception of the divine, it is not so easy to understand why he distanced himself from Plato/Diotima's definition of beauty as a Form. Could it have been because Plato had not been univocal on the relationship between the good and the beautiful, either in the *Symposium* or elsewhere?[14] Although he had consistently presented them as separate Forms, albeit internally linked, Plato had sometimes intimated that they are identical (*Meno*, 77b6–7 and *Timaeus*, 87c4–5) while, at other times,

[12] Carlo Marsuppini (1399–1453), author of poems and letters, became Chancellor of the Republic of Florence. His brother, Cristoforo Marsuppini, is the fictional author of Alcibiades, *Speech* 7. For information on the structure of the *De amore*, see Robichaud's detailed account (2018: 113–22).

[13] For a sound and readily accessible translation of Plato's *Symposium*, see Plato (1999). For the Greek text, see Plato (1995b).

[14] See, e.g., Barney (2010) and Riegel (2014).

implying that they are different (*Philebus*, 64e5–6),[15] and leaving the Beautiful out of account in his description of the role of the Good in book VI of the *Republic*.

Perhaps because of Plato's lack of clarity on the matter, Plotinus had not conceived of the good and the beautiful as Forms.[16] In this Ficino followed him. He made Marsuppini remark that common usage (cf. *dicimus*) takes the beautiful and the good to be separate properties; while the beautiful is assumed to stem from outer perfection or harmony (*perfectio exterior*) between perceptible component parts, the good consists in inner perfection or harmony (*perfectio interior*) between states of the soul. Through a series of examples, which include perceptible and non-perceptible objects at the peak of their beauty, Ficino had Marsuppini challenge common usage and argue that beauty in its purest form cannot but be the outward manifestation or blossom (*flos*) of goodness.[17] In thus unobtrusively building a normative element into his concept of beauty, Ficino/Marsuppini paved the way for the defence of what would be the central claim of his speech, namely that beauty, once it is conceived as an incorporeal property, leads the soul to the transcendental fount of all goodness. Although reminiscent of Diotima's *scala amoris*, the move required delicate adjustments on Ficino's part, who had to make it compatible with both Agathon's pagan view of love and Christian doctrine. The consummate skill with which he modifies Agathon's thesis constitutes the main source of interest in a speech that might otherwise have been an insipid piece of rhetoric.

3. The Incorporeal Nature of Beauty

The issue was delicate. Had it not been for his commitment to the defence of Agathon's conception of love as a deity, Ficino/Marsuppini could have turned for (limited) philosophical support to Diotima's claim that the quality of love is proportionate to the worth of its object and that worth, in this case, is to be measured by the degree of detachment from physical nature. Syncretism, however, supplied Ficino with alternative, more serviceable, arguments. As his belief in the monolithic nature of the corpus encouraged him to do, he turned to the *Timaeus*, a dialogue likely to have been composed later than the *Symposium*. In that dialogue Plato had drawn a distinction between, on the one hand, sight and hearing and, on the other, touch, taste and smell (47a–d).[18] While the first two senses, he had argued, enable us to apprehend objects at a distance, the other three confine us to the immediate vicinity; while the first two senses serve the august function of empowering reason

[15] For a sound and readily accessible translation of the *Philebus*, see Plato (2001). For the Greek text, see Plato (1995b).

[16] On this issue see Stern-Gillet (2000).

[17] In so far as *flos* is the Latin equivalent of the Greek *anthos*, it is a likely borrowing from the *Orphic Hymns*, 59 or the *Chaldean Oracles*, 34, 35, 37, 42 and 49 (see Des Places 1971).

[18] For a sound and readily accessible translation of the *Timaeus*, see Plato (2008). For the Greek text, see Plato (1905).

and fostering the development of learning, the other three play the humbler role of enabling the body to function as its nature dictates. From the *Timaeus*, therefore, Marsuppini could infer that sight and hearing have a natural affinity to the soul and that, like truth and virtue, they hold intrinsic worth for it. By contrast, the value that the soul in us attaches to the other three senses is merely instrumental to the fulfilment of its role as minister of the body. In line with the negative theorisation of the body that Plato had defended in early dialogues, the *Phaedo* particularly, Ficino/Marsuppini concluded:

> odours, savours, heat, and the like either harm the body a great deal, or help it, but they present little either to the admiration or to the censure of the soul, and are only moderately desired by it. On the other hand, the reasons present in incorporeal truth, colours, shapes and sounds move the body either not at all or with difficulty and very little. But they greatly sharpen the edge of the soul for inquiry and research (*indagandum*), and they attract its desires to themselves.[19]

Natural allies of the soul, the specific objects of sight and hearing foster its ability to think beyond the here and now. In so doing, they sharpen its desire to ascend to greater degrees of beauty. The step was crucial to Ficino/Marsuppini's aim to demonstrate that true beauty is an incorporeal light of divine origin.

Plotinus's description of the formation of aesthetic judgements provided Ficino with the next step in his argument. In *Ennead* I 6 [I], Plotinus had argued that aesthetic judgements are the products of the application of principles (*logoi*) held in the soul to physical objects perceived by the sense organs. Judgements of beauty are formed, he wrote, 'by fitting the beautiful body to the form in itself and using this for judging beauty as we use a ruler for judging straightness' (I 6 [I] 3.3–5). More generally, he continued:

> When sense-perception, then, sees the form in bodies binding and mastering the nature opposed to it, which is shapeless, and shape riding gloriously upon other shapes, it gathers into one that which appears dispersed and brings it back and takes it in, now without parts, to the soul's interior and presents it to that which is within as something in tune with it and fitting it and dear to it. (3.9–15, Plotinus 1966–88) [20]

In the emanative ontology of the *Enneads*, the *logoi* in question are traces (*typoi*) left in the soul by the higher reality from which it is emanated, namely Intellect and its constituent Forms. The Forms, as Plotinus conceived them, are archetypes of objects in the world of sense and paradigms for the human soul to imitate on its way to virtue. According to Plotinus's conception of aesthetic judgements, therefore, the embodied soul that apprehends beauty, even in its humblest form, brings itself closer to the archetype of beauty. It served Ficino's strategy, therefore, to agree with

[19] V 2, 42, trans. Jayne (Ficino 1985), modified. Other translations from Ficino's Latin are mine, sometimes indebted to Arthur Farndell.

[20] All quotations from Plotinus's *Enneads* are in Armstrong's translation (Plotinus 1966–88), which, depending on the particular *Ennead*, are based on either Henry and Schwyzer's *editio maior* (Plotinus 1951–73) or Henry and Schwyzer's revised *editio minor* (Plotinus 1964–82).

Plotinus that the focus of aesthetic interest lies, not in the materiality of its object, but in such reflected properties as are received by the soul of the beholder. As he had Marsuppini conclude:

> The beauty of any person pleases the soul not insofar as it lies in external matter, but insofar as an image (*imago*) of it is apprehended or grasped by the soul through sight ... The soul can only like the beauty which it has taken in. Though this beauty may be an image of an external body, it is nonetheless incorporeal in the soul. (V 3, 43–44)[21]

As Ficino knew better than anyone else in his time, Plotinus's conception of aesthetic judgments has deep roots in his system, stemming as it does from a combination of a highly complex theory of sense-perception[22] and a concept of matter that is inimical to the view that beauty can be predicated of sensory objects. Taking the first point first, I shall now suggest that Plotinus's theory of sense-perception, as well as the principle of causation from which it derives, were decisive in leading him to conceive of beauty as a metaphysical property first and foremost. No emanated entity, he taught, can initiate changes in the reality from which it is emanated. The paradoxical implication of this principle is that the embodied soul is impassible (*apathēs*) and cannot therefore receive affects (*pathē*) coming from the world of sense. To lessen the paradox and account for the everyday reality of sense-perception, Plotinus postulated the existence of judging agencies, vested in the imagination (*phantasia*) and the sense organs themselves, to function as go-betweens and process the data of sense so as to make them accessible to the soul in us. Only when so processed, he held, can sensory objects be assessed for their aesthetic merit by the soul. Although Plotinus's conception of sense-perception would have been of direct help to Ficino in his attempt to demonstrate the incorporeality of beauty, he may have thought it too abstruse and counter-intuitive to be included in the relatively light-hearted context of a sympotic speech. Conceivably, he may also have judged it to be philosophically fragile if not flawed, as did many a later reader of the *Enneads*. Whatever his reason for ignoring that particular aspect of the philosophy of the *Enneads*, Ficino endorsed Plotinus's view that the judgement of beauty bears, not on physical objects, but on abstracted or 'spiritualised' versions of them. The view provided additional support for Marsuppini's contention that beauty is not of this world.

In focusing the speech on the incorporeality of beauty, Ficino was also drawing on Plotinus's disparagement of the world of sense. Our world, Plotinus taught, is not a metaphysically independent entity which can be understood as such, but the product of the formative action of soul upon matter. In so far as matter is produced at the point at which the emanative process has all but exhausted itself, it is inherently sterile in the sense of altogether being deprived of emanative power. As such,

[21] 'Placet animo persone alicuius speties, non prout in exteriori iacet materia, sed prout eius imago per visum ab animo capitur vel concipitur ... Placet utique animo ea dumtaxat speties que ab illo suscipitur. Hec autem licet exterioris corporis simulacrum sit in eo tamen est incorporea.'

[22] On this issue, see Emilsson (1988).

it is the 'contrary' (*to enantion*) of the power of all things, namely the One or Good. Shapeless, formless, indeterminate and altogether without quality, matter is the passive recipient of such *logoi* as the descending soul retains within itself at that stage and projects upon it as *typoi* (traces). In presenting the world of sense as resulting from the projection of images of the Forms onto insubstantial matter, Plotinus in effect ruled out that it could be beautiful in itself. As he conveyed the point in one of his most telling metaphors, the world of sense is but 'a corpse adorned'.[23]

The action of the Plotinian Soul upon matter, it should be noted at that point, is not to be understood either on the model of Aristotle's efficient cause or, even less, as an act of creation. Unlike Aristotle's efficient cause, the descending soul of the *Enneads* does not transform matter into something that it had not been before, and, contrary to the teachings of the Abrahamic religions, soul does not bring matter into being. All the Plotinian soul does is to emanate matter as part of an eternal and necessary process that unfolds from the One. Covering matter with such traces of the Forms as it retains at that point, the descending soul makes matter the substrate of a world of semblance. So doing, the soul may well disguise the abjectness of matter and thus fool a superficial eye, but the truth is that soul can never make matter into anything other than a mere image deprived of ontological density.

As a committed Christian and, since his ordination in 1473, a priest, Ficino could not endorse Plotinus's metaphysical and aesthetic depreciation of the world of sense. To have done so would have amounted to blasphemy since he regarded that world as the product of divine creation through the successive intermediary of the Angelic Mind and the Soul.[24] However, if Ficino did not follow Plotinus in questioning the beauty of the world of sense, he agreed with him in holding that although Forms (or Angels) are paradigms of beauty, they are not the ultimate fount of it. Plotinus had reserved that role for the One, generator of being (*gennētēs*, V 2 [11] 1.7), from which all things are eternally emanated. In Ficino's Christianised version of the One, the fount and origin of universal beauty (*pulchritudo universalis*) is God the Father, creator of both the visible and the invisible universe, and whose power transcends all. 'Beauty', he wrote, 'is the name we give to the grace of the divine face (*divini vultus*)' (V 4, 47). In keeping with the emanative structure that he had taken over from Plotinus, Ficino distinguished stages in God's diffusion of beauty into his creation. The divine creative ray, he taught, makes its power and radiance felt in descending order of luminosity, first in the souls of the angels, then

[23] *On Matter* (II 4 [12]) 5.18. However, as testified by the more positive view of the physical world that he presents throughout *Ennead* IV 8 [6], Plotinus does not unfailingly disparage the world of sense.

[24] Ficino was aware of having altered Plotinus's terminology: 'The Platonists call this kind of pictures in Angels forms or ideas, in souls reasons and concepts, in the matter of the world forms and images' (V 4.46). Let it here be noted, parenthetically, that in making Forms or Angels exemplars of which the human soul bears the traces within itself and uses in the formation of aesthetic judgements, Plotinus and Ficino introduced into Western philosophy an idealist theory of beauty which was to prove influential on both Renaissance and post-Renaissance art theory as well as on later philosophical aesthetics, from Kant to Collingwood.

in those of human beings, before reaching the constituents of the world of sense: 'In its mercy, the divine power, transcending all, imbues the cosmos, the angels, and the souls it has created (as if they were his children) with its ray, in which there is the fertile power to create anything' (V 4, 46). What we take to be beauty in the physical world, therefore, Ficino/Marsuppini regarded as mere reflections of the 'grace of the divine face', which is incorporeal by definition. As Ficino wrote with typical stylistic flourish, 'those who thirst for beauty ... must look elsewhere than in the river of matter or the rivulets of quantity, shape, or colours of any kind, to find the sweetest drink of the beauty that would assuage their thirst' (V 3, 46). Shorn of its connections with the physical world, Ficino's concept of beauty was now ready to be enlarged so as to include beauties within the soul or, more specifically, the virtues.

This brought Ficino, once again, in agreement with Plotinus. Despite their doctrinal differences on the origin of the world of sense, the two philosophers were at one on the normative implications for individual human souls of the incorporeal nature of beauty. Being twice removed from the divine source of light and burdened by their function as ministers of body, human souls, Ficino held, are prone to yield indiscriminately to the demands of the physical nature and thus to make themselves oblivious of their own higher nature. Confining themselves to the here and now of the world of appearances and labouring under the mistaken assumption that beauty lies in physical appearances, they fail to notice the presence in their inner self of a spark of the higher reality from which they come. Self-forgetfulness was the diagnosis that both philosophers gave of such malfunctioning of the human soul. Plotinus's presentation of the point begins with a question: 'What is it, then, which has made the souls forget their father, God, and be ignorant of themselves and him, even though they are parts which come from the higher world and altogether belong to it?' (V 1 [10] 1.1–3). To answer the question, Plotinus undertook to enlighten the soul on its own nature before recommending it to engage in a process of self-purification that would liberate it, so far as possible, from its association with the body and thus enable it to acquaint itself with its higher self.[25] While keeping the body functioning, a purified soul, he was confident, would become conscious of the traces of the higher realities that it bears within itself and of its own role in the emanative process.[26]

Like Plotinus, Ficino identified care of the body as the main cause of the apostasy of the human soul. More explicitly than Plotinus, however, Ficino maintained that the use of reason would enable it, not only to understand that the beauty of the world is but a reflection of its divine creator, but also to strive to contemplate the divine principle itself:

> our soul, being *created* in a state so as to be enveloped by an earthly body, tends downwards to serve the body; and once it is weighted down by this tendency, it neglects the

[25] For the moral advice that Plotinus gives to embodied human souls, see the famous purple passage in the tractate *On Beauty* (I 6 [1] 9) on the theme of 'working on your statue', as well as the tractate *On Virtues* (I 2 [19]) in its entirety.

[26] See, e.g., *Ennead* V I [10] 2 and 12.

> treasure hidden in the deepest part of itself ... As a result, it comes about that the soul fails to see the light of the divine face which shines unceasingly within it, *until the body becomes fully grown and reason is awakened: then it contemplates in thought the face of God which is reflected in the structure of the world and is obvious to the eyes*. Through such contemplation, the soul is led to apprehend the face of God which shines within it.
>
> (V 4, 47, emphasis added)

In these lines, we hold the core of Ficino/Marsuppini's speech, both thematically and exegetically. For the claim that over-attentiveness to the body makes the soul oblivious of its true self, Ficino, as the lines from *Ennead* V I [10] quoted earlier, make clear, is indebted to Plotinus. However, as his third-level, trans-doctrinal, syncretism enabled him to do, Ficino had re-interpreted the Plotinian reference along Augustinian lines. In Augustine's heavily Christianised version of Plotinus's conception of the soul, human souls, as created by God, are illuminated from within by a spark of the divine ray. While Ficino's phrase 'treasure in its heart' brings to mind Augustine's famous apostrophe to the deity: 'You were deepest within me and higher than the highest part in me',[27] his reference to the downward pull that the body exerts on the soul echoes Augustine's advice to resist 'the somnolence of the body' and to 'lift the invisible eyes of the spirit to the divine source of light and norm of beauty'.[28] As for the remedy that could reverse the self-oblivion of the soul, Ficino, still in Augustine's footsteps, proved to be more optimistic than Plotinus had been.[29] Rational maturation, he held, can lead the soul to the realisation that the physical beauty it admires is in truth immaterial since it is received through the intermediary of an immaterial medium, namely light:

> Therefore, since the light of the sun is incorporeal, whatever it receives, it receives according to the mode of its own nature, and so it receives the colours and shapes of physical objects in a spiritual way. It is in the same way that light is received by the eyes. And so it is that the whole beauty of this world, which is the third face of God, presents itself to the eyes as incorporeal, through the incorporeal light of the sun.
>
> (V 4, 48)[30]

As is evident from these lines, Ficino had taken over Plotinus's assumption that light is immaterial.[31] Whether he could have known that the assumption was erroneous is uncertain. What, at any rate, is certain is that he drew metaphysical mileage from the analogy since he concluded at that point that the focus of aesthetic interest

[27] For further medieval sources of this Ficinian view, see Laurens's notes in Ficin (2002: 285, n. 26).

[28] Both quotations come from the *Confessions* (Augustine 2002), the first from III, 6, 11, the second from X, 35, 54.

[29] On the theme of divine illumination, see also Augustine (1995).

[30] 'Cum igitur solis lumen incorporeum sit, quicquid suspicit nature sue suscipit modo. Propterea colores et figuras corporum modo suscipit spiritali. Eodemque pacto ipsum ab oculis susceptum inspicitur. Quo factum est ut totus hic mundi decor, qui tertius est dei vultus, per incorpoream solis lucem incorporeum sese oculis offerat.' For Plotinus's statement of the same view, see, e.g., tractates II 1 [40] 7 and VI 4 [22] 7.

[31] For a comprehensive list of Plotinus's references to light, see Ferwerda (1965: 46–55).

is not the object in its materiality or corporeality, but the representation or image of it that is received in the beholder's soul.

4. Agathon Redux

Ficino's reinterpretation of Agathon's speech was nearly complete at that point. All that remained for him to do was to explain that beauty, as he had theorised it anew, can be a force of attraction and an object of love. This had presented no difficulty for Agathon in whose view *Erōs* is a young and physically attractive individual deity. Ficino, who must have known that his conception of beauty as incorporeal made it more difficult to account for the pull it exerts on human souls, enlisted the help of etymology, philosophical tradition and theological doctrine in his attempt to deal with the issue.

He turned first to etymology and had Marsuppini remind his fellow symposiasts that in the *Cratylus* Socrates had been made to note that *kallos* (beauty) derives from *kalein* (to call). Making Marsuppini trust the etymology,[32] Ficino had him claim that true beauty calls the soul to itself, as is testified by the intrinsic value that most human beings attach to harmonious sequences of sounds, graceful bodily proportions and, more crucially, moral virtue (V 2.42). Having granted incorporeal beauty the capacity to urge the soul onto the path of moral goodness, Marsuppini was then able to argue that it also has the power to attract love. As he had already noted earlier on in the *De Amore*, 'When we say "love," understand "the desire for beauty, for this is the definition of love among all philosophers"' (II, 4). By 'all philosophers', Ficino meant 'all philosophers in the Platonic tradition', which he regarded as emblematic of philosophy.

At this point, the elements were in place for Ficino to clinch the main argument of *Speech V*. He made Marsuppini argue that since each individual human soul is a mirror reflecting the divine face, it is naturally drawn to the original of which it bears the traces in its inner self in the way in which 'a father's face is a welcome sight to his children' (V 4, 47). When the soul has achieved sufficient intellectual and spiritual maturity to detach itself from the care and concerns of the body, he continued, it will understand that the beauty it is drawn to in the physical universe is nothing other than 'the grace of the divine face' (V 4, 47), and that what it truly loves is God, Father and creator of all things, fount and norm of beauty. The argument is circular and Ficino, who cannot but have realised this, sought to bolster it by turning even more explicitly to Christian doctrine. He made the human ability to love into a gift from God who, in his providential goodness (*benignitas providentiae*, V 10), eternally bestows it on his creatures, from the Angels to individual human souls.

[32] For a sound and readily accessible translation of the *Cratylus*, see Plato (1998). For the Greek text see Plato (1995a). The use of the etymology has no backing in Plotinus, who may have suspected it to be fanciful. Chantraine (1968–80: III, 487) describes it as 'unknown'.

Those who love true beauty, therefore, have the capacity to elevate themselves to the divine principle and fulfil the ideal of god-likeness, which Plato had famously expressed in a text that Ficino knew well, the interlude in the *Theaetetus*: 'a man should make all haste to escape from earth to heaven; and escape means becoming as like God as possible; and a man becomes like God when he becomes just and holy, with understanding' (Burnyeat 1990: 176a9–b2).[33] While Plato had left unclear the identity of the divine principle, Ficino, as his trans-doctrinal syncretism enabled him to do, had identified it with the God of Christianity.

And so, finally, the question may be asked as to whether Ficino had succeeded in vindicating Agathon's conception of love. 'Partially but not entirely', must be the answer. To the extent that he successfully combined canonical texts in the Platonic tradition with the teachings of Scripture, he can be said to have mounted an argument that exceeded in cogency and sophistication the Platonic Agathon's own efforts to demonstrate a similar thesis. More specifically, in presenting love as a divine gift to humankind, he made Agathon emerge partially vindicated from the re-interpretation of his speech. However, Ficino had had to make too many adjustments to Agathon's original position for the vindication to be complete or indeed convincing. The *Erōs* of the young playwright's description had to be transformed almost beyond recognition; no longer a youthful and physically attractive deity dwelling on Mount Olympus, he had become at Ficino's hand a gift to humankind from the Creator and a manifestation of His providence; no longer a paradigm of beauty conceived on the human model, he had become a light of preternatural beauty; no longer 'the leader in festival, chorus and sacrifice' (*Symp.* 197d3), fêted in pagan rituals, he had become the deity to whom human souls are to pray.

Syncretism would never go further or be more historically fruitful.[34]

References

Augustine, St. (1995), *Against the Academicians* and *The Teacher*, trans., with introduction & notes P. King (Indianapolis/Cambridge, Hackett).

Augustine, St. (2002), *The Confessions*, trans. M. Boulding (New York, New City Press).

Barney, R. (2010), 'Notes on the *Kalon* and the Good in Plato', *Classical Philology*, 105.4: 363–77.

Burnyeat, M. (1990), *The Theaetetus of Plato*, with the translation of M.J. Levett, revised by M. Burnyeat (Indianapolis/Cambridge, Hackett).

Chantraine, P. (1968–80), *Dictionnaire étymologique de la langue grecque*, 4 vols (Paris, Éditions Klincksieck).

[33] For an account of the ideal of god-likeness in the *Theaetetus* and in Plotinus, see Stern-Gillet (2019). For Ficino's use of the theme in both his conception of the soul as mirror of the divine light and his philosophy of friendship, see Robichaud (2018: chapter 3 *passim*).

[34] I should like to express my gratitude to Kevin Corrigan, Arthur Farndell, Valery Rees and Christopher Strachan for their readiness to discuss with me various aspects of Ficino's *De amore* and its sources, Platonic and Neoplatonic. I should also like to thank Stefan Sperl for his editorial vigilance and the very learned anonymous referee commissioned by the editors of this volume.

des Places, E. (ed. & trans.) (1971), *Oracles Caldaïques avec un choix de commentaires anciens* (Paris, Les Belles Lettres).

di Dio, R. (2016), '*Selecta Colligere*: Marsilio Ficino and Renaissance Reading Practices', *History of European Ideas*, 42: 595–606.

Emilsson, E.K. (1988), *Plotinus on Sense-Perception* (Cambridge, Cambridge University Press).

Ferwerda, R. (1965), *La signification des images et des métaphores dans la pensée de Plotin* (Groningen, Wolters).

Ficin, M. (2002), *Commentaire sur le Banquet de Platon, 'De l'Amour'*, ed. & trans. P. Laurens (Paris, Les Belles Lettres).

Ficino, M. (1985), *Commentary on Plato's 'Symposium On Love'*, trans. with introduction & notes by S. Jayne, 2nd edn (Woodstock, Spring Publications).

Ficino, M. (2016), *On the Nature of Love: Ficino on Plato's 'Symposium'*, trans. A. Farndell (London, Shepheard-Walwyn Ltd).

Gentile, S. (1984), *Marsilio Ficino e il ritorno di Platone. Mostra di manoscritti, stampe e documenti 17 maggio-16 giugno 1984: Catalogo* (Florence, La Lettere).

Hankins, J. (1990), 'Cosimo de' Medici and the "Platonic Academy"', *Journal of the Warburg and the Courtauld Institutes*, 53: 144–62.

Henry, P. (1941), *Études Plotiniennes: II. Les Manuscrits des Ennéades*, Museum Lessianum. Section Philosophique, no. 21 (Paris, Desclée de Brouwer & Brussels, L'Édition Universelle).

Magnard, P. (ed.) (2001), *Marsile Ficin: Les Platonismes à la Renaissance* (Paris, Editions Vrin).

Marcel, R. (1958), *Marsile Ficin (1433–1499)* (Paris, Les Belles Lettres).

Pascal, B. (1963), *Œuvres Complètes*, présentation & notes L. Lafuma (Paris, Éditions du Seuil).

Plato (1905), *Platonis Opera*, tomus IV, ed. J. Burnet (Oxford, Clarendon Library).

Plato (1995a), *Platonis Opera*, tomus I, eds E.A. Duke, W.F. Hicken, W.S.M. Nicoll, D.B. Robinson & J.C.G. Strachan (Oxford, Clarendon Press).

Plato (1995b), *Platonis Opera*, tomus II, ed. J. Burnet (Oxford, Clarendon Library).

Plato (1998), *Cratylus*, trans. C. Reeve (Indianapolis, Hackett).

Plato (1999), *The Symposium*, trans. C. Gill (London, Penguin Books).

Plato (2001), *Philebus*, trans. R. Waterfield (London, Penguin Books).

Plato (2008), *Timaeus* and *Critias*, trans. & annotated by D. Lee, revised, introduced & further annotated by T.K. Johansen (London, Penguin Books).

Plotinus (1951–73), *Plotini Opera*, ($H\text{-}S^1$), ed. P. Henry & H.-R. Schwyzer (Paris, Desclée de Brouwer & Bruxelles, L'Édition Universelle).

Plotinus (1964–82), *Plotini Opera*, revised edition ($H\text{-}S^2$), ed. P. Henry & H.-R. Schwyzer (Oxford, Oxford University Press).

Plotinus (1966–88), *Enneads*, volumes I to VII, trans. A.H. Armstrong (Loeb Classical Library; Cambridge MA, Harvard University Press).

Riegel, N. (2014), 'Goodness and Beauty in Plato', *Archai: Journal on the Origins of Western Thought*, 12: 147–58.

Robichaud, D. (2017), 'Ficino on Force, Magic and Power: Neoplatonic and Hermetic Influences in Ficino's Three Books on Life', *Renaissance Quarterly*, 70: 44–87.

Robichaud, D. (2018), *Plato's Persona: Marsilio Ficino, Renaissance Humanism and Platonic Traditions* (Philadelphia, University of Pennsylvania Press).

Saffrey, H.-D (1996), 'Florence, 1492: The Reappearance of Plotinus', *Renaissance Quarterly*, 49.3: 286–508.

Stern-Gillet, S. (2000), 'Le Principe du Beau chez Plotin: Réflexions sur *Enneas* VI 7 32 et 33', *Phronesis*, 45.1: 38–63.

Stern-Gillet, S. (2011), 'Proclus and the Platonic Muse', *Ancient Philosophy*, 31.2: 363–80.

Stern-Gillet, S. (2019), '*Homoiōsis theōi* in the *Theaetetus* and in Plotinus', *Ancient Philosophy*, 39: 89–117.

12

'A Man within a Woman, or even a God': Vittoria Colonna and 16th-Century Italian Poetic Culture

ABIGAIL BRUNDIN

1. Introduction: Vittoria Colonna and Michelangelo

THIS CHAPTER HAS as its focus a famous friendship, one that was much discussed during the 16th century, and frequently commemorated in subsequent eras.[1] The aristocratic poet Vittoria Colonna (1492–1547) met the artist Michelangelo Buonarroti (1475–1564) some time in the 1530s in Rome, and their friendship continued for around a decade until Colonna's death. Michelangelo needs little introduction, especially in a Neoplatonic context: his work has long been a key critical reference point in discussions of 16th-century Italian Neoplatonism, both in relation to his production in the plastic arts and to his poetry.[2] Vittoria Colonna, on the other hand, is not as well known as she ought to be, or used to be. Famed during her lifetime as an impeccable poetic stylist writing in the Petrarchan genre, in subsequent centuries she was chiefly known for her friendship with Michelangelo, cast as his muse and even as his lover.[3] Colonna's fame as a poet began to grow across Italy from 1525, when she was left widowed and still childless at the relatively young age of 33 and began to write poetry of mourning in memory of her deceased husband.[4] Her poems were published in numerous printed editions in her lifetime and after, and she also wrote a number of devotional prose meditations that had

[1] On the friendship between Colonna and Michelangelo see the recent biography of Colonna by Targoff (2018). Spiritual aspects of their friendship are explored in Campi (1994) and Forcellino (2016). The mythologising of the friendship during the 19th century is documented in Martorelli (1997).
[2] See for example the discussions in Robb (1935: 239–69); Panofsky (1939: 171–230); Tolnay (1964: 31–55). A more recent discussion of Michelangelo's poetic Neoplatonism is Moroncini (2010).
[3] It is significant that there has been no up-to-date and accurate biography of Vittoria Colonna until Targoff (2018).
[4] On Colonna's early poetry, see Cox (2008: 45–75) and McHugh (2013).

Proceedings of the British Academy, **240**, 292–305, © The British Academy 2022.

wide circulation in print.[5] Much of her poetry was also set to music by some of the preeminent composers of the period.[6]

The precise details of Colonna's early education remain uncertain. She came from a wealthy family, and certainly knew some Latin and classical literature. As a young married woman she spent time at the court on the island of Ischia in the Bay of Naples, presided over by her aunt-by-marriage, Costanza D'Avalos, a powerful patron and intellect.[7] On Ischia the young bride had access to the excellent library assembled by Costanza, and she also met many literary and intellectual figures who came to the island to wait out periods of plague in Naples.[8] We can hypothesise with some conviction that she at some point read Marsilio Ficino's Italian translation of, and commentary on, Plato's *Symposium*,[9] but other less direct Neoplatonic influences are also important in Colonna's formation, including the courtly air that she lived and breathed, the Petrarchan poetic model that she adopted, the religious views she encountered, and the other kinds of vernacular and humanistic literature she consumed.[10] Like any other vernacular poet of her period and class, she had an implicit awareness of Neoplatonic models.

In its earlier stages, Colonna's poetry followed a relatively standard Petrarchan model of longing for an absent beloved.[11] Clearly, however, it was far from standard in significantly altering the gender norms of the genre, by citing as the absent beloved the idealised figure of the poet's deceased husband, Francesco d'Avalos, Marquis of Pescara, who died after fighting for the Imperial troops against the French in 1525.[12] The first edition of Colonna's *Rime* was published in 1538, making her the first published secular woman poet in Italy.[13] While the Petrarchan formula was by this stage very familiar and widely practised, due to the immense popularity of Francesco Petrarca's *Rime sparse* as a model and source text, its appropriation by

[5] A full history of the print publication of Colonna's poetry is provided in Crivelli (2016). The most recent Italian edition is Colonna (1982), and a parallel-text translation of the collection of devotional sonnets prepared for Michelangelo is Colonna (2005). Carinci (2016) analyses her devotional prose works, one of which is translated into English in Haskins (2008).

[6] Colonna's poetry was a particularly important source for spiritual madrigals in the second half of the 16th century by composers such as Perissone Cambio, Nicolò Dorati, Pietro Vinci and Philippe de Monte: see Piejus (2016).

[7] Costanza D'Avalos and her role at the court in Ischia is discussed in Leone de Castris (1997).

[8] On Colonna's early life in Naples and on Ischia, see Thérault (1968).

[9] Ficino (2011). English translations are Ficino (1985) and Ficino (2016). For a close analysis of Ficino's philosophical method, see the analysis of his commentary by Suzanne Stern-Gillet in this volume.

[10] On the influences of Colonna's Neapolitan environment, see Ranieri (1996; 2000).

[11] See for comparison the poetry of Pietro Bembo, the primary practitioner in the Petrarchan genre in 16th-century Italy, whose poetry provided the model for linguistic and stylistic best practice: Bembo (1960). Notably, Bembo greatly admired Colonna's poetry, particularly its quality of *gravitas*: Brundin (2016a: 64–7).

[12] A contemporary biography of Francesco D'Avalos is Giovio (1931). See also Targoff (2018: 11–25) for an account of the circumstances surrounding his death.

[13] Erdmann (1999) discusses the comparative European data and Cox (2008) adds much to the picture for Italy.

a woman was unprecedented.[14] Notably, Colonna was greatly helped by the actual circumstances in which she wrote: she was wealthy, widowed and childless, and therefore had the time and means to write. Her husband was dead, so that she was able to long for him with complete decorum.[15] Colonna's longing for her deceased husband is framed in these early, mourning sonnets as a Neoplatonic aspiration upwards, or a constant desire for flight: she bemoans her earthbound state and seeks to rise towards her 'sun', D'Avalos, the source of much-needed heat and light. In his absence the poet's life is represented as a prison, a trap, or a knot that binds her to earth and a life she no longer desires:

> How can it be that this frail body,
> tangled in human garb to my detriment,
> pulls it to earth, when it is united in Heaven
> with its glorious and noble light;
> If there it is gratified, nurtured and fed,
> and living in this prison would always
> be torture, or more, a living death?[16]

2. A Spiritual Friendship

Vittoria Colonna and Michelangelo met some time in the late 1530s in Rome, after her poetry was already circulating in print and manuscript, and they kept up a correspondence until Colonna's death in 1547. They seem to have been close and met regularly. Contemporary dialogues by the Portuguese artist Francisco de Hollanda describe the pair meeting in a Roman church to discuss questions of art and faith.[17] When Colonna was living outside Rome for periods, contemporary accounts record her journeys back to Rome to see her friend.[18]

A significant aspect of the friendship between these two intense individuals was an engagement with the reformist doctrinal ideas that were under discussion in certain circles in Italy in the period. Both Colonna and Michelangelo were drawn to the Lutheran doctrine of *sola fide* or Justification by faith alone, which, drawing on the writings of St Paul and St Augustine, rejected the efficacy of good works and taught

[14] On the reception and circulation of Petrarch's lyric poetry in Renaissance Italy, see Jossa (2015).

[15] Colonna's absolute decorum is stressed in a contemporary account of the court at Ischia by Paolo Giovio, in which she is described as always accompanied by two elderly virgins who keep watch over her virtue: Giovio (2013); Gouwens (2015: 78).

[16] 'Or come avien che questa fragil salma, / di mortal gonna per mio danno ordita, / la tiri in terra, essendo in Ciel unita / con la sua luce gloriosa ed alma? / S'ivi s'appaga, si nudrisce e vive, / e l'abitare in questo carcer sempre / le saria grave, anzi pur viva morte' Colonna (1982: 30) (author's translation). See, for a discussion of these motifs, Sapegno (2016).

[17] Hollanda (2013) is a recent English translation of the dialogues. See also Bury (1981), Forcellino (2016) and Targoff (2018).

[18] Forcellino (2016) provides details of this, including citing Michelangelo's biographer, Condivi, who describes Colonna's frequent journeys from Viterbo back to Rome.

that salvation could not be earned through merit but was freely given to those with faith.[19] They were in close contact with some high-placed members of the Roman Church who argued for the legitimacy of this doctrine, before it was definitively rejected during the opening sessions of the Council of Trent and declared heretical.[20] This is not to say that either Colonna or Michelangelo was themselves a heretic of course – they lived through a period of great doctrinal uncertainty, but it is clear that both sought to be the best Christians they could be, and shared an interest in developing their faith. After her husband's death, Colonna spent most of the rest of her life lodging in various convents, although she never took religious vows to become a nun. Her deep piety was a key aspect of her public profile as a poet.

Colonna and Michelangelo frequently exchanged gifts. Michelangelo made three devotional drawings for Colonna – identified as a *Pietà* now in the Isabella Stewart Gardner Museum in Boston, a *Crucifixion* now in the British Museum, and a drawing of the Samaritan Woman meeting Christ at the Well, which is lost but exists in numerous copies.[21] He also composed numerous poems, many of which were addressed to her. In return, Colonna compiled a manuscript of poems that she gave to Michelangelo in around 1540, representing her most recent and mature lyric compositions.[22] It is worth stressing that Colonna's gift of sonnets was an extremely unusual move for her: although her poetry was widely copied and circulated, as well as being issued in numerous printed editions during her lifetime, the poet herself only very rarely sanctioned or organised its direct transmission.[23] The preparation of a collection of 103 sonnets, in an unembellished manuscript, as a private gift, was a sign of the importance of this friendship for Colonna. Michelangelo duly treasured the gift, turning down requests to loan it out to other readers.[24]

In the context of the friendship between this pair, despite Michelangelo's towering reputation as a sculptor and painter, Vittoria Colonna was the dominant partner. Michelangelo looked to her for spiritual guidance and openly acknowledged his need for her support. This is clearly expressed in a famous madrigal, composed by Michelangelo in the mid-1540s when his friendship with Colonna was at its most intense, in which he re-genders her and assigns her a godlike role (Buonarroti 1991: 398, [illegible]):

> A man within a woman, or rather a god
> speaks through her mouth, so that I,

[19] On Luther's doctrine of *sola fide*, see Wriedt (2003: 88–94).

[20] On the movement for reform in Italy, see Bowd (2002), Bozza (1976) and Caponetto (1999). On Colonna's religious beliefs, see Ranieri (1992), Brundin (2008), Bowd (2016) and Campi (2016).

[21] Michelangelo's drawings for Colonna have generated much scholarship as well as a recent debate about their status as drawings or paintings. See as a starting point Nagel (1997) and D'Elia (2006), as well as the up-to-date case for a new approach to the works presented by Forcellino (2016).

[22] On Colonna's gift manuscript, identified as the work now in the Biblioteca Apostolica Vaticana in Rome (Codice Vaticano Latino 11539), see Colonna (2005) and most recently Copello (2017).

[23] On the circulation of Colonna's works in manuscript during her lifetime, see Brundin (2016a); on her print circulation in the same period, Crivelli (2016).

[24] Michelangelo's refusal to loan his manuscript is discussed in Brundin (2016a: 54).

by having listened to her,
have been made such that I'll never be my own again.
I do believe, since I've been
taken from myself by her,
that, being outside myself, I'll take pity on myself;
her beautiful face spurs me
so far above vain desire
that I see death in every other beauty.
O lady who pass souls
through fire and water on to days of joy:
Pray, make me never turn back to myself again.

Colonna's transformative effect on Michelangelo is clearly portrayed in this poem: he has been taken from himself by the lady, and 'being outside myself, I'll take pity on myself'. He longs never to return to his previous earthbound state.

In another of the poems he addressed to her, Michelangelo adds a notably concrete element to the impact that he hopes Colonna's advice and support will have on him. The poet compares the act of hacking away the 'hard alpine stone' to reveal the 'living figure' contained within it, to the stripping off of the 'coarse, rough, hard bark' of flesh that hides the trembling soul within his own form (Buonarroti 1991: 305,):

Just as, by taking away, lady, one puts
into hard and alpine stone
a figure that's alive
and that grows larger wherever the stone decreases,
so too are any good deeds
of the soul that still trembles
concealed by the excess mass of its own flesh,
which forms a husk that's coarse and crude and hard.
You alone can still take them out
from within my outer shell,
for I haven't the will or strength within myself.

In this madrigal Michelangelo is describing the work of revelation that he undertook with such skill and confidence in his day job as a sculptor: the process of 'scultura per forza di levare', 'sculpting by taking away', that allowed him, through the power of his divine ability, to reveal the perfect form that was hidden in the rough block of marble, the block that he had carefully selected because he knew that the form was already there, contained within it. The role of art, according to Plotinus in the *Ennead*, is to impose form, and therefore beauty, on matter. In *Ennead* V 8, he describes two stones, one untouched, the other 'mastered by art' into a statue: 'The stone which has been brought to beauty of form by art will appear beautiful not because it is a stone – for then the other would be just as beautiful – but as a result of the form which art has put into it' (V 8 [31] 1, A: 237).[25] In *Ennead* I 6, the reader is

[25] Grateful thanks to Cristina D'Ancona for her advice about this and other passages in Plotinus. See Plotinus (1969) for quotations from volume I of the *Ennead*, and Plotinus (1984) for those from volume V.

urged to beautify his own soul through a process akin to sculpting, 'just as someone making a statue' (V 8 [31] 9, A: 259).[26] Yet whereas in the plastic arts Michelangelo was powerful and unerring in his work, when it came to the work of 'revealing' the goodness and beauty in his own soul he was inept, 'trembling', and begged his friend for help, asking that she take up the chisel and sculpt him via the medium of her own art form, that of poetry: 'You alone can still take them out / from within my outer shell, / for I haven't the will or strength within myself.'

It should be clear from these two brief examples that the Neoplatonic emphasis in Michelangelo's poems addressed to Vittoria Colonna is loud and unmistakable. Michelangelo bemoans the crude bark that encrusts his soul, but believes there is 'good work' hidden within. Similarly, Plotinus relates, in *Ennead* V 8, that the inside can be beautiful even if the outside is ugly, giving the example of a hideous man who possesses a beautiful soul.[27] Michelangelo longs to be a better Christian and draw closer to the example of Christ. With Colonna's help he can leave his earthbound state, rise above it and never return to it. The onus he places upon his friend to work upon his rough 'bark' and reveal his beautiful soul is a serious duty.

3. Colonna's Neoplatonic Poetic Vision

How did Colonna respond to Michelangelo's plea? We can find at least some of the answer in the manuscript collection of 103 sonnets that Colonna sent to him around 1540. The manuscript is, as mentioned earlier, simple and unadorned: it has no illumination or coat of arms, no decoration of any kind: the front cover bears only the annotation 'sonetti spirituali della Signora Vittoria' ('spiritual sonnets by the Lady Vittoria'). Michelangelo prized his gift manuscript so highly not because it was precious or valuable in material terms, but because it contained the most recent, mature and deeply thought out work of a poet at the height of her powers, directed to him as its first intended reader.[28]

There is a strong sense, from the opening poem of Michelangelo's manuscript collection, of a marked shift in Colonna's poetic stance: 'love' is still the dominant frame, but this is not the courtly love of standard Petrarchan lyric verse, nor the marital love found in Colonna's earlier mourning poems. Instead this love is spiritual, raw and corporeal. Notably, the figure of the poet's husband has disappeared entirely. Christ is now the poet's only beloved, but the transition is accomplished

[26] I am grateful to Stefan Sperl for pointing to this consonance in *Ennead* I. See also the discussion in this volume by Stern-Gillet of the similarities between Ficino's and Plotinus's theories of the nature of beauty. For more on Michelangelo's theory of art, see Clements (1963); Summers (1981).

[27] 'But the beauty also in studies and ways of life and generally in souls makes clear that what is pursued is something else and that beauty does not lie in magnitude: it is truly a greater beauty than that when you see moral sense in someone and delight in it, not looking at his face – which might be ugly – but putting aside all shape and pursuing his inner beauty' (V 8 [31] 2, A: 245).

[28] On Michelangelo as Colonna's first reader, see Brundin (2016b).

smoothly through the retention of the moniker 'sole' (sun): the beloved remains the source of heat and light. The poet's tools, her pen, quill and paper in place of the marble and chisel that Michelangelo uses, are the nails of the Crucifixion, dipped in the blood dripping from Christ's wounds and used to inscribe her verse on his pale, lifeless body to teach others about his suffering (Colonna 2005: 57,):

> Since my chaste love for many years
> kept my soul aflame with the desire for fame, and it nourished
> a serpent in my breast so that now my heart languishes
> in pain turned towards God, who alone can help me,
> let the holy nails from now on be my quills,
> and the precious blood my pure ink,
> my lined paper the sacred lifeless body,
> so that I may write down for others all that he suffered.

By insisting on a new frame for her poetry, emphasising that 'from now on' she will write in Christ's blood, the poet demonstrates that she is already far advanced on her ascent towards God. Although she is beset constantly by doubts and fears that she will not have the capacity to complete her journey, her manuscript opens self-assertively, with the claim that she has left her worldly love far behind (Colonna 2005: 57,):

> It is not right here to invoke Parnassus or Delos,
> for I aspire to cross other waters, to ascend
> other mountains which human feet cannot climb unaided.
> I pray to the sun, which lights up the earth and the
> heavens, that letting forth his shining spring
> he pours down upon me a draught equal to my great thirst.

It is worth emphasising that this is a striking departure from previous Petrarchan poetic production, as well as a striking attitude for a woman poet to adopt. Petrarch himself never overcame his earthly love for Laura, but Colonna, the first woman Petrarchist, does manage to rise beyond her earthly union with her husband, Francesco D'Avalos, using it as a springboard to bring her closer to Christ.[29] She has succeeded where Petrarch failed, and she advertises this success clearly in the opening sonnet of her manuscript for Michelangelo: 'let the holy nails from now on be my quills'.[30] Although Colonna does not address Michelangelo directly in the poems in his manuscript, she is clearly offering her own example as a model for spiritual ascent. From poem to poem she enacts a gradual, often painful process

[29] On Petrarch's failure to rise beyond earthly love in the *Rime Sparse*, see Barolini (2009).

[30] Targoff (2018: 75) has argued recently that Colonna was 'certainly no Neoplatonist', and that she 'actively resisted the very idea that she might reconcile her earthly and divine love'. My own interpretation would be to see the move from poetry celebrating a love of D'Avalos to poetry celebrating a love of Christ as a continuum rather than a break and change of direction.

of self-reflection in search of greater understanding and deeper faith. The stress is on the individual's responsibility for nurturing an active faith, one which finds resonances in both Neoplatonic and reformist religious thought.[31]

The poet's progress is slow: the poems in the collection draw us forward inch by inch but often she has a loss of heart and falls back again, defeated by the task. She is worried by the inadequacy of human language to describe her visions: the Dantean image of a 'sphere lit up around by a thousand stars, and a sun which shines amongst them with such brightness', becomes only 'a dark shadow' when the poet tries to write it down with her 'broken and inadequate words' (Colonna 2005: 115,):

> Thus I inscribe upon these pages a dark shadow
> to represent that dazzling sun, and I speak to others here
> of heavenly things with broken and inadequate words.
> Our minds can only see as much as he chooses
> to reveal of himself, and can only fly if he lends wings
> and if he clears and banishes the fog for us.

In another example, the poet's vision is of a wall blocking her path (Colonna 2005: 113,):

> A high wall in the form of a mosaic
> of lively sparks flying rapidly
> and so tightly bound by chains of love,
> that one casts upon the other a pure light
> without any shadows to give *chiaroscuro*,
> but only resplendent light from the heavenly sun
> which decorates, colours, arranges and adorns them.

The perfection of this vision is depleted by the frailty of the poet's human capacities (Colonna 2005: 115,):

> … no living thought
> could ever draw, nor could memory ever commit it
> to paper, much less the intellect describe it in verse.

The poet's vision here is strongly Neoplatonic. The chains of love she describes evoke the *vinculum animae* or chain of the soul that binds mortals to God.[32] The sparks remind us of *archon*, described by Marsilio Ficino in his work of 1489, *De vita coelitus comparanda*, as the process of light joining matter and being transformed, creating sparks of life specific to each individual being.[33] The repeated

[31] Although Neoplatonists stress the dignity of man and reformers acknowledge instead his irreversible depravity, they share a belief in salvation through progress in knowledge ('knowledge' as synonymous with 'faith') which is slow and gradual. Both also emphasise the role of choice in directing the will towards God. These shared resonances are discussed further in Brundin (2008).

[32] See Walker (2000: 96–106).

[33] The imagery is also notably Dantean: see for example *Paradiso* 28.88–93.

references to a failure of human capacity to record or remember what it sees in heaven evokes Dante's similar struggle in the *Paradiso* to describe or even perceive heaven.[34] The poet at all times keeps in play both her soul, *alma*, and her intellect, *intelletto*, as two distinct qualities but both implicated in her search for God through poetry. Her soul aspires upwards, but it is her intellect that allows the traces of God to be conjured in words, albeit broken and inadequate ones.[35] While the Neoplatonic roots of this dualism are clear, notably they also allow the poet both to keep in play the non-intellectual (feminised) spirituality traditionally associated with female saints and mystics, and to claim for herself a place in the (masculine) intellectual culture of learned poetry and piety.[36]

In another poem, the poet produces 'rough uncultivated verses', despite herself, because (Colonna 2005: 137–9,):

> the divine fire, which through its mercy
> inflames my mind, sometimes gives out
> these sparks of its own accord,
> and if one such spark should once warm
> some gentle heart then a thousand times
> a thousand thanks I owe to that happy mistake.

Although the prevalent attitude in all these examples is of humility, note that the poet is thankful that one such spark might 'warm some gentle heart' – subtly she is claiming a role for herself as leader and instructor, a role which seems more significant when we think about the poet's relationship with the intended reader of this collection of poems.[37]

Elsewhere in Michelangelo's manuscript, although the poet represents herself as 'weak and ill', 'blind' and 'naked', her tone is rapturous and she begins to imagine a time when her journey towards God will reach its culmination (Colonna 2005: 73,):

> Weak and infirm I run towards true salvation,
> and blindly I call out to the sun which alone
> I worship, and naked I burn for his heavenly gold,
> and approach his flames fashioned in pure, cold wax;
> and however much I distrust myself, so much more
> then does my soul trust in his wondrous gift,
> which has the great healing power to make me
> healthy, enriched, and whole in his loving fires.
> Thus once armed with these gifts and this burning ardour

[34] For a full discussion of Dante's failure of memory in the *Paradiso*, see the contribution by Cristina D'Ancona to this volume.

[35] For an example of the intellect's exhortation of the soul in medieval Hebrew poetry, see the contribution by Adena Tannebaum to this volume.

[36] For a discussion of the spiritual power of women in early modern Europe, as intellectuals as well as beings endowed with a 'sacred charisma', see Furey (2004).

[37] For a more developed discussion of Colonna's aspiration to fulfil the role of spiritual teacher, see Brundin (2001).

> I may behold him not through my own powers of vision but through his,
> and may love and worship him through the power of his love for me.
> Thus my deeds and my desires will no longer be my own,
> but lightly I will move upon celestial wings
> wherever the force of his holy love might fling me.

Notably, the poet as she runs towards salvation describes herself as 'fashioned in pure, cold wax'. Where Michelangelo's trembling soul is encased in a rough bark, requiring strong blows on a chisel to begin to chip it away, wax will be easily melted in the heat of proximity to God. Colonna is seemingly far more confident than Michelangelo about her potential release from the human bonds of sin. This is in line with the reformed doctrine of *sola fide*, which teaches that Faith is passive, merely receiving Christ and all his benefits without seeking to earn them, so that the poet abandons herself joyfully to her helplessness. It is not her own powers of vision but God's that will allow her to see, and his love for her will allow her in turn to love. She longs to be tossed hither and yon by 'the force of his holy love'.

In *Ennead* I 6, Plotinus states that in order to perceive God we must first ourselves become Godlike: 'you must first become all godlike and beautiful if you intend to see God and beauty' (I 6 [1] 9, A: 261). While we might expect the attitude of the female poet in particular to be one of abject humility when faced by the enormous task of spiritual renewal that she faces, instead in this last example what we find is a far more strident and confident voice, one that begins to assume a godlike and beautiful attitude. The poet is naked and burning, she runs towards the flames and knows that the wax impeding her ascent will begin to melt. Once it does, she will be 'healthy, enriched and whole'. What is more, she assumes a teaching role, leading her friend Michelangelo by example on the path of spiritual understanding. Implicitly, we understand that she is equipped to succeed in her journey in part precisely because she is a woman, thus naturally endowed with the kind of pure, non-intellectual spirituality that allows her to absorb the sparks of heat and light towards which she strains. By keeping her intellect at all times in play, however, the poet also lays claim to much more than this, by insisting on a higher authority that she earns through the power of her impeccable poetry.

Notably, in the very last sonnet of the manuscript that Colonna made for her friend, the 103rd poem in the cycle, her attitude of confidence once again wavers and the poet is attacked by a fear that her verses have become too slick and polished, no longer possessing the raw spirit that they need in order to draw her closer to God (Colonna 2005: 139,):

> I am afraid that the knot, with which for many years
> I have kept my soul bound up, now orders my verses
> only through long habit, and not for that first reason
> that they are turned towards God and inflamed by him.
> I am afraid that they are knots tied tightly
> by one who works badly with a dull file,
> so that fired with false esteem I believe
> that my days are useful when in fact I waste them.

Out of fear, the poet longs for silence to replace her poetry, and a return to the 'pain and hoarse cries' that are a true representation of her soul. This might be deemed a surprising move: as she draws her collection of poems to a close, the poet undermines its value or usefulness and worries that she may even be doing harm through her writing. Perhaps, however, the lack of conclusion is entirely necessary. The closing sonnet imposes a sense of circularity on the collection. Nothing is resolved or completed: instead the process of soul-searching must begin again and the reader must return to the first poem and restart their reading. The spiritual work is never done and while language remains to express it the poet's work is likewise unending, cyclical and painfully slow.

4. Conclusion: A Model for Imitation

In this chapter I have taken as my focus the poetic relations between Vittoria Colonna, a highly aristocratic widow, and Michelangelo, one of the most famous artists of his day. Yet it is worth pausing for a few moments, finally, on the question of dissemination, a key consideration of this volume as a whole. As other chapters in this collection aim to demonstrate, Neoplatonism was a poetic system that spanned centuries, languages and countries, connecting cultures and peoples that might at first glance appear to have little in common. In conclusion, therefore, we need to pose the question, did the Neoplatonic, poetic conversation between these two close friends reach beyond them to touch others? And if so, in what ways?

While her manuscript for Michelangelo was a private gift which he guarded closely, Colonna's spiritual sonnets were available in numerous printed editions in 16th-century Italy, some of high quality and some extremely cheap, printed on poor paper in small format and designed to be sold as widely as possible.[38] As well as the 24 discreet editions of her *Rime* published in the 16th century, Colonna's poetry was also included in the many poetic anthologies that were one of the newly fledged publishing industry's best sellers in the period.[39] They were also, as previously mentioned, set to music multiple times. In other words, Colonna's poetry – extremely popular, widely circulated and respected – was consumed by large numbers of ordinary readers and listeners, well beyond the courts, and was hugely influential. In her wake, many other secular women picked up a pen and began to write and print their work: in Italy, over 250 works by women were printed before the end of the 16th century, which is over 200 more than in any other European country in the period.[40] But not only women: many other male poets were also hugely influenced by the example of Colonna's wholly spiritualised

[38] For a full survey of Colonna's print history, see Crivelli (2016).

[39] On the role of Colonna's poetry in the anthologies published by Gabriele Giolito, see Robin (2016). More generally on Renaissance anthologies, see Quondam (1974).

[40] The most complete data are provided in Cox (2008).

Petrarchism, so that she was described by an admiring successor as 'the first to have begun to write with dignity in verse of spiritual things'.[41]

In this way, what may have begun as an esoteric, inward-looking phenomenon, courtly Petrarchism with its strongly Neoplatonic flavour, was transformed via the poetry of Vittoria Colonna and its reception in 16th-century Italy first into serious spiritual work, and second into a nationwide phenomenon that extended its influence far beyond her own elite circles to reach entirely new kinds of readers. The desire for this reach and influence seems to be implicit in the poetry itself: she tells us that if one of her poetic 'sparks' can enflame another mind she will be happy. In the most discreet manner possible, she embraces and even insists on her status as a model for imitation, and on the utility of courtly Petrarchism as a tool in the search for the divine.

References

Barolini, T. (2009), 'The Self in the Labyrinth of Time: *Rerum vulgarium fragmenta*', in V. Kirkham & A. Maggi (eds), *Petrarch: A Critical Guide to the Complete Works* (Chicago/London, University of Chicago Press), 33–62.

Bembo, P. (1960), *Prose e rime*, ed. C. Dionisotti (Turin, Unione Tipografico-Editrice).

Bowd, S. (2002), *Reform before the Reformation: Vincenzo Querini and the Religious Renaissance in Italy* (Leiden, Brill).

Bowd, S. (2016), 'Prudential Friendship and Religious Reform: Vittoria Colonna and Gasparo Contarini', in Brundin *et al.* (2016), 349–70.

Bozza, T. (1976), *Nuovi studi sulla Riforma in Italia. I. Il Beneficio di Cristo* (Rome, Storia e letteratura).

Brundin, A. (2001), 'Vittoria Colonna and the Virgin Mary', *Modern Language Review*, 96: 61–81.

Brundin, A. (2008), *Vittoria Colonna and the Spiritual Poetics of the Italian Reformation* (Aldershot, Ashgate).

Brundin, A. (2016a), 'Vittoria Colonna in Manuscript', in Brundin *et al.* (2016), 39–68.

Brundin, A. (2016b), 'Poesia come devozione: leggere le rime di Vittoria Colonna', in M.S. Sapegno (ed.), *Al crocevia della storia: Poesia, religione e politica in Vittoria Colonna* (Rome, Viella), 161–75.

Brundin, A., Crivelli, T. & Sapegno, M.S. (eds) (2016), *A Companion to Vittoria Colonna* (Leiden, Brill).

Buonarroti, Michelangelo (1991), *The Poetry of Michelangelo: An Annotated Translation*, ed. & trans. J.M. Saslow (New Haven/London, Yale University Press).

Bury, J.B. (1981), *Two Notes on Francisco de Holanda* (London, Warburg Institute).

Campi, E. (1994), *Michelangelo e Vittoria Colonna: un dialogo artistico-teologico ispirato da Bernardino Ochino, e altri saggi di storia della Riforma* (Turin, Claudiana).

Campi, E. (2016), 'Vittoria Colonna and Bernardino Ochino', in Brundin *et al.* (2016), 371–98.

[41] The citation is from Fiamma (1570: unpaginated dedicatory letter). On Colonna's status as a model, see Rabitti (2000) and, most recently, Cox (2016).

Caponetto, S. (1999), *The Protestant Reformation in Sixteenth-Century Italy*, trans. A.C. Tedeschi & J. Tedeschi (Kirksville, Thomas Jefferson University Press).
Carinci, E. (2016), 'Religious Prose Writings', in Brundin *et al.* (2016), 399–430.
Clements, R. (1963), *Michelangelo's Theory of Art* (New York, New York University Press).
Colonna, V. (1982), *Rime*, ed. A. Bullock (Rome/Bari, Laterza).
Colonna, V. (2005), *Sonnets for Michelangelo*, ed. & trans. A. Brundin (Chicago, University of Chicago Press).
Copello, V. (2017), 'Il dialogo poetico tra Michelangelo e Vittoria Colonna', *Italian Studies*, 72: 271–81.
Cox, V. (2008), *Women's Writing in Italy, 1400–1650* (Baltimore, The Johns Hopkins University Press).
Cox, V. (2016), 'The Exemplary Vittoria Colonna', in Brundin *et al.* (2016), 467–501.
Crivelli, T. (2016), 'The Print Tradition of Vittoria Colonna's *Rime*', in Brundin *et al.* (2016), 69–139.
D'Elia, U.R. (2006), 'Drawing Christ's Blood: Michelangelo, Vittoria Colonna, and the Aesthetics of Reform', *Renaissance Quarterly*, 59: 90–129.
Erdmann, A. (1999), *My Gracious Silence: Women in the Mirror of Sixteenth-Century Printing in Western Europe* (Lucern, Gilhofer & Rauschberg).
Ferino Pagden, S. (ed.) (1997), *Vittoria Colonna: Dichterin und Muse Michelangelos* (Vienna, Kunsthistorisches Museum and Skira).
Fiamma, G. (1570), *Rime spirituali del R.D. Gabriel Fiamma, Canonico Regolare Lateranense, esposte da lui medesimo* (Venice, Francesco de' Franceschi Senese), dedicatory letter.
Ficino, M. (1985), *Commentary on Plato's Symposium on Love*, ed. & trans. S. Jayne, 2nd edn (Woodstock, Spring Publications).
Ficino, M. (2011), *El libro dell'amore* (Bologna, Zanichelli).
Ficino, M. (2016), *On the Nature of Love: Ficino on Plato's* Symposium, trans. A. Farndell (London, Shepheard-Walwyn Ltd.).
Forcellino, M. (2016), 'Vittoria Colonna and Michelangelo: Drawings and Paintings', in Brundin *et al.* (2016), 270–313.
Furey, C. (2004), '"Intellects Inflamed in Christ": Women and Spiritualized Scholarship in Renaissance Christianity', *The Journal of Religion*, 84: 1–22.
Giovio, P. (1931), *Le vite del gran Capitano e del Marchese di Pescara*, trans. L. Domenichi (Bari, Laterza).
Giovio, P. (2013), *Notable Men and Women of Our Time*, ed. & trans. K. Gouwens (Cambridge, MA, Harvard University Press).
Gouwens, K. (2015), 'Female Virtue and the Embodiment of Beauty: Vittoria Colonna in Paolo Giovio's *Notable Men and Women*', *Renaissance Quarterly*, 68: 33–97.
Haskins, S. (ed & trans.) (2008), *Who is Mary? Three Early Modern Women on the Idea of the Virgin Mary* (Chicago, University of Chicago Press).
Hollanda, F. de (2013), *On Antique Painting*, trans. A.S. Wohl, introduction J.O. Caetano & C. Hope, ed. H. Wohl (University Park, Pennsylvania State University Press).
Jossa, S. (2015), 'Bembo and Italian Petrarchism', in *The Cambridge Companion to Petrarch*, ed. A.R. Ascoli & U. Falkeid (Cambridge, Cambridge University Press), 191–200.
Leone de Castris, P. (1997), 'Kultur und Mäzenatentum am Hof der D'Avalos in Ischia', in Ferino Pagden (1997), 67–76.
Martorelli, L. (1997), 'Die Fortuna Vittoria Colonnas im 19. Jahrhundert', in Ferino Pagden (1997), 479–85.

McHugh, S. (2013), 'Rethinking Vittoria Colonna: Gender and Desire in the Rime Amorose', *The Italianist*, 33: 345–60.

Moroncini, A. (2010), 'La poesia di Michelangelo: un cammino spirituale tra Neoplatonismo e Riforma', *The Italianist*, 30: 352–73.

Nagel, A. (1997), 'Gifts for Michelangelo and Vittoria Colonna', *Art Bulletin*, 79: 647–68.

Panofsky, E. (1939), *Studies in Iconology: Humanistic Themes in the Art of the Renaissance* (New York, Oxford University Press).

Piejus, A. (2016), 'Musical Settings of the *Rime*', in Brundin *et al.* (2016), 314–45.

Plotinus (1969), *Ennead, Volume I: Porphyry on the Life of Plotinus: Ennead I*, trans. A.H. Armstrong (Cambridge, MA, Harvard University Press).

Plotinus (1984), *Ennead, Volume V*, trans. A.H. Armstrong (Cambridge, MA, Harvard University Press).

Quondam, A. (1974), *Petrarchismo mediato: per una critica della forma 'antologia'* (Rome, Bulzoni).

Rabitti, G. (2000), 'Vittoria Colonna as Role Model for Cinquecento Women Poets', in L. Panizza (ed.), *Women in Italian Renaissance Culture and Society* (Oxford, Legenda), 478–97.

Ranieri, C. (1992), 'Vittoria Colonna e la riforma: alcune osservazioni critiche', *Studi latini e italiani*, 6: 87–96.

Ranieri, C. (1996), 'Premesse umanistiche alla religiosità di Vittoria Colonna', *Rivista di storia e letteratura religiose*, 32: 531–48.

Ranieri, C. (2000), 'Imprestiti platonici nella formazione religiosa di Vittoria Colonna', in V. De Caprio & C. Ranieri (eds), *Presenze eterodosse nel Viterbese tra Quattro e Cinquecento* (Rome, Archivio Giodo Izzi), 193–212.

Robb, N.A. (1935), *Neoplatonism of the Italian Renaissance* (London, Allen & Unwin).

Robin, D. (2016), 'The Lyric Voices of Vittoria Colonna and the Women of the Giolito Anthologies, 1545–1559', in Brundin *et al.* (2016), 433–66.

Sapegno, M.S. (2016), 'The *Rime*: A Textual Conundrum?', in Brundin *et al.* (2016), 140–94.

Summers, D. (1981), *Michelangelo and the Language of Art* (Princeton, Princeton University Press).

Targoff, R. (2018), *Renaissance Woman: the Life of Vittoria Colonna* (New York, Farrar, Straus and Giroux).

Thérault, S. (1968), *Un cénacle humaniste de la Renaissance autour de Vittoria Colonna châtelaine d'Ischia* (Paris and Florence, Didier and Sansoni Antiquariato).

Tolnay, C. de (1964), *The Art and Thought of Michelangelo* (New York, Pantheon).

Walker, D.P. (2000), *Spiritual and Demonic Magic: From Ficino to Campanella* (London, Sutton Publishing).

Wriedt, M. (2003), 'Luther's Theology', in D.K. McKim (ed.), *The Cambridge Companion to Martin Luther* (Cambridge, Cambridge University Press), 86–119.

13

The Ascent of the Soul: Neoplatonic Themes in the Literature of Golden Age Spain

COLIN P. THOMPSON

SUSAN BYRNE'S RECENT book *Ficino in Spain* begins by setting the record straight:

> A consistent presence in Spanish letters in the centuries following his death, Marsilio Ficino was decisively written out of that literary history at the end of the nineteenth century as those who began to fashion what would come to be the Spanish literary canon excised his voice in favour of a purist, all-Spanish approach.
>
> (Byrne 2015: 3)

She shows that copies of Ficino's work, in Latin, Italian and Spanish, were found in many royal, aristocratic, university and ecclesiastical libraries, alongside his influential translations of Plato and Plotinus into Latin. The humanist current in Spanish Golden Age culture, as she persuasively demonstrates, flourished long after the fall from grace of Erasmus or the imposition of a narrow version of Catholic orthodoxy after the Council of Trent, and she provides many examples of the ways in which Ficino was regarded as an *auctoritas* in a wide range of areas, in a necessary and long overdue corrective to the intellectual history of the period.

I have chosen what I hope may be the complementary approach of looking at how Neoplatonic ideas were adapted by a number of writers in a variety of genres to suit a changed philosophical and theological culture.[1] Two important works will be my guides, the *Enneads* of Plotinus from Late Antiquity and the Renaissance *Diálogos* of León Hebreo. I include Hebreo because his later years in Italy brought him into close contact with the Florentine Academy, because his work was well known in early modern Spain, and because he also cites the works of Jewish and Islamic philosophers such as al-Fārābī, Avicenna, al-Ghazālī, Averroes and Maimonides.[2]

[1] Space forbids inclusion of the vibrant drama of the period: on this, see Byrne (2015: 155–8) and Parker (1985: 174–215).

[2] Educated Spaniards would have read him in Italian; he was translated into Spanish by the Inca Garcilaso de la Vega (1539–1616).

Proceedings of the British Academy, **240**, 306–322, © The British Academy 2022.

1. Human Love: Poetry

One could hardly find a better summary of the relationship between human and divine love than the one offered at the end of the *Diálogos*:

> Since our soul is formed in the image of the highest beauty, and by its nature desires to return to its divine origin, it is ever impregnated with this natural desire. When, therefore, it sees a beautiful person whose beauty is in harmony with itself, it recognises in and through this beauty, divine beauty, in the image of which this person also is made. And the image of this beloved in the mind of the lover quickens with its beauty the latent divine beauty which is the very soul, and gives it actuality, as if it were to receive it from the beauty of the divine original itself. Therefore the [image] is made divine and its beauty is increased, even as divine beauty is greater than human. And the love of it becomes so intense, ardent and active that it steals away sense, imagination and the whole mind, as if it were divine beauty withdrawing the human soul to itself in contemplation. And the image of the beloved person is revered in the mind of the lover as divine in so far as the beauty of the soul and body of the beloved is more excellent and more similar to divine beauty and as it reflects the highest wisdom most clearly.
>
> (Hebreo 1937: 465–6)

The soul recognises divine beauty in a beautiful individual and the more beautiful that individual is, the greater the degree of recognition. Unlike Diotima's account of love human and divine as remembered by Socrates in the *Symposium*, Hebreo's text does not assume the same progression from the ephemeral beauty adored in the human form to the eternal Beauty which is its source.

Nor, on the whole, does Golden Age love poetry, even when its language suggests otherwise. We see this clearly in the first and greatest of the Spanish Renaissance poets, Garcilaso de la Vega (*c.* 1501–36), when he confesses that the beloved's sparkling eyes communicate directly with his soul (sonnet 8; *De aquella vista pura y excelente*) (Rutherford 2016: 39,):

> Out from those eyes, so pure and excellent,
> come vapours that are burning and alive,
> and into my own vision being sent
> they make for where grief's felt, and there arrive.

Plato himself called the eyes the windows of the soul (*Phaedrus* 255), but there is no sign here of its being raised to contemplate a higher beauty.[3] Indeed, Garcilaso is quite capable of sending the whole thing up. In sonnet 22 the poet expresses his ardent desire to see what his lady has hidden in her breast, but confesses that his

[3] The proximate source of this eye to soul communication is Bembo's closing speech in Castiglione's *Il Cortegiano*, where 'those vivacious spirits shining from her eyes … constantly add fresh fuel to the fire' (*quei vivi spiriti che scintillan fuor per gli occhi … aggiungan nuova esca al fuoco* [Castiglione 1766: 289; translation from Castiglione 1967: 334]). The *Cortegiano* was translated into Spanish at Garcilaso's urging by his close friend and fellow-poet, Juan Boscán; Garcilaso himself wrote the prologue.

eyes are unable to pass beyond her external beauty into her soul. Its ending turns a line from Petrarch (*Canzionere* 23, 34), in which the poet speaks of a time when love's arrow had not yet pierced his clothes, into a playful complaint to the lady, that 'I couldn't see beyond your gown'. Even when Garcilaso adopts a more serious tone, the shepherd Nemoroso's lament for the death of his beloved, Elisa at the end of the first eclogue, envisages only an eternity when he can be with her, not God, for ever (Dent-Young 2009: 145,):

Divine Elisa, for now it is the sky
you tread and measure with immortal feet,
and watch its changes while remaining still,
have you forgotten me? Why do you not ask
for that time to come more quickly when this veil
of the body will be torn and I be free?
Then in the third heaven,
with you hand in hand,
we will seek another plain,
other mountains, other flowing rivers,
other flowering shady valleys,
where I can rest forever and ever have you
before my happy eyes,
without the fear and shock of losing you.

The 'third heaven' is the sphere of Venus; it is Elisa who is divine, and the poet speaks only of an eternal enjoyment of her presence. Nemoroso aspires to the immortality of their earthly love, beyond the world of time and flux, not to the contemplation of supreme, unchanging beauty.[4] Such articulations are entirely characteristic of Golden Age love poetry, which is inspired by Petrarchan love poetry rather than the more metaphysical aspects of Neoplatonism. This tendency to apply Neoplatonic language to purely corporeal love is raised to a fine art in the poetry of Francisco de Quevedo (1580–1645). 'If my eye-lids, Lisi, were lips' (*Si mis párpados, Lisi, labios fueran*) follows the initial hypothesis through with sustained double-entendre: if such were the case, the rays proceeding from his eyes towards Lisi would be kisses by which his lips would drink in her beauty, and 'would live by nourishing their death'. The verb 'to die' (*morir*) is a common metaphor for orgasm, and the first tercet continues the play (Rutherford 2016: 187):

By unseen intercourse sustained and fed,
my body-naked sense and faculties
would feast upon your favours …

'Unseen' (*invisibles*) and 'body-naked' (*desnudos de cuerpo*) ought to refer to the unseen world of the soul as it ascends free from the body, but the context demands a more literal nakedness, while 'intercourse' (*comercio*) and 'feast' (*gozar*) both

[4] On Garcilaso's Neoplatonism, see Parker (1985: 43–52).

have strong sexual overtones.[5] Likewise, in 'In a curly storm of wavy gold' (*En crespa tempestad del oro undoso*), the poet's heart may be 'thirsty for beauty', but he likens himself to Icarus, who 'burns his wings to die a glorious death' and in that orgasmic moment 'attempts to make his death engender lives', that is, conceive new life through intercourse. When the language is overtly Neoplatonic, it still looks for an eternity of physical love. In another sonnet the poet confesses that he has spent ten years loving Lisi, since first he glimpsed the light of her eyes 'Ten years of my life have passed' (*Diez años de mi vida se ha llevado*), before concluding (Quevedo 2006: 480):

> Enough to see but once beauty so great;
> for once it is seen, it is eternally kindled,
> and lasts eternally within the soul.[6]

Physical beauty may leave an eternal impression in the soul, but it does not raise it to the realm of the unchanging.

In the most celebrated of his love sonnets Quevedo appears to be remembering a passage from Hebreo about the survival of love after physical dissolution. Philón declares that he will continue to love Sofía 'until Charon ferries me over the river of oblivion; and that, if the soul takes any feeling with it into the world beyond, mine should retain even there its love and crown of thorns' (Hebreo 1937: 67). Quevedo turns this into (Rutherford 2016: 191,):

> The final shades may come to shut my eyes
> and steal the white of day away from me,
> and an indulgent hour that gratifies
> my soul's anguished desire may set it free.
> My soul shall not, though, on that further shore,
> abandon all its burning memories:
> my flame can disrespect a rigid law
> and through cold water swim with greatest ease.
> A soul imprisoned by a god, no less,
> veins that have fed so great a conflagration,
> and marrow that has burnt in wondrousness,
> will quit its body, not its adoration,
> will be cold ash, but ash that feels, and will
> be driest dust, but dust that loves her still.

In a complete reversal of Platonic *anamnesis* the soul in the hereafter remembers its earthly passion, while the dust and ashes to which the body has returned still retain their love for the lady, in a memorable restatement of the *topos* of love stronger than death.

Neither Garcilaso nor Quevedo were intentionally undermining or mocking the Platonic concept of beauty and love. Quevedo himself, whose range of writing in

[5] Quevedo's sonnet 'Ah, Floralba, I dreamt that I ... should I say?' (*¡Ay Floralba!, soñé que te ... ¿diré lo?*) is even more playfully erotic and distinctly non-Neoplatonic.

[6] All unattributed translations are mine. The references provided relate to the Spanish original.

both poetry and prose stretched from the scatological to the deeply serious, is also the author of many fine philosophical poems, in which the dominant voice is neo-Stoical. They were simply adopting the conventions of that part of Neoplatonic tradition which informed Courtly Love and passed into Petrarchan love poetry; their aim was to produce new and striking versions of its commonplaces, and their first-person voice is an artistic construct rather than an autobiographical statement.

2. Philosophical Poetry[7]

A more substantial engagement with Neoplatonism is found in the philosophical poetry of the period, whose most accomplished practitioner is the Augustinian Fray Luis de León (1527–91). First, however, I should clarify something which is also germane to the mystical writing I shall look at in due course. As Paul Henry explains, images of movement and of spatial relations are metaphors for the spiritual journey towards the One: 'The road is an ascent, a movement upwards from below ... "high" and "low" express not spatial relations ... but a scale of values ... This "movement" is not local, but metaphysical and moral ... The supreme presence is at the summit of the ascent ... It is also within' (Plotinus 1991: lxxvi–vii). When poets and mystics write of the ascent from the earthly to the heavenly, of movement from the outward to the inward, they are using different metaphors to describe exactly the same process. To ascend is to look within, to leave behind attachments to earthly values in search of more enduring, heavenly ones.

Music can inspire the soul to remember its divine origin (Platonic *anamnesis*). For Plotinus, its ravishing quality raises the hearer to the harmony of the Intellectual World and Absolute Beauty (I 3 [20] 1): 'For who that truly perceives the harmony of the Intellectual Realm could fail, if he has any bent towards music, to answer to the harmony in sensible sounds?' (II 9 [33] 16, M: 129). All earthly music represents the rhythm of the Ideal Realm (V 9 [5] 11). The soul has a memory of its true home, outside time (IV 3 [27] 25), while the movement of the celestial spheres is like the melody sung by the tuned strings of a lyre (IV 4 [28] 8). Hebreo takes up these ideas, noting that Pythagoras taught how 'as they move, the heavenly bodies emit exquisite sounds, conforming one to the other in harmonious concordance' (1937: 107). Apollo with his lyre is the god of music, 'as the harmony of heaven is composed of the divers movements of all the spheres' (1937: 161). Fray Luis's Ode to the blind musician Francisco de Salinas moves in the same world, except that it is the effect of Salinas's playing which awakens the soul to the lost memory

[7] I do not include Luis de Góngora's famously controversial *Solitudes* (*Soledades*) of 1613, written in an extremely learned, Latinate syntax and lexis, despite his claims in a letter in defence of the poem that its obscurity functions as a sign of 'the first truth' (see Jones 1963). The poem's epic sweep of human love in the natural world appears to offer a more Lucretian vision, in which the natural world is constantly renewing itself, while human endeavour is at best fleeting.

of its 'illustrious first origin' (line 10) and frees it to rise through the spheres to hear 'another kind of music, imperishable, which is the source and the first' (Fray Luis 1986: 81–2).

Several of Fray Luis's poems end with the poetic voice coming crashing back down to its earthly bondage, as if the ascent could not be sustained. Plotinus speaks in a similar manner of his own mystical experience:

> Many times it has happened: lifted out of the body into myself; becoming external to all other things and self-encentred; beholding a marvellous beauty; then, more than ever, assured of communion with the loftiest order; enacting the noblest life, acquiring identity with the divine ... yet, there comes the moment of descent from intellection to reasoning, and after that sojourn in the divine, I ask myself how it happens that I can now be descending, and how did the Soul ever enter into my body, the Soul which, even within the body, is the high thing it has shown itself to be.
>
> (IV 8 [6] 1, M: 334)

Augustine's reading of Plotinus was immensely influential in the Western Christian tradition. As an Augustinian, Fray Luis would certainly have read the saint's vision of Ostia (*Confessions* ix.10), when, in conversation with his mother Monica, their souls are lifted up and for a moment touch the realm of uncreated Wisdom before returning to earth.[8] Fray Luis expresses the rapturous effects of the earthly, time-bound music of Salinas lifting him to hear the music of the Creator himself in three exclamatory mystical paradoxes (Fray Luis 1986: 83):

> Oh happy swoon!
> Oh death which gives life! Oh sweet forgetfulness!

But the exclamation which follows counters any sense that the poet has reached such bliss for more than an instant (Fray Luis 1986: 84):

> could I but stay in your repose
> without ever being restored
> to this coarse, lowly sense!

The unfulfilled desire (*durase*; imperfect subjunctive) is followed by the wish 'May it [your music] sound continually' (line 46; *suene*, present subjunctive), so that my senses can be permanently awake to the 'divine good' (*bien divino*; line 48). In another poem, 'Beloved region of shining light' (*Alma región luciente*), Fray Luis imagines the Good Shepherd leading his flock to rest in the heavenly pastures and playing immortal music to them, but once again the last two stanzas come back down to earth with a bump (Fray Luis 1986: 143–4):

> Oh voice! Oh music! Might
> but some faint strain descend into my sense
> in transports of delight,
> that my soul, journeying hence
> might lose itself in you, oh Love immense!

[8] See Louth (1981: 132–58 [on the Ostia vision, 134–41]), Turner (1995: 75–8).

then I would truly know,
my soul's sweet Spouse, the place where you abide,
and freed from prison woe
live ever at your side
and never wander far from you, my guide![9]

The imagery combines Platonic and biblical symbols (the prison of the body; Psalm 23, Song of Songs, Matthew 18.12–14/Luke 15.3–7) to express a longing for what cannot be sustained, expressed once more in a series of imperfect subjunctives.

By contrast, Fray Luis's 'Calm night' (*Noche serena,*) poem ends on a high point.[10] It is constructed around two sets of antithetical images. Earth is associated with sleep, oblivion, imprisonment, darkness, folly, vanity, deception, shadow, exile and the relentless passage of time; the heavens, with light, beauty, truth, the divine, awakening, contentment, peace, sacred love and the eternal. Gazing upwards at the night sky, the image of the eternal realm of God (line 38) the poet wonders why humans prefer to remain in their dark prison. The pattern of the ascent is similar to that set out by Hebreo, from earth, through the celestial spheres, to the fount of all beauty:

> We may ascend through a hierarchy of beauty, from the lesser to the greater and from the pure to the purest, [as if a ladder were set up] leading to the knowledge and love, not only of the most beautiful intelligences, souls and motors of the heavenly bodies, but also of the highest beauty and of the supremely beautiful, the giver of all beauty, life, intelligence and being.
>
> (1937: 426)

Much of the poem's thought can be found in Plotinus: the night sky as a prompt to ascend from the earth (III 8 [30] 11), the longing to break free of the body (I 6 [1] 5), the ascent from the body out of sense, slumber and shadow (III 6 [26] 6), the visible universe as an image or copy of the unseen eternal realm.[11] The 'true fields', 'meadows fresh and pleasant with truth' (*campos verdaderos* and *prados con verdad frescos y amenos*) of the last stanza of the *Noche serena* are surely descended from Plato's *Phaedrus* (248b) and its 'plain of truth' and 'meadow' which produces 'fit pasturage' (1973: 53–4).

3. Love Human and Divine: The Mystics

The ascent to the source of all beauty and truth, which is imagined but never wholly attained by Fray Luis, finds fulfilment in the mystical tradition, represented above all by the poetry and prose of St John of the Cross (San Juan de la Cruz, 1542–91).

[9] 'Not going astray' (*sin vagar errada*) may also echo Plotinus's reference to 'The "Meadow of Truth" from which it [the soul] does not stray' (VI 7 [38] 13, M: 483).

[10] For a parallel evocation of the night sky as revealing the harmony and order which creates peace, see the opening of 'Prince of Peace' (*Príncipe de paz*) in his *On the names of Christ* (*De los nombres de Cristo*); Luis de León (1997: 404–6).

[11] A frequent image in later *Enneads*, see II 9 [33] 8, III 2 [47] 3, III 7 [45] 11, V 8 [31] 7, V 8 [31] 12.

Union with the divine becomes possible even in the realm of earthly transience. There are striking correspondences between Plotinus, Hebreo and San Juan, in both the imagery they share and the mystical theology it represents. All three emphasise the inadequacy of human language to speak of the transcendent divine. In Plotinus it is found in statements like: 'The One is in truth beyond all statement' (V 3 [49] 13, M: 380); 'The One, as transcending Intellect, transcends all knowing' (V 3 [49] 12, M: 379);[12] 'no words could ever be adequate or even applicable to that from which all else – the noble, the august – is derived' (VI 8 [39] 8, M: 520). Hebreo writes: 'we can only speak of God and incorporeal things in words which in some sense are incorporeal, since our tongue and speech are corporeal in themselves' (1937: 315).[13] This language of negation and paradox, associated with pseudo-Dionysian apophatic theology, is strongly marked in San Juan: 'what God communicates to the soul in this intimate union is utterly beyond expression and nothing can be said of it, just as nothing can be said of God which is anything like him' (CB26.4).[14]

Despite this, each habitually turns to the language of image and symbol in order to communicate something of the inexpressible. One such is the fountain. Plotinus writes of the Principle which is the cause of life:

> Imagine a spring that has no source outside itself; it gives itself to all the rivers, yet is never exhausted by what they take, but remains always integrally what it was; the tides that proceed from it are at one within it before they run their several ways, yet all, in some sense, know beforehand down what channels they will pour their streams.
>
> (III 8 [30] 10, M: 245)

One of the saint's best-loved poems, 'How [or For] well I know the fountain' (*Que bien sé yo la fonte*), imagines such a fountain by night. Its source is hidden yet is the origin of everything; it is beautiful, unfathomable, unfordable and clear; its current is omnipotent and the streams that proceed from it are equal to it (an echo of the Nicene Creed); and it calls out to creation to drink its waters and be satisfied. But it is also different: the poem's language, woven around symbols of night, water, light and bread is also Johannine, while at the end of the poem the fountain is identified with 'this bread of life', that is, with Christ, seen veiled in the Eucharistic bread.[15]

Other examples show the same pattern of similarity and difference. An image common to Hebreo and San Juan is that of lamps and the shadows they cast: 'many lights do not form one single light: you will see that if you walk by the light of two lanterns there will be two shadows and that the number of shadows will always

[12] This is echoed in the refrain of San Juan's *copla* 'I entered I knew not where' (*Entréme donde no supe*), 'transcending all knowledge' (John of the Cross 1982: 35–7).

[13] See also Hebreo (1937: 34; 1986: 123–4).

[14] I follow the second redaction of the *Spiritual Canticle* (*Cántico espiritual* = CB); see also *Living Flame of Love* (*Llama de amor viva* = L) 3.8, 4.10; *Dark Night of the Soul* (*Noche oscura del alma* = N) 2.17.5. N2.17 is an important chapter which explains why the soul cannot express anything but the vaguest approximation of what it knows; see Thompson (2002: 234–8).

[15] For a fuller analysis of this poem, see Thompson (2002: 70–80).

correspond to the number of lanterns' (Hebreo 1937: 211). But what is merely illustrative of the sun's light for Hebreo becomes part of a more theological interpretation of this imagery in San Juan's commentary on the third verse of his 'Llama' poem (L3.12). The 'lamps of fire' of the first line of the stanza are interpreted in the commentary as representing the attributes of God, and the 'shadows' they cast touch the soul and become, paradoxically, radiance: not the divine light itself, but as much of it as the soul can bear (L3.14). This exegesis turns on the 'overshadowings' (*obumbraciones*) cast by the lamps, a neologism San Juan has invented from the narrative of the Annunciation in Luke 1.35, when Mary is told that the Holy Spirit will overshadow her (Vulgate Latin *obumbrabit*; L3.12) in order to impregnate her with the divine Word. The imagery may be similar but for San Juan all the lamps and, by extension, their bright shadows, are but one lamp and represent the divine attributes flowing from the Godhead. Hebreo's image has become theologically charged.

There are elements in the writing of San Juan which, naturally enough, are alien to Plotinus and León Hebreo, notably the doctrine of the Incarnation, the theology of grace, and the teaching so specific to the saint, the dark night of the soul, in which God appears to withdraw from the soul and plunge it into spiritual anguish.[16] The language of darkness derives ultimately from the negative theology of Pseudo-Dionysius, where its primary purpose is to refer to the unknowability of God. San Juan, however, turns it into a symbol for the various stages on the soul's mystical journey, through what the soul in its sensual and spiritual parts does (the active night) and how God works within it (the passive night). His dark night is experiential rather than ontological, an immanent reality rather than a Dionysian symbol of transcendence.

The repeated emphasis in these writers on the gulf between Creator and creature suggests the impossibility of any kind of union between them, yet all three speak of unitive states. Plotinus can write that 'unable to state it, we may still possess it' (V 3 [49] 14, M: 381), and that 'the soul takes another life as it draws nearer and nearer to God and gains participation in Him' (VI 9 [9] 9, M: 546). Hebreo is more explicit. For him, it is by love that 'inferiors unite with superiors, the corporeal world with the spiritual, the corruptible with the eternal, and the whole Universe with its Creator, through the love it bears Him and its desire to unite with Him and be blessed in His divinity' (1937: 191). This unitive state is one: 'the intellect, transformed and united with the Divinity' (1937: 447). For San Juan, it is divine love which alone can bridge the ontological gulf between creature and Creator, so that he can boldly speak of the soul's 'possession of love' (N2.24.3); and of how 'the soul becomes deiform and God by participation' (CB39.4). As we look further

[16] As noted, for example, by Henry (Plotinus 1991: lxxx) and Louth (1981: 51, 144–5, 155–6). As Louth points out, for Plotinus the One is self-sufficient: it 'has no concern for the soul that seeks him; nor has the soul more than a passing concern for others engaged on the same quest' (51); and the soul is not united with the One, but with the *nous*, which emanates from the One.

into the nature of such possession and participation we shall find further instances of how San Juan takes Neoplatonic theology in a new direction.[17]

Beauty is a central theme of all three, as indeed of St Teresa of Ávila in her short poem 'Oh Beauty surpassing | all forms of beauty!' (*¡Oh, Hermosura que excedéis | a todas las hermosuras!*), which neatly encapsulates the distinction between the ultimate beauty of the Creator and the derived beauty of every creature (Teresa of Ávila 1967: 500).[18] San Juan's 'Cántico' poem refers to 'beauty' (*hermosura*) four times, in stanzas 5, 11, 33, 36, while in his commentary on the last of these, 'and let us go to see in your beauty', the word becomes a kind of mantra, repeated 25 times in a single paragraph, as the soul asks for the beauty of her beloved to become her beauty (CB 36.5). Plotinus is almost as obsessive in his repetitions:

> Its beauty, too, will be unique, a beauty above beauty: it cannot be beauty since it is not a thing among things. It is lovable and the author of beauty; as the power to all beautiful shape, it will be the ultimate of beauty, that which brings all loveliness to be; it begets beauty and makes it yet more beautiful by the excess of beauty streaming from itself, the source and height of beauty.
>
> (VI 7 [38] 32, M: 501)

He follows this with four further uses of the noun in the next sentence. Hebreo writes in similar terms:

> Those who participate the most in the intellectual beauty of the supremely beautiful have a greater knowledge of how much of the beauty of their Creator is lacking in even the most perfect of His creatures. And their love and desire is accordingly strengthened that they may enjoy to all eternity the highest degree of participation and union possible to them; and in this their ultimate happiness consists.
>
> (1937: 312)

He makes a strong distinction between original and derived beauty: 'the beauty of the Creator cannot in any way be proportionate to that of any created thing, and those perfections which are found in His creatures are not comparable to His beauty, wisdom and every other perfection' (1937: 314); and again, 'the lack of beauty of every creature relative to that of the Creator is infinite' (1986: 317). The same language is found in San Juan (1982), at the beginning of his commentary on the 'Noche oscura' poem, the *Ascent of Mount Carmel* (*Subida del monte Carmelo* = S), where he writes in severely antithetical terms of creaturely beauty and wisdom as absolute ugliness and ignorance compared with the divine: 'all the attachments [the soul] has to the creatures are pure darkness before God' (S1.4.1), and that 'all the being of the creatures, compared with the infinite [being] of God, is nothing' (S.1.4.4).

[17] Louth sees Pseudo-Dionysius as inheriting the Iamblichian rather than the Plotinian version of Neoplatonism (1981: 161–4). Likewise, he contrasts Origen's 'mysticism of light' with the 'mysticism of darkness' associated with Gregory of Nyssa (1981: 179–89).

[18] San Juan's *glosa* 'I shall never lose myself | for any beauty' (*Por toda la hermosura | nunca yo me perderé*) clearly refers to created beauty, as he searches for 'an I know not what | which is gained by good fortune' (John of the Cross 1982: 38–9; compare the last line of stanza 7 of the 'Cántico').

On the other hand, in both authors the whole creation depends absolutely for its existence on divine love: 'Without love not only can there be no felicity; but the world would not exist nor would anything be found therein, if there were no love' (Hebreo 1937: 190); '[God] continually supports them throughout their existence, for if He were to abandon them for one instant they would all be changed to naught' (1937: 252). San Juan makes the same point: 'And this kind of union is ever made between God and all the creatures, in which he is keeping them in the being they have; so that if he were to fail them [in this way] they would at once be annihilated and cease existing' (S2.5.3). If the creatures depend absolutely on the Creator's love for their existence, they are to be counted as 'nothing' (*nada*) in terms of the soul's affections, not because they are evil in themselves (they are not) but because the soul's attachment to the creaturely can never truly fulfil its desires: it will be united with 'nothing'.

This is not, however, San Juan's last word on the created order: far from it. His vision of creation as God sees it, rather than seeing God through the creatures (L4.4–5) finds a parallel in Plotinus:

> For all There is heaven; earth is heaven, and sea heaven; and animal and plant and man; all is the heavenly content of that heaven: and the gods in it, despising neither men nor anything else that is there where all is of the heavenly order, traverse all that country and all space in peace.
>
> (V 8 [31] 3, M: 414)

> The sky There must be living and therefore not bare of stars … Earth too will be There, and not void but even more intensely living and containing all that lives and moves upon our earth and the plants obviously rooted in life; sea will be There and all waters with the movement of their unending life and all the living things of water; air too must be a member of that universe with the living things of air as here.
>
> (VI 7 [38] 12, M: 481)

Hebreo writes of knowledge of God through the creatures as one of effect, not cause: 'Our human intellect perceives the incorporeal in the corporeal, and though it knows the first cause to be measureless and infinite, this knowledge is derived from the effect of this cause, which is the corporeal universe: thus the Master is known by His works, and not by direct perception of Himself' (1937: 323). San Juan's vision is remarkably consistent with this, as he explains the meaning of 'you recall' (*recuerdas*) in line 20 of the 'Llama' poem:

> This remembrance is a movement made by the Word in the substance of the soul, of such grandeur, majesty and glory, and so intimate and gentle, that it seems to the soul that all the balsams and fragrant spices and flowers of the world are moving and mingling together as they turn and give off their sweet fragrance; that all the kingdoms and realms of the world and all the principalities and powers of the heavens are moving; and not only this, but all the virtues and substances and perfections and graces of every created thing are shining as together they move, each to the other and in each other.
>
> (L4.4; 1982: 859)

He also follows Hebreo's distinction between knowing God through the creatures and knowing the creatures through God. In his version, though, 'knowing the effects through their cause and not the cause through its effects' (L4.5), he makes the bolder claim that the soul in union with God sees creation no longer as a distant glimpse of the divine presence in its manifold beauties but as God himself sees it.

These, then, are some of the parallels and differences in the shape of the soul's journey to union in Plotinus, Hebreo and San Juan. But the saint's teaching on union with the divine has one important emphasis absent from them. Plotinus, or Augustine after him, conceive of union with the *nous* or God as an ascent away from the earthly which is at the same time a journey within, towards light, knowledge and beauty in their everlasting state, and the philosophical poetry of Luis de León follows this tradition. But a more affective form of spirituality developed in the Western mystical tradition in the Middle Ages, associated above all with St Bernard of Clairvaux (1090–1153) and evident in his 86 sermons on the Song of Songs, and it strongly marks San Juan's account.[19]

Hebreo has much to say about the love creation feels towards its Creator. But San Juan's insistence on the unitive work of love through the dark nights of sense and spirit leads him to an understanding which at first sight appears to contradict everything he and his predecessors have said about the vast gulf fixed between Creator and creature. If there is an infinite ontological gulf between them, love alone is capable of bridging it and bringing about union, because its property is to create 'likeness between what loves and what is loved' (S1.4.3). He grounds the unitive life in what he terms 'equality of love' (*igualdad de amor*) between the two extremes, a teaching elaborated in his exposition of these mysterious lines from stanza 37 of his 'Cántico' (1989: 257):

> There you would show me
> what my soul was claiming.

This 'claim', he explains, is to equality of loving in the unitive state. How is it possible for the creature to claim any kind of equality with the Creator? The reason such a bold assertion can be made is that in this transformed unitive state the soul's faculties, emptied of all creaturely affections, are now occupied solely by the gifts which God has given them, so that the whole content of the soul's thinking, willing and loving is what God thinks, wills and loves. The argument is dense:

> and so the soul will love God as she is loved by him, since her understanding will then be the understanding of God, her will the will of God, and her love the love of God. Because although the soul's will is not lost here, she is so firmly united with the stronghold of the will of God by which she is loved by him, that she loves him as strongly and perfectly as he loves her, for both wills are united in one will and love, which is God's; and so the soul loves God with the will and the strength of God

[19] See Louth (1981: 183); Thompson (2002: 139).

> himself, united with the same strength of love as the love by which he loves her ... She loves in some manner through *the Holy Spirit which has been given her* (Rom. 5.5) in this transformed state.
>
> (C38.3; 1982: 719–20)

There is, moreover, a significant linguistic difference between Hebreo and San Juan in the terminology used for the divine and human lovers. Hebreo writes that 'the lover is transformed and converted into the beloved' (1937: 259). He also speaks of an equal love between two lovers, but only between two human souls, not the soul and God: 'My affection and love, has transformed me into you, begetting in me a desire that you may be fused with me, in order that I, your lover, may form but a single person with you, my beloved, and equal love may make of our two souls one' (1937: 57).

San Juan's version of the transformation of the lovers in (or into) each other in the fifth verse of his 'Noche oscura' poem does seem remarkably similar, until attention is paid to the terms he uses for the lovers (1989: 262, ):

> Oh night, you that united
> beloved with lover,
> lover transformed in the beloved!

For Hebreo, the soul is the active seeker, hence the 'loving one', the noun formed from the present participle (*amante*). God is 'the one beloved', from the past participle (*amado*). San Juan departs from this tradition by using past participles for both: a male and a female beloved (*amado*, *amada*), their linguistic identity acting as a marker of the equality of loving between them, in that the soul is returning to God the very love which he has already given her – divine love, unmixed by any creaturely affection at all.

When the creature becomes aware of the supreme wisdom and beauty of the Creator and of its own distance from union with them, Hebreo writes:

> it loves and desires to enjoy Him in perfect union, as the lover seeks to be wholly transformed into the most beautiful beloved. By means of this love and desire for God it attains to that ultimate and perfect union which is the final and most perfect activity; and in this consists not only the beatitude of the intellect, transformed and united with the Divinity, but also the ultimate perfection and happiness of the whole created universe ... And through the intellect alone the whole is made worthy of union with its high beginning, and of achieving perfection and lasting happiness in enjoyment of this union with the Divinity.
>
> (1937: 447)

San Juan shares this language of transformation and participation but his consistent parity of terminology for the lovers embodies the equality between them. Creator and creature, though distinct as such, are united by the love which binds together the Persons of the Trinity, and which has been poured into the lover entirely transparent to the divine will. The Plotinian pattern of emanation from the One and return to the One, which Hebreo hints at, is reinterpreted as the love which flows from the Trinity into the soul made in its image and returns to its source. This specifically Christian vision is also seen in the soteriological focus of his popular retelling of the Prologue to St John's Gospel (*Romances sobre el Evangelio 'In principio erat Verbum'*), in lines such as 'that God would be man | and man would be God' (ballad 4) and 'and God, there in the manger | was weeping and groaning' (ballad 8). Remembering the altruism of Achilles, Philón asserts that 'the beloved is under no obligation to the lover, nor is he constrained by love to die for him' (Hebreo 1937: 273). In San Juan's christological world that cannot be. The Father has sent the Son to redeem the world by his incarnation and his sacrificial death, as his 'Little Shepherd-Boy' poem (*Un pastorcico solo está penando*) makes clear. The shepherd-lad in love with his shepherdess willingly suffers and dies for her out of love (1989: 281):

> And after a long time he climbed
> a tree, where he opened wide his fair arms,
> and died clinging to it with them,
> his breast sorely wounded by love.

Such sentiments are unthinkable in a properly Neoplatonic discourse. Humans may make the ascent to union with the divine, but the unmoved Mover does not willingly take flesh, suffer and die for the sake of the creature. San Juan may speak the same language but his theology is unambiguously Christian.

My final example comes from another Spanish mystic, St Teresa of Ávila (1515–82), and represents the complex and layered way in which Neoplatonic ideas crossed centuries and cultures. Her most mature treatise on prayer, *The Mansions of the Interior Castle* (*Moradas del castillo interior* = M; 1577), begins with a vivid picture of the soul as a diamond or crystal castle formed of concentric rooms, with the light of God radiating through them from the centre. Much scholarly ink has been spilled in an attempt to locate a source for this architectural and spiritual wonder: suggestions have ranged from biblical, medieval, and Renaissance iconography to Islamic texts, which do indeed provide close parallels, though it is hard to imagine that Teresa can have known them.[20] But there may be a common tradition behind them all, which could have reached Teresa in a number of ways, most probably through oral transmission in spiritual conversations or sermons.[21] Two passages from the *Enneads* suggest that this may be so; neither provides an exact parallel but each comes close:

> There is, we may put it, something that is centre; about it, a circle of light shed from it; round centre and first circle alike, another circle, light from light; outside that again, not another circle of light but one which, lacking light of its own, must borrow.
>
> (IV 3 [27] 17, M: 270)

> Or imagine a small luminous mass serving as centre to a transparent sphere, so that the light from within shows upon the entire surface, otherwise unlit: we surely agree that the inner core of light, intact and immobile, reaches the whole field ... We can no longer

[20] See Chorpenning (1991: 138–47) and López-Baralt (1985: 73–97).
[21] López-Baralt herself suggests this (1985: 95).

> speak of the light in any particular spot; it is equally diffused within and throughout the entire sphere.
>
> (VI 4 [22] 7, M: 446)

Teresa imagines the soul as 'a castle made wholly of diamond or very clear crystal, in which there are many rooms', 'and in the centre and middle of all these dwelling-places is the principal room, where things of great secrecy pass between the soul and God' (M1.1.3). Moreover, 'the fount and that radiant sun which is in the centre of the soul does not lose its radiance, because it is always within her and nothing can take away its beauty' (M1.2.3). Unlike Plotinus, she warns that 'almost none of the light which comes from the palace where the king has his abode reaches these first mansions' (M1.1.14). But the fundamental image of an unchanging light at the centre radiating outwards through a transparent sphere is common to both.

Crystal castles feature in chivalric romance, a genre to which the young Teresa was, by her own confession, addicted (*Vida* 2.1).[22] Virtually the first thing Don Quixote sees in his adventure in the Cave of Montesinos is 'a magnificent royal palace or fortress whose walls seemed made of clear and transparent crystal' (Cervantes 1998: II. 23). Teresa cannot have read Plotinus, and Cervantes is writing more than three decades after her death, but such structures were staples of the fantasy literature of her age. Though she could not read Latin, her vision is also inspired by biblical passages she would certainly have known – the 'many mansions' of John 14.2, which provide the title of her work, and St John the Divine's vision of the heavenly city in Revelation with 'the glory of God and a radiance like a very rare jewel, like jasper, clear as crystal' (Rev.21.11, Vulgate *et lumen eius simile lapidi pretioso tanquam lapidi iaspidis, sicut crystallum*).[23] The Plotinian transparent sphere has morphed into a crystal castle with biblical motifs attached, and Teresa's account is based on the indwelling of the Trinity in the soul, differently from Plotinus's account.[24] This process of accretion seems to me characteristic of the way in which earlier Neoplatonic writing may lie behind both Christian and Islamic elaborations of the image.

4. Conclusion

I have not attempted to trace, even were it possible, the precise means by which the writers I have examined acquired Neoplatonic ideas. The more learned would have been able to consult the works of Plato and Plotinus in Latin translation and those of Ficino and León Hebreo in Italian; they would also have had access to the works

[22] There is, for example, a crystal castle in the Middle English metrical romance *Sir Orfeo* (see Whitaker 2016: 393) and a palace of clearest crystal in chapter 30 of the pseudo-historical 15th-century *Sarracen Chronicle* (*Crónica sarracina*; Viña Liste 2000: 569).

[23] The English text follows the New Revised Standard Version.

[24] For an account of the Augustinian origins of this concept, see Louth (1981: 146–8).

of other significant intermediaries of the tradition, such as Augustine, Boethius, Castiglione and Bembo. Others, whose reading was limited to the vernacular, may have encountered them mediated through secondary sources and oral traditions. I cannot say, for example, that Fray Luis de León had read and assimilated the *Enneads* and that is why his poetry is so full of echoes of that work; even less so that St John of the Cross knew Hebreo's *Dialogues*: the history of transmission, even if it could be charted in every detail, is too complex. I have concentrated instead on the remarkable continuity found between the writings of Plotinus and León Hebreo, representing the Neoplatonism of the ancient world and its Renaissance revival in the Florentine Academy, and those of a range of Spanish Golden Age authors, and also on identifying some of the ways in which this long tradition evolved to reflect changed perspectives. Sometimes writers borrow its elevated language to speak of the hopes and fears of human lovers; sometimes they follow its ascent beyond the visible world into the realm of the eternal; and sometimes its voice is clearly heard in the mystical search for union with the divine. One way or another, what cannot be doubted is its persistent and pervasive presence.

References

Byrne, S. (2015), *Ficino in Spain* (Toronto/Buffalo/London, University of Toronto Press).

Castiglione, B. (1766), *Il Cortegiano del conte Baldessare Castiglione* (Padua, n.p.), Bodleian Digitized Books Project, accessed 1 August 2017, http://dbooks.bodleian.ox.ac.uk/books/PDFs/590209360.pdf

Castiglione, B. (1967), *Castiglione: The Book of the Courtier*, trans. G. Bull (Harmondsworth, Penguin).

Cervantes, M. de (1998), *Miguel de Cervantes. Don Quijote de la Mancha*, ed. F. Rico, introduction F. Lázaro Carreter, 2 vols (Barcelona, Crítica).

Chorpenning, J.F. (1991), 'The Pleasance, Paradise, and Heaven: Renaissance Cosmology and Imagery in the *Castillo interior*', *Forum for Modern Language Studies*, 27: 138–47.

Dent-Young, J. (2009), *Selected Poems of Garcilaso de la Vega* (Chicago/London, University of Chicago Press).

Hebreo, L. (1937), *The Philosophy of Love (Dialoghi d'Amore)*, trans. F. Friedeberg-Seeley & J.H. Barnes (London, The Soncino Press).

Hebreo, L. (1986), *León Hebreo. Diálogos de amor*, trans. C. Mazo del Castillo, ed. J.M. Reyes Cano (Barcelona, Promociones Publicaciones Universitarias).

John of the Cross, St (1982), *San Juan de la Cruz. Obras completas*, 11th edn (Madrid, Biblioteca de Autores Cristianos).

John of the Cross, St (1989 edn), *San Juan de la Cruz. Poesía*, ed. D.Ynduráin, 5th edn (Madrid, Cátedra).

Jones, R.O. (1963), 'Neoplatonism and the *Soledades*', *Bulletin of Hispanic Studies*, 40: 1–16.

López-Baralt, L. (1985), *Huellas del Islam en la literatura española de Juan Ruiz a Juan Goytisolo* (Madrid, Hiperión).

Louth, A. (1981), *The Origins of the Christian Mystical Tradition from Plato to Denys* (Oxford, Clarendon).

Luis de León, Fray (1986), *Fray Luis de León. Poesía*, ed. J.F. Alcina (Madrid, Cátedra).
Luis de León, Fray (1997), *Fray Luis de León. De los nombres de Cristo*, ed. C. Cuevas (Madrid, Cátedra).
Parker, A.A. (1985), *The Philosophy of Love in Spanish Literature 1480–1680*, ed. T. O'Reilly (Edinburgh, Edinburgh University Press).
Plato (1973), *Plato. Phaedrus & Letters VII and VIII*, trans. W. Hamilton (Harmondsworth, Penguin).
Plotinus (1991), *Plotinus: The Enneads*, trans. S. MacKenna, introduction J. Dillon (Harmondsworth, Penguin).
Quevedo, F. de (2006), *Francisco de Quevedo. Poesía original completa*, ed. J.M. Blecua (Barcelona, Planeta).
Rutherford, J. (2016), *The Spanish Golden Age Sonnet* (Cardiff, University of Wales Press).
Teresa of Ávila, St (1967), *Obras completas de Santa Teresa*, ed. E. de la Madre de Dios & O.Steggink, 2nd edn (Madrid, Biblioteca de Autores Cristianos).
Thompson, C.P. (2002), *St John of the Cross: Songs in the Night* (London, SPCK).
Turner, D. (1995), *The Darkness of God: Negativity in Christian Mysticism* (Cambridge, Cambridge University Press).
Viña Liste, J.M. (ed.) (2000), *Textos medievales de caballerías* (Madrid, Cátedra).
Whitaker, M.A. (2016), 'Otherworld Castles in Middle English Arthurian Romance', in R. Liddiard (ed.), *Late Medieval Castles* (Woodbridge, Boydell and Brewer), 393–408.

14

The Christian Neoplatonism of Francisco de Aldana in the *Carta para Arias Montano*

TERENCE O'REILLY

THE WRITERS IN 16th-century Castile whose works show the influence of Neoplatonism include the Carmelite mystics, Teresa of Ávila (1515–82) and John of the Cross (1542–91). Both wrote extensively about the encounter with God in contemplation, an experience they termed *teología mística* (mystical theology).[1] The phrase had a long pedigree, stretching back to the *Mystical Theology* of Denys the Pseudo-Areopagite (*c.* 500), who combined a Christian theology with the late Neoplatonism of Iamblichus (*c.* 245–325) and Proclus (412–85).[2] The approach to prayer associated with Denys was made known in Spain partly by translations of medieval works on which it had left its mark. The meditation manual of García de Cisneros, for instance, the first of its kind to be printed in Spain (Montserrat, 1500), contained an extensive *florilegium* on contemplation drawn from late medieval works, including the influential *Theologia mystica* of Hugh of Balma (late 13th century) which expounded and developed Denys's thought (Baraut 1967). A vernacular version of Balma's treatise was printed subsequently in Toledo.[3] The Dionysian tradition was made known as well by original works in Spanish, among them a number of books by Franciscan authors on *recogimiento* (recollection), a meditation practice designed to prepare the soul for contemplation (Andrés Martín 1975). One of the most popular

[1] St Teresa uses the term on four occasions in her *Libro de la vida* (in chapters 10.1, 11.5, 12.5 and 18.2): see Álvarez (2006: 429–46). St John uses it once in the *Subida del Monte Carmelo* (Book 2, chapter 8.6), four times in the *Noche oscura* (Book 2, chapters 5.1, 12.5, 17.26, 20.6), thrice in Version B of the *Cántico espiritual* (Prólogo.3; chapters 27.5 and 39.2), and once in Version B of the *Llama de amor viva* (chapter 3.49): see Pacho (2009: 1114–25).

[2] On the writings of Denys and their reception in the Christian mystical tradition, see Knowles (1975), Pelikan (1987), Turner (1995) and Rorem (1996).

[3] The translation, entitled *Sol de contemplativos*, was printed in Toledo in 1514 by Juan Varela de Salamanca. There is a modern edition (Martín 1992). On Balma's treatise and its influence on subsequent writers, see Ruello & Barbet (1995).

Proceedings of the British Academy, **240**, 323–335, © The British Academy 2022.

of such books was the *Tercer abecedario espiritual* (Third Spiritual Alphabet) of Francisco de Osuna (1492–1541) which St Teresa read at a formative stage (a point to which I shall return).[4] These writings, disseminated by the printing press, fed an interest in contemplation that flourished not only among clergy and the religious, but among laypeople too. A case in point is the poet Francisco de Aldana (1537–78), who was a soldier. In September 1577, writing from Madrid, he sent a friend, the humanist Benito Arias Montano (1527–98), a magnificent verse-epistle entitled *Sobre la contemplación de Dios y los requisitos della* (On contemplation of God and its requirements) (Aldana 1985: 437–58). The date is significant: in November of that year, in the convent of San José in Ávila, Teresa finished writing *Las moradas del castillo interior* (The Mansions of the Interior Castle) (Álvarez 2006: 133), while a few months later, in the early part of 1578, John of the Cross composed in Toledo the first 31 stanzas of his *Cántico espiritual* (Spiritual Canticle) (Pacho 2009: 195). Aldana, it seems, knew neither Carmelite. The subject of contemplation was in the air.

Like Teresa and John, Aldana was familiar with the Neoplatonic themes and images that the Western mystical tradition had absorbed during the Middle Ages, but he drew inspiration as well from another source: in Florence, where he was raised,[5] he came to know the writings of the Florentine Academy, including those of its founder, Marsilio Ficino (1433–99), whose understanding of contemplation was shaped by Denys and the broader Neoplatonist tradition.[6] Aldana's close reading of Ficino is apparent in three features of the poem. First, in its description of the journey from meditation to the beginnings of contemplation, and from there to transforming union with God. Second, in the links it establishes between human friendship and divine love. And third, in the nature of its metaphors. The pages that follow explore each of these features in turn.

1. Contemplation

Aldana's poem begins with a cry of anguish. Looking back on his life at the age of 40, he finds in it two sources of pain. One is his experience of war; the other, not named, appears to be his experience of sexual love. These have induced in him a sense of disorder that is unbearable. But now at last he is breaking free. He is

[4] The *Tercer abecedario espiritual* was printed in Salamanca in 1527 by Remón de Petras. There is a recent modern edition (López Santidrián 2005).

[5] Aldana spent the first two decades of his life in Florence, where his family had close links with the Medici court: see Lara Garrido (Aldana 1985: 21–3), who comments (22): 'Etapa crucial, pero indocumentada, la de estos años toscanos … de la que sólo entrevemos una formación intelectual corta, pero intensa.' Aldana's friendship in Florence with the Neoplatonist Benedetto Varchi (1503–65) is noted in Ruiz Silva (1981: 12).

[6] See Kristeller (1964: *passim*), Marcel (1958: 602–78), and the introductions to Allen & Hankins (2001) and Allen (2015). On the influence on Aldana's poem of Denys and the medieval mystical tradition, see Lefebvre (1953: 127–52).

moving inwards, towards his true self, and at the same time outwards, towards the freedom and joy of the divine (Aldana 1985: 439, ll. 43–8,):

> But now (thank Heaven!) I am breaking free,
> now I am cutting loose from the tether
> in which obsequious hope had me twice bound:
> I am resolved to quit the common path
> followed by the crowd, and to travel straight
> towards the homeland that is truly mine.[7]

Aldana's approach to contemplation, which then unfolds, differs in some respects from the descriptions of it that we find in devotional works of his time. There is no mention, for instance, of the three Ways through which the soul passes: purgative, illuminative and unitive. Instead he proposes for meditation two topics dear to the Neoplatonist tradition: the beauty of God and his goodness, reflected in the natural world. He pictures these attributes of the divine as inspiring in the soul a flight upwards, from the world of the senses to the realm of the spirit. There it encounters God and is transformed. In the meditation on divine beauty, the process by which the soul comes to love God is compared, in a vivid image, to the making of scent (Aldana 1985: 440–1, ll. 70–81,):

> and just as through a still a fire draws out
> fragrant dew from the centre of a rose
> whose body has been placed within its heat,
> so will she distil, readied by love's fire,
> a beauty varied and intangible
> from the world's expansive countenance;
> and from there she will soar to such a height
> that finding she is lifted now so high
> she will lose awareness of her nature,
> and come to see that its capacity
> has there expanded almost to the point
> of transformation into her first Cause.

The journey heavenwards, as Aldana recounts it, draws the soul through the five hypostases that Ficino, following Proclus (Allen 2006: 13–14), defined in his *Theologia Platonica*: 'let us … assemble things on five levels, placing God and angel at the summit of nature, body and Quality at the foot, but soul halfway between those on high and those below'.[8] Aldana alludes to this hierarchy in the meditation on divine goodness, when he observes that the power to bring things into existence belongs to God, and is denied to the other levels of being (Aldana 1985: 445, ll. 160–8,):

> and be aware that God's generous hand
> fashioned things so numerous and varied,

[7] The translations of the poem cited in this chapter are my own.

[8] 'in quinque gradus … omnia colligamus, deum et angelum in arce naturae ponentes, corpus et qualitatem in infimo; animam vero inter illa summa et haec infima mediam' (Allen & Hankins 2001–6, I: 230–3).

including the most sordid and the least,
without granting Principal Qualities,
the heavens in their luminous beauty,
or angelic choirs in the Empyrean,
a power sufficient for them to make
the least and most repugnant of creatures
that mud conceals; such exploits none can do.

To make the point that the soul resides half-way between matter and spirit, Ficino uses the image of a horizon: 'The rational Soul ... is placed on the horizon, that is, on the borderline between eternity and time, since it possesses a middle nature between eternal and temporal things'.[9] Aldana affirms, similarly, that the soul will realise in the course of her journey that she lies between the worlds of matter and spirit like a horizon (Aldana 1985: 445, ll. 151–6,):

she will see herself as a line produced
from the eternal centre, and lowered
in a mortal self to rule human life
from within the prison of the body,
set there as the horizon of two worlds,
this changing one and one unblemished, pure.

A further way in which Aldana's poem differs from most contemporary treatments of contemplation is the absence within it of references to Christ and the Trinity. Such references abound in devotional writings of the time. An example is the popular book on prayer and meditation (*Tratado de la oración y meditación*) composed by Pedro de Alcántara, a relative of Aldana (Rivers 1966: xii), which was printed in Lisbon at some point between 1556 and 1558 (Sanz Valdivieso 1996: 210–11). The topics it proposes for meditation focus on the saving death of Jesus, and his identity as both God and man. We know from his other poems that Aldana was an orthodox Catholic, with a devotion to the Passion of Christ, the incarnate Word (Rivers 1966: xxxvii–xxxviii), but there is no direct reference to Jesus here. It may be that there is an indirect reference to him at one point, when the poet notes that the enfleshed soul cannot go to God unaided (Aldana 1985: 443, ll. 109–17,):

It is indeed true that the happy flight
to a peak so sublime is often checked
by the terrestial weight of the body,
but Jacob's ladder none the less comes down
to the lowly earth, and so we may climb
to the castle fortress of high heaven,
for as we rise we will no doubt receive
the help of more than one caring angel
to ensure our journey is delightful.

[9] 'Anima rationalis ... in orizonte, id est, in confinio aeternitatis et temporis posita est, quoniam inter aeterna et temporalia naturam mediam possidet' (Ficino 1962: 657–8). The middle position of the soul in Ficino's view of the cosmos is discussed in Lauster (2002: 48–9, 51) and Allen (2006: 112).

The image of Jacob's ladder, uniting heaven and earth (Genesis 28:12), calls to mind the passage in St John's Gospel where Christ applies the figure to himself: 'You will see heaven open and the angels of God ascending and descending upon the Son of Man' (John 1:51). Arias Montano, a renowned biblical scholar, would have been aware of the connection, which was standard in biblical exegesis of the time.[10] But the New Testament resonance, if intended, is left for the reader to infer. The absence of an explicit Christology is a feature also of Ficino's writings. In the words of Jörg Lauster: 'Ficino conspicuously neglects certain basic elements of the Christian doctrine of Christ. The Cross of Christ, the Atonement of human sin and the Resurrection have no important roles in his thought' (2002: 58; cf. 68–9). In this respect, it could be said, Ficino reflects a tendency apparent earlier in the tensions between Classical philosophy and Christian theology in Late Antiquity (Drobner 2008).[11]

The point is crucial for the reception of Neoplatonism in Counter-Reformation Spain, as the example of Teresa of Ávila makes clear. When she read the *Tercer abecedario espiritual* of Osuna as a young nun, she was uncertain how to proceed in prayer. The book taught her that to prepare for the gift of contemplation one should empty the mind of images of Christ in his humanity. For 20 years she struggled, often against her inclinations, to obey, before concluding that Osuna was mistaken (O'Reilly 2018: 112–13). The issue, as she saw it, was not a matter of technique, but of principle: faith in Christ's role as the one mediator between God and humankind (1 Timothy 2:5). In the account of her life she wrote:

> I can see clearly, and since that time have always seen, that it is God's will, if we are to please Him and He is to grant us great favours, that this should be done through His most sacred Humanity, in whom, His Majesty said, He is well pleased (Matthew 3:17). Very, very many times have I learned this by experience. The Lord has told it me. I have seen clearly that it is by this door that we must enter (John 10:9) if we wish His Sovereign Majesty to show us great secrets.[12]

Teresa's break with this aspect of the Neoplatonist tradition had a decisive influence on devotional writing in Spain. Osuna's book was a bestseller in the early 1500s (we know of seven editions between 1527 and 1555), but though it was not included by the Inquisition in the Indices of Prohibited Books, it faded into the background later: no further edition in the 16th century is recorded (Wilkinson 2010: 360–1). Meanwhile, Teresa's account of her life, first printed in 1588, went

[10] See, for instance, the commentaries on John 1:51 by Juan Maldonado (1533–83) and Cornelius a Lapide (1567–1637): Maldonado (1874: 2, 451–2), Lapide (1868–76: 16, 324–5).

[11] On Ficino, see also Suzanne Stern-Gillet's chapter in this volume.

[12] *Libro de la vida* 22:6, in Mediavilla (2014: 160): 'Y veo yo claro, y he visto después, que, para contentar a Dios y que nos haga grandes mercedes, quiere sea por manos de esta Humanidad sacratísima, en quien dijo Su Majestad se deleita. Muy, muy muchas veces lo he visto por esperiencia. Hámelo dicho el Señor. He visto claro que por esta puerta hemos de entrar si queremos nos muestre la soberana Majestad grandes secretos.' For further discussion of this issue, see Álvarez (1980), O'Donoghue (1989: 27–41) and Castro (2009: 300–8).

through seven more editions (two of them in French and one in Latin) before her beatification in 1614 (Diego Sánchez 2008: 82–3, 91–2). Her canonisation eight years later in Rome (1622) established her teachings as authoritative. After the Council of Trent, Ficino continued to be read in Catholic Europe generally, but he was rarely cited as an authority in matters theological.[13] An example is the *Traité de l'amour de Dieu* (Treatise on the Love of God) by St François de Sales (1567–1622), which was published in Lyon in 1616. It shows a keen engagement with the writings of Teresa, whom the author praises (O'Reilly 2015). His debt to the writings of Ficino is apparent too, as recent research has shown, above all in the themes of God's beauty and goodness and in the imagery of God as light (Mellinghoff-Bourgerie 2014). Ficino himself, however, is not mentioned by name. Aldana's description of the soul's journey to God marks a moment in the reception in Spain of Ficino's understanding of contemplation. It was a moment that passed when the Dionysian tradition was integrated in a different way into the culture of the Counter-Reformation Church.

2. Friendship

Aldana's poem, written in the form of a letter to Arias Montano, is suffused with the esteem and affection that unites them. Towards the end, their closeness is referred to explicitly when the poet describes Montano as 'the best part of myself' (l. 338: 'eres de mí lo que más vale'), and writes of them forming together a whole (ll. 446–7), but it is apparent also from the start, and in each of the three sections into which the poem falls.[14] The opening lines, for instance, evoke Montano's first cognomen, Arias, by alluding to the constellation of Aries that the sun enters at the beginning of the year (Aldana 1985: 437, ll. 1–6,):

> Montano, whose name is the first starred sign
> through which the sun proceeds as it revolves
> around the oblique circle of its sphere,
> named thus by will divine to indicate
> that in you Apollo begins to shine
> the light of his heavenly instruction.

Here, following Ficino and the Neoplatonic conventions on which he drew, the sun is a figure of God, and Montano the privileged recipient of his teachings. Later, a second image comes to the fore, that of a mountain, reflecting the friend's second cognomen (Aldana 1985: 453, ll. 319–21,):

[13] The reception of Ficino in Spain is traced in Byrne (2015). On Ficino and Catholic orthodoxy, see Allen (2008). Cf. Lauster: 'Looking for Ficino in theological manuals is generally a fruitless task. This may simply illustrate the fact that the early Renaissance does not play a great role in the historical self-understanding of Catholic and Protestant theology' (2002: 47).

[14] On the structure of the poem, see Lefebvre (1953: 93, 101–2), Archer (1988), Grande Quejigo (2006) and O'Reilly (2008).

> You, Montano, resemble the great peak
> of this huge mountain, for living with you
> spells the death of all heaviness of heart.

Now the moral qualities of Montano are emphasised, as before his learning: his virtues give life to Aldana's soul. Finally, the poem ends with a description of the contemplative retreat that Aldana imagines them occupying together: a verdant landscape, under a blue sky and beside the sea, where they will be united in heart and in mind.

The love of friends is a central theme also in the writings of Ficino, especially his letters. His understanding of it is based, as Paul Kristeller showed, on a classical tradition established by Plato and Aristotle and summarised memorably by Cicero, but to this antique wisdom Ficino added a further dimension: a connection between friendship and the love of God (Kristeller 1964: 278–87). In a letter to Giovanni Cavalcanti he affirmed:

> Since friendship strives by mutual consent of the lovers to cultivate the soul by virtue, it is apparently nothing but a perfect concordance of two Souls in the worship of God. Those who worship God with a pious mind, however, are loved by God. Therefore, there are not two friends only, but always necessarily three, two human beings and one God ... He unites us into one; He is the insoluble bond and perpetual guardian of friendship.
>
> (Kristeller 1964: 279)[15]

In his poem for Montano, Aldana develops the contemplative dimension of friendship to which Ficino points. When, in the first part, he describes the journey of the soul to God, he is not telling his friend things he does not know: on the contrary, because Montano indwells Aldana, his learned understanding of contemplation is at the poet's disposal.[16] Their shared knowledge includes familiarity with the Bible, to which there are regular allusions, not only in the first part but throughout the text.[17] Similarly, in the second part, it is from the virtues of Montano that Aldana draws what he needs to overcome the moral weakness impeding his own ascent to God. In the last part, the two friends are pictured walking by the shore of the sea, and delighting in the play of sunlight on thousands of seashells gathered there (Aldana 1985: 445–6, ll. 373–90,):

> We will go down that way from time to time,
> talking of great marvels we have pondered,

[15] Ficino (1962: 634): 'Amicitia igitur cum duorum consensu ad animum virtute colendum nitatur, nihil utique aliud videtur esse, quam duorum animorum summa in Deo colendo concordia. Amantur autem a Deo quicumque Deum pia mente colunt. Ideo non duo quidem soli, sed tres necessario amici sunt semper, duo videlicet homines unusque Deus ... Hic nos in unum conciliat, hic indissolubilis est amicitiae nodus.'

[16] Parallels between Aldana's poem and the writings of Montano are discussed in Gómez Canseco (2007: 152–63).

[17] The biblical allusions are annotated in the translation of the poem which appears in the Anthology *Lyrics of Ascent* that accompanies the present volume.

united in reciprocated love;
you will see waves on the shores of the sea
polish and shine in foam as they retreat
a thousand white shells lying in the sand,
which when the sun strikes them with serene light
send back, as it were, new suns of their own
that stop in its course the ray of vision.
You will see a thousand spiralled conches,
a thousand fluted molluscs, with the marks
and the tints of radiant sunsets and dawns:
among them some the colour of coral,
others the colour of light that the sun
captures in the hues of painted rainbows,
varied in their activity, diverse
in design, discharging what look like sparks
in a rich mix of turquoise and gold.

The detailed description of the scene is itself a token of friendship, for Montano was a collector of seashells and a keen student of their intricacies (Lara Ródenas 1998: 357–66), but read with the preceding sections in mind, it has a religious meaning too. The identification of the divine with light, established at the start, indicates that by the sea the friends will be allowed a glimpse of the beauty of God in Nature. Here we have an echo of the *Theologia Platonica* of Ficino, where the beauty of individual things is described as a hook that secretly lifts up the beholder 'in order to become God', a transformation that fulfils the soul: 'Happy indeed are those whom the universe's beauty, that is, the lustre of the good itself, transforms by love into the good itself.'[18]

At the close of the poem Aldana promises to say more, on another occasion, about 'our contemplative solitude' (l. 440: 'nuestra soledad contemplativa'). The phrase draws attention to something remarkable in what he has described. In the Spain of his day it was customary to define contemplation as a private and individual experience. That, certainly, is how it is understood by Teresa of Ávila and John of the Cross. Here, however, Aldana presents it as something shared in the context of human love. Precedents for what he evokes are not easy to find, but one does exist in the tradition of Christian Neoplatonism: the conversation between Augustine of Hippo and Monica, his mother and 'supreme friend' (Chadwick 1986: 69), shortly before her death.[19] In a passage of the *Confessions* (Book 9:10) suffused with phrases of Plotinus, he tells how one day in Ostia they stood at a window overlooking a garden: 'Alone with each other', he relates, 'we talked very intimately ... We asked what quality of life the eternal life of the saints will

[18] Allen & Hankins (2001–6, IV: 41): 'Beati nimium quos universi pulchritudo, boni ipsius splendor, in ipsum bonum amore transformat' (I have modified the translation slightly).

[19] Cf. Jennings (1996: 21, 23): 'It is a unique experience among those related by the mystics since it depicts a *shared* moment of ecstasy and illumination ... It is an indication of the extraordinary closeness and affinity of these two people that they could reach and sustain *together* so lofty an experience.'

have', and 'our minds were lifted up by an ardent affection towards eternal being itself'. Their souls then rose through the universe to the region of the eternal, where they experienced a brief moment of ecstasy, before returning to the world of time (Chadwick 1991: 170–1). The experiences that Augustine and Aldana relate are not identical: in one the friends soar heavenwards, only to return a while later to everyday life, in the other they probe the depths of the ocean in a regular and customary way; but in both accounts the contemplation that they share is informed by their mutual love and described in Neoplatonic terms.

3. Metaphor

Mention was made earlier of Ficino's notion of a hierarchical universe composed of five levels of being: at the summit there is the spiritual realm, God and then the angels; at the bottom, the corporeal realm, the body and Quality; and in the middle, uniting both realms, the soul. This notion underlies his understanding of metaphor, for he held that the levels of being were connected in their innermost identity, and thus reflective of each other's nature. When he uses a metaphor, therefore, with a philosophical end in view, the relationship between the two terms of the comparison is often more than rhetorical, it is substantive too: the image, that is to say, and what it refers to are linked by a hidden connection that makes their relationship real (Kristeller 1964: 93–4).[20] Light, for example, is for him more than a figure of the divine: it is a manifestation of God's truth and goodness in each level of being. The luminous beauty of the natural world is linked intrinsically to the greater splendour of the angels by an affinity that links the angels in turn with the unsurpassed glory of the One:

> When you look upward, the celestial entities tell you the glory of God through the rays of the stars, like the glances and signs of their eyes, and the firmament announces the works of His hands. But the sun can signify to you God Himself in the highest degree. The sun will give you the signs; who would dare to call the sun false? So the invisible things of God, that is, the angelic divinities, are seen and understood particularly through the stars, and God's eternal power and divinity through the sun.
>
> (Kristeller 1964: 98)[21]

In Aldana's poem metaphor functions in this way. To evoke contemplation and its impact on the soul, for instance, Aldana draws in the first part on images of water,

[20] On Ficino's use of metaphor, see also Cassirer (1945: 493–8) and Garin (1989), and on Ficino's approach to language more generally, Allen (2002).

[21] Ficino (1962: 966): 'Coelestia igitur tibi sursum conspicienti, statim per ipsos stellarum radios tanquam oculorum suorum aspectus atque nutus errant gloriam Dei, et opera manuum eius nuntiat firmamentum. Sol uero maxime Deum ipsum tibi significare potest. Sol tibi signa daret, Solem quis dicere falsum audeat? Ita demum inuisibilia Dei, id est angelica numina per stellas potissimum intellecta conspiciuntur, per Solem uero sempiterna quoque Dei virtus atque diuinitas.' The passage quoted occurs in his treatise *De comparatione solis ad Deum*.

air, earth and fire, the four elements that for Plato constitute the corporeal realm (ll. 220–31). When later he describes the natural landscape in which he and Montano will dwell, the four elements recur, but now charged with the connotations of the spiritual realm established earlier. As they walk along the seashore, the friends will observe, he says, little fish hidden inside shells and conches that they leave, on occasion, to explore the sea. The description, no doubt, is meant to be taken literally, but the reader is invited to recall as well that earlier the body was compared to a cave, and the soul to a fish in the great ocean of the divine. The subject of their conversation, in other words, will be not just the beauty of the corporeal realm, but the wonders of the spiritual realm that it signals (Bergamín 1973: 162–3; O'Reilly 2008: 51–6). Another instance of the technique is the image of a ship that Aldana applies in the first part to his own writing (Aldana 1985: 443, ll. 124–9,):

> But since my bark, Montano, with sail spread,
> is racing over this enormous sea,
> seeking in the infinite a landfall,
> I shall, to weave a tapestry so rich,
> consider from far back what can be done
> by the soul that flies to attain its Cause.

Here the bark crossing the sea is his attempt to navigate the Ocean of God. Later, the divine realm is compared to a New World that the contemplative is called to explore, like a *conquistador* (Aldana 1985: 450, ll. 274–6,):

> O great, o most richly endowed conquests
> of the Indies of God, of that great world
> so hidden from the gaze of worldly eyes!

Later still, at the poem's close, the image returns, when it is said that the friends, walking together beside the sea, will see a ship sailing fast towards distant lands (Aldana 1985: 457, ll. 415–17,):

> You will see also the ship running fast
> across the sea, its air-blown sails aslant
> and speeding, on its way to distant climes.

The implication is, once again, that in their shared solitude they will ponder the marvels of the spiritual realm that contemplation opens up.

In the verse-epistle of Aldana, poetry and Neoplatonism come together in a most powerful way to evoke contemplation and its transforming effects. In this respect it bears comparison with the great poems on the same subject by John of the Cross. There is, admittedly, a contrast also: John, like Teresa before him, writes of an experience that has been fully lived, Aldana of an experience to which he aspires, and that he yearns fully to know. Aldana's contemplative dream, moreover, was never realised: a year after completing his epistle, he was killed in action in North Africa (Aldana 1985: 38–9). He remains, none the less, a significant figure in the history of Spanish mysticism. As Alexander Parker, a perceptive reader of his work, remarked, 'Aldana's poetry … demonstrates indisputably that a longing for ideal [human] love, sincerely felt and sought for, could lead under the prevailing influence of Renaissance Platonism to the search for God, and that the love of God, while representing the same human need to break down the isolation of the individual, leads beyond the physical to the spiritual' (1985: 71).

References

Aldana, F. de (1985), *Poesías castellanas completas*, ed. J. Lara Garrido (Madrid, Cátedra).

Allen, M.J.B. (2002), '*In principio*: Marsilio Ficino and the Life of the Text', in E. Kessler & I. Maclean (eds), *Res et Verba in der Renaissance* (Wiesbaden, Harrassowitz Verlag), 11–28.

Allen, M.J.B (2006), 'Paul Oskar Kristeller and Marsilio Ficino: e tenebris revocaverunt', in J. Monfasani (ed.), *Kristeller Reconsidered: Essays on His Life and Scholarship* (New York, Italica Press), 1–18.

Allen, M.J.B. (2008), 'At Variance: Marsilio Ficino, Platonism and Heresy', in D. Hedley & S. Hutton (eds), *Platonism at the Origins of Modernity: Studies on Platonism and Early Modern Philosophy* (Dordrecht, Springer), 31–44.

Allen, M.J.B. (ed. & trans.) (2015), *Marsilio Ficino: On Dionysius the Areopagite*, 2 vols (Cambridge MA, Harvard University Press).

Allen, M.J.B & Hankins, J. (trans. & ed.) (2001–6), *Marsilio Ficino, Platonic Theology*, 6 vols (Cambridge MA, Harvard University Press).

Álvarez, T. (1980), 'Jesucristo en la experiencia de Santa Teresa', *Monte Carmelo*, 88: 335–65.

Álvarez, T. (ed.) (2006), *Diccionario de Santa Teresa. Doctrina e historia*, 2nd edn (Burgos, Monte Carmelo).

Andrés Martín, M. (1975), *Los Recogidos. Nueva visión de la mística española (1500–1700)* (Madrid, Fundación Universitaria Española).

Archer, R. (1988), 'The Overreaching Imagination: The Structure and Meaning of Aldana's *Carta para Arias Montano*', *Bulletin of Hispanic Studies*, 65: 237–49.

Baraut, C. (1967), 'La bibliothèque ascétique de García de Cisneros, Abbé de Montserrat', *Studia Monastica*, 9: 327–39.

Bergamín, J. (1973), *Beltenebros y otros ensayos sobre literatura española* (Barcelona/Madrid, Noguer).

Byrne, S. (2015), *Ficino in Spain* (Toronto, University of Toronto Press).

Cassirer, E. (1945), '"Ficino's Place in Intellectual History", a Review of the First Edition of Kristeller (1943)', *Journal of the History of Ideas*, 6.4: 483–51.

Castro, S. (2009), *Cristología Teresiana* (Madrid, Editorial de Espiritualidad).

Chadwick, H. (1986), *Augustine* (Oxford, Oxford University Press).

Chadwick, H. (trans.) (1991), *Saint Augustine: Confessions* (Oxford, Oxford University Press).

Diego Sánchez, M. (2008), *Santa Teresa de Jesús: Bibliografía sistemática* (Madrid, Editorial de Espiritualidad).

Drobner, H.R. (2008), 'Christian Philosophy', in S. Ashbrook Harvey & D.G. Hunter (eds), *The Oxford Handbook of Early Christian Studies* (Oxford, Oxford University Press), 672–90.

Ficino, M. (1962), *Opera omnia* (Turin, Bottega d'Erasmo).

Garin, E. (1989), 'Images et symboles chez Marsile Ficin', in E. Garin, *Moyen Age et Renaissance* (Paris, Gallimard), 218–34.

Gómez Canseco, L. (2007), *Poesía y contemplación. Las 'Divinas Nupcias' de Benito Arias Montano y su entorno literario* (Huelva, Universidad de Huelva).
Grande Quejigo, F.J. (2006), 'La *Carta a Arias Montano* de Francisco de Aldana, epístola horaciana de *amicitia*', in J.M. Maestre Maestre *et al.* (eds), *Benito Arias Montano y los humanistas de su tiempo*, vol. 2 (Mérida, Editora Regional de Extremadura), 837–47.
Jennings, E. (1996), *Every Changing Shape: Mystical Experience and the Making of Poems* (Manchester, Carcanet Press).
Knowles, D. (1975), 'The Influence of Pseudo-Dionysius on Western Mysticism', in P. Brooks (ed.), *Christian Spirituality: Essays in Honour of Gordon Rupp* (London, SCM), 79–94.
Kristeller, P.O. (1964), *The Philosophy of Marsilio Ficino*, trans. V. Conant (Gloucester MA, Peter Smith; the first edition was published in 1943).
Lapide, C. a (1868–76), *Commentaria in Scripturam Sacram*, 21 vols (Paris, Vivès).
Lara Ródenas, M.J. de (1998), 'Arias Montano en Portugal. La revisión de un tópico sobre la diplomacia secreta de Felipe II', in L. Gómez Canseco (ed.), *Anatomía del humanismo. Benito Arias Montano (1598–1998)* (Huelva, Universidad de Huelva), 343–66.
Lauster, J. (2002), 'Marsilio Ficino as a Christian Thinker: Theological Aspects of His Platonism', in M.J.B. Allen, V. Rees & M. Davies (eds), *Marsilio Ficino: His Theology, His Philosophy, His Legacy* (Leiden, Brill), 45–69.
Lefebvre, A. (1953), *La Poesía del Capitán Aldana (1537–1578)* (Concepción, Chile, Universidad de Concepción).
López Santidrián, S. (ed.) (2005), *Francisco de Osuna. Tercer abecedario espiritual* (Madrid, Biblioteca de Autores Cristianos).
Luibheid, C. (trans.) (1987), *Pseudo-Dionysius: The Complete Works* (London, SPCK).
Maldonado, J. (1874), *Commentarii in quatuor evangelistas*, 2 vols (Mainz, Kircheim).
Marcel, R. (1958), *Marsile Ficin (1433–1499)* (Paris, Les Belles Lettres).
Martín, T.H. (ed.) (1992), *Hugo de Balma. Sol de contemplativos* (Salamanca, Sígueme).
Mediavilla, F.S. (ed.) (2014), *Santa Teresa de Jesús. Libro de la vida* (Madrid, Real Academia Española).
Mellinghoff-Bourgerie, V. (2014), 'Soleil et Amour divin. François de Sales lecteur de Marsile Ficin', *Travaux de Littérature*, 27: 125–36.
O'Donoghue, N. (1989), *Mystics for Our Time: Carmelite Meditations for a New Age* (Edinburgh, T. & T. Clark).
O'Reilly, T. (2008), 'Friendship and Contemplation in the *Carta para Arias Montano*', *Calíope*, 14.1: 47–60.
O'Reilly, T. (2015), 'The Mystical Theology of Saint Francis de Sales in the *Traité de l'amour de Dieu*', in L. Nelstrop & B.B. Onishi (eds), *Mysticism in the French Tradition: Eruptions from France* (Farnham, Ashgate), 207–20.
O'Reilly, T. (2018), 'St Teresa and Her First Jesuit Confessors', in T. O'Reilly, C. Thompson & L. Twomey (eds), *St Teresa of Ávila: Her Writings and Life* (Oxford, Legenda), 108–23.
Pacho, E. (ed.) (2009), *Diccionario de San Juan de la Cruz* (Burgos: Monte Carmelo).
Parker, A.A. (1985), *The Philosophy of Love in Spanish Literature 1480–1680*, ed. T. O'Reilly (Edinburgh, Edinburgh University Press).
Pelikan, J. (1987), 'The Odyssey of Dionysian Spirituality', in Luibheid (1987), 11–24.
Rivers, E.L. (ed.) (1966), *Francisco de Aldana. Poesías* (Madrid, Espasa-Calpe).

Rorem, P. (1996), 'The Uplifting Spirituality of Pseudo Dionysius', in B. McGinn, J. Meyendorff & J. Leclercq (eds), *Christian Spirituality: Origins to the Twelfth Century* (London, SCM), 132–51.

Ruello, F. & Barbet, J. (eds) (1995), *Hugues de Balma. Théologie mystique*, 2 vols (Paris, Cerf).

Ruiz Silva, C. (1981), *Estudios sobre Francisco de Aldana* (Valladolid, Universidad de Valladolid).

Sanz Valdivieso, R. (ed.) (1996), *Vida y escritos de San Pedro de Alcántara* (Madrid, Biblioteca de Autores Cristianos).

Turner, D. (1995), *The Darkness of God: Negativity in Christian Mysticism* (Cambridge, Cambridge University Press).

Wilkinson, A.S. (ed.) (2010), *Iberian Books: Books Published in Spanish and Portuguese or on the Iberian Peninsula before 1601* (Leiden, Brill).

15

A Poetics of Difference: Neoplatonism and the Discourse of Desire in the Early Modern Spanish Love Lyric

JULIAN WEISS

NEAR THE END of his dialogue, *Il Cortegiano* (the *Book of the Courtier*), which defined courtly ideals for Renaissance Europe, Baldassare Castiglione invites us to imagine an extraordinary scene. He has us picture one of the leading humanists of the day, Pietro Bembo, explaining the true nature of love to the assembled noble men and women of the refined court of Urbino. As the author of a treatise on Neoplatonic love, *Gli Asolani*, first published in 1505, Bembo must have seemed the perfect choice to expound the intricacies of love's ascent towards a transcendent Truth, despite (or perhaps because of) his adulterous passion for Lucrezia Borgia. Castiglione depicts Bembo following the by now conventional upward rise of the soul as it passes from physical attraction, through the sensuous kiss that conjoins lover and beloved in spiritual union, and ever upwards towards the contemplation of cosmic beauty. Bembo does not just describe the trajectory; he experiences it: for by the end of his discourse, he is left in a state of ecstasy, 'silent and still, looking towards heaven, as if dazed'.[1] A moment's stunned silence. Then, Emilia Pia, an aristocrat famed for her wit, brings him back down to earth with a tug on his sleeve and a wry comment: 'Take care, Pietro, that with these thoughts of yours you too do not cause your soul to leave your body' (343).

Emilia's ironic aside epitomises the capacity of the Renaissance dialogue to represent 'process rather than affirmation of elusive truths', enabling readers to explore ideas from multiple perspectives, shaped by the lives and circumstances of the speakers.[2] These perspectives, like the participants themselves, are not static; they evolve and change. In this way, Castiglione's dialogue stages the spectacle of

[1] I follow the translation by George Bull (Castiglione 1967: 342–3).

[2] Kushner (2004: 240–1); for Renaissance dialogues in Italian, French, German, English and Neo-Latin, see Heitsch & Vallée (2004), and their bibliography for other languages. The dialogue's encounter with Spanish and Portuguese censors is explored in Vian Herrero *et al.* (2016).

ideas in action, in a world of contingency and lived experience. And it is this lived experience that gives Emilia's intervention its critical edge. Her comment provokes the misogynist of the group, Gaspare Pallavicino, to declare that women could not possibly follow the spiritual ascent described by Bembo because their passionate nature hinders their powers of contemplation: 'I think to travel this road would be difficult for men, but impossible for women ... The souls of women are not as purged of the passions as those of men or as versed in contemplation as Pietro has said those which are to taste divine love must be' (343). It is late – dawn has broken – so the debate is postponed until the following evening. But that evening never comes, because Castiglione brings his work to a close, leaving the question hanging in an eternal dawn.

Though the question has an uncertain future, its past is clear. The noble gathering had already debated how the ideal courtier's values and conduct might be compatible with the nature and experiences of women. The entire third book is dedicated to a discussion about the ideal court lady, which broadens into a wide-ranging debate over the nature of woman (Castiglione 1967: 207–78). The detractors' arguments have their ideological roots in the medieval *querelle des femmes* ('debate over women') and in physiological theories that stretch back to Antiquity. For example, Aristotle's belief that the female provides the matter and the male the generative form helped shape centuries of patriarchal thought that emphasised how, while men and women were spiritual equals in the eyes of the Christian God, woman's earth-bound frailty meant that she lacked man's potential for intellectual perfection.[3] This philosophical proposition is countered by an alternative one: 'namely, that those who are weak in body are able in mind. So there can be no doubt that being weaker in body women are abler in mind and more capable of speculative thought than men' (218). The debate staged in book III interweaves a variety of topics and perspectives, but a prominent thread is love and the way it shapes the relations between men and women. In this way, Castiglione lays the basis for Pietro Bembo's discourse that, positioned at the end of book IV, serves as the dialogue's climax.[4]

By grafting theories of Neoplatonic love onto a long-standing gender debate, Castiglione illustrates how Renaissance Neoplatonism was the product as well as the facilitator of an open-ended dialogue between philosophical and ideological positions. It provided a framework for writers to move to and fro between

[3] Scholarship on the *querelle* and pre-modern theories of the body is vast. Fenster & Lees (2002) offer a wide range of approaches and case studies, while Blamires *et al.* (1992) provide representative texts. For the debate's Hispanic context see Weiss (2002, esp. 256–81 for a Baroque nun's riposte), Archer (2005), Solomon (2010), Vélez Sainz (2015) and Francomano (2018). Solomon's account of the medical underpinning of misogyny complements Cadden (1993) and MacLean (1980), who survey physiological, scholastic and theological perspectives on pre-modern gender.

[4] Not that Castiglione planned the connection: the work evolved from manuscript drafts to its 1528 edition in a complex 15-year process. In tracing its gestation Pugliese (2004) notes how Castiglione altered his treatment of women, toning down defamatory statements to give Emilia Pia a more prominent role.

Plato and Aristotle, Galen, and a host of Islamic, Jewish and Christian thinkers. In Castiglione's case, the conversation radiates outwards beyond the boundaries of his text: the *Book of the Courtier* was a widely travelled and translated book.[5] Readers and writers could continue the unresolved debate between Pietro Bembo, Emilia Pia and Gaspare Pallavicino by putting it into creative dialogue with other European best-sellers that engage, directly or indirectly, with Neoplatonism and the battle between the sexes. I am thinking in particular about that other great polyphonic and multifaceted best-seller, Leone Ebreo's *Dialogues on Love*, which was roughly contemporary with Castiglione's dialogue and which also travelled through Europe and beyond in multiple editions and translations.[6] This incomplete work is structured by a questioning, unresolved exchange between a male teacher, Philo, and his female student, Sophia. 'Ebreo's philosophical system', Rosella Pescatori points out, 'is strongly based on gender/sexual polarity' (Ebreo 2009: 44). It is also very playful: Ebreo interweaves philosophical inquiry with a sexual game, in which Sophia resists Philo's desperate desire to seduce her, not only by rationally challenging his arguments (just because you desire me, why should I comply?) but also by questioning his language (if you talk about desire and reason, you need to define these terms). She also reminds him of his own worldliness and humanity: at the start of the third dialogue, 'On the Origin of Love', Philo walks straight past Sophia without recognising her, and when she chides him, he answers coyly that he was 'attending to some needs of the part of lesser value' (Ebreo 2009: 301). When prodded – 'Lesser value? It cannot be of little value to you if it deprives your eyes of seeing and your unclosed ears of hearing' – he tries to clarify: 'My mind, bothered by worldly business and the necessity of such base pursuits, has withdrawn into itself for refuge'. Eventually, Sophia manages to worm out of him a more concrete explanation of these vague 'needs' and 'base pursuits': he was so distracted by the mental image of Sophia (the Petrarchan motif of *alienatio amorosa*) that he failed to notice the real woman standing in his path. Whatever the actual cause of his distraction – an urgent call of nature, erotic fantasy, Neoplatonic contemplation? – is beside the point. Playfully, Ebreo here uses Sophia to summon Philo back into the real world, and to ask unsettling questions about the relation between the living woman and her idealised image.[7]

If we put Castiglione and Ebreo into conversation with each other, aligning them on the literary horizon of Renaissance Europe, the symbolism of Emilia

[5] See Burke (1995) for translations, adaptations, and responses from the 16th through the mid-19th centuries.

[6] Castiglione reworked his first draft (1513–1518) in the early 1520s, publishing it in 1528, a year before his death. Leone Ebreo (Judah ben Isaac Abravanel) began his book around 1505. The compositional process and original language – Hebrew or Italian – cannot be confirmed; the first Italian edition (1535) appeared 15 years after the author's death. The best overview, with a list of early modern and modern translations, is the English translation by Bacich & Pescatori (Ebreo 2009).

[7] On this aspect of Sophia's rhetorical and philosophical role, see Sommer (1996: 403). Ebreo thus subverts the Ovidian seduction manuals of medieval 'erotodidactic schooltexts', on which see Cantavella (2015).

Pia's gesture comes more clearly into view. Like Sophia, she is the one to bring Neoplatonic desire down to earth, because although (for a man) Woman offers the material means – the body – through which he might embark on his spiritual ascent, she is also the earthbound obstacle to that journey and the reminder of his own bodily nature. The image of Emilia Pia tugging the hem of Bembo's robe and her mordant words combine to create a piece of 'emblem literature': that coupling of visual symbol and epigrammatic motto – 'picta poesis' – that was so popular from the 1530s onwards.[8] And the meaning of the emblem is this: man uses language not just to describe an external reality, but to conjure it up in heightened form: 'by the power of his imagination', says Bembo, 'he will also make [his beloved's] beauty far more lovely than it is in reality' (Castiglione 1967: 338). As Bembo's ecstasy demonstrates, he then inhabits this newly fashioned world, which is made possible by female beauty yet denied to real women. Then, from the edges of that world, female wit – the intuitive by-product of their cold and wet bodies – challenges the male-centred order, breaks its illusory spell, and brings man back down to earth.

It is worth dwelling for a moment on the physicality of Emilia Pia's contestation. According to some early modern natural philosophers, women's cold and moist complexion rendered them incapable of serious intellectual or scientific activity; at the same time, it also predisposed them to a particular kind of bristly, frivolous wit. This much was conceded, with evident condescension, by the Spanish physician Juan Huarte de San Juan (1529–88), whose *Examen de ingenios para las ciencias* (1575) had a wide European circulation, with 55 editions in six languages. 'Quedando la mujer en su disposición natural', he declares, 'todo género de letras y sabiduría es repugnante a su ingenio' ('Whilst a woman abideth in her natural disposition, all sorts of learning and wisdom carrieth a kind of repugnancy to her wit'). However, if a woman's complexion is cold and wet 'in the first degree', she will certainly display signs of an 'ingenio agudo', but this will make her an uppity woman, 'arisca, áspera y desabrida' ('froward, cursed and wayward').[9] When all is said and done, women 'cannot be endowed with any profound judgment. Only we see that they talk with some appearance of knowledge in slight and easy matters' (Huarte de San Juan 2014: 292; original, 1989: 627). In the following century, the great novelist María de Zayas (1590–1661) turned this argument on its head and used it to justify her creativity and insight as a *novelera*. The human soul, she writes, is neither male nor female, and the only reason why men are wise and presume that we are not is because they have locked up us with our needlework. With access to books and teachers we too could become professors, 'perhaps of sharper wit, since our disposition is colder, given that understanding is humid, as can be

[8] The first and most influential collection is Andrea Alciato's *Emblemata* (1531). Daly's introduction to theory and practice (2014) includes a critical review of previous approaches.

[9] Huarte de San Juan (1989: 615–16). I quote Richard Carew's English translation (1594); see Huarte de San Juan (2014: 284), with excellent introduction and bibliography by Rocío G. Sumillera. For the treatise's international reception, see pp. 23–30.

seen in quick wit and calculated deceit, for everything done with skill, although it be not virtue, is ingenuity'.[10]

In the remainder of this chapter I examine three poetic versions of these emblematic encounters between Emila Pia, Pietro Bembo, Sophia and Philo, to show how Spanish sonnets, written both by male and female poets from the Renaissance and the Baroque, exploited Neoplatonic discourse as a means of thinking about – and thinking beyond – the boundaries of gender identity. My poets are the Spanish soldier Francisco de Aldana (1537–78), the provincial noblewoman Catalina Clara Ramírez de Guzmán (1611–*c.* 1680), and the Mexican nun Sor Juana Inés de la Cruz (1651–95).[11] I have chosen the sonnet form deliberately. Like Neoplatonism itself, it enabled writers to practise what in the spirit of this volume we might call a 'poetics of difference'. Sonnets constitute a technology of the self, a formal mechanism for constructing a highly mobile selfhood, a subjectivity that unfolds through the verbal and syntactic patterns of the poem itself. This mobility is enhanced by the sonnet's intertextuality: its conventionalised motifs and language constitute a dialogue between the lyric subject and other selves from different times and places. So, in what follows I am less concerned with the source of the Neoplatonic components of a sonnet than in what the sonnet is doing with, and to, Neoplatonic theories of love.

I begin with the most explicit instance of how the sonnet works with Neoplatonic discourse, Francisco de Aldana's famous sonnet 12 (1985: 201–2, ):

> 'What is the cause, my Damon, that as
> we together in love's tussle are combined
> with tongues and arms and feet, and all enchained
> like grapevines that in jasmine get entwined,
> and, taking both of us the breath of life
> in through our lips, worn out from sips sublime,
> amidst such joy we find ourselves compelled
> to groan and sigh out loud from time to time?'
> 'Love, my Phyllis fair, who deep inside
> our souls did bind, within his forge aspires
> our bodies to conjoin with force as great,
> and since it can't — like water with a sponge —
> pass into the beloved soul's sweet core,
> the mortal veil bemoans its shabby fate.'[12]

Aldana does not versify a Neoplatonic commonplace, producing philosophy in metrical form. Like Castiglione, he chooses the dialogue structure to question and

[10] See her address 'To the reader' ('Al que leyere') that prefaces her first collection of tales, *Novelas amorosas y ejemplares* (Zayas 2000: 159–61; English translation, Zayas 2009: 48); for its feminist implications, see Greer (2000: 61–83).

[11] For Aldana's Neoplatonism see the contributions in this volume of Colin Thompson and Terence O'Reilly, who provide further bibliography.

[12] The translation is by Alix Ingber: www.poesi.as/fas012uk.htm

unsettle. And like Castiglione, he has a woman, Phyllis, initiate doubt through her body, in this case her recollection of 'love's tussle', or 'la lucha de amor'. She remembers, in the two quatrains, her physical experience of erotic sensuality, picturing how her limbs entwine with those of her lover as naturally and as beautifully as the entanglement of jasmine and vine.[13] The movement conveyed by the progressive present of the Spanish – 'se va enredando' – is diminished by the English 'get entwined'. Nonetheless, the translation preserves that dynamism through the enjambment at the end of the first quatrain, which keeps our thoughts moving in an upward spiral, passing from tangled limbs to the kiss that, in its turn, compels lips to sigh and eyes to weep. Phyllis's question, 'What causes this joyful sorrow?' reflects her inability to see beyond her body and beyond her intuition to grasp the higher Truth of their shared desire. Damon provides the Neoplatonist's answer: love has united two souls, which were split asunder in life. The sighs and tears remind us that true union cannot be found while we exist in this world, while our bodies are clothed in our mortal veil.

The sonnet's binary structure splits the female question from the male answer. But countering this dichotomy is the equal distribution of syntactic intricacy, which, like love's vine, still binds Damon and Phyllis together in grammatical unity. Although sonnet quatrains tend to have greater syntactic complexity, Aldana continues it into the tercets. Damon has the capacity to act as Phyllis's tutor, certainly, but the syntax keeps him symbolically entwined with the object of his desire. And desire itself has the final word: the English 'shabby fate' fails to convey the semantic range of the Spanish 'avara suerte'. Like its Latin etymon, *avarus*, the adjective *avaro* denotes a material craving that is never satisfied.[14] Thus, Damon acknowledges their shared experience of lack in a gesture that is at once a marker of difference and of reciprocity. Even as he rationalises his own desire by viewing it from the perspective of eternity, his words return him full circle to the start of the poem and to the bodily yearning that ties him to Phyllis.

This coupling of masculine and feminine perspectives echoes the dialogues of Castiglione and Ebreo. In fact, as numerous scholars have observed, Aldana bases his poem on a passage in the first of Leone Ebreo's *Dialogues on Love*.[15] What inspires Aldana, however, is not Ebreo's philosophical position on the body/soul dichotomy, but the way that this Jewish exile uses Neoplatonism to represent what it means to live between polarities. Thus, the focal point of Aldana's sonnet is not the

[13] Contrast the image of the vine as clinging and fertile wife in Psalm 128, verse 3: 'Your wife will be like a fruitful vine within your house.'

[14] As defined, for example, by Sebastián de Covarrubias in his *Tesoro de la lengua castellana* (1611): 'Avariento y avaro. Lat. *avarus*, quasi *avidus aeris*, *tenax*, *parcus*, *restrictus*: del verbo latino *aveo*, *-es*, por dessear, atento que el avaro, quanto más tiene, más desea.' John Stevens, in his *New Dictionary, Spanish and English, English and Spanish* (1726), cites a variant proverb that underscores the lack that lies at the heart of the miser's desire: '"El avaro, quanto más tiene, está más menguado": the covetous man, the more he has, the more wretched he is. Because he still covets and is never satisfy'd.'

[15] See, for example, Lara Garrido (Aldana 1985: 201) and Terry (1982: 239).

start or endpoint of love's ascent, but what lies in between, the lived experience of moving back and forth between body and mind. As Arthur Terry (1982) pointed out over 30 years ago, although Neoplatonism could compound the body/soul dualism, this sonnet illustrates how Renaissance poets also recognised the interdependence of thought and feeling and explored the close relationship between the intellect and the senses. Fernando de Herrera, in his famous *Anotaciones* (1580) on the poetry of Garcilaso de la Vega, paraphrases Plotinus to underscore how all the senses must work together with the intellect to form a 'common sense' where thoughts are formed, just like lines converging in the centre of a circle.[16] But this does not mean that mind and body operate on equal terms. In the gendered economy of this poem, masculine thought is privileged. Phyllis's tongue, like her arms and feet, the metaphoric tendrils of vine and jasmine, is an instrument of her clinging sensuality. Her name evokes the Greek myth of Phyllis, popularised by Ovid's *Remedia amoris* and *Heroides*. Abandoned by Demophon, the love-lorn princess committed suicide and her body was metamorphosed into a tree. Damon's tongue, on the other hand, is linked to his penis. This might appear a strange connection to make, were it not for the fact that Leone Ebreo himself makes it in his second dialogue on love: 'The penis', Philo explains,

> is analogous to the tongue in position, shape and power of extension and retraction; it is placed in the middle of all, and it works in the same way as the penis, its movement generates physical progeny; the tongue generates them spiritually with specific speech, and it gives birth to spiritual offspring just as the penis does with physical offspring. The kiss is common to both, one often provoking the other.
>
> (Ebreo 2009: 175)

Aldana's Damon and Leone Ebreo's Philo may still be locked in a sensual 'tussle of love', but at least their tongues can generate 'spiritual offspring': the men have the privilege of tutoring the objects of their desire. Castiglione's Bembo declared that the male lover should guide his beloved and

> be at pains to keep her from going astray and by his wise precepts and admonishments always seek to make her modest, temperate and truly chaste … And in this manner, our courtier will be most pleasing to his lady, and she will always be submissive, charming and affable and as anxious to please him as she is to be loved by him.
>
> (Castiglione 1967: 335)

Their explanations – 'mansplaining' – operate within a phallogocentric world. What, then, of the perspectives of female poets, the flesh and blood versions of Leone Ebreo's Sophia, Castiglione's Emilia Pia and Aldana's Phyllis?

[16] See Herrera's notes on Garcilaso's Sonnet VIII: 'Como dize Plotino, en tanto que nosotros pensamos atentamente en alguna cosa, conviene que todos los otros sentidos recorran al sentido común, donde se forman los pensamientos; no de otra suerte que suelen hazer las líneas tiradas de la circunferencia al centro.' Both Terry (1982: 238) and Herrera's editors (2001: 336) suggest he culls ideas from *Enneads* IV. Herrera also cites Plotinus in a Neoplatonic excursus on love, probably alluding to *Enneads* V, 3 (not III, 5 as Herrera's editors suggest: 2001: 318–27, at p. 320).

Catalina Clara Ramírez de Guzmán was a noblewoman from Extremadura, who never seems to have left her provincial town of Llerena. Yet she was one of the most distinctive female poets of the Spanish Baroque, at a time when women were striving to consolidate their position within a predominantly masculine literary world.[17] Her extant work includes eight surviving 'portrait poems': a well-established poetic theme that explores the relation between visual and verbal artifice. Though poems about portraits could be written in a variety of metres, the fixed form of the sonnet was especially appropriate because its tight structure could serve as a frame for the representation of the (usually) female face depicted and eulogised by the (usually) male poet. Whether explicitly or mediated by Petrarchism, these portrait poems have deep roots in Platonic notions, not least in the way that the Neoplatonic lover transforms the physical body of his beloved into a mental portrait.[18] If this volume of essays reminds us that Neoplatonism entails a struggle to glimpse the 'Faces of the Infinite', the following sonnet reminds us that what we glimpse of that allegedly infinite face is contingent upon gendered ways of seeing (Olivares & Boyce 2012: 129,):

To a portrait of a lady

Portrait, if you are a shadow, how can you imitate
the brighter splendours of the sun?
Dead, how can your colours be so alive?
Lacking life, how can you steal so many lives?
   Lacking body, you lend strength to many souls;
lacking soul, where is your rigour forged?
If Clori's favours have no peer
why do you strive to surpass her?
   You are an apparition that recreates
(enjoyed only by the eyes),
a joyful illusion of the idea;
   a deceit that fashions through appearances,
a fiction that flatters taste,
a lie, finally, that gives the lie to truth.[19]

Like Aldana, Ramírez de Guzmán divides her sonnet into question and answer, distributed between quatrains and tercets. Unlike him, however, the enigma and its solution are uttered by the same disembodied voice. Initially, at least, there is no reason to identify the speaker as either male or female; indeed, the challenge to the portrait could also be uttered by the poem itself, staging a rivalry between verbal and visual art. Readers would be aware that the rhetorical concept of *enargeia*,

[17] For a valuable anthology of Hispanic women poets, see Olivares & Boyce (2012), and Olivares (2009) for representative samples of critical approaches. For broader guides, see Mujica (2004), Baranda & Cruz (2018) and the online *Bibliografía de escritoras españolas* (BIESES).

[18] For their rhetorical conventions, philosophical premises, and antecedents see McLaughlin (2010: 192–232) and Rabin (1997).

[19] The literal translation is mine. For her complete works, see Ramírez de Guzmán (2010); Borrachero Mendíbil (2009) and McLaughlin (2010: 228–9) examine her verse portraits.

the capacity to bring a representation to life before our very eyes, was shared by word and image alike – *ut pictura poesis*. Beginning with the blunt, accusatory apostrophe – 'Portrait' – the poem expresses puzzlement that an object so lacking life, body and soul manages to emulate Clori's peerless beauty, which shines like the life-giving rays of the sun. Yet the copy does indeed exert its affective sway over souls and appears to have a life and agency of its own. The puzzlement of the two quatrains then modulates first into understanding (tercet one) and then, in the final three lines, into the disillusion (*desengaño*) so characteristic of the Hispanic Baroque. Here we discover that the pleasurable illusion that recreates the Platonic Idea is nothing more than a deceit (*un engaño*), a fiction fashioned out of appearances according to artistic convention (*gusto*, or taste). The final line generates an apparent paradox: this lie (the painting) reveals the Truth itself to be a lie – the alleged Truth here being the belief that Clori is the Platonic Idea itself; she is not, and she never can be. Although she appears to embody this life-giving force, that is merely the effect of the two poetic conceits deployed by Catalina herself: the lady's name recalls the classical nymph Chloris, associated with fecundity and new growth (Botticelli depicted the roses spouting from her lips in his painting 'Primavera'); and the metaphor of the sun derives ultimately from the sixth book of Plato's *Republic*, where it is used by Socrates as an analogy for the idea of goodness, illuminating the world with truth. The closing paradox – 'the lie that gives the lie to Truth' – returns us to the poem's start and invites us to consider how the woman is doubly fashioned: not just by the pictorial art of the portrait, but by the verbal artifice of the sonnet.

I suggested that the poem's voice is disembodied: it is not marked male or female. Therein lies its power and, paradoxically perhaps, its feminist potential. Words do not speak on their own: they lack agency outside their discursive context, where they are uttered and heard, written and read. Catalina's critique emerges when we relocate her poem among other portrait poems written by women, secular and religious, including by Catalina herself. Take her *Coplas* or 'verses' about a nobleman's request for a pen-portrait. Written in a lower, more conversational register, she paints a self-mocking picture of an utterly average face and physique, with a large nose sitting – astonishingly – between her two eyes, perhaps with spectacles perched on top, and with a generally maladroit appearance (Olivares & Boyce 2012: 145–9,):

Portrait of the author, because one of her suitors requested it

If my forehead's more
of a lily or a rose
is hard to say;
and I don't know that I can render
flowers I don't really understand, anyway.
. . .
About my nose, sometimes I think
that I have been lucky,

> Or perhaps that's just a whim[20]
> But I persuade myself that it is so,
> because I have always borne it
> between my eyes.[21]

Refusing the idealisation of feminine beauty so common in the Petrarchan tradition, Catalina challenges the reification of woman by masculine representational conventions. In doing so, she reveals how a convention is no mere formal device: it is the place where social position and literary practice meet; for conventions naturalise assumptions about how to see, speak and think in a particular way and render them tacit.[22] By refusing to wear one mask, Catalina ironically unmasks a social reality embedded in the representational convention she is invited to adopt: in Berger's lapidary formulation, 'Men act and women appear' (1972: 47). By 'humanising the courtly icon' (Olivares & Boyce 2012: 41), she asserts her agency as a woman.

What does this 'humanity' entail? Borrachero Mendíbil explains how Catalina's *Coplas* draw on contradictory ways of seeing, interlacing them in a poetic whole (2009: 91). Its compositional elements swing elusively between compliance and resistance: subject to the discourse of others, she is the subject of her own. Although it is not a philosophical poem, it lays claim to the humanist selfhood most famously articulated by Pico della Mirandola. His *Oration on the Dignity of Man* (2012 [1486]) declared that Man (here, read Woman) was God's only creature not assigned a fixed place in the ladder of creation: this being was uniquely capable of self-fashioning, of moving up and down that ladder, for better or for worse. In the *Coplas*, Catalina reclaims her humanity by refusing to be assigned a fixed role in the conventions of masculine lyric discourse. In her sonnet, she turns the fossilised residue of Neoplatonic tradition back upon itself and recovers its creative potential to think between polarities. Although its discursive context makes it a deeply oppositional gesture, the sonnet also opens onto a horizon that transcends gender.

The desire to escape the patriarchal constraints of femininity was most forcefully expressed by the Mexican nun Sor Juana Inés de la Cruz. In her poetry, drama and polemical writings – most notably the *Respuesta a sor Filotea*, or *The Answer to Sor Filotea* – she launched the most sustained attack on patriarchal thought in the Hispanic Baroque.[23] Like Catalina, though in a more pervasive and intellectually

[20] This is a pun on 'anteojos/antojos': spectacles/whim.

[21] McLaughlin (2010: 222–5) points out that although male poets satirised courtly or Petrarchan motifs, this is 'possibly the first of its kind by a female poet in Spain, a groundbreaking composition, which may have set a trend for others to follow' (224). See also Borrachero Mendíbil (2009), Olivares & Boyce (2012: 38–42) and Powell (2011: 153–4); I adopt her translation of the rubric and the first stanza quoted.

[22] For Raymond Williams, 'Within any social theory of art and literature, a convention is an established relationship, or ground of a relationship, through which a specific shared practice – the making of actual works – can be realized' (1977: 173–9, at p. 173). See also John Berger's pioneering critique of the conventionalised 'surveyed female' (1972: 45–64).

[23] See Merrim (1991, 1999); Anglophone readers will find excellent introductions, with further bibliography, in the translations by Sayers Peden, Arenal and Powell, and Grossman (Juana Inés de la Cruz 1997, 2009, 2016), and Bergmann and Schlau's companion to Sor Juana studies (2017).

challenging manner, she refused to be categorised. In her love sonnets, for example, she constantly shifts voice and addressee, writing now as man to woman, now as woman to man, and at other times as woman to woman.[24] This play of perspectives structures her well-known version of the conventional portrait sonnet, which is numbered 145 in the first edition of 1689, and is introduced by an explanatory rubric: 'Procura desmentir los elogios que a un retrato de la poetisa inscribió la verdad, que llama pasión' ('She attempts to minimise [give the lie to] the praise occasioned by a portrait of herself inscribed by Truth – which she calls Ardor [passion]') ():

> This that you gaze on, colorful deceit,
> that so immodestly displays art's favors,
> with its fallacious arguments of colors
> is to the senses cunning counterfeit,
> this on which kindness [flattery] practiced to delete
> from cruel years accumulated horrors,
> constraining time to mitigate its rigors,
> and thus oblivion and age defeat,
> is but an artifice, a sop to vanity,
> is but a flower by the breezes bowed,
> is but a ploy to counter destiny,
> is but a foolish labor, ill-employed,
> is but a fancy, and, as all may see,
> is but cadaver, ashes, shadow, void.[25]

The printed text is built around the same key words employed by Catalina: while the rubric signals the poet's aim to *desmentir la verdad* ('give the lie to truth'), successive verses expose the portrait's *lisonja* ('flattery'), *primores* ('beauty', or 'favours'), *engaño* ('deceit') and *sombra* ('shade', or 'shadow'). But Sor Juana's perspective is different, almost the reverse. Whereas Catalina addresses the portrait directly, the Mexican nun turns her gaze to the viewer, who is also the poem's reader. Her deictic 'este que ves …', 'this thing that you see', is a refusal to look at her painted self full in the face.[26] Rhetorically, her most powerful move is to reject even the word *retrato*, 'portrait', in the poem itself. She has cast it into the void, the *nada* or 'nothingness', of the final line. Evading its gaze, she intercepts the gaze of the onlooker, who is asked to look more closely ('bien mirado'), using her own verbal art as a prism that refracts the portrait's 'fallacious arguments of colors'. The sonnet's structure, with its uncompromising alliterative tercets, damns the truth claims of the pictorial art. The poem shares the same concern with gendered optics

[24] See Sabat de Rivers (1995), Bergmann (2017); Powell (2011; 2017) situates Sor Juana's Sapphic verse in its broader feminist context.

[25] Trans. Sayers Peden (Juana Inés de la Cruz 1997: 169).

[26] I take the phrase 'this thing that you see' from Grossman's translation. The addition of the noun 'thing' to the demonstrative adjective and pronoun 'este' underscores the reification that Sor Juana attacks.

that underwrites her great *Primero Sueño*, which, in creative dialogue with the infamous Baroque poet Luis de Góngora, also explored the relation between visual perception, knowledge and power (Bergmann 2013).

In the final line, Sor Juana refuses to be misrecognised; in doing so, she repudiates the misrepresentations of female beauty fashioned by earlier male poets.[27] Her conclusion paraphrases the final line of Góngora's sonnet: 'Mientras por competir con tu cabello' ('While the sun shines in vain to compete with the burnished gold of your hair'). This sonnet had rewritten the Horatian *carpe diem* motif into a dark vision of human beauty and poetic art annihilated by time: Góngora's anonymous young woman, together with the Petrarchan imagery that represents her, will be transformed into 'earth, smoke, dust, shadow, nothingness' ('en tierra, en humo, en polvo, en sombra, en nada'). The structure of Góngora's poem glosses, in its turn, an equally well-known sonnet by that most iconic of Spanish Renaissance love poets, Garcilaso de la Vega: 'En tanto que de rosa y azucena / se muestra el color en vuestro gesto' ('Whilst the colour of your complexion is of rose and lily'), which may also have been evoked by Catalina's *Coplas*, discussed above. Perhaps that intertextual network also extends to the famous sonnet by Francisco de Quevedo, 'Cerrar podrá mis ojos la postrera / sombra' ('The final shades may come to shut my eyes'), which, inspired perhaps by Leone Ebreo, offers a more hopeful Neoplatonic vision of love's persistence beyond death: Quevedo's body may be reduced to ashes, but these ashes will still love.[28]

As Sor Juana joins this network, her poem becomes a site of confluence, a place where voices meet. Her poem does not operate on a purely philosophical level, and nor is it a means to force entry into someone else's conversation; it brings that conversation into the orbit of her own literary and social world, extending its transnational and transhistorical scope. Her poem enables her, from the margins of Colonial Mexico, to speak to the culture of the Spanish metropolis; to add her distinctive voice to the general hubbub of verses about human mortality, including her own (the portrait, after all, is of her); and, finally, to enter debates about 'the nature of visual art and about the art object as a vehicle of representation … and of signification' (Clamurro 1986: 30). And it is this last point – the art object as a vehicle of signification – that takes us back to Emilia Pia's emblematic gesture, the tug on the sleeve that brings the Neoplatonic lover back to earth. This sonnet echoes other works in which she criticises the value judgements embedded in words, notably the gendered inequality of language. The rubric sees through the masquerade of Truth to reveal its origins in Passion: this flattering portrait is the product of 'una necia diligencia errada'. The translation 'foolish labor, ill-employed' inevitably loses the resonance of these words in Sor Juana's lexicon. The key terms *pasión*, *error* and especially *necio* link this sonnet to her corruscating *Sátira filosófica*, addressed

[27] For further details, and for the sonnets by the male poets mentioned below, see Clamurro (1986) and Prendergast (2007).

[28] See Colin Thompson's chapter in this volume, and the bibliography cited there.

to 'Hombres necios' ('Stupid men'). This poem decries the utter vacuity of male knowledge and language that place women in a double bind. Having turned women into the objects of desire, men condemn them whether or not they reciprocate their passion: 'Queredlas cual las hacéis / o hacedlas cual las buscáis' ('Either love what you create / or else create what you can love').[29]

Sor Juana's sonnet draws strength from one of Neoplatonism's underlying assumptions about the materiality of human language. Yet while she recognises that language is always doomed to betray Truth, she will not reject it: language continues to operate powerfully in the world as it is lived. Her final word – *nada* – is not nihilism but a symptom of her desire to rise above masculine representation and its traps. By voiding the stylised conventions of the portrait, which have turned her into a reified icon (the 'Tenth Muse' as she was labelled on the title page of the 1689 edition of her works), the term suggests that her truth lies elsewhere, in a universality where man-made gender distinctions do not operate. Her sonnet is one example of the ways in which women's counter discourses could be, as Amanda Powell explains, 'grounded ideologically in Christian Neoplatonist philosophy' (2011: 160; see also 2017: 71, 75).

A brief epilogue: gender is not the only human difference negotiated through Neoplatonism, and nor are sonnets the only literary medium for that negotiation. María de Zayas engaged with Neoplatonic motifs and modes of thought in her *Desengaños amorosos*, her tales of female disillusion and resistance (1646). The sixth story in this collection, 'Amar solo por vencer' ('Love for the Sake of Conquest'), holds out the possibility of a desire that transcends heterosexuality only to become 'an implicit rejection of the Neoplatonic philosophy of love as one among many amorous discourses men use to portray women' (Greer 2000: 75–6, at p. 76). Near the start of Lope de Vega's famous play about class conflict, *Fuenteovejuna* (*c.* 1612), peasants engage in a debate that pits Neoplatonic ideas of altruism and cosmic harmony (inevitably via Leone Ebreo) against Aristotelian notions of love as a natural desire for self-preservation (Act I, 366–444). Their rustic philosophy may provoke condescending laughter; as the drama unfolds, it provides the moral and political legitimacy for their resistance to seigneurial oppression and underpins their claim to a human dignity that straddles class frontiers.

To gender and class, we might add race. The most poignant feature of Leone Ebreo's *Dialogues on Love* is the fact that it was written by one of the first victims of Europe's emerging taxonomy of race, a discourse of violence that was configured in 15th-century Iberia through the bodies of real and imagined Jews (Nirenberg 2009). And what did this prominent member of the Abravanel family do, when his family and community had been torn apart by institutionalised hatred and sent into exile? He wrote a book about love. Its Neoplatonic terms enabled him to integrate (though never to assimilate) into a new social and intellectual community,

[29] Trans. Sayers Peden (Juana Inés de la Cruz 1997: 148–50, at p. 149). For another nun's critique of this double bind, see Weiss (2002: 256–81).

and to assert the interconnectedness of Jewish, Islamic and Christian thought at a time when Jewish, Muslim and Christian lives, beliefs and polities were in conflict. Towards the end of the 16th century, the *Dialogues* were translated into Spanish by Garcilaso de la Vega, *El Inca* (Gómez Suárez de Figueroa, 1539–1616), son of an Incan princess and Spanish *conquistador*, who left his native Peru to seek fortune in Spain. When it was published in Madrid in 1590, his copiously annotated translation was the first work authored by a native of the Americas to appear in print. Several scholars have found parallels between the lives of the exiled Jewish author and his uprooted *mestizo* translator.[30] Indeed, when he dedicated his translation to King Philip II, he hints at an analogy between the *Dialogues*' vision of the noble genealogy and universality of love and his own hybrid lineage, which combined conflicting cultures, worldviews and histories into a potentially new way of life. Ebreo's Neoplatonism provided 'an available set of terms for collating interpersonal love and worldly issues of the present day' (Greene 1999: 208) and given the controversies surrounding the conquest of the New World it is perhaps unsurprising that El Inca's translation was put on the Spanish Index of prohibited books in 1632.[31]

Zayas, Lope, and El Inca Garcilaso encounter Neoplatonism in much the same way as the poets surveyed here. As appropriated and deployed in these sonnets, Neoplatonism constitutes the grounds of a poetics, a way of thinking and writing dialogically. It is transformed into a malleable conceptual frame for thinking across binaries in search of the place where seemingly incommensurable elements meet. It provides the structure for what Raymond Williams called 'structures of feeling': elusive social experiences that stand 'on the edge of semantic availability', neither fully formed nor in total flux (1977: 128–35). In this way, however much Neoplatonism lures us into a higher contemplative region, it never loses its capacity to bring us back down to earth and to imagine and reimagine our material worlds otherwise.

References

Alciato, A. (1531), *Emblemata* (Lyons, G. Rouillium, M. Bonhomme).

Aldana, F. de (1985), *Poesías castellanas completas*, ed. J. Lara Garrido (Madrid, Cátedra).

Archer, R. (2005), *The Problem of Woman in Medieval Hispanic Literature* (Woodbridge, Tamesis).

Baranda, N. & Cruz, A. (eds) (2018), *The Routledge Research Companion to Early Modern Spanish Women Writers* (Abingdon, Routledge).

Berger, J. (1972), *Ways of Seeing* (London, BBC; Harmondsworth, Penguin).

Bergmann, E. (2013), 'Sor Juana, Góngora and Ideologies of Perception', *Calíope*, 18.2: 116–38.

[30] See Sommer (1995; 1996), Greene (1999: 203–13) and Nelson Novoa (2006). The four early modern Spanish translations are surveyed by Cosmos Damian Bacich (Ebreo 2009: 621–39).

[31] Bacich (Ebreo 2009: 639).

Bergmann, E. (2017), 'Sor Juana's Love Poetry: A Woman's Voice in a Man's Genre', in Bergmann & Schlau (2017), 142–51.

Bergmann, E. & Schlau, S. (eds) (2017), *The Routledge Research Companion to the Works of Sor Juana Inés de la Cruz* (Abingdon, Routledge).

BIESES: *Bibliografía de escritoras españolas*, accessed 7 February 2018, www.bieses.net/

Blamires, A., Pratt, K. & Marx, C.W. (eds) (1992), *Woman Defamed and Woman Defended: An Anthology of Medieval Texts* (Oxford, Clarendon).

Borrachero Mendíbil, A. (2009), 'El autorretrato en la poesía de Catalina Clara Ramírez de Guzmán', in Olivares (2009), 81–122.

Burke, P. (1995), *The Fortunes of the 'Courtier': The European Reception of Castiglione's 'Cortegiano'* (University Park, Pennsylvania State University Press).

Cadden, J. (1993), *Meanings of Sex Difference in the Middle Ages: Medicine, Science, and Culture* (Cambridge, Cambridge University Press).

Cantavella, R. (2015), 'The Seducer's Tongue: Oral and Moral Issues in Medieval Erotodidactic Schooltexts', in T.V. Cohen & L.K. Twomey (eds), *Spoken Word and Social Practice: Orality in Europe (1400–1700)* (Leiden, Brill), 393–420.

Castiglione, B. (1967), *The Book of the Courtier*, trans. G. Bull (Harmondsworth, Penguin).

Clamurro, W.H. (1986), 'Sor Juana Inés de la Cruz Reads her Portrait', *Revista de Estudios Hispánicos*, 20.1: 27–43.

Covarrubias, S. de (1611), *Tesoro de la lengua castellana* (Madrid, Luis Sánchez).

Daly, P.M. (2014), *The Emblem in Early Modern Europe: Contributions to the Theory of the Emblem* (Farnham, Ashgate).

Ebreo, L. [Judah ben Isaac Abravanel] (2009), *Dialogues of Love*, trans. C.D. Bacich & R. Pescatori, introduction and notes by R. Pescatori (Toronto, University of Toronto Press).

Fenster, T. & Lees, C.A. (eds) (2002), *Gender in Debate from the Middle Ages to the Renaissance* (New York, Palgrave).

Francomano, E.C. (2018), 'The Early Modern Foundations of the *Querella de las mujeres*', in Baranda & Cruz (2018), 41–60.

Greene, R. (1999), *Unrequited Conquests: Love and Empire in the Colonial Americas* (Chicago, University of Chicago Press).

Greer, M.R. (2000), *María de Zayas Tells Baroque Tales of Love and the Cruelty of Men* (University Park, Pennsylvania State University Press).

Heitsch, D.B. & Vallée, J.-F. (2004), *Printed Voices: The Renaissance Culture of Dialogue* (Toronto, University of Toronto Press).

Herrera, F. de (2001), *Anotaciones a la poesía de Garcilaso*, ed. I. Pepe & J.M. Reyes (Madrid, Cátedra).

Huarte de San Juan, J. (1989), *Examen de ingenios para las ciencias*, ed. G. Serés (Madrid, Cátedra).

Huarte de San Juan, J. (2014), *The Examination of Men's Wits*, trans. R. Carew, ed. R.G. Sumillera (London, Modern Humanities Research Association).

Juana Inés de la Cruz, Sor (1997), *Poems, Protest, and a Dream*, trans. M. Sayers Peden, introduction I. Stavans (Harmondsworth, Penguin).

Juana Inés de la Cruz, Sor (2009), *The Answer: Including sor Filotea's Letter and New Selected Poems = La respuesta / Sor Juana Inés de la Cruz*, trans. E. Arenal & A. Powell, 2nd edn (New York, Feminist Press at the City University of New York).

Juana Inés de la Cruz, Sor (2016), *Selected Works: A New Translation, Contexts, Critical Traditions*, trans. E. Grossman, ed. A. More (New York, W.W. Norton).

Kushner, E. (2004), 'Renaissance Dialogue and Subjectivity', in Heitsch & Vallée (2004), 229–41.

MacLean, I. (1980), *The Renaissance Notion of Woman: A Study in the Fortunes of Scholasticism and Medical Science in European Intellectual Life* (Cambridge, Cambridge University Press).

McLaughlin, K.P. (2010), '"Defragmenting the Portrait": Catalina Clara Ramírez de Guzmán, Extremadura's *No Conocida Señora* of the Golden Age. A Critical Multidisciplinary Reappraisal of the Work of Catalina Clara Ramírez de Guzmán (Llerena, 1618–c.1684)' (unpublished Ph.D. thesis, University of Bradford).

Merrim, S. (ed.) (1991), *Feminist Perspectives on Sor Juana Inés de la Cruz* (Detroit, Wayne State University Press).

Merrim, S. (1999), *Early Modern Women's Writing and Sor Juana Inés de la Cruz* (Liverpool, Liverpool University Press).

Mujica, B.L. (2004), *Women Writers of Early Modern Spain: Sophia's Daughters* (New Haven, Yale University Press).

Nelson Novoa, J. (2006), 'From Incan Realm to the Italian Renaissance: Garcilaso el Inca and the Voyage of his Translation of Leone Ebreo's *Dialoghi d'Amore*', in C.G. Di Biase (ed.), *Travel and Translation in the Early Modern Period* (Amsterdam, Rodopi), 187–201.

Nirenberg, D. (2009), 'Was There Race before Modernity? The Example of "Jewish" Blood in Late Medieval Spain', in M. Eliav-Feldon *et al.* (eds), *The Origins of Racism in the West* (Cambridge, Cambridge University Press), 232–64.

Olivares, J. (ed.) (2009), *Studies on Women's Poetry of the Golden Age: 'Tras el espejo la Musa escribe'* (Woodbridge, Tamesis).

Olivares, J. & Boyce, E.S. (2012), *Tras el espejo la musa escribe*, 2nd edn (Madrid, Siglo Veintiuno).

Pico della Mirandola, G. (2012 [1486]), *Oration on the Dignity of Man: A New Translation and Commentary*, ed. F. Borghesi, M. Papio & M. Riva (Cambridge, Cambridge University Press).

Powell, A. (2011), 'Baroque Flair: Seventeenth-century European Sapphic Poetry', *Humanist Studies & the Digital Age*, 1.1: 151–65, accessed 14 October 2019, http://journals.oregondigital.org/hsda/

Powell, A. (2017), 'Passionate Advocate: Sor Juana, Feminisms, and Sapphic Loves', in Bergmann & Schlau (2017), 63–77.

Prendergast, R. (2007), 'Constructing an Icon: The Self-Referentiality and Framing of Sor Juana Inés de la Cruz', *Journal for Early Modern Cultural Studies*, 7: 28–56.

Pugliese, O. Zorzi (2004), 'The Development of Dialogue in *Il libro del Cortegiano*: From the Manuscript Drafts to the Definitive Version', in Heitsch & Vallée (2004), 79–94.

Rabin, L. (1997), 'Speaking to Silent Ladies: Images of Beauty and Politics in Poetic Portraits of Women from Petrarch to Sor Juana Inés de la Cruz', *Modern Language Notes*, 112.2: 147–65.

Ramírez de Guzmán, C.C. (2010), *Obra poética*, ed. A. Borrachero Mendíbil & K. McLaughlin (Mérida, Editora Regional de Extremadura).

Sabat de Rivers, G. (1995), 'Veintiún sonetos de Sor Juana y su casuística de amor', in S. Poot Herrera (ed.), *Sor Juana y su mundo: una mirada actual* (Mexico City, Universidad del Claustro de Sor Juana), 397–445.

Solomon, M. (2010), *Literature of Misogyny in Medieval Spain: The Arcipreste de Talavera and the Spill* (Cambridge, Cambridge University Press).

Sommer, D. (1995), 'Mosaic and Mestizo: Bilingual Love from Hebreo to El Inca', *Jewish Studies Quarterly*, 2.3: 253–91.

Sommer, D. (1996), 'At Home Abroad: El Inca Shuttles with Hebreo', *Poetics Today*, 17.3: 385–415.

Stevens, J. (1726), *A New Dictionary, Spanish and English, English and Spanish* (London).

Terry, A. (1982), 'Thought and Feeling in Three Golden-Age Sonnets', *Bulletin of Hispanic Studies*, 59: 237–46.

Vélez Sainz, J. (2015), *La defensa de la mujer en la literatura hispánica. Siglos XV–XVII* (Madrid: Cátedra).

Vian Herrero, A., Vega, M.-J. & Friedlein, R. (eds) (2016), *Diálogo y censura en el siglo XVI (España y Portugal)* (Madrid, Iberoamericana; Frankfurt am Main, Vervuert).

Weiss, J. (2002), '"¿Qué demandamos de las mujeres?" Forming the Debate About Women in Late Medieval Spain (with a Baroque Response)', in Fenster & Lees (2002), 237–81.

Williams, R. (1977), *Marxism and Literature* (Oxford, Oxford University Press).

Zayas y Sotomayor, M. de (2000), *Novelas amorosas y ejemplares*, ed. J. Olivares (Madrid, Cátedra).

Zayas y Sotomayor, M. de (2009), *Exemplary Tales of Love and Tales of Disillusion*, ed. & trans. M.R. Greer & E. Rhodes (Chicago, University of Chicago Press).

Part IV

Neoplatonism in Modern Poetry: Splintered but Vibrant

16

An Equivocal Echo: Eugenio Montale

PETER ROBINSON

1. A Poet and His Muse

Il Corriere della sera, the Milanese daily, reported on its front page for Monday 14 September 1981 that Giovanni Spadolini, the President of the Republic, had attended Eugenio Montale's funeral 'to render homage to a poet who was not only a "lyric voice" of 20th-century European culture, but an ethical protagonist in the life of Italy'. Fourteen years earlier, the poet had received an honorary degree from the University of Cambridge and, in Italy, been made a Senator for life. He was awarded the Nobel Prize for Literature in 1975. Montale's international reputation, though, would follow quickly upon the success of his first book, *Ossi di seppia* (Cuttlefish Bones), which had appeared 50 years before. An article on his work by G.B. Angioletti was featured in T.S. Eliot's *Criterion* in 1927. The following year saw Mario Praz's first English translation, of 'Arsenio' (Montale 1984: 83–4), in the same journal. Montale's poetry was introduced to the United States through an 'Italian Letter' published by *The Saturday Review of Literature* in July 1936. Its author was Irma Brandeis.

Writing to Brandeis on 14 April 1985, Gianfranco Contini allusively began by addressing her as 'Cara Clizia' (Brandeis & Contini 2015: 22), adopting the *senhal* – the 'signal' or codename used by Provencal troubadours for their loves – first employed by Eugenio Montale in his poem 'La primavera hitleriana' (1939–46). Brandeis's reply, dated 22–23 May, firmly rejects this poetic flattery:

> If I had so beautiful a name I would permit no nicknames, or other forms of address. As for me, I must certainly not be called Clizia. I have spent sleepless nights codifying the reasons why I am not she. But in the end there is one that holds and makes me shudder. Clizia, ever-faithful to her love, was a murderess. I think the whole story suits better someone else. I am tired of reading that C. was an American who went back to her own country. I did not want to go.
>
> (Brandeis & Contini 2015: 24)

Brandeis is referring to the source of Montale's nickname in Ovid,[1] and remembering in her final hand-written addition ('I did not want to go') that the Racial Laws of 1938 – Brandeis being American Jewish – and the outbreak of war had made it impossible for her to stay in Italy, or to return for many years. These public and other private reasons on Montale's side were behind the end of their actual involvement, which had begun in the summer of 1933. On 28 June 1985, Contini wrote back in defence of Montale's naming her thus, as he had done some 40 years before: 'He wasn't thinking of Ovid, but of the verses (Dantescan? in my Dante *Rime*, 1939), "the unchanged love you, changed, preserve", independently of the changes of place, and of situations, something that, I'm persuaded of it, was meaningful above all for him' (Brandeis & Contini 2015: 30).

Montale echoes the line ('e 'l non mutato amor mutata serba' – and, changed, the unchanged love preserves) from the sestet of sonnet 74 among poems attributed to Dante. Addressing Clizia by name for the first time in the final stanza of 'La primavera hitleriana', he appears to assert by means of this allusion that the love she bears is to be sacrificed, in a Christ-like act, for the good of humanity (1984: 257, [illegible]):[2]

Look once again
high above, Clizia, it's your fate, you
who, changed, the unchanged love preserves,
until the blind sun you bear in you
is dazzled in the Other and destroyed
in Him, for everyone.

But in May 1985 Irma Brandeis was not to be appeased:

> When I wrote to you I knew the sonnet and the line that led E. M. to choose that name. Indeed, I only learned who Clizia was from your footnote … But I did learn who she was, and the name remains for me somehow an irony. In any case, it is not mine; I was never called by it nor could have been; it belongs only to a figure of poetry.
> (Brandeis & Contini 2015: 32)

The dating of 'La primavera hitleriana' to those seven years from 1939 to 1946 further indicates that her words ('I was never called by it') are quite literally true: Montale never called Brandeis thus either in their correspondence or face-to-face. He had written and posted to her earlier poems, such as the first three 'Mottetti' (1984, 139–41) and 'Costa San Giorgio' (1984: 173–4), which address or evoke her but where she is not signalled by means of this name. Her last visit to Florence, when the two met, happened during the summer of 1938, some months, that is, after the actual Hitlerian spring of the poem which alludes to the tour of Florence

[1] See Ovid, *Metamorphoses*, Bk. IV, ll. 234–73. Contini's note (see Alighieri 1939: 267), describes Clizia as 'daughter of the Ocean and lover of the Sun, who, having with her jealousy provoked the death of Leucothoe, was abandoned by the Sun and turned into a heliotrope or sunflower'. Drusilla Tanzi's threatening suicide on hearing of his intentions towards Brandeis may have contributed to Montale's choice of *senhal*.

[2] Translated quotations from Montale's poetry are referenced to their originals. All renderings are mine.

by the Italian and German dictators on 9 May previous. Moreover, by insisting that 'it belongs only to a figure of poetry' Brandeis puts Montale's equivocal poetics firmly in their place.

Writing to her on 10 December 1934 about the first three of his 'Mottetti', which, strictly speaking, she only partly inspired, Montale assures her that 'by now the liaison [trait-d'union] San Giorgio-Costa S. Giorgio has made [of it] a single mysterious woman', exclaiming 'Mysteries of autobiographism! Beatrice and the Donna Velata' (Montale 2006: 116). Within a year and a half of their first meeting, then, Montale had recruited Brandeis as a Dantescan spiritual guide. By 1985, though, she had outlived her poet by four years, and his equivalent of Bice di Folco Portinari, or the Raphael 'Veiled Woman' in the Pitti Palace, writes back to dissociate herself from the 'figure' that she had been metamorphosed into for the purposes, albeit lofty ones, of his wartime poetry. If these unforeseen consequences result in irony, then it is much to the purpose of this chapter, for here the real person in a real place writes to reject a spiritualisation of herself – and not only on account of the inappropriateness of the Ovidian source, but for whatever thoughts could produce sleepless nights codifying the reasons why there has occurred, as it were, a case of mistaken identity.

What's more, Montale had not begun by thinking of her as a sublimated, a spiritualised messenger or guide, even if he quickly found himself embracing the terms for doing such a poetical thing. Irma Brandeis had read the poet's first book *Ossi di seppia* (1925) when hoping to meet Montale in 1933 at his workplace, the Gabinetto Vieusseux in Florence. From their subsequent six-year involvement the poet would adapt her into a 'donna amata', as in Dante, and employ this 'figure of poetry' for an aesthetic wrestling with his times, the results of which would appear in his second and third books, *Le occasioni* (1939) and *La bufera e altro* (1957), as well as inspiring epilogues such as 'Clizia dice' and 'Nel '38' (see 1984, 712–21) in *Altri versi* (1981). Elaborated over the years after their first encounter, until plans to be united were abandoned during the 12 months or so after their final meeting in that summer of 1938, Montale's love poetry would be conceptualised as a spiritual resistance to Fascist Italy, a resistance in which the poet's being driven inwards by events, both public and private, would drive on his poetry's spiritual ascent.[3]

The two allusions to Plato in his correspondence with Brandeis between 1933 and 1939 – when, aside from a brief note in the last year of his life, it ceased – are both strongly negative. A letter dated 9 May 1934 explains that because 'I have *never* been near for long the women I have loved', Brandeis must not think him 'un cold lover', as Montale puts it in his macaronic Italo-English, and he continues:

> This has made of me a being capable of a sort of enormous compelled Platonism; capable of living for an idea even for years and years and to anticipate a minute

[3] Thirty years after his definitive separation from Brandeis, Montale reflected on earthly brushes with divine presences in 'Divinità in incognito' (1984: 376–7), dated 28 October 1968, and composed in his plain-spoken, editorialising later style.

> for centuries and to prolong it without end. I say 'compelled', 'obliged', because in reality *I hate* Platonism and believe that in life there exists nothing other than 5 September with variants and additions.

Montale's letter continues in his own English: 'if I dream you I don't dream your Soul, I dream your lips, your eyes, your breast, and the rest which is *not* silence. I dare say that the rest is the best and Shakespeare knew it' (2006: 77). Though Rosanna Bettarini (Montale 2006: xv) thinks that '5 September' refers to an especially romantic evening on the Rampe from Piazzale Michelangelo, Florence (the setting of 'Costa San Giorgio'), David Michael Hertz (2013: 61) believes that Montale and Brandeis spent the night together on 5 September 1933 at the Hotel Bristol in Genoa before she boarded ship for her return to New York. The poet's 1 June 1934 letter may confirm this latter view, for when looking forward to further intimacy he jokily asks her to 'bring something in order not to build many Arsenii or Irme' (2006: 85), 'Arsenio' being one of his self-names, as in the early poem of that title (1984: 83–4)

The poet's expressed hatred of Platonism is based on its 'compelled' and 'obliged' (words in English in the original) nature for him – a tribute to the idea, alive during their separation through the winter and spring of 1933–4, that they would eventually enjoy a full physical relationship, and be together either in Italy or America in the not distant future. But by the time of the second reference to Plato, the possibility of their being able to enjoy such a life, then or in the future, had been severely tested by the revelation that Montale was already complexly involved with Drusilla Tanzi, who had threatened suicide in the winter of 1934–5 on hearing of Montale's intentions towards Brandeis. In English on 7 March 1936, he attempts to explain a situation that would not evolve as he imagines here:

> On a point only I never was contradictory with me and with Her: telling to me, telling to her that it was impossible in my mind to live without you. I hope, I am almost sure when she'll be entirely convinced of this point she will make the first step toward my freedom. I hope, I am almost sure that this moment is not far. What I try is to let not a bloody trace behind me, not to create a ghost between us when our life will begin difficult and hard.
>
> (2006: 208)

The continuing presence of the suicide-threatening Drusilla in the poet's life would be one reason why he would be obliged to elaborate the Clizia figure and to evolve her role in his poetry through the following decade.

That second reference occurs in a 17 July 1935 letter where Montale writes: 'I hated Platone, the old greek pederast. I hated sexual business without love. I hate i medioevali costumi di questo paese [the mediaeval customs of this country] in love affairs' (2006: 161). Yet, as we have seen from his borrowing for 'La primavera hitleriana', aspects of such customs would immediately attract him. On 5 December 1933 he writes asking her for negatives of snapshots: 'I speak of *negatives* – because I'll take care of the enlargement. Do me this pleasure, Irma … like Guido Cavalcanti "molto di ciò ten preco"' (2006: 38), citing line 25 of the canzone 'Perch'i' no spero di tornar giammai'. But for Brandeis's *negatives* read the *soul* or *spirit* of Cavalcanti's love object, and for the allusion to Cavalcanti's exile *from* Florence, read Montale's exile *in* that same city.[4]

On 24 April 1965, Montale delivered the final presentation at a conference in Florence on the seventh centenary of Dante's birth. Eventually entitled 'Dante ieri e oggi' (Dante yesterday and today), this essay asserts that for the contemporary poet Dante's era is definitively over: 'If we consider the *Commedia* as a "summa" and an encyclopedia of understanding the temptation to repeat and emulate the prodigy will always be irresistible; but the conditions for success no longer exist' (1996a, II: 2687). In asserting this, Montale echoes Benedetto Croce's influential *La poesia di Dante* (1921), in which the unity of *La divina commedia* is 'quite irrelevant to the poetic experience' (Brandeis 1960: 11) – as Irma Brandeis puts it in the introduction to *The Ladder of Vision: A Study of Dante's Comedy*.[5] It is as if the poem's 'period' structure provides an extended trellis for the blossoms of its poetry: we can enjoy the verse and ignore the woodwork.

Yet Montale's lecture is speckled with indications of ways in which his listeners, by 1965, might have understood him to be acknowledging consciously undertaken debts to a poet supposedly no longer usable as an exemplar. He mentions, for example, the 'merely academic' question '*de mulieribus*', of who the women evoked in Dante's *Rime* and *Vita Nuova* may have been (1996a, II: 2678), and alludes positively to that same book, *The Ladder of Vision: A Study of Dante's Comedy* by the object of his romantic aspirations from 30 years before, a book which had first appeared five years earlier and is a respectful refutation of Croce's theory in its emphasis on the integral artistic and theological purpose of Dante's poem.

Outlining Brandeis's governing metaphor for his Florentine audience, Montale notes that this book 'is the most suggestive account I have read of the ladder which leads to God, and not for nothing is it placed under the patronage of St Bonaventura'. He then translates the book's epigraph by this 'Seraphic Doctor': 'Since, then, one must climb Jacob's ladder before descending it, let us place the first step of the ascent far down, putting the whole of the sensible world before us as it were a mirror through which we may pass to God' (Brandeis 1960: title page). And Montale adds: 'Ladder or mirror or ladder mirrored?' (1996a, II: 2686) Brandeis had in effect answered his question in her first chapter called 'Substance and Idea' when she describes St Bonaventura as discovering God 'diversely mirrored in each rung' (1960: 16).

[4] Cavalcanti's lines (1967: 61) beg: 'se tu mi vuoi servire, / mena l'anima teco / (molto di ciò ti preco) / quando uscirà del core' (if you wish to serve me, / lead your soul / (much of that I beg you) / when it issues from the heart).

[5] Brandeis's title, and her book's shadowy dispute with Montale, could have been suggested by the opening line of his 'Siria' (1951–2): 'Dicevano gli antichi che la poesia / è scala a Dio' (The ancients would say that poetry / is a stairway to God). But 'Forse non è così / se mi leggi' (Perhaps it's not so / if you read me), he adds (1984: 240).

Brandeis's study grazes the Neoplatonic theme when she evokes the 'idea of the world as a theophany – a shifting play in time and space of tangible forms, each realising some infinitesimal portion of the divine immaterial principle', which, she adds, 'was not new when Dante wrote'. She believes he may have encountered it in 'the Arabian Sufi poets' (1960: 15) as well as 'forecast in Thomas Aquinas' doctrine that the ideas of all things existed in the mind of God in anticipation of the Creation' (1960: 15). She suggests that Dante will have known 'such teachers as Honorius of Autun and Hugh of St Victor' who 'had read the life of each beast and plant as a living allegory' (1960: 16), while a study of *Platonism and Poetry in the Twelfth Century* notes that 'Hugh of St. Victor inspired ... Bonaventure' (Wetherbee 1972: 66) – from whom Brandeis took the ladder image for her title. With the aid of these variously Neoplatonic sources she argues, *pace* Croce, for the *Commedia* as an integrated poetic and ethical structure to which the inspirational muse-figure, Beatrice, is central for her poet, who is finally 'reunited with the beloved lady through whom he had caught his first glimpses of the truth, and with her help sees the life of perfected being' (1960: 19). Underlining the Platonic sign under which she is writing, Brandeis cites for the epigraph to her final chapter, called 'The Ladder of Vision', the explanation of why 'God invented and gave us sight' from the *Timaeus* (1960: 168).

Echoing his old love, who notes that like 'Osiris, Odysseus and Aeneas, the hero of the *Comedy* enters the country of the dead' (1960: 19), Montale underlines the importance of Dante's making himself the *personaggio* of his visit to the underworld, so that, for the first time, the writer of the poem is the central character of its drama: 'the personage-hero of a project reserved until then to an Aeneas and a Saint Paul, is, albeit with the assistance of Virgil, the writer himself, the Poet' (1996a, II: 2680). This too, in his way, Montale takes on, not so much by producing the *Vita di un uomo* (Life of a man) like Ungaretti, or a *Canzoniere* (Songbook) of his life and loves, as Saba would, but by dramatising his times in the light of his own attenuated amatory interlocutors, of whom Brandeis (both as and as not Clizia) was by far the most important – so that the 'Xenia I and II' elegies (1984: 287–318) that he dedicated to his eventual wife, Drusilla Tanzi, after her death on 12 October 1963 resemble a Hardy-like too-late reparation.[6]

Even the poet's six-year hesitation, about whether his future would keep him in Italy with Drusilla or take him to America with Irma, can be seen as a wavering between the earthly possibilities which could be characterised by his saying 'in reality *I hate* Platonism' and the emergence of just such an equivocally Platonism-derived role for the latter woman, transformed, in his poetry. Towards the end of that spiritualising human hesitation, one which prompted many of the finest poems from his second book, *Le occasioni* (1939), Montale included in a 31 July 1938

[6] In the Dante essay, Montale cites *Purgatorio* 30, 46–8, lines adapting Virgil's 'veteris vestigia flammae' (*Aeneid*, IV, 23), the phrase Hardy used as epigraph to his 'Poems of 1912–13', which the Italian poet knew.

letter in his faulty English this echo of the Platonic theory of love: 'you are my half or you are nothing, you have present the link that unites our lifes, that link I have forced and worn but not broken' (2006: 225), and concludes: 'If I am a third rade [*sic*] poet no one can make a genius of me; but I have to breath and to discover in you the breath of God, the work of a Divinity!' (2006: 226)

2. A Memory of the Absolute

'In margine alle "occasioni" ', Vittorio Sereni's 1940 review of Montale's second book, identifies an 'initial attitude of the minor poet, one would say; without ambitions to eternal poetry', but, the younger writer adds, on the contrary, 'the configuration of his images, the echo of his words leaves in us a memory of the absolute' (2013: 818). *Le occasioni*, published the previous year, would serve Sereni as a spiritual companion throughout the war – which, for him, was to include two years of imprisonment as a POW of the Allies mostly spent in North Africa. Meeting Montale in Florence during July 1942, when expecting to be posted to North Africa to join the Axis forces halted within striking distance of Cairo, Sereni would recall in 'Ognuno conosce i suoi':

> Montale asks me (and it seems a pure question of politeness): 'What are they saying in the regiment?' What did he want them to be saying? Rommel at El Alamein, the Germans in the Caucasus and on the Volga ... 'Seeing as,' he says 'you're just in time to enter Alessandria with parade-ground step ... But in the regiment, how do they see it?' I'm embarrassed once more, knowing I'll displease him by responding that in the regiment it looks ... good. 'Which doesn't mean,' I hasten to add, 'that the Axis have won the war' ('But ... [who] with you at the burning mirror / that blinds the pawns can deploy / your steely eyes') was the irresistible and, naturally, unexpressed, thought. (2013: 1011)

Sereni's unspoken thought-allusion here cites the closing two and a half lines of 'Nuove stanze' (New Stanzas), a poem whose occasion was provided by Brandeis's visit to Florence in that summer of 1938; and, though Sereni could not have known this while reviewing *Le occasioni* in 1940, or when remembering lines from this poem at his meeting with Montale in 1942, those 'steely eyes' are those of *I. B.* – the book's mysterious dedicatee first identified thus in the 1949 Mondadori edition. Their role in Montale's poem, and in the life of that young poet in uniform about to be posted to the front just before what Churchill would call 'the end of the beginning', points towards the connection between Montale's 'compelled' Platonism and the employment of that 'echo' and 'memory of the absolute' as a form of resistance to the times through which they were compelled to live.

Yet Montale had divined the terms for just such a deepening and engaging of his art when still a young poet on the Ligurian coast at Monterosso. To Brandeis on 10 January 1934, he wrote in English: 'Surely, it's not possible to pick up a philosophy in my poems. But there is a sort of philosophy: perhaps idealism in the first poems' (2006: 47).[7] When in 'I limoni' (The Lemon Trees), composed in November 1922, Montale finds himself hesitating on the threshold of discovering 'a mistake of Nature' which, if followed out, will place us 'nel mezzo di una verità' (in the middle of a truth) and in touch with 'some disturbed Divinity', he had, in effect, already prepared the terms for addressing Brandeis as a divinity in his 31 July 1938 letter – which may even be a memory of his own poem, a poem in which he characterises the paradoxical concretion of his mature poetry (1984: 11):

> You see, in these silences where things
> abandon themselves and seem close
> to betraying their ultimate secret,
> at times you wait here
> to discover a flaw in Nature,
> the dead point of the world, the link that won't hold,
> the thread to unravel that finally puts us
> in the middle of a truth.

The passage combines a sense of lack or damage (the 'sbaglio di Natura' and the 'punto morto del mondo'), and a pessimism in this 'sbaglio', this 'punto morto', but then revalues it as a means to place us 'nel mezzo di una verità'. Given what sounds like a Dantescan allusion here ('nel mezzo del cammin'), it is difficult not to think that this 'verità' must be a transcendental truth, and an indication of the poet's ongoing temptation to imitate his forebear's prodigious exploit. This intuition seems underlined when, in the next stanza, Montale introduces the terms of an overtly transcendent dimension (1984: 12):

> The gaze rummages around,
> the mind inquires, accords, divides
> in the spreading scent
> when the day weakens further.
> They're the silences where you see
> in every human shadow growing distant
> some disturbed Divinity.

But, as Montale would spell out in his 1965 comments on the modern poet and Dante, the conditions for such an imitation no longer exist, and lyric poets in the 20th century, or perhaps at any time, cannot be expected to have a coherent philosophical position to which their every poem coheres; rather, in magpie fashion, these lines from 'I limoni' articulate a disjunction, and a stretching, between the concrete experience of the Ligurian coast and an ulterior spiritually validated reality. In doing so they may constitute an initial contact with a dualistic and equivocally Neoplatonic strain in his evolving poetics.

In 'Intenzioni (immaginaria)' of 1946 Montale discusses the idea that poetry is no longer a mode of representation but of understanding, and describes, with reference to the poems of *Ossi di seppia*, his sense of living under a glass bell

[7] For indications of Benedetto Croce's place in Montale's philosophical and poetic development, see 'L'estetica e la critica' (1996a, II: 2523–40), and for an account of Croce's influence at this time, see La Penna (2016).

(1996b: 1480). This image had already been used in a 30 November 1934 letter to Brandeis: 'I live in a glass bell like a fish in an acquarium' (2006: 114); but by this post-war stage, it has been self-identified with a brand of idealism in which the world of perception is separated, as a thin veil, from a form of idealist *quid*, or, perhaps, *Ding an sich*. The idea that the material world could provide the rungs on a ladder, mirrored for spiritual ascent, is not a huge step away. This other reality is, Montale asserts, unreachable – but he also suggests that, for him, immanence and transcendence cannot be disentangled, and the musicality that he pursues in his poetry appears to be his instinctive attempt to approximate an arrival beyond the glass bell in which he is spiritually and philosophically enclosed.

Yet the material conditions in these early poems, their earthly occasions, are especially important in Montale's placing the ladder at the lowest possible and this-worldly level – the poet's technique engaged in coordinating the employment of a *rime petrose*, stony rhyme, in musically attuned lyric lines – coordinating in such lines both terms of the dualism articulated in the early poems. Montale's poetry is intent not so much on finding the 'anello che non tiene' (the link that won't hold) as in imitating its holding by collocating the resistant 'things' of his immediate surroundings, figured in his unusually consonantal vocabulary, with that intuited spiritual dimension, by means of his rhythm and melody. In the 'Intenzioni (intervista immaginaria)' he expressed the wish to 'wring the neck of our old aulic language, even at the risk of a counter-eloquence' (1996b: 1480). His distinctive concretion, both of perception and vocabulary, might then be emblematically represented by the hard, glassy rhymes ('abbaglia ... meraviglia ... travaglio ... muraglia ... bottiglia') of his earliest published poem's final stanza (1984: 30):

> And going on in the sun that dazzles
> to feel with a sad marvelling
> how all of life and its travail
> is in this following a wall
> that's topped with sharp shards of bottle.

Thus the images and linguistic detail in Montale's poetry do not appear as the 'no ideas but in things' of a William Carlos Williams, but as mysteriously animistic, suggesting spiritual 'things-in-themselves', however concretely and specifically rendered, because their immanent significances turn out to be forms of 'varco' (passage) or gap through which momentary glimpses of a transcendent elsewhere may be articulated. Even when casual physical things, such as intimate personal objects and attributes, are listed in his poetry, they are presented as giving access to significances other than themselves. This is the fundamental 'doubleness' of Montale's work, providing what Sereni had described as an echo of the absolute.

3. A Historical Role for the Muse

Again in his 'Intenzioni', Montale applies that image of himself as compelled to live under a glass bell not only to the philosophical disposition of his early poetry, but to his daily life in Florence (having moved there from Genoa in February 1927). Thus, the philosophical 'idealism' of his early poetry is extended to figure as a symbol for living as an 'inner emigré' under the Fascist regime – in the style of, as he puts it, Browning in the same city. Thus we find a poet ready to meet someone in Florence, as Dante had done, who will set him on his own spiritual trajectory, and this doubling of the philosophical and political predicaments makes it possible for him to conceive of his attention to immanence in the evocations of scenery as a training in his own 'vocazione trascendente' (1996a, II: 2676).

As early as 30 April 1936, Montale could write to Brandeis in Italian that 'your presence is still grown gigantic in my heart, like a sacred thing' (2006: 218). To Gianfranco Contini on 15 May 1939, he describes the experience of composing a recent poem, the very one that Sereni would silently recall when meeting Montale some three years later:

> *Listen*; fallen into a state of trance (something which rarely comes to me, because usually I write in conditions of cynical self-control) I have given a follow-up to the old STANZAS ...
>
> Follow-up in a manner of speaking. These, that could be entitled 'Love, chess and war vigil', but they will rather bear a 2 and no more, they are a little different. They're more Florentine, more inlaid, harder; but they seem to me good and I hope they seem so to you, above all on a re-rereading. The Martinella, as you know, is a Palazzo Vecchio bell; it only rings, according to Palazzeschi, to indicate 'insult'. *Inter nos* I have heard it even on certain occasions that you understand ...
>
> (Isella 1997: 48)

Here, in the final sentence, Montale uses the very word 'occasioni' that would become the title for his second book, including this poem, not eventually called '2' but 'Nuove stanze', still linking it with the earlier 'Stanze' (1984: 169–70), both of which would be collected in *Le occasioni* later that year. The word translated as 'insult' here, or perhaps 'blame' is 'vituperio', and the bell tolls in the poem's final stanza, frightening the 'ivory shapes' ('sagome d'avorio'). 'Between ourselves', Montale adds with the Latin tag, 'I have also heard it even on certain occasions that you understand'. These 'occasions' will silently allude to that meeting between Hitler and Mussolini in Florence on 9 May 1938, but also, perhaps, to the meeting between Brandeis and Montale in the same city the month after the first indication of the coming Racial Laws had occurred in newspaper articles on the supposed ethnic purity of the Italians.

'Nuove stanze', written in a trance if the poet is to be trusted, begins in an earthly occasion, an interior, which it etherealizes and draws upwards in its opening and over the course of four stanzas (1984: 184):

> Then as the final threads of tobacco
> are spent with your gesture
> in the glass plate, towards the ceiling
> slowly rises the spiral of the smoke
> the chess bishops and knights

regard stupefied; and new rings
follow, more changeable than those
on your fingers.

The scene is the studio apartment at 54 Costa San Giorgio in the Oltr'arno area of Florence, probably in August 1938, and the addressee has just put out a cigarette, which starts rings of smoke rising towards the ceiling above the bishops and knights of a chess game. The upward motion of these symbols of love and marriage, associated with the actual rings on her fingers at the close of the verse, figures the trajectory of the poem's subsequent stanzas. Though everything has gone up in smoke, as it were, the way it has gone up signifies a spiritualised ascent, and foreshadows what Montale would be more or less compelled to do if he was to maintain connection with the woman evoked.

Montale explicated the movement of this poem between its four stanzas as an ever-greater spiritual abstraction. In a 22 May 1939 letter to his friend Bobi Balzen Montale speaks of a certain *fantaisiste* tone in the first stanza which rises to that 'classic' one in the second: 'With the 3rd stanza the tone rises again; and to the 4th we are in a zone where the word "classicism" has no more sense. In this progress is the secret of the *Stanze*' (1996c: 203). In the second verse this rising spiral of smoke is troubled by a breath from outside, from an opened window, which occasions a glimpse of the political realities that are also disturbing this love and its meanings: 'a swarming / of men not knowing this incense of yours, / on the chessboard for which only you / can assemble the sense'. In the third, the poet recalls an earlier doubt about whether she was unaware of this 'game' of black and white played out beyond that room with its chessboard, and imagines how her look might call 'beyond the thick / curtains that, stood by, the god / of chance, he stirs for you'.

Then, in the final stanza the tone rises once more into a confirming revelation, one instigating a further purpose granted to the poet (1984: 185):

Now I know what you want; la Martinella
strikes its weak peal and frightens
the ivory shapes in a spectral
snow-fall light. But it's him resists
and wins the lonely vigil's prize,
the one with you at the burning mirror
that blinds the pawns who can oppose
your steely eyes.

'Nuove stanze' is a founding poem in the conversion of Irma Brandeis from a human person with whom the poet was in regular epistolary contact, and with whom he had sustained the near-fiction of a possible life together, into a visiting angel who could be used, in poetry, to figure a spiritual resistance to the shaming degradations and horrors that he and those around him would then have to endure from the 'swarming /of men' on the political chessboard outside. This same role can also be detected in a poem added to the second edition of *Le occasioni* and dated 1940, 'Il ritorno' (The Return), which, through their correspondence, can now be securely associated with a visit paid to Bocca di Magra, indicated as the location of the poem beneath its title, by the poet and his American love in September 1934. For though critics had associated this poem with a woman Montale had known on his summer holidays at Monterosso, and who may well have contributed to the poem's verbal density, nevertheless, his correspondence underlines Brandeis's role. In a 26 September 1934 letter he writes in Italian: 'that day, and the following one at Bocca di Magra you were very hard with me, and everything seemed useless and impossible (at least to you)' (2006: 94).

The occasions of Montale's second book have, then, what appears to be an 'onlie begetter', in the form of the book's eventual dedicatee, given with her initials as if imitating the dedication to Shakespeare's *Sonnets*. They also have '*Grund und Boden*' (ground and foundation), as Goethe put it when telling Eckermann that all of his poems were occasional poems ('*Gelegenheitsgedichte*').[8] Yet Montale's occasions again contain a bifurcation, one suggested by the further implications of the word 'occasioni' – for not only do these poetic moments befall, or chance to happen, as in the 'dio / del caso' (the god of chance) from the third verse of 'Nuove stanze', as the Latin root in 'cadere', shared with 'cadence', would suggest, but they are also 'opportunities', or even 'bargains' (in which mutual loss and gain must be accepted), as when the word is pasted on the windscreens of Italian second-hand car dealerships. What is thus revealed by the publication of the correspondence between Montale and Brandeis is that the poet was caught in this bifurcation, only able fully to take advantage of the opportunity provided by their meetings in one direction, namely poetry; or, put more sharply, it was only because he was not able to resolve his dilemmas and take the earthly, human opportunity offered, was unable to strike a non-Platonic bargain, that he was both compelled and enabled to exploit these poetic occasions in a direction that, I am suggesting, contains such an equivocally Neoplatonic echo.

4. From Real Woman to Visiting Angel

Finisterre, a 15-poem postscript to the thwarted love story in *Le occasioni*, had to be published, given the conditions in Italy, with Contini's help in Lugano, Switzerland, in 1943. It was described by Montale as encapsulating his 'Petrarchan' experience, by which he may have meant that the definitive loss of Irma in 1939–40 was, for him, like the death of Laura, which prompted the so-called 'in morte' part of the *Canzoniere*. Montale spelled this out in his comments to Glauco Cambon on 'Giorno e notte' (Day and Night), the book's thirteenth poem: 'But who is she? Certainly, at first, real woman; but here and elsewhere, everywhere rather, *visiting angel*, barely or not material.' Then, explaining the characteristically double imagery (both

[8] 'All my poems are occasional poems, they have been prompted by reality and thus have ground and foundation. I don't hold with poems plucked out of the air' (Eckermann 1948: 48).

present thing and sign of other significance), he adds: 'Feather, glint in the mirror and other signs (in other poems) are no more than the enigmatic announcements of the event about to occur: the "privileged" instant (Contini), often a visitation.' This figure, who Montale would soon name Clizia, 'cannot return in flesh and bone' since 'she has ceased for a long time to exist as such. Perhaps she's been dead for some time, perhaps she'll die elsewhere in that instant' (1996b: 1498). 'Giorno e notte' also contains the image of an 'antro / incandescente' (incandescent cave) which is glossed in Jonathan Galassi's notes as 'a reference to the myth of the cave in Plato's *Republic*' (Montale 2000: 550), though it may equally be an image of insomnia, and an invocation of the space in which the spirit of love may visit him. While it promises to overcome the violence and disturbance of wartime Florence, it may also report on the 'fight to the death', as it were, between the two women in his life.

Montale wrote in his 1946 'Intenzioni (Intervista immaginaria)' that 'art is the form of life of those who don't truly live' (1996b: 1476). Significantly, though, however much Goethe's *Gelegenheitgesdichte* contributed to the title and thinking behind Montale's *Le occasioni*, the German poet was of quite the opposite opinion, writing in 'Dreistigkeit' (Boldness) from his *West-Oestlicher Divan* that 'Before he sings and before he ceases, / the poet must live' (1974: 20). If it is the case that the correspondence with Irma Brandeis and the poems Montale wrote under the spell of that involvement follow a thread leading from an insisted on anti-Platonic position, though one which strongly acknowledges its terms, through to the projection of an imagined spiritual support that communicates with the poet through rendered moments of immanence, then a distinct difference between Goethe's and Montale's 'occasions' emerges.

Yet the 'compensation' or 'surrogate' that the Italian poet takes art to be may then go into the lived lives of others, such as the young Sereni, and accompanies them through sometimes extremely testing situations – as *Le occasioni* had done for him and his wartime generation. By adding its spiritualising to life, in this fashion, Montale's echo of the infinite had helped at least one younger poet to live, and indeed survive, so that he too could sing and cease, as Goethe would put it, in the post-1945 world of Italy's economic miracle. Thus, if the experience and composition of *Le occasioni* enacts a spiritualising move from Goethe's sense of life and art to Montale's as expressed in his imaginary interview, his poetry's reception by readers may serve as a re-instigation of the German poet's priorities.

5. A Heretic's Dream of Salvation

In his 1981 interview with Geoffrey Hill, John Haffenden asks: 'do you actually practice any faith? Would you class yourself as an agnostic, or would you assent to Harold Bloom's term "desperate humanist"?' The poet replies:

> I would not wish to describe myself as an agnostic. There is a phrase by Joseph Cary in his book *Three Modern Italian Poets* – I forget which poet he's referring

> to – that, if it were applied to my own poetry, might seem to be not wholly irrelevant, 'a heretic's dream of salvation expressed in the images of the orthodoxy from which he is excommunicate'. That seems to me an apt phrase to describe the area in which my poetry moves.
>
> (1981: 97–8)

The phrase appears in the discussion by Cary of Montale's poem 'Iride' (Iris), a work that opens the section of *La bufera* including 'La primavera hitleriana':

> A heretic's dream of salvation, expressed in the images of the orthodoxy from which he is excommunicate – that would be one of the ways of describing what is going on here. 'Iris,' the title of the poem and the *donna*'s newest *senhal*, is not only a flower and thus part of the company of the floral presences with which the poem is tissued, not only synecdoche for the eye of *coscienza* [conscience] which is one of her main signs, not only the name of the rainbow goddess and messenger for the Olympians, but also and above all – as the poem will say – *Iri del Canaan*, the rainbow of the Promised Land, the Lord's own sign of covenant with the lost and wandering.
>
> (Cary, 1969: 316–17)

Cary's words ask whether Montale was, as Hill imagines, a heretical excommunicate, longing for the forms of salvation that he cannot have, or whether he is, rather, a non-believing poet making use of the ancient structures as a form of serious game (more like a Stevens or Arnold), by which he is able to articulate the idea that Christ's task can be forwarded despite formal Christianity, and despite the non-existence of the teleology that would support it. Reviewing a bilingual edition of Stevens's poetry in 1954, Montale noted that 'Sunday Morning', the title poem of the collection, is 'a portrait of a woman prismatically decomposed, which has cosmic implications and celebrates an absolute pantheism' (1996a, I: 1649).

The Christian imagery in 'Iride', which begs the question of whether its poetic fiction parasites off such religious beliefs or supports them, is evident. Montale's poem evokes 'the bloodied Face on the shroud / which divides me from you', and then continues (1984: 247 [illegible]):

> this and little else (if your sign
> is little, a wink, in the struggle
> that pushes me into a charnel-house, back
> to the wall, where celestial sapphires
> and palms and storks on one leg can't
> close off the atrocious view from
> the poor, lost Nestorian).

Nestorius (386–450) believed that the human and divine persons of Christ were separate, a view declared heretical at the Council of Ephesus in 431. In the course of discussing the contribution of *Thaïs* (1890), the novel by Anatole France, to Montale's 'Nubi color magenta' (Magenta-Coloured Clouds), Franco Fortini insists that we 'need also to ask ourselves if the "Nestorian", that's to say he who would not see the unity of the contradiction, the anti-dialectic (in reality, the gnostic and the Neoplatonic tempted by a demiurgic vision of the universe as a system of emanations), if we don't find ourselves here in a condition very similar to that of Paphnutius' (2003: 624). For Fortini, Christ's double existence as both human and divine is understood as a form of dialectics, so that the Nestorian is a denier both of the Christian mystery and the Hegelian structure in Marxist thought. The machinery of Montale's political and spiritual deliverance is found thus to be thwarting that aspirant release. In the third verse of 'Nubi color magenta', Montale admits to being 'Like Paphnutius in the desert, too / intent on conquering you, I'm conquered' (1984: 269). Fortini takes this to be emblematic of the political, cultural and spiritual predicament in Montale's poetry, defeated by its own best intentions.

The role of this analysis in Fortini's criticism is, from his socialist perspective, to reinterpret the equivocally Neoplatonic echo in Montale's poetry as a displacement. Fortini can then see Montale as an exemplary and instructive instance of how his culture had attempted to oppose Fascism, on grounds of taste, without identification with the class struggles that had been the focus of this poet and critic's lifelong commitments. Montale, he had earlier observed 'anticipated those works in images which are the only *nekyia* of the Italian bourgeois intellectual class, its only authentic descent into the hells of its own inauthenticity' (2003: 615, n. 2). By characterising Montale's poetry as a 'rite by which ghosts were called up and questioned about the future' (ἡ νέκυια), he allows himself to celebrate the genuine poetic and historical engagement of the poet's art while simultaneously preserving a Marxist critique of the Italian middle-class's aesthetic resistance to Fascism.

In this light, however gnostic or Neoplatonic Montale's echo might be, his art is no longer pretending to a love it cannot have, but rather attempting to use poetry's own resources in relation to Neoplatonic thought as a means for resisting the barbarism and irrationality of the politics through which he lived. Yet the high cultural terms for this form of resistance had then been, themselves, subjected to a criticism by Fortini, which sought, as it were, to save Montale's poetry from himself, and from its use as an alibi for what he would believe an evasion.

In the context of Christian heresy here in 'Iride', the relation of the body to the spirit, Montale's associating himself with this figure from the early church leads on to a spiritual invocation plainly articulated and italicised at the poem's close (1984: 248):

> If you appear, here you return me, under the pergola
> of bare vines, beside the landing-stage
> of our river – and the ferry not come back,
> the St Martin's sun dissolves, black.

Again in his 'Intenzioni' Montale accepted the charge of obscurity in this poem (1996b: 1483–4), which derives from the heretical theology employed to give significance to this transcribed dream visitation, one in which a poet with a strongly agnostic, even nihilistically pessimistic streak, would go about attributing to his

Jewish-American spiritual guide, a Christ-like role in the re-establishment of a civil society in the aftermath of war in Europe (1984: 248):

> But if you return you're not you, your
> earthly story's changed, you don't
> wait for the prow at the ferry,
>
> you don't have looks, yesterday or tomorrow;
>
> *because His work* (which is transformed
> in yours) *has to be continued.*

The poem's conclusion collocates the spiritual visitations of his Clizia figure with the salvific role of Christian sacrifice. It is as if as a strictly 'lay' poet without any religious affiliations he nonetheless sees, in the aftermath of the war, no other alternative for humanity than to use its deep cultural traditions – such as the role of a beloved woman in troubadour poetry and its Italian adaptors – as a defence against barbarism. He is not so much a heretic longing for salvation as an atheist seeking to deploy his spiritualised sexual feelings as a transformed religion.

In the only book dedicated to relations between Italy's greatest mediaeval and modern poets, Ashi Pipa follows up on the core point of Montale's lecture on Dante at the present time, identifying crucial differences between the roles of the two most inspiring women in their works:

> We have thus the divine Beatrice on the one hand and the numinous Clizia on the other. This longing for angelic womanhood is essentially the mythic translation of a metaphysical urge to sound the 'sea of being' with a plumb line, as it were, in the hands of a privileged woman. The real conception takes place within a womb, after all, and the poet may hope to learn something of his own mental conception by committing himself to a woman possessed with divinatory powers. It is the underlying theme of Plato's *Symposium*, in which Socrates takes lessons from Diotima concerning the mystery of love.
>
> (1968: 141)

The story of Montale's poetry might then be seen as first expressing a propensity to an idealist dualism derived from an early reading of Croce, which, in his relations with Irma Brandeis, he can be seen attempting to contest and escape. But the obstacles to that escape occasion a recidivism of sorts, and the narrative of his relations with her between 1933–4 and 1938–9 see him in effect compelled to live that dualism by both losing her and keeping her in another form: 'You know: I've to lose you again and I can't', as the first of the 'Mottetti' begins (1984: 139). If this was originally a means for helping him endure what he appears to have hoped would be their temporary separation, it would become, after 1938–9, a means for her recruitment to another poetic purpose. The frustration of that earthbound link across the Atlantic drives his poetic consciousness inward, within that glass bell, and then upwards towards what were in those political times disparaged spiritual values, as in the ascending structure and smoke-rings-like Dantescan circles of his 'Nuove stanze'.

Nevertheless, without this frustrated secular love and its forcing in a different direction, it would not have been possible for him to use this imaginative transition as a resistance to the world in which he lived, and which had played its part in the thwarting of that love. Equally, this resistance would then not have been able to function either as a talisman and support for the young soldier-poet Vittorio Sereni during the wartime, or as a preeminent instance of the inauthenticity authentically diagnosed that Franco Fortini finds in Montale's poems – and it was at a discussion of his post-war legacy that in 1946 these distinguished younger poets first encountered each other (Colli & Raboni 2004: 113). The Neoplatonic echo in Montale's poetry, if that is what it is, survives, then, as a means for turning the thwarted feelings of two people into a form of resistance to temporal powers intent on, in their turn, 'weaponising' race and sexuality in the interests of an exclusive nationalist will. Montale deployed all the accuracy and skill and integrity of his poetry to set his own intuitions of immanence, and tacit transcendence, against that political 'faccia di bronzo', against that brazen face.

References

Alighieri, D. (1939), *Rime*, ed. G. Contini (Turin, Einaudi).

Brandeis, I. (1960), *The Ladder of Vision: A Study of Dante's Comedy* (London, Chatto & Windus).

Brandeis, I. & Contini, G. (2015), *'Questa stupida faccia': Un carteggio nel segno di Eugenio Montale*, ed. M. Sonzogni (Milan, Archinto).

Cary, J. (1969), *Three Modern Italian Poets: Saba, Ungaretti, Montale* (New York, New York University Press).

Cavalcanti, G. (1967), *Rime*, ed. G. Cattaneo (Turin, Einaudi).

Colli, B. & Raboni, G. (2004), *Un tacito mistero: Il carteggio Vittorio Sereni-Alessandro Parronchi (1941–1982)* (Milan, Feltrinelli).

Croce, B. (1921), *La poesia di Dante* (Bari, Laterza).

Eckermann, J.P. (1948), 'Gespräche mit Goethe in den letzten Jahren seines Leben', in J.W. von Goethe, *Gedenkausgabe der Werke, Briefe and Gespräche*, xxiv, ed. E. Beutler (Zürich, Artemis).

Fortini, F. (2003), *Saggi ed epigrammi*, ed. L. Lenzini (Milan, Mondadori).

Goethe, J.W. von (1974), *West-Eastern Divan / West-Oestlicher Divan*, trans. J. Whaley (London, Oswald Wolff).

Haffenden, J. (ed.) (1981), *Viewpoints: Poets in Conversation with John Haffenden* (London/Boston, Faber & Faber).

Hertz, D. Michael (2013), *Eugenio Montale, the Fascist Storm, and the Jewish Sunflower* (Toronto/Buffalo/London, University of Toronto Press).

Isella, D. (ed.) (1997), *Eusebio e Trabucco: Carteggio di Eugenio Montale e Gianfranco Contini* (Milan, Adelphi).

La Penna, D. (2016), 'The Rise and Fall of Benedetto Croce: Intellectual Positionings in the Italian Cultural Field, 1944–1947', *Modern Italy*, 21.2: 139–55.

Montale, E. (1984), *Tutte le poesie*, ed. G. Zampa (Milan, Mondadori).

Montale, E. (1996a), *Il secondo mestiere: Prose 1920–1979*, ed. G. Zampa, 2 vols (Milan, Mondadori).

Montale, E. (1996b), *Il secondo mestiere: Arte, musica, società*, ed. G. Zampa (Milan, Mondadori).

Montale, E. (1996c), *Le occasioni*, ed. D. Isella (Turin, Einaudi).

Montale, E. (2000), *Collected Poems 1920–1954*, ed. J. Galassi (New York, Farrar, Straus & Giroux).

Montale, E. (2006), *Lettere a Clizia*, ed. R. Bettarini, G. Manghetti & F. Zabagli (Milan, Mondadori).

Pipa, A. (1968), *Montale and Dante* (Minneapolis, The University of Minnesota Press).

Sereni, V. (2013), *Poesie e Prosa*, ed. G. Raboni (Milan, Mondadori).

Wetherbee, W. (1972), *Platonism and Poetry in the Twelfth Century: The Literary Influence of the School of Chartres* (New Jersey, Princeton University Press).

17

Eroticism of the Infinite: Neoplatonism, Kabbalism and Sufism in the Work of José Ángel Valente

CLAUDIO RODRÍGUEZ FER*

THE PURPOSE OF this volume is to try to put into context and counteract the conflict and mutual incomprehension that ethnic, cultural and religious divisions are playing out across Europe, Asia and Africa with so much intolerance and violence in our present century by looking back to the ancestral philosophical links of antiquity that unify them; these are to be found in the Neoplatonism of the Greek-Egyptian thinker Plotinus and his followers. However, we will also consider poets as contemporary as the Spaniard José Ángel Valente, who struggled all his life to breathe, write and study in depth, according to his own words, 'in the uninterrupted air of a poetic tradition where East and West must meet one another once more' (Valente 2008: 369).

The Galician poet José Ángel Valente, who was born in Ourense in 1929 and died in Geneva in 2000, is without doubt one of the most important writers in Hispanic literature in the 20th century. He is also one of the most European of Spanish intellectuals (he taught at Oxford and was an international civil servant in Geneva and Paris) and most open to universal otherness due to his life experience (he travelled through Europe, Africa, Asia and America) and his ideological calling (he always defended interculturalism), and to his literary assimilation of the world's diverse mystical traditions (from the Middle East and Far East passing through India). This was reflected in his excellent creative work, both poetic and narrative, and in the lucid intellectual deliberations to be found in his rigorous essays or his thoughtful meta-literature, a Kabbalistic expression of a true comprehensive avant-garde and of a demanding ethical and aesthetic critical awareness.

Moreover, the richness of content, form, genre, languages and multi-artistic dialogues that his work offers, as various as it is coherent, is founded on the profound

* The editors are grateful to Caroline Maldonado for her translation of this chapter from Spanish.

assimilation of the most canonical tradition, the most exceptional heterodoxy, and the most open-minded avant-garde. It somehow assumes the bringing together of Spanish Renaissance and Baroque mastery; the art of meditation of the ascetics and Christian, Jewish and Muslim mystics, and the spirit of rupture of the most radical German Romanticism, French and English symbolism, and the European avant-garde of the 20th century. In this way, Valente's creative production is a palimpsest of the literature of all ages. He absorbs the initial teaching of the Spanish poet Francisco de Quevedo (1580–1645) and the English Metaphysics of the 17th century and the later meta-poetics of modernity represented by Lautréamont and Rimbaud, by Cernuda and Lezama,[1] or by Celan and Jabès, in the constant company of St John of the Cross or the discoveries of Hölderlin, the Jewish Kabbalah, Sufi mysticism and the haiku of the East.

As a result, the poetry of José Ángel Valente transcended absolutely the narrow margins of post-war Spanish literature, firstly through the rigorous elaboration of an ascetic discourse and then by cultivating a subversive counter-discourse that led him to the radicalism with which he finally approached the dissolution of discourse, opening the way to his final non-discourse, as demonstrated by the four cycles – three in Castilian and one in Galician – in which he brought together all his poetic work: *Punto cero* (Point Zero, 1953–79), containing his first works; *Material Memoria* (Material Memory, 1977–8), containing his mature works; *Cantigas de alén* (Songs of Long Ago, 1989), containing his poems in the Galician language; and *Fragmentos de un libro futuro* (Fragments of a Future Book, 1991–2000), containing his posthumous work. And to that can be added the compilation of his narrative works, of no less poetic rigour, under the title *El fin de la edad de plata, seguido de nueve enunciaciones* (The End of the Silver Age, followed by Nine Enunciations, 1973).

Valente's openness towards mysticism directed his poetry and essays to the search for, and the discovery of, universals of being that demonstrated, as the author himself said, 'the existence of homogeneous structures within mystical phenomena, whatever their time and place. Certain extreme experiences tend towards analogous forms of language (or of the suspension of language) and towards analogous forms of symbolism' (2008: 371–2). This occurs especially in the expression of eroticism, as he would try to show.

Starting from this point, Valente's creative work and essays became an intercultural space where, both diachronically and synchronically, Platonism, Neoplatonism, Christian mysticism, the Kabbalah and Sufism can be found together.

[1] Luis Cernuda (1902–63), Spanish poet of the 1927 Generation who lived in exile after the Spanish Civil War. He taught in the UK for a while (from 1938) before moving to the United States (1947) and finally Mexico (1952) where he died. He is now considered one of the three great Spanish poets of the 20th century, alongside Antonio Machado and Federico García Lorca. José Lezama Lima (1910–76) was a Cuban poet, who had a great influence on Latin American literature.

1. Neoplatonism and Interculturalism

The poet himself asserted: 'There is Platonism or Neoplatonism in the Sufis, as there is in St John of the Cross, despite his Thomist training' (2008: 316) as well as 'that, despite its evident Neoplatonic premises, the Kabbalah might differ from them in the vision they bring of the catastrophe of materialisation' (2008: 390).

In any case, Valente's Neoplatonism led him somehow to be a neo-Sufi in Al Ándalus, where he lived, for after his retirement from Unesco he settled in Almería, and to be a neo-Kabbalist in Jerusalem, a city that he visited to perform his *Tres lecciones de tinieblas* (Three Lessons of Tenebrae, 1980), composed with reference to the Hebrew alphabet. In this way he converted himself into an authentic advocate of interculturalism. In fact, a large part of his public lectures and his essays propose a harmonious meeting through dialogue and the reclaiming of historical links between cultures of the Middle East and the Mediterranean, always insisting on the need to be aware of the undeniable mystical and poetic connections between Judaism and Islam and Spanish literature.

As a consequence of this theoretical position, he denounced the intercultural impasse in Europe, including polemical statements in the press: 'Interculturalism is only an idea on paper. We continue to be Eurocentric. We don't know other cultures and we are frightened of the other.' And he did so recalling the best moments in inter-Mediterranean relationships, arguing for a more welcoming approach towards immigrants: 'Earlier, the two Mediterranean coasts were praised for their hospitality. The foreigner was a protected species' (1996: 48).

However, focusing on the universal correspondences in the language of the mystics, Valente distinguishes between convergence and transmission, following Rudolf Otto (1932). So, he considers that 'Otto's fascinating work alone shows the existence of homogenous structures within the mystic phenomenon, whatever its time and place'; then, he establishes a 'surprising system of affinities between Sankara (800 CE), the Hindu master of non-duality, and Eckhart (1260–1327), the Rhineland master of simple unity', whose 'possible chain of transmission' is not pertinent. Naturally, 'that homogeneity does not exclude difference. On the contrary, "the essence of mysticism – writes Otto – is only obtained by the totality of its possible distinctions"' (2008: 371–2). In fact, Valente states:

> The different manifestations of the mystical phenomenon are determined by different religious or cultural contexts, but they also go beyond them. For this reason, a German Dominican of the thirteenth century might turn out to be in certain essential aspects closer to Vedanta mysticism or Mahayana mysticism than to the mysticism of Plotinus, despite the obvious constraints of his own tradition. For the same reason, in the work of the 'Germanic Prophetess', Hildegard of Bingen, written more than a century before that of Eckhart, Hans Liebeschuetz draws attention to the presence of factors particular to Iranian cosmologies. Or Swami Siddheswarananda can write: 'When the numerous Indianised visitors who call on us, with a sense of inferiority deplore that no equivalent of the Raja-yoga (supreme yoga of realisation) exists in the Christian

> tradition, we advise them to read the complete works of St John of the Cross several times, as we have ourselves; we are able to state without any doubt that we consider St John of the Cross to be the Patanjali of the West.'
>
> (2008: 372)

However, although Valente maintains 'that the comparatist would need to separate the phenomena of convergence and the phenomena of transmission with great sensitivity' (2008: 372), he does not deny, in fact he precisely restates, the possibilities of dialogue, common identity and universal correlations between ethnic groups, cultures and religions.

Moreover, it is clear that Valente was particularly interested in the correlations between East and West by means of Neoplatonism, Judaism and Sufism, as he said very clearly: 'Without prejudice to their specificity and differing elements, the mystical tradition of the three religions demonstrates from the start the obvious phenomenon of a radical correlation' (2008: 374). For this reason, he was a continuous theoriser on Orientalism in Europe and vice versa:

> There is, on the other hand, Orientalism as a root. Christian mysticism finds its defining forms of expression in the spirituality of the desert, the seeds of monasticism, and the works of the first Fathers. That element, supported by the subsequent dissemination of work by Pseudo-Dionysius, at the heart of which are the works of Origen and Plotinus, is present in all the great founders of Western spirituality from John Cassian to St Benedict or St Bonaventure. Without the *Vitae Patrum* and Cassian's commentaries, we would understand neither Benedictine spirituality nor the asceticism of the Cistercian or Carthusian orders that in France, as Gilson recalls, reproduce the life of the cenobitic and eremitic Egyptian monks. From this we can conclude, in a way, that the more Western mysticism tends towards its more extreme form, the more it finds its origins again and converges towards its natural Orientalism.
>
> (2008: 375)

In this context there is a strong link between Valente and Ibn ʿArabī of Murcia, whom he studied closely, praised and quoted, making use of the Arabist Miguel Asín Palacios's translation of his *Futuḥāt* (1931: 166):

> Maybe nobody has described this convergence more generously or more beautifully, nor with more relevance to the theme that concerns us here, than the man who was called by the Muslims 'son of Plato', the Sufi of Murcia Ibnʿ Arabī: 'I believe everything that the Jew and the Christian believes, and everything that exists in their respective religions and in their revelatory books ... as much as I believe in my own book of revelation ... And truly, my book contains their book and my religion their religion. And so, their religion and their book are implicit in my book and in my religion.'
>
> (2008: 374)

Ibn ʿArabī of Murcia, a Muslim philosopher and Andalusian poet from the period of Sufi mysticism, is without doubt one of the greatest Islamic presences in Valente's vast archive and rich library, donated by him to the University of Santiago de Compostela and in the custody of the 'Cátedra José Ángel Valente de Poesía e Estética'. In fact, the poet collected around 20 of Ibnʿ Arabī's works, mainly in French but also in English and Spanish.

However, if Ibn ʿArabī is Valente's principal example of mysticism, the first and most permanent of his Christian references was Juan de Yepes, canonised by the Catholic Church – after being persecuted by it – as St John of the Cross, whose biblical sources he highlights, mainly following Colin P. Thompson from Oxford University whom, by the way, he frequently quotes and praises in his studies of John of the Cross. Valente and Thompson had actually met one another in Oxford when the former became aware of Thompson's research and analysis for his edition of the heterodox mystic Miguel de Molinos's *Guia espiritual* (Spiritual Guide, 1974), as the poet himself related:

> My work was finishing at the start of 1974. In the spring of that same year I disseminated its results in a graduate seminar led by P.E. Russell in Oxford. Curiously, the person charged with responding to my contribution was Colin P. Thompson, who was then working on what was soon to be one of the best contemporary studies of St John of the Cross's *Cántico espiritual* (Spiritual Canticle).

Moreover, despite the explicit recognition of the biblical sources of St John of the Cross's poetry demonstrated by Thompson (1977), Valente also alludes explicitly to the Neoplatonic sources, above all in relation to desire and its infinity:

> The dynamism of the infinity of desire is the engine and axis of *Canciones de la esposa* (Songs of the Spouse): the theory of a union that consumes itself and the desire for a new more overwhelming union. Perhaps it is clear that the internal impulse of *Cantar de los cantares* (Song of Songs) is no more than that, without it having been compromised and contaminated (naturally, apart from the introduction of a line of thought on Philo and Plotinus) by the spirituality of some of his major commentators, as in the cases of Gregory of Nyssa in the Greek church and Bernard of Clairvaux in the Latin.
>
> (2008: 403)

In his essay 'Eros and divine fruition' Valente begins to highlight how divisions can be overcome by means of mystic union:

> What constitutes mysticism is the extreme experience of union. Beyond visionary rapture, where the *propagatio fidei* has tended to fix the imagery of Christian mystics, mysticism sustains itself with the simple and profound experience of unity: *simplificatio* of the ancients, Meister Eckhart's simple unity, Sankara's *advaita* or state of non-duality.
>
> (2008: 290)

This would be the true interpretation of Eros: 'In the ultimate substance of the soul (*scintilla, apex*, intimate interior) where union occurs, the unification of opposites occurs: human-divine, spouse-beloved, exterior-interior, body-soul, feminine-masculine. This unifying activity of the split being is an activity that, according to a long tradition, corresponds to Eros.'

And with this decisive interpretation Valente refers to the *Enneads* of Plotinus (VI 7 [38] 34):

> The mystic draws the total unifying potential of Eros into the higher states of his experience. From here, strictly speaking, there is no difference of expression between

> divine and loving physical union. *Fruitio, delectatio, dulcedo, voluptas*: the expression of both experiences becomes indivisible, as both experiences are experiences of immersion within a sole unity. 'Lovers who wish to merge together to make themselves one – writes Plotinus – imitate on earth this celestial union.'
>
> (2008: 291)

For Valente, 'There can be no opposition between divine and carnal love (nor sexuality and sacred), just as in poetry the – unique – expression of one or other love should not be split' (2008: 295).

Ample evidence of this lies in his erotic book *Mandorla* (1982), a collection of poems that takes its title from the mystical almond and from the sculpted representations of Christ and the God Pantocrator in an oval of circles cut out and very apparent in Romanesque architecture and Byzantine art, often designed in a shell or associated with a fish shape (like *vesica piscis* already present in Mesopotamia and other ancient civilisations). Already, in the poem that opens the collection, such a sacred mandorla seems to represent to Valente the vulva matrix, showing the dissolution of the Christian divisions between body and soul or between spirit and matter (2006: 409,):

> *Mandorla*
> You are dark in your concavity
> and in your secret shadow contained,
> inscribed within yourself.
>
> I caressed your blood.
>
> You entered me to the depths of your drunken night
> of clarity.

The book, as well as the actual poem 'Mandorla', shows the mystical communion between the erotic and the religious through the female body, conceived as matter in which all divisions actually dissolve, reverting back to their primordial origin. The same happens in the poem 'Graal' [Holy Grail], in the same book, where a woman, or perhaps a welcoming vulva, is the symbolic sacred chalice in which the poet seems to lose himself, confuse himself, fill and empty himself, dissolve and integrate himself until he reaches the centre, that is to say a Neoplatonic unity (2006: 417,):

> *Graal*
> Vulva's dark breath.
>
> In its pulsing the silt fish pulsed
> and I pulsed in you.
> You breathed me
> in your full emptiness
> and I pulsed in you and inside me
> the vulva, word, vertigo and the centre pulsed.

Valente delved into this poetry of origin in his next erotic collection, significantly titled *El fulgor* (Radiance, 1984), a unique poem, in a way, composed of

36 fragments about the body. In poem VII, the dead body drags itself into obscurity without hope before, in an epiphany, encountering the day in sacred woods. He sees the flame, hears the call, and his soul resurrects like Lazarus in the Bible, but with a turning towards the life of the body in the manner of César Vallejo's poem 'Masa',[2] although here it is the body that revives the soul (2006: 446,):

Radiance VII
He hauled his body
like a blind ghost
of his never tomorrow.

All at once,
in the sudden woods
the day burned.
He saw the flame,
recognised the call.

His body raised up his soul,
he started to walk.

Poem XIII draws simultaneously on biblical and Neoplatonic traditions. Thus, the symbol of the stag or the hind thirstily approaching water merges with the motif of the beloved woman who surrenders herself to her own water, identifying herself in it, revealed in the limitless depths of transcendence through her own eyes (2006: 448,):

XIII
In the liquid depths of your eyes
your body leaps the water
like a transparent deer.

In his book *Al dios del lugar* (To the God of Place, 1989) Valente seems to follow traces, by way of dissolving origins and compressing speech, that bring him close to the body as a place of sacred and physical enclosure, like a sacred dithyramb. In it is a metaphysical dawn in which absorption and suction generate light and word, but they can only arise from the primordial darkness of origin and the natural animality of desire once again in the midst of living waters. And, thus, the poet brings us to 'the frontier where awakening warbles', that is to say to the limit where light is made and becomes incarnate in the poetic word, already identified with knowledge and life (2006: 472,):

I drank from you, I drank, I sucked you,
animal submersed in the folds
of your flooded clarity.

Incessantly
the waters lowered

[2] César Vallejo (1892–1938) was a Peruvian poet, writer, playwright and journalist. Although he published only three books of poetry in his lifetime, he is considered one of the great poetic innovators of the 20th century.

towards the trembling throats of light.
Entrails, birds, palpitating
bubbles from your body
entering me.

I drank from you
until day broke from my mouth,
like a dark vacuum on the frontier
where awakening warbles.

Valente thus enters the Neoplatonic tradition that tries to harmonise opposing concepts like light and darkness. In it, visible and deceptive reality contrasts with another, more inapprehensible and mysterious but transcendent, that only appears accessible through poetry, thought and above all love fully realised in the union of bodies, when the dichotomies of life and death or humanity and divinity dissolve in unity and the infinity of the universe. Thus, One can be Everything and Diversity can be One.

One reaches the glowing light facing the dark shadow like a radiant centre equivalent to a solar image, the 'point zero' that Valente speaks of as the infinite's unifying fusion. In this awakening of light, the body of the woman is the bearer of luminous revelation, as the following erotic dawn in the book *Mandorla* shows from its beginning (2006: 416,):

Sunrise is your body and all
the rest still belongs to shadow.

Your slow waves force
the delicate membrane
to waken.

You announce something: not the day
but the quiet
duration of the pulse
in the shadow matrix.

You announce yourself,
advancing and continuous
like duration.

Lasting, like the hard night,
for the night is only the submerged body
of your visible light.

If in Plato the transcendental Good is now identified with Beauty and represented as Light that generates itself as well as being the creator of the Sun, the Neoplatonic tradition tended in poetry to be embodied in the woman. As the object inspired by Love, she was called Light, Beauty and Good. Moreover, in Valente the Good and Beauty embodied in the loved and desired Woman converge spiritually and bodily in the same centre as the one that rises and the one that sets, because reality is everywhere, like a feminine sun illuminating both darkness and elusive but consistent matter. It is unfathomable in its permanence, and like the shortest poem, actually called 'Centre' (from *Fragmentos de un libro futuro*), summarises, a cipher for the erotic in the cosmic infinite (2006: 557,):

> Around the solar female the universe still continues to turn darkly.

However, the infinity of the beloved provoking the epiphany of totality simultaneously creates an infinite desire for the loved person that can only be embodied in the eroticism of the infinite in its free transcendental otherness, without capture or possession. For that reason, it should not surprise us that among Valente's aphorisms, always a highly significant part of his most established and profound thought, is found the following note, absolutely definitive in this respect: 'In a particularly intense book, *Totalité et infini,* Enmanuel Lévinas wrote: "Nothing distances us more from Eros than possession"' (2008: 466).

In reality, Valente has identified himself ever more creatively with the *anima* of femininity than with the *animus* of masculinity, as he made clear in his meta-poetics:

> Maybe the supreme and only radical practice of art is in the exercise of withdrawal. To create is not an act of power (power and creation negate one another); it is an act of acceptance or recognition. To create carries the mark of femininity. It is not an act of penetration into the material, but the passion of being penetrated by it.
>
> (2006: 387)

This attitude led Valente to highlight the importance of symbolic androgyny in the mysticism of all traditions:

> The experience of original unity, the re-absorption of the many into the one, the mystical experience leads to the re-unification of the indivisible, original creature where Eros was formed. According to Clement of Alexandria (quoted by Schubart), Christ said to Mary Salome: 'Men will not see the truth until two have become one and man and woman have given birth to a third being neither man nor woman'. The text quoted by Schubart repeats the words of Thomas the Apostle: 'When you have made of two one … of the male and female one being, so that the male is not male nor the female female … then you will enter the Kingdom'. The theme can be found everywhere. In the yogic context, according to Mircea Eliade, the ritual coupling represents: 'the concurrence of time and eternity' and, on the purely *human* level, 'it is the integration of primordial androgyny, the conjunction in the being itself of the male and female: in short, the restoration of the plenitude that precedes all creation.' The importance of androgyny in Jacob Boehme's mystical system is known. Should we remind ourselves that, in one of the most supreme mystical expressions of all time, St John of the Cross assumes the soul's feminine voice in his *Cántico espiritual*, the first – and, strictly speaking, more apt – title of which was *Canciones de la esposa* (Songs of the Spouse). Curiously, certain mystics such as Sister Katrei,[3] Hildegard of Bingen, or Elisabeth of Schönau, have thought of themselves as masculine at times, as M.-M. Davy has noted. This floating between *animus* and *anima* occurs in many different traditions. Along the mystical path called *rāga*, Krishna's

[3] Sister Catherine (Schwester Katrei) was the supposed spiritual daughter of Meister Eckhart; it is also the title of an early 14th-century mystical treatise declared heretical because it was seen as representative of the Heresy of the Free Spirit.

> devotee on his spiritual journey completely adopts the feminine behaviour of Radha. Eros raised, then, to its extreme unifying potential, Eros not excluding sexual activity (we have already seen elsewhere how naturally it is incorporated in the movement of the spirit), but exceeding it. Excessive and immersive eroticism perhaps more characteristic of the woman than the man, which perhaps explains why the erotic impulse is so under attack in the West's feminine mystical tradition.
>
> (2008: 292)

2. Between the Kabbalah and Sufism

It was in Geneva that Valente discovered the Jewish Kabbalah and where he attended the classes of the Jewish Kabbalist of Sephardic origin, Carlo Suarès, a meeting that we have already touched on in the corresponding section of *Valente vital (Geneva, Savoy, Paris)* (Rodríguez Fer 2014: 272–4). It was also during this period that Valente wrote about the foundation of the Hebrew alphabet, *Tres lecciones de tinieblas* (Three Lessons in Tenebrae; 2006: 393–404). And that was the time when he entered the Islamic Mystical tradition in greater depth. Two encounters, the Jewish and Muslim, would decisively influence his poetic works and essays when he was dissatisfied with the limitations of an exclusively Christian realm. And so, already in his book *Las palabras de la tribu* (The Words of the Tribe), he wrote:

> Hermeneutics is established with the naturalness of the essential in traditions different from those I previously considered to be part of the core of Western Christianity, that is to say, in traditions where language is the depository of occult content that is only manifested in the language itself. The topic of compression of speech seems substantially to do with very different forms in those traditions where language as a whole has not lost its sacred status. As is hardly worth mentioning, I am referring to the Semitic tradition and languages that identify with the language of first naming (the language of Syria or 'language of solar illumination' for Islam) or are considered close to it. The Kabbalah, which most condensed that tradition, has been imbedded in the world of Western Christianity (that strictly speaking lacked a sacred language), not only at the time when the latter set itself up as a great political power, but also in its contemporary form. As indicated by Scholem, whose books on *La Cabala* (The Kabbalah) and *Las grandes corrientes de la mistica judia* (Major Trends in Jewish Mysticism) are in so many ways indispensable. One of the particular characteristics of the Kabbalists is their metaphysically open approach to language, considered to be the actual instrument of divinity. The secret world of divinity is for the Jewish mystic a world of language.
>
> (2006: 88–9)

From that moment on, the discovery of the Jewish Kabbalah led Valente to a whole new philosophical and creative approach, as can be seen in the extraordinary symbolic secrecy of *Tres lecciones de tinieblas*, consisting of a series of monads corresponding to the first letters of the Hebrew alphabet and inspired by the musical rendering of the Tenebrae service celebrated before Easter in the Catholic Church. The work starts from nothingness represented by the first letter, that is to say the Aleph, the absence: 'the point where breath starts' (2006: 397). Furthermore, the poet himself undertook a critique of his work which is essential to understanding his meaning as a 'song about germination and origin or about life as imminence and closeness' (2006: 403–4).

On this journey towards the seeds of Semitism, his close intellectual and ideological relationship with the writer Juan Goytisolo was of supreme importance. Goytisolo was the main representative of cultural and literary Spanish Arabism at that time and also, of course, a close friend, as they both were to Edmond Amran el Maleh. The importance of these two relationships, consolidated in France in Valente's life as well as his work, is faithfully recorded by María Lopo in *Valente en Paris: Fragmentos recuperados* (Valente in Paris: Recovered fragments; Lopo 2014: 363–491).

Juan Goytisolo dedicated to his friend the lucid and illuminating writings collected in his book *Ensayos sobre José Ángel Valente* (Essays on José Ángel Valente) published in 2009 by the Cátedra Valente, with an introduction by the Mexican poet and scholar Luis Vicente de Aguinaga. His point of departure was always the freedom of thought and freedom to create expressed in the essays and poetry of the author in question:

> Both in his essays and in his poetry, José Ángel Valente traced the origins of common intolerance back to most religions. Faced with rigid orthodoxy, the Galician poet asserted the freedom of thought of history's great persecuted men, from St John of the Cross to Spinoza, via Miguel de Molinos, to the Jewish and Muslim mystics. Accused of heresy and persecuted, they sustained the spirit's flame against the 'bureaucratisation of the divine'.
>
> (Goytisolo 2009: 77)

Edmond Amran el Maleh himself is the author of an early study of *Tres lecciones de tinieblas* in which the distinguished teacher identifies the poet's perspective in relation to the Kabbalistic beginnings of original migration and so defines his poetry correctly as an overture song. Precisely because of his training in the Kabbalah, El Maleh would always insist on the impossibility of any task of deconstruction and on the necessary avoidance of any possible interpretation of Valente's poetry (El Maleh 1992). As for Frank Savelsberg (2008), he undertook his thorough approach to *Tres lecciones de tinieblas* starting from its contexts, and, as will be seen, Fatiha Benlabbah (2008b) and Jorge Machín-Lucas (2010) placed him in between the Christian and Islamic traditions. Savelsberg emphasised the open nature of the poetry collection without denying its affiliation:

> Moreover, the polysemic nature of Hebrew letters is also found in Valente's texts which can be understood as representations of different meanings and functions of the letters: the consonantal sign, the numeric values and meaning by way of pictographic symbols … This archetypical character of the letters refers to the Kabbalah's interpretation of the act of Creation and its beliefs can also be found in *Tres lecciones de tinieblas* by resorting to the Tetragram and all the linguistic thought associated with it in the Kabbalah.
>
> (Savelsberg 2008: 128)

In fact, the Kabbalah and Sufism are complementary sources of Christian mysticism and of Valente's intercultural spiritual development. Accordingly, as Jorge Machín-Lucas has set out, they are the breeding ground for the secular poetry of the author of Mandorla:

> We also depend on the Jewish Kabbalah's sources relating to letter and word being sources of the creation of human beings and the world, just as those of Muslim Sufism are pertinent with their songs of divine love and their natural, almost erotic, symbolism. He has revitalized all of them and redirected them, fertilised by his own poetic imagination, towards a secular poetry, in the form of pagan theophanies, visions of the fragmentation of being, an expression of his own sense of futility and inability to reach the radiating centres of his life.
>
> (Machín-Lucas 2010: 291)

In a spirit of reciprocity, Valente approached the work of Edmond Amran el Maleh, with the same openness, shown in the latter's article 'The cypresses of the absurd'. His aim was to publish a Spanish translation of the Moroccan Jewish writer's first novel *Parcours immobile* (Motionless Journey, 1983), which was in fact prefaced by Juan Goytisolo. There, according to Valente, 'personal memory' comes together with 'the struggle of the Moroccan people for their independence' during the years 1948–59, but in a manner characteristic of the man, activist and writer, in a prose that appears to breathe its own life towards enlightenment: 'the loss and rediscovery of identity' (2008: 1462–3).

He mentions and quotes Edmond Amran el Maleh in his writings and already in his first lesson on *Tres lecciones de tinieblas* uses as an example 'Abraham Abulafia, father and guardian of the flame, Kabbalist, poet of Zaragoza', referring to him in the same way as does Maleh (El Maleh 1992: 217). And from that point on Abraham Abulafia de Zaragoza also becomes an important reference point in Valente's own literary creation. He makes him the protagonist of the story 'Abraham Abulafia against Portam Latinam' (2006: 693–5), where he confronts the simoniacal power of the Roman Pope with the liberating message of Maimonides of Cordoba, a confrontation that announces the arrival in Rome of a pilgrim to the East, Abulafia himself, with the apocalyptic words: 'He has no land and is of every land'. And this is how Valente tells it, with an ironic touch at the end about the repression that follows messages of liberation:

> The same night, at the same hour, a man on foot arrived at the gates of Rome, covered with the dust of the whole earth. When interrogated, he said he was called Raziel or Zacharias or Abraham Abulafia de Zaragoza. No documentation was found on him. The only baggage he carried was a book entitled *Guía de descarriados* (Guide for the Perplexed) by the doctor from Cordoba, Moses Maimonides. The police, avid for culture, seized the text. They burnt the book.

Moreover, Valente's interest in the Hebrew contribution to contemporary European poetry and to the tradition of the art of knowledge led him to an extraordinary identification with the Jewish, Romanian-born, German language poet, Paul Celan, whom he translated extensively. Celan's impact on Valente's poetry coincided with his first translations, illustrated by the title of the first poem of his book *Mandorla* that starts with a quote from the Romanian writer – 'In der Mandel – was steht in der Mandel. Das Nichts' – in fact taken from his poem similarly titled 'Mandorla'. Celan would be Valente's permanent companion until his final work, *Fragmentos de un libro futuro* (Fragments of a Future Book), and, in his articles on Celan in the 1990s, he defines the tormented and suicidal poet as 'the European poet who has marked his century most definitively' (2008: 759).

From then on, the francophone writer Valente most identified with was the Jewish French poet, born in Cairo, Edmond Jabès, several versions of whose work he also published, and about whom he wrote various articles. In addition, the friendly personal relationship and mutual poetic admiration sustained by Jabès and Valente is confirmed in statements made by both. For example, Jabès stated that Valente 'is interested in many of the questions that interest me. He's always questioning himself about language, often through particular Hebrew traditions' (see Quiñonero 1987). And as for Valente, he came to consider Jabès 'one of the central figures of world poetry' (2008: 662–73).

The essential analogies between them are already implicit in the first essay that Valente dedicated to the Jewish poet, 'Jabès o la inminencia' (Jabès or Imminence; 2008: 639–42), apropos of the 'eternal openness' of the desert and the 'voluntary exile's mystical practice', both fundamental in reaching the 'most accessible and receptive condition of writing characterised by the extreme tension between absence and imminence that so profoundly marks the entire Jewish tradition'. Later, Valente would demonstrate his connection with the Jewish writer in his important essay 'Edmond Jabès: Judaísmo e incertidumbre' (Edmond Jabès: Judaism and Uncertainty; 2008: 662–73): 'My contact with Jabès's poetry did not just determine the basic direction of my subsequent writing. It determined something far more decisive for me: a new perspective from the one I had adopted until then. After meeting Jabès I recognised myself, I gave myself an identity, a lineage, an ancestry.'

In addition, Valente, who was always anti-dogmatic, also dealt with Jabès's difficult reception in Spain, in this regard specifically vindicating the element of Jewishness that is lost yet retrievable through 'being *Jewish*, as essential *uncertainty*, as questioning' (2008: 1456), and specifically in relation to this poet 'of Sephardic ancestry' (2008: 1455), Valente himself speculated about 'the hypothetical origins of the Sephardic surname Jabès' (2008: 666). Valente, always interested in the culture of diaspora and exile that is so evident in both his poetic and narrative work, could not exclude it from his essays and drafts about the poetry of the author of *Le livre des Questions* (1963): 'It is from there that the image which touches us most in Edmond Jabès's poetry is that of exile or foreignness, the figure of the foreigner in which the face of the other is outlined' (2008: 637).

Mariá Lopo made a detailed analysis of the Jabès–Valente literary relationship with the meaningful title *José Ángel Valente e Edmond Jabès. Reconocerse en la palabra* (José Ángel Valente and Edmond Jabès: Recognising One Another through the Word; Lopo 2008) and returned to it more biographically in *Edmond Jabès y la resonancia* (Edmond Jabès and Resonance; Lopo 2014: 463–71), where she clearly demonstrates both poets' engagement with Jewishness: 'Just as Valente took on the role of mediator in bringing back the Jewish voice that had been expelled from the Spanish literary system and promoting its revival through the work of Jabès, so Jabès concerned himself with the promotion of Valente and his work in the French literary system' (Lopo 2014: 466–7).

In addition, Jabès introduced Valente to other relationships with Jews, such as the one with the French-Israeli philosopher Stéphane Mosès, whom the author of *Tres lecciones de tinieblas* would get to know in a meeting to celebrate the former in Cerisy-la-Salle in August 1987. In Valente's library there are two of his works of great interest to the poet: *Système et révélation: la philosophie de Franz Rosenzweig* (1982) and *L'ange de l'Histoire: Rosenzweig, Benjamin, Scholem* (1992). The impression Mosès made on Valente was reflected in the letter which he sent to Valente on 6 December 1987 in his own name and that of his wife, Liliane Klapisch:

> Nous serions très heureux de pouvoir vous revoir, si vos projets prévoient un séjour à Paris cet hiver ou au printemps. Comme je te l'ai dit à Cerisy, ton travail a été pour moi une véritable révélation. Il y a longtemps qu'une poésie ne m'avait aussi profondément touché.[4]

Everything that has been said about Judaism comes together in Valente's own poetic work. Starting with the exile of Spanish Jews in 1492 and of the Spanish Republicans in 1939, he dedicated his important essay 'Poesía y exilio' (Poetry and Exile) to the state of exile of all true creation:

> The Kabbalah of the sixteenth century was Judaism's response to expulsion from Spain. The Kabbalists who, following their Spanish exile, set up the Safed school in Galilee which was initially filled with nostalgia for Sefarad, finished by envisaging the exile of the people of Israel as the exile of the whole world and the redemption of the nation as the redemption of the world, as a cosmic redemption.
>
> (2008: 682)

Valente's poetry also comes out of this 'original or primordial exile', this 'ontological exile' (2008: 683), irrespective of his own intellectual migration or the council of war which was the subject of his story 'El uniforme del general' (The general's uniform) and his own political exile during the Franco dictatorship.

A poetic exile, finally, who was to integrate roots and seeds as he searched for his personal and communal Galician origins, and in his European and universal pilgrimage, his crucial personal and social commitment and his most libertarian thought and poetry.

Carmen Blanco, in her comprehensive analyses of the presence in Valente's work of the Galician poet Rosalía de Castro, highlighted the profound fellowship throughout the world between Jewish and Galician immigrants as a sublime space of poetic clarity. She was referring to her reading of Edmond Jabès at his most

[4] Unpublished letter. Cátedra José Ángel Valente de Poesía e Estética, Universidade de Santiago de Compostela.

Valentinian and his statements such as 'Sur l'étranger, le juif a la supériorité d'une lecture' (Jabès 1989: 81) together with that of José Angel Valente at his most pro-Jewish, with quotes such as 'Jew is the word we choose to wound the other – frequently to death – for his difference' (Valente 2011: 258), as well as to Valente's profound re-appropriation of the poetry of migration, strangeness, foreign status and exile from the author of the book *Cantares gallegos* (Galician Songs) and the poem 'Estranxeira na súa patria' (Foreigner in her own country) in *Follas novas* (New Leaves) (Blanco, 2011: 141–56; 2013: 23–31):

> Rosalía de Castro's Galician songs and her book *Cantares gallegos* reveal a profound experience of this reality and its hardships that became the origin of 'the Rosalian book', committed to the Galician cause from start to finish and to the challenge of migratory exodus caused by poverty; in particular 'I am alone in a foreign land / Where everywhere I look / They call me foreign / Everything says to me: foreigner!' (Castro 1992: 92–3). But Rosalia is also an exceptional writer on the general state of the foreignness of human beings in the world and more especially of women (Blanco 2005). A foreignness that allows itself a distance in which to open up thoughts and feelings and paths towards a better understanding of life. This, among other meanings, is suggested by Jabès's quote 'Sur l'étranger, le juif a la superiorité d'une lecture' (Jabès 1989: 81).[5]

As Carmen Blanco suggests, Rosalía, poet of liberty and independence in her post-romantic poetry 'Lieders', where, by the way, she declares herself 'as free as Arabs in the desert', is like Albert Camus, like Jabès and Valente, foreign, free, solitary, and supportive of profound inclusive human openness:

> Valente, writer of verses in radical solidarity with heterodoxy 'foreign, fathered by your land / foreign, like all of us' (2006: 316) and translator of *L'étranger* by Camus, draws attention to these quotes from Jabès in different ways ... and, once or twice, asserts his own foreignness: 'L'étranger te permet d'être toi-même, en faisant de toi, un étranger ... Juif errant, dont l'ombre se profile sur chaque page du livre un bâton à la main' (Jabès 1989: 9, 31, 42). The Galician poet who writes in Castilian and Galician Spanish, but mainly in Galician, joins the foreign fellowship of Spanish and Galician exiles: the Spanish *Galicianism* of emigration and Iberian exile.
>
> (Blanco 2013: 27)

It is clear that, out of all the Islamic traditions, Valente paid particular attention to Sufi mysticism, and his withdrawal to Almería was not unrelated to this, 'the principal focus of esoteric Sufism in Andalusia' and 'spiritual metropolis of all Spanish Sufis', according to Asín Palacios in a quote specifically picked up by the poet in his essay *Variaciones sobre el pájaro y la red* (Variations on the Bird and the Net; 2008: 428). In the same book Valente himself noted that Spanish literary contact with Sufism had its eminent antecedents: 'The teacher Asín Palacios was the first to set out a wide range of connections between Sufi mysticism, in particular Spanish Muslim Sufis such as Ibn ʿArabī of Murcia and Ibn ʿAbbād of Ronda, and Spanish

[5] In the original Spanish version of this paper, this quotation was in Galician.

mysticism, above all in the two towering figures of Teresa de Ávila and St John of the Cross' (2008: 376–7).

And to that must be added the range of connections stretching just as wide in contemporary times between Sufism and Valente, set out by the Moroccan scholar Fatiha Benlabbah in her first article 'Sufi traces in the poetry of José Ángel Valente' (2008a), in her brilliant doctoral thesis (2005) and in the book that came out of it, *En el espacio de la mediación. José Ángel Valente y el discurso místico* (*In the Space for Mediation: José Ángel Valente and Mystical Discourse*; 2008b), demonstrating how a contemporary poet opened himself up to such opportunities, and reached from the depths to the culmination of his art. Already, in her first published piece Fatiha Benlabbah understood the Sufi affiliation of the author of *Variaciones sobre el pájaro y la red*:

> The traces of Sufism, in particular, can be identified from the multiple quotes and references to great Sufi figures such as Husayn Mansur Al-Hallaj, Ibn ʿArabi, Suhrawardi, Tumi, Shabestari, Ibn al-Arif and others. There is no doubt that Valente, without knowing the Arabic language, was able to access the content of Sufi works through translations, those of Massignon and Sami Ali, for example, and through important studies such as those of Asín Palacios, Titus Burckhardt – author of *Du soufisme. Introduction au langage doctrinal du soufisme* – and others.
>
> (Benlabbah 2008a: 135)

But it was in her doctoral thesis that Benlabbah was to develop her theory on the *barzakh*[6] as applied to Valente's poetry:

> In fact, we consider the Valente poetic vision to be *barzakh* inspired in the sense that it places the poetic experience between speaking and staying silent, in the same way that he placed erotic and mystical experiences between the visible and invisible. The *barzakh* is a theosophical concept belonging to Ibn ʿArabī. As we have seen, he raised it into a supreme science and a way to know the Absolute.
>
> (Benlabbah 2008b: 411)

The Moroccan researcher's Sufi interpretation of Valente profoundly clarifies Valente's interpretation of Sufism: 'Valente expresses the same vision of mystical experience: a vision that we term *barsikhyiana*, by reclaiming and affirming the union of opposites: the corporal and spiritual as we have just shown, the visible and invisible, the sayable and unsayable' (Benlabbah 2008b: 414).

It is clear from his quotations and essays that Valente was interested in other Islamic mysticisms, and in other religious communities, such as the syncretic, pacifist and those as ethnically diverse as the Bahāʾīs, based in Israel, on whom he published a monographic journal and brief glossary. Juan Goytisolo set out with a fraternal cogency the mystical and poetic syncretic heterodoxy of his poet friend, with whom he so identified from the side of prose, for:

[6] The *barzakh* (Arabic for 'barrier, obstacle') is a Qur'anic term used by Ibn ʿArabī to denote the boundary between the physical and the spiritual worlds, between God and Creation, which is embodied by the Perfect Man.

> the careful appropriation by Valente not only out of his own tradition – that of Teresa de Ávila, John of the Cross and Miguel de Molinos, whom he salvages in some luminous pages from impoverished ideological-religious readings and scholastic treatises – but also from Meister Eckhart, the Kabbalah, Hindu mysticism and Arabic and Iranian Sufism, and from his bonds with the few contemporary fellow poets whose neglect and alienation he shares.
>
> (Goytisolo 2009: 92)

3. The Infinite Heterodoxy of the Universe

Valente valued many diverse traditions, appreciating 'poetic as much as religious experience' in them, but distinguishing between 'both experiences which we can call respectively the order of the literary and the order of the ecclesiastical' (2008: 305). However, he felt very alien to any formality and orthodoxy. In fact, Valente denounces authoritarian and totalitarian orthodoxies in the story 'Informe al Consejo Supremo' (Report to the Supreme Council), which is about how established authorities deny the existence of thinkers they condemn, since they prefer to silence them rather than refute their ideas.

In this story, the bishops Irenaeus and Cyril each represent power confronting dissent, concretely the Gnostic and the Neoplatonic. The victims of reprisal by the first are the Gnostic Valentinus, denier of the resurrection of the flesh, and the mathematician, astronomer and Egyptian geographer, Ptolemy, while the one sacrificed by the second is the 'Neoplatonic virgin Hypatia':

> Such is the blatant case of Irenaeus, who, in his *Anatropé tes pseudonimou gnoseos*, in the very heart of what for that reason was an aborted history, asserted that Valentinus and Ptolemy never existed, protecting himself to this end with the massive artillery of the Gnostic deniers. Even more blatant and more serious was the case of the bishop Cyril, who in order to rebut the Alexandrians created the beautiful, desired body of the Neoplatonist virgin Hypatia and then unleashed the sexual fury of the Christians who tore her apart.
>
> (2006: 707–8)

Valente sang through his poetry, set out in his essays and also edited many heterodoxies that were persecuted or crushed by religious orthodoxy. Among others, he came across one such heterodoxy connected to the Neoplatonic tradition, that of Giordano Bruno of Nola, about whom he eventually composed an opera libretto. And thus, in his essay 'La infinitud de los soles' (The Infinity of Suns), where Valente recalls Bruno's conviction and torment in fire, he relates Infinity to Neoplatonism from the start: 'The spirit is the metaphor for the infinity of matter' (2008: 712). And he adds, about the polymath from Nola:

> He believed in the infinity of the universe, in the uninterrupted multiplication of beings and in worlds continually transformed. The infinity of the world is the infinity of God. The role of man is to be enthused by the extreme infinity of worlds and suns.

> Only in this way can he approach a perception of the divine. And this perception is a journey where memory is our guide. But the symbol of this journey – in its depths and heights – is the sunflower which meets its final destiny in light, light born out of this immense and secret labour pain that is enclosed in night's lair.
>
> (2008: 713)

Paradoxically and metaphorically, Valente converts Bruno into a 'luminous flame' in his writing (2008: 713). Burning philosophical fire and dazzling mystical light that somehow identifies itself with the no less dazzling double flame of erotic union. Not in vain, in poem XXXVI with which he concludes the book *El fulgor* he finishes by setting fire to the body burnt by the eroticism of the infinite with 'absolute radiance' (2006: 458,):

> And everything which exists in this hour
> of absolute radiance
> is scorched, burns
> with you, body,
> in the torched mouth of night.

References

Asín Palacios, M. (1931), *El Islam Cristianizado. Estudio del 'Sufismo' a través de la obra de Abenarabi de Murcia* (Madrid, Plutarco).

Benlabbah, F. (2005), *José Ángel Valente y el discurso místico* (unpublished doctoral thesis, University Mohammed V–Agdal, Rabat, Morocco).

Benlabbah, F. (2008a), 'Huellas sufíes en la poética de José Ángel Valente', in Rodríguez Fer (2008), 133–8.

Benlabbah, F. (2008b), *En el espacio de la mediación. José Ángel Valente y el discurso místico*, introduction in Galician, Castilian Spanish, French and Arabic by C. Rodríguez Fer (Cátedra José Ángel Valente de Poesía e Estética; Santiago de Compostela, Universidade de Santiago de Compostela).

Blanco, C. (2005), 'Extranjera en su patria', in R. de Castro, M. Antonio, L. Pimentel & L. Pozo Garza (eds), *Extranjera en su patria. Cuatro poetas gallegos* (Círculo de Lectores; Barcelona, Galaxia Gutenberg), 7–24.

Blanco, C. (2011), 'Valente Rosalía: aire e lama', *Revista de Estudos Rosalianos*, 4: 141–57.

Blanco, C. (2013), 'Valente Rosalía: Cantares gallegos no Diario anónimo', *Cadernos Ramón Piñeiro*, 26: 23–31.

Castro, R. de (1992), *Poesía galega completa I: Cantares gallegos*, ed. A. Pociña & A. López (Santiago de Compostela, Sotelo Blanco Edicións).

El Maleh, E.A. (1992), 'Lecciones de tinieblas', trans. M. Arancibia, in C. Rodríguez Fer (ed.), *José Ángel Valente, El escritor e la Crítica* (Madrid, Taurus), 215–20 (first published in Quimera (1987), 58: 46–9).

Goytisolo, J. (2009), *Ensayos sobre José Ángel Valente* (Cátedra José Ángel Valente de Poesía y Estética; Santiago de Compostela, Universidade de Santiago de Compostela).

Jabès, E. (1963), *Le livre des questions* (Paris, Gallimard).

Jabès, E. (1989), *Un Étranger avec, sous le bras, un livre de petit format* (Paris, Éditions Gallimard).

Lopo, M. (2008), 'José Ángel Valente y Edmond Jabès. Reconocerse en la palabra', in *Referentes europeos en la obra de José Ángel Valente* (Cátedra José Ángel Valente de Poesía y Estética; Santiago de Compostela, Universidade de Santiago de Compostela), 149–84.
Lopo, M. (2014), 'Valente en París: Fragmentos recuperados', in Rodríguez Fer *et al.* (2014), 363–516.
Machín-Lucas, J. (2010), *José Ángel Valente y la intertextualidad mística postmoderna. Del presente agónico al presente eterno* (Cátedra José Ángel Valente de Poesía y Estética; Santiago de Compostela, Universidade de Santiago de Compostela).
Molinos, M. de (1974), *Guía espiritual seguida de la Defensa de la contemplación*, ed. J.Á. Valente (Barcelona, Barral Editores).
Mosès, S. (1982), *Système et révélation: la philosophie de Franz Rosenzweig* (Paris, Éditions du Seuil).
Mosès, S. (1992), *L'ange de l'histoire. Rosenzweig, Benjamin, Scholem* (Paris, Éditions du Seuil).
Otto, R. (1932), *Mysticism East and West: A Comparative Analysis of the Nature of Mysticism*, trans. B.L. Bracey & R.C. Payn (New York, Macmillan & Co.).
Quiñonero, J.P. (1987), '"Valente es el poeta más importante de su generación", Edmond Jabès, presentador del escritor español', *ABC*, 14 November: 45.
Rodríguez Fer, C. (ed.) (2008), *Valente: el fulgor y las tinieblas* (Lugo, Editorial Axac).
Rodríguez Fer, C. (2014), 'Valente en Ginebra: Memoria y figuras', in Rodríguez Fer *et al.* (2014), 13–361.
Rodríguez Fer, C., Blanco de Saracho, T. & Lopo, M. (2014), *Valente vital (Ginebra, Saboya, París)* (Cátedra José Ángel Valente de Poesía y Estética; Santiago de Compostela, Universidade de Santiago de Compostela).
Savelsberg, F. (2008), 'Aproximaciones a Tres lecciones de tinieblas', in Rodríguez Fer (2008), 63–131 (revised version of a paper published in *Moenia, Revista Lucense de Linguística & Literatura* (2000), 6: 51–125).
Thompson, C.P. (1977), *The Poet and the Mystic: A Study of the 'Cántico espiritual' of San Juan de la Cruz* (Oxford, Oxford University Press).
Valente, J.Á. (1996), 'La interculturalidad es solo una idea. Seguimos siendo eurocéntricos', *Ideal*, 12 December: 48.
Valente, J.Á. (2006), *Obras completas I. Poesía y prosa*, ed. & introduction A. Sánchez Robayna (Barcelona, Galaxia Gutenberg–Círculo de Lectores).
Valente, J.Á. (2008), *Obras completas II. Ensayo*, ed. A. Sánchez Robayna & introduction C. Rodríguez Fer (Barcelona, Galaxia Gutenberg–Círculo de Lectores).
Valente, J.Á. (2011), *Diario anónimo 1959–2000*, ed. & introduction A. Sánchez Robayna (Barcelona, Galaxia Gutenberg–Círculo de Lectores).

18

Body and Soul in the Arabic Literature of the Americas

ROBIN OSTLE

1. The Syro-Lebanese Diaspora

THE COMBINATION OF circumstances which led to the large scale migrations of Syro-Lebanese in the latter decades of the 19th century has been well documented (Hourani & Shehadi 1992): these included the sectarian tensions which led to the violent disturbances between the Maronite peasantry and their Druze landlords in and around 1860, the oppression of Ottoman rule which largely increased during the reign of ʿAbd al-Ḥamīd (1876–1909), and above all severe economic pressures. For those who struggled to support themselves and their families on the beautiful but relatively barren slopes of Mount Lebanon, the dreams of greater wealth and liberty which might be available in Europe or North and South America were powerful incentives to leave the insecurities and hardships of Greater Syria. One of the favoured migration routes was to Egypt and the Sudan, especially after the establishment there of British control, while other groups settled in West Africa and as far afield as Australia, but by far the greatest numbers travelled to North and South America where they established thriving communities in the major cities of New York, Rio de Janeiro and Sao Paulo (see Ostle 1992a: 95–6). It was in New York in particular that a number of Arab writers and poets came together between 1900 and 1920 to form the literary group known as the *Mahjar* (émigré) writers who were important both in their own right and for their impact on modern Arabic literature in general (Ostle 1992b: 209–11). Unsurprisingly, the focal points of their activities were the publications of the Arabic language press of the Syro-Lebanese community in New York. The monthly literary periodical *al-Funūn* first appeared in 1913 and became an important outlet for their poetry, criticism, translations and general discussion of ideas and theories. The other significant publication for these *Mahjar* authors was a twice-weekly paper entitled *al-Sāʾiḥ* founded in New York in 1912. *Al-Funūn* appeared only sporadically before its final demise in 1918, and

Proceedings of the British Academy, **240**, 392–403, © The British Academy 2022.

in an attempt to preserve themselves as a literary movement, in 1920 the writers formed a group named *al-Rābiṭa al-Qalamiyya* ('The Pen Club').

2. Ibn Sīnā and Jibrān Khalīl Jibrān

The first president of the Pen Club was Jibrān Khalīl Jibrān (1883–1931) who was undoubtedly the most famous of the *Mahjar* writers but who is also difficult to evaluate in literary terms. Outside the Arab world, Jibrān is probably the most widely known modern Arab author but paradoxically this is primarily because of the works which he wrote in English such as *The Madman* (1919), *The Prophet* (1923), *Sand and Foam* (1926) and *Jesus Son of Man* (1928) which have had wide popular appeal, especially in North America. Yet in spite of the great popularity of books such as *The Prophet*, they appear to have had no durable impact on serious literary activity elsewhere in English. Jibrān's most significant contribution to literature has been within Arabic literature from those works which he wrote originally in Arabic, and it is here that the impact of Neoplatonism started to become apparent. One of his articles in the miscellaneous collection *al-Badāʾiʿ waʾl-Ṭarāʾif* / *Rare Wonders* (Jibrān 1964: 542–5) is entitled 'Ibn Sīnā and his Poem' referring to the poem in which the medieval philosopher describes how the soul was sent down to earth by God (van Gelder 2013: 73–4,):

> There fell upon you from on high a dove, glorious, inaccessible,
> Hidden from every knowing gaze, yet she is unveiled and unconcealed.

In fact, the attribution of the poem to Ibn Sīnā (d. 1037) was questioned as early as the 13th century (van Gelder 2013: 73), although Jibrān was obviously not aware of this and indeed no other specific attribution has ever been established. Jibrān writes with enthusiasm that no other author in pre-modern Arabic has expressed ideas which are as close to his own as those of Ibn Sīnā on the nature of the soul, and being somewhat carried away in admiration he praises the manner in which this philosopher had anticipated by centuries similar images and ideas of Shakespeare and some of the major figures of European Romanticism (Jibrān 1964: 542, 545; Khoury 2004: 269–73). Of course, the majority of the *Mahjar* writers were Christian, usually Maronite or Orthodox, and as such they would have a general familiarity with the idea of the duality of body and soul which had been a feature of Christian Platonism ever since St Augustine of Hippo. Although Jibrān was in no sense an educated philosopher, what seems to have struck a particular chord with him was Ibn Sīnā's insistence that the human soul is a separate intelligence which leads its own spiritual existence while being united only temporarily with the body. Furthermore, the soul is immortal and cannot be touched by corruption because it is immaterial (Goichon 1971: 943–4).

These ideas were rehearsed and developed constantly by Jibrān from the beginnings of his writing in Arabic and thereafter throughout most of his career.

Some of his earliest pieces were published in the newspaper *al-Muhājir* in New York during the years 1903–8, and were subsequently published as a book in 1914 with the title *Dam'a wa-Ibtisāma* (*A Tear and a Smile*) by Jibrān's colleague Nasīb 'Arīḍa who was also the editor of *al-Funūn*. Most of these compositions are typical of Jibrān's early Arabic style of poetic prose which has strong echoes of the parallelism of biblical texts. One such piece is simply entitled 'The Soul' (Jibrān 1964: 256):

> And the God of gods separated from His essence a soul and created within it beauty. He gave it the delicacy of the gentle breezes of the dawn, the perfume of the flowers of the meadow, the gentleness of moonlight …
> And He gave it a cup of joy and He said: 'You will not drink of it until you have forgotten the past and neglected the future.' And a cup of sadness and He said: 'You will drink of it so that you know the treasure of the joy of life' … And He brought down upon it knowledge from heaven to guide it to the paths of truth. And he put in its depths perception to see the unseen … And the God of gods smiled and wept, and felt His boundless infinite love, and created a link between man and Himself.

This theme expressed in a style of religious incantation is maintained in another passage from the same collection which bemoans the darkness and suffering of the body in stark contrast to the light and beauty of the soul (Jibrān 1964: 269):

> Have mercy, oh my soul. You have given me a burden of love which I cannot bear. You and love are a unified power while I and matter are in disunited weakness. Will the struggle be long between strong and weak? You have created beauty for me and I have hidden it. You and beauty are in light, whilst I and ignorance are in darkness. And will the light mingle with the darkness? You, my soul, rejoice in the hereafter before its coming, but this body suffers with life while it is living …
> You hurry towards everlasting life, while this body takes slow steps towards the void; you do not tarry while it makes no haste, and this, my soul, is the ultimate misery. You ascend to the heights while this body falls to the depths under the lure of the earth. You give it no consolation, while it gives you no good wish, and this is real misery.

This painful relationship between body and soul became a prominent motif in some of the earliest stories written by Jibrān in the collections *'Arā'is al-Murūj / Brides of the Meadows* (New York, 1906) and *al-Arwāḥ al-Mutamarrida / Rebellious Spirits* (New York, 1908). These are in effect proto-novellas and as such are of particular interest in the history of modern Arabic narrative prose. A striking example is *Martha from Ban* (Jibrān 1964: 58–68) which chronicles the downfall of the teenage Martha who is abducted from a life of harsh but pure rural simplicity and reduced to a state of degrading prostitution in the sordid back-alleys of Beirut. In a melodramatic deathbed scene, the narrator seeks to reassure Martha that in spite of all the injustices which have been perpetrated against her and the sins which have been committed against her rather than by her, her essential purity remains inviolate and her redemption will be ensured through her immortal soul (Jibrān 1964: 65):

> The soul, Martha, is a golden ring which has slipped from the divine chain, and the glowing flame may melt this ring and change its form and destroy the beauty of its roundness; however it will never change its gold to any other substance, but will increase its lustre.

This Neoplatonic concept of the dualism of body and soul feeds indirectly but no less powerfully into the other stories in these early collections which narrate the usually unhappy destinies of simple virtuous people who are victimised by the traditional mechanisms of social control, whether these are ecclesiastical, legal or economic. As illustrated in *Martha from Ban*, Jibrān believed that the immortal soul cannot be tainted in its essence by the corruption of the lower material world, and for him one such form of corruption was promoted by the hierarchies and institutions of the Maronite Church. Thus, in the same collection of stories, *John the Madman* (Jibrān 1964: 69–81) is a simple shepherd boy in the mountains of Lebanon who spends his days tending his animals in the unspoiled beauty of the countryside, and his nights reading the Gospels, being completely inspired by the example of Christ on earth. When his animals strayed onto the land of the local monastery, the monks seized the animals and imposed a fine on John. He was bold enough to accuse them of being anti-Christian, whereupon he was seized and flogged. When he repeated the accusation on the occasion of the dedication of a new cathedral, he was again seized and thrown into prison and the only way his father could obtain his release was to claim that John was stricken by madness. A similar narrative of the oppression of a simple virtuous individual by the power and wealth of the established church is found in *Khalil the Unbeliever* (Jibrān 1964: 121–66) and Jibrān also rails against the secular legal system in *Crying from the Tombs* (Jibrān 1964: 100–10) in which three humble people are arbitrarily and cruelly put to death. For Jibrān, it is clear that such laws have nothing in common with the heavenly realms which redeem these victims of earthly injustice (Jibrān 1964: 105):

> The law? What is the law? Who saw it descending with the light of the sun from the depths of the sky? And what human being saw the heart of God and knew His will for mankind? In what generation did the angels come against men and say: 'Deprive the weak of the light of life and destroy the lowly with the edge of the sword and crush sinners with feet of iron?'

With his regular insistence on the virtual sanctity of individuals, especially humble individuals who are oppressed and abused by the institutions and conventions of society, Jibrān in common with other *Mahjar* writers was doubtless influenced by the Protestantism which had been preached by American missionaries in Greater Syria in the 19th century. Through his characters of *John the Madman* and *Khalil the Unbeliever*, it is clear that Jibrān upholds the principle of individual liberty to interpret the Scriptures against the authority of the established Church, although it is equally clear that he does not subscribe to the doctrine of original sin and man's fall from grace. Rather, he believes in the original goodness of man and in spite of the blemishes and injustices which may be the consequences of the corruption of the lower material world, salvation is possible through the spiritual power of the individual and through the indissoluble link of the soul with divine immortality (Hawi 1972: 169–70).

Jibrān's insistence on the corruption of the lower material world leads to a constant antithesis in his writing between the pastoral purity of nature, and the laws and institutions of man-made society. By extension, those individuals who retain their instincts for good through remaining in the closest possible communion with nature, are the regular victims of the injustice, repression and degradation of the material world. Their only relief will come through death when they will be reunited with peace and calm (Jibrān 1964: 250). Unsurprisingly the city, which for Jibrān is the ultimate reality and symbol of earthly corruption, is a regular focal point of the rural–urban antithesis. In *Lament in the Meadow*, the breeze, the flowers, the stream and the birds all weep at the wickedness and unhappiness of men (Jibrān 1964: 283):

> Oh pure stream, why do you lament? And it replied: 'Because I am going against my will to the city, where men despise me and exchange me for the juice of the vine, and make use of me to transport their filth. How should I not lament when soon my purity will become filth and my clearness squalor?'

3. Romantic Ensoulment

There are obvious pantheistic extensions to Jibrān's view of the soul and the manner in which it redeems the wronged and the oppressed. When the soul is separated from the divine essence it is invested with beauty and granted the properties of the delicate dawn breezes, the scents of meadow flowers and the gentleness of moonlight. The characters of John, Martha and Khalil are all in close harmony with their natural surroundings which become extensions of their pristine virtues and noble spirits, even as these are challenged by the coercion and corruption of the material world. Just as the soul is the indissoluble link between the human and the divine, so also the beauties of natural phenomena are manifestations of that soul (Jibrān 1964: 34).

Given that Jibrān sees presences of the soul in countless forms of natural beauty, it is significant that throughout his voluminous writings, one can detect echoes of European Romanticism, although it is difficult to assign specific sources to his own works. Equally Jibran and other of his colleagues in the *Mahjar* would surely be aware of the latter-day romanticism and transcendentalism of the writings of Emerson, Thoreau, Longfellow and Whitman (Badawi 1975: 180), but precise links are not easy to find. What is clearer is that the concept of the 'ensoulment' of nature was a mediated form of Neoplatonism for the European Romantics and that it was assimilated readily by Jibrān, as it was by his other colleagues in the *Mahjar* such as Mikhā'īl Nu'ayma and Nasīb 'Arīḍa.[1] The most that one can say

[1] The significance of Platonism and Neoplatonism for the poetry of the European Romantics is exemplified in the papers on Blake, Coleridge, Wordsworth and Shelley in Baldwin & Hutton (1994). See also Lewisohn (2009).

about the origins of such Romantic influences is that during his sojourn in Paris (1908–10), he read the works of Rousseau and responded to his anti-clericalism, his belief in the natural innocence of man and the corrupting influences of material society (Hawi 1972: 167–8). There also appear to be clear resonances from the English Romantics such as Blake, Keats and Shelley (Hawi 1972: 171–7), as well as from certain German Romantics and some of the works of Nietzsche (Hawi 1972: 206–14). Blake in particular, for whom the visual image was an integral part of his written creations, must have been a powerful model for Jibran in his own fusions of the written and the visual, but it remains difficult to establish with any precision the points at which Jibrān may have read these authors and their works at first hand. However, his enthusiasm for what he believed to be the ideas of Ibn Sīnā on the dichotomy of body and soul and the constant recurrence of this theme throughout his work, make a persuasive case for the continuing relevance of this particular Neoplatonic concept for Jibrān himself and for other of his colleagues in the *Mahjar*. In terms of his own lasting contribution to the history of Arabic literature in the 20th century, it is clear that his early writings represent significant stages in the development of narrative prose, yet despite the poetic nature of much of his prose output, his talents as a poet were unremarkable. His own unconventional life and his championing of the individual challenged by the conventional forces of social control made him something of an iconic hero for later writers in the 20th century who sought to confront through their art the boundaries of the conventional and the permissible. For the *Mahjar* writers, and particularly those concentrated in New York, Jibrān was a pivotal charismatic personality who provided themes, inspiration, encouragement and general education for the other members of the Pen Club who did not possess his range of knowledge and experience, and not the least of those ideas to strike chords with his colleagues was the often painful relationship of body and soul, and the belief that the soul pervaded the beauties of natural phenomena.

4. Mikhāʾīl Nuʿayma and the Russsian Tradition

Amongst Jibrān's close colleagues in the *Mahjar*, Mikhāʾīl Nuʿayma (1889–1988) is of particular significance. Apart from Jibrān himself, he was probably the most cultured and widely read member of the Pen Club and the most able of them as a literary critic. Although not a prolific poet, a number of his poems were the subject of debate in the Arab world, as were his articles of literary criticism. He is also unusual amongst the Arab writers of his generation in that the first broadening of his literary knowledge came through his exposure to 19th-century Russian literature. Nuʿayma was an Orthodox Christian and attended the Russian primary school which had been opened in his home town of Baskinta in Lebanon in 1899, from where he went on to attend the Russian Teachers' Institute in Nazareth in 1902 (Naimy 1967: 68ff.). Thanks to his exceptional academic talents in 1906 he was chosen to continue his studies at an Orthodox seminary in Poltova in the Ukraine where he remained until 1911. After returning to the Lebanon he migrated to the United States in 1912, initially to the University of Seattle, and he subsequently joined the *Mahjar* group in New York in 1916.

While in Poltova, Nuʿayma developed increasingly anti-clerical attitudes and left the seminary under something of a cloud although he was allowed to graduate. Interestingly Nuʿayma's anti-clericalism was based not on Jibrān's Rousseauism but on the writings of the elder Tolstoy after his spiritual crisis of 1876 (Nuʿayma 1959–60, I: 269):

> I was attracted more by the Tolstoy who sought after the truth of himself and the truth of the world around him than by the author of *War and Peace* and *Anna Karenina*. So I myself began in great earnest to seek the truth of myself and the truth of the world in which I lived. The one light by which I guided myself is the light which Tolstoy followed. I mean the Gospels. It disturbed him as it disturbed me that the Church should hide the rays of that light from the faithful with thick clouds of rites and dogma, and that it should create a Christianity which was devoid of Christ, and differing from idolatry only in name.

These lines recall Jibrān's characters John the Madman and Khalil the Unbeliever. They are victims of the worldly corruption of the Church and the injustice of its laws, they are closer to the spirit of Christ than the Church authorities, but they are cast out and reviled. Tolstoy himself struggled to regain the original purity of Christianity and was excommunicated by the Russian Church. Even more striking is the debt which Nuʿayma acknowledged to the poetry of Mikha'il Lermontov (1814–41). According to the diary in his own handwriting which is still kept in his home in Baskinta, Lermontov's poem 'The Angel' was to have a lasting impact on his life and his writing: the poet's infant soul is carried down to earth in the arms of an angel, but the soul struggles in its earthly existence and cannot recapture the bliss of its divine origins (Naimy 1967: 89–91). Only through the different manifestations of pure untainted nature can the poet catch glimpses of heavenly beauty, but the soul is blocked from its ethereal homeland by the lower man-made world and its corrupt institutions and moralities. Thus, both Jibrān and Nuʿayma adopt the Neoplatonic antithesis of body and soul, but from totally different sources of inspiration, just as both celebrate the pantheistic manifestations of the soul through pristine natural phenomena unsullied by material corruption. Such themes recur throughout the vast corpus of Nuʿayma's prose writings, and in his poetry nowhere more clearly than the poem 'Who are You, My Soul?' written in 1917. These are lines of gentle musing on the mysteries of the soul and its numerous manifestations: it is everywhere in nature and undoubtedly of divine origin (Nuʿayma 1966: 21,):

> My soul! You are a melody whose echo sounds within me
> Played by an artist's hands who is hidden, unseen.
> You are wind, breeze, wave, sea,
> Lightning, thunder, night, dawn.
> You are divine emanation.

The close contacts which the Pen Club writers maintained with each other in New York led to the regular interchange of themes and ideas between them, to the extent that it is reasonable to suggest that they constitute the first genuine literary school in modern Arabic literature. As seen above, the Neoplatonic view of Soul and Body and their corresponding dimensions of spiritual purity and material corruption can be traced to different origins in Jibrān and Nuʿayma, but it was primarily Jibrān himself who was the major source for these themes which appeared in the works of other *Mahjar* authors.

5. Nasīb ʿArīḍa

Nasīb ʿArīḍa (1887–1946) had been a colleague of Nuʿayma in the Russian Teachers' Institute in Nazareth. He emigrated to New York in 1905, and in 1912 founded the Atlantic Press which was to publish the literary periodical *al-Funūn* (ʿAbbās & Najm 1967: 193). He was also responsible for collecting into book form Jibrān's miscellaneous articles which appeared as *A Tear and a Smile* in 1914, and for him and for other of the *Mahjar* authors this is the most likely source for what were to become familiar Jibrānian themes. ʿArīḍa's single volume of verse, *al-Arwāḥ al-Ḥāʾira / Perplexed Spirits*, was published in New York in 1946, the year of his death, but most of the poems it contains were written between 1912 and 1930. Much of his verse is focused on the suffering and loneliness of the exile, nostalgia for Lebanon and the hardships and humiliations suffered by Syria and Lebanon during the First World War, but he finds his most frequent and preferred means of escape from such misery in communion with his soul, rising above the lower world. As in much of Jibrān's and Nuʿayma's work, the soul finds its closest affinities with the purest aspects of unspoilt nature (ʿArīḍa 1946: 54):

> In the air clouds run along, moving with the spirits of flowers.
> The river seeks to join with them, the soul yearns to unburden itself.
> The south wind sang ... the south wind.
> The soft wind whispered ... the soft wind.

ʿArīḍa 's poem 'On the Grave of a Prostitute' (ʿArīḍa 1946: 205–8) recalls Jibrān's proto-novella *Martha from Ban*. Like Martha, the fallen woman of this poem succumbed to sin more through force of circumstances than any inherent evil of her own:

> The beauty of the body is but skin deep, the soul has an eternal beauty, higher,
> And many a virgin harbours a tainted soul, though she has preserved her body.

While initially the soul is a companion for the poet with whom he can share his problems and misgivings, or a companion who holds out the promise of blissful immortality, unusually the relationship which develops between ʿArīḍa and his soul becomes more fractious rather than a source of solace and relief. The soul suffers and complains about the fact that it is forced to dwell in the earthly body with all its contaminations and imperfections. It yearns and aspires towards its natural state of eternal purity, and rails against the unpleasant prison of the body which it has to endure. Two poems in particular present the most complete statements of this conflicted relationship: “Soul!” (‘Arida 1946: 87–90,) and “To My Soul” (‘Arida 1946: 104-6). In the opening lines of the latter, ‘To My Soul’, the poet exclaims in pain and amazement at the soul’s constant complaints and discontent (ʿArīḍa 1946: 104):

> Pity, oh my soul. You have moaned long. Softly, alas how you complain.
> How you call for aid! What do you seek? Enough struggle. Are you not
> weary, rebellious one?

The poet chides the soul for its apparent inability to appreciate the saving graces of the lower life such as beauty or the music of poetry. This is hard for the poet to bear when he considers that the soul is but a passing visitor (ʿArīḍa 1946: 106):

> Pluck the flowers of this life. Discover its secrets.
> You have blamed life without knowing it. Have you not learned, you are
> only a passing visitor here?

More typically Jibrānian is the long poem ‘On the Road to Iram’ (ʿArīḍa 1946: 179ff.), the fabulously rich city of Arab legend which here is a symbol of the poet’s yearning for a spiritual Eldorado. The fifth section is subtitled ‘The Caravan’ (ʿArīḍa 1946: 189ff.), and uses desert imagery to great effect as the poet journeys on, his companions being all the crucial elements which make up his world: his heart and soul, his intellect and love, his dreams and desires, his memories and his poetry. The powerful force, which makes all these elements combine to attempt to break out of the prison of his lower life and to seek the mystical state of perfection represented by Iram, is like a camel driver urging them on with songs. And yet the poet remains blind and fettered (ʿArīḍa 1946: 189):

> My longing urges them on
> With the camel song of one blind and fettered.
> He sees without eyes
> A vision which inspires love and enamours.

6. *Mahjar* Poets, North and South

The most prolific of the Arab poets in the northern *Mahjar* was Ilyā Abū Māḍī (1889–1957), but his work was in no sense dominated by the ideas and themes of Jibrān and Nuʿayma, close colleagues though they were. Before his migration to the United States in 1911, Abū Māḍī’s formative years were spent in Egypt and unlike a number of the other *Mahjar* writers he had a solid grounding in the Arab literary tradition. According to the Lebanese critic ʿAbd al-Laṭīf Sharāra, the Egyptian intellectual and cultural climate were to remain with him throughout his career (Sharāra 1961: 6–9). By contrast some of the lesser poets of the group such as Rashīd Ayyūb

(1881–1941) and Nadrah Ḥaddād (1887–1950) demonstrate how the members of the Pen Club functioned as a definable literary school, transferring ideas and themes from one to the other, while the critics Iḥsān ʿAbbās and Yūsif Najm wrote of the bewitching effect which Jibrān's work and ideas had upon Ayyūb's poetry in particular (ʿAbbās & Najm 1967: 229). So too did the impact of Jibrān reach to the Arab poets of South America who formed their own version of the Pen Club in Sao Paulo in 1933 with the title *al-ʿUṣba al-Andalusiyya / The Andalusian Group* (see Ostle 1992a: 108–9). One member, Fawzī al-Maʿlūf (1899–1930), attained fame largely as a result of his long poem 'On the Carpet of the Wind' consisting of 14 sections which reiterate many of the themes familiar from Jibrān and Nuʿayma. Section three, 'The Slave', describes the struggle between the poet's spirit and his body, the latter being enslaved in an environment where all emphasis is placed upon material values (al-Maʿlūf 1929: 53):

> Between my spirit and my imprisoned body was a distance whose
> bitterness I tasted.
> I am earthbound and the spirit is above the ether. I am enslaved,
> and she is free.

The fourth section sees the poet transported to the realms of the spirits by means of some strange flying machine, a device which somewhat strains poetic credibility. After initial rejection by the spirits, he is finally accepted after explaining the essentially spiritual nature of his mission and being as a poet. There is a moment of ecstatic union between the poet and his spirit, but ultimately he has to descend again to earth to resume his struggle with the conflict between body and soul (Badawi 1975: 201).

7. The *Mahjar* Heritage

The first three decades of the 20th century were the key period for the production of this Arabic literature of the *Mahjar*; thereafter the Syrian and Lebanese migrants and their descendants were largely assimilated into American culture and the English language. Given that theirs was a pocket of immigrant culture, in spite of the independent value of their work its impact on the modern literature of the Arab world could have been minimal. In fact, the opposite was the case for this Arabic *Mahjar* literature was to be a source of stimulation and inspiration most particularly for Arabic poetry. Two publications were highly significant in this context. Mikhāʾīl Nuʿayma's critical writings first appeared in book form in Egypt in 1923 with the title *al-Ghirbāl / The Sieve*, with an introduction by the Egyptian critic and intellectual ʿAbbās Maḥmūd al-ʿAqqād. Although Nuʿayma and al-ʿAqqād disagreed on matters of prosody and the nature of the language of poetry (al-ʿAqqad in Nuʿayma 1964: 11–12), this sparked off regular and lively debates on such issues. Even more influential was the enthusiasm of the important Egyptian critic Muḥammad Mandūr for the *Mahjar* literature in general and its poetry in particular. In his seminal book

Fī 'l-Mīzān al-Jadīd he coined the term '*al-adab al-mahmūs* – the quiet voice in literature' in analyses of poems by Nuʿayma and Nasīb ʿArīḍa, praising the qualities of their restrained language of poetry as opposed to the loud declamatory rhetoric which was still characteristic of much contemporary Arabic verse at the time (Mandūr nd: 69–91). The best of the *Mahjar* poets were amongst the most important members of the Romantic movement in Arabic poetry (Ostle 1992a: 95–110) and their impact can be traced clearly in the work of poets such as the Egyptian ʿAlī Maḥmūd Ṭaha (1902–49) and the Tunisian Abū 'l-Qāsim al-Shābbī (1909–34) (Badawi 1975: 137ff., 157ff.). What they achieved in the development of the language of poetry and prosody, and the manner in which they treated themes such as the duality of body and soul, and the pantheistic manifestations of divine beauty in ensouled nature, was to change the face of modern Arabic poetry between the two world wars.

References

ʿAbbās, I. & Najm, M. (1967), *Al-Shiʿr al-ʿArabī fī 'l-Mahjar* (Beirut, Dār Ṣādir).
ʿArīḍa, N. (1946), *Al-Arwāḥ al-Ḥāʾira* (New York, Maṭbaʿat Jarīdat al-Akhlāq).
Badawi, M. (1975), *A Critical Introduction to Modern Arabic Poetry* (Cambridge, Cambridge University Press).
Baldwin, A. & Hutton, S. (eds) (1994), *Platonism and the English Imagination* (Cambridge, Cambridge University Press).
Goichon, A.M. (1971), 'Ibn Sīnā', in B. Lewis, V.L. Ménage, Ch. Pellat & J. Schacht (eds), *The Encyclopaedia of Islam, Second Edition*, vol. 3 (Brill, Leiden), 941–9.
Hawi, K. (1972), *Kahlil Jibran: His Background, Character and Works* (Beirut, The Arab Institute for Research and Publishing).
Hourani, A. & Shehadi, N. (eds) (1992), *The Lebanese in the World* (London, Centre for Lebanese Studies and I.B. Tauris).
Jibrān, K. (1964) *Al-Majmūʿa al-Kāmila li-Muʾallafat Jibrān Khalīl Jibrān* (Beirut, Dār Ṣādir).
Khoury, R.G. (2004), 'Avicennismus, Neuplatonismus und Weltbürgertum im Werke des Djubrān Khalīl Djubrān (1883–1931)', in R.G. Khoury & J. Halfwassen (eds) with F. Musall, *Platonismus im Orient und Okzident: Neuplatonische Denkstrukturen im Judentum, Christentum und Islam* (Heidelberg, Universitätsverlag Winter), 265–80.
Lewisohn, L. (2009), 'Correspondences between English Romantic Poetry and Persian Sufi Poets: An Essay in Anagogic Criticism', *Temenos Academy Review*, 12: 185–226.
Maʿlūf al-, F. (1929), *ʿAlā Bisāṭ al-Rīḥ* (Rio de Janeiro).
Mandūr, M. (nd), *Fī 'l-Mīzān al-Jadīd* (Cairo, Maktabat Nahḍat Miṣr).
Naimy, N. (1967), *Mikhail Naimy, An Introduction* (Beirut, American University of Beirut) [e-book].
Nuʿayma, M. (1959–60), *Sabʿūn*, 3 vols (Beirut, Dār Ṣādir).
Nuʿayma, M. (1964), *Al-Ghirbāl* (Beirut, Dār Ṣādir).
Nuʿayma, M. (1966), *Hams al-Jufūn* (Beirut, Dār Ṣādir).
Ostle, R. (1992a), 'The Romantic Poets', in M. Badawi (ed.), *The Cambridge History of Arabic Literature: Modern Arabic Literature* (Cambridge, Cambridge University Press), 82–131.

Ostle, R. (1992b), 'The Literature of the *Mahjar*', in A. Hourani & N. Shehadi (eds), *The Lebanese in the World* (London, Centre for Lebanese Studies and I.B. Tauris), 209–25.
Sharāra, 'A. (1961), *Ilyā Abū Māḍī* (Beirut, Dār Ṣādir).
van Gelder, G.J. (2013), *A Library of Arabic Literature Anthology: Classical Arabic Literature* (New York/London, New York University Press).

19

Neoplatonist Echoes in Modern Arabic Poetry: The Case of Muḥammad ʿAfīfī Maṭar

FERIAL J. GHAZOUL

> As speech is the echo of the thought in the Soul, so thought in the Soul is an echo from elsewhere: that is to say, as the uttered thought is an image of the soul-thought, so the soul-thought images a thought above itself and is the interpreter of the higher sphere.
>
> Plotinus (Ennead I 2 [19] 3, M: 19)

ECHOING NEOPLATONISM IN poetry does not mean finding direct influences of Plotinus; rather it signifies that an image or a verse or a poem carries the resonance of Plotinus's thought. Neoplatonism is not a defined school of thought, but a fluid set of orientations and *The Enneads* of Plotinus were written down (by his student Porphyry) based on his oral teaching and were translated into various languages, permeating different cultures starting with the Mediterranean world and moving further West and East, reaching the New World. With each move, the thought of Plotinus coloured diverse cultures and was coloured by them. Neoplatonism, and specifically Plotinus, left a profound impact on various cultural aspects of the medieval world directly or indirectly, impacting philosophy, literature and even cultural practices.

In the medieval Arab world, Plotinus was known through fragments and partial texts, attributed to Aristotle and dubbed as 'Theology'. The work of Plotinus as it circulated in Arabic among scholars in the Middle Ages came to be known in modern studies as the Arabic Plotinus (see Adamson 2002; D'Ancona 2004). The process of the discovery of the Arab Plotinus in the 20th century was started by ʿAbd al-Raḥmān Badawī who edited and published these medieval fragments and sayings of Plotinus – called in the manuscripts the Greek sage, *al-shaykh al-yunānī* – in 1955 in Cairo, under the heading of *Aflūṭīn ʿind al-ʿArab* (Plotinus of the Arabs). These writings were known and circulated in the Middle Ages as *Uthulūgiyā Arisṭūṭalīs,* or *Rubūbiyyāt Arisṭūṭalīs*. In 1970, Fuʾād Zakariyya translated the fourth *Ennead* into Arabic under the title *Al-Tisāʿiyya al-Rābiʿa li-Aflūṭīn fī ʿIlm al-Nafs*. More recently, Farīd Jabr translated the complete *Enneads* directly from Greek into Arabic as *Tāsūʿāt Aflūṭīn*; it was published in Lebanon in 1997.

Proceedings of the British Academy, **240**, 404–418, © The British Academy 2022.

To seek the impact of Plotinus one should not confine one's search to that of the philosopher by name. Whatever he was called in Arab culture and whatever extracts of his were known, he left his imprint on medieval Sufi thought and philosophical endeavours, particularly through the concepts of the unity of being, emanation, and multiplicity in unity. The influence of Plotinus and Neoplatonism can be detected in the *Epistles of the Brethren of Purity* as well as in the works of Ibn ʿArabī, Ibn al-Fāriḍ, and al-Suhruwardī, among others. Illumination and imagery of light – key metaphors in Plotinus (Schroeder 1996: 341) – are detected in the mystic discourse in the East and the West.

1. Arabic Poetry and the Challenges of Modernism

In the 20th century, modern Arabic poetry was trying to break away from the restrictive mould of classical Arabic poetics with its mono-rhyme and rigid metre restrictions in order to express emotions and reflections more freely. 20th-century Arabic poetry was seduced by the appeal of new modes of expression and tempted to risk a rupture with the poetic past. However, new exciting untrodden paths implied the loss of cultural identity and poetic continuity. Torn between new modes of writing poetry in the modern world on the one hand and literary continuity on the other hand, poets embarked on varied paths of experimentation. There were efforts to revive the Arabic poetic legacy (*al-turāth al-shiʿrī*) by putting new content in old forms. Other attempts aimed at easing the restrictions of established norms of writing poetry by accommodating subjectivity, romanticism and symbolism. The revivalists (*al-iḥiyāʾiyyūn*), sometimes called the neoclassicists, attempted to resurrect the pre-Islamic qasida (ode) but failed to be part of the contemporary worldwide poetic scene. The few early modernists who turned their back entirely on the literary tradition in writing their poetry became cultural anomalies. The solution to the dilemma was to look for precursors of modernity in Arab literary culture who relaxed restrictions or revolted against traditional modes. The well-known Sufis with the richness and ambiguity of their language offered a way to meet the challenge of being both part of one's own culture and also a modernist. The Sufi works represented both *aṣāla* (cultural authenticity) as the texts are part of the heritage, and *hadātha* (modernism) in the sense that they offered new modes of expression often highly personal and symbolic. It was as if 'the return to the roots in order to promote the present is attained through the employment of the Sufi masks and literary techniques' (Assadi & Naʿamneh 2011: 1). The use of Sufi poetics in the new poetry offered a connection with the Arab poetic heritage as well as highlighting figures who were cultural rebels presenting existential themes in their writing (al-Yūsufī 1985: 156–7).

Thus, the literary past was excavated to find models of alternative poetics. Nāzik al-Malāʾika in her groundbreaking critical work, *Qaḍāyā al-Shiʿr al-Muʿāṣir* (Issues of Contemporary Poetry) offered a genealogy of her innovative *tafʿīla* poetics (commonly known as 'free verse') in the historically marginalised Arab modes of poetry (1962: 195–212). Adonis (ʿAlī Aḥmad Saʿīd) as a poet and critic pointed out the repressed elements in Arab culture that came to flourish in modern times and sought to create affinities between modern trends and Arabic literature. In *Al-Ṣūfiyya wa'l-Suriyaliyya*, 1995 (*Sufism and Surrealism* 2005), Adonis touched on the elements of Sufism that match surrealistic manifestoes, without erasing the difference between the two: 'God in Sufism is not only the one but also the many. He is part of existence, the high point (as Breton calls it), the point at which what we call matter and what we call spirit come together and all contradictions between the two are eliminated' (2005: 8). Both Sufis and Surrealists believe in an invisible world that cannot be grasped by reason, he adds (2005: 12).

While the Sufis use figurative language to relate the visible to the invisible, the Surrealists use wild metaphors to relate the unconscious to consciousness. The non-discursive and the assimilationist approach to textuality deployed by Plotinus and Neoplatonists (see Rappe 2000: 45–66) is what brings them into alliance with Islamic Sufis specifically, and with mystics in general.

Dozens of critical works have analysed the dissemination of Sufi diction and poetics in modern and contemporary Arabic poetry in the oeuvres of such well-known poets as the Iraqi ʿAbd al-Wahhāb al-Bayātī, the Syrian Adonis, the Palestinian Maḥmūd Darwīsh, and the Egyptians Salāḥ ʿAbd al-Ṣabūr and Muḥammad ʿAfīfī Maṭar. Clearly, each poet has his take in bringing the Sufi universe into his poetics and has his favourite mystic to highlight – al-Ḥallāj for Salāḥ ʿAbd al-Ṣabūr; ʿAṭṭār for Mahmūd Darwīsh; and Ibn ʿArabī for Muḥammad ʿAfīfī Maṭar.

The other invisible impact of Plotinus on modern Arabic poetry might be sought in reading Western poetry that has been influenced by Neoplatonism. Several poems by William Butler Yeats as well as 'Howl' by Allen Ginsberg refer to Plotinus. Modern Arab poets[1] – many of whom majored in English Literature – read William Wordsworth, Samuel Coleridge and W.B. Yeats among others who were impacted by Thomas Taylor's translations of Plotinus (O'Meara 1993: 116). Some Arab poets read French poetry – Charles Baudelaire, Stéphane Mallarmé, André Breton, René Char – in French or in translation. Academic studies have been undertaken on the impact of Romantic and modernist writers on Arabic poetry (see for example Faddul 1992; Motawy 2003). We can postulate that the Neoplatonic vision was present to some degree in the works of modern Arabic poetry in general, and more specifically in the writings of a poet like Maṭar who was an avid reader of philosophy and of mysticism.

2. Maṭar's Poetry and Poetics

Muḥammad ʿAfīfī Maṭar (1935–2010), born in the Egyptian Delta, studied Philosophy at Ain Shams University, and authored dozens of collections of poetry, a short memoir about his coming of age, short stories for children and critical studies. He is

[1] Among them is Khalīl Jibrān whose work is discussed in Robin Ostle's contribution to this volume.

known as a 'poets' poet' with his complex diction, rich allusions, startling syntax, and intersecting of the sensual with the mystical. Not easy to decipher on a first reading, Maṭar has been dubbed an enigmatic poet. His creative intertextual use of Qur'anic verses and diction (Abū al-Najāt 2017: 278–326) adds a sublime aura to his worldly poems dealing with the flesh (al-Masri 2012: 151–4). The ambiguity is caused by the multiplicity of frames of reference used in his poetry, coupled with poetic economy, thus creating a density that needs to be unpacked. Often a single word (such as a neologism based on a philological derivation) encompasses a micro-world that is dialectically related to the macro-world of the entire poem (Tu'aylib 2007: 156).

Maṭar, in his introduction to a poetry collection by the young and brilliant poet 'Alī Qandīl (1953–75), published in 1976, provides what amounts to his poetic manifesto in nine points: (1) creating existential unity between means and goals on every level, including in art, where form and content are inseparable; (2) breaking away from homogeneity to create art that engages with the human condition; (3) a radical, but not nostalgic, revisiting of cultural memory to uncover figures of the past who can illuminate the present; (4) recalling texts of Islamic Sufism that liberate the language from its shell, without turning them into idols; (5) rejecting the politicised application of the theory of mimesis; (6) moving from organic unity to the unity of the poetic climate, taking into consideration the silences of the poem; (7) dismantling models including those of modernism since each poem has its own poetic structure; (8) posing questions rather than offering ready-made answers; and (9) constructing a poetic method based on dreams, free association and the rejection of Aristotelian unities (Maṭar 1976b: 5–17).

How did Maṭar combine high-brow philosophy with his peasant life, modernist poetry within the ethos of Lower Egypt? In other words, how did he manage the dissonance between his sophisticated worldview and his everyday village context? In an interview that raised this issue, the poet explained at length the coexistence of his village affiliation with the quest of the early Greek philosophers. Maṭar outlines first the appeal of philosophy to him:

> The problematic which has preoccupied the poet-philosophers before Socrates was the relationship of being to becoming. Being is the most important quality of beings which can be extracted by reason; and in order to comprehend it and define it, it has to be permanent and final, not changing. Beings are in a state of constant flux and continual change. Therefore, there must exist an '*aṣl*' (principle) which stays as such beneath becoming. The mode of search for this *aṣl*, the forms of its transformation, the logic of this transformation, in the philosophy of the early naturalists and in European thought from Socrates to Heidegger – tend to be a search into nature and its primordial principles. As for Heidegger, he offers a radically different interpretation and orients the search to ontology, or to the exposition of the self to the call of Being, not beings. Anyhow, I tend strongly towards Heidegger's interpretation.
>
> (1980: 69)

Maṭar goes on to link his interest in philosophy to that of his own community:

> As for me, my readings, my early specialisation in philosophy, and my intense admiration for the spirit of adventure in Greek thought made me very interested in the

> question of the spirit of the community (*al-jamāʿa*), the meaning of civilisation, and the forms of national manifestations in intellectual, scientific, and architectural phenomena as well as the vision of the cosmos and life and death. The community that is closest to me and most touching to my senses is my village community and its forms manifested in everyday life. This is how I started and how I was brought up. I used to see everything, hear the language, receive modes of expression and behaviour, and consider it all coming out from a total, comprehensive significance which wore the paleness of faces and the rending of worn garments … This search has led me all along and I have considered it the foundation of knowledge, the definition of poetry, the theory of life, and the responsibility and task of a citizen named Muḥammad ʿAfīfī Maṭar.
>
> (1980: 69)

This shows that Maṭar did not see in Greek philosophy a foreign intervention into the fabric of Egyptian culture, but viewed it as corresponding to the collective quest for being in Maṭar's own community. He was able to detect the analogical relation between philosophical knowledge and living experience.

3. Maṭar and Neoplatonism

Though Maṭar does not make a direct reference to Plotinus in his poems, he refers to him in his interviews and prose writing. There is a direct reference to Plotinus when an interviewer accuses him of vagueness and lack of focus since his poetry is 'based on Plotinus's concept of emanation'. Miffed by the idea of Plotinus's emanation causing incoherence, Maṭar redefines the concept to his interlocutor as 'the theory that tries to solve potential philosophical problems concerning the One in relation to the Many, the Perfect Creator to imperfect creatures' (1980: 69). In his memoir, *Awāʾil Ziyārāt al-Dahsha: Hawāmish al-Takwīn* (First Instances of Wonder: Notes on Coming of Age), Maṭar mentions reading about 'the Alexandrian School and Neoplatonism' (1997a: 74) and speaks admiringly of the valuable book he read, *Durūs fī Tārīkh al-Falsafa* (Lessons in the History of Philosophy), a textbook on the history of Philosophy from its Greek dawn to Kant (1997a: 123).

It is almost certain that Maṭar who was a student of philosophy in the 1960s and an instructor of philosophy in Egypt in the late 1960s and 1970s had read and was imbued with Neoplatonism. After all, the Arabic Plotinus texts were edited by his professor and mentor, ʿAbd al-Raḥmān Badawī. It was probably on the syllabus of Philosophy majors at Ain Shams where Maṭar studied and where Badawī taught. Maṭar's infatuation with philosophy was the outcome of reading Badawī on Nietzsche at the age of 17 and then reading other works the prolific Badawī penned or edited.

Maṭar refers in interviews and in his poetry to his affinities with the *Muʿtazila* (the more philosophical approach to Islam) and the *Mutaṣawwifa* (the more hermeneutic approach to Islam). As Maṭar explains in one of his interviews:

> What helped me personally to come away from the political framework and common language, what helped me deepen and broaden my personal experience was the

relation between mysticism (*taṣawwuf*) and philosophy. It turned me to the language of the Qur'an and manifests itself specifically in my two collections *Quartet of Joy* (*Ruba'iyyāt al-Faraḥ*) and *You Are Its One* (*Anta Wāḥiduhā*).

(al-Shībānī 1989: 116)

Among the markers of Maṭar's consciousness were the Qur'an and Qur'anic language, particularly in its shorter Meccan chapters with their captivating melody, amazing syntax and poetic density. The power of the Qur'anic style as recited by Maṭar's mother marked him since childhood. He contrasts her melodic recitation with the masculine articulation of the Qur'an by the shaykh instructor. His memoir begins with that opposition, under the heading of 'Motherly Intoning':

When my mother used to ask me to repeat what I had memorized of the short suras of the Qur'an up to the long ones, from the *'amma* section to the *tabārak* section,[2] and correct my mistakes with her melodious voice – her face illuminated with joy, her eyes shut – the lofty rhythm would embrace everything with its purity and the world would take the shape of an enthralling rosary of voices and taut harmony.

On the morning of the first day I attended the kuttab, a cloud of intertwined rhythms gathered at a distance above the house of Sayyidna, our master. As my steps came closer, the intertwining and resonance of these rhythms increased. The kuttab was a large room in the house of Sayyidna. When I took my place on the mat among a group of beginners, I became frightfully and alarmingly aware of Sayyidna's voice as he scolded his wife and young daughter, who were behind the door. Then he raised his hoarse and harsh voice with the verses of the short suras. I said to myself: The Qur'an must be a woman, and the verse unadulterated motherhood, unknown to men. I realized that everything I had learned from the Qur'an by heart had dropped out of my memory ... and I cried.

(Maṭar 2008: vi)

It is the fluidity and the sensual reading of the mother as opposed to the rigid and harsh reading of the shaykh in the Qur'anic school that prepared Maṭar for absorbing and assimilating the language of Ibn 'Arabī and al-Niffarī, with their philosophical and lyrical dimensions. From his earliest childhood, Maṭar equated the Qur'an, synecdoche of the One, with the female essence and its tenderness and motherliness.

Even though Maṭar's themes vary, from philosophically informed reflective poems to political protest poetry, the personal and the experiential dimensions lurk behind the lyrical structure. Maṭar was keenly aware of his Egyptian, Arab and Islamic identities. He has a collection that specifically poeticises local myths of his region, the Delta of Egypt, *Yataḥaddathu al-Ṭamyi: Qaṣā'id min al-Khurāfa al-Sha'biyya* (The Silt Speaks: Poems of Popular Myths). The fact that Plotinus was a Hellenised Egyptian (or a Greek resident in Egypt) from Lycopolis in the Delta, from where Maṭar hails, must have created a sense of kinship. Like Plotinus, the

[2] For purpose of recitation and prayer the Qur'an has been divided into 30 sections (*ajzā'*) of which section *'amma*, consisting of suras 78–114, is the last, and section *tabarāka*, consisting of suras 67–77 is the penultimate. Their names are derived from the first words of suras 78 and 67 respectively.

frame of reference of Maṭar is both Egyptian and Greek (Ghazoul 1994). He upheld both the Greek Athena and the ancient Egyptian Thoth as deities of knowledge – the latter standing for gnosis and illuminative knowledge and the former standing for reasoning and more strictly philosophical thinking (Maṭar 1972: 113):

> Between the eyes of Thoth
> And the Sun of Athena
> My drowned heart desired
> The sun of visions and serenity

In his poetry, we come across Greek figures – mythological and historical – such as Athena, Aphrodite, Oedipus, Empedocles, Socrates, Alexander (Ghazoul 1994). Maṭar was enamoured with Greek culture and particularly with the Pre-Socratics. He has an entire collection on Empedocles, *Malāmiḥ min al-Wajh al-Imbadhuqlīsī* (Features of the Empedoclesean Face, 1998). In this collection, Maṭar presents the philosophy of Empedocles as the struggle between Love and Strife and his dramatic ending in the volcanic Etna. The theory of the classical elements – earth, air, fire and water – was formulated by Empedocles and was adhered to by Islamic and Western philosophy for two millennia, including its presence in the philosophy of Plotinus. Maṭar develops what Empedocles called the four 'roots' into an entire poetic collection entitled *Rubaʿiyyāt al-Faraḥ* (Quartet of Joy). Maṭar's 'Earth Joy', 'Fire Joy', 'Water Joy' and 'Air Joy' present the classical elements viewed lyrically as ontological stations of being (1997b: 3):

> Here is the river changing itself
> into a vegetal being teeming with bodies,
> with water moss, lotus, the foam of the verdure,
> and odour of death.

Eros is a fundamental theme in both Plotinus and Maṭar. For Plotinus, Eros is the desire to unite the individual with the One, while making a distinction between heavenly love (There) and earthly love (here):

> That our good is There is shown by the very love inborn with the soul; hence the constant linking of the Love-God with the Psyches in story and picture; the soul, other than God but sprung of Him, must needs love. So long as it is There, it holds the heavenly love; here its love is the baser; There the soul is Aphrodite of the heavens, here, turned harlot, Aphrodite of the public ways: yet the soul is always an Aphrodite. This is the intention of the myth which tells Aphrodite's birth and Eros born with her (*Ennead* VI 9 [9] 9, M: 546).

It is this union of souls, without necessarily raising the communion with the One, that Maṭar presents as the apotheosis of being. Duality is banished between lover and beloved and alterity is erased. In the following poetic excerpt, there is a dialogue between the poetic persona and the beloved about union in death. Their love turns them into one even though the onlookers fail to see the oneness (1997b: 63, ):

> I become light; you become light;
> neither are you from you,

nor I from me;
we have ripened into one blood …

— One dead,
how will death be split
into two corpses?

—It is one corpse.

— What if the kin fought to fill
two dust holes with one dust
gathered by love in the prostration
of passion?

This union in death is also a return to Earth 'beneath the hand of God', to use the expression of Maṭar. It is not exactly the Plotinian merging with the Divine, but it is a merging with the World created by the Divine. For Maṭar the material world partakes in divinity as it was created by the One; it is an extension of the divine (1997b: 63, [illegible]):

—Soft is the clay step in the clay:
beneath us the earth gathers into a carpet,
dust flinging upon dust;
and in the passion prostration
the blood of the man prostrating
does not reveal the blood of the woman prostrator;
one blood runs aground in the darkness
of the earth
beneath the hand of God,
then tossed by the wind
in the hand of the omnipotence;
it rises lightly, taking its course
in the radiant mystery
of its nocturnal journeys,
largely, as the frame
of the universe exacts,
narrower than the sigh of spirit
in spirit.

The first things that draw attention to Plotinus–Maṭar affinities is the view of the one and the multiple, the unity in multiplicity, and the union of the fragmented. Maṭar strikes his readers with his fondness for numbers – 4, 7, 40, 50, 1,000, etc. – only to reveal that they are faces of the one, one in a lower case to start with; but soon we recognise that the one points to the One in an upper case. The titles of Maṭar's collections written in the 1970s and 1980s point indirectly to the Infinite. In *Quartet of Joy* (Rubaʿiyyāt al-Faraḥ), Maṭar refers to the four elements: 'Earth Joy', 'Fire Joy', 'Water Joy' and 'Air Joy', yet all of them reflect and interpenetrate each other. In his collection *Wa'l-Nahru Yalbas al-Aqniʿa* (And the River Wears Masks, 1976a), we are presented with a favourite technique of Maṭar where he wears the masks of past figures – Ghaylān al-Dimashqī and al-Ḥasan ibn Haytham (known in medieval Europe as Alhazen). Masks are variations on the same identity; they exemplify multiplicity within unity. It is the same river, to use Maṭar's metaphor, but it changes faces or rather changes masks. But the most telling title of Maṭar's collections is *Anta Wāḥiduhā wa-Hiya Aʿḍāʾuka Intatharat* (You Are Its One and It is Your Parts Dispersed, 1986). This sense of acknowledged fragmentation in the title yearns for the unity of the One. Like the 99 attributes/names of God, *Asmāʾ Allah al-Ḥusnā*, the many point to the One.

To give an example of Maṭar's simultaneous use of numbers (40), Greek philosophy (Zeno of Elea) and Islamic mysticism (al-Niffarī), I cite the opening of the Second Prelude of 'Earth Joy' (1997b: 2–3, [illegible]).

Forty doors …
Circles looping out upon circles
and corridors meshing,
and the trees of stairs branch up
and down …

My friend Zeno of Elea surprises me
by showing me the space between the arrow
and the horizon
and fills the void of paper
with the savagery of the race
between me and the tortoise of beginning
and the word of revelation.

And my friend al-Niffari surprises me
with the rose of crimson water
and the glare of sea
and taste of salt air…
I end up craving bread,
and wait for time
and the childhood
of evening talk
and the disclosure
and the moment that stuns.
I who am born of forty women,
I look out for the ravings of memory
and the defiance of forms,
for the earth is arched over
the harvests of death
and the decanters of aged thirst.

Seven, the number often related to the eternal return, is associated with Empedocles and with ancient Egyptian and Indian thought. Maṭar would have read his mentor's book, Badawī's *Rabīʿ al-Fikr al-Yūnānī* (The Spring of Greek Thought), in which the cyclical nature of changes in the world are spelled out in the section on Empedocles (1943: 194–202). In an interview, Maṭar points out the impact of majoring in Philosophy where he studied with Badawī among others, dedicating years to exploring Greek and Islamic philosophy and reading seminal medieval and modern texts (ʿAbd al-Amīr 1980: 140). The number seven occurs in a stanza in a poem entitled the 'Traveler' in the collection *Malāmiḥ min al-Wajh al-Inbadhuqlīsī* (1998: 42):

> I entered through seven doors
> the Kingdom of the rocks
> I heard from the throat of the inanimate world
> its painful desire to generate.

4. Close Reading of 'Recital'

In several poems of Maṭar, we encounter echoes of Plotinus. The one I would like to concentrate on is entitled in Arabic *Qirāʾa* which I have rendered into English as 'Recital' (see Maṭar 1987, [illegible]). Let me explain before delving into the interpretation that this poem was written in November 1975 and first published in July 1977 in an Iraqi literary journal, *Al-Aqlām*; it was reprinted as a single poem in the above-mentioned collection *Anta Waḥiduhā wa-Hiya Aʿḍāʾuka Intatharat* (1986). Though it stands by itself as a self-sufficient poem, Maṭar chose to juxtapose it later to a poem he wrote in 1968 entitled 'Kitāb al-Madīna wa 'l-Manfā' (Book of the City and Exile). What he intended with the 'city' was the Greek term *polis* which stands for a self-governing community or state. In this 1968 poem on the City he bemoans the dramatic defeat that Egypt suffered in 1967. The 1975 poem 'Recital' is an effort to transcend this trauma. The relation between the two poems that Maṭar juxtaposed in his collected poetic works was analysed by a critic under the heading of 'The Textual Equivalent' (ʿUbayd 2002). 'Recital' by itself has been analysed by several critics, including Ghazoul (1984), Glover (1996) and ʿAbd al-Ḥamīd (2017: 313–18).

The poem takes the form of a mystical dream or rather an ascension to the One. Maṭar refers to is as a *miʿrāj* and so evokes a parallel with the *miʿrāj* of the Prophet Muḥammad who went on a night journey using the winged mare al-Burāq to travel from Mecca to Jerusalem and then to the seven levels of Paradise where he encountered God after seeing the prophets. Al-Burāq is often pictured as a winged white horse with a woman's face – not that its female sex or handsome looks are given in the Qur'an which mentions the journey only briefly in *Sūrat al-Isrāʾ* (Qur'an 17:1). These details were provided by biographers of the Prophet who added supplementary information which in turn inspired painters and carvers in representing the transporting mare. Whether literal or metaphorical, the beatific vision and night journey of the Prophet function as an intertext in Maṭar's 'Recital'. The poem links itself with that prophetic paradigm and supplements it with erotic motifs, recalling Islamic mystics and specifically Ibn ʿArabī who used eroticism and its ecstasies as a metaphor of union with the divine.

The poem's title '*Qirāʾa*' literally means 'reading' and by extension alludes to the recitation of the Qur'an, the central text of Islam. It also conjures up the first verse revealed to the Prophet Muḥammad, which begins with the words 'Recite in the name of thy Lord who created' (*Iqra' bi-'smi rabbika alladhī khalaqa*, Qur'an 96:1).[3] As the poem progresses, a sense of dispersal overtakes the reader, only to be reorganised into a structured format thanks to the refrain *salāmun hiya hattā mashriq al-nawmi … salāmun* (Peace it stays until nightfall … Peace). This recurring line brings the varied and rich parts of the poem together as if in a prayer or in a spiritual rite. It does not remain the exact same refrain as in ballads or songs, but changes slightly. The refrain occurs in the poem seven times, varying from 'Peace it stays until nightfall … Peace', to 'Peace it stays until sunrise … Peace', to 'Peace; that mask of merciful night', to 'Peace, a spider of blood, clothed by the feature's similarity … Peace'. The word 'Peace' is what is repeated and the refrain is an intertextual reference to a Qur'anic verse: 'Peace it stays until sunrise' (Qur'an 97:5). This Qur'anic verse refers to a special night; it is a night better than a thousand months where the angels bring down mercy. This night is associated with the night of revelation of the Qur'an to Muḥammad, thus it is the night of *tanzīl* or Revelation. The word in Arabic for Revelation, *tanzīl*, means literally bringing down, as in the first verse of the Power sura of the Qur'an: 'Behold, We brought it down on the Night of Power' (97:1). In Revelation thus a divine text is brought down to earth; in *mi'rāj*, ascension, a creature from earth is taken up to heavens. Thus, we have in both *tanzīl* and *mi'rāj* movements that imply God and Man; in the first there is descent, in the second ascent. The poet's ascension then necessarily recalls the verses about the seven heavens and the Prophet's ascension – a scene that has inspired mystic visions. This intertextual and interactive use of Qur'anic verses by Maṭar and his allusion to Paradise reveals a yearning to link the poem with the primary text of Islam. This invariably invokes a desire to embrace the divine presence, the One of Plotinus. The unity of being, *waḥdat al-wujūd*, associated with Ibn 'Arabī is hinted at by the poetic line between brackets indicating a citation: 'The letters, a nation among nations, are addressed and entrusted' (Maṭar 1987: 350). This is directly borrowed from Ibn 'Arabī in his *Al-Futuḥāt al-Makiyya* ('Meccan Revelations', Ibn 'Arabī 1972, I: 260).

The poem goes on to assert (1987: 351, [illegible]):

> I knew I walked the way of Ascension. I dwelt in the lodge of ultimate certitude.
> The circumference of the earth expanded.
> The heavens appear as garments ripping at the waistline of the living river.

This ascension brings the vision of the poetic persona into the company of Sufis of all kinds and into the emanation of Plotinus (1987: 351, [illegible]):

> The Oriental Sages, the Hermetists and Gnostics partake of the banquet of luminous dialogue.

[3] All translations of the Qur'an in this chapter are derived from Arberry (1955).

> Al-Suhrawardi breathes in the fullness of space, divides bread and the silvery fish of the Nile. He eats in the plenitude of anarchy and drinks in the profusion of ceaseless emanation.
> The Hermetists weave the cape of chants and enchantments. They unfold it for the noble tribe, the beasts and the birds at resting, sheltering space for initiating and linking creatures twice, thrice, four times and up to the last number memory may retain.

Apart from the vertical dream journey to heaven, the poet presents the journey undertaken by village women to fetch water from the river. The horizontal journey of women takes place before sunrise and after sunset so that they would not be exposed as darkness hides their features. The poet calls them 'river women' and what he means is that they are on their way to the river. As the sun sets, the women rise and make their nocturnal journey to the Nile. Metonymically, they are identified in the scene as 'Anklets of grass twist circlets of / Silver and silt, desire wet with the water's foam' (1987: 349). The roundness of their anklets and the circlets of silt, associated with fertility and cultivation in the Nile Valley and complemented by 'desire wet with water's foam', inevitably touch on the erotic. The translation loses the alliteration and the rhyme effects of the original Arabic, which associates desire (*raghba*) with foam (*raghwa*).

The poem moves forward to describe a pastoral scene of sleeping nature – fields, birds, bulls and serpents all slumbering. The night is merciful and that is when the poet's 'mortal self' is asleep while his 'living half' is awake. The body is still, but the spirit is awakened. By God's bounty the mortal diurnal half allows the nocturnal living half to be freed. Like al-Burāq miraculously transporting the Prophet, the poetic persona is transported by 'An imperial mare' – an Arabian steed that crosses the stretches of Arab lands from Granada to what is Beyond the River, a nomenclature that stands for Central Asia and what used to be called Transoxiana. In other words, the mare covers the land of the Islamic empire stretching from Western Europe to Central Asia.

The swift mare has all the characteristics of a desired woman. She wears kohl on her eyes. She gallops along and 'Space is folded for her'. The innovative metaphoric interlocution here inspires wonder. Instead of a mare racing in immense distances, it is the distances that collapse as if folded for her. The sky above is invoked through the star Canopus (*Suhayl*) which was used by the ancient Arabs for navigation at night. This nocturnal dream has a plethora of juxtaposed images: horses springing out of section *ʿamma* of the Qur'an; writing on the face with green leaves; birds breaking away from the dome – all of which suggest an ecstatic and surrealistic scene so typical of dreams. That is when, as the poet puts it, 'heavens came to me'. That is when joy is mingled with bewilderment and when the poet joins the Oriental sages and al-Suhrawardī in 'the banquet of luminous dialogue'. This is also the moment when all creatures are joined together, over and over, 'twice, thrice, four times and up to the last number memory may retain'. It is an infinite mode of connecting and reconnecting, including not only humans but also beasts and birds in this unending heavenly feast.

Now that the nocturnal journey of the poet has taken place, we are re-introduced to the river women who announce by their horizontal journey the end of the night as they go fetching water just before sunrise. The poet also comes down from his vertical journey to his earthly being (1987: 352, ):

> He descends to the murmur of vermin, the clinging of insects, the slither of reptiles.
> The steps shorten.
> I wrapped myself in the tatters of the diurnal half.

As the poet regains his earthly Self, the poem refers to his body being drained from its water – a water that is devoid of memory. He is back to matter after the transcendental journey has ended.

How does this heavenly journey relate to Plotinus? Here is an excerpt of Plotinus which is in tandem with Maṭar's poem, 'Recital':

> For all There is heaven; earth is heaven, and sea heaven; and animal and plant and man; all is heavenly content of that heaven: and the gods in it, despising neither men nor anything else that is there where all is of the heavenly order, traverse all that country and all space in peace.
>
> (*Enneads*, V 8 [31] 3, M: 414).

The new book-length study of the universe of Maṭar, *Al-Ḥilm wa'l-Kimiyā' wa'l-Kitāba* (Dream, Alchemy and Writing) by Shākir ʿAbd al-Ḥamīd asserts that Maṭar's poetics can only be grasped though Plotinus's theory of emanation and its presence in the illuminationist Islamic philosophers (2017: 295). Citing Plotinus as rendered into Arabic in the *Theology of Aristotle*, he sees the parallelism between the philosopher and the verses of 'Recital':

> I may keep to myself, put my body aside, and become a gem stone without body. I then enter into myself, coming back to it, and coming out of various things. I become simultaneously the knower, the known, and knowledge. I see in myself beauty, radiance, and light.
>
> (Badawī 1955: 22)[4]

Neoplatonism seems to be latent in the consciousness of Maṭar. He was prepared to see the latent becoming manifest in the texts of Plotinus which he read – whether directly in the course of his studies or indirectly through their impact on Sufi figures and mystical quests. This overlap between the inner and the outer, the Egyptian and the Greek, becomes a key in understanding the philosopho-mystical poetics of Maṭar.

[4] This corresponds to *Ennead* IV 8 [6] 1, a famous passage in which Plotinus gives an account of his own religious experience.

References

ʿAbd al-Amīr, K. (1980), 'Ḥiwār maʿa al-Shāʿir Maṭar, Muḥammad ʿAfīfī', *Al-Ṭalīʿ al-Adabiyya*, 6.7 (July): 136–49.

ʿAbd al-Ḥamīd, S. (2017), *Al-Ḥilm waʾl-Kimiyāʾ waʾl-Kitāba fī ʿĀlam Muḥammad ʿAfīfī Maṭar* (Cairo, Battana).

Abū al-Najāt, ʿA. (2017), *Al-Ṣūra al-Adabiyya ʿinda Shuʿarāʾ al-Jīl al-Thānī fī Ḥarakat al-Shiʿr al-Jadīd fī Miṣr* (Cairo, Maktabat al-Adab).

Adamson, P. (2002), *The Arabic Plotinus: A Philosophical Study of the 'Theology of Aristotle'* (London, Duckworth).

Adonis (2005), *Sufism and Surrealism*, trans. J. Cumberbatch (London, Saqi).

Arberry, A. (1955), *The Koran Interpreted* (New York, George Allen and Unwin).

Assadi, J. & Naʿamneh, M. (2011), *The Road to Self-Revival: Sufism, Heritage, Intertextuality and Meta-Poetry in Modern Arabic Poetry* (New York, Peter Lang).

Badawī, ʿA. (1943), *Rabīʿ al-Fikr al-Yūnānī* (Cairo, Maktabat al-Nahḍa al-Miṣriyya).

Badawī, ʿA. (ed.) (1955), *Aflūṭīn ʿind al-ʿArab* (Cairo, Maktabat al-Nahḍa al-Miṣriyya).

D'Ancona, C. (2004), 'The Greek Sage, The Pseudo-Theology of Aristotle and the Arabic Plotinus', in R. Arenzen & J. Thielmann (eds), *Words, Texts and Concepts Cruising the Mediterranean Sea: Studies on the Sources, Contents, and Influences of Islamic Civilization and Arabic Philosophy and Science* (Leuven, Peters Publishers), 158–78.

Faddul, A. (1992), *The Poetics of T.S. Eliot and Adunis: A Comparative Study* (Beirut, Alhamra Publishers).

Ghazoul, F. (1984), 'Fayḍ al-Dalāla wa-Ghumūḍ al-Maʿnā', *Fuṣūl*, 4.3 (April–June): 175–89.

Ghazoul, F. (1991), 'The Greek Presence in Modern Egyptian Poetry: The Case of Muḥammad ʿAfīfī Maṭar', in Kavafis International Committee, *Proceedings of the First Kavafis International Symposium*, 37–51.

Ghazoul, F. (1994), 'The Greek Component in the Poetry and Poetics of Muḥammad ʿAfīfī Maṭar', *Journal of Arabic Literature*, 25: 135–51.

Glover, M. (1996), 'Qirāʾa: A Re-Reading (A Comparative Study of Maṭar's "Qirāʾa" Touching on Problems of Reception and Semiotics)', *Journal of Arabic Literature*, 27.2: 125–42.

Ibn ʿArabī, Muḥyi al-Dīn, (1972), *Al-Futūḥāt al-Makiyya*, ed. ʿUthmān Yaḥyā, 14 vols (Cairo, Al-Hay'a al-Miṣriyya lil-Kitāb).

al-Malāʾika, N. (1962), *Qaḍāyā al-Shiʿr al-Muʿāṣir* (Beirut, Dār al-ʿIlm lil-Malāyyīn).

al-Maṣrī, S. (2012), *Shiʿriyyat al-Jasad* (Cairo, Al-Hayʾa al-Miṣriyya lil-Kitāb).

Maṭar, M.ʿA. (1972), *Kitāb al-Arḍ waʾl-Dam* (Baghdad, Mudīriyyat al-Thaqāfa al-ʿĀmma).

Maṭar, M.ʿA. (1976a), *Waʾl-Nahru Yalbasu al-Aqniʿa* (Baghdad, Wizārat al-Iʿlām).

Maṭar, M.ʿA. (1976b), 'Sharāra Khāṭifa ʿalā Qaws al-Ḥayāt waʾl-Mawt', in ʿAlī Qandīl, *Kāʾināt ʿAlī Qandīl al-Ṭāliʿa* (Cairo, Dār al-Thaqāfa al-Jadīda), 3–20.

Maṭar, M.ʿA. (1977), 'Qirāʾa', *Al-Aqlām*, 10.12 (July): 54–7.

Maṭar, M.ʿA. (1980), 'Al-Lahẓa al-Shiʿriyya Shajāʿa Inqilābiyya Nādira', *Al-Mustaqbal*, 4.169: 68–9.

Maṭar, M.ʿA. (1986), *Anta Wāḥiduhā wa-Hiya Aʿḍāʾuʾka Intatharat* (Baghdad, Dār al-Shuʾūn al-Thaqafiyya al-ʿĀmma).

Maṭar, M.ʿA. (1987), 'Recital', trans. F. Ghazoul & D. O'Grady, in S. Khadra Jayyusi (ed.), *Modern Arabic Poetry: An Anthology* (New York, Columbia University Press), 349–52.

Maṭar, M.ʿA. (1997a), *Awāʾil Ziyārāt al-Dahsha: Hawāmish al-Takwīn* (Cairo, Dār Sharqiyyāt).

Maṭar, M.ʿA. (1997b), *Quartet of Joy*, trans. F. Ghazoul & J. Verlenden (Fayetteville, The University of Arkansas Press).
Maṭar, M.ʿA. (1998), *Malāmiḥ min al-Wajh al-Inbadhūqlīsī* (Cairo, Dār al-Shurūq).
Maṭar, M.ʿA. (2008), 'Early Awakenings', trans. F. Ghazoul, in A. Parker, *Twilight Visions in Egypt's Nile Delta* (Cairo, The American University in Cairo Press), vi–xix.
Motawy, Y. (2003), 'Time, Nature, and the Body: Sufi Dimension in Muḥammad ʿAfīfī Maṭar's *Quartet of Joy* and T.S. Eliot's *Four Quartets*' (unpublished MA thesis, The American University in Cairo).
O'Meara, D. (1993), *Plotinus: An Introduction to the Enneads* (Oxford, Clarendon Press).
Plotinus (1991), *The Enneads*, trans. S. MacKenna (London, Penguin Classics).
Rappe, S. (2000), *Reading Neoplatonism: Non-discursive Thinking in the Texts of Plotinus, Proclus, and Damascius* (Cambridge, Cambridge University Press).
Schroeder, F. (1996), 'Plotinus and Language', in L. Gerson (ed.), *The Cambridge Companion to Plotinus* (Cambridge, Cambridge University Press), 336–55.
al-Shībānī, K. (1989), 'Ḥiwār maʿa Muḥammad ʿAfīfī Maṭar', *Al-Ḥayāt al-Thaqāfiyya*, 52: 113–17.
Tuʿaylib, A. (2007), 'Al-Mughāmara al-Islūbiyya wa-Taʾsīs al-Ḥuriyya fī al-Khiṭāb al-Shiʿrī al-Muʿāṣir', in Ḥ. Sālim (ed.), *Shāʿir Miʿdhanat al-Damʿ: Dirāsāt fī Shiʿr Muḥammad ʿAfīfī Maṭar* (Cairo, Al-Majlis al-Aʿlā lil-Thaqāfa), 125–82.
ʿUbayd, M.Ṣ. (2002), 'Al-Muʿādil al-Naṣṣī: al-Qirāʾa al-Shiʿriyya lil-Qaṣīda', *ʿAmmān*, 84: 20–5.
al-Yūsufī, M.L. (1985), *Fī Binyat al-Shiʿr al-ʿArabi al-Muʿāṣir* (Tunis, Dār Sirās).

20

Shards of Infinitude: Neoplatonist Relics in Modern Persian Poetry

AHMAD KARIMI-HAKKAK

When the fox – in truth a fennec or African fox – tells the Little Prince 'what is essential is invisible to the eye' she is giving expression to an idea in human experience with a pedigree that stretches through much of the history of early man, at least to many thousands of years ago. In our modern historical understanding we habitually assign the origins of the idea to ancient Greek thought, which later seeped through many cultural walls and fences, jumped over or sneaked under many barriers, to become something akin to a principle of our knowledge of life and the world as well as our speculations about the limits of its reach, dynamics of its operations, and fit the texture of the cultures it entered at one point or another. In exploring such perennial ideas and the course of their movement, we need to keep in mind that certain historical occurrences stood between us and our perceptions of such ideas: that in the opening years of the 16th century in his 'School of Athens' fresco Raphael depicted the gestures of Aristotle and Plato in a way that we think of as etched in binary opposition, that some centuries before Raphael the Latin culture had lost much of its power to distinguish between the two most celebrated Greek philosophers, and that, even before them by several centuries, Arab and Persian Muslims, men like al-Kindī, al-Fārābī and Ibn Sīnā had translated, interpreted and commented upon or otherwise investigated the works of these seminal forebears and set them well within the evolving terms of the early Islamic thought that had been lost to them, turning Aristotle and Plato into archetypes of Renaissance speculations about heaven and earth, with human destiny and the human story hanging in the balance.

Still, we must remember at least that these ideas had aged through travel in time, that some of the works that were by one were attributed to the other, and that the practice of translating Greek or Greco-Roman ideas into Arabic and Persian was performed with certain assumptions and with latitudes and limitations inherited from the native traditions of Islamic Fiqh, or Kalām, plus an amalgam

Proceedings of the British Academy, **240**, 419–432, © The British Academy 2022.

of philosophical ideas that had survived Islam as relics of Zoroastrian or Buddhist or Hindu thought components. What I am pursuing here, in other words, has to do with the conscious or unconscious practice of Neoplatonism, or some of its elements, in Persian poetry, not so much with the expounding of it.

To begin this pursuit at the most basic level, let us think of the words that Muslim thinkers gave to ideas they came across when studying ancient Greek texts. The word philosophy and the concept behind it were gradually changed to words more familiar to Muslims, *ḥikma* in Arabic and *ḥekmat* in Persian. The choice – and the change – which were hugely consequential to classic Arabic and Persian thinkers are not of small relevance to our concerns here. The Arabic word *ḥikma* is used several times in the Qur'an, and its Persian version *ḥekmat*, as the practical equivalent for the word *falsafeh* derived from the ancient Greek word 'philosophia', was expressive of a concept that formed the word for the activity in which Plato and Aristotle as well as later Greek philosophers, including Plotinus and Porphyry, were known.

In his introduction to a ground-breaking work on Suhravardī's *Ḥikmat al-Ishrāq*, the Iranian scholar Ja'far Sajjādī devotes a section to 'Definition or Definitions of Philosophy', which he opens with a discussion of ancient Greek philosophy going back to pre-Platonic times. In mentioning the process of Greek philosophy's arrival in Islamic Iran, he observes:

> And in the process the word *falsafah* 'philosophy' has been changed to the word *ḥekmat*, following the example of the noble Qur'anic verse where we read *yu'tī al-hikmata man yashā'*. With this shift to a word that has an Islamic root the definition of philosophy changes to the activity in which, instead of research into the truth of existence, emphasis is placed on enlightening the heart of whoever God pleases. As such, Greek philosophy comes to stand face to face with Islamic *ḥekmat* (wisdom) and Iranian *ḥekmat-e zowqī*. This last word enshrines a complex idea that ranges from grasping an idea to being enlightened by it through divine grace.
>
> (Suhravardī 1988: 8)

Nor should it be surprising that elements of Greek philosophy would find their way to Islamic jurisprudence and other strands of Islamic intellectual thought as they were evolving in the early centuries of Islam's presence in non-Arab civilisations. It is important to note, for instance, how receptive the Persians were to these strands in the cultural zone of Khurasan as the region began to be steeped in the gnostic tradition.[1] Over the centuries when Persian poetic practice was dominated by increasingly diffused and attenuated discourses of a gnostic or mystic colouring, active awareness of the strands of thought that connected the vision behind that practice to what we may relate to Neoplatonism was gradually but steadily dimmed. Sufism was, after all, perceived more and more as a manifestation of a brand of mysticism indigenous to Islam, and this was particularly

[1] For explorations of this vision in two major poets from Khurasan, Sanā'ī Ghaznavī and Farīd ad-Dīn 'Aṭṭār, see Shāfi'ī-Kadkānī (1994; 1999).

evident in the development of Persian poetry on the Indian subcontinent.[2] In pre-Moghul times, the migration of many Sufi leaders from Iran to India in general, and from Khorasan in particular, had loosened connections between India and Greece or increasingly mediated them through Sufism as conceptualised in the heartland of Iran. And when through the 18th and 19th centuries medieval Islamic culture began to give way to various forms of native drive towards a modern world, most widely conceived trends such as nationalism and secularism had acted as further and increasingly more powerful motivating forces towards indigenisation. That, incidentally, may well be related to the inclination, while identifying historical trends running through modernising attempts in various non-Western cultures, to find ways of divesting modern trends of almost all metaphysical tendencies, such as portrayals of the afterlife or acknowledgments of the challenges of the human soul as distanced from perennial or archaic ideas, akin to those that may be found in medieval articulations with Neoplatonist links.[3]

In our search for more complex relationships between the kinds of change within the amalgam of ideas which we associate with that ancient Greek philosophy and other currents and forces within the respective poetic cultures we are discussing here, we tend to minimise various forms of Neoplatonic presence in modern poetic traditions. We may also view poetic practice in modern times as more related to the Theories of Evolution, or Modernism, or Postmodernism. Words like relics, vestiges, traces and others with similar senses or practical implications are used regularly to define what is left of Neoplatonism in our modern cultures, and what use they might or might not have for the creative processes at work in our cultures.

With the spread of modernism in the Persianate world in the late 19th and early 20th centuries not only much contemplative poetry of the past, but all manner of philosophical poetry, began to be regarded as outdated or backward or anachronistic, and was thus pushed to the margins of poetic praxis.[4] Much scholarly debate still attends the discussion of modernism in Persian poetry and poetics, but the question of modern and modernist poetry's thematic thrust remains one of the thorniest of issues in studying that evolving tradition. By and large, we can say that an observable shift has taken place from meditative or mystical discourses to those more amenable to poetic discussions of social or political concerns. Given that, almost all practice of something as occult-like or esoteric or metaphysical as Neoplatonism by definition would force the poet to the margins of his or her culture. In recent decades, however, many such poets – i.e. those who had kept aloof of the urge to be engaged and to practise committed poetry, whose principles dominated discourses of modernism – have moved more to the centre than they were in much of the earlier decades of the 20th century.

[2] For a fuller discussion of this development, see Karimi-Hakkak (2012).

[3] In recent decades, scholarship on the history of Persian poetry in India has been enriched by a series of insightful explorations of its history and culture. For brilliant examples of this, see Orsini & Sheikh (2014), Kinra (2015) and Sharma (2017).

[4] For a discussion of modernity in Persian poetry, see Karimi-Hakkak (1995).

1. Bījan Elāhī

It is within that context that I would like to introduce a few modern poets of Iran in whose work traces of a Neoplatonist vision – i.e. on the nature of love, on the place of beauty beyond mundane reality, on a variety of silences and/or contemplative utterances, and lastly on the many struggles of the human soul as it attempts to purify itself – can be seen, grasped or expressed in poetry. The first of these is Bījan Elāhī (1945–2010),[5] the modernist Iranian poet most thoroughly immersed in the heritage of Persian Sufism and its legendary inaugurating archetype Manṣūr al-Ḥallāj; he would have been far better known if he had demonstrated more personal interest in seeing his compositions through to publication in his lifetime. He was fairly uninterested in processes of submission to literary journals and temperamentally indifferent to both the dominant discourse in the modernist poetry of Iran in the second half of the 20th century and to the resistance against that tendency. His true passion was total immersion in al-Ḥallāj, the man as well as the mystic, and the mightiest of nay-sayers who lost his life because his unmasked statements had begun to shake the foundations of the emerging Islamic orthodoxy in the early centuries of the religion. Besides, in his youth Elāhī was far more successful as an artist and painter than he was as a poet, and even though his involvement with that art stopped after a brief few years, it coloured his poetry for the rest of his life. Elāhī did publish at least one collection of poetry and several single or series of poems in his lifetime, but the bulk of his work remained unpublished at his death in 2010, and has only now begun to attract some attention.[6] The Manā'ī, a series of three short poems, was first published informally, later republished in *Ḥallāj al-Asrār* (Carder of Secrets) and is now available online. It was presumably set for type by the poet himself, and is dedicated to his wife Jāleh Kāẓemī. In the undated online edition the following note can be seen before the poems: 'my Manā'ī is neither a translation (*tarjomeh*) nor a composition (*ta'bieh*); it is, rather, "a variation or adaptation of his '*annī ilayk*" (in Arabic/Persian: "from me to you"), that is, what he, presumably al-Ḥallāj, uttered on the last night of his imprisonment'.[7]

1.1. The Three Poems: 'Death Announcements' (Manā'ī)

The three poems, entitled 'Death Announcements' (Manā'ī) and numbered 1, 2 and 3 respectively, represent something of an exception in their own time and have now begun to invite much appreciative discussion. In Manā'ī 1, lamenting the absence of a meaningful humane world without any attention to the infinite, to the One, the speaker as the poet's second self proclaims (Elāhī 2015: 15,):

[5] For a biography of Bījan Elāhī, see Ganjavī (2016).

[6] Three of Elāhī 's poetic collections have been published since his passing in 2010 (see Elāhī 2013; 2014; 2015).

[7] My discussion of Elāhī's 'Death Announcements' is based on the version included in the posthumous *Ḥallāj al-Asrār* (Elāhī 2015: 15–17), to which, however, I have added the poet's note from the online version.

What's up? The death of a lonely world
its mind dormant, its beloved gone.
Soul of all souls, where to? Beyond where?
He addressed the star of the dawn sarcastically.

What's up? Demise of the heart. No flowers rising
from the earth to taste the celestial mystery.
Without the grace of the air, tears of a cloud,
the grief of fresh tulips was renewed.

What's up? The death of He is the Truth, the One, the He!
Birds have grown dumb, forgotten their songs
so the dumb ones with ten duplicitous tongues
display their inebriated coquetry, their showy manifestations.

The demise of a silent world where hearts are dead, flowers no longer grow, and the Truth, the One and the He have ceased to exist provides mute testimony to the dimensions of the cataclysm that has descended upon the earth. Yet, the fact that there is a herald to spread the word, and someone to receive it, leaves the gates open to some sort of possible remedy to be thought of and devised. And as we proceed into the poem, we see that the event that is being heralded with such alarm is not an actual apocalypse, but the perception of all – or most – good things deserting the earth, and that the possibility of renewal through a basic revival is not to be completely negated. The poem's lexicon may indeed be more sparing in the original than I have been able to render in this translation. To begin, the all-important line that closes each of the three four-line stanzas, and the rhyme that makes this structure a feature of all three poems in question, make it more or less clear that we are not witnessing a finality but a perceptibly degraded condition of wholesale decay and degeneration. The Persian words at the ending line of the first stanza, *gūsheh zad bā setāreh-ye saharī*, which I have translated as 'he addressed the star of the dawn sarcastically', are ambiguous or equivocal in the original Persian. It is not clear what the compound verb *gūsheh-zadan* means in reporting the apostrophe that contains the news of the death of a lonely world; it might harbour a hint that someone is nudging the star of dawn, as if to make it aware or warn it of an impending catastrophe. Similarly, in the second stanza fresh tulips can be seen as taking on new blemishes or receiving fresh news that renders them mournful. In Persian the sentence might also mean that the grief of the newly blossomed tulip was renewed. Only the last stanza seems to take on a clearly mournful tone where dervish calls to besiege God by repeating his name in the chants of *ḥaqq ḥaqq* (truth truth) and *hū hū* (He He) seem commensurate with the ascendance of duplicitous pretenders full of multiple two-faced tongues signalling a verbose pretence, empty of all substance. On the whole, though, the poem clearly sets up a wretched end-of-existence where birds have forgotten their songs against the background of an original purity which caused birds to sing their songs. Manā'ī 2 speaks in the same vein (Elāhī 2015: 16, ):

What's up? The death of all address, apostrophe, edict.
All speech makers have let down their shields:

a flame has been lit, what response now
how would a tree begin to breathe?

What's up? As He began to draw the bow of an ogling,
happy tidings spread from the jasmine to the grass,
the honey hive shrank and nobody saw an impress
but dust upon the garden's pages.

To heave out the smoke of a heartfelt pain,
the dew disappeared, no memory was left of the rosebud:
thank God that some idea was left of the purity of paradise,
of that Night of All Light.

What we have in Manā'ī 2 seems to be the logical conclusion and a most definitive instance of the situation we have witnessed in the previous Manā'ī, that is what is likely to happen after the news of the final apocalypse has spread, the end of all seen with any degree of certainty or finality has been declared, and makers of invocations with any certainty have let down their shields. Then it seems the lighting of a kindling, such as we have in the story of Moses and the Burning Bush of Sinai, has received no response, and no reason has been given for a tree to begin breathing. In Persian the mention of the word *qabas* (kindling) also evokes at once a line in Hafiz where the speaker expresses his joy at seeing the fire from the secure realm (*vādi-ye imān*), so much so indeed that he imagines himself in exactly the same hope in a spring moment as may have been experienced by Moses. It is as if the speaker in this poem is wondering how, given the death of all definitive or authoritative speech, even a tree would have the ability to 'begin to breathe'.

The second stanza places us at the precise moment of creation on the day of *Alast*, the momentous inaugurating occasion when the as yet unborn souls, in response to the question 'Am I not your Lord?' (*a-lastu bi-rabbikum?*), affirm their allegiance to the Creator (see Qur'an 7:172).[8] The notion of a pre-eternal ogling, a loving glance from God, an amorous look that can only emanate from God, with as much effulgence as we see here, is immediately followed by two contrasting concepts: the good tidings (*bishārat*) that God has spread over the universe and the gradual decay (*pusidan*) that man has initiated and that has resulted in the leaves of the orchard being turned into dust at this end of the universal moment.

Manā'ī 3, the shortest of the three poems, is also the sharpest in terms of the speaker's articulation of a doomsday scenario in a world totally devoid of spirituality (Elāhī 2015: 17, [illegible]):

The story was renewed but my mind was not refreshed.
What's the use? None! The fair ones of the garden
have now departed, and love has arisen sweetly,
wrapped in the tinsel of a brand-new vision.

The world has turned into a desert, no beginning, no end
Filled with countless flies, a whole horde of asses

[8] For a detailed discussion of this theme in classical Persian poetry, see Karimi-Hakkak (2012: 231–42).

> who mingle, speak, see, and hear, putting airs on display,
> repeating: 'wonderful, well-done, bravo.'

Stories fail to refresh minds, beauties of a celestial garden have departed, and love, sweet love, is wrapped in a covering of lace and tinsel. That mental landscape finds its analogous vision of the world as an expanse of a wasteland where flies and asses thrive by putting themselves on display and praising themselves endlessly. Hope has definitively deserted the world here; the speaker seems to imply through the total negation of any reason for it: 'What's the use? None', he exclaims! And there may well be more reasons for his desperate tone, if we consider the 'fair ones' having departed and love now 'wrapped in lace and tinsel'.

Taken together, the three poems cited and briefly discussed here leave little space or hope for renewal of the kind that is amply articulated in the gnostic discourses of early Persian mystic visions. The question begs to be asked: is that a consequence of secularism or nationalism, is it a condition of modernity? I tend to view the near total negativity of Elāhī's posture in these poems as a consequence of the loss of knowledge about the background that inspired poetic practice in a culture, saturated by gnostic poetic practice over many centuries, which is now engaged in an attempt to leave its past behind. While it does not present systematised accounts of the contents of the religious predilections of ancient Iran or India, nor of Qur'an and the hadith, Persian poetry of medieval times is permeated by multiple systems of thought, therefore receiving ideas about a supreme deity, or of the fate of the human soul, or of the contours of afterlife from Neoplatonism as filtered through native religious visions of the sacred and the worldly. Yet, Persian poetry did not view Neoplatonism as observably opposed to the more seemingly timely notions of a 'modern world'. Extending this into other poetic cultures, where modernity in itself presents a challenge to all gnostic visions, we can say that a whole gamut of speculative heterodox religious thought, which lies outside all faith-based orthodoxies and which includes such cultural phenomena as Cabalism, Neoplatonism and a variety of Gnosticisms expressed through Sufi poetry, is more compatible with a belief in gnosis or direct awareness of the Divine through mythosis.

2. Sohrāb Sepehrī

None of the other modern Iranian poets to whom I turn now is as directly or manifestly involved with Neoplatonic ideas as Elāhī. Still, to the extent that their work reveals aspirations that reach beyond manifest reality to touch something of the infinite and the invisible, they can be said to partake of a perennial tradition in Persian poetry where, after all analysis, something more or less ineffable remains that cannot be related to mundane or quotidian reality as we know it. Sohrāb Sepehrī (1930–80) is perhaps the best example of a modernist nature poet in whose works the natural world seems to possess a soul all its own. He is certainly unique in expressing an ever-present concern with the course of modern civilisation as it seems to move forward heedless of those aspects of human existence that cannot be contained in material reality as we know and sense it. The clearest and most direct and elaborate expression of this tendency occurs, I believe, in the long autobiographical poem titled 'The Sound of Water's Footstep' (Ṣedā-ye Pā-ye Āb) where the speaker recounts in specific detail his pedigree, names the city of his birth, revealing many specific traits of his physical surroundings, and recounts the stages of his life from childhood to the time of the composition of the poem in question. He has a diversified ancestry that may have included an unknown plant in India, a prostitute from the fabled medieval city of Bukhara, and some clay pottery from the ancient settlement in Sialk near his birthplace of Kashan. At the same time, he is sure that Kashan is the city where he was born and grew up. He then tells us how, having emancipated himself from all these 'belongings', he now has built himself a city 'on the other side of the night', presumably the night that has come to signify the presence of certain undesirable socio-political situations in the dominant poetry of his time.

His profession of faith is perhaps one of the most pronounced aspects of the life the speaker recounts and recalls, and it stands as explicit testimony to the poet's tendency to posit a living soul in nature as the final arbiter of the beauty that points to some metaphysical space beyond all organised religion or faith-based practice that we might imagine (Sepehrī 1985: 90–1,):

> I am a Muslim
> pray facing a red rose
> over a jetting fountain
> and press my forehead against a shaft of light,
> sensing that the whole plain is a prayer rug.
> I do my ablutions along with pulsating lattices,
> the moon flows in my prayer, as does an apparition
> and as does a rock through it.
> And the particles of my prayer glow and turn luminous.
> I pray after the wind has made its call from the minaret that is the cypress
> I pray after the grass has uttered its 'God is glorious' chant,
> after the billowing of the surge.
> My sacred sanctuary stands at the edge of the sea
> moves through the acacias
> flows from garden to garden, from one city to the next,
> much like the breeze.
> My Black Stone is the glowing of a little flower-bed.

As this final anomaly, playing on the opposition of 'The Black Stone' or Ka'ba, indicates, declarations of a faith with a difference or as a binary option abound in those Persian poets who, in one way or another, entertain a gnostic vision of life, either in discourse or as a matter of belief. It is exemplified in passages such as Sa'dī pointing to the purposeful and emblematic beauty in nature that signals the kind of superior intelligence which recalls the grandeur of God's design for humanity, as in his famous opening line: 'To the intelligent mind a leaf upon green trees / is but a sign carrying a book on the knowledge of the divine.' What is distinct, in the manner in which the sentiment is expressed in modernist Persian poetry, has to do with the difference in the departures far more typical of modernity, where the link between the apparent beauty as evident in nature finds little expression in contemporary scientific approaches emblematic of social life in its dominant form in many modern Muslim-majority societies. As such, secularism of the type that is prevalent in modern Iran has been almost entirely incapable of envisioning a realm superior to manifest reality, but corresponding to it in spheres higher than that of the mundane sense-based world, we are reduced to religious beliefs in an afterlife superior to the present but still bound to it by the force of orthodox belief, rather than faith.

What we see in Sepehrī's excerpt, is, rather, an individual ceremony of worship that involves a red rose, a jetting fountain, and a shaft of light, each registering a basic difference that separates them from objects of mass observances emblematic of Islam as an organised religion. Revolving around such subtle natural phenomena the exact meaning and function of the worship may not be familiar to masses of believers, but they do lead the observant speaker along a personal pathway to the heavens.

Conceptualised and practised as a requirement for being a Muslim, the actions described through the speaker's profession of faith may not satisfy the prescribed rituals for such an appellation or communicate a sense of belonging to an organised religion. Yet, the excerpt begins with as frank and emphatic an expression of being Muslim as possible. How can one be a Muslim and not pray in the direction of the Ka'ba as the *qebleh* or pivot of the world, or have any Ka'ba other than the solid *Ḥajar Aswad* in Mecca, the famous black stone around which Muslims are supposed to do the ceremonial circumambulations of the Hajj, but one that emanates light, moves breeze-like from one garden to the next or even from city to city? And how can one profess to be a Muslim, so deeply immersed in nature's beauty, and yet not move to thoughts of the one God that is the greatest of them all? The conclusion seems inevitable, somehow the speaker here has arrived at a plane of the truth about the relationship between natural beauty and that of the one and only God which others are pitifully unaware of.

3. Forūgh Farrokhzād

Distinctly different in shape from this is the poetry that Forūgh Farrokhzād (1935–67) wrote towards the end of her life, where the same impulse for personal discovery gives rise to an aspiration to touch the face of infinitude. This impulse may not constitute a staple of the poet's concern but, when it does, it almost invariably takes on a much more intense and passionate tone of utterance, and may well signal a far greater arena of inclusion. In a poem composed towards the end of her brief poetic career, titled 'Only the Voice Remains', she imagines herself – or is it her soul? – experiencing an upward ascent that can be said to constitute a modernist analogue to a Rumi ghazal where the speaker depicts the human soul's upward journey as a fully-fledged ascension story; these two poems certainly thematise the foundational Islamic ascension story – i.e. the Prophet Muḥammad's nocturnal journey to the heavens – recalled and celebrated time and again by medieval Persian poets. The modern element in her poem, however, is rooted in an abiding tendency in Farrokhzād's poetry to feature speakers who find themselves caught in a confining environment but somehow discover within themselves an intense desire, and sometimes an overriding will, to seek higher planes. Farrokhzād's poem opens with an ascent motivated by the impatience that results from this feeling of confinement (Farrokhzād 2004: 90,):

> Why should I stop, why?
> the birds have flown off through the breadth of the blue
> the horizon looks vertical
> the horizon looks vertical and motion looks like lifting up.
> Shining planets revolve
> at the edge of my sight.
> From that height, the earth begins to multiply,
> pockets of air
> turn into tunnels reaching down,
> and the day is an enormity
> that cannot be contained in the mind of the worm
> that is the daily paper.

The initial image of contemplating the birds who 'have flown off through the breadth of the blue' compels us to sense or even see the swelling of that motivating desire and, once having begun the avian journey, the poem describes aspirations that take the ascending speaker all the way to an ultimate union with the sun. Glancing down, Farrokhzād's speaker is repulsed by what she observes not just on the surly face of the earth as a whole, but, more precisely, in the very environment that has nurtured her former self; only now that environment appears to her as 'the land of the midgets', social standards look like those that have forever 'revolved around zero', and individuals appear like sightless subjects in 'the fiefdom of the blind': those to whom she is now beginning to appear determined not to leave any part of her being, especially something as precious as her heart's protocol (Farrokhzād 2004: 91–3,):

> In the land of the midgets
> standards of measurement
> have forever revolved around zero.
> Why should I stop?
> I pledge allegiance to the four elements
> and shall not leave the task of drafting my heart's protocol
> to the fiefdom of the blind.

Building on this initial narrative of distancing from a lowly earth, a path towards the skies that lies through what the speaker calls 'the capillaries of life', the speaker describes the voice as something 'that will be absorbed into atoms of time', and asks again: 'why should I stop?' And as she looks down at the earth, viewing it as a swamp that can only be 'the spawning ground for petrifying vermin', a nurturing ground for 'the mind of the morgue' that is 'measured by bloated corpses', as well as a few choice descriptions of this kind before coming to a final realisation anchored in a kind of certainty that would just not be possible without that distancing (Farrokhzād 2004: 91,):

> The end of all forces is union, union
> with the sun's luminous essence
> flowing into the intellect of light.
> It is only natural
> for wooden windmills to fall apart,
> why should I stop?

What we have in 'Only the Voice Remains' is a modern poetic experience of ascent where we too, as readers, clearly witness a process of distancing where all that is devoid of any good is left behind in its putrid earthly existence, while at the same time seeing the speaker approach 'the sun's luminous essence / flowing into the intellect of light'. It is from that celestial vantage point that the speaker – and the poet, and we – can view the unity invisible to all eyes and minds that can only scan the surly surface of the earth. Our speaker here definitely now seems totally detached from life as we know it and all that it may hold. Even an innocuous mating call seems to her to be, not the expression of a desire that can ultimately ensure the survival of the species, but as 'the long howl of savagery in a beast's sexual organ', and the human activity of love-making finds expression in an animal act analogous to the movement of 'a puny worm inanely penetrating a fleshy vacuum'. In separating herself from all this, aspiring instead to be connected to life by the 'bloodstained lineage of red roses', the speaker is now seen as the pure soul of the bird whom we have seen in the act of taking flight at the poem's opening (Farrokhzād 2004: 93,):

> What have I to do with the long howl of savagery
> in a beast's sexual organ?
> What have I to do with a puny worm inanely penetrating a fleshy vacuum?
> The bloodstained lineage of red roses ties me to life
> the bloodstained lineage of red roses, you know!

Are these 'red roses' of the same species of 'red rose' which the speaker in Sepehrī's biographical poem discussed above has made the object of worship, much in the way that a Muslim in worship presses his forehead against a piece of clay, preferably from some holy ground? I have no answer, but the coincidence seems striking.

4. ʿAbbās Kiarostami [Kiyārostamī]

It is this ensouled world at various stages of its movement towards infinite perfection that we see in ʿAbbās Kiarostami's (1940–2016) minimalist poetic vision which the internationally acclaimed Iranian film-maker arrived at in the latest stages of his lifelong artistic peregrinations.[9] What he adds to Sepehrī and Farrokhzād's artistic accomplishments, one which he cherished and has memorialised in several of his films as well, is the depiction of many poetic agents and themes in his first poetry collection titled *Hamrāh bā Bād* (1999), translated into English as *Walking with the Wind* (2001). There we see personages more or less as phenomenologically direct manifestations at once of specific states of being and of the chain that connects them all in an infinite continuum ranging from the lowly and the mundane to the invisible and incomprehensible. The pine and the box-tree, the sycamore and the oak, the mulberry and the cherry, the weeping willow and the towering cypress all grow and decay side by side with the rattan, the cotton, the poppies, the violets and the begonia. All are there to relay single messages from an infinite number of entities and states, both local and global, and far larger, so much so, indeed, that they remain utterly unimaginable and shall, therefore, stay forever unexpressed. This full assembly of vegetation, animals winged or not, and humans high and low, are described as moving or being moved, observing and being observed at the same time, and as part of single acts of concentrated attention defying human categories: nuns young and old walk seemingly directionless, mostly arguing and disagreeing, while small children play their seemingly unimportant games. Nearby pregnant women cry next to their sleeping men, soldiers march to and from nameless battlefields. Meanwhile, the scarecrow acts and is acted upon in every conceivable way except scaring the crows, a snowman melts under the wishful eyes of a child nursing a fever and a doll is handled far more gently by the child than by her mother.

In one poem that Michael Beard and I, as translators, highlight in our introduction, we are invited to contemplate how the contrast between the heavy and the light serves the purpose of advancing the vision behind that ensouled existence (Kiarostami 2001: 44,):

> How merciful
> That the turtle doesn't see
> The little bird's effortless flight.

The fact that the three vantage points we have here – the turtle's, the bird's and the human observer's – 'may leave us wondering where we stand, both literally and metaphorically', leads us to conclude that 'somewhere beyond the three viewpoints we sense a vision that lights the flame of an impossible desire'. In another instance, we discuss how an obvious event, perhaps even a mundanely obvious one, may invite a sharper eye, a closer, more wholesome observation (Kiarostami 2001: 57,):

> Autumn afternoon
> A sycamore leaf
> falls softly
> and rests
> on its own shadow.

Here we begin with the premise that 'The aesthetic of close observation is akin to the aesthetic of familiar objects: the imperative to pause and look more closely at

[9] See my Persian essay on Kiarostami the poet (Karimi-Hakkak 2017).

daily experience'. Applied to the instance of the sycamore leaf and its shadow poetically observed, the impression is inescapable:

> Strictly speaking, it is obvious that a leaf falls on its shadow. It is a process so logical it should bear no comment, except, of course, that the observer may forget the logical conclusion that the shadow and the leaf are connected. Observation corrects consciousness. It is our unscientific selves who are capable of surprise at how exactly the two match up.
>
> (Kiarostami 2001: 8)

At the centre of this sacred journey, as the pilgrim-narrator's constant companion, the wind impresses us as a vocable of breathing, an echo of a voice that seems to be saying: I will be your guide, passer-by; for I am vast and invincible. Come with me, let me calm your fears, let me lead you far from the anguish of daily life.

Towards the end of our Introduction, we devote some time to placing the poet within his aesthetic tradition, especially in reference to the mystical trend, both medieval and modern, within it. We conclude with these words:

> Habitually, nonchalantly, Kiarostami combines the supple lexicon of the Persian language with the vast aesthetic potential of Persian poetry to make that august aesthetic tradition new. Characteristically, he throws the spotlight on the object rather than on the perceiving mind to keep our attention fixed on the poetic nature of our world. In this way, his poetry embodies and exhibits the most abiding concerns of the entire tradition: the structure of the ineffable, those relations that cannot be reduced to human logic ... [His] poems ... often acknowledge and celebrate the presence of mystery in our midst. Whether explicitly ... or more subtly, ... they place the human within a world of nature, but nature widened to emphasize the mundane and the quotidian as well as the supernatural. Kiarostami has thus grafted the most abiding aspirations of the best of Persian poets, both classical and modern, to contemporary concerns. If he can be said as a film-maker to have led the art form of the twentieth century to new aesthetic heights, these restless, airy walks with the wind may guide us step by step to a new verbal kinetic.
>
> (2001: 13)

The whole journey, and the sacred silence, that is thus communicated through Kiarostami's poetic world appears attentive to ordinary life and acts, ultimately, as a recognition of some sort of ineffable intelligent universe. Tellingly, the process means that rather than renouncing power, wealth and honour in a noble sacrifice, we simply discover that they no longer hold such interest for us. This *via negativa* rids the self of worldly contrivances, resulting in true peace, an astonishing refreshment, a sense of a heart enlarged. In that state of contemplation, all souls, all potentially divine, begin to manifest the divine.

Certainly, Elāhī's engagement with matters that relate directly or indirectly to the Neoplatonic understanding of the world is unique in many ways and, therefore, appears as most striking in the context of modern and modernist Persian poetry. Read against the background of the classical tradition, his poems strike us as the ultimate illustration of 'divestiture' of the most dispiriting type – indeed part of the trend that I have described here as distancing of all metaphysical tendencies. When it comes to the other poets included in my discussion they seem to be searching for some ulterior, non-material essence, one that rises above all dogma to present glimpses of a secular spirituality whose aesthetic and moral worth has yet to be recognised. Taken together, these four modern Persian poets, and many others along with them, continue to carve a sacred space, much resembling an altar in a celestial temple, in the universe of Persian poetry for the presence, at once lovingly wholesome and embracing, yet forever invisible, ineffable but essential to the wholeness, of that very universe. There reigns a silence that seems to speak forever to the whole of the human race.

References

Elāhī, B. (2013), *Dīdan* (Tehran, Bidgol).

Elāhī, B. (2014), *Javāniha* (Tehran, Bidgol).

Elāhī, B. (2015), *Ḥallāj al-Asrār* (Tehran, Bidgol).

Farrokhzād, F. (2004), *Remembering the Flight: Twenty Poems, A Parallel Text, Selected and Translated with an Introduction by A. Karimi-Hakkak*, 3rd edn (Los Angeles, Ketab Corporation).

Ganjavī, M. (2016), 'Elāhī, Bījan', in *Encyclopædia Iranica*, online edition, accessed 19 October 2018, www.iranicaonline.org/articles/Elāhī-Bījan

Karimi-Hakkak, A. (1995), *Recasting Persian Poetry: Scenarios of Poetic Modernity in Iran* (Utah, University of Utah Press).

Karimi-Hakkak, A. (2012), 'Love, Separation, and Reunion: The Master-Narrative of the Human Condition in Persian Mystical Poetry', in W. Ahmadi (ed.), *Converging Zones: Persian Literary Tradition and the Writing of History, Studies in Honor of Amin Banani* (Costa Mesa, Mazda Publishers), 220–45.

Karimi-Hakkak, A. (2017), 'Abbas Kiarostami, the Belated Poet: Evaluation and Appreciation', *Arman, Journal of the Arman Cultural Foundation*, 4: 56–82.

Kiarostami, ʿA. (1999), *Hamrāh bā Bād: Majmūʿeh-ye Sorūdehhā-ye ʿAbbās Kiyārostamī* (Tehran, Nashr-e Honar-e Īrān).

Kiarostami, ʿA. (2001), *Walking with the Wind: Poems by Abbas Kiyarostami*, bilingual edition, trans. from the Persian by A. Karimi-Hakkak & M. Beard (Cambridge MA, Harvard Film Archive).

Kinra, R. (2015), *Writing Self, Writing Empire: Chandar Bhan Brahman and the Cultural World of the Indo-Persian Secretary* (Oakland, University of California Press).

Orsini, F. & Sheikh, S. (eds) (2014), *After Timur Left: Culture and Circulation in Fifteenth-Century North India* (New Delhi, Oxford University Press).

Sepehrī, S. (1985), *Montakhab-e Ashʿār* (Selected Poems: Selections by A.-R. Aḥmadī) (Tehran, Tahuri).

Shāfiʿī-Kadkānī, M.-R. (1994), *Dar Eqlīm-e Rowshanāʾī: Tafsīr-e chand Ghazal az Ḥakīm Sanāʾī Ghaznavī* (Tehran, Agah).

Shāfiʿī-Kadkānī, M.-R. (1999), *Zobūr-e Parsī: Negāhi beh Zendegī va ghazalhā-ye ʿĀṭṭār* (Tehran, Agah).

Sharma, S. (2017), *Mughal Arcadia: Persian Literature in an Indian Court* (Cambridge MA, Harvard University Press).

Suhravardī, S. ad-Dīn (1988), *Ḥīkmat al-Ishrāq*, trans. with commentary by J. Sajjādī (Tehran, Tehran University Press).

21

The New Image of the Beloved in the Old Mirror: Reflections on the Neoplatonic Tradition in Modern Turkish Poetry

NESLIHAN DEMIRKOL AND MEHMET KALPAKLI*

THIS EDITED VOLUME includes two other chapters dealing with the traces of Neoplatonism in Ottoman poetry, those of Walter Andrews and Didem Havlioğlu. In this chapter, we will be talking even more about Turkish poetry – modern poetry in particular, and we show how modern Turkish poets have embraced a Neoplatonic cosmology of an Islamic character, one specifically exemplified by the Ottoman poetic tradition. To do this, we use a sample of poems by several modern Turkish poets: Asaf Hâlet Çelebi (1907–58), Behçet Necatigil (1916–79), Sezai Karakoç (b. 1933), Hilmi Yavuz (b. 1936) and Birhan Keskin (b. 1963). Through a close reading of the thematic structure of these poems, we show how several key themes – namely those of the beloved–lover dynamic; the symbolism of mirror, light and unity; and spiritual journeys for the sake of the ascent to the One – are re-shaped, reclaimed and represented in modern Turkish poetry, especially following the strong rejection of Ottoman mysticism in the cultural politics of the Republic of Turkey. This chapter maps out the diverging and new forms of Neoplatonic imagery and themes re-emerging even in secular poetry. Hence, we seek to reveal the significant role Neoplatonic cosmology continues to play in defining the aesthetic codes, the hierarchical dynamic between the lover and the beloved, and the rules of spirituality in modern poetry.

We start with a brief introduction about the relationship between Neoplatonic thought and Islamic mysticism. Then we touch upon the Ottoman poetic tradition and the role of Neoplatonic cosmology in it. This is followed by a short overview of the transition from the Ottoman state to the Turkish Republic and the consequences of this transition in the cultural and literary fields from the perspective of the poetic tradition and its Neoplatonic sources. In light of the latter, we analyse our selection of poems to assess the 'continuity' or 'discontinuity' of Neoplatonic thought in modern Turkish poetry.

* We would like to thank Hugh J. Turner for helping with proofreading.

We will not offer an extensive discussion of Neoplatonic cosmology or of its founding exponent, Plotinus, for these points are covered in the introduction to this volume.[1] Nor will we offer an extensive treatment of the influences of Neoplatonism on Islamic mysticism or Ottoman poetry, which subjects are well covered in the chapters by Walter Andrews and Didem Havlioğlu.

Nevertheless, a few additional words on this latter subject are necessary to contextualise our discussion here in this chapter. Ottoman poetry produced sublime and sophisticated examples of Neoplatonic cosmology.[2] This version of Neoplatonic cosmology had an Islamic character inherited from Arabic and Persian literary cultures. Neoplatonic images and themes, such as divine and profane love, converge throughout as reciprocal mirror images. 'Light' and 'mirror' symbolism and the concepts of 'purification' and 'unity of being' pervade the lyrical tradition and constitute the conceptual and aesthetic backbone of Ottoman poetry.

Ottoman poetry, as Andrews states in his chapter in this volume, was an indispensable element of Ottoman cultural life, which was, in essence, a Neoplatonic narrative. In Ottoman society, the figures of the ruler and religious leader merged in the person of the sultan-caliph. Accordingly, in poetry, the beloved, the ruler and the Divine are represented in the same figure. In this regime, the ruler/Divine becomes the source of all interpretations (Andrews 2004: 15). Thus, when we refer to the Ottoman poetic tradition, whether in terms of classical or folk poetry, what should be understood is an Islamic mysticism with Neoplatonic features. Accordingly, in dealing with the traces of Neoplatonism in modern Turkish poetry, we are mainly looking for the marks of the Ottoman poetic tradition rather than overt references to Plotinus, because – much as Ferial J. Ghazoul argues in her contribution to this volume concerning the Neoplatonic echoes in Arabic culture and modern Arabic poetry – the names of the philosopher and his works are absent in modern Turkish culture.[3]

The Ottomans had a strong poetic tradition; however, Turkish literature, and Turkish poetry specifically, went through a profound epistemological and aesthetic transformation during the transition from empire to nation-state. Beginning with the modernisation project during the 19th century, this break in tradition left behind an extremely polarised political and cultural milieu. During the rise of nationalism among the various ethnic and religious communities of the Ottoman Empire

[1] For an analysis of Neoplatonism and the Islamic tradition, see Morewedge (1992) and Schimmel (1975). For mysticism and Islamic poetry, see Schimmel (1982).

[2] For more about Ottoman poetry and its Neoplatonic features, see Andrews (1985), Andrews & Kalpaklı (2005) and Ayvazoğlu (2002).

[3] The first partial translation of Plotinus's *Enneads* into modern Turkish was published only in 1975, see Eralp (1975), while the first complete translation was almost 20 years later, see Özcan (1996). This information is based on our search in the catalogues of Milli Kütüphane (National Library), İBB Atatürk Kitaplığı (Atatürk Library of Istanbul Metropolitan Municipality), To-Kat (a national catalogue of library collections) and WorldCat (a global catalogue of library collections). We would also like to express our gratitude to Asst. Prof. Dr Filiz Cluzeau (Ancient Greek Language and Literature Department, Istanbul University) for confirming our findings.

during the 19th and early 20th centuries, each newly emerging 'national' community needed a figure of the 'other' against which to frame its own identity. For the minorities of the empire, it was a rather easy process: 'We are not Ottoman, and what is Ottoman is not us' was the motto of their nation-building process. But for the new Turkish Republic, the process was one of self-denial. As Victoria Holbrook states, the process was a schizophrenic act by the state which ended up creating an 'other' through itself (1998: 12–13). The Ottoman Empire and anything related to it – especially Ottoman poetry – became controversial.[4]

The mainstream historical narrative about the modernisation of Ottoman-Turkish literature is one of binary oppositions: Ottoman versus Turkish, court poetry versus folk poetry, centre versus periphery, East versus West, new versus old, and modernity versus tradition. Thus, the attitude of a scholar, poet or intellectual towards Ottoman poetry is often as political a stance as it is an academic or aesthetic one. To avoid falling into the trap of these essentialist binaries, Andrews suggests focusing instead on 'becomings'.

A 'becoming', a conceptual tool offered by Deleuze and Guattari to help move beyond binary oppositions, is an area where concepts are not seen as being in hierarchy with one another. In the process of 'becoming', a culture can be both Western and Eastern, central and peripheral, and modern and traditional. Rather than oppositions, the elements of these binary sets are considered more as simultaneous 'becomings' (Andrews 2004: 13). In this chapter, we follow the footsteps of Andrews's reading of three modern Turkish poets as possible examples of 'Turkish-becoming-Ottoman-becoming-modern'.

The emerging Turkish nation constructed its identity against an Ottoman 'other'. As Andrews puts it, this led to a 'cataclysmic discontinuity' in the culture that was triggered by the encounter of 'Turkish-culture-becoming-Persian-becoming-European' with European culture and ultimately resulted in the dissolution of the Ottoman state (2004: 14). Starting from the 19th century, the most frequently criticised aspects of Ottoman literature were its mystic and 'unrealistic' features – elements stemming from the mystical character of its poetry. In a political environment where the intellectuals of the period considered scientific approaches in society and realism in literature as the pillars of the European-like state they longed for, they strongly opposed Islamic mysticism and the classical forms of Ottoman poetry as symbols of belatedness that needed to be purged from literature. This sets the Turkish case quite apart from that of Arabic culture, where, as Ghazoul details in her chapter in this volume, a solution to the dilemma of modernisation was found in a return to poetic roots with new themes and old but relaxed forms.

Nevertheless, despite the cultural policies of rejecting Ottoman mysticism, it found its way back into modern Turkish poetry. The re-emergence of mystical features in modern Turkish poetry coincides with the transition to multi-party politics in Turkey. Parallel to Andrews, we claim that a similar process occurred in

[4] For more about the history of Turkish poetry and its modernisation, see Özgül (2018).

the literary field and that poetry became more heterogeneous. In his article, based on Deleuze and Guattari's concepts of a signifying regime and a post-signifying regime, Andrews defines Ottoman society as a signifying regime, where the sultan-caliph was at once the ruler and the Divine, as well as the centre of meaning and interpretation in poetry (2004: 15–16). We claim that the single-party regime of Turkey between 1923 and 1946 created a similar atmosphere for the literary field; thus, in this period, meaning and interpretation were mostly generated according to the ruling power and the ideologies of the new republic.[5]

After 1946, the transition to multi-party politics created a paradigm shift and paved the way for a de-centralisation and multiplication of meaning and interpretation in the cultural field. We argue that this change made the period after 1950 a post-signifying regime. In this new regime, with its multi-party and capitalist system,[6] needs and meaning were 'subjectivised', thereby liberating meaning and interpretation for both Islamic-mystic poets and secular poets.[7] For mystical poets, there was no longer a need to identify the Divine subject of the poem with a ruling power. Mystical poetry referred directly to the Divine. For more secular poets, the dissolution of the centre of meaning was more a process of individuation, one in which the poet needed only love as a companion and mediator on the road to self-realisation and enlightenment.

1. Four Stances towards the Neoplatonic Tradition

As a comprehensive review of all modern Turkish poets and their poems would have been impossible in a chapter of this size, we have had to be selective. But we believe that the sample of Turkish poetry we analyse here is, if not perfectly representative of the whole, at least illuminating for the stimulating view it provides regarding different 'becomings' in the Turkish cultural field.

We analyse modern Turkish poets starting from the late 1940s under four categories based on their attitudes towards the mystical poetic tradition to determine how elements of the mystical tradition once again came to flourish in Turkish poetry.

The first category is composed of poets who are neutral towards mysticism. The poets of this group manifest a form of continuity with and an awareness of the mystical poetic tradition through their use of Neoplatonic terminology, but they do not deliberately appropriate it. They therefore lie beyond the scope of the chapter,

[5] Pertinent examples of this include the poems written for Atatürk by such well-known poets as Fazıl Hüsnü Dağlarca, Ümit Yaşar Oğuzcan and Orhan Seyfi Orhon, as well as the famous minstrel Âşık Veysel in the field of folk literature.

[6] For more on the economic history of Turkey after the 1950s see Tokatlıoğlu & Öztürk (2008), Altuğ *et al.* (2008), Aydın & Taşkın (2018).

[7] For more about the profiles of Muslim intellectuals of Turkey, see Meeker (1991; 1994), and Mardin (1994b). Meeker's and Mardin's arguments provide a solid basis for our interpretation of the 1950s as a paradigm shift in the history of Turkish poetry. We would like to thank the reviewer for drawing our attention to these studies.

but nevertheless warrant a brief mention. They include such figures as Nazım Hikmet, Oktay Rifat, Turgut Uyar, Cemal Süreya, İlhan Berk, Ece Ayhan, Atillâ İlhan and Enis Batur.[8] Most are considered members of 'İkinci Yeni' (Second New Movement – the Turkish Avant-Garde), a poetry movement founded in the mid-1950s by a group of young poets. Though neutral towards mysticism, they nevertheless use certain concepts of Islamic mysticism and its poetic tradition. İkinci Yeni poets were aware of the philosophical background and poetic tradition of mysticism. Despite this, they did not include mystical elements as an organic part of their poems, instead merely providing nominal references to them in the titles of poems that have nothing to do with traditional mystical forms, themes or symbolism.[9] Andrews and Kalpaklı discuss, in a similar vein, the position of the traditional *kaside* form in the late Ottoman and republican periods: 'naming some poem a "kaside" in the post-Ottoman age becomes a way of establishing a relation to the past, a relation ... independent of any prior rules of form or genre conventions. The character of that relation is open and dynamic' (1996: 324–5).

In the second category are poets we identify as modern representatives of institutionalised Islamic mysticism – that is, modern-day analogues, or 'disciples' (*murid*), of the Ottoman-era poets of the religious orders (*tarikat*). The leading figure of this group is Necip Fazıl Kısakürek, and other representatives include Sezai Karakoç, Cahit Zarifoğlu, Erdem Bayazıt, Rasim Özdenören, Nuri Pakdil, Mehmet Akif İnan and Alaeddin Özdenören.[10] These poets consider themselves a link in the chain of Islamic tradition and devote their poetry to producing a modern version of Islamic mysticism. Their poetry is largely defined by themes of the mystical tradition. Generally, their poetry is part of an ideological and political effort to 'resurrect' Islam and can be viewed as an outgrowth of political Islam. In this category, we are going to examine Sezai Karakoç.

Laurent Mignon argues that Necip Fazıl Kısakürek and Sezai Karakoç introduced the theme of mystical love to modern poetry (2003: 66). Although we agree with

[8] For more on Turkish avant-garde poetry, see Hızlan (2006).

[9] Murat Nemet-Nejat, a translator and an essayist, views such references as harking back not to the Ottoman mystical tradition, but instead to a pre-Islamic, pagan, shamanistic Sufism deriving from Central Asian Turkic culture (2004: 325). Nemet-Nejat's praise of the allegedly pre-Islamic source of Sufism reflects the continuities of the imagined historical narrative introduced by the new republican project, which was determined to eliminate Arabic, Persian and Islamic influences in cultural identity, and exemplifies how the modern Turkish nation-building project misinterprets Ottoman lyric poetry.

[10] These seven poets are referred to as the 'yedi güzel adam' (seven good men) in Turkish literary circles and by their readers. In an interview, Rasim Özdenören states that 'Yedi Güzel Adam' is the title of Cahit Zarifoğlu's poem published in 1974, and they are named after this poem. He refers to the above-mentioned seven poets as the 'original seven good men' (see Anon. 2014b). Except for Karakoç, six of them attended the same high school in the south-eastern Turkish province of Kahramanmaraş. The 'seven good men' have been the subject of cultural policies, too. The national public broadcaster of Turkey, the Turkish Radio and Television Corporation (TRT), aired a TV series with the same title in 2014. The Kahramanmaraş Metropolitan Municipality, also, inaugurated the Yedi Güzel Adam Edebiyat Müzesi (Seven Good Men Literary Museum) on 6 March 2019. See the website of Kahramanmaraş Metropolitan Municipality. Both the museum and the TV series were praised by the national press. See Anon. (2014a; 2014b; 2019a; 2019b; 2019c).

Mignon's classification of these poets under the category of the 'new Sufi poetry' (2002a: 129), we feel the need to emphasise their ties with the ideology of political Islam. We argue that these two poets not only write modern Sufi poetry but also express their political and ideological engagements through the images of Neoplatonism. In their poetry, they search not only for God and spiritual love but also for ways of constructing a world order conducive to the experience of the spiritual love they describe. We believe this aspect popularised their poetry among the leaders of political Islamic movements and made it a convenient tool for their campaigns.[11]

In the third category are poets who adopt and reclaim the mystical tradition but who are neither members of an institutionalised Islamic cult nor necessarily in search of an Islamic divine. We call them modern-day dervishes, as their poetic attitude recalls the dervishes of Ottoman times. Unlike the mystic ideologists in the previous category, the poets of this category do not pursue the traces of the tradition for the sake of ideology, but for the sake of mystical experience and the poetic tradition. These poets aim not to re-establish an Islamic civilisation or resurrect the past, but to reclaim the mystical tradition and to pursue their spiritual journey beyond the influence of binary oppositions and without an ideological engagement with an Islamic worldview. Their poetry is a modern-age guide for the soul's self-realisation without reference to any specific religion, but simply to the One. In this category, we are going to examine Asaf Hâlet Çelebi and Hilmi Yavuz.

In the last category are the poets we call secular dervishes. On the level of belief, their poetry is neither mystical nor Islamic. The essence and the subjects of their poetry are profane and worldly. However, the poetic cosmos they craft between the lines is rooted in a Neoplatonic theory of human conditions and emotions. Their poetry deals with earthly matters through a Neoplatonic perspective and symbolism. Of all the poets examined here, it is those in this group who best exhibit how Neoplatonic philosophy in modern poetry can serve in the world of a post-signifying regime, where there is hardly ever a centralised focal point of interpretation or meaning. In this category, we are going to examine Behçet Necatigil and Birhan Keskin.

2. Ideologist in Exile: Karakoç's 'From the Land of Exile to the Capital of Capitals'

Sezai Karakoç (b. 1933) defines himself as a mystic and describes mysticism, religion and civilisation as the fundamental concepts of his poetry and ideology

[11] Karakoç was himself the leader of a political party, Diriliş (Diri-P / Party of Resurrection), established in 1990. Diri-P was dissolved in 1997, and Karakoç founded a new party a decade later: the Yüce Diriliş Partisi (Party of Supreme Resurrection) (http://yucedirilis.org.tr/). The poem we analyse in this chapter was publicly read by Recep Tayyip Erdoğan, then prime minister (and now president) of Turkey, in 2012, even though Karakoç was the leader of another political party (Anon. 2012). Erdoğan seems to be a fan of Kısakürek as well (Anon. 2013).

(2012: 6–7). In his writings on poetics, he emphasises the relationship between the poet and metaphysics. With the term metaphysics, he points to not only the source of artistic creation but also the link between the artist and the Divine. To Karakoç, a poet sits outside the world, somewhere unknown to us, and is always inclined towards God, even if sometimes unwillingly. Throughout history, poets have always dealt with the idea of the infinite, and the Necessary Being, and modern times are no exception; hence according to Karakoç, when the resurrection of the 'civilisation of Truth' is completed, the reign of metaphysical/mythical literature will also be restored (2012: 31–54).

Andrews argues that Karakoç's poetry contains a longing for a metaphysical world under a centralised Ottoman rule (2004: 19). The problem for Karakoç lies in the lack of a single signifying regime as a reference point for all the interpretations in the world today, a lack which he hopes to remedy by a 'return' to an Ottoman order. Hilmi Yavuz, too, in his Marxist reading of Karakoç's 'From the Land of Exile to the Capital of Capitals', concludes that the poet desires an Ottoman rule based on Islamic civilisation (2010: 47). While we do not oppose these claims, we aim to provide a different perspective on the poem.

The poem is a very long one and is composed of four parts. Here we address the fourth and final part. The first two parts of the poem start with the verse (1995: 20, 22):

> Following the tradition of our ancestors[,]
> let's begin the poem with the roses.

This is a clear reference to Ottoman classical poetry, where the rose is one of the main symbols of the beloved, the ruler and God. Karakoç thus invites us into the poetic world of Ottoman mysticism. However, as the poet is situated in a post-signifying regime, there is no way that we can interpret the 'rose' as a symbol of a central ruler. As he is a mystic poet, it is also hard to read the 'rose' as signifying a beloved other than God. Therefore, in this post-signifying regime, Karakoç, as a mystical poet, can only speak to God, because in this modern era God is the only central power that can define meaning.

The third part of the poem begins as follows (Karakoç 1995: 24):

> The dead ones have arrived with hackberries and ivies
> They have climbed up my walls and towers.[12]

Who are 'the dead ones' in these lines? After the arrival of the dead, the poet hears the voice of the One, thus indicating that the 'dead ones' are the poets of the old signifying regime echoing the central meaning of their times. In Karakoç's time, there is neither an ideal figure to serve as a role model for society nor a mediator for the protagonist in her or his spiritual journey. Thus, to find the right meaning and right

[12] All translations are ours except where otherwise noted.

expression in his poetry, he needs the cosmology of the old poets, and it is upon the artefacts of that cosmology that he constructs his poem.[13]

The fourth part of the poem emphasises a pure asceticism for the poet, since life on earth is described as an exile (Sılay 1996: 496,):

First I was banished from your heart
And in a way all my exiles continue that banishment
Beyond all ceremonies, feasts, services, holy days
I came to you, came to you on my knees
I came to beg forgiveness, though I don't deserve forgiving
Don't prolong my worldly banishment.[14]

Life on earth is nothing more than an exile and source of pain. Also, its elements – time, reflection and light – are just a crooked image of the truth and are not helpful at all (Sılay 1996: 496,):

The lamps are crooked
Mirrors scorpion angels
Time, a last vision of the stricken horse.

The symbol for the beloved in the old poetry, Leylâ, cannot represent or symbolise the One anymore. The poet is unable to create the meaning or construct the symbolic universe of the old poetry using the same image. Hence the lover again asks for the mercy of the beloved (Sılay 1996: 496,):

Oh tenderest and most profound of hearts
Beloved
Most beloved
Oh, beloved
Don't prolong my worldly banishment.

For the poet, there is no place of refuge, because the house of the ruler has collapsed and meaning has been lost. The poet/lover can no longer find peace in the profane space of the ruler, as there is nothing left behind of the one ruler, the single signifier of all meaning: 'A home is no inheritance but inheritance's phantasm' (Sılay 1996: 496). The poet cannot survive in this new order, and he cannot produce meaning as his ancestors did. That is why he is obliged to refer to the Divine subject, God, without any references to the ruling power. The lover is weak, in constant pain, longing for the beloved, the One, and his or her forgiveness (Sılay 1996: 497,):

In your breast there is a vein that summons your exiles to return
I won't give up hope in you, there's a tree called mercy in your heart
Beloved
Most beloved
Oh, beloved.

[13] The image can also be interpreted as an invasion by the ivy and hackberries surrounding the poet's walls, and thus as implying the isolation of the poet. Although we prefer our interpretation, we would like to thank the reviewer for reminding us of this alternative reading of the verses.
[14] This translation is by Walter G. Andrews.

3. Modern-Day Dervishes: Asaf Hâlet Çelebi and Hilmi Yavuz

Asaf Hâlet Çelebi (1907–58), a unique figure in modern Turkish poetry and a contemporary of Nazım Hikmet, won little praise for his poetry in Turkish literary circles. Nevertheless, in his poetry, he achieved a very liberal interpretation of the tradition of which he was a part, an interpretation that revised and reinvented the traditional mystical cosmos (İnam 1996: 148–9). Mysticism, wrapped in a folkloric mode of expression, constitutes the essence of his poetry. Compared to his other mystic contemporaries like Neyzen Tevfik and Necip Fazıl Kısakürek, Çelebi was the only poet of the early Turkish Republic who managed to write mystical poems without using the old poetic forms (İnam 1996: 170). Treating mysticism as part of everyday life and poetry, his poems present refined and aestheticised examples of mystic thought without veering into ideology.

Although literary critics emphasise the Islamic aspect of his poetry, Çelebi's understanding of mysticism was a complex one in which the philosophies of the East and the West commingled. He was an avid reader and researcher of different mystical teachings. Çelebi worked on the 15th-century poems of Eşrefoğlu Rûmî, whom he considered the first representative of institutionalised mysticism in Anatolia, as well as on such well-known figures of mystical poetry as Omar Khayyam and Jami. He also studied the Malamatiyya and Mawlawiyya, and published a book on Rûmî. In addition, he studied and published on Buddhism and Gautama Buddha based on the Pali canon, and the traces of this study are apparent in both his poems and his understanding of the Islamic concept of unity.

His interest in other forms of spirituality is reflected in his works. His first collection of poems was published under the title *Om Mani Padme Hum*, a six-syllable Sanskrit mantra, in 1953 (Çelebi 2013: 7). Buddha was the protagonist in some of his poems, such as 'Sidharta' (Siddhartha) and 'Ayna' (Mirror) (2013: 28):

> it is me looking into the mirror
>   son of my imaginary mother
>   bodhisattva gautama.[15]

In his writings, he defines his poetry as mystical but does not confine his understanding of mysticism to Islam. He says 'without fear or hesitation, I confess that mysticism plays an important role in most of my poems' (Çelebi 2004: 'Şiirlerimde Mistisizm Temayülü'). Instead of the Sufi term *fanâ' fî-Allâh* (losing/annihilating oneself in God), he appropriates the Buddhist term Nirvana, describing his poems as an invitation to or a guide for attaining Nirvana. He defines the state of Nirvana as the self's transcending of its limits, as a diffusion of the self beyond time and space, and as a void or emptiness. Nirvana is the moment where

[15] In our translations we preserve the misalignment of lines, as well as the idiosyncrasies, of the poets who do not use capitals in their original texts.

there is no time, no space and no thought, only the faint light of the sun and the one spirit ruling the universe (Çelebi 2004: 'Şiirlerimde Mistisizm Temayülü').

Çelebi's poem 'Cüneyd' is a narration of the soul's journey to *fanâ' fî-Allâh* or Nirvana. The eponymous protagonist of the poem is a famous 9th-century Sufi figure, Junayd of Baghdad. The poem recalls the plain but straightforward style of Turkish folk poetry, as exemplified in the poems of the 14th-century poet Yunus Emre. The poem is a pure expression of mystic thought but without any mystical terminology. Its simple language displays Çelebi's attitude towards mystic thought: it is the foundation of his worldview, it is the essence of everyday life, and it is open equally to everyone (İnam 1996: 170).

The poem can be divided into three parts. In the first, Cüneyd says (Çelebi 2013: 9, ):

those who look at me
see my body

But the audience is deceived, because 'I am elsewhere'. The body is there, interacting with the people around it, but the mind and the heart are no longer located in the body. In the second part, we witness a dialogue between Cüneyd and others which provides further support for this interpretation: the robe Cüneyd wears is just an empty cover:

throw open your robe cüneyd
                    what do you see
                              the invisible

When the robe is thrown open, we expect to see Cüneyd but do not. We then witness the confusion of Cüneyd's interlocutors asking what has become of Cüneyd, like the confusion of the uninitiated before the act of a mystic. However, the explanation is not a mystical one, but the simple yet cryptic:

what happened to me and you
happened to him, too

The last part of the poem then explains what happened to Cüneyd and declares his physical annihilation:

beneath his robe
cüneyd disappeared into the blue

But what does this disappearing act symbolise for the poet? There is no doubt that the answer is *fanâ' fî-Allâh* or Nirvana. But the ordinariness of this as something that happens to 'me and you' seems to belie this reading. Hence, we argue that what Çelebi means by *fanâ' fî-Allâh* or Nirvana – or the void or the emptiness of the body – is in fact death, because what happens to everyone is not Nirvana or *fanâ' fî-Allâh* but death. The ordinary life of ordinary people is thus depicted as a spiritual journey – again, one that is open equally to everyone – that ends in the annihilation of the body.

Of the two poets we discuss in this category, Hilmi Yavuz (b. 1936) is not only a student of Behçet Necatigil and a follower of Asaf Hâlet Çelebi, but also a literary critic and an intellectual engaged in philosophy. For Yavuz, who focuses on specific themes in his poems like 'the mirror', 'time' and 'evening', poetry is tradition. Yavuz argues that to define cultural identity, one must detect what of the past is left today (the essence) and what has changed (accidents). Yavuz believes that religion necessarily involves a conservative attitude, and he says that he is not conservative. He thus does not aim to develop a religious approach towards tradition, for he does not believe it is possible to construct a cultural identity based solely on religion. He accepts, however, that religion is without question a part of cultural identity.

Defining tradition as a matter of relations, Yavuz embraces a relation pattern which can be observed in both Turkish literature and other literary traditions and which derives from Islamic mystical thought: the relation between the perceiver and the perceived. In different traditions, we witness different manifestations of this pattern: in Greek mythology, Narcissus sees himself when he looks into the water. In Ottoman lyric poetry, Necati can see nothing but a glimmer in the mirror, while Fuzuli sees the face of Leylâ everywhere. Thus Yavuz argues that his poetry becomes a part of this poetic tradition by maintaining the essence of this poetic relation, since from Yavuz's point of view, 'as tradition can be defined as a web of relations and images, what needs to be done to reproduce the tradition is to change its objects while preserving its essence, and [thereby] to tell a new story through this web of relations' (Yavuz & Armağan 2003: 23–5).

Yavuz argues that reproducing tradition in poetry is accomplished through 'appropriation' (*temellük*), an idea which he develops based on the teachings of his mentor Behçet Necatigil. For Yavuz, 'one should appropriate whatever was produced in the past' with an awareness of what and whom to appropriate. It is through proper appropriation that both poem and poet derive their strength (Akbayır 2011: 267).

Yavuz defines himself as 'bound but not limited to the [Ottoman poetic] tradition' and considers the Western tradition an element of his poetry as well (Yavuz & Armağan 2003: 29). The symbols and traces of Islamic mysticism and Neoplatonism in Yavuz's poems are a reflection of his philosophical readings, and they are drawn from world traditions as well as Ottoman lyric poetry. Thus, similar to Asaf Hâlet Çelebi, Yavuz's poetry also refers to different traditions; however, his poetry is much more ambiguous than that of Çelebi, as Yavuz does not make use of culture- or tradition-specific terms, but instead draws on a pool of common concepts.

This pool of common concepts makes his poetry hard to follow for the reader. As Andrews notes, all these references from different poetic traditions create an ambiguity about what is coming from where (2004: 24–6). Through this act of strategic disconnecting and the deliberate ambiguity it produces, meaning, image, symbol, self, signifier and signified are all de-centralised in Yavuz's poetry. In a post-signifying regime, Yavuz's poetry offers no fixed point of interpretation or any comment on modern-day society. In Andrews's words, he 'suggest[s] no compensatory program, no revival of a regime of the spirit, no revolution in the name of social justice' (2004: 26).

In light of Andrews's interpretations and Yavuz's comments on his own poetry, we argue that 'the identity sonnet' of Yavuz is a microcosm of his poetic attitude. This microcosm encompasses the ambiguity of his poetry. It is ambiguous because it is hard to determine who 'the other' is in the poem. Is it the One, the object of *waḥdat al-wujūd* (the Islamic mystical notion of unity of being) (Yavuz 2007: 75, [illegible]):

> this journey of ours ... but the stopping place, the road where?
> which of us is a mystery to the other or silvering even?[16]

Or is 'the other' the protagonists in the rewriting of an appropriated Echo and Narcissus story where the vanishing of the former leads to the destruction of the latter?

> while the fine sand of passions, in storm-battered
> hours, piles over me, in the twilight if it fade—
> with grief and afternoons as if having made
> love—and fail, i am the one who is shattered

In Yavuz's poetry, a heterogeneous Neoplatonic cosmos is the only universe that allows him to construct a poetic identity where his existence is in unity with the images of the past and the One in the present: 'the mirror dissolves in the skin, this skin is lost in the mirror' (2007: 75).[17] The mirror encompasses the reflections, the essence of the Eastern and Western traditions; and for Yavuz, constructing a poem should go through an act of freeing poetry from those characteristics that are deceptive or fleeting – namely 'the skin', the cultural identity we put on – and merging it with the essence of the poetic traditions on which he draws in a way that makes it impossible to tell which symbols derive from which tradition. In a similar vein, at the end of the poem, the poet creates a new poetic universe where he keeps the essence (the Neoplatonic symbols of the mirror and unity) but changes the objects (the accidents):

> my identity has died, i renounced my name long before
> alas, now i am my mirrors and am nothing more ...

4. Secular Dervishes: Behçet Necatigil and Birhan Keskin

Behçet Necatigil (1916–79) was not only a poet, translator and playwright but also a literature teacher and Hilmi Yavuz's high-school teacher. Thus, the essence of the poetic attitude for which Yavuz coined the term 'appropriation of the poetic tradition'

[16] The translations of Yavuz are by Walter Andrews who preserves the idiosyncrasies of the poet, including his avoidance of capitals.

[17] The image can also be interpreted as the dissolution of any possibility of identity. Although we prefer our interpretation, we would like to thank the reviewer for reminding us of this alternative reading of the verses.

is also apparent in Necatigil's poetry. Necatigil believes that there is an ageless essence rooted in folk poetry, Ottoman classical poetry and Sufi poetry which also nurtures modern poetry (2012c). For Necatigil, writing a poem is like constructing a house using old stones (Necatigil 2009: 229). Thus, half of his poetry is new, but the rest is rooted in tradition, as he writes in 'Köşebent' (Necatigil 2009: 232):

> There are callings in similar centuries, hear them out!
> The pain of my half face is Hayyam [Khayyam] and Fuzuli

However, as Kalpaklı states, the result of this blending of traditions and of old and new is not the gauche display of an artificial 'Oriental corner' in an otherwise Western home, but rather a natural synthesis (2010: 25). The elements from Turkish and other poetic traditions form an organic whole: 'You can find foreign threads here and there, but the pattern is ours, the composition is ours; we melted the raw material into new combinations as we wished, we took away its independence and made it ours' (Necatigil 2012b).

In Necatigil's poetry, the 'slavishness of mundane life' and the 'melancholic delights' of ordinary people constitute the main theme, but he makes use of mystical metaphors and symbols to express it. Can Bahadır Yüce claims that it is impossible clearly to express Necatigil's stance on mysticism in his poetry; the best we can say is that his poetry shares the same emotional universe as mysticism (2010: 162). Ahmet İnam argues that the mysticism in Necatigil's poetry is an implicit, disguised one, one wrapped in the material world and its worries (1996: 172). We agree with both critics. For Necatigil, life and existence are a mystical struggle: 'To live is a torment for most of the time' ('Yel Değirmenleri'; Necatigil 2009: 17). For this reason, Mahmut Temizyürek (2010: 166–7) defines Necatigil's poetry as one of imprisonment. Necatigil feels trapped on the earth, between the ground and the sky. However, in the same poem 'Yel Değirmenleri', he puts up with life with the patience of a dervish, and never gives up the struggle (Necatigil 2009: 17):

> There is no one standing ready to save me
> Death, yet far behind, follows
> Don suffering as a garment,
> And attack the windmills one more time

For Necatigil, who considers earth a place of exile, it is not light but darkness that symbolises salvation ('Haltercümesi'; Necatigil 2009: 18):

> From the lights turned towards me,
> Night – save me!

Darkness is a metaphor for death, the end of the torments of life ('Kabul Günü'; Necatigil 2009: 24):

> He waits for death as if awaiting a pleasant guest at home:
> I know bliss
> will not come to me on earth
> I wait for death

For Necatigil, light represents the outer world, social life; however, he claims (2012c) that: 'What gives us [poets] our true nature is getaways, stepping-asides – maintaining our solitude amid the crowd and developing a cocoon to maturity. All study requires its own solitude. Those who heed what has accumulated within them, who listen to that "inner" sound, hear more than what has been said aloud.' Thus darkness, which provides a shelter from the crowd, is a friend, while light is a troublemaker, a disturber ('Köşebent'; Necatigil 2009: 232):

> The razor cut off one side of my face
> Take away your lamp, let me stay in the dark

According to Necatigil, who says in 'Doğa', 'The day is extinguished, I am heading into the light of darkness', lamps are not a source of peace, and death is the cure for loneliness: 'I had two lamps, yet the eyes of the dead are enough' (Necatigil 2009: 228). In Necatigil's poetic universe, he can find refuge in death and darkness ('Lambalar'; Necatigil 2009: 385):

> All lamps suppress a fear
> A corpse puts an end to loneliness
> What about now, without a lamp, without death
> In what peace will I rest?

Similar to the inversion of the symbol of the lamp, the symbol of the mirror is also generally not a welcome image in this poetic universe. Mirrors, which are responsible for reflecting the beauty of the beloved and the truth, do not serve the same purpose in this modern world ('Maskeli Balo'; Necatigil (2009: 74):

> Don't look at the mirrors, mirrors are dirty
> your face is lost in the mirrors

In fact, they distort and reflect an ugliness, as the title of another poem ('Turning Ugly') implies; mirrors are no longer friends of the poet ('Çirkinleme'; Necatigil 2009: 277,):

> If you are not around, I am relaxed
> You, the mirrors, magnifying my shrinking

Another representation of the poet's earthly exile is Necatigil's poem 'Abdal' (Sılay 1996: 478–9,). In it, we witness the walk of an *abdal* (dervish) on the streets of a modern city and his search for meaning. Alphan Akgül, in his comparative textual analysis of the poem, focuses on its use of metaphors and themes from three different cultural and literary traditions: the Ottoman literary tradition, the Hero and Leander story in Greek mythology, and romantic expressionism. According to Akgül, this constitutes a using and adapting of the fundamental sources of the Ottoman literary tradition but also a 'contradicting' of some elements of these fundamental sources (using the metaphors and themes of cultures other than the poet's own) on the same metaphoric level (2010: 135–6). But instead of interpreting it as a 'contradiction', we think it is more meaningful to understand Necatigil's poetry as multi-layered and multifaceted, as was Ottoman poetry.

Akgül points out that by using words related to 'water' and 'light', Necatigil exhibits symmetry (proportion-*tenâsüp*), as common in traditional Ottoman poetry. He thus follows tradition, and in this way composes a poem that transforms the Islamic mystical tradition from within. As Akgül (2010: 141–2) rightly comments, the main theme of this poem is the reaching of 'the One' in the formulation of lover–path–beloved – or, in other words, lover–guide/mentor/sheikh/mystical path–the One/God. Just as a ship is lost in the dark when the beam of the lighthouse fails, and just as Leander was lost in a stormy sea while trying to reunite with his beloved, without the guidance of a mentor/sheikh (the light-emitting lighthouse) one (a Sufi) cannot reach the beloved/God (Sılay 1996: 476, ):

> In ages when fire was still new-found
> So were those lamps wont to burn
> And then, on the asphalt plains
> Were flowing torrents and the Abdal

As George Messo, the English translator of Birhan Keskin's *& silk & love & flame* (2013), points out, 'in an artistic culture traditionally dominated by men, Birhan Keskin is one of a growing number of women poets … who have risen to prominence since the mid-1990s for their bold, challenging verse' (Keskin 2013: 10–11). Considering that studies on mysticism, love and poetry have long neglected the women poets of modern Turkish literature (İnam 1996; Mignon 2002a; 2002b; 2003), here in this chapter we should perhaps have focused not on the many male poets we have discussed so far but instead on a single modern woman poet, Birhan Keskin – as Didem Havlioğlu has done with Mihrî Hatun, an Ottoman woman poet, in her contribution to this volume.[18] Focusing exclusively on Keskin would have not only offered insights into the appropriation of the poetic tradition among contemporary poets but also enabled us to observe the transformation of such a strictly gendered cultural and artistic field into a realm of new possibilities of expression. However, as Turkish poetry has limited representation in the English language on a global level, we have opted to forgo that opportunity for the sake of providing

[18] The Neoplatonic influence is quite different in the two cases. In the Ottoman case, as Havlioğlu makes clear in her chapter, it would have been unthinkable for a woman to express her love for a man, let alone another woman, in her poetry. The only fitting object for such an expression of love was God. In this context, the gender-neutral ideal of the Neoplatonic beloved provided a shield of ambiguity that made such expression possible, allowing a poet to write of love for the divine – the One – in a way that could simultaneously express love for a more earthly object (see pp. 193–4). However, in the modern Turkish case, and certainly in the case of Keskin, the Neoplatonic tradition no longer seems to play the same role. Writing about more mundane sorts of love is no longer taboo, for women or for men. Even in cases of homosexual love (still a taboo subject in certain quarters of society), gay poets often write freely, and even when they do so more surreptitiously, they do not turn to the Neoplatonic tradition to give voice to their sentiments. Keskin, too, is openly gay, but does not try to hide her sexual identity in real life or her beloved's identity in her poetry, as can be seen, for instance, in her poem 'Taş Parçaları', the story of the breakup of two lovers whose gender is revealed without any hesitation. See Keskin (2016: 23).

a more comprehensive picture of modern Turkish poetry and its relations to the Neoplatonic tradition.[19]

To put it bluntly, Birhan Keskin is not a mystical poet. Indeed, she seems almost the opposite. Amanda Dalton describes Keskin's poems as 'paradoxical' because her poetry includes incompatible elements in the same poetic universe and yet manages to create poetic harmony (Keskin 2013: 13–14). It is this poetic paradox that serves our purposes for a Neoplatonic reading of Keskin's poetry – namely the profound Neoplatonic expression of the themes of this pure materialist, naturalist and profane poetic universe: 'My poems have always had their roots in the earth and the human starting from the beginning' (Keskin 2010).

The main theme of Keskin's poetry appears to be love and pain, and despite her tight relation with the earth and the human, she chooses to express them in a Neoplatonic universe through the images of Ottoman lyric poetry. Keskin's poetry overlaps with Ottoman poetry in three categories: the necessity of love as the meaning of life, the dichotomy between the lover and the beloved, and the constant suffering of the poet.

Love is one of the main themes of Keskin's poetry. According to her, human beings, as a species aware of their own mortality, need meaning in life. And that meaning can only be found in love. But love, in turn, requires a vessel, an object. In her words, 'There is always an object of love: someone, ourselves or God' (Erdoğan 2012: 117–18). And therein lies the tension, for our love, and therefore the meaning in our lives, can never exist independently of that object, the beloved, yet neither can it be entirely confined to that object. Indeed, sometimes Keskin even creates the beloved for the sake of meaning (Keskin 2013: 63, 🎧):

> I gave birth to you…
> from my inner spring, my bitter flow
> I gave birth to you, for a dream
> from a season on loan[20]

The search for meaning leads the poet to love, and it is impossible to make a life meaningful without it. In accordance with this, the poet always needs an object of desire, an 'other', to construct her poetic universe. In Keskin's poems, the object of desire or the lost beloved appears not only as the similar 'other' of the poetic self but also as a supreme being. We need 'the other' as the object of desire in poetry because, as Keskin states, 'everything about the human exists in the form of binary oppositions. If love is a search for completion, and so we believe it to be, then it carries with it its opposite, in other words, separation. Love exists thanks to separation' (Erdoğan 2012: 117) (Keskin 2013: 85):

> I lived like a whole split in two
> One side an enemy to the other[21]

[19] Having said that, it is a pleasure to see another translation of Birhan Keskin's poetry into English, by Murat Nemet-Nejat (see Keskin 2018).

[20] 'Leaf', translation by George Messo.

[21] 'Winter of Murder', translation by George Messo.

But despite this dichotomy, what we find is the cohesion of these opposing ends in a symbiotic form, as in her poem 'Sun… Star' (2013: 35,):

The road is long, the path difficult; what should I say?
My graceful friend, I took you to my side, as if walking with my twin.
Should I call you star or sun,
I wanted surprise in my nights, surprise in my days
I'm like you sometimes, sometimes like me myself[22]

In this poetic universe, pain and suffering – generally caused by the departure or loss of the objects of desire in Keskin's poems – are presented as transcendental in nature, beyond the realm of knowledge and experience. It seems so natural to write about pain, because 'what can you write when you're happy?' (Keskin 2009). As this suffering also constitutes the meaning of life, in partnership with love, it is impossible for her to abandon this suffering or the 'other' who causes it. This never-ending suffering and the addiction to it create an affinity between Keskin and Fuzuli, a prominent figure of Ottoman lyric poetry (2013: 75, 77):

I understood there's no sense apart from pain
let evening's blind darkness beat my brow

as always
as always[23]

Keskin's poems display her knowledge of the semiotic world of Ottoman lyric poetry. In her 'casting pebbles', aware of the hierarchical relation between the lover and the beloved in Ottoman lyric poetry, she writes (2018: 53):

Love, between two people is what is never =
I am not a Divan poet darling
to chisel lines for you nevertheless, on the spur of the moment,
I'd like people to know my attraction for your eyes, your hands, your feet.
I'm of this mad times, this venomous moments
the poet, in smithereens. What can I say,
still, in me, from very ooold times,
Ah, Lei… Ah, Leilaaaaa
I left your name on a cold desert night.[24]

For Keskin, her words are not sufficient to write the best poem for her beloved; she cannot write as the poets of Ottoman lyric poetry did. She does not belong to those days, but to the unfortunate modern times of poetry and humanity. She does not feel at home; she feels she is in the wrong place and in the wrong time (2016), yet she still believes in poetry and hopes that while improving her poetry she can also complete her mental and spiritual development (2006).

Keskin explains the purpose of her existence on earth as 'to look': 'I came [to earth] to look because I will linger here for a time, and then move on' (2006).

[22] Translation by George Messo.
[23] 'The Traveller's Black Suitcase', translation by George Messo.
[24] Translation is by Murat Nemet-Nejat who preserves the idiosyncrasies of the poet.

This is a symbol we are familiar with from the poetics of Hilmi Yavuz, one that he describes as the core dynamic of the lyric poetry of all traditions. And what is she looking at? It is the mirror, another familiar image, because regardless of the nature of the beloved, 'there should be a mirror showing us ourselves' (Erdoğan 2012: 118). According to Keskin, when we are in love, 'we need a mirror. A mirror to show us our love, the width of our heart and our language' (Erdoğan 2012: 118). This reference connects Keskin to the master of modern Turkish poetry we discussed earlier in this section: Behçet Necatigil. A verse from 'Nilüfer' (Water Lily) by Necatigil goes as follows: 'It was a mirror to show me myself, they took it' (2009: 209). In Necatigil's poem, there are three versions of the verse, and each refers to the object that 'they took' in a different way: as a mirror, as meaning, and as a lamp. Keskin argues that our mirror, our meaning and our lamp all come into being in the beloved (Erdoğan 2012: 118).

In a state of constant suffering and lacking the necessary tools to express her love, the poet needs patience to be able to survive and ends up with the merging of the self with nature (Keskin 2013: 43, 53,):

> I spread myself, flat on flat, me, I am a plain.
> As the wind stirs me, let the grass resound.[25]
>
> I was told, there's a ripe fruit behind the curtain of patience,
> the world will teach you both patience, and the ripe fruit's taste.
>
> They said, you waited like these trees, a vision like these trees,
> sorrowful like these trees.[26]

And she gives meaning to life by sacrificing her existence and telling the 'other' to give up on her (2013: 43, 53,):

> I met with absolute desolation,
> I was the absolute detachment from memory.
> I'm nothing, me,
> pass on.[27]
>
> Pass through me, I'll remain, I'll wait, pass through me,
> but where you pass through me I cannot know[28]

5. Conclusion

The essence of the history of literature is generalisation, but it is always difficult to define a whole poetic tradition based on merely a small sample of poets and poems.

[25] 'Plain', translation by George Messo.
[26] 'Door', translation by George Messo.
[27] 'Plain', translation by George Messo.
[28] 'Door', translation by George Messo.

With this difficulty in mind, in this chapter we have tried our best to bring together a representative sample of modern Turkish poetry to show that the Neoplatonic tradition – heavily loaded with Islamic influences and deeply rooted in Ottoman classical poetry – still plays an important role in the expression of emotions in the post-signifying regime of modern Turkey. The Neoplatonic expression of emotions is put to use not only in cases of pure belief and mysticism but also in the cases of profane love and worldly torment. Thus, we infer that despite the catastrophic rupture in Turkish society in republican times and that period's endeavours to centralise the definition of meaning, the backbone of the older poetic tradition is still there – sometimes disguised, sometimes transformed, but always lively. Walter Andrews writes in his chapter in this volume (pp. 185–6) that we can think of 'Ottoman life as being … scripted by a mystical narrative influenced by or analogous to Neoplatonism' and that this served as 'an attitude toward the world and an "emotional ecology" that grounded the lives of individuals in Ottoman society'. We claim that not only modern Turkish poetry but modern life itself retains the essence and the tools of that Neoplatonic 'emotional ecology'. We believe that in Turkey today, this Neoplatonic, mystical essence inherited from Ottoman classical poetry continues to define our relation to the beloved, whispering the way to express our love and providing the tools for coping with the suffering of mundane life. We still live and find meaning in this 'emotional ecology', a composition of Eastern and Western lyric and mystical traditions.

References

Akbayır, S. (2011), *'Ne kadar gitsem o kadar uzak', Hilmi Yavuz* (Istanbul, Ferfir Yayınları).

Akgül, A. (2010), '"Abdal"da Mesnevi Geleneği, Mitoloji ve Romantik Dışavurumculuk', in İnal & Tunç (2010), 135–8.

Altuğ, S., Filiztekin, A. & Pamuk, Ş. (2008), 'Sources of Long-term Economic Growth for Turkey, 1880–2005', *European Review of Economic History*, 12.3: 393–430.

Andrews, W.G. (1985), *Poetry's Voice, Society's Song: Ottoman Lyric Poetry* (Seattle, University of Washington Press).

Andrews, W.G. (2004), 'Stepping Aside: Ottoman Literature in Modern Turkey', *Journal of Turkish Literature*, 1: 9–32.

Andrews, W.G. & Kalpaklı, M. (1996), 'Across Chasms of Change: The Kaside in the Late Ottoman and Republican Times', in S. Sperl & C. Shackle, *Qasida Poetry in Islamic Asia and Africa* (Leiden, Brill), 301–25.

Andrews, W.G. & Kalpaklı, M. (2005), *The Age of Beloveds: Love and the Beloved in Early-Modern Ottoman and European Culture and Society* (Durham NC, Duke University Press).

Anon. (2012), 'Erdoğan okuduğu şiir salonu ağlattı', *Yeni Şafak*, 30 September, accessed 15 September 2018, https://bit.ly/2CQFCNB

Anon. (2013), 'Üstad Necip Fazıl'ın Erdoğan'dan istediği şiir', *Yeni Şafak*, 25 September, accessed 18 September 2018, https://bit.ly/2CSoreS

Anon. (2014a), '7 güzel adam 7 derin hikaye', *Sabah*, 19 April, accessed 5 April 2019, https://bit.ly/2XFfagb

Anon. (2014b), 'Yedi güzel adam: Bir Türkiye hikayesi', *Yeni Şafak*, 27 April, accessed 5 April 2019, https://bit.ly/2KUTlrH
Anon. (2019a), 'Kahramanmaraş'ta "7 Güzel Adam Edebiyat Müzesi" açıldı', *HaberTürk*, 6 March, accessed 5 April 2019, https://bit.ly/2GAvPMq
Anon. (2019b), 'Yedi Güzel Adam Edebiyat Müzesi açıldı', *CNNTürk*, 6 March, accessed 5 April 2019, https://bit.ly/2UQHYpp
Anon. (2019c), 'Yedi Güzel Adam Edebiyat Müzesi Tamamlandı', *Sabah*, 12 February, accessed 5 April 2019, https://bit.ly/2W8dGLr
Aydın, S. & Taşkın, Y. (2018), *1960'dan Günümüze Türkiye Tarihi* (Istanbul, İletişim Yayınları).
Ayvazoğlu, B. (2002), *Aşk Estetiği: İslam Sanatlarının Estetiği Üzerine Bir Deneme* (Istanbul, Ötüken Neşriyat).
Çelebi, A.H. (2004), *Bütün Yazıları*, ed. H. Sazyek (Istanbul, Yapı Kredi Yayınları) [e-book].
Çelebi, A.H. (2013), *Bütün Şiirleri* (Istanbul, Yapı Kredi Yayınları).
Eralp, V. (trans.) (1975), 'Ennead'lar I-IV: Hayvan nedir? İnsan nedir?', *Felsefe Arkivi*, 19: 81–111.
Erdoğan, V. (2012), *Aklın Azabı: Birhan Keskin Şiirinde Hatıra Medeniyeti* (Istanbul, Granada Yayınları).
Hızlan, D. (2006), 'İkinci Yeni'nin Estetik Açılımı', in T.S. Halman, M. Kalpaklı *et al.* (eds), *Türk Edebiyatı Tarihi* (Ankara, Kültür ve Turizm Bakanlığı), 48–62.
Holbrook, V.R. (1998), *Aşkın Okunmaz Kıyıları: Türk Modernitesi ve Mistik Romans*, trans. E. Köroğlu & E. Kılıç (Istanbul, İletişim Yayınları).
İnal, A.A. & Tunç, G. (eds) (2010), *Asfalt Ovalarda Yürüyen Abdal: Behçet Necatigil* (Ankara: İş Bankası Kültür Yayınları).
İnam, A. (1996), *Ararken: Edebiyat yazıları (1967–1975)* (Ankara, Suteni).
Kalpaklı, M. (2010), '"Bir Çağ Günümüze": Necatigil ve Divan Şiiri', in İnal & Tunç (2010), 25–39.
Karakoç, S. (1995), *Şiirler IV: Zamana Adanmış Sözler* (Istanbul, Diriliş Yayınları).
Karakoç, S. (2012), *Edebiyat Yazıları I: Medeniyetin Rüyası Rüyanın Medeniyeti* (Istanbul, Diriliş Yayınları).
Keskin, B. (2006), 'Yeryüzüne bakmaya geldim ben', interviewed by Can Bahadır Yüce for *Zaman Kitap Eki*, 1 May, accessed 18 September 2018, www.metiskitap.com/catalog/interview/2955
Keskin, B. (2009), 'Birhan Keskin'le birkaç saat', interviewed by Hacer Yeni for *Elle*, September, accessed 18 September 2018, www.metiskitap.com/catalog/interview/302
Keskin, B. (2010), 'Her şey tüccarların elinde', interviewed by Figen Şakacı for *Radikal Kitap Eki*, 9 April, accessed 18 September 2018, www.metiskitap.com/catalog/interview/3034
Keskin, B. (2013), *& silk & love & flame*, trans. G. Messo, introduction A. Dalton (Todmorden, Arc Publications).
Keskin, B. (2016), 'Burası değil, burası değil, böyle değil', interviewed by Çağlayan Çevik for *IAN Edebiyat*, March, accessed 18 September 2018, www.metiskitap.com/catalog/interview/6235
Keskin, B. (2018), *Y'ol*, trans. M. Nemet-Nejat (New York City, Spuyten Duyvil).
Mardin, S. (ed.) (1994a), *Cultural Transitions in the Middle East* (Leiden, Brill).
Mardin, S. (1994b), 'Cultural Change and the Intellectual: A Study of the Effects of Secularization in Modern Turkey', in Mardin (1994a), 189–213.

Meeker, M.E. (1991), 'The New Muslim Intellectuals in the Republic of Turkey', in R. Tapper (ed.), *Islam in Modern Turkey: Religion, Politics and Literature in a Secular State* (London, I.B. Tauris), 189–219.
Meeker, M.E. (1994), 'The Muslim Intellectual and His Audience: A New Configuration of Writer and Reader among Believers in the Republic of Turkey', in Mardin (1994a), 153–88.
Mignon, L. (2002a), *Çağdaş Türk Şiirinde Aşk, Âşıklar, Mekânlar* (Istanbul, Hece Yayınları).
Mignon, L. (2002b), *The Beloved Unveiled: Continuity and Change in Modern Turkish Love Poetry (1923–1980)* (unpublished Ph.D. thesis, SOAS, University of London).
Mignon, L. (2003), *Elifbâlar Sevdası* (Istanbul, Hece Yayınları).
Morewedge, P. (ed.) (1992), *Neoplatonism and Islamic Thought* (Albany, State University of New York Press).
Necatigil, B. (2009), *Bütün Yapıtları / Şiirler*, ed. A. Tanyeri & H. Yavuz (Istanbul, Yapı Kredi Yayınları).
Necatigil, B. (2012a), *Düz Yazılar II* (Istanbul, Yapı Kredi Yayınları) [ebook].
Necatigil, B. (2012b), '"Arada", "Dar Çağ"... Necatigil'de "İkinci Yeni" mi?', in Necatigil (2012a).
Necatigil, B. (2012c), 'Necatigil Şiiri Yol Ayrımında mı?', in Necatigil (2012a).
Nemet-Nejat, M. (2004), *Eda: An Anthology of Contemporary Turkish Poetry* (Jersey City, Talisman House).
Özcan, Z. (trans.) (1996), *Enneadlar* (Bursa, Asa Kitabevi).
Özgül, K. (2018), *Dîvan Yolu'ndan Pera'ya Selâmetle – Modern Türk Şiirine Doğru* (Istanbul, Yapı Kredi Yayınları).
Schimmel, A. (1975), *Mystical Dimensions of Islam* (Chapel Hill, University of North Carolina Press).
Schimmel, A. (1982), *As Through a Veil: Mystical Poetry in Islam* (New York, Columbia University Press).
Sılay, K. (ed.) (1996), *An Anthology of Turkish Literature* (Bloomington, Indiana University Turkish Studies).
Temizyürek, M. (2010), 'Azaplıktan Şiir ile Kurtulan', in İnal & Tunç (2010), 165–86.
Tokatlıoğlu, İ. & Öztürk, F. (2008), '1950–1980 Yılları Arasındaki Dönemde Türkiye'de Uygulanan Para Ve Maliye Politikalarının Etkinliği', *Ekonomik Yaklaşım*, 19.66: 155–74.
Yavuz, H. (2007), *Seasons of the Word*, trans. W.G. Andrews (Syracuse, Syracuse University Press).
Yavuz, H. (2010), *Okuma Biçimleri* (Istanbul, Timaş Yayınları).
Yavuz, H. & Armağan, M. (2003). *Hilmi Yavuz ile Doğu'ya ve Batı'ya Yolculuk* (Istanbul, Ufuk Kitaplar).
Yüce, C.B. (2010), '"İçe Dönük Bir Kapı": Necatigil Mistik Miydi?', in İnal & Tunç (2010), 155–63.

22

Neoplatonists in Modern Greek Poetry

DAVID RICKS

OTHER CONTRIBUTORS TO this volume have analysed in rich detail the extent to which a cluster of ideas and motifs with real or purported Neoplatonic antecedents or of a Neoplatonic cast have, over the centuries, permeated poetry and poetics at the confluence of Africa, Asia and Europe. It might be a natural inference that poetry written in the modern form of the Greek language – in the ablest hands, an elastic instrument of expression, which can draw on multiple historical strata – would be an especially propitious place to look. I have the impression that this is not in fact the case. At the same time, a number of poems by important Greek poets since 1880 have found inspiration from revolving around, not so much Neoplatonic doctrine or tradition, as flesh-and-blood (though often fictional) people who live out the drama of a life inspired by, or connected to, something of the Neoplatonic in its different phases and guises. I hope that the varied texture of this cast of characters will illustrate how Neoplatonism has still had life through individual lives as recorded, or invented, by individual modern Greek poets.

But it would be only appropriate to begin by acknowledging how Greek identity – inextricable from Orthodox identity, even for those who resist this – is founded on a confrontation with Platonism. The greatest religious poet in the Greek language in the Byzantine period, Romanos the Melode, exclaims in one of his verse sermons from the 6th century: '*Ti planontai pros Platona*?' ('Why do men vainly wander after Plato?') (Romanos 1963: 265). Only an historically speaking temerarious view to the effect that, if you scratch a Greek, you will find a pagan underneath, and that Platonic survivals in the Greek mind operated pervasively over many centuries, in a subterranean way at odds with institutional Christianity, could offset this. Furthermore, the varied and distinguished productions of Greek poets since the Revolution of 1821 have had little time for philosophy and philosophers: Andreas Kalvos (Andrea Calbo), writing in 1824, has his ode 'To the Muses' (Ricks 1997a) restoring the Greek poetry of the past to the insurgent nation

Proceedings of the British Academy, **240**, 454–468, © The British Academy 2022.

but has no poem on a dreamed-of return of the philosophers. We can add to this a couple of further points of context.

The first is the lack in the Greek tradition, not of any contact with the Renaissance, to be sure, but of what might be called a line of metaphysical poets such as this volume examines from other languages, this despite the existence of three Neoplatonist Academies in Crete (Bancroft-Marcus 1982). And just as the major modern Greek poets have tended to have an oblique relationship to religious questions (Hirst 2004), they have not, in general, been much given to abstraction, and in particular have rarely had a philosophical training. (In this important respect, there is no equivalent to T.S. Eliot in Greek.) If, accordingly, the prospects for a sustained Neoplatonic dimension to modern Greek poetry appear poor, one exception is an acclaimed poet who will find but a marginal place in this chapter: Odysseus Elytis (1911–96).

Elytis drew on Plotinus glancingly in his poetry and prose (Iakov 1983: 74; see also Taylor 1998) and in a short prose piece, 'The divine light according to Plotinus' (Elytis 2011: 311–13; see Pourgouris 2011: 121–2), giving salience to him in the last triumphant section of his longest poem, *To Axion Esti* (1959) with the phrase 'the nine steps Plotinus climbed' (Elytis 1977: 84; for discussion of this poet and philosophy see Tempridou 2016). But even in this case, the Neoplatonic aspect has something of a walk-on part in the rich texture (or, to those less impressed, the indigestible soup) of Elytis' debts to the past. It is noteworthy that in the shortest list of his heroes or mages which the poet gave in his essays (Elytis 2011: 9), the poet both places Plotinus first in a quasi-apostolic 12, and also associates him with such culturally remote figures as Fra Angelico and Mozart; a sign, it might be thought, that Plotinus is more a resonant name than a person, let alone part of a historical Neoplatonic tradition. In a late longer poem Plotinus once again appears as part of a group of elective affinities, and it is both symptomatic and of course deliberate that the great philosopher there appears perhaps subordinate to the eternal feminine (Elytis 1982: 15, [illegible]):

> Whether he was right or no
> Plotinus will one day appear
> the great eye with its transparency
> and with a sea behind him like Helen
> tying up the sun
> along with other flowers in her hair[.]

In any case, with one significant exception among Greek poets, with which I shall end, Elytis seems to me an outlier in his overt though sporadic borrowing from Neoplatonic tradition. It is other philosophical traditions (in the case of German thought, a tradition with a debt to Neoplatonism) that have had a deeper influence on modern poets writing in Greek: German Idealism in the national poet Dionysios Solomos and the sonneteer Lorentzos Mavilis (along with a debt to the Sanskrit sacred texts in the latter); a loose Epicureanism in C.P. Cavafy's celebrated 'Ithaca'; the millenarian doctrine of Marxism in Yannis Ritsos and others; and the

Pre-Socratics (Heraclitus, Empedocles and Parmenides, especially) in a range of 20th-century and later poets, among them Antonis Fostieris today (Loulakaki 2014). With the massive exception of Marxism here, the poets' encounters with these philosophical currents are notably eclectic and even attracted to, or characteristically issuing in, the fragmentary. If there is an 'underground' tradition of Neoplatonism in Byzantium (Athanassiadi 2015) it does not seem to surface much in modern Greek poetry – if we except a Sufi flavour to some of the *rebetika* popular songs originating in Asia Minor that dwell on the joys of intoxication in the *tekke*, as the hashish den was called.

Beyond this, if we can speak of a governing myth that haunts Greek poetry since independence, it is one which is the very opposite of *anagoge*: the myth of the Dead Brother in the ballad of that name, who returns from the Underworld to this world only to descend once more (Ricks 1997b). Modern Greek poetry in general has a chthonic tendency, above all in the hands of its greatest mystic, Angelos Sikelianos (1884–1951). (Widely if unsystematically read, Sikelianos was pervasively indebted to the chaotic writings and example of Edouard Schuré (1841–1929).) The title of his poem 'From the Prologue to *Plethon*' – a tragedy he was, symptomatically, never to complete – (Sikelianos 1981: 143–4) misleads the reader who goes in search of a thoroughgoing Neoplatonic text. In some ways, of course, George Gemistos Plethon's story (*c.* 1355–*c.* 1452) is the great romantic tale of Neoplatonism, and beyond numerous scholarly studies (see recently and soberly Siniossoglou 2011) was the treatment of a rollicking anti-Western novel, *The Gypsy Girl* (1884) by modern Greece's greatest writer of fiction, Alexandros Papadiamantis (1851–1911) (Papadiamantis 1981: 345–658, with discussion in Peckham 1998). Sikelianos's poem, published in 1914, and supposedly written at Mistra in 1912 (Savidis 2012: 83–4), in fact has nothing to say of Plethon specifically. Rather, it is a terse and subtle conjuring up of the Blessed Virgin Mary – and, at the same time, Helen of Sparta – from Mistra's ruined churches among which Plethon had lived.

1. Kostis Palamas: Neoplatonism and the Hellenic Identity

Yet some Greek poets, since the time of the Second Athenian School of the 1880s, have shown an intermittent yet keen interest in Neoplatonists *as people*; often, if not always, in surprising ways. Let me start with one of the less surprising, though a forceful one enough: the translation of Leconte de Lisle's 'Hypatie' (1847) by the first of the three poets I shall address here, Kostis Palamas (1859–1943).

It is not unreasonable – though in the case of Greece still unusual – to treat a volume of collected translations as an integral part of a poet's production as with, in this case, Palamas' *Music Transposed* (1930) (on which see now Stylianidou 2015). But the Greek poet's version of the 19 fervent quatrains of 'Hypatia' may be seen as reflecting his outlook just as much as a poem of his own, 'The Triumph' (1915), makes a tragic hero out of a thinker of a different time and school. That thinker, who himself lends himself to a robust anti-Christian message, is Lucretius (discussion in Ricks 2014). Leconte de Lisle's perfervid denunciation of the Christianity which could inspire the Alexandrian rabble to murder Hypatia on 8 March AD 415 turns the language of the *Acts of the Christian Martyrs* against itself. Let me quote the closing lines of Palamas's translation, generally close to the French original, and with some success reproducing its alexandrines in the staple metre of modern Greek poetry (Palamas nd, XI: 255–7,):

> The base Galilaean struck you, cursed you,
> but you were greater as you fell to ground;
> and now Aphrodite's body and Plato's mind are gone,
> have taken flight from the Hellenic sky for ever.
>
> Sleep, spotless victim, in the depths of our soul,
> in your virginal shroud crowned with lotus;
> sleep, for filth and ugliness now rule the world
> and we have lost the way that leads to Paros.
>
> Ashes are the gods and the dumb earth will never speak
> as before in your ruined heavens.
> But live in the poet's heart, sing there
> the melodious hymn of holy Beauty.
>
> But she above all things lives on, immutable and eternal.
> Death scatters the shaken universes,
> but beauty flames out and moulds all things anew;
> beneath her white feet whirl the worlds around.

A few points here call for comment. The first thing to note is the fact, evident elsewhere, that Neoplatonism is always liable to be opposed to Christianity when viewed retrospectively – something natural when we think of this celebrated confrontation between Hypatia and the Patriarch (later Saint) Cyril of Alexandria, but by no means so clear overall when we think about the shifting and elusive nature of Neoplatonism's followers and their various intellectual and spiritual affinities, from Plotinus to Plethon. When Palamas writes of 'the Galilaean' here, he will be thinking, not only of Julian the Apostate's reputed last words: 'Vicisti, Galilaee', but also of Swinburne's much-quoted line from his 'Hymn to Proserpine' (1866) and this carries Leconte de Lisle's animus further still: 'Thou hast conquered, o pale Galilaean; the world has grown grey from thy breath.' Palamas admired Swinburne for his neo-pagan ardour but in particular for his fervent poem on the Cretan rising of 1866 (Palamas nd, X: 368–85) – a further sign that the modern tradition's relation to antiquity is (as, for example, Carl Ernst's contribution to the present volume notes) often closely bound up with modern causes and allegiances.

The point can be refined with reference to three deviations by Palamas from his original (which is otherwise closely rendered). The first is his recasting of 'Le souffle de Platon et le corps d'Aphrodite' as '*Tes Aphrodítes to kormí, tou Platona ho nous*'

(Aphrodite's figure, Plato's mind), the inversion of which accentuates Hypatia's beauty in a way characteristic of the Greek poet. Again, the reference to 'les beaux cieux d'Hellas' comes across as the more wistful in the phrase 'have taken flight from the Hellenic sky for ever'; not least because the Greek reader reads Palamas's poem under that same sky. And, were a reader to ask once more whether the poem is in fact Palamas's own, the answer is ready from the date appended to the poem: ' 23.3.15' marks the translation as very much of its own time: 1,600 years almost to the week after Hypatia's murder, and in the last week of Great Lent, a time of keen religious observance for pious Greeks. I read the appended date as having a clear element of coat-trailing, and it is of course the same year in which Palamas published his poem on Lucretius, 'The Triumph'. At this time when Greece was violently divided about whether or not to enter the Great War, Palamas set himself with the liberal reformer Eleftherios Venizelos against the monarchy and the forces of reaction.

The other protagonist of Neoplatonism to appear prominently in Palamas's work is of a different type and in a very different setting, one with which the sedentary Palamas preoccupied himself for much of this career: Athens. The protagonist is Proclus (AD 412–485) as he appears in Athens in Palamas's epic, *The Emperor's Reedpipe* (1910). That uneven and often bombastic work, fuelled by the irredentist Great Idea which was to collapse in the Asia Minor Disaster of 1922, attempts to create a synthesis of Greek identity in which the jarring contrasts between pagan antiquity and the Christian inheritance (in sources well documented by Kasines 1980) become a kind of asset for a modern sensibility. Proclus, arriving in Athens in 431, about a century before the final closure of the Schools, stands for Palamas at a turning point. In Book VII, the Rock (the Acropolis, but masculine in grammatical gender and personification) laments the collapse of the gigantic lamps of Wisdom and Energy and their replacement by a third lamp, that of 'another worship, of the lawless foreign Jewess' – the Virgin Mary. Turning on its head the tropes of the *Akathistos Hymn to the Panagia*, she is here the one who is (Palamas nd, V: 96, [illegible]):

> denier of all,
> and all have been chased away by thee, and last of all, alas, those
> seven last philosophers, flesh of thy flesh,
> frail scions, one day, just like that, fled
> with the change of times to the Persian king
> (land that broke Xerxes and moulded Aeschylus!),
> the seven last philosophers, flesh of thy flesh,
> among the Persians.

The School of the Persians is presented here, not as the saving of Wisdom by her translation to the East, and her incubation for some later return, but rather as a deluded enterprise: no ageless Hellas, this, but a worn-out idol.

Book VIII, however, represents to some extent a palinode, in the sense that Proclus during his sojourn in Athens can still be receptive to an Athena now banished from her own Parthenon. Here Palamas repeats the story once told by Marinus in his life of Proclus, with much detail from that text (Kasines 1980: 235–42) and makes it his own (Palamas nd, V: 101, [illegible]):

> And one tale tells
> a wandering tale long passed on among men,
> that as the sun set once there came from Xanthus,
> sacred to Apollo and from Alexandria,
> to the Lady's land, and having drunk from the stream
> that quenched the thirst of Socrates and which is still
> called Socrates' stream, he ascended to thee,
> as pilgrim to the Guardian Goddess and votary of the Virgin Goddess,
> Lycian Proclus, last prophet of the pagans,
> so fair he brought to mind the god of day when
> he came to live here below, a king's herdsman.
> But he found thy castle shut and sentinels round.

To the storks who ask his identity, Proclus announces grandly that he is:

> Chaldee, Orphic, in search of Pallas
> undefiled pilgrim with the eyes of the soul,
> threefold, of Athena, of Athens, and of
> all the world, philosopher, poet, hierophant.
>
> (Palamas nd, V: 101)

This identity is a thinly disguised version of Palamas's own – Proclus was, of course, both a close student of ancient poetic texts (especially Homer and Hesiod) and a prolific versifier himself. What grips the modern poet in the figure of Proclus is not so much any doctrine he possesses or transmits – he is, as he appears here, more the voice of the pagan than of anything specifically Neoplatonic – as his prophetic fervour and his willingness to renounce all by living in a hut at the foot of the Acropolis. His reward is an ambiguous one: at dead of night an apparition of Athena appears seeking a night's refuge; but at dawn she disappears like a puff of smoke. She has been driven out by the Virgin, her avatar and foe, and must now seek a new life among barbarous peoples of the East. In a sudden twist, the modern poet turns from Athena-Sophia, the goddess in whom he would love to believe, and from the whole Platonic and Neoplatonic tradition, to her who is indeed venerated by the Greek race today, the Virgin Mary. For Palamas, Proclus is (as he historically was) a poet, and above all a poet: he exemplifies the prophetic strain which, if it altogether fails, must leave the poetic vocation empty – and at the same time the ascetic commitment to something which may be no more than a delusion. The role of Proclus here, as of the Christian monk whose story immediately follows, is left hard to fathom (Hirst 2004: 107–12). Neoplatonism for Palamas seems to be a chimera, however beautiful; perhaps the more beautiful for being just that. In fact, it could be said without injustice – and with acknowledgement of the poet's formidable breadth of reading (see, e.g., Palamas 2018: 174 and 363–4) – that Palamas lights on the Neoplatonic simply as one of many exemplars of the poetic-prophetic vocation.

There was one sequel to Palamas's translation: a partisan poem by Zisis Oikonomou (1911–2005), 'The Death of Hypatia, AD 415'. This poem inveighs against what it calls the 'Greeklings' as false Christians: here Hypatia prophesies that she and her pupils will one day return to a 'jungle of subhumans'; and the eye-witness to her death speaks in the poem's last line of a 'robot-population'. For Oikonomou, it seems that Hypatia (though he misspells her) still possesses a salvific power centuries on.

2. C.P. Cavafy: Neoplatonism and History

From such meditations, abstract enough even when grounded in historical sources, the world of the second poet discussed here, C.P. Cavafy (1863–1933), is remote; and this reflects a conscious strategy on the part of this ambitious, patient contemporary less heralded in his own time. Cavafy is at once Palamas's rival, especially where the intellectual territory of Byzantium is concerned (Hirst 1998), and a mind whose receptivity to different schools of thought and outlooks on life is less schematic – less hitched to the 'march of mind' – and more elusive; nor are the personae of his poems typically or uncritically to be identified with his own. This is particularly true of his relationship with Christianity (Ricks 2001). Nor, despite Cavafy's long-standing (and perhaps generally Paterian) preoccupation with Plato (Zamarou 2005), does he make overt reference to the persons of Plotinus, Proclus or Plethon. Yet the Neoplatonic presence is significant in his poetry, and it lies outside the category of those (relatively early-career) poems which he perhaps unwisely called 'philosophical'. To get an idea of how complex an exercise the modern poet is engaged in, we can do worse than begin with Cavafy's only poem (1917) in which the word 'Platonic' appears[1] (Cavafy 2007: 92,):

In a City in Osrhoene
From a tavern brawl they brought him wounded,
our friend Rhemon last night around midnight.
Through the windows that we left wide open
his lovely body on the bed was lit up by the moon.
We are a mixture here: Syrians, Greeks, Armenians, Medes.
Such too is Rhemon. Yet yesternight as the moon
lit up his sensuous face,
our minds turned to the Platonic Charmides.

The poem's last word alerts us to the title of an early poem (essentially, a Keats pastiche) by Wilde, 'Charmides' (1881), and the rhyme scheme (not, alas, visible in my English version; but see the version by Cavafy's brother John: J.C. Cavafy 2003: 58) is akin. On the face of it, this might seem to be a poem which simply reflects Cavafy's penchant for the hybrid; or which (to another type of reader) seeks

[1] The three Cavafy poems appear in translations of my own, but with reference to the originals in brackets.

to discern an authentic enduring Hellenism behind the contingencies of time. Yet there are further layers of complexity here. The first relates to the Platonic figure named, Charmides, who gave Cavafy the working title of his poem (1916) (Zamarou 2005: 43). Plato's dialogue of that name has as its subject temperance (*sophrosyne*), something rather at odds with Rhemon's involvement in a bar fight (Mendelsohn 2009: 409). And what the poem does not tell us, but which may be inferred from its presence in Cavafy's thematic collection of his *Poems (1916–1918)*, surrounded by 'tomb' poems, is that the poem is best read as an epitaph: it is as if Rhemon can only attain to the sublime Platonic order in death. Here Rhemon's identity is not merely a miscegenated one, but one which has drawn strength from a confluence of traditions – of which he himself may well be unaware, unlike the narrator – which have preserved the wine of the old Platonism in new bottles. In Osrhoene, and specifically in its capital, Edessa, teachers from various linguistic traditions – those traditions are named in this poem, but the names of Neoplatonic teachers themselves, from Bardaisan (154–222 CE) on, do not appear – had operated as exegetes, developing Platonism into what we now know as Neoplatonism. For Cavafy, it is as if the One is to be discerned only with and through the multiplicity attendant on historical development. The poem, then, revolves around Neoplatonism at least as much as the Platonic original with which it might seem to end.

In the next two poems discussed, we move from a milieu in which Neoplatonism flourished to overt mention of specific teachers in the Neoplatonic line. Once again, though, this takes place with a degree of obliquity which makes it clear that Cavafy's interest lies in men as historical actors, more than with their actual teachings – and which is a long way from the doctrinaire and ringing formulations of Palamas:

> *Of the School of the Eminent Philosopher*
> He spent two years as a student of Ammonius Saccas;
> but philosophy became a bore and so did Saccas.
>
> Then he went in for politics.
> But he threw it in. The Eparch was a fool;
> and those around him officious, pompous puppets;
> their Greek worse than barbarous, a wretched set.
>
> His curiosity was attracted
> to some degree by the Church; to be baptized
> and pass for Christian. But he soon
> changed his mind. There would be bad blood undoubtedly
> with his parents, ostentatious pagans;
> and they would – horrible thought – immediately
> cut off his extremely generous allowance.
>
> Yet he had to find something to be going on with. He became an habitué
> of the disorderly houses of Alexandria,
> of every clandestine den of iniquity.
>
> Fortune smiled on him in this at least.
> She had endowed him with a form most comely.
> And he revelled in the god-sent gift.

For another ten years at least
his good looks would last. And after that –
perhaps he'd go back to Saccas.
And if the old boy had died in the meantime,
he'd go with some other philosopher or sophist;
a ready one is always to be found.

Or, if it came to it, he might go back
to politics – commendably mindful
of family tradition,
duty to country, and other high-sounding guff.

Here is a poem (Cavafy 2007: 134,) which mentions philosophy in its title and names an illustrious Neoplatonist in its first line and towards the end. But how like Cavafy to choose Ammonius Saccas (d. 243): a great name, to be sure, but an author none of whose works (if he wrote any) are extant. Slyly, the modern poet, focalising the narration through the musings of an anonymous young man, and adding a note of detachment through indirect speech, draws our attention, not to Neoplatonic teachings at all, nor to the force of personality exerted by their expositors, nor even to the allure of the Neoplatonic milieu, but rather to the crooked timber of humanity which Neoplatonism's teachers were, often vainly, seeking to straighten out. Ammonius's students, tradition tells, included a Plotinus and an Origen: Cavafy's poem reminds us that not all young men had such intellectual gifts or so strong a vocation, whether philosophical or Christian or both. We thus become alert, not to the content of what the school taught, but, so to speak, to its business model: how to retain for years of arduous study those who have other options in life, those for whom the distinction between sage and sophist is meaningless? (See Keeley 1976: 91–3 for a slightly different emphasis.) It is not that Cavafy himself is corrosively sceptical of all teachers of strange doctrines – consider his various poems that relate to Apollonius of Tyana (Bowersock 1983) – but he is a realist. Our anonymous speaker here is nowhere close to *Bildung*, let alone *anagoge*. And we don't dislike him for it.

The third and last of the Cavafy poems discussed here (Cavafy 2007: 144,) once again shows the world of Neoplatonism as embedded in history and in contact – here, conflict – with the now ascendant doctrine of Christianity. It concerns Julian the Apostate, an enduring subject of interest to Cavafy, from at least the time of his close reading of Gibbon in the 1890s (Bowersock 1981):

Julian in Nicomedia
A misguided business and a perilous.
Praise for Hellenic ideals.

Theurgies and visits to the temples
of the pagans. Transports of enthusiasm for the gods of old.

Frequent colloquies with Chrysanthius.
The contemplative teachings of the philosopher – an able one, to be sure – Maximus.

And here's what comes of it. Gallus is starting to show considerable
anxiety. Constantius has his suspicions.

Well, those who had taken counsel had been less than circumspect.
The whole story has – in Mardonius' view – been going on long enough,

and the stir caused must cease once for all.–
Julian the lector is off once again

to church in Nicomedia,
where in ringing tones and with profound

devotion he reads from Holy Writ,
and his Christian piety arouses the admiration of the people.

As with Cavafy's historical poems in general, this one from 1924 dwells on 'how it strikes a contemporary' – to adopt the title of Browning's celebrated poem. The Church now knows Julian as the Apostate – and in the Orthodox Church as the Transgressor (*Parabates*) – but Cavafy knows that history has many cunning passages, contrived corridors.

Such passages are inhabited by competing persons, among whom we find here – jostling for influence among men closer to the levers of power, such as Julian's brother Gallus and his tutor Mardonius – the two Neoplatonists Chrysanthius of Sardis and Maximus of Ephesus, who did so much to infuse the old-time imperial paganism in Julian's mind with pervasive Neoplatonic elements. The two philosophers themselves reflect different tendencies as people, even though each was committed to theurgy. On the one hand, Chrysanthius, pupil of Iamblichus, quietist, irenic – who, as Eunapius reports (1921: 444–6), refused to be recruited to Julian's project to reverse the Christian régime. On the other, Maximus of Ephesus, who appealed to Julian's love of *theoria*, is marked here by the word 'able' (*deinos*), which carries the too-clever-by-half colouring which marked Maximus' chequered career and eventual execution after Julian's own death.

Once again Cavafy situates his Neoplatonists in historical context (Ephesus in 351, ten years before Julian ascended the imperial throne) and as part of a range of preferences. If we think of the poem's terse and gossipy idiom as being that of the imperial court, then the initial form which the anxieties about Julian take might be no more than a hint at Greek love in the opening lines, exacerbated by reference to pagan rituals, indeed ritualism, in the lines that follow. But the specifically Neoplatonic element seems to raise such political anxieties to a higher pitch: it is as if Julian's connection with the two philosophers is more dangerous than simply deluded: are these private meetings on abstruse subjects perhaps a cover for political stratagems? That is certainly how Julian's brother Gallus thinks – but he himself will be executed, by Constantius in 354. It is not that Cavafy is an enemy of abstract thought or indeed mysticism. But he is circumspect about the sorts of abstraction which – depending on taste – permeate or befog the poetry of

Palamas: for the Alexandrian poet, it is as if men (he would never have written on Hypatia, despite the Alexandrian setting), not laws, are the key.

3. Zissimos Lorenzatos: Neoplatonism as Living Tradition

From the preceding discussion of these two most important rivals in Greek poetry of the late 19th century and the first half of the 20th – and despite the fact that each was well-read, and with a good sense of how Neoplatonism figures in the story of the Greek mind – one might conclude that a more mystical and heartfelt engagement with that school of thought, or its offshoots, is – beyond Elytis's impressionistic mode of collage – nowhere to be found in the poetry of the language which has succeeded ancient Greek. And an irreverent reader might be tempted to recall with a chuckle something Palamas once wrote about his own work, satirising the philosophical over-readings to which critics are known to succumb: 'A poem that came out of an emotional adventure in my personal life was taken to have been born from study of Plotinus's *Enneads*' (Palamas 2018: 85).

So it is salutary to turn, for our last example, to the essayist and poet Zissimos Lorenzatos (1915–2004), an author of (consciously) Coleridgean breadth and, like Coleridge, well versed in the Neoplatonic tradition, as in much else.

Lorenzatos was hesitant about his poetic gifts, but towards the end of his life he turned once more to poetry, to integrate in a smaller compass the sorts of concerns addressed in what is now the large three-volume edifice of his collected essays. Steeped in Greek poetry and thought from Homer to the present day, he was always at pains to link his native tradition to wider horizons, and the poem cited here (Lorenzatos 2006: 168–70,) is a classic example. For here, in this late poem (1991), the Neoplatonic figure, so to speak, comes from far to the West, in al-Andalus, and appears in the form of a thinker prominent in this volume, Ibn ʿArabī (1165–1240):

The Stranger
Evening came on in Tunis.
Alone in
The Great Mosque in his dim place of prayer
Drawn by devotion into a corner
He fashions a poem he will never utter to anyone
Or even write down
But rather as with a pair of oxen yoked
In the field of memory, deep in the furrows of his brain
It is engraved there for ever day and night.

And now a few months later in Seville
He is accosted in the street by a young fellow he is not acquainted with
And hears a recitation, as if it were a set of beads in an ascetic's hands
Of the entire poem stanza and verse
Ibn Arabi turns white as a sheet.

Shaken
He asks who wrote the poem? And he is shaken
Once more to hear these words:
'Ibn Arabi' – when the other man does not know who he is
Or that he is right before his eyes.
Well, how could he have learned stanza and verse?
Some months
Ago – the very day and time

The Prophet's faithful one was fashioning
His poem in Tunis – there fell in with
A bunch of young fellows right here
In Seville a stranger, some unknown pilgrim
And drew from his sheath before them as a horseman
His slashing sword through air, a poem.
So taken with it were those young fellows
They begged him to tell it out again and again
Until at length they knew it all by heart.
Later the stranger went the way he came
And disappeared – never to be seen again.

***

King or footsoldier rich man or poor
Whosoever seeks to know with certitude
With the aid of ruler and compass
Just who the stranger was will
Never for the life of him learn anything about poetry (let alone things
More deeply hidden in the mind of man) – that is the tale's point –
However he may search for the needle in the haystack
In beetling libraries
Seeking to tame wild books
However adept he is at reading the world
However wise he is
and even if he speaks
(As in the last verses I harvest here)
In the tongues of men and of angels…

A notable feature of Lorenzatos's 1991 collection is its extensive section of notes – now at the back of the collected volume, but originally in a separate volume in the slipcase – and the title this section bears: 'Sources'. Such is this writer's range of reference that any reader is grateful for the help the notes provide; but in calling this section 'Sources', rather than 'Notes', Lorenzatos is also thinking of tradition as a wellspring. (Compare the 'ancient springs' to which Kathleen Raine gave her allegiance: see Messenger 2019.) But it is characteristic here that, rather than turning right back to, say, Proclus direct – as Palamas had done – Lorenzatos chooses to see the inner essence of the Neoplatonic through its very transmission or, as he would prefer to think of it, transfusion in the thought-world of Islam. In fact, the whole first section of the poem is at one level a versification of a paragraph in a book by the student of Sufism (and, as a shadow behind that, of Proclus), Henry Corbin (1903–78), *L'imagination créatrice dans le soufisme d'Ibn ʿArabi* (1958), a paragraph printed in its entirety in the note (Lorenzatos 2006: 198).

Now this method, of the 'found poem', is a perfectly respectable one. But why has the Greek Lorenzatos chosen it over recourse to an overtly Neoplatonic figure? Lorenzatos's preoccupation with the *philosophia perennis* leads him to deflect the story from being solely or primarily a Greek one to being universal – it is not a tale of transmission, whereby Greek thought is merely curated by Arabic, but one of permeation, whereby a certain outlook, in subterranean or subaqueous mode, moves across the Mediterranean. Anxious to seek the essence of esoteric doctrine, Lorenzatos sidesteps the Neoplatonism of the textbooks in order to record this parable; and he takes it from a modern authority committed to exploring the sorts of wide cultural connections which are the subject of this volume. There is also historical justice to this, in that some of the founding Neoplatonists were themselves native Arabic-speakers (Goutas 2007). But both the first section of the poem and the second – the latter an authorial comment on the first – show the Greek poet polishing and resetting the enigmatic and precious story so as to make of it something slightly different.

Two insertions in the first part contribute to distinguishing it from what Corbin, reporting Ibn ʿArabī, writes. The first is the recurrent term 'fashions', *mastorevei*, which endows the protagonist's act of making with more of a material sense: the word is one we would use, say, of a stonemason. The second, a related point, is the oxen-simile, evoking the ancient Greek practice of writing *boustrophedon*. Both of these processes are painstaking and recursive – quite unlike the rapid-fire recitation of the poem as gushing from the lips of the first mysterious stranger. But all three are of a different order from the reason-hobbled, book-bound seeker admonished in the poem's second section.

Lorenzatos has one last thought, however, which seeks to create a bridge between this Sufi tradition he is so attracted by and the Orthodox Christianity of which he was throughout his life and work so ardent an adherent; and this comes in the opening and concluding lines of the second section. The final quotation, of course, is from 1.Cor. 13; and by implication what the Sufi tale then has to teach us is, for Lorenzatos, nothing less than *agape*. But the opening lines of the section, less visibly to the Western reader, quote (in Modern Greek translation) from the Eastern service for the dead (Lorenzatos 2006: 226). The tension between Neoplatonism and Christianity which our earlier poets explored is here reconciled.

To conclude. The world of the Platonic dialogues continues to present to the West (and beyond) the most compelling (Western) picture of the teacher–student relationship that exists; and, through many intellectual and worldly vicissitudes, this remained a large part of the mystique of Neoplatonism, with its careful (if not always by modern standards historical) attention to the lines of teacher and student over the years. In the first of the cases discussed here, however, the poetry of Palamas, such a focus is deliberately occluded by the sense that the eternal voice of Plato issues forth in the exceptional and the solitary: it is as if the One must have just One, at any given time, who gives it expression. Proclus, for Palamas, is the lonely hymnode rather than the head of the Platonic school at Athens; and this despite the fact that Palamas draws so closely on Marinus's life of Proclus. With Cavafy things are otherwise: Rhemon can live among Platonists without having any idea of what they know or even what they think; the anonymous pupil of Ammonius Saccas is but a weak vessel for the transmission of any stable doctrine; Julian's Neoplatonic theurgy may be no more than a striving for effect, a playing to the gallery, a dallying with conspiracy – in all these cases, the master–pupil relationship is seen as inauthentic at best. In such cases we may speak of faces of the finite: the flawed individuals drawn into contact with the current of Neoplatonism. To such examples, and in full knowledge of them, Lorenzatos counters an historically and geographically remote successor who, in his view, restores to our vision a full-throated idea of what authentic teachings are and how they operate in the mind, some sense of the mystery which Neoplatonism set out to explore and which it continues to exemplify.

References

Athanassiadi, P. (2015), *Mutations of Hellenism in Late Antiquity* (Farnham, Ashgate).

Bancroft-Marcus, R. (1982), 'Literary Cryptograms and the Cretan Academies', *Byzantine and Modern Greek Studies*, 8: 47–76.

Bowersock, G.W. (1981), 'The Julian Poems of C.P. Cavafy', *Byzantine and Modern Greek Studies*, 7: 89–104.

Bowersock, G.W. (1983), 'Cavafy and Apollonius', *Grand Street*, 2.3: 180–9.

Cavafy, C.P. (2007), *Collected Poems*, ed. A. Hirst, trans. E. Sachperoglou (Oxford, Oxford World's Classics).

Cavafy, J.C. (trans.) (2003), *Poems by C.P. Cavafy* (Athens, Ikaros).

Corbin, H. (1958), *L' imagination créatrice dans le soufisme d' Ibn 'Arabî* (Paris, Flammarion).

Economou, Z. (2004), 'The Death of Hypatia', trans. Kimon Friar, in P. Bien, P. Constantine, E. Keeley & K. Van Dyck (eds), *A Century of Greek Poetry, 1900–2000* (River Vale, Cosmos Publishing), 354–7.

Elytis, O. (1977), *To Axion Esti* (Athens, Ikaros).

Elytis, O. (1982), *Tria poiemata se semeio eukairias* (Athens, Ikaros).

Elytis, O. (2011), *En Leuko* (Athens, Ikaros).

Eunapius (1921), *Lives of the Philosophers*, in Philostratus and Eunapius, *Lives of the Sophists etc*, trans. Wilmer C. Wright (Cambridge MA, Loeb Classical Library).

Goutas, D. (2007), 'Greek and Arabic: Early Contacts', in A.-F. Christidis (ed.), *A History of Ancient Greek* (Cambridge, Cambridge University Press), 244–50.

Hirst, A. (1998), 'Two Cheers for Byzantium: Equivocal Attitudes in the Poetry of Palamas and Cavafy', in D. Ricks and P. Magdalino (eds), *Byzantium and the Modern Greek Identity* (Aldershot, Ashgate), 105–17.

Hirst, A. (2004), *God and the Poetic Ego: The Appropriation of Biblical and Liturgical Language in the Poetry of Palamas, Sikelianos and Elytis* (Bern, Peter Lang).

Iakov, D.I. (1983), *He archaiognosia tou Odyssea Elyti* (Athens, Polyptycho)

Kasines, K.G. (1980), *He hellenike logotechnike paradose sten* Phlogera tou Vasilia (Athens, Palamas Foundation).

Keeley, E. (1976), *Cavafy's Alexandria*, 2nd edn (Princeton, Princeton University Press).

Lorenzatos, Z. (2006), *Poiemata* (Athens, Ikaros).

Loulakaki, I. (2014), 'The Dark Philosopher and the Post-Modern Turn: Heraclitus in the Poetry of Seferis, Elytis and Fostieris', *Byantine and Modern Greek Studies*, 38.1: 91–113.

Mendelsohn, D. (ed. & trans.) (2009), *C.P. Cavafy, The Collected Poems* (New York, Knopf).

Messenger, J.L. (2019), *The Inspired Intellect: Neoplatonism and its Reception in Robert Graves, Jorge Luis Borges, Suzanne Lilar, and Kathleen Raine* (unpublished Ph.D. thesis, University of St Andrews).

Palamas, K. (nd), *Hapanta*, 16 vols (Athens, Biris).

Palamas, K. (2018 edn), *Semeiomata sto Perithorio*, ed. M. Psalti (Athens, Patakis).

Papadiamantis, A. (1981), *Hapanta*, vol. 1 (Athens, Domos).

Peckham, R.S. (1998), 'Papadiamantis, Ecumenism and the Theft of Byzantium', in D. Ricks and P. Magdalino (eds), *Byzantium and the Modern Greek Identity* (Aldershot, Ashgate), 91–104.

Pourgouris, M. (2011), *Mediterranean Modernisms: The Poetic Metaphysics of Odysseus Elytis* (London, Routledge).

Ricks, D. (1997a), 'The Progress of Poesy: Kalvos, Gray and the Revival of Ancient Literary Language', *Modern Greek Studies/Australia/New Zealand*, 4: 111–32.

Ricks, D. (1997b), 'Tradition and the Individual Talent: Remarks on the Poetry of Michalis Ganas', *Byzantine and Modern Greek Studies*, 21: 132–53.

Ricks, D. (2001), 'Cavafy and the Body of Christ', *Journal of the Hellenic Diaspora*, 27.1–2: 19–32.

Ricks, D. (2014), 'Lucretian Moments in Modern Greek Poetry', in Dimitris Tziovas (ed.), *Re-imagining the Past: Antiquity and Modern Greek Culture* (Oxford, Oxford University Press), 252–65.

Romanos (1963 edn), *Sancti Romani Melodi Cantica Genuina*, ed. P. Maas and C.A. Trypanis (Oxford, Oxford University Press).

Savidis, G.P. (2012), *Semeioseis ston Lyriko Vio tou Angelou Sikelianou* (Athens, Hermes).

Sikelianos, A. (1981) *Lyrikos Vios*, vol. 2 (Athens, Ikaros).

Siniossoglou, N. (2011), *Radical Platonism in Byzantium: Illumination and Utopia in Gemistos Plethon* (Cambridge, Cambridge University Press).

Stylianidou, M. (2015), *Kostis Palamas as Verse Translator and Anthologist: A Study of* Xanatonismene Mousike (unpublished Ph.D. thesis, King's College London).

Taylor, J. (1998), 'Odysseus Elytis: The Innate Passion and the Apotheosis', *Poetry*, 172.5: 295–9.

Tempridou, P. (2016), *To Amoiasto tes Poieses kai to Isoposo tes Philosophias: Ho Diplos Heautos tou Odyssea Elyti* (unpublished Ph.D. thesis, Aristotle University of Thessaloniki).

Zamarou, R. (2005), *Kavaphes kai Platon* (Athens, Kedros).

Index of References to the *Enneads* of Plotinus

Ennead I

I 1 [53] 8 9, 53n3
I 1 [53] 12 136n7
I 2 [19] 25n46, 94, 286n25
I 2 [19] 3 404
I 2 [19] 7 94
I 3 [20] 1 61, 310
I 4 [46] 10 53n3
I 6 [1] 10, 296, 312
I 6 [1] 2 31, 156
I 6 [1] 3 283
I 6 [1] 5 158, 312
I 6 [1] 6 59, 162n16
I 6 [1] 7 154
I 6 [1] 8 53n4, 57, 59, 136n8, 157, 161
I 6 [1] 9 53n2, 57, 59, 63, 73, 157, 159–60, 164, 286n25, 301

Ennead II

II 1 [40] 7 287n30
II 2 [14] 2 37n61, 63n19, 122n62
II 3 [52] 7 101
II 4 [12] 5 285n23
II 9 [33] 163
II 9 [33] 4 63
II 9 [33] 8 312n11
II 9 [33] 16 161, 310
II 9 [33] 17 162n16

Ennead III

III 2 [47] 3 312n11
III 4 [15] 3 9
III 5 [50] 1 155
III 5 [50] 9 10, 271n67
III 6 [26] 6 312
III 6 [26] 7 57
III 7 [45] 11 312n11
III 8 [30] 10 313
III 8 [30] 11 312

Ennead IV

IV 3 [27] 10 8n9
IV 3 [27] 11 53n1, 58
IV 3 [27] 12 53n4, 57, 63
IV 3 [27] 17 319
IV 3 [27] 25 310
IV 3 [27] 26 63
IV 3 [27] 30 69n43
IV 4 [28] 1 261n25
IV 4 [28] 1–2 21n37
IV 4 [28] 5 108
IV 4 [28] 8 310
IV 7 [2] 13 132n2
IV 8 [6] 285n23
IV 8 [6] 1 11n15, 29n49, 63n19, 103, 136n9, 203, 212n7, 261n27, 311, 416n4
IV 8 [6] 6 153
IV 8 [6] 8 155

Ennead V

V 1 [10] 1 9n12, 261n27, 286
V 1 [10] 2 61, 286n26
V 1 [10] 6 7
V 1 [10] 12 286n26
V 2 [11] 1 285
V 2 [11] 2 135n6
V 3 [49] 342n16
V 3 [49] 12 313
V 3 [49] 13 7, 104, 313
V 3 [49] 14 314
V 3 [49] 17 44
V 5 [32] 108, 121
V 5 [32] 3 108
V 5 [32] 6 152
V 5 [32] 8 61
V 5 [32] 12 164n18, 165–6
V 5 [32] 13 221n17
V 8 [31] 10, 164n18
V 8 [31] 1 12, 58, 60–1, 73, 296
V 8 [31] 2 162, 297n27
V 8 [31] 3 316, 416
V 8 [31] 6 6
V 8 [31] 7 312n11
V 8 [31] 9 297
V 8 [31] 12 312n11
V 8 [31] 13 57, 158
V 9 [5] 2 61
V 9 [5] 11 61, 110, 310

Ennead VI

VI 4 [22]	103
VI 4 [22] 7	287n30, 320
VI 5 [23]	103
VI 5 [23] 1	104
VI 5 [23] 12	103
VI 5 [25] 2	260n20
VI 7 [38] 3	60
VI 7 [38] 8	8n10
VI 7 [38] 10	101
VI 7 [38] 12	8n9, 316
VI 7 [38] 13	312n9
VI 7 [38] 14	13, 114n45
VI 7 [38] 15	11, 122
VI 7 [38] 32	315
VI 7 [38] 33	121n60
VI 7 [38] 34	123, 377
VI 7 [38] 35	138
VI 8 [39] 8	313
VI 8 [39] 15	10n14
VI 8 [39] 18	122n62
VI 9 [9] 1	8
VI 9 [9] 2	8
VI 9 [9] 6	11
VI 9 [9] 7	8
VI 9 [9] 8	68
VI 9 [9] 9	1, 10, 11, 314, 410
VI 9 [9] 11	13, 31, 81

Index of Citations from the Qur'an

Sura: Verse

2:31	160
2:115	104
2:152	102
2:197	99
5:54	114
6:32	101
7:172	103, 154, 424
7:180	163
17:1	103, 413
17:110	163
20:8	163
23:14	150
24:35	15, 137
26:224–7	100n13
26:227	35n58
40:39	101
41:10	107
42:11	104
45:34	102
55:27	104
59:24	163
88:25–6	139
89:27	31
97:1	414
97:5	414

Index of Names and Places

The names of authors whose poems are reproduced in this volume and the corresponding page references are printed in **bold**. References to names that appear in the poems are marked as '**in cited poetry**'.

Aaron ben Elijah of Nicomedia 244n23
Abarbanel, Isaac 22
Abarbanel, Judah *see* Ebreo, Leone
ʿAbd al-Laṭīf Shams b. Ṣadr al-Dīn Rūzbihān Thānī 150–1
ʿAbd al-Ṣabūr, Salāḥ 406
Abū Māḍī, Ilyā 400
Abū Tammām 105–12, 125
Abulafia, Abraham 22, 384
al-ʿAdawiyya, Rābiʿa 20n36, 113, 190n4
Adonis (ʿAlī Aḥmad Saʿīd) 406
Africa 3–4, 148, 373, 419; North Africa 22, 56, 220, 332, 361; West Africa 17n28, 392
Agathon 281–2, 288–9
Albert the Great 255n1, 266n51
Alcántara, Pedro de 326
Alḍāhirī, Zechariah 23, **223–32**
Aldana, Francisco de 26, 29, **323–33**, **340–1**, 343
Alexandria 14, 16n24, 41, 65, 79, 239, 389, 408, 457, 464; **in cited poetry** 459, 461
Alḥarīzī, Judah 223, 225, 230–2, 243n19
Amasya 179, 195, 196
Amelius 67–8, 75n64
America 358, 360, 373, 392–402
Ammonius Hermeiou 65
Ammonius Saccas 14, 41, 467; **in cited poetry** 461–2
Anatolia 16, 169–70, 172n4, 441
Andalusia, al-Andalus 5, 22–3, 34, 37, 102n16, 217–23, 238, 243–9, 387, 464
Aphrodite 410
Apollonius of Tyana 56, 462
al-ʿAqqād, Abbās Maḥmūd 401
Aquinas, Thomas St 144n29, 256n1, 256n10, 267–8, 360
Arabia 22, 360, 416; **in cited poetry** 211
ʿArīḍa, Nasīb 394, 396, **399–400**, 402
Aristotle 15, 60n13, 71, 102, 117, 133, 256n10, 268, 285, 419; *for Theology of Aristotle see* Index of Subjects *Plotiniana Arabica*
Asia 3–4, 17n28, 212, 373; Central 148, 169, 415; Asia Minor 56, 456, 458
Astarābādī, Fażlullāh 176
Athena 41, 410, 458–9; **in cited poetry** 410
Athens 458; School of 16n24, 65, 77, 136, 210, 419, 458, 467; **in cited poetry** 410
al-ʿAttābī 144
ʿAṭṭār, Farīd ad-Dīn 19, 32, 406, 420
Augustine of Hippo 24, 256, 279, 287, 294, 311, 317, 321, 330–1
Australia 392
Avicenna *see* Ibn Sīnā
Ayhan, Ece 437
Ayyūb, Rashīd 400–1

Bacchylides 54
Badawī, ʿAbd al-Raḥmān 39, 404, 408, 412
Baghdad 19, 24, 105, 113, 223n25, 442
Baqlī, Rūzbihān 20, 28, **148–66**
Bar Hiyya, Abraham 223n23
Bardaisan 461
al-Baṣrī, Ḥasan 113
Batur, Enis 437
al-Bayātī, ʿAbd al-Wahhāb 406
Bayazıt, Erdem 437
Bayezid II, Sultan 195–6
Bektaş, Ḥacı 172n4
Bembo, Pietro 293n11, 307n3, 321, 336–40
Ben Aharon, Shelomo 245n26
Ben Samuel, Joseph 37, **247–9**
Berk, İlhan 437
Bernard of Clairvaux, St 317, 377
Bessarion, Cardinal 85–6
al-Bisṭāmī, Bayazid 113
Blake, William 396n1, 397
Bocca di Magra 366
Boethius 24, 256, 268, 321
Borgia, Lucrezia 336
Brandeis, Irma 36, 355–67, 370
Bruno, Giordano 389–90

al-Buḥturī 113, 140–3
Buonarroti, Michelangelo *see* Michelangelo
Byzantium 4–5, 26, 71, 73, 79–86, 237–40, 244, 456, 460

Cairo 23, 239, 248, 361, 385, 404
Calcidius 24n42, 265–6
Câmî *see* Jāmī
Capella, Martianus 24
Careggi 278, 280
Castiglione, Baldassare 307n3, 321, 336–42
Castro, Rosalía de 386–7
Catalonia 223, 238n3
Cavafy, C.P. 455, **460–4**, 467
Celan, Paul 374, 384–5
Çelebi, Asaf Hâlet 433, **441–3**
Çelebi, Caʿfer 20, **179–85**, 199n12
Çelebi, Müʿeyyedzâde Abdurrahman *see* Hâtemî
Celsus 67
Cervantes 320
Christodorus of Coptus 77
Chrysanthius of Sardis 463
Cisneros, García de 323
Clement of Alexandria 381
Clizia 36–7, 355–8, 360, 367, 370; **in cited poetry** 356; *see also* Brandeis
Colonna, Vittoria 21, 26, 28, 33–4, **292–303**
Constantinople 16, 23, 77, 82, 85–6, 170, 238, 244, 248
Contini, Gianfranco 355–6, 364, 366
Covarrubias, Sebastián de 341n14
Crimea 169, 244, 248n33, 249
Cüneyd *see* Junayd

Damascius 15, 16n24, 65, 68, 82–3
Dante 4, 25, 33–4, 36, 40, **255–71**, 356–64, 370
Darʿī, Moses ben Abraham 239–44, 248–9
Darwīsh, Maḥmūd 406
D'Avalos, Costanza 293–4
D'Avalos, Francesco 293–4, 298
al-Daylamī, Abū al-Ḥasan 149n2
Denys *see* Dionysius the Areopagite
al-Dimashqī, Ghaylān 411
Diocletian, Emperor 64
Dionysius the Areopagite 16, 20n36, 24, 41n64, 72, 79, 256, 279, 314, 315n17, 323–4, 376
Diotima 20n36, 188–201, 281–2, 370
Duncan, Robert 133–4

Ebreo, Leone (Judah Abarbanel) 22, 26–7, 34–5, 306–21, 338, 341–2, 347–9
Eckhart, Meister 24, 375, 381n3, 389
Edessa 461
Egypt 5, 14–15, 56, 169, 218n5, 238–40, 248, 392, 400–1, 406–16
El Maleh, Edmond Amran 383–4
Elāhī, Bījan 36, 39, **422–5**, 431
Eliot, T.S. 355, 455
Elytis, Odysseus 455, 464
Empedocles 149, 270, 410, 412, 456
Eriugena, John Scotus 24
Eros/*Erōs* 281, 288–9, 377, 381–2, 410
Europe 3–4, 14n21, 228n45, 300, 328, 338, 370, 375–6, 392, 412; Eastern 22, 169, 237–40, 248; Western 16, 23, 25, 85, 415
Eusebius of Caesarea 17n26, 53n5, 67, 75n64

al-Fārābī 100, 110, 192, 209, 306, 419
Farrokhzād, Forūgh 39, **427–30**
Fazıl, Enderunlu 199
Ficino, Marsilio 5, 23, 25–6, 29, 35, 85, 276–89, 293n9, 299, 306, 324–31
Firdawsī 204
Florence 26, 36, 85, 276, 280n11, 281n12, 324, 356–9, 361, 364–5, 367
Fortini, Franco 368–9, 371
Fostieris, Antonis 456
François de Sales, St 328

Galen 149, 210, 338
Gallienus, Emperor 55, 64
Garcilaso de la Vega 27, **307–8**, 342, 347
Gaza 78–9
Genoa 169, 358, 364
George of Pisidia 78–9
al-Ghazālī, Abū Ḥāmid 19–20n36, 104n21, 149n2, 192–3, 224n27, 306
al-Ghazālī, Aḥmad 114
Góngora, Luis de 310n7, 347
Gordian, Emperor 15, 55, 64
Goytisolo, Juan 383–4, 388–9
Granada 415
Greece 18, 41, 169, 209, 421, 456, 458; **in cited poetry** 85
Gregory of Nazianzus 16, **79–80**
Gregory of Nyssa 16, 73, 81, 315n17
Gwāliyārī, Muḥammad Ghawth 212

Ḥaddād, Nadrah 401
Hafez 1
Hagia Sophia 77–8
Halicz (Halych) 248
al-Ḥallāj/al-Ḥallâc 20n36, 43, 114, **131–45**, 149n2, 388, 406, 422
Hanım, Leylâ 190n5
Hanım, Nigâr 190n5
al-Ḥarīrī, Abū 'l-Ḥasan 225
Hâtemî (penname of Mü'eyyedzâde Abdurrahman Çelebi) 195–6, 198

Hatun, Mihrî 20–1, 26, 190, 192, **195–201**, 440
Hatun, Zeynep 191
Ḫayâlî 20, 31, **173–9**
Hebreo, León *see* Ebreo, Leone
Hecate 66, 76
Hermias 68, 278
Herrera, Fernando de 342
Hikmet, Nazım 437, 441
Hill, Geoffrey 367–8
Hollanda, Francisco de 294
Homer 58, 61–2, 70–1, 135–7, 459, 464
Hugh of Balma 323
Hypatia 16n24, 389, 456–7, 460, 464; **in cited poetry** 457

Iamblichus 15, 66–7, 71, 73, 243n20, 278, 323, 463
Iberia 22, 348
Ibn ʿArabī 20, 22, 33, 35, 38, **118–25**, 246n27, 376–7, 406, 466; **in cited poetry** 464–5
Ibn Ezra, Abraham 32n53, 244–6, 249
Ibn al-Fāriḍ 33, **116**, 118
Ibn Gabirol, Solomon 22–3, 25, **220–3**, 226–7, 228n42, 229–30, 242n13, 247
Ibn al-Haytham, al-Ḥasan 411
Ibn Jaʿfar, Qudāma 94n2
Ibn Masarra of Cordoba 22
Ibn Paquda, Baḥya 226n35, 230
Ibn Rashīq 144n25
Ibn al-Shahrazūrī 115–16, 118
Ibn Shuhayd 35
Ibn Sīnā 18, 21, 26, 38, 100, 138, 193, 206, 209–10, 220; *Ode to the Soul* 31, 115n49, **393**
Ibn Ṭufayl 22
İlhan, Atillâ 437
Immanuel of Rome 223
İnan, Mehmet Akif 437
India 4, 15, 113n40, 148, 203–13, 224n27, 373, 421, 425–6
Iran 18, 148, 213, 420–32; *see also* Persia
Iraq 94, 145, 169
Isaiah 243n17, 247n30
Ischia 293
Israeli, Isaac 22, 24, 220
Istanbul 170, 173, 177, 179, 180; *see also* Constantinople
Italy 5, 85–6, 190n2, 238n3, 292–5, 302–3, 306, 355–60, 366–7

Jabès, Edmond 385–7
Jabr, Farīd 404
Jāmī/Câmî 32n53, 170–1, 441
Jerusalem 239, 375, 413
Jibrān, Jibrān Khalīl 37, **393–7**, 399, 401
John of the Cross, St *see* Juan de la Cruz, San
John of Damascus 59–60
John of Gaza 16, **78**
Jones, Sir William 212
Juan de la Cruz, San 27, 31, 43, 312–19, 323–4, 374–7, 381, 383, 388–9
Juan de Yepes 377
Juana Inés de la Cruz, Sor 21, 190–1, 340, **345–8**
Julian the Apostate, Emperor 57, 86, 462–3
Julian the Chaldean 65
Julian the Theurgist 65–6
Junayd/Cüneyd 113, 442
al-Jurjānī, ʿAbd al-Qāhir 143

Kaʿba 20, 112, 119–20, 122–4, 426–7; **in cited poetry** 118, 120
Kalvos, Andreas (Andrea Calbo) 454
Kāmrān of Shiraz 210
Karakoç, Sezai 433, **437–40**
Karo, Joseph 229
Kashan 426
Kayvān, Āẕar 21, 25, 28, **203–13**
Kāẓemī, Jāleh 422
Keskin, Birhan 40, 43–4, 433, **447–50**
al-Kharrāz 15
Khudājūy ibn Nāmdār 204
Kiarostami, Abbas 39, 429–31
al-Kindī 18, 24, 108, 110–11, 113, 121, 149n2, 419
Kısakürek, Necip Fazıl 437, 441
Klapisch, Liliane 386

Laylā/Leylâ 115–16, 440, 443
Lebanon 15, 37, 392, 395, 397–9, 404
León, Fray Luis de 27, 33, 76, 111n36, **310–12**, 321
León, Moses de 22
Lermontov, Mikha'il 398
Leylâ *see* Laylā
ha-Levi, Judah 217n2, 222, 240, 244, 246–9
Levinas, Emmanuel 12–13, 381
Lope de Vega 348–9
Lorenzatos, Zissimos 464–7
Lowell, Robert 132–3, 134
Luther, Martin 295n19
Luzatto, Moshe 23n41

Macrobius 24–5, 257, 268–71
Maimonides, Moses 22, 223n23, 224, 228, 231, 244, 306, 384
al-Majnūn 115–16
al-Malāʾika, Nāzik 38n63, 405
Maleh, Edmond Amran El 384

al-Maʿlūf, Fawzī 401
Mandūr, Muḥammad 401–2
Mann, Thomas 237
Marcus Aurelius, Emperor 65
al-Marghīnānī, Abū al-Ḥasan Naṣr b. Ibn al-Ḥasan 139–40, 143
Marinus 73, 74n58, 86, 459, 467
Marsuppini, Carlo 281–8
Marsuppini, Cristoforo 281n12
Maṭar, Muḥammad ʿAfīfi 38–9, 43, **406–16**
Mavilis, Lorentzos 455
Maximus of Ephesus 463
Mecca 119–20, 120, 122, 124, 172n4, 413–14, 427
Medici, Cosimo de' 278, 279n6
Mehmed II, Sultan 179
Menander Rhetor 141–2
Michelangelo Buonarroti 26, 33, **292–8**, 300–2
Mirandola, Pico della 345
Mobad *see* Mīr Ẕūl-fiqār Āẕar Sāsānī
Mongus, Peter 65
Monica, mother of Augustine of Hippo 311, 330
Montale, Eugenio 36, 40, 43, **355–71**
Montano, Benito Arias 26, 29, 323–32
Mosès, Stéphane 386
Muḥammad, Prophet 19n34, 33, 150, 160–1, 185; ascension of 39, 103, 203, 209, 413–14, 428
al-Musayyab ibn ʿAlas 96–7
al-Mutanabbī 113, 137, 143
al-Muʿtaṣim, Aḥmad ibn 106, 111
al-Muʿtaṣim, Caliph 106, 110

Najara, Israel 23n41
Naples 293
Nāṣir-i Khrusraw 19n33
Necatigil, Behçet 433, 438, **443**–7, 450
New York 392, 394, 397–9
Niccoli, Niccolò 279n6
al-Niffarī 409; **in cited poetry** 412
Niẓāmī 32n53, 115n47
Nonnus of Panopolis 74–9
Nuʿayma, Mikhāʾīl 38, **396–9**, 401
Numenius of Apamea 55n9

Odysseus 133, 135–6, 360
Oikonomou, Zisis 460
Origen 67n31, 315n17, 376, 462
Osrhoene 460–1
Osuna, Francisco de 324, 327
Otto, Rudolf 375
Ottoman Empire 169, 171, 181, 185–6, 195, 434–5
Ovid 356
Özdenören, Alaeddin 437
Özdenören, Rasim 437

Pakdil, Nuri 437
Palamas, Kostis 41, **456–61**, 464–7
Palamas, St Gregory 41n65
Palestine 22, 79, 238n3
Pallavicino, Gaspare 337–8
Pamprepius of Panopolis 77
Paul the Silentiary 16, **77–8**
Paul, St 56, 262, 294, 298, 360
Persia 2, 16n24, 64–5, 148, 209–10, 213; **in cited poetry** 211
Petrarca, Francesco (Petrarch) 25, 294n14, 292, 293n11, 298, 303, 308, 343
Pia, Emilia 336–40, 342, 347
Pindar 54
Plato 54, 61, 136, 357–8, 420, 460–1; *Cratylus* 288; *Meno* 281; *Phaedo* 57, 71n52, 218n3, 259; *Phaedrus* 54, 68, 70, 83, 166n20, 246n28, 259, 307, 312; *Philebus* 282; *Republic* 53–4, 58, 60, 63n18, 81–3, 142, 259n17, 344, 367; *Symposium* 20n36, 58, 188–9, 200–1, 259, 271, 276, 280–9, 293, 370; *Timaeus* 24, 82, 218n3, 256–70, 281–3; *Theaetetus* 63, 289; *see also* Plotinus
Pletho, George Gemistus 16, **84–86**
Plotinus, ascension 11n15, 39, 67–8, 103, 203, 212n7, 261n27, 311, 416n4; on gender 13–14, 189; language 7, 11, 104, 156, 164n18, 313; life 2, 13–15, 64, 210; and Plato 8n10, 9n11, 10–11, 43n66, 57, 63, 158n12, 164n18, 259, 271, 278–80; thought 6–14; *see also* Index of References to the *Enneads*, Index of Subjects, *esp.* aesthetics, art, beauty, body, intellect, love, Neoplatonism, *Plotiniana Arabica*, soul
Plutarch 54n7, 65
Poland 5, 23, 238, 247
Porphyry 2n3, 15, 24, 53, 56–7, 64, **66–8**, 71, 280n11, 404, 420
Portinari, Beatrice 33, 36, 257, 259, 263–4, 267, 360, 370
Proclus 15–16, 34–4, 53, 57, **62–86**, 136, 280n11, 323, 458–60, 465–7
Provence 22, 223, 238n3
Psellos, Michael 16, **82–3**
Pseudo-Dionysius *see* Dionysius the Areopagite
Ptolemy 389

Qandīl, ʿAlī 407
al-Qaʿqāʿ 96–8
Qazvīnī, ʿAbbās Kayvān 213
Quevedo, Francisco de 308–9, 347, 374

al-Rāghib al-Iṣfahānī 135, 137–8, 145
Ramírez de Guzmán, Catalina Clara 190–1, 340, **343–5**

Rifat, Oktay 437
Ritsos, Yannis 455
ha-Rofe, Aaron ben Joseph 238n3, **244**–7, 249
ha-Rofé, Zechariah 224n28
Romanus the Melode 454
Rome 15, 56, 86, 292, 294, 328, 384
Rûmî, Eşrefoğlu 441
Rūmī/Rûmî, Jalāl al-Dīn 20n36, 39, 170, 192, 427

Safed 223, 229, 386
Sajjādī, Ja'far 18n32, 420
Samarra 110
San Juan, Juan Huarte de 339
Sana'a 225
Sao Paolo 393
Sāsānī, Mīr Ẕūl-fiqār Āẕar 208, 211
Selim I, Sultan 179–80
Selmân-ı Sâvecî 197
Sepehrī, Sohrāb 40, **425**–7
Sereni, Vittorio 37, 361, 363–4, 367, 371
Sergius of Constantinople 79
al-Shābbī, Abū 'l-Qāsim 402
Shankaracharya 210
al-Shushtarī 117–18
Sibyls 67
Sidney, Sir Philip 33n54
ha-Ṣidoni, Mordecai 225
Sikelianos, Angelos 456
Silvestris, Bernardus 25, 266n54
Simonides 54
Socrates 117, 164n18, 188–9, 281, 288, 307, 344, 370, 407; **in cited poetry 459**
Solomos, Dionysios 455
Spain 18, 29, 217, 242n13, 248, 306–21, 323, 330, 345n21, 349, 385–6; *see also* Andalusia
St John of the Cross *see* Juan de la Cruz, San
Suarès, Carlo 382
Suhrawardī/Suhravardī 21, 39, 204, 210–12, 224n28, 300, 415, 420
Süreya, Cemal 437
Symeon the New Theologian 16, **80–1**
Syria 15, 79, 144n31, 382, 392, 395, 399
Syrianus 15, 66, 68; **in cited poetry 86**

Ṭaha, 'Alī Maḥmūd 402
Taher Saifuddin, Sayyidna 19n33
Tanzi, Drusilla 358, 360
ha-Teimani, Abner ben Helek 225–7, 229, 231
Teresa of Ávila, St 27, 116, 315, 319–20, 323–4, 327–8, 330, 332, 388–9
Tevfik, Neyzen 441
Theodosius, Emperor 64
Titianus/Ṭūṭiyānūsh 210
Transoxiana 415
Trent, Council of 295, 306, 328
Turkey 40, 186n21, 190n5, 195, 433, 435–8, 451; *see also* Ottoman Empire
al-Tustarī, Sahl 113
Ṭūṭiyānūsh *see* Titianus
Tyre 15
Tzvi, Sabbatai 23n41

Ukraine 248, 398
Urbino 336
Uyar, Turgut 437

Valente, José Ángel 37, 40, 43, **373–90**
Vallejo, César 379
Venice 169, 244n25
Vyasa 210

Wilde, Oscar 460
William of Conches 25, 264n41, 266
Williams, William Carlos 363
Wordsworth, William 38

Yavuz, Hilmi 39, 433, **443–4**
Yemen 5, 23, 34, 223–32, 238n3

Zakariyya, Fu'ād 404
Zaragoza, Abraham Abulafia de 22, 384
Zarifoğlu, Cahit 437
Zayas, María de 339, 340n10, 348–9
Zeno of Elea 412; **in cited poetry** 412
Zeus 12, 60, 84–5; **in cited poetry** 71, 84–5

Index of Subjects

Page references to the text of poems reproduced in this volume are marked as '**in cited poetry**'.

Alast, Day of 103, 154, 424
'aql 121, 137–8, 219, 246n27; *see also* Intellect, reason
aesthetics, Islamic 99, 192–4; of Judaism 26; Neoplatonic/Plotinian 27, 32, 35n59, 53–61, 72–4, 79, 82, 285n24; of poetry 196, 198, 244, 249; *see also* art
allegory 27, 29–30, 34, 70, 115, 131–45, 206, 263n34, 360; Platonic 81, 83, 246
alliteration 112, 116, 415
anagoge 39, 66, 68, 456, 462; *see also* ascension, ascent
analogy 100, 107–10, 123, 135, 175n9, 219, 344, 349; in the *Enneads* 60, 271, 287
anamnesis 309, 310; *see also* memory
Arabic Plotinus corpus *see Plotiniana Arabica*
art 11–12, 53–63, 72–3, 77–8, 110–11, 169, 296–7, 343–7, 367, 407, 431
ascension 61, 103, 111, 203–5, 211–13, 414, 427; *see also* ascent
ascent 59, 72, 95–6, 148, 192, 203, 255, 298, 310–12, 339, 357, 427–9, 433; *see also anagoge*, ascension, God, goodness, the One, Soul, in Index of Names: Muḥammad, Plotinus
attributes, of God 104–7, 121, 125, 221n17, 152–3, 160, 164–5, 209, 269

badī' style 94, 105, 110–13, 116, 125
beauty 9–10, 148–68, 276–91; of art 11–12, 35n59, 53, 57, 59–61, 73, 110–15, 296–7, 310; corporeal/physical 172, 286, 309, 315, 380; feminine 339–47; and God/the One 7, 30, 116, 150–7, 161, 193, 285–6, 301, 312, 315, 325; and the good/goodness 10, 163–6, 223, 281–2, 288, 297, 325, 380; incorporeal/intelligible 156–7, 179, 259, 282–8, 394, 398, 426, 457; innate in the soul 10n13, 57n11, 156–7, 158; of nature 26, 162, 330–1, 396, 402, 427; and truth 312, 446; **in cited poetry** 78, 116, 154, 242, 296, 309, 325–6, 399, 457; *see also* longing, love
Bible 102n16, 134, 217, 238, 239n6, 329, 379
body (as opposed to soul) 81–3, 206–12, 217–19, 229–30, 237–49, 283–8, 331–2, 341–4; in the *Enneads* 9, 59, 81, 108, 136, 155, 203, 283, 311, 416; **in cited poetry** 83, 85, 197, 241, 245, 247, 294, 298, 308–9, 326, 343, 379–80, 390, 442, 460
Brethren of Purity, Epistles of 110–11, 152n6, 220, 405

Chaldean Oracles 66–7, 73, 76, 82, 136, 144, 279, 282n17
Christianity 19n34, 59, 64–5, 67, 82, 368, 382, 398, 454, 460; *see also* Neoplatonism, theology
circle metaphor 26n48, 68n35, 37, 77, 122, 178, 259, 319, 328, 342; circular motion 20n36, 63–4, 76n66, 68n35, 53, 83, 192
contemplation 29, 51–78, 102, 123, 219, 307, 323–32, 336–8, 431; *see also* God, the One
creation (of the world) 101, 106, 110, 132, 152–3, 221–2, 226–7, 285, 316–17, 383–5; divine 79, 132, 285; *see also* emanation

darkness, as an image 29, 58, 64, 312, 315, 379–80, 394, 445–6; **in cited poetry** 75, 79, 83, 115, 411, 449
discursiveness, in language 11, 28; in reason 69, 121, 270–1; in thought 7, 44, 63, 117, 259–61, 270
'doubleness' 17, 30, 101, 174–6, 180, 183, 363; *see also* language

emanation 58, 69–71, 152–3, 178, 218, 228–9, 245, 280, 318, 408, 416; and creation 222; and light 185; **in cited poetry** 398, 415
Enneads 2, 9–10, 15; in Arabic 18, 24, 105, 136, 153n8, 404; in Latin 23–5, 279n6; and the Qur'an 100–4; in Turkish 434n3; *see also* Index of References to the *Enneads* of Plotinus

evil 9, 102, 159–60, 163, 165n19, 178, 230–2, 316, 399; **in cited poetry** 242, 245

face(s), beauty/ugliness of 160–3, 285–6, 296, 297n27, 344, 446; of God 99, 104, 116, 122–3, 263, 280, 285–6, 287–8, 368, 411, 443; of the infinite 9, 11–12, 153, 343, 427; of the Other 12–13, 385
femininity 116, 190–2, 194, 198, 200–1, 345, 381
figure (rhetorical) 27, 131–45
forgetfulness, of the soul 9, 29, 102, 108, 258n14, 259, 261–2, 286; **in cited poetry** 72, 107, 311
Form(s), Platonic 8, 11, 69, 71, 82, 110, 133–4, 164–5, 172, 177, 259–60, 281–3, 285
form(s), poetic 16, 17n28, 31–3, 35, 38, 62–4, 97–9, 211, 223, 227n38, 407, 435

gazel *see* ghazal
genre 27, 32, 131–45, 225, 232, 249n34, 320; norms/conventions of 293, 437
gender, feminine 116, 191, 219, 242; masculine 458; norms of 26–7, 189–201, 293, 337–48; and Plotinus/Neoplatonism 13–14, 21, 32, 43, 189–90, 201, 348, 447n18
ghazal/gazel 20, 32, 98n10, 114–15, 174, 175n9, 181, 195, 427
God 99–110, 359–61, 379; approximation/proximity to 113, 114, 301; ascent/return to 31, 102, 178, 329; assimilation to 73, 94–5, 107, 118n57, 123, 125, 219; contemplation of 116n50, 324; love of 1, 30, 154, 194, 230n50, 317–18, 439, 447–8; and the One 104, 124, 280; search for 300, 333, 438; union with 21, 68, 80, 204–6, 313–21, 324; **in cited poetry** 67, 75, 79, 80–1, 109, 131–2, 207, 211–12, 241–2, 264, 295, 298, 301, 309, 325, 332, 394, 411, 424, 426; *see also* attributes, beauty, contemplation, face, god-likeness, goodness, light, love, the One, praise, truth
god-likeness 29, 31, 59, 81, 85, 104, 107, 160, 205, 256, 289, 301, 314, 317, 320, 330
goodness/the Good 118, 166n20, 269, 330, 344, 395, 410; ascent to 66, 72, 78, 81; and God 107, 331; and the One 7, 10, 61, 84, 104, 285; participation in 85
Gospel 17n26, 137; of St. John 74–5, 319, 327, 398

heart (as organ of perception) 119–24, 138, 170, 181–4, 230, 300, 364, 400, 450; eye(s) of the 120, 245–6, 193; **in cited poetry** 79, 83, 118, 120, 133, 181–4, 196, 211, 245, 300, 359, 410, 423, 428, 440, 457
Hekhalot 203
hesychasm 41n64, 170
hierarchy, of being 8–9, 17, 29, 69, 71, 106–9, 112, 172, 257n12, 312, 325
Hurufism 176–7; *see also* letter(s)
hypostasis, 8, 36, 66, 70, 81n78, 152, 164–5, 325; *see also* Intellect, Soul
hymn(s) 34, 68, 73–7, 79–81, 84–5, 227, 229, 279, 457–8; to the Muses 71–3, 77; Orphic 76, 136, 279, 282n17; of the Pearl 32, 205; to Plotinus 15, 67–8; **in cited poetry** 245, 457

identity (cultural/political) 1, 8, 21, 36–7, 39–42, 97, 376, 384–5, 435, 443–4, 454–9
imagination 145, 193, 198, 204, 246n27, 269, 339; and *phantasia* 60, 69, 85, 284; **in cited poetry** 151, 154
immanence 9, 26, 102, 109, 159, 364, 367; and transcendence 17, 20, 29, 43, 99–100, 103–4, 121–2, 124, 363, 371
infinite, the 11–13, 33, 40–1, 43, 153, 228, 343, 367, 373–90, 425, 439; *see also* face(s)
Intellect/intellect, as a guide 61, 72, 117, 137–8, 152, 206, 230, 243; limitation of 36, 80–1, 121, 154, 256–7, 300; Universal 8–9, 36, 58, 122, 132–3, 222, 226, 248, 269, 280; **in cited poetry** 28, 39, 70–2, 80, 82–4, 151, 154, 206, 241, 258, 299, 429; *see also* *ʿaql,* reason
Islam 15–17, 79, 108, 123–4, 375, 427, 437–8, 465; *see also* Ismāʿīlī Shīʿa, Muʿtazila, Neoplatonism, Qu'ran, Sufism, theology, Index of Citations from the Qur'an
Ismāʿīlī Shīʿa 18–19n33

Judaism 4, 30, 203, 238–9, 375–6, 385–6; *see also* Kabbalah, Karaites, Neoplatonism, Rabanites

Kabbalah 5, 22, 23n41, 224–6, 228, 373–5, 382–6, 409; *see also* mysticism
Karaites 238–49; *see also* Judaism

ladder 58, 312, 345, 363; Jacob's 327, 359–60; **in cited poetry** 326
language, figurative 32–3, 63, 125, 406; inadequacy of 11, 25, 28, 80–1, 104, 221n16, 256–71, 299; nature of 143–5, 177, 339, 348, 382; poetic 101, 180, 184, 198; *see also* allegory, discursiveness, 'doubleness', metaphor, wordplay
letter(s) (of the alphabet) 115–17, 132, 134, 176–7, 238n2, 382–3, 414
light 72, 204–6, 221n17, 243, 287, 312–20, 331, 379–80, 394, 405, 446; divine 78, 185, 263, 283, 289n33, 455; of God 15, 109, 137, 193, 319, 328; intelligible 11,

75, 83; **in cited poetry** 71–2, 75, 78, 81, 82–3, 133, 184, 207, 241, 245, 247, 258, 294, 299, 328, 330, 365, 380, 424, 426
Logos/*logos* 13, 73–5, 143–4
longing 132, 145, 157, 247, 312, 368, 370, 439; for beauty 154–5, 172; for love/the beloved 197, 293–4, 332–3; for the One 44, 440; primordial 114, 120; for union 10, 172; **in cited poetry** 96, 132, 400; *see also* love
love 1, 10, 42–44, 113–25, 183–5, 312–21, 448–50; and beauty 30, 148, 153–5, 281, 288–9, 309; courtly 194, 297, 310; earthly/profane 27, 37, 179, 182, 308–9, 371; earthly versus heavenly 10, 175, 182, 378, 410, 434; and God/the One 1, 10n14, 114, 132, 152, 193, 288, 301, 317–18, 325, 328–30, 410, 424; heavenly/divine 15, 30, 172, 180, 197, 259, 297, 312, 324, 384, 438; Neoplatonic 98, 181–2, 198–9, 201, 331, 336–7, 340–1, 348, 369, 380, 451; Platonic 179, 201, 361; **in cited poetry** 1, 120, 122, 131–2, 153, 175, 181–5, 298, 299, 301, 311, 318, 330, 340, 356, 400, 411, 424, 444; *see also* longing, God, poetry

macrocosm 101, 125, 197
man, divine 56, 73; and God 102, 134, 144, 289, 319, 326–7, 389, 394, 414; as a microcosm 218, 256; poetic 61; wise 56; and woman 188–9, 195–8, 292, 339, 345–6, 381–2, 447n18; **in cited poetry** 133, 242, 295, 411, 465
Man, the Perfect 118, 388n6
maqāma 223–32, 239
meadow, of truth 312, 312n9; **in cited poetry** 131, 183, 394, 396
memory/remembrance 21, 29, 69n43, 102, 157, 259–61, 361–2, 390, 416; of the soul's divine origin 9, 12, 30, 103, 108n27, 155, 310–11, 316; **in cited poetry** 67, 207, 211, 258, 299, 412, 415, 424, 450, 464; *see also anamnesis,* recollection
men, divine 68; godlike 81, 85; persecuted 383; poetic 61; wise 6, 77, 209; as opposed to women 188–201, 336–48, 381, 409, 447, 464; **in cited poetry** 72, 75, 85, 86, 182, 191, 200
metaphor 29, 54, 63–4, 105–20, 175n9, 182, 248, 268, 331–2, 359, 445–6; in the *Enneads* 11, 43, 53, 59–61, 285, 310, 405; *see also* circle, mirror, sun
metaphysics 6–7, 11, 14, 22, 29–33, 63–4, 69–74, 84, 132, 374, 439; Neoplatonic 16–19, 35n59, 66, 217, 279
metre 79, 86, 97, 99, 204, 208, 231, 240n11, 457
microcosm 101, 125, 219, 197, 256, 444
mimesis 53–4, 60, 219, 407
mirror 29, 40, 53–4, 57–8, 63–4, 69n43, 179, 219n7, 359, 433–4, 446, 450; soul as 9–11, 20, 73n54, 219, 288, 289n33; **in cited poetry** 365, 440, 441, 446
moon 193, 205, 243n17, 263; and the soul 83; **in cited poetry** 76, 82, 83, 426, 460
multiplicity *see* Unity, the One
music 3, 44, 110–11, 171, 192, 293, 302, 310–11, 400
Muʿtazila 105–6
mysticism 15, 72, 204, 374–88, 406, 463; Christian 24, 27, 41n65, 79, 258n14, 315n17, 332, 374; Islamic 22, 149n1, 170, 177, 192–3, 387, 412, 420, 433–43; Jewish 22, 203, 221n14; Neoplatonic 26, 64, 80–1; secular 40, 444–51; *see also* Kabbalah, Sufism

nafs 102n16, 219, 241, *see also* Soul
name(s), of God 76, 104, 105n25, 120, 160, 163, 176, 312n10, 412
nefesh 102n16, 219, 226, 228n42, 229–31, 242, *see also* Soul
Neoplatonism 2, 217n1, 278n5, 279; and the arts 53–62, 110–13; and Christianity 15–16, 23–7, 74–6, 276–89, 297–302, 312–21, 323–33, 375, 457, 462, 466; in India 210–12; and Islam 17–22, 98, 99–104, 110, 113–15, 192–5, 375, 404–5, 434n1; and Judaism 22–3, 26, 217–21; and modernity 33–44, 374, 376, 393, 416, 421, 434, 438, 443, 466–7; Ottoman 171–2, 185–6, 189–90; Persian 420–5; and poetry 27–36, 62–9, 125, 131–45, 256n9, 349, 396n1, 406; Renaissance 4, 16, 25–7, 30, 321, 333, 327; transmission of 14–27, 268–71, 277–80, 302; *see also* love, poetics, poetry
nous 83–4, 152, 219, 269, 314, 317, 457; *see also* Intellect, reason

One, the 7–13, 31–3, 43–4, 53, 103–4, 152–3, 185, 189, 218–19, 280; ascent to 12, 60, 68, 80, 413–14, 433; assimilation to/union with 10, 37, 73, 94, 197, 410; beyond reach 422, 440; contemplation of 61, 78; emanation from 10, 31, 58, 218–19; female 116; ineffable 40, 104, 256; and Intellect 133, 164–5; and the Many 76, 97–8, 105n25, 116n51, 117, 119, 122, 125, 380, 408, 412; participation in 33, 43, 71, 81; return/reversion to 63, 75, 192, 243; transcendent 104, 313, 409; **in cited poetry** 80, 82, 84, 241, 245, 423; *see also* beauty, God, goodness/the Good, hypostasis, longing, love, Plotinus

Parsis 203n1, 212–13; *see also* Zoroastrianism
participation 8, 58–9, 69–71, 80–1, 85, 314–15, 318; **in cited poetry** 83; *see also* the One
Petrarchism, *see* Index of Names: Petrarca
philosophy, function/purpose of 9, 12, 28, 44, 208–10, 420–1; Indian 15; Neoplatonic 7, 22, 42, 101, 110, 348, 438; and poetry 28, 54, 61, 82, 143, 171, 217, 259, 270, 340, 361, 407–12, 455; *see also* Neoplatonism
piyyut 23, 217, 230, 243n18
Platonism 2n4, 82–5, 143, 217n1, 263, 278–9, 357–8, 360–1, 396n1, 454
Plotiniana Arabica/Arabic Plotinus corpus 18–22, 108, 113, 150, 404; *Epistle on Divine Science* 110–11, 121, 165, 218; *Theology of Aristotle* 35, 105–6, 114, 118n57, 132, 136, 153–62, 210n6, 218–20, 416
poetics 60, 109, 240, 340, 357, 374, 381, 405–6; Neoplatonic 3, 25, 27–37, 62–9, 73–4, 79, 85, 131–45, 349, 362
poetry, love 114, 115n47, 119, 173, 175, 179, 185, 190n2, 240, 307–8, 310, 357; mystical 10, 17, 99–100, 115, 179–80, 436, 441; panegyric 94, 105–13, 117; Sufi 19, 34, 93–4, 113–24, 142, 425, 438, 445; *see also* Neoplatonism, philosophy, praise
praise 67, 140–2, 206, 227, 346; of God 106, 112, 206, 220–1, 246; of the One 80; **in cited poetry** 67, 80, 207, 245, 462; *see also* hymn, poetry/panegyric
purification 9, 29, 113n42, 155n11, 158, 160, 219, 434; *see also* Soul

qasida/kaside 20, 32, 34, 94–9, 105–13, 115–25, 142, 405, 437
Qur'an 99–105, 124, 135, 137–40, 142–5, 150–63, 176, 409, 413–15, 420; and the *Enneads* 100–4; *see also* Index of Citations from the Qur'an

Rabanites 239–40
reason (i.e. intellect) 15, 58, 195, 228n41, 282; discursive 69, 271; limitation of 120, 121n60, 172, 181–2, 193, 200, 286–7, 406, 466; **in cited poetry** 120, 181, 200; *see also* *'aql*, Intellect
recollection 159, 166, 243, 323; of the soul's divine origin 43n66, 157, 259; **in cited poetry** 258; *see also* memory
Renaissance 6, 225, 285n23, 307, 336, 340, 347, 374, 419, 455; *see also* Neoplatonism
rhyme 139, 196, 208, 231, 363, 415, 423, 460; mono-rhyme 97–8, 106, 116–17, 123–5, 240n11, 245n26, 248n33, 404; *redif* (post-rhyme refrain) 98, 174, 181

sonnet(s), English 366; Hebrew 23n41; Italian 32, 34, 293–302, 356; Spanish 32, 191, 307–9, 340–9; Turkish 444
Soul/soul, ascent of 59, 63, 205, 317, 325, 336, 427; beautified 57, 157, 158n12, 160, 286n25, 296–7; dance of 20n36; feminine 98, 219, 242; human 8–9, 15, 62, 113, 155, 246, 259–64, 288, 307, 339, 393, 421; journey of 19, 81, 178, 100–3, 329, 217, 329, 442; and poetry 54, 70, 113, 217–49, 393–402; purified 9, 43, 102–3, 113n42, 286, 422; Universal 8–9, 11, 36, 155, 209, 219, 226, 246, 248; **in cited poetry** 67–8, 72, 80–3, 85, 183–4, 206–7, 212, 222, 229–32, 241–2, 245, 247, 264, 296, 298, 300–1, 309, 311–12, 317, 332, 340, 343, 379, 398–400, 423, 457, 459; *see also* beauty, God, hypostasis, Intellect, memory, mirror, *nafs*, *nefesh*, purification
Suda 65, 68
Sufism 19–20, 43, 93, 113–25, 148–66, 171–85, 192, 204, 382–89, 406–7, 420–1, 437, 466; *see also* Islam, mysticism
sun 60, 78, 83, 205, 287, 294, 298, 320, 331, 344, 428, 442; in Plato 269, 380; in Plotinus 160; **in cited poetry** 78–9, 81n78, 82–3, 207, 298–300, 328, 330, 343, 347, 356, 363, 369, 395, 410, 449, 455, 459
symmetry 110–13, 116, 219, 447

theology 18, 76, 134, 171, 210, 256n9, 369; Christian 72, 79, 319, 323, 327; Muslim 102, 149, 151, 163; mystical 85, 313–14, 323; negative 79, 124, 150, 256, 314–15; Proclian 84–5
Theology of Aristotle, *see Plotiniana Arabica*
theurgy 34, 54, 65–6, 73, 76, 463, 467
transcendence 41, 94n3, 101, 151, 159, 205–6, 211, 221, 314, 362, 379; *see also* immanence
Truth/truth 6–7, 99, 360; and appearances 269–70, 285, 287, 341, 440; and God 171, 177, 193, 336, 423; and literature/poetry 33–5, 100, 136–44, 229, 266, 269, 344–7; and nature 362, 427; **in cited poetry** 132, 176, 343, 362, 394, 423; *see also* beauty, meadow

ugliness 156, 158, 160–2, 193, 315, 446, 457
union, of lovers 37, 42, 114, 120, 123, 182, 198, 336, 380, 390, 410; with fire 59, 154; with light 72; of opposites 180, 388; mystical 68, 377–8, 413; with the sun 428; **in cited poetry** 182, 429; *see also* God, the One

Unity/unity, of being 405, 414, 434, 441, 444; in the *Enneads* 31, 58, 103; experience of 377–8, 429; formal/organic 32, 60, 98–9, 359, 407; and multiplicity 71, 73, 97, 123, 380–1, 405, 411–2; Primal/absolute 53, 72, 84, 121, 171–85, 221

virtue 61, 73n54, 96–7, 105–7, 113–14, 125, 188, 280, 288, 329; Plotinus on 57–8, 94, 157, 160, 283

woman 188–201, 242, 265, 292–5, 301, 337–47, 366–70, 379–82, 409; **in cited poetry** 295, 411; *see also* femininity, gender, man, Soul
women 13–14, 116n50, 179, 181, 188–201, 247, 300, 302, 336–48, 357, 370, 415–16; poets 4–5, 21, 27, 190–3, 295, 343, 447; **in cited poetry** 200, 412; *see also* femininity, gender, men
wordplay 107, 243n15, 246–7, 249

Zoroastrianism 21, 28, 203–13, 420